UMI ANNUAL COMMENTARY

PRECEPTS
FOR
LIVING®

MISSION STATEMENT

*W*e are called
of God to create, produce, and distribute
quality Christian education products;
to deliver exemplary customer service;
and to provide quality Christian
educational services, which will empower
God's people, especially within the Black
community, to evangelize, disciple,
and equip people for serving Christ,
His kingdom, and church.

Urban Ministries, Inc.
The African American Christian Publishing
& Communications Co.

UMI ANNUAL SUNDAY SCHOOL LESSON COMMENTARY
PRECEPTS FOR LIVING® 2011–2012
INTERNATIONAL SUNDAY SCHOOL LESSONS
VOLUME 14
UMI (URBAN MINISTRIES, INC.)

Melvin Banks Sr., Litt.D., Founder and Chairman
C. Jeffrey Wright, J.D., CEO

All art: Copyright © 2011 by UMI.
Bible art: Fred Carter

CONTRIBUTORS

Editor
Vincent Bacote, Ph.D.

Vice President of Editorial
Cheryl P. Clemetson, Ph.D.

Developmental Editor
Evangeline Carey, M.A.

Copy Editors
Mary Lewis
Marjorie Vawter
Kyle Waalen, M.S.

Cover Design & Layout
Trinidad D. Zavala, B.A.

Bible Illustrations
Fred Carter

Contributing Writers
Essays/In Focus Stories
Evangeline Carey, M.A.
Lisa Crayton, B.A.
Rukeia Draw-Hood, Ph.D.
Judith St.Clair Hull, Ph.D.
Barbara Carr-Phillips
Rosa Sailes, Ed.D.
Kyle Waalen, M.S.

Bible Study Guide Writers
Allyson D. Nelson Abrams, Ph.D.
J. Ayodeji Adewuya, Ph.D.
Evangeline Carey, M.A.
Jimmie Wilkerson-Chaplin, M.B.A.
Lisa Crayton, B.A.
Jay D. Ganger, B.S.
Jean Garrison, M.A.
Charlesetta Watson-Holmes, M.Div.
Judith St.Clair Hull, Ph.D.
Jennifer King, M.A.
Angela Lampkin, M.S.
LaTonya Mason, M.A.
Beverly Moore, M.S.
Eric Pazdziora, B.Mus.
Evonne Thompson, M.B.A.
Kim Varner, M.Div.
Kyle Waalen, M.S.
Faith Waters, M.Div.

More Light on the Text
J. Ayodeji Adewuya, Ph.D.
Evangeline Carey, M.A.
Moussa Coulibaly, Ph.D.
Clay Daniel, M.Div.
Richard Gray, Ph.D.
Angelo Hill, Ph.D.
Kevin Hrebik, D.Min.
Judith St.Clair Hull, Ph.D.
Nathan Munn, M.Div.
Anthony Myles, M.Div.
James Rawdon, Ph.D.
Philip & Jerii Rodman, M.Div.
Louis Wilson, Ph.D.

Dear *Precepts* Customer,

It is our privilege to present the 2011–2012 *Precepts For Living*®. While your exposure to and embrace of God's Word grows through these lessons, we are very confident that you will find this resource to be indispensable.

Precepts For Living® comes to you in three versions: the *Personal Study Guide* (the workbook), the CD-ROM version of *Precepts*, and a large-print edition. You will also notice that the biblical text for each lesson continues to include the New Living Translation in addition to the King James Version; this contemporary translation will enhance your textual understanding when you compare it side by side with the classic English translation.

Precepts For Living® is designed to be a witness through our learning and sharing of the Bible. Our intent is to help facilitate innovative ways to pursue a deeper understanding and practice of God's Word. One of the ways we are doing this is by making more of our lessons highlight the larger narrative of God's work in salvation as a key part of understanding each biblical passage. We believe it is important to help you understand not only the particulars of the text, but also the broad sweep of God's revelation to us, as well. This panoramic approach enhances our ability to witness to others about the saving power of Jesus Christ.

This year we explore the following themes: "Tradition and Wisdom," "God Establishes a Faithful People," "God's Creative Word," and "God Calls for Justice." Each year of Bible study offers great potential for a more intimate and transformative walk with God.

We want to keep refining *Precepts For Living*® as we strive to meet our customers' needs. We are always looking for ways to enhance your study of the Bible, and your comments and feedback are vital in helping us. We encourage you to help us. If you have questions or suggestions, please e-mail us at precepts@urbanministries. com or mail your comments to UMI, *Precepts For Living*®, PO Box 436987, Chicago, IL 60643-6987.

May God draw you closer to the fullness of life with Him through this book.

God's blessings to you,

Vincent E. Bacote, Ph.D.

Vincent E. Bacote, Ph.D.
Editor

Uncovering the Benefits of Precepts

It is a great privilege to participate in Christian education and play a significant role in the spiritual formation of fellow Christians in our churches. *Precepts For Living®* is a resource that is designed to help you lead others toward greater knowledge and practice of following Jesus Christ. To that end, I would like to help you take advantage of the resources provided to you in this year's commentary.

From the standpoint of your vocation as a teacher, it is very important to be aware of the great responsibility that goes along with your position. James 3:1 reminds us that we have such a great opportunity in front of us that we run the risk of greater judgment if we are derelict in our duties. This is a strong word to us that helps us understand the great influence that we have when we help our students learn about God's Word. To be a teacher means that we are participating in one of the church's greatest tasks, one that the ancient church called "catechesis." While this word is often associated with particular denominations and with a form of teaching that relies upon a systematic question and answer format, the central meaning of the word is "teaching," and it carries with it the idea of teaching the entirety of the faith to Christians. While many Sunday School teachers might not be familiar with this word, the truth is that every time any of us helps others learn about God's Word and ways, we are participating in this great task of the church, which has been with us from the beginning. Our participation in catechesis is central to the life of the church, and at times this function of the church gets lost in the midst of other concerns. As a teacher, you have an opportunity to energize and/or revitalize this aspect of your church's ministry. Are you up for the challenge?

What is the goal when you are using *Precepts For Living®* to open up the riches of the Bible to your students? It is more than merely the acquisition of "spiritual data." Certainly we want our students to grow in knowledge, but the knowledge we seek to pass on is not merely Bible facts, but a larger sense of knowledge where the information and doctrine conveyed is oriented toward a faithful life of discipleship. The People, Places, and Times; Background; In Depth; and More Light on the Text sections are there to help you with providing insight and understanding of the text. But the lesson is about more than simply compiling information. In each lesson, you will also see that we have In Focus stories and the sections Lesson in Our Society and Make It Happen. These sections are there to serve as catalysts for bringing the biblical text to our life situations. It is very important that we as teachers pass on knowledge that will enable our students to deepen their devotion to God in an "upward" focus and help them to be able to better embody that devotion in a way that makes their lives a living witness to the world. In each lesson, our goal should be one of helping our students become better at being living examples of the Scriptures, because their lives may be the only Bible some people ever read.

In order to best take advantage of this commentary, you will find it beneficial to utilize the essays which highlight notable African Americans and quarterly themes, and they also help you to become a better teacher by providing insight on enhancing the classroom experience and ways to convey the lesson across a range of learning styles. We believe that this commentary is a great tool which can help the church form fully devoted followers of Christ, and we invite you to take advantage of the variety of resources provided here. May God be glorified as you play your part in this great task of the church!

Creative Teaching

• **Energizing the Class.** If the class does not seem as enthusiastic or energy is low, after you open with prayer, have everyone stretch to the sky or outward. Then tell the class to shake off the low energy, and open up their hands to receive the love of God that is right there. You can always have a 30-second meet and greet time. This usually helps to wake people up so that you can begin class on a higher energy level.

• **Two Teachers in One Class—Bring Out the Best in Both.** Taking turns works in some classes, but in others it creates tension and favorites. Encourage teachers to study together, and then divide the segments of the lesson. Perhaps one will teach the introduction while the other teaches a section of the text. Encourage them to also become a true team with each contributing throughout the lesson.

• **Remember.** Everyone cannot read or write on the same level. Use different teaching techniques and styles when teaching. How you learn affects how you teach, so be open and willing to learn and teach through various mediums.

• **Avoid Study in Isolation.** People often "get it" when they are involved with more than talking about the lesson. Why not allow the class to see the connections themselves? Try using a chart to have adult students work in pairs or groups to compare and contrast Bible persons such as David and Solomon or Ruth and Orpah, Naomi's daughters-in-law. To help the students get started, suggest specific categories for comparisons such as lifestyles, families, or public ministry. As class members search the Scriptures, they will learn and remember much more than if you had told them about either person.

• **Group Studies.** Have the class form groups, and have each group read the Scripture lesson and a section of the Background for the text. Have each group create a two-minute skit about the Scripture to share with the class. Encourage the groups to use their imaginations and energy. You may want to have at least one "leader" in a group if you have more than two or three reserved persons in your class.

• **Volunteers.** Many classes begin with reading the lesson. When class members have studied, this activity is more "bringing minds" together than about the actual lesson. Still some classes can benefit from dramatic and creative reading of Bible passages at any point in the lesson. When the passage under study lends itself, assign parts to volunteers. This need not be formal—standing up isn't even critical. This strategy works best in passages that have a story such as the conversation between Moses and his father-in-law, Jethro, or Paul confronting the merchants in Thessalonica. Assign one person to each speaking character in the Bible text. Feel free to be creative with giving the class roles as "the crowd." Make sure to assign a narrator who will read the nonspeaking parts. It is fun, it is fast, and it makes for memorable Bible reading.

• **Alternatives.** Select one or two persons from the class to read the Scripture lesson with enthusiasm and drama. Ask a few persons to develop a newspaper or magazine headline with a brief story that explains the headlines. Have another group write the headlines and a story that will be used in a cell phone video. (Let the class know that they should bring their cell phones—with video recording—so that most people can share in this activity. Presently, there is technology available for cell phone videos.)

2010–2014 Scope and Sequence—Cycle Spread

	FALL	WINTER	SPRING	SUMMER
YEAR ONE 2010–11	GOD **The Inescapable God** Exodus Psalms 8, 19, 46, 47, 63, 66, 90, 91, 139	HOPE **Assuring Hope** Isaiah Matthew Mark	WORSHIP **We Worship God** Matthew Mark 1, 2 Timothy Philippians 2 Jude Revelation	COMMUNITY **God Instructs the People of God** Joshua Judges Ruth
YEAR TWO 2011–12	TRADITION **Tradition and Wisdom** Proverbs Ecclesiastes Song of Solomon Matthew	FAITH **God Establishes a Faithful People** Genesis Exodus Luke Galatians	CREATION **God's Creative Word** John	JUSTICE **God Calls for Justice** Exodus Leviticus Deuteronomy 1, 2 Samuel 1, 2 Kings 2 Chronicles Psalm 146 Isaiah Jeremiah Ezekiel

YEAR THREE 2012–13	FAITH
	
	A Living Faith
	
	Psalm 46
	1 Corinthians
	  13:1–13
	Hebrews
	Acts
		GOD: JESUS CHRIST
		
		Jesus Is Lord
		
		Ephesians
		Philippians
		Colossians
			HOPE
			
			Beyond the Present Time
			
			Daniel
			Luke
			Acts
			1, 2 Peter
			1, 2
			  Thessalonians
				WORSHIP
				
				God's People Worship
				
				Isaiah
				Ezra
				Nehemiah

YEAR FOUR 2013–14	CREATION **First Things** Genesis Exodus Psalm 104	JUSTICE **Jesus and the Just Reign of God** Luke James	TRADITION **Jesus' Fulfillment of Scripture** Zechariah Malachi Deuteronomy Matthew	COMMUNITY **The People of God Set Priorities** Haggai 1, 2 Corinthians

THE MIGHTY JUSTICE OF GOD

by Evangeline Carey

In Amos 5:24 (KJV), we find these words: "But let judgment run down as waters, and righteousness as a mighty stream." In the New Living Translation, this same verse reads, "Instead, I [God] want to see a mighty flood of justice, an endless river of righteous living." The picturesque waterfall on our front cover should remind you of this passage of Scripture, and that a righteous God values justice and righteousness in the here and now—in our everyday relationships—in our day-to-day living. They are essential in His plans and purposes to advance His kingdom. God's inerrant Word tells us that He will not let injustice flourish always. In fact, His essential command is that we work to bring justice—a mighty flood of justice to this world. We as obedient believers must do our Father's will.

During these four new quarters, we will see that indeed a sovereign God is in control of His universe, and He is moving it toward an expected end—His justice and righteousness ruling for ever and ever. We learn that He did not just create His universe and forget about it, but plays an active role in controlling the course of history as He brings it to His final conclusion.

Therefore, in our study for the fall quarter, we will survey some of the Old Testament's "Wisdom Literature" with the theme of "Tradition and Wisdom" from Proverbs, Ecclesiastes, and Song of Solomon, and then culminate with the Gospel of Matthew. Our survey should help us gain insight from the theme "God Establishes a Faithful People" from Genesis, Exodus, Luke, and Galatians for the winter quarter, and then go into our spring quarter of 2012 with an in-depth study of John's gospel through the theological lens of creation. From John's gospel, we should learn that God's one-time action of bringing the world into existence not only involves God's ongoing action of reconciling and re-creating (in His image) now, but also in eternity. In fact, Almighty God created His Holy Word which was, is, and shall make all things good. Not only was His Word in the beginning, but it is in the here and now, and will be forever more. We also examine God's promises to us of not only life, but also security, resurrection, and the way to God.

Finally, from our studies, a foundation should be laid to help us delve into a challenging discussion of "God's Calls for Justice" from the books of Exodus; Leviticus; Deuteronomy; 1, 2 Samuel; 1, 2 Kings; 2 Chronicles; Psalm 146; Isaiah; Jeremiah; and Ezekiel. In all of these books, we are looking at relationships and the lessons we should learn from experience and tradition—words of wisdom passed on from generation to generation by parents and teachers on how to *justly relate* to others. We cover the themes of "Justice Defined," "Justice Enacted," and "Justice Promised." Not only will we look at God's coming judgments, but we will also examine an omniscient (all-knowing) God's teachings on wisdom. In God's frame of reference, to do justice and be just are paramount to being wise. It is being obedient to God's Word.

Remember that Holy God is concerned about how we live as His people, forgive as His people, love as His people, and pray as His people. He is concerned about how we help to build His kingdom where Jesus will reign with His Bride, the Church, forever and ever.

So look at the waterfall repeatedly and be refreshed and reminded that God is a just God, and His justice and mercy will rule the day! Let the waterfall be an exhortation to excellent, powerful Christian living. Be moved to let others see the Jesus—the justice in you.

Evangeline Carey is the Developmental Editor for Precepts For Living®, *has been an Adult Sunday School Teacher for more than 25 years, and holds a Master of Arts in Biblical Studies from Moody Bible Institute, Chicago, IL.*

Tradition and Wisdom

The study of this quarter is a survey of Old Testament wisdom literature, as well as an examination of Jesus' teachings on wisdom.

UNIT 1 • TEACHING AND LEARNING

As is characteristic of wisdom literature, these books make little reference to covenant or religious life. Instead, they are focused on human wisdom and transmit lessons learned from experience and tradition. They are the words of a teacher to a student, or a parent to a child, words of wisdom passed on from one generation to another. The first five lessons draw on the wisdom collected by the writers of Proverbs. The next two lessons consider the wisdom of Ecclesiastes. The final lesson comes from the Song of Solomon.

Lesson 1: September 4, 2011
Righteousness and Wisdom
Proverbs 3:1–12

When we choose to live in obedience to God, He grants us wisdom. Proverbs 3 describes wisdom as a value that protects and brings well-being. Trusting in God's wisdom and guidance helps develop strong faith, as well as offers purpose and meaning in life.

Lesson 2: September 11, 2011
From Generation to Generation
Proverbs 4:10–15, 20–27

Using the model of parental teaching, that has been handed down from one generation to the next, the author encourages people to walk the path of righteousness and wisdom.

Lesson 3: September 18, 2011
Teaching Values
Proverbs 15:21–33

The author offers advice that contains wise and godly principles for living, which helps strengthen one's trust in God. Heeding and practicing the advice offered in Proverbs lead to positive outcomes.

Lesson 4: September 25, 2011
Wisdom and Discernment
Proverbs 25:1–10

In this lesson, the proverbs of Solomon were collected by King Hezekiah. While they originally meant to help those who dealt with a king, these verses have positive applications for a wide variety of relationships. They offer wisdom on values such as humility, honesty, discretion, and respect.

Lesson 5: October 2, 2011
An Ordered Life
Proverbs 29:16–27

Wisdom is provided for living an ordered life. Wickedness and unrighteousness affect the entire community. However, God and God's laws are the ultimate sources of justice, and righteousness will prevail. God wants people to revere Him and obey Him by ordering their lives in the way of God.

Lesson 6: October 9, 2011
The Superiority of Wisdom
Ecclesiastes 9:13–18

The parable of a poor man who saved a town is shared as an example of quiet, thoughtful wisdom. Wisdom is greater than strength, and soft-spoken wisdom is better than loud words of foolishness.

Lesson 7: October 16, 2011
Wisdom for Aging
Ecclesiastes 11:9–12:7, 13

This lesson gives wisdom about aging. It is not only important to enjoy life while being young, but to remember that we belong to God, live in fear (reverence) of Him, and keep His commandments.

Lesson 8: October 23, 2011
Tradition and Love
Song of Solomon 4:8–5:1a

Solomon expresses his feelings of love for his bride. He cherishes her love. While traditional interpretations see this book as an allegory of the relationship between God and Israel, and Christ and the church, people today can find encouragement in these words as they contemplate love and commitment.

UNIT 2 • JESUS TEACHES WISDOM

These five lessons examine Jesus' Sermon on the Mount and its relationship to the traditional teaching of Mosaic Law. The first four lessons, taken from Matthew 5 and 6, give attention to what Jesus says to disciples about living, forgiving, loving, and praying. The final lesson invites the participants to hear anew Jesus' words about worry-free living.

Lesson 9: October 30, 2011
Living as God's People
Matthew 5:1–12

Jesus shares the Beatitudes as part of the Sermon on the Mount. In it, He identifies traits that are pleasing to Him and notes ways that God blesses those who seek Him first and strive to live as His people.

Lesson 10: November 6, 2011
Forgiving as God's People
Matthew 5:17–26

Jesus teaches wisdom as it applies to our attitude toward Him and in the way we relate to others. Specifically, keeping the law requires more than outward obedience. It requires a change of heart.

Lesson 11: November 13, 2011
Loving as God's People
Matthew 5:43–48

It is easy to love a neighbor and hate an enemy, but Jesus teaches that love and prayer are to be extended to our enemies.

Lesson 12: November 20, 2011
Praying as God's People
Matthew 6:5–15

It is important to recognize and appreciate effective prayer. Jesus presents a model prayer that teaches how to pray effectively and intimately to God.

Lesson 13: November 27, 2011
Facing Life without Worry
Matthew 6:25–34

Jesus teaches disciples not to worry about daily necessities, as God supplies our needs. It takes faith to trust in God's provisions. When one puts his or her life in God's hands, worry and anxiety diminish.

The Original Self-Help Guru

by Kyle Waalen

God is in the self-help business, but unlike most self-help gurus, God is not trying to sell you something. There are no gimmicks or profit-driven agendas. Instead, He offers everyone a gift that comes with an everlasting-life guarantee. There is no need to redeem any coupons or rebates; God offers us all of the redemption we need. But this is a limited time offer and may expire at any time. That's why it's important to act now!

Being the original self-help guru, God also wrote the biggest selling self-help book of all time, the Bible. In His Book, He reveals His wisdom through tips, guidance, and instructions on how to live according to His will. God even dedicates an entire section of the Bible, called Proverbs, to providing nuggets of wisdom for us to follow. "For the foolishness of God is wiser than man's wisdom, and the weakness of God is stronger than man's strength" (1 Corinthians 1:25, NIV).

Five Beneficial Qualities of the Bible

1. Instructional—Non-Christians often see God's Word as prohibitive, but believers see it (or should see it) as instructive. The Bible instructs people on how to live, but they aren't forced to live that way. People can live any way they want, but if they defy God's commands, there will be consequences. God knows what is best for us, and His Ten Step Plan to Proper Living (aka The Ten Commandments) is meant to benefit us. "The fear of the LORD is the beginning of wisdom; all who follow his precepts have good understanding. To him belongs eternal praise" (Psalm 111:10, NIV).

God is in the self-help business because He's ultimately in the people business. God loves people. We are all His children. As our Creator, God knows what we need. Obedience and righteous living may not always be entertaining, but there are serious benefits. "All Scripture is God-breathed and is useful for teaching, rebuking, correcting and training in righteousness" (2 Timothy 3:16, NIV).

2. Traditional—God's Word is one of the oldest written documents in history. It has been passed down from generation to generation. Christians throughout history have faced persecution in order to preserve and practice the teachings of the Bible. With this rich history, God's Word has influenced millions of people throughout the existence of humankind. Typically, many traditions and cultures fade away, but the Bible has survived the test of time. It continues to be a hot topic in the media, society, and the world today. People still turn to it for guidance and seek the wisdom it contains. Unlike fad diets and motivational programs, the information in the Bible is just as current as it was thousands of years ago.

Unlike Oprah, who continually updates her media empire in order to stay relevant, or Dr. Oz and Dr. Phil, who must keep up with the latest health practices, God is omniscient. He knows everything! "Do not forsake wisdom, and she will protect you; love her, and she will watch over you. Wisdom is supreme; therefore

3

get wisdom. Though it cost all you have, get understanding" (Proverbs 4:6–7, NIV).

3. Personal—God's Word is for the individual. God wants to have a personal relationship with each person, regardless of worldly status. He is concerned for the well-being of every individual and wants to nurture and protect every single one. But just because the Bible is *for* you does not mean it is *all about* you. Instead, it's all about Christ and our need for Him. "It is because of him that you are in Christ Jesus, who has become for us wisdom from God—that is, our righteousness, holiness and redemption" (1 Corinthians 1:30, NIV).

Everyone has problems in life, but not everyone's problems are the same. The Bible addresses all of life's troubles in one way or another. Instead of having to purchase separate books on relationship advice, healthy living, and financial planning, God's Word contains all of these things and more within the pages of one book. It's the one-stop-shop for guidance about righteous living and wisdom. For example, Suze Orman may offer advice on financial planning, but she is not an expert on physical health. God, on the other hand, can tackle any issue at any time.

4. Universal—God's Word is for everyone. It is full of universal truths that apply to all people. "But the wisdom that comes from heaven is first of all pure; then peace-loving, considerate, submissive, full of mercy and good fruit, impartial and sincere" (James 3:17, NIV). The times change, but God's Word does not. The information is never outdated. It applies to the here and the now, the way back when, and to things yet to come. The Bible has been translated into dozens of languages and has crossed racial, political, and national borders.

In order to understand why God's wisdom is universal, people must understand that He created the entire universe from scratch. Beat that, Martha Stewart! He's an expert in every field that there ever was, is, and will be, and He's been in the industry literally since the dawn of time. Nobody knows people better than God. He has never let us down before; therefore, there is no reason why we shouldn't trust in His Word.

5. Transformational—God's Word not only helps people, but it transforms them. People are always looking for fulfillment, meaning, and improvement in their lives. God offers all of these and more. On the TV show *The Biggest Loser*, fitness experts attempt to change people's lives by addressing their physical, emotional, and psychological issues. While this is a worthy goal, the show's main objective is for the individual to find it within him- or herself to change his or her life. We can strive for excellence and perfection on our own, but without Jesus Christ, we will surely fail.

By following God and His Word, we are changed from the rest of the world. Nobody can transform lives like God can. "And be not conformed to this world: but be ye transformed by the renewing of your mind, that ye may prove what is that good, and acceptable, and perfect, will of God" (Romans 12:2).

As Christians and imperfect human beings, we know that there is no such thing as self-help; there is only God's help. "Trust in the LORD with all thine heart; and lean not unto thine own understanding. In all thy ways acknowledge him, and he shall direct thy paths" (Proverbs 3:5–6). The next time you're in need of some wisdom, don't pick up a self-help book at your local bookstore when you haven't even opened your copy of God's Book at home. Instead of seeking worldly advice, seek God's advice first. It will not only save you a lot of time and trouble, but it will save your very soul. "If any of you lacks wisdom, he should ask God, who gives generously to all without finding fault, and it will be given to him" (James 1:5, NIV).

Kyle Waalen *is a freelance editor and writer. He holds a Master of Science in Written Communication.*

Wisdom for All People!

As we survey some of the "wisdom literature" found in the Old Testament, which includes the books of Proverbs, Ecclesiastes, and Song of Solomon, there is much we can learn to positively impact our everyday living for our just God. As we focus on human wisdom—transmitted lessons from generation to generation through parents and teachers—let us, too, learn from experience and tradition and become doers of God's inerrant Word. Even as we end our study with the Gospel of Matthew in the New Testament, and explore where Jesus teaches wisdom in His Sermon on the Mount and its relationship to the traditional teaching of the Mosaic Law, let us also see what principles we can draw from the discussion to enhance our daily walk with God. From this study, we will learn about living, forgiving, loving, and praying for each other. These lessons can help us in our daily living—our daily interaction with others. They can help us live an ordered life, even to face life without worry. To whet your appetite, look at what Proverbs tells us about the "sound" wisdom that all people should embrace and practice.

PROVERBS 10, NLT

Proverbs of Solomon:

1 A wise child brings joy to a father; a foolish child brings grief to a mother.

2 Ill-gotten gain has no lasting value, but right living can save your life.

3 The LORD will not let the godly starve to death, but he refuses to satisfy the craving of the wicked.

4 Lazy people are soon poor; hard workers get rich.

5 A wise youth works hard all summer; a youth who sleeps away the hour of opportunity brings shame.

6 The godly are showered with blessings; evil people cover up their harmful intentions.

7 We all have happy memories of the godly, but the name of a wicked person rots away.

8 The wise are glad to be instructed, but babbling fools fall flat on their faces.

9 People with integrity have firm footing, but those who follow crooked paths will slip and fall.

10 People who wink at wrong cause trouble, but a bold reproof promotes peace.

11 The words of the godly lead to life; evil people cover up their harmful intentions.

12 Hatred stirs up quarrels, but love covers all offenses.

13 Wise words come from the lips of people with understanding, but fools will be punished with a rod.

14 Wise people treasure knowledge, but the babbling of a fool invites trouble.

15 The wealth of the rich is their fortress; the poverty of the poor is their calamity.

16 The earnings of the godly enhance their lives, but evil people squander their money on sin.

17 People who accept correction are on the pathway to life, but those who ignore it will lead others astray.

18 To hide hatred is to be a liar; to slander is to be a fool.

19 Don't talk too much, for it fosters sin. Be sensible and turn off the flow!

20 The words of the godly are like sterling silver; the heart of a fool is worthless.

21 The godly give good advice, but fools are destroyed by their lack of common sense.

22 The blessing of the LORD makes a person rich, and he adds no sorrow with it.

23 Doing wrong is fun for a fool, while wise conduct is a pleasure to the wise.

24 The fears of the wicked will all come true; so will the hopes of the godly.

25 Disaster strikes like a cyclone, whirling the wicked away, but the godly have a lasting foundation.

26 Lazy people are a pain to their employer. They are like smoke in the eyes or vinegar that sets the teeth on edge.

27 Fear of the LORD lengthens one's life, but the years of the wicked are cut short.

28 The hopes of the godly result in happiness, but the expectations of the wicked are all in vain.

29 The LORD protects the upright but destroys the wicked.

30 The godly will never be disturbed, but the wicked will be removed from the land.

31 The godly person gives wise advice, but the tongue that deceives will be cut off.

32 The godly speak words that are helpful, but the wicked speak only what is corrupt.

Source:

Life Application Study Bible. New Living Translation. Tyndale House Publishers, Inc. Wheaton, IL. 1996. 992.

Wisdom Literature: Perpendicular Path

by Barbara Carr-Phillips

I am a perpetual goal setter. I'm always charting a path to where I want to be. I teach others how to use a personal journal to help them meet their goals. It's important to define a clear path by writing it down.

Last summer, my journalized goals included accomplishing tasks at the law firm where I worked, and helping abused and neglected children as a volunteer of the court. The family vacation was my husband's idea, or so we thought. If my husband hadn't insisted I schedule some vacation time, I wouldn't be alive today. Looking back, we both feel God called us away.

God's nature is to care for His children. I see His love through wisdom literature, the tangible evidence of His deep and infinite knowledge. My nature as a child of God is to go about my business and call on God if I fall. Last summer, God did not allow me to fall. "Thou compassest my path and my lying down, and art acquainted with all my ways" (Psalm 139:3). The path I designed went straight to my goals, but after a few quiet days at the ocean, I noticed another path emerging—a path perpendicular to mine. Indeed, God did chart another path for me, and He eliminated the distractions of my daily schedule with a vacation so that I would find it.

I remember sitting alone on the balcony of our rented beach apartment. I opened my prayer journal and was surprised that my last entry was dated three weeks ago—no wonder my life felt so unmanageable. Time alone with God had been replaced with excuses: "I'll make one more call, and then I'll spend time in prayer. I'll squeeze in one more appointment, and then maybe I'll have time for Bible study." Of course, I was usually too tired to do either by the end of the day.

I began to pray and ask the Lord to direct me. I thought of my mother, who had just finished treatment for breast cancer. I wrote in my journal that I'd schedule a mammogram when I returned home. I surprised myself when I wrote the words. After all, my mother's doctor said a hormone treatment she took years ago probably initiated her cancer. I'd never taken any type of medicine other than an occasional aspirin. I had no reason to believe I was at risk for breast cancer.

As I soaked up a few minutes alone with God each day, I knew He wouldn't allow the mammogram to weigh on my mind without reason. Psalm 145:14–15 illustrates that God gives me what I need as I need it--not before and not after. "The LORD upholdeth all that fall, and raiseth up all those that be bowed down. The eyes of all wait upon thee; and thou givest them their meat in due season" (Psalm 145:14–15).

Each day of my vacation, I spent time alone with the Lord in prayer and study. I did not know why I felt such urgency to schedule the mammogram as soon as I returned home; I just knew I needed to do it. I revised my goals, adding the mammogram appointment and daily time with God to my list. Returning home, I felt very relaxed and energized, confident in my written goals. I scheduled and completed a mammogram, but my resolution to spend time each day with the Lord was quickly replaced with soccer schedules, overtime, and volunteer work. At the office, I was annoyed when I was interrupted by a call from the mammogram technician. "We need you to come in for a follow-up test," she said. "It's no big deal, but you have some dense tissue we need to look at more closely since you have a family history of breast cancer."

If it's no big deal, why bother? I wondered. Reluctantly, I added the follow-up appointment to my schedule.

The second test was inconclusive. An ultrasound was scheduled just to be "on the safe side." The dense tissue appeared as a tiny spot on the ultrasound screen. I couldn't understand all of the concern over a one-centimeter spot, but my doctor encouraged me to have a biopsy. I hesitated to add another appointment to my schedule, but I remembered the urgency I felt at the beach to schedule the first appointment. I decided to go ahead with the procedure.

I can't remember exactly what the doctor said to me when he called me at the office with the biopsy results. I heard the words "malignant," "chemotherapy," "radiation"—strange, unbelievable words that floated around my thoughts and spilled out in silent tears across my pillow that night.

How could a tiny spot be cancer? How could it be that it was already starting to spread to my other organs? I was only 41, and my youngest child was only 4! I focused on the diagnosis and that focus increased my fear. I had accepted Jesus in my heart as a young child, yet I refused to lift my eyes from the disease, so I could not see down the path. Ecclesiastes 3:11 (NIV) teaches: "He has made everything beautiful in its time. He has also set eternity in the hearts of men; yet they cannot fathom what God has done from beginning to end."

I learned that cancer treatment is much more debilitating to the human body than cancer itself. Chemotherapy kills bad cells, but it kills good cells, too. My immune system was wiped out, and I couldn't be around people because they could unintentionally infect me with a virus that could kill me. I took a leave of absence from work. There were many days my husband would carry me from the bathroom floor to my bed because I was too weak to stand. When my 4-year-old daughter stroked my hair, it crumbled and fell out into her hand.

As a lifelong Christian, I believed I would be exempt from such pain. If only I had paid attention to Job 1:7: "And the LORD said unto Satan, Whence comest thou? Then Satan answered the LORD, and said, From going to and fro in the earth, and from walking up and down in it." The enemy was always awake, looking to attack. I was unprepared.

Isolated from my friends and family, I turned to my journal more and more, praying and recording Scripture. I knew from God's Word that He would receive my questions. Proverbs 2:2–3: "So that thou incline thine ear unto wisdom, and apply thine heart to understanding; Yea, if thou criest after knowledge, and liftest up thy voice for understanding." One day, my body broke out into a cold sweat and I was trembling in my bed. I could not lift my head from my pillow nor could I lift a phone to call for help. I shut my eyes and asked God if I was going to die.

God answered my question, just as He said He would in Proverbs 8:17: "I love them that love me; and those that seek me early shall find me." Once again, God had set aside a time just for the two of us when He would plant a small seed of knowledge for what was ahead. I felt a warm rush of blood through my veins. Uncertainty vanished. I could breathe without pain for the first time in weeks. I knew I had received His healing touch because He allowed me to see a bit farther down the path, which He had prepared for me last summer. Physical healing began.

I learned that the meaning of life is not revealed by my job or my good intentions. The meaning of life is revealed to me in the Easter (Resurrection) story. When faith begs for renewal, the resurrection of Jesus provides the answer. When I am not listening, my ever-present Father will bring me to a place where I will have no choice.

Staying grounded through wisdom literature reminds me of God's faithfulness, even during the attack of the enemy (as in Job's story). My responsibility is to focus on His Word so that I will understand He is not only with me through every season of life, but He will also prepare the correct path for me. I never want to forget that His infinite knowledge lies ahead of me on this path, waiting to receive me through every circumstance. I am a cancer survivor. As much as I believe in the power of journalizing my path to success, ultimate success is achieved by staying on a path paved by the wisdom of God's Word—God's perpendicular path.

Barbara Carr-Phillips *is a freelance writer and has published many short stories, articles, and essays.*

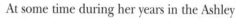

Elizabeth Freeman

The year was 1780. The residents of Massachusetts gathered in the town square to hear the reading of their new state constitution. It started out sounding very much like the United States Declaration of Independence. A young female slave called Mum Bett was listening.

"All men are created free and equal, and have certain natural, essential, unalienable rights; among which may be reckoned the right of enjoying and defending their lives and liberties; that of acquiring, possessing, and protecting property; in fine, that of seeking and obtaining their safety and happiness."

As Mum Bett returned to the Ashley household, she thought about the implications for all people—men, women, slaves, Black people. Yes, freedom is a God-given right, since God created all people equal.

Bett was probably born about 1742 as a slave in the Peter Hogenboom family in Claverack, New York. But, at some point in her life, she and her sister, Betsy, were sold to the John Ashley family in Sheffield, Massachusetts. Bett was a strong woman. When John's wife, Hannah, tried to strike Betsy with a heated shovel, Bett put up her arm to prevent the blow to her sister. As Bett's wound healed, she refused to roll down her sleeve, but left it up as a reminder to all of the cruel treatment that Hannah Ashley gave to her slaves.

At some time during her years in the Ashley household, Bett married and had a daughter named Betsy. Her husband fought in the Revolutionary War and died.

In 1780, she went to see Theodore Sedgwick, a lawyer who believed in the abolition of slavery. Sedgwick enlisted the support of Tapping Reeve, the founder of the first American Law School. Together they defended both Bett and Brom, another Ashley household slave. The lawyers argued that "all men are born free and equal" meant that no one should be enslaved. The court in Great Barrington, Massachusetts, agreed, thus abolishing slavery in the state of Massachusetts. John Ashley was ordered to pay Bett and Brom for their labor and to pay damages, as well.

Mum Bett became the first African American woman to be freed under the Massachusetts constitution, which helped lead Massachusetts to be the first state in the union to abolish slavery. Slaves had no last names, so Bett changed her name to Elizabeth Freeman. She was probably 85 when she died in 1829.

Source:
Africans in America/Part 2/Elizabeth Freeman (Mum Bett). http://www.pbs.org/wgbh/aia/part2/2p39.html (accessed July 26, 2010).

Teaching Tips

September 4
Bible Study Guide 1

Words You Should Know

A. Depart (Proverbs 3:7) *cuwr* (Heb.)—Avoid, shun.

B. Firstfruits (v. 9) *re'shiyth* (Heb.)—Beginning, best, chief.

Teacher Preparation

Unifying Principle—Wisdom for Living.
Proverbs 3 teaches that trusting in God's wisdom helps develop strong faith and reveals purpose and meaning in life.

A. Pray for your students and lesson clarity.

B. Study and meditate on the entire text.

C. Complete the companion lesson in the *Precepts For Living Personal Study Guide®*.

D. Use a dictionary to compare and contrast *knowledge* and *wisdom*. Be prepared to discuss.

O—Open the Lesson

A. Open with prayer, including the Aim for Change. After prayer, introduce today's subject.

B. Read the Aim for Change and Keep in Mind verse in unison.

C. Then compare and contrast *knowledge* and *wisdom*.

D. Ask students to share times they've leaned *on their own* understanding and the results.

E. Have students read the In Focus story, and ask them how they relate to the characters in the story.

P—Present the Scriptures

A. Have volunteers read the Focal Verses.

B. Now use The People, Places, and Times; Background; Search the Scriptures; At-A-Glance outline; In Depth; and More Light on the Text to clarify the verses.

E—Explore the Meaning

A. Dividing the class into groups and assigning one or two questions to each, answer questions in the Discuss the Meaning, Lesson in Our Society and Make It Happen sections. Representatives can report their responses.

B. Read through the Focal Verses and list the benefits of wisdom.

N—Next Steps for Application

A. Write some take-away principles under the Follow the Spirit and Remember Your Thoughts sections.

B. Close with prayer.

Worship Guide

For the Superintendent or Teacher
Theme: Righteousness and Wisdom
Song: "I Will Trust in the Lord"
Devotional Reading: Psalm 115:3–11
Prayer

Righteousness and Wisdom

Bible Background • PROVERBS 3:1–35
Printed Text • PROVERBS 3:1–12 | Devotional Reading • PSALM 115:3–11

———— Aim for Change ————

By the end of the lesson, we will: IDENTIFY God's principles for living purposeful lives; TRUST that God's wisdom reveals purpose and meaning of life; and SEEK God's wisdom when making choices in daily life.

———— In Focus ————

"We can do this together," Sonyia offered.

Yolonda didn't know how to respond. She was hurt that her business partner branched off into another area of business without consulting her, especially a business Yolonda didn't believe in. "So, what do you say?" Sonyia asked.

"First, let me say congratulations. Unfortunately, I won't be joining you. I love *this* business. This is where I'm supposed to be."

"Yeah, but we're financially struggling. We chase checks every day. Aren't you tired of living like this?"

While Yolonda's answer was an affirmative, she knew going into a business just to make money was the wrong thing to do. As far as she was concerned, there were too many people in the business for the wrong reasons. She knew people who'd opened those kinds of businesses without any experience in the field and were now driving luxury cars and living in expensive houses. One company in their office complex shut down when the owner was charged with fraud. Yolonda knew it was her conviction to stay put.

"Yes, I'm tired of being broke, but I believe in the business we started. This business will be around long after the state stops funding the others," Yolonda said.

Today's lesson teaches that wisdom protects, preserves, and provides.

———— Keep in Mind ————

"Trust in the LORD with all thine heart; and lean not unto thine own understanding" (Proverbs 3:5).

"Trust in the LORD with all thine heart; and lean not unto
thine own understanding" (Proverbs 3:5).

13

Focal Verses

KJV **Proverbs 3:1** My son, forget not my law; but let thine heart keep my commandments;

2 For length of days, and long life, and peace, shall they add to thee.

3 Let not mercy and truth forsake thee: bind them about thy neck; write them upon the table of thine heart:

4 So shalt thou find favour and good understanding in the sight of God and man.

5 Trust in the LORD with all thine heart; and lean not unto thine own understanding.

6 In all thy ways acknowledge him, and he shall direct thy paths.

7 Be not wise in thine own eyes: fear the LORD, and depart from evil.

8 It shall be health to thy navel, and marrow to thy bones.

9 Honour the LORD with thy substance, and with the firstfruits of all thine increase:

10 So shall thy barns be filled with plenty, and thy presses shall burst out with new wine.

11 My son, despise not the chastening of the LORD; neither be weary of his correction:

12 For whom the LORD loveth he correcteth; even as a father the son *in whom* he delighteth.

NLT **Proverbs 3:1** My child, never forget the things I have taught you. Store my commands in your heart,

2 for they will give you a long and satisfying life.

3 Never let loyalty and kindness get away from you! Wear them like a necklace; write them deep within your heart.

4 Then you will find favor with both God and people, and you will gain a good reputation.

5 Trust in the LORD with all your heart; do not depend on your own understanding.

6 Seek his will in all you do, and he will direct your paths.

7 Don't be impressed with your own wisdom. Instead, fear the LORD and turn your back on evil.

8 Then you will gain renewed health and vitality.

9 Honor the LORD with your wealth and with the best part of everything your land produces.

10 Then he will fill your barns with grain, and your vats will overflow with the finest wine.

11 My child, don't ignore it when the LORD disciplines you, and don't be discouraged when he corrects you.

12 For the LORD corrects those he loves, just as a father corrects a child in whom he delights.

The People, Places, and Times

Solomon. He is the author of the majority of the book of Proverbs and the son of King David of Israel by Bathsheba. As David's life was full of turmoil and darkness (though with many triumphs and blessings), he wanted a different life for his lastborn. His hope for a calmer life began with naming the child; Solomon's name means *the peaceful one.*

Solomon's life was much more peaceful and affluent than his father's life. Perhaps that can be attributed to the way Solomon lived. When God gave him a choice, Solomon chose wisdom over riches (1 Kings 3:4–9), and was known as the wisest man ever to live.

Like his father, Solomon chronicled his life through his writings—David through the book of Psalms, and Solomon through Song of Songs, Proverbs, and Ecclesiastes. In Proverbs 3, Solomon is persuading his own son on the benefits of living wisely.

Proverbs. A proverb can be defined as a brief and to-the-point saying that expresses a basic truth or practical precept. Teaching by proverbs was an ancient way of teaching among the Greeks, and it was popularly used because of its plain and simple methodology.

Background

Though many regard the book of Proverbs as a collection of wise sayings from primarily King Solomon, we would do well to regard the Holy Spirit as the ultimate source. The proverbs are just as timely to be practiced today as when they were first given.

The first chapters of Proverbs are looked upon as a preface—an introduction that explains the book's scope, intention, and background. In most Bibles, Proverbs 1 is labeled as "The Purpose of Proverbs," and chapter two is considered as an invitation to the benefits of wisdom. Chapter three outlines the benefits of wisdom when they are applied because of one's trust in God.

At-A-Glance

1. Three Regards (Proverbs 3:1–6)

2. Three Exhortations (vv. 7–12)

In Depth

1. Three Regards (Proverbs 3:1–6)

King Solomon advises his son with three regards. The first—to have a continual regard for God's precepts—can be found in verses 1 and 2. Verse 1 reads, "My son, forget not my law; but let thine heart keep my commandments." Solomon admonished his son to do more than memorize the Scriptures. Knowing that God's Word can be forgotten as quickly as it is memorized, Solomon encouraged his son to keep God's commandments in his heart. While the mind records words, the heart paints pictures with detail and emotions, and gives purpose and inspiration to mere words. There is an often-quoted adage, "People will forget what you said, they will forget what you did, but they will never forget how you made them feel." It is true that the heart retains what the mind forgets.

The second concern that Solomon encouraged his son to keep was a regard for God's promises, as found in verse 3. "Let not mercy and truth forsake thee: bind them about thy neck; write them upon the table of thine heart." Solomon made sure to let his son know that life wouldn't always be rosy. He encouraged his son to depend on God's promises and faithfulness during difficult times. He urged him to wear God's promises and faithfulness as one wears a treasured necklace, never meant to be removed by its owner.

Solomon taught that his son must also have a continual regard for God's providence. Verse 5 reads, "Trust in the LORD with all thine heart; and lean not unto thine own understanding." Though Solomon was wise and rich and had many forms of success, he taught that none of these things would have been possible without God. So Solomon encouraged his son to seek God's will, direction, and provision for his life through prayer.

Just as David desired a more peaceful life for his son Solomon, Solomon wanted the same for his own son. Solomon knew that if his son kept a persistent and continual regard for God's precepts, promises, and provision, he would lead a life of unspeakable advantages.

2. Three Exhortations (vv. 7–12)

Solomon was an exhorter, one who inspired others to action through encouragement. In verses 7 through 12, he gave his son three exhortations, each enforced with a good reason. The first can be found in verse 7, "Be not wise in thine own eyes: fear the LORD, and depart from evil." To fear the Lord is to live humbly and dutifully before Him. Some people who consider themselves as wise are self-reliant, prideful, conceited, and arrogant. It is impossible to fear the Lord and be wise in your own eyes. In verse 8, Solomon cited the advantage of fearing the Lord. It is good health and strength of the body, or "health of thy navel and marrow to thy bones."

"Honour the LORD with thy substance and with the firstfruits of all thine increase," is the second exhortation, and is found in verse 9. Solomon lived in luxury but recognized that it was poor substance if he had not honored the Lord with it. Solomon was known for dedicating his belongings to the Lord, and he encouraged his son to do the same. The blessing of giving back to the Lord what He gives us is "increase," as indicated in verse 9.

Verse 11 contains the third exhortation, wherein Solomon advises his son not to disregard God's correction. Solomon knew that hating, ignoring, or hardening oneself, while under affliction, prolongs it. While being corrected by God is hard, it is necessary. Solomon taught his son that God's correction

is not vindictive or for punishment. It is for grooming and producing, and is done out of love. The advantage of being receptive to God's correction includes sharing a close, delightful, and loving relationship with God.

Search the Scriptures

1. What are the advantages of keeping God's Word in the heart (Proverbs 3:2, 4)?

2. Whose path is directed (v. 6)?

3. Whom does the Lord correct (v. 12)?

Discuss the Meaning

Read verses 11 and 12 and consider this: If God gives to those who give back to Him, then why are so many tithing Christians financially struggling?

Lesson in Our Society

The cares of life are choking the strength out of families. Financial challenges, underemployment, depression, and addictions are just a few of the things that pull parents away from their families. Today, many parents are too worried, too busy, and too overwhelmed to take time with their children. As a result, we find many children sexting, murdering, failing school, doing drugs, and having babies. In Proverbs 3, we find Solomon—a busy king with 700 wives and 300 concubines—making time to teach his son how to live. How can the Black church as a spiritual community empower parents to become active participants in their children's lives, in spite of life's challenges?

Make It Happen

If it is not us personally, then we all know people who are struggling to raise their children. Try your best not to judge yourself or them as bad parents, and commit to do better yourself, or to help them do better. Pray for direction, and ask God for help. Do something productive this week: find a counselor, attend a parenting support group, talk with your pastor or other godly parents, get active in your child's school, and definitely talk to your child. With God, it is possible to restore and resurrect parent-child relationships.

Follow the Spirit

What God wants me to do:

_____

_____

_____

_____

Remember Your Thoughts

Special insights I have learned:

_____

_____

_____

_____

More Light on the Text

Proverbs 3:1–12

1 My son, forget not my law; but let thine heart keep my commandments;

The writer of Proverbs begins the chapter with the affectionate and familial language of endearment, "my son." He exhorts his "son" and, by implication, the reader not to forget his "law" (Hebrew *torah,* **to-RAW**) or the teachings and commandments that are to follow. To "forget" (Hebrew *sakach,* **shaw-KAKH**) does not merely refer to the natural slippage of memory that can result from drinking alcohol as in 31:7. Here, "forget" refers to willful, deliberate neglect and

diversion of attention (cf. 2:17). The author of Hosea conveys this latter sense more clearly in Hosea 4:6 where God threatens to "forget" Israel's sons because of their sins. The deliberateness in Proverbs 3:1 is also present in the word "keep" or, literally, "retain" (Hebrew *natsar,* **naw-TSAR**). The word occurs in Proverbs about 25 times. "Keep" is more than mere rote memory or passive retention. The father (teacher) states the reason and reward of obedience in 3:2. Obedience will bring a long and peaceful life. Just like there is a price to pay when we forget important things, there is a reward for obedience and remembering to do the right things. Although this passage applies to the Scripture as we now have it, the law and commandments to which the writer alludes are those that immediately follow, from verse 3 onward. The admonition, "let thine heart keep my commandments," implies, of course, spiritual obedience, that is, an obedience which arises from the inward principles of the heart being in harmony with the spirit of the Ten Commandments, but it implies, further, external conformity to their requirements: we are "to observe to do" them (Deuteronomy 8:1).

2 For length of days, and long life, and peace, shall they add to thee.

The expression, "length of days" (Heb. *'orek yowm,* **o-REK yowm**), literally means "extension of days" and signifies the prolonging of life; its duration to the appointed limit. It occurs again in verse 16 and in Job 12:12 and Psalm 21:4. It is important to note that "length of days" is represented as a blessing in the Old Testament, depending, however, as in these verses present, on the fulfillment of certain conditions. Thus in the fifth commandment, God added a long life to the honoring of parents (Exodus 20:12), and God promised "length of days" to Solomon at Gibeon, on the condition that he walked in the ways, statutes, and commandments of God (1 Kings 3:14). The Jewish expression "long life" (Heb. *shaneh chay,* **shaw-NEH KHAH-ee**), literally means "years of life," although containing the thought of longevity stated in the previous expression "length of days," amplifies it. It is life in a qualitative sense—a life worth living, the good life, indicated by "peace" or *"shalom"* (cf. also v. Proverbs 3:17). The teachings also bring a state of wholesome, peaceful well-being primarily realized in relations among people. In 3:2, peace is not just a matter of inner tranquility or absence of trouble; peace includes material "prosperity" (NIV) or wholesomeness. One could live long without truly living. So the idea of the years of life is that there will be many years in their fullest sense—true happiness and enjoyment. However, we must be careful not to understand "prosperity" only as having money to pay bills, buy food, etc., as a financial enticement to righteousness.

3 Let not mercy and truth forsake thee: bind them about thy neck; write them upon the table of thine heart:

Verse 3 actually shows how far removed Proverbs is from an ethic of external obedience and reward. "Mercy" (Heb. *cheçed,* **KHEH-sed**) and "truth" (Heb. *'emeth,* **EH-meth**) are the two basic covenant terms in Israel. *Cheçed* in this context is essentially fidelity to obligations arising from a relationship while *'emeth* is essentially that upon which one can rely, that which is stable. However, the exhortation to hold on to mercy and truth is more than an emphasis on trust in God's fidelity to the covenant. It includes internal character. It is firmness and constancy in keeping and executing one's promise, hence the NIV translation, "faithfulness." Obedience is more than lip

service or outward show. Instead, it must become an integral part of the disciple—internal character of the heart. The author looks for inner integrity that manifests itself in all interactions with God and people. The command to "bind them about thy neck; write them on the table of thine heart" further indicates that the character of the reader is in view rather than just his/her behavior. By "binding" and "writing" the teacher is stressing that the teachings become a part of the disciple's nature. A disciple is to hold the teachings permanently in memory; make them an indelible part of his/her character. We require more than being reminded. Writing on the tablet of the heart (cf. Proverbs 7:3; Jeremiah 17:1) signifies permanency (Isaiah 30:8; Jeremiah 31:33b).

4 So shalt thou find favour and good understanding in the sight of God and man.

The verse states the outcome and provides the final motivation: "favour and good understanding." The Hebrew word for "understanding" (*sekel,* **SHE-kel**), although capable of different meanings, here refers to regard and reputation. As in 2 Chronicles 30:22, it denotes the judgment awarded to anyone, the favorable opinion one has concerning him or her. Both God and humans will approve such a person. To find favor "in the sight of God" is to be acceptable to God and enjoy a sense of His approval. Favor "in the sight of . . . man" is that which others feel toward those whose character can be found blameless. For example, Genesis claims Joseph to have found favor in the sight of his keeper while in prison (Genesis 39:21). In Proverbs 3:4 "good understanding" indicates the way others see us—their perspective or attitude. Although godly people suffer at first where they are not fully known or when among those opposed to God, a truly godly and benevolent character will, in general, be prized wherever it is well known.

5 Trust in the LORD with all thine heart; and lean not unto thine own understanding.

There are two commands in verse 5. The first is to trust God with all one's heart. The word "trust" (Hebrew *batach,* **baw-TAKH**) carries the force of relying on someone for security; one's confidence is to be in the Lord and not in human understanding. "Trust" in God does not mean faith as a mental assent to a theological proposition. Trust actively negates any thoughts of passivity or resignation. It connotes a feeling of security and confidence in the fulfillment of expectations. To trust in God is to believe that He can and will do what He has promised and is supposed to do. Realizing that we are, in and of ourselves, incapable of assuring our own success and happiness, we should trust God and not for a moment doubt His wisdom to discern what is ultimately best for us. The call here is for a trust characterized by total commitment—"with all your heart" (v. 5, NIV) and "in all your ways" (v. 6, NIV). We, like Abraham, must be fully persuaded that He is faithful to fulfill what He has promised (Romans 4:21). From this conviction, we are to commit all our concerns to Him so that we can be directed, ordered, and overruled as His infinite wisdom sees best. "Trust in God" (Hebrew *biynah,* **bee-NAW**), means giving up one's confidence or trust in one's own understanding exclusively. The command to trust God "with all your heart" (Proverbs 3:5) means that the total personality is to be committed to God's care, although it emphasizes the mind and volition. The prohibitions are against depending on one's own understanding and against intellectual pride (vv. 5b, 7a). We are to use our understanding, but we must not transfer to it any measure of dependence that should

be placed on God alone. These expressions call for absolute obedience and surrender in every realm of life. Relying on one's own human (natural) understanding, or setting a high value on one's own wisdom are the opposites of a trusting dependence on God. The commitment of the heart to God means that all the beliefs and decisions of life are to be submitted to God. Every practical decision of life is in view here. Human wisdom is inadequate, but divine wisdom is sufficient for guidance in life.

6 In all thy ways acknowledge him, and he shall direct thy paths.

Verse 6 literally translates as "in all your ways, know Him." To know God in all our ways means giving constant attention to the divine will and presence. We often consider some things important and some less important; some small and some casual, but we must acknowledge God in all things, even in those that we sometimes consider accidental. When obedient faith is present, the Lord will direct or, literally, "make straight" the believer's paths in spite of difficulties and hindrances. James Moffatt paraphrases the verse nicely: "Have the mind of him wherever you may go, and he will clear the road for you" (*A New Translation of the Bible*). We are to acknowledge God: (1) by referring everything to Him; (2) by praying for and expecting His divine guidance; and (3) by consulting and applying His will as revealed in His Word. This trust and acknowledgment do not exclude or preclude our own individual endeavor. We must think well, consult wisely, act diligently, and trust wholly. The assurance in this verse is that God will direct our lives and enable us to reach our destination.

7 Be not wise in thine own eyes: fear the LORD, and depart from evil.

Verses 7 and 8 are essentially a repetition of verses 5 and 6, where the writer urges the reader to trust in the Lord. Here the author urges us not to take ourselves too seriously, but to reverence the Lord and avoid evil. The admonition is a warning against self-sufficiency, self-conceit, and self-reliance. This verse formulates the principle of relying on God rather than on one's intellectual resources and wisdom. To be "wise in thine own eyes" is to be in an utterly hopeless situation. According to 26:12, there is more hope for a fool than for such a person! Trust in God means giving up confidence in oneself, honoring God with one's material wealth and allowing God to become one's teacher and father. Even when one acquires wisdom, one must hold to humility and not allow confidence in his or her intellect and learning to displace the demands of confidence in God and faith. Here, too, there is a difference between human wisdom and divine wisdom (cf. Isaiah 5:21). There must be a higher source, and Proverbs 3:7b clarifies it: "fear the LORD and shun evil" (NIV).

8 It shall be health to thy navel, and marrow to thy bones.

Compliance with the wisdom of verse 7 is therapeutic: it will bring health to the body and nourishment for the frame. The healing that the fear of the Lord and avoidance of evil bring is first spiritual. The benefit of true wisdom is physical health and vigor. The navel and the bones are symbols for the whole body. Knowledge of God that leads to spiritual well-being has its effects on psychological and physical aspects of human personality. As health to the navel and marrow to the bones represent physical strength, so the fear of the Lord is the spiritual strength of God's children.

9 Honour the LORD with thy substance, and with the firstfruits of all thine increase:

An important element in a person's relationship with God is honoring Him with one's wealth and firstfruits—to give back to God some of one's wealth as a sacrifice in recognition that God is our source. Many scholars have noted the uniqueness of these verses that command a liturgical (worship, ritual) offering (see Exodus 23:19; Numbers 28:26–27; Deuteronomy 18:4; 26:1–2). The admonition reminds the faithful of their religious duties to God. "Honour" (Hebrew *kabad*, **kaw-BAD**), as in this Scripture, sometimes implies giving gifts or benefits (Numbers 22:37; 24:11; Judges 9:9). Nevertheless, "honour" here also signifies, as usual, showing respect and paying homage. Kidner poignantly states, "To 'know' God in our financial 'ways' is to see that these *honour* Him" (*Proverbs*, 64). The Hebrew word *hôwn* (**hone**), here translated as "substance" or literally, wealth, refers to the product of one's righteous labors (see the Septuagint, LXX). "Firstfruits" refers to topmost, first in its kind, or simply, the best. "Increase" or abundance translates the Hebrew word *tebûw'âh* (**teb-oo-AW**), which refers to the produce of the earth—one's own crops and husbandry. The implication of these words is that one must give to the Lord from the entire range of one's possessions. Our profession of faith in Christ is a mockery unless it affects how we spend our money as well as all other concerns of life. Our possessions ought to be consecrated to God, spent in conscious obedience to His will and used for His glory—as in the sustenance of worship, the support and extension of missions, the relief of the poor, the sick, the needy, the widow and orphan (cf. James 1:27).

10 So shall thy barns be filled with plenty, and thy presses shall burst out with new wine.

The command to give is followed by the promise of blessings in the "barns" (Hebrew *'açâm,* **aw-SAWM**) or storehouses and the "presses" for making wine. When one honors God with a portion of one's increase, he or she will receive material blessings. We can and should trust God with our gifts and for our material needs. These verses show a principle of stewardship rather than a guarantee of material wealth and prosperity. The promise held out to encourage the devotion of one's wealth to Jehovah's service, while appearing at first sight as selfish and questionable is in reality a trial of faith. The promise echoes the language of Moses in Deuteronomy 28:1–8, where, among other things, he promises that in return for full obedience to God, Jehovah will command a blessing upon the "storehouses" (v. 8) and industry. The principle is otherwise expressed in Proverbs 11:25 and is exemplified in other passages in the Old Testament (Haggai 1:3–11; 2:15, 19; Malachi 3:10–12), and in the New Testament (2 Corinthians 9:6–8; Philippians 4:14–19).

11 My son, despise not the chastening of the LORD; neither be weary of his correction:

The final specific instruction warns the disciple not to rebel against the Lord's discipline, because it is evidence of His love. Abundant prosperity shall flow from honoring Jehovah, but He sometimes sends affliction and indeed, without this life would be incomplete. The verb "despise" (Hebrew *ma'ac,* **maw-AS**) is "to reject" and "to condemn." "Chastening" (Heb. *muwcar,* **moo-SAWR**) means "correction" not by reproof only (as in Proverbs 6:23; 8:30) but by punishment also (13:24; 22:15). The meaning here is expressed by the Greek word *paideia* (**pahee-DI-ah**), and is found in the Septuagint LXX, which is "instruction by punishment," discipline, or schooling. To "be weary" means to loathe, abhor, feel disgust, or vexation toward someone. So the expression "neither be weary" reinforces the previous phrase "despise not" and represents a more deeply seated aversion to Jehovah's plans. The word "correction", like *muwcar* in Proverbs 3:11, has a twofold meaning of either punishment or chastening, as in Psalm 73:14; or reproof or rebuke, as in Proverbs 1:23; 5:12; and 15:31. It is here used to mean "chastening" or "punishment." To loathe the correction of Jehovah is to allow the aversion to estrange us completely from Him. If we are spiritually "weary of his correction"— if we "resent his rebuke" (3:11, NIV)—we ignore our belief in the truth that "all things work together for good to them that love God" (Romans 8:28, KJV).

12 For whom the LORD loveth he correcteth; even as a father the son in whom he delighteth.

The verse provides the motive for submissiveness to God's corrections—they are the corrections of covenantal love. The writer employs the familial relationship of father and son in order to reconcile us to God's corrections. God corrects those whom He loves after the same manner as a father corrects the son whom he loves—an idea that is taken from Deuteronomy 8:5. The idea of the paternal relationship of God to humankind is found elsewhere (Jeremiah 31:9; Malachi 2:10) and especially finds expression in the Lord's Prayer. When we learn the truth of this passage, we shall be drawn to, rather than repelled from, God by His corrections. Proverbs 3:12 finds its parallel in Job 5:17, "Behold, happy is the man whom God correcteth: therefore despise not thou the chastening of the Almighty." The gracious end of earthly trials appears also in Hebrews 12:2–6; compare this with Romans 5:3–5 and 2 Corinthians 4:17. One must accept suffering as an act of divine love, not repudiate it and rebel against one's condition. One must not engage in indignant questioning, scornful rebellion, and proud efforts of stoical (indifference to pain or pleasure) fortitude.

Sources:

Baltes, A. J., ed. Biblespeech.com. http://biblespeech.com (accessed July 6, 2010).

Clarke, Adam. *Clarke's Commentary, Vol. 2: Job–Malachi.* Nashville, TN: Abingdon, n.d.

Clifford, Richard J. *Proverbs.* Louisville, KY: Westminster John Knox Press, 1999.

Garrett, Duane A. *Proverbs, Ecclesiastes, Song of Songs. New American Commentary, Vol. 14.* Nashville, TN: Broadman, 1993.

Hebrew and Greek Lexicons. Bible Study Tools.com. http://www.biblestudytools.com/lexicons (accessed September 16, 2010).

Horton, Robert Forman. *The Book of Proverbs.* New York: A. C. Armstrong, 1891.

Kidner, Derek. *Proverbs: An Introduction and Commentary.* Downers Grove, IL: InterVarsity Press, 1964. 64.

Merriam-Webster Online Dictionary. Merriam-Webster, Inc. http://www.merriam-webster.com (accessed July 6, 2010).

Moffatt, James. *A New Translation of the Bible: Containing the Old and New Testaments.* London: Hodder and Stoughton, 1935. 695.

Strong, James. *New Exhaustive Strong's Numbers and Concordance with Expanded Greek-Hebrew Dictionary.* Seattle, WA: Biblesoft, and International Bible Translators, 1994.

Say It Correctly

Chronicles. KRO-ni-kəlz.
Septuagint. Sep-TOO-ə-jint.
Torah. TO-ra.

Daily Bible Readings

MONDAY
The Sun of Righteousness
(Malachi 4:1–6)

TUESDAY
Remember All the Commandments
(Numbers 15:37–41)

WEDNESDAY
God Is Our Help and Shield
(Psalm 115:3–11)

THURSDAY
God's Abundant Blessings
(2 Corinthians 9:6–12)

FRIDAY
Wisdom in Relationships
(Proverbs 3:27–35)

SATURDAY
The Profit from Wisdom
(Proverbs 3:13–26)

SUNDAY
Trust in the Lord
(Proverbs 3:1–12)

Teaching Tips

September 11
Bible Study Guide 2

Words You Should Know

A. Incline (Proverbs 4:20) *natah* (Heb.)—To stretch out, extend, offer.

B. Perverse (v. 24) *lezuwth* (Heb.)—Deviant, crooked.

Teacher Preparation

Unifying Principle—The Wise Path. Proverbs 4 suggests that to live life to the fullest, we must make good choices and keep a righteous path.

A. Pray for lesson clarity.

B. Study and meditate on the entire text.

C. Complete the companion lesson in the *Precepts For Living Personal Study Guide®*.

O—Open the Lesson

A. Begin class with prayer, including the Aim for Change.

B. Explain that today's lesson is about living life to the fullest by choosing to walk on God's righteous paths.

C. Read the Keep in Mind verse in unison.

D. Then ask students to share times when they refused godly instruction and their outcomes.

E. Tell students that today's lesson refutes the belief that life (or parenting) doesn't come with instructions.

F. Read and discuss the In Focus story.

P—Present the Scriptures

A. Analyze the Focal Verses.

B. To clarify the verses, use The People, Places, and Times; Background; Search the Scriptures; At-A-Glance outline; In Depth; and More Light on the Text.

E—Explore the Meaning

A. Assign a question from the Discuss the Meaning section to three groups. After ten minutes of discussion, have each report their responses.

B. Read the Lesson in Our Society. Discuss.

C. After reading the Focal Verses, identify points of instruction that promote wise living.

N—Next Steps for Application

A. Write insights you've gained under the Follow the Spirit and Remember Your Thoughts sections.

B. Remind students to complete the Daily Bible Readings.

C. Close with prayer and praise.

Worship Guide

For the Superintendent or Teacher
Theme: From Generation to Generation
Song: "Order My Steps"
Devotional Reading: Jeremiah 31:7–11
Prayer

From Generation to Generation

Bible Background • PROVERBS 4:27
Printed Text • PROVERBS 4:10–15, 20–27 | Devotional Reading • JEREMIAH 31:7–11

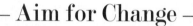

———— Aim for Change ————

By the end of the lesson, we will: EXPLAIN how the teachings from the proverb promote wise living; CONSIDER living wisely and following a straight path; and DEVELOP a strategy for making good choices and living a godly life.

———— In Focus ————

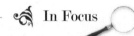

Kim had gone to three stores looking for the colorful bracelets her 8-year-old daughter, Destiny, wanted. She chastised herself for waiting until today to look for them. Sunday after church was not the best time to shop for anything.

When Kim and Destiny went into the fourth store, Destiny ran right to the bracelets. "Mom, they're here!"

Kim snatched a couple of bags of bracelets and led her daughter to the counter. "Praise the Lord," she told the cashier.

"Praise Him, sister," the cashier responded. "So, you're a believer?"

"Yes, ma'am."

"Well, you should know what these bracelets mean. Your daughter is too young to know, but girls her age like them because they're colorful and are cute animal shapes. But older girls give them to boys because the colors stand for certain sexual acts. I know it sounds crazy, but what is innocent today might mean meet-me-behind-the-bleachers tomorrow."

Kim didn't hesitate to put the bracelets back, and she allowed Destiny to take her time choosing another gift.

In today's lesson, we will find a father teaching his son the importance of making good choices and staying on the right path.

———— Keep in Mind ————

"Take fast hold of instruction; let her not go: keep her; for she is thy life"
(Proverbs 4:13).

"Take fast hold of instruction; let her not go: keep her; for she is thy life"
(Proverbs 4:13).

Focal Verses

KJV **Proverbs 4:10** Hear, O my son, and receive my sayings; and the years of thy life shall be many.

11 I have taught thee in the way of wisdom; I have led thee in right paths.

12 When thou goest, thy steps shall not be straitened; and when thou runnest, thou shalt not stumble.

13 Take fast hold of instruction; let her not go: keep her; for she is thy life.

14 Enter not into the path of the wicked, and go not in the way of evil men.

15 Avoid it, pass not by it, turn from it, and pass away.

4:20 My son, attend to my words; incline thine ear unto my sayings.

21 Let them not depart from thine eyes; keep them in the midst of thine heart.

22 For they are life unto those that find them, and health to all their flesh.

23 Keep thy heart with all diligence; for out of it are the issues of life.

24 Put away from thee a froward mouth, and perverse lips put far from thee.

25 Let thine eyes look right on, and let thine eyelids look straight before thee.

26 Ponder the path of thy feet, and let all thy ways be established.

27 Turn not to the right hand nor to the left: remove thy foot from evil.

NLT **Proverbs 4:10** My child, listen to me and do as I say, and you will have a long, good life.

11 I will teach you wisdom's ways and lead you in straight paths.

12 If you live a life guided by wisdom, you won't limp or stumble as you run.

13 Carry out my instructions; don't forsake them. Guard them, for they will lead you to a fulfilled life.

14 Do not do as the wicked do or follow the path of evildoers.

15 Avoid their haunts. Turn away and go somewhere else,

4:20 Pay attention, my child, to what I say. Listen carefully.

21 Don't lose sight of my words. Let them penetrate deep within your heart,

22 for they bring life and radiant health to anyone who discovers their meaning.

23 Above all else, guard your heart, for it affects everything you do.

24 Avoid all perverse talk; stay far from corrupt speech.

25 Look straight ahead, and fix your eyes on what lies before you.

26 Mark out a straight path for your feet; then stick to the path and stay safe.

27 Don't get sidetracked; keep your feet from following evil.

The People, Places, and Times

Way of wisdom. The way of wisdom might be synonymous with "the paths of righteousness" identified in Psalm 23:3, but it is not an actual path or walkway. It is metaphorical for choosing a godly lifestyle. A person who walks in the way of wisdom or chooses a godly lifestyle rejects peer pressure, avoids making bad and uninformed decisions, and lives by God's Word. The way of wisdom is a narrow and tight road. Not many take it. It is restrictive and can be difficult to stay on. Its walkers believe that life is too short to mess up.

Background

In our lesson text, we find Solomon teaching his children how to shun peer pressure.

He taught them to be mindful of the places they go, the company they keep, and the words they speak. It may be hard for us to imagine the kind of trouble kids in Solomon's day got into, and we probably don't believe it was anything like the trouble kids get into today. Today, we see and hear of reports about youth violence, ungodly youth trends, and crimes perpetrated against youth. But as Solomon wrote in Ecclesiastes 1:9 (NIV), "There is nothing new under the sun." Youth then were not exempt from trouble.

At-A-Glance

1. Two Paths, Two Different Outcomes (Proverbs 4:10–15)

2. Practice Makes Perfect (vv. 20–27)

In Depth

1. Two Paths, Two Different Outcomes (Proverbs 4:10–15)

Simply put, Solomon taught that life is a two-way street and that his children could go the right way (the way of wisdom) or in the wrong direction (the path of the wicked). Similar to God, Solomon allowed his children to choose by telling them in effect, "I have led you in the right paths; the rest is up to you." Solomon taught his children by example and showed them how to hide God's Word in their hearts, how to recognize ungodliness, and how to shun evil. Though he was not a perfect man, his children were witnesses to the blessings of God upon Solomon's life.

He warned that the way of wisdom would not always be easy, and that it was not a popular road. When parents know what they put into their children, they can usually know what to expect out of them. Solomon stressed the importance of choosing the way

of wisdom so that his children's lives would be different from their aunts and uncles. Their uncle Absalom had his half-brother Amnon killed for raping his sister Tamar, and he later tried to steal his father's kingdom but instead was killed. Then when David was advanced in years, their uncle Adonijah tried to have himself declared king instead of Solomon. Solomon knew that adherence to God's Word could break the cycle of violence and sexual sins among the men in his family. He taught that the way of wisdom is a path to long life, prosperity, and happiness.

2. Practice Makes Perfect (vv. 20–27)

To Solomon, it was not enough to tell his children to choose the way of wisdom and not give them practical tips on doing so. In these verses, he advised them to: (1) guard their hearts, (2) set a guard over their mouths, (3) attend to what they see or look upon, and (4) be considerate in all they do.

As verse 23 points out, the heart must be guarded as the issues of life flow from it. To keep one's heart undefiled by sin, we must keep up good thoughts and keep out bad ones. The heart is defiled by sinful and evil thoughts and desires. A well-kept heart produces glory unto God and goodness toward others. Out of a poorly kept heart comes murder, lust, lying, envy, and other sins.

Verse 24 includes another practical tip: to set a guard over one's mouth. Negative words slip out of a perverse and "froward" (distorted, crooked—evil speaking) mouth, but a mouth that is well-guarded is careful not to curse, swear, lie, or slander.

Solomon warns against having a roving eye. In verse 25, he tells his children to only look straight ahead—not behind, not to the sides, not even above. Be focused only on what is in front of you. Keep your eye on the Lord. A wandering eye (as Eve had when she saw that the forbidden fruit was pleasing to the eye) can lead to ensnarement.

Make no decisions rashly is what Solomon taught in verse 26 when he wrote, "Ponder the path of thy feet." He tells them to weigh their actions. If they were to put God's Word on one balance of a scale and their actions on the other, they would easily be able to make right and informed decisions (see v. 27). He teaches his children to take the steady direction and the sure paths so that their ways might be successful.

Search the Scriptures

1. According to Solomon's teaching, what would give life (Proverbs 4:13)?

2. What advice did Solomon give regarding the path of wickedness (v. 14)?

Discuss the Meaning

Read verse 26 and consider this: If you continue to work for the next 10 years as you do today, what will you have gained?

Lesson in Our Society

When related to teenagers, it is called peer pressure, but concerning adults, it's called keeping up with the Joneses. Using peers as a benchmark for where one should be is dangerous and leads to other evils. Keeping up with the Joneses has plagued African American communities and many others with debt, depression, and fear.

Make It Happen

Read the Focal Verses again. What if Solomon was talking to his children about their financial lives? Evaluate your finances. Which path are you taking—the wide one that leads to poverty, or the narrow, tight one that leads to prosperity? What financial plan can you put together, based on the Focal Verses, to get or keep you on the right road?

Follow the Spirit

What God wants me to do:

_____

_____

_____

_____

Remember Your Thoughts

Special insights I have learned:

_____

_____

_____

_____

More Light on the Text

Proverbs 4:10–15, 20–27

Introduction

Proverbs 4 is essentially divided into three parts. Verses 1 through 9 focus on a father's relaying of advice to his "children" (v. 1) that he received from his father. This is followed by verses 10 through 19, which are dominated by the doctrine of two ways and where language of taking a journey occurs frequently. The third section, which ends chapter 4, focuses primarily on achieving a holistic sense of health. Throughout the first and second sections, the father guides his son in "the way of wisdom" and "along straight paths" (v. 11, NIV). The son's "steps will not be hampered," and he "will not stumble" if he follows the father's instruction (v. 12, NIV). In addition, the father warns him not to "set foot on the path of the wicked," or head their way (v. 14, NIV). The righteous walk in the safe light of day. "But the way of the wicked is like deep darkness; they do not know what makes them stumble" (v. 19, NIV). Verses 10 through 15—the core of this advice—begin this week's text.

10 Hear, O my son, and receive my sayings; and the years of thy life shall be many.

The section starts with the admonition to "hear" (Hebrew *shâmà*, **shaw-MAH**), which not only means to listen carefully but also to obey. The importance and the link between listening and obedience is heightened by the Hebrew word *lâqach* (**law-KAKH**), translated "receive," which also means "to accept" and "take to instruction." There must be attentiveness and a willingness to appropriate what is taught. The consequence is that the life of the pupil "shall be many," which means he or she will be given a long life. Adam Clarke sums up the second part of the verse very well. He writes, "Vice and intemperance impair the health and shorten the days of the wicked; while true religion, sobriety, and temperance, prolong them. The principal part of our diseases springs from 'indolence, intemperance, and disorderly passions.' Religion excites to *industry*, promotes *sober habits*, and destroys *evil passions*, and *harmonizes* the soul; and thus, by preventing many diseases, necessarily prolongs life" (Clarke, 712). How true those words are even today.

11 I have taught thee in the way of wisdom; I have led thee in right paths. 12 When thou goest, thy steps shall not be straitened; and when thou runnest, thou shalt not stumble.

Beginning from verse 11, the father/teacher gives additional reasons why his authority should be respected and the teaching followed, so that his commands may not be judged as harsh and arbitrary. He uses the figure of a road to make a comparison. Living according to wisdom is like walking or running on a safe road, a road that is well defined, where the feet can tread on good surface and take a course that will be free of unnecessary obstacles, so that progress will be certain. On such a road, one can move along with easy strides and be sure of smooth progress. "Thy steps shall not be straitened" means the journey will not encounter restraint, confinement, or rebuke. It is a metaphor taken from those who walk in a straight (narrow, troubled) and uneven path, where they are apt to stumble and fall. When one lives by this teaching—"thou shalt not stumble"—nothing will impede progress. Those under the influence of sound biblical teachings ponder their paths and carefully examine circumstances as they occur; the fear of God leads them to act in an upright, honest manner, and thus their way in business and life is both clear and large. They are without fear of being tripped up by unpredictable, seemingly insurmountable obstacles.

13 Take fast hold of instruction; let her not go: keep her; for she is thy life.

The admonitions of this verse challenge the believer to urgent faithfulness. Not only is wisdom the means of making progress in life, it is life itself. Anything so essential must be enthusiastically maintained. This is the import of the Hebrew word *châzaq* (**khaw-ZAK**) translated here as "take fast hold of," "cleave to," and "be obstinate about" something. The believer must not let go of the truths of God's words and must not allow God's words to go unheeded. Elsewhere, "instruction" (Heb. *muwcar*, **mo-SAWR**) also means "self-discipline," or "moral religious education" (see Proverbs 1:3). Here it refers to discipline, such as parental counsel. It is our duty to hold to the truth that God has revealed to us and to attend to the commandments that He has sent us. But it is also for our own soul's profit. Divine truth is not a mere luxury; it is a necessity of life.

14 Enter not into the path of the wicked, and go not in the way of evil men. 15 Avoid it, pass not by it, turn from it, and pass away.

Here begins a command to avoid evil association, which is a source of mischief to everyone, but especially to the young, who are more imitative and whose habits are undergoing development. "Evil men"—primarily as were noted in chapter 1—are bloodthirsty men of violence. The warning is to avoid evil ways and evil men by not starting on the wicked path of life. The rapid sequence of imperatives in verse 15 stresses the urgency of the matter. In addition, the expressions used continue the comparison of lifestyle with traveling along a path—only now the lifestyle to consider is evil. Phrases such as "avoid it" and "pass not by it" state in the strongest terms to get as far away from evil as possible. Whether for the sake of worldly gain, or through a desire to please others, never approach the pathway along which you would not wish to be found when God calls you into the eternal world. The serious purpose of our soul should be to shun every appearance of evil.

4:20 My son, attend to my words; incline thine ear unto my sayings. 21 Let them not depart from thine eyes; keep them in the midst of thine heart.

The rest of the chapter consists of warnings, which are permeated by a metaphorical use of body parts. The ear is to remain keen for listening to wise advice (v. 20); the eyes are to stay fixed on right teaching (vv. 21, 25), and the feet are to stay on the right path (vv. 26–27). The mouth and lips must shun using twisted words (v. 24). Above all, the heart must be guarded by sound doctrine (vv. 21, 23). If the son listens to his father, his whole body will be healthy (v. 22). By using ears, eyes, and heart, the teacher is exhorting the whole person to receive the teaching.

The son is first advised to heed the wise words of the father. The word "attend" translates the Hebrew word *qâshab* (**kaw-SHAB**), which means to incline the ear attentively. The restating of this phrase in the same verse underscores its importance.

22 For they are life unto those that find them, and health to all their flesh.

The reason for heeding the instruction is that the father's words of wisdom are the means of life and health. The human condition apart from God is regarded as a condition of death or enfeebled by sickness, but obeying wise advice can restore the listener to life, health, and soundness. This brings up the old Latin quotation, *"mens sana in corpore sano,"* which means "a sound mind in a sound body." The Hebrew verb *mâtsà* (**maw-TSAW**), "to find," implies an activity and suggests a deliberate effort to get possession of and procure wisdom. It does not automatically come to a person. The "health" that is promised here is physical, emotional, and spiritual—the whole person. God's words bring deliverance from the evils that harm and hinder life. Nothing preserves soul and body in a healthier state than when we always keep before our eyes and carry in our hearts good doctrine. "All their flesh" implies the completeness of the restoration; it is not confined to one part, but pervades the whole body.

23 Keep thy heart with all diligence; for out of it are the issues of life.

Verse 21 instructs the believer to guard wisdom in the heart for it is the wellspring of life. The heart is the starting point of life's activities (23:19); it determines the course of life. "Heart," here as elsewhere, refers not to the physical organ but to the mind and the entire personality of the individual. The capacity to live with joy and vigor ultimately comes from within and not from circumstances. The corrupt heart draws one down to the grave, but wisdom protects the heart from that corruption. John Flavel, in his book *Keeping the Heart*, very wisely observed, "The greatest difficulty in conversion is to win the heart to God; and the greatest difficulty after conversion is to keep the heart with God" (Flavel, 2). As the living stream "issues" from the physical heart in its normal, healthy condition, to vitalize and nourish every part of the body, so in spiritual things the heart is the seat of the Lord of life and glory. The streams of spiritual life proceed from Him to all the powers and faculties of the soul. We must, therefore, be vigilant about our treatment of wisdom. The Hebrew term for "diligence" (*mishmar,* **mish-MAWR**) is very emphatic; it means "to set double guards" such as those which provide high-level security. This forcefulness of expression plainly implies how difficult it is to "keep" our hearts, and how dangerous to neglect them! Care must be taken that the fountain not be stopped up nor injured. We must be circumspect and careful with the thoughts we express.

24 Put away from thee a froward mouth, and perverse lips put far from thee.

After the father challenges his son to store wisdom in his heart and watch over his heart with all diligence, he gives the son a series of instructions involving his mouth, eyes, and feet. Centuries later, Paul referred to our bodies as "members of Christ" that we can use either as instruments of righteousness or unrighteousness (1 Corinthians 6:15–20). The commands in Proverbs 4:24–27 concerning our mouths, eyes, and feet can be obeyed only when we are watching over our hearts with full vigilance. Otherwise, we will have a type of external obedience only (such as that of the Pharisees in the days of Jesus). The heart works in tandem with the tongue and as such, starts with it. As the source of life, the heart sends up the thoughts that the tongue expresses in words. Words flow out of the heart. A believer must avoid the words that swerve from truth and purity to lies, prevarication, deceit, and wrong discourse of every kind. Instead, righteousness must control the tongue, and twisted and crooked speech must be shunned. Truthful speech is the product of wisdom (see 8:13; 10:32).

25 Let thine eyes look right on, and let thine eyelids look straight before thee.

The final exhortation returns to the imagery of the path (vv. 25–27). The idea is that one should not be distracted from the way of wisdom (v. 25). "Look straight before thee" is an expression of unswerving directedness toward a goal. The person who does this pursues wisdom single-mindedly, not looking to the right or the left to check out other options and is not distracted by temptation to leave the correct path. The foolish person is always looking around for different objects of desire. As the story of John Bunyan in *Pilgrim's Progress* well illustrates, temptations lie on both sides of the way, requiring one to focus directly ahead and walk without deviating to either side, without even glancing at them. As the author of Proverbs often states, winking or squinted eyes are symptoms of unreliability and guile (6:13; 10:10; 16:30). The wise person will have an unswerving directness, but the fool is easily distracted (17:24).

26 Ponder the path of thy feet, and let all thy ways be established.

Here the warning is not to allow our feet to take us down the wrong path. Proverbs speaks of the foolish as having "feet that are quick to rush into evil" (6:18, NIV; see also 1:16). By contrast, the wise stay on the path of life, the path of righteousness. Proverbs 15:21 says that "a man of understanding keeps a straight course" (NIV). By contrast, the foolish man follows paths that are "crooked" (2:15). Having feet that stay on the path of righteousness demonstrates a single-minded pursuit of wisdom. The word "ponder" (Heb. *pâlaç*, **paw-LAS**) means "to make level," "to weigh," and metaphorically, "to consider, to deliberate." The sense is that one must consider undertakings well by examining them thoroughly beforehand and pondering whether they are right and proper, so that one may have confidence in the righteousness of conduct and the providential ordering of the result (Psalm 119:133; Hebrews 12:13).

27 Turn not to the right hand nor to the left: remove thy foot from evil.

Proverbs 4:27 repeats the warning in verse 25 in a manner reminiscent of Deuteronomy 5:32; 17:11; 28:14; and Joshua 23:6. Proverbs 4:27 is closely connected with verse 26, which it more fully explains. As in verse 25, the gaze is to be concentrated; the feet are not to deflect nor turn aside to byways. Nothing is to be permitted to divert the believer from the right way, neither adversity, nor prosperity, nor anything that can possess the power of temptation. The disciple must not allow anything to turn him or her aside the path of virtue, honesty, and fair dealings in all matters of faith.

Sources:

Baltes, A. J., ed. Biblespeech.com. http://biblespeech.com (accessed July 6, 2010).

Clarke, Adam. *Clarke's Commentary, Vol. 2: Job–Malachi.* Nashville, TN: Abingdon, n.d. 712.

Clifford, Richard J. *Proverbs.* Louisville, KY: Westminster John Knox Press, 1999.

Flavel, John. *Keeping the Heart.* http://www.the-highway.com/heart1_Flavel.html (accessed June 7, 2010).

Garrett, Duane A. *Proverbs, Ecclesiastes, Song of Songs. New American Commentary, Vol. 14.* Nashville, TN: Broadman, 1993.

Hebrew and Greek Lexicons. Bible Study Tools.com. http://www.biblestudytools.com/lexicons (accessed September 16, 2010).

Merriam-Webster Online Dictionary. Merriam-Webster, Inc. http://www.merriam-webster.com (accessed July 6, 2010).

Plaut, W. Gunther. *Book of Proverbs.* New York, NY: Union of American Hebrew Congregations, 1961.

Strong, James. *New Exhaustive Strong's Numbers and Concordance with Expanded Greek-Hebrew Dictionary.* Seattle, WA: Biblesoft, and International Bible Translators, 1994.

Notes

Say It Correctly

Deuteronomy. D(y)oō-tə-RAH-nə-mē.
Pharisee. FA-rə-sē.

Daily Bible Readings

MONDAY
Guard Your Heart and Mind
(Proverbs 23:15–19)

TUESDAY
Walk Uprightly
(Psalm 84:8–12)

WEDNESDAY
Keep God's Commandments
(Joshua 23:1–8)

THURSDAY
Lifelong Protection
(Psalm 91:9–16)

FRIDAY
Walk in Your Parents' Paths
(Proverbs 1:8–15)

SATURDAY
Prize Wisdom
(Proverbs 4:1–9)

SUNDAY
Walk the Straight Path
(Proverbs 4:10–15, 20–27)

Notes

_____

_____

_____

Teaching Tips

September 18
Bible Study Guide 3

Words You Should Know

A. Abomination (Proverbs 15:26) *towèbah* (Heb.)—A disgusting thing.

B. Reproof (vv. 31, 32) *towkechah* (Heb.)—Rebuke, correction, punish, chastisement.

Teacher Preparation

Unifying Principle—Good Advice. Proverbs 15 emphasizes the importance of obtaining godly wisdom in order to live well and succeed.

A. Pray for lesson clarity.

B. Study and meditate on the entire text.

C. Complete the companion lesson in the *Precepts For Living Personal Study Guide*®.

D. Collect photographs of sources people use to seek advice such as counselors, horoscopes, palm readers, etc.

O—Open the Lesson

A. Open with prayer, including the Aim for Change.

B. After prayer, introduce today's subject—"Teaching Values."

C. Then read the Aim for Change and Keep in Mind verse in unison. Afterward, have students identify sources where people seek advice. Share the photographs you collected.

D. Ask students to share times they've taken someone's bad advice, and the results—differentiate between accepting good and bad advice.

E. Read the In Focus story. Discuss.

P—Present the Scriptures

A. Have volunteers read the Focal Verses.

B. Now use The People, Places, and Times; Background; Search the Scriptures; At-A-Glance outline; In Depth; and More Light on the Text to clarify the verses.

E—Explore the Meaning

A. Instruct the class to silently read the Discuss the Meaning section and answer the questions.

B. Evaluate the Lesson in Our Society and Make It Happen.

N—Next Steps for Application

A. Summarize today's lesson.

B. Write important notes under the Follow the Spirit and Remember Your Thoughts sections.

C. Close with prayer.

Worship Guide

For the Superintendent or Teacher
Theme: Teaching Values
Song: "Speak to My Heart, Lord"
Devotional Reading: Proverbs 1:1–7
Prayer

Teaching Values

Bible Background • PROVERBS 10:1–15:33
Printed Text • PROVERBS 15:21–33 | Devotional Reading • PROVERBS 1:1–7

—————— Aim for Change ——————

By the end of the lesson, we will: DISCUSS the advice given in the lesson that promotes godly wisdom; REFLECT on experiences of following both good and bad advice; and DECIDE to follow the advice offered in the proverb.

———— In Focus ————

Keisha was trying to keep her cool, but her toddler-niece, Jasmine, was getting into everything and her sister Tasha wasn't doing anything about it. Keisha refused to intervene because Tasha didn't like for anyone to tell her how to raise her child. But when Jasmine almost fell, Keisha couldn't resist.

"Tasha, do you see Jasmine? She's climbing all over the coffee table."

"Get down, Jasmine."

Keisha rolled her eyes at her sister. She could've told the baby not to do that, she thought. Keisha got up and peeled Jasmine away from the table. "If you do that again, I'm going to pop your behind," she scolded.

"You ain't gonna hit my baby."

"That's what's wrong with her now. Our parents whupped us and we turned out decently," Keisha assessed.

"Whupped? We got beat, and I'm not treating my child like an animal."

"But she's acting like one."

Tasha took Jasmine from Keisha. "Well, how about me and my animal go home then."

"That's not what I meant. I'm just trying to give you some advice. If you don't discipline her now, you'll be sorry later."

Without advice and support, the path of life is downward. In today's lesson, the advantages of good advice are outlined.

—————— Keep in Mind ——————

"He that refuseth instruction despiseth his own soul: but he that heareth reproof getteth understanding" (Proverbs 15:32).

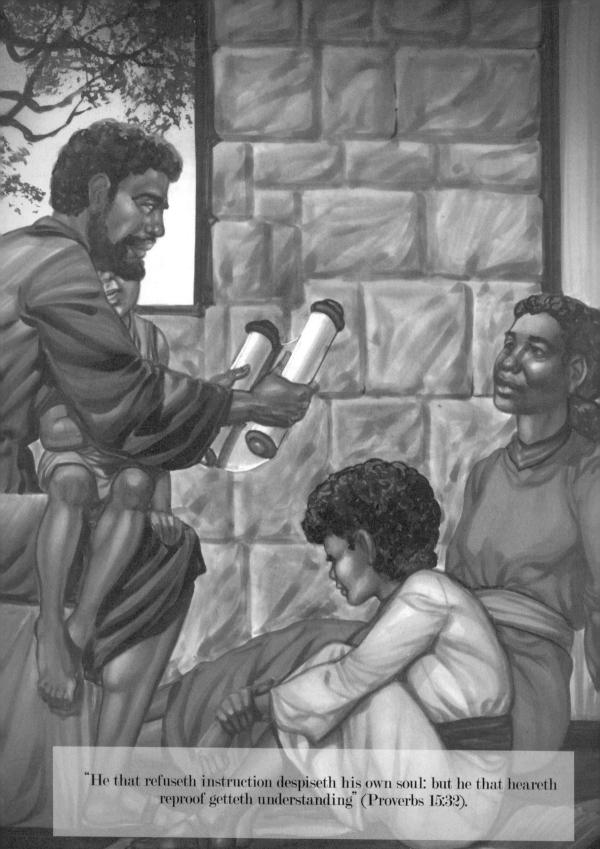

"He that refuseth instruction despiseth his own soul: but he that heareth reproof getteth understanding" (Proverbs 15:32).

Focal Verses

KJV **Proverbs 15:21** Folly is joy to him that is destitute of wisdom: but a man of understanding walketh uprightly.

22 Without counsel purposes are disappointed: but in the multitude of counsellors they are established.

23 A man hath joy by the answer of his mouth: and a word spoken in due season, how good is it!

24 The way of life is above to the wise, that he may depart from hell beneath.

25 The LORD will destroy the house of the proud: but he will establish the border of the widow.

26 The thoughts of the wicked are an abomination to the LORD: but the words of the pure are pleasant words.

27 He that is greedy of gain troubleth his own house; but he that hateth gifts shall live.

28 The heart of the righteous studieth to answer: but the mouth of the wicked poureth out evil things.

29 The LORD is far from the wicked: but he heareth the prayer of the righteous.

30 The light of the eyes rejoiceth the heart: and a good report maketh the bones fat.

31 The ear that heareth the reproof of life abideth among the wise.

32 He that refuseth instruction despiseth his own soul: but he that heareth reproof getteth understanding.

33 The fear of the LORD is the instruction of wisdom; and before honour is humility.

NLT **Proverbs 15:21** Foolishness brings joy to those who have no sense; a sensible person stays on the right path.

22 Plans go wrong for lack of advice; many advisors bring success.

23 Everyone enjoys a fitting reply; it is wonderful to say the right thing at the right time!

24 The path of life leads upward for the wise; they leave the grave behind.

25 The LORD tears down the house of the proud, but he protects the property of widows.

26 The LORD detests evil plans, but he delights in pure words.

27 Greed brings grief to the whole family, but those who hate bribes will live.

28 The heart of the godly thinks carefully before speaking; the mouth of the wicked overflows with evil words.

29 The LORD is far from the wicked, but he hears the prayers of the righteous.

30 A cheerful look brings joy to the heart; good news makes for good health.

31 If you listen to constructive criticism, you will be at home among the wise.

32 If you reject discipline, you only harm yourself; but if you listen to correction, you grow in understanding.

33 Fear of the LORD teaches wisdom; humility precedes honor.

The People, Places, and Times

Hell. In the Old Testament, the Hebrew word for hell is *sheol*, and it is defined as a grave, pit, an underworld, and an abode of the dead. Hell is characterized as a place of no return, a place of punishment for the wicked. In the New Testament, the word for hell is translated *Hades* and *Gehenna*. While *Hades* still means grave and underworld, *Gehenna* (translated as "lake of fire") is known as a place of future punishment and torment.

Multitude of Counselors. Separately, the translated words for "multitude" and "counselors" mean a great number of people who advise and consult.

Background

As pointed out in lesson one, the beginning of the book of Proverbs is a preface, an introduction to the actual proverbs. The proverbs—short but weighty sentences—begin in chapter 10. Most of them are *distichs*, two-sentence couplets in each verse that illustrate each other. Each proverb sets before us the advantages and disadvantages, the blessings and curses, and the difference between the wise and foolish.

The verses in our lesson text outline the blessings of good advice. The author points out that plans created by one person tend to be less effective than they could be. Wise planning encourages participation and counsel from a variety of people.

At-A-Glance

1. Right Actions
(Proverbs 15:21–22, 24–25, 27)

2. Right Speaking (vv. 23, 26, 28)

3. Right Thinking (vv. 31–33)

In Depth

1. Right Actions (Proverbs 15:21–22, 24–25, 27)

Solomon offered that it is easier to know what to do when one seeks the advice of others. He encouraged his children to shy away from making decisions alone and to avoid hasty decision-making. Obtaining counsel from others promotes sound judgment, support, and success.

Because fools isolate themselves when they make decisions, their overconfidence will lead them to failure, and they may stumble when they come upon defeating circumstances that they could have foreseen and prepared for, if they had used wisdom.

The language of 15:24 possibly anticipates what later Scripture will clearly teach about the ultimate destination of the wise and righteous way of life. The writer means primarily that leading such a life preserves the wise and good from a disastrous death (14:32). The path may be steep, hard, and painful, but the good man's path leads heavenward (Philippians 3:20). The believer's affections are set "on things above" (Colossians 3:2).

According to verse 27, bribery, direct and indirect, is the bane of public men and the curse of a country. Those who make the most of their position for their own pockets, who make laws and administer them for their own selfish ends, ought to remember these words—they are laying up trouble for their own families.

2. Right Speaking (vv. 23, 26, 28)

While speaking well is a strength, speaking right is vital. An articulate person speaks well—he knows how to express himself, pronounces his words precisely, and is verbally captivating—but a wise person speaks right. According to Proverbs 15:23, 26, and 28, right speaking includes knowing when to speak, speaking with pure motives and good intentions, and speaking profitably, truly, and pertinently.

A fool speaks wrongly. His words are ill-timed, and he says whatever comes to his mind. He speaks with evil intent, and he dishonors the hearers of his words.

Thus, it is the right word spoken at the right time. It may not be the word that is sought and asked for. It may even be an unwelcome word, a startling word, a word of rebuke. Whether by way of advice and counsel, or of exhortation and instruction, or of comfort, the Lord provides such words to His people. As someone once said, "Wisdom is not just speaking your mind but your speech." It is of great importance not only to consider the *matter*, but also the *manner* of our utterances.

3. Right Thinking (vv. 31–33)

The hinge on which right speaking and right actions swing is right thinking. Solomon teaches the necessity of developing and maintaining a mind that is God-centered. Such a mind is the wellspring of life. A person who thinks right can accept rebuke. Because he has an open mind, he is teachable and is able to gain understanding. He is directed in good ways.

A foolish person on the other hand is easily offended, despises correction, and is stiff-necked. He thinks he is smarter than others and believes he is above reproach. Yet he fears trouble, his mind rehearses his failures and mistakes, and he is often anxious.

Search the Scriptures

1. What kind of man has joy (Proverbs 15:23)?

2. Whose house will be destroyed (v. 25)?

Discuss the Meaning

Read verse 22 and consider this: If plans fail without counsel, then why do so many people start businesses, ministries, and families without consulting others with relevant experience? Identify barriers to seeking counsel.

Lesson in Our Society

Some families in urban African American communities have been raised to keep quiet about their plans, pregnancies, dreams, and goals for fear of being jinxed, ridiculed, or talked about. It's no wonder disparities exist in education, entrepreneurship, and home-ownership. If plans fail without counsel, then how can we encourage African American churches and communities to seek support and guidance from others?

Make It Happen

Are you one to seek advice from others? If so, with whom do you consult? Sometimes family and friends may not be the best people to consider when you need advice. This is especially true if they are not supportive or experienced in the area about which you have questions. Do you have an important decision to make? If you are on the cusp of entrepreneurship or thinking about launching a ministry, identify at least two to three supportive and experienced people you can talk to about your plans.

Follow the Spirit

What God wants me to do:

_____

_____

_____

_____

Remember Your Thoughts

Special insights I have learned:

_____

_____

_____

_____

More Light on the Text
Proverbs 15:21–33

21 Folly is joy to him that is destitute of wisdom: but a man of understanding walketh uprightly.

Merriam-Webster defines *folly* as "lack of good sense," which leads to terrible results and, in some cases, tragic outcomes. Therefore, the focus of this week's lesson contains serious urgency. The fool delights in folly and does not seem to comprehend the outcome of an immoral deed. He or she follows any whim and finds delight in impulsive behavior because he or she "is destitute of wisdom" (Hebrew *chacer leb*, **khaw-SARE labe**) to see the foolishness in it. To find joy and satisfaction in folly is definitely a sign of stupidity since folly can bring disaster. The senselessness of the fool, paradoxically, gives him joy. In contrast, the wise person has insight, appreciates the potential for danger, and, therefore, walks "uprightly" (Hebrew *yashar*, **yaw-SHAR**), that is, in a "straight course." The verse underscores the importance of good judgment (in Hebrew *tebuw'ah*, **teb-oo-AW**) and suggests that a valuable lifestyle must be maintained by wise decisions.

22 Without counsel purposes are disappointed: but in the multitude of counsellors they are established.

A successful plan requires using good advice; this general observation has value on the personal and national level. Imprudent action brings disaster; prudent action gives security. In contrast to 11:14, where the national interest is at the forefront, consultation here is advised for more personal matters. Failure to seek advice is associated with pride in 13:10. Here, and in 11:14, seeking advice from many counselors can avert disaster. If a person determines the nature of a matter, and goes about its resolution hastily and precipitously, without mature deliberation, without consulting and taking the advice of others in forming a strategy to bring about desired results, it generally comes to nothing.

23 A man hath joy by the answer of his mouth: and a word spoken in due season, how good is it!

As this verse points out when it comes to advice, content and timing have synonymous importance. The well thoughtout and appropriate instruction requires knowledge and wisdom. Obviously good advice and good timing do not always coincide. One of the ideals of the sage was to have the right word at the right time, as this verse indicates. "A word spoken in due season" is advice given at the right moment and in the most suitable manner, when the occasion and the interests at stake demand it (comp. Proverbs 25:11).

24 The way of life is above to the wise, that he may depart from hell beneath.

The meaning in the NLT of "upward" in Hebrew (*ma`al*, **MAH-al**) is not entirely clear. As such, the verse generally is taken to mean that "upward" refers to this physical life and contrasts with "departing from hell beneath," or literally going down to "hell" (Heb. *sheol*, **sheh-OLE**) or "the grave" (NLT), because the idea of immortality is not clearly revealed in Proverbs. Such an upward life tends to material and spiritual health. Primarily, a long and happy life is promised to those who fear the Lord, as stated in Proverbs 3:16; additionally, the promise includes avoidance of the downward course, which ends in hell. The point here would be that the righteous expect to live long and healthy lives (2:20–22; 3:18; 5:6).

25 The LORD will destroy the house of the proud: but he will establish the border of the widow.

The Lord administers His justice through righteousness. He brings down the proud but protects the needy. The proud, self-confident man shall be uprooted along with his family, his household, and his wealth. The second part of verse 25 refers to the particular vulnerability of the widow in Israelite society, since she had none but herself to mount a defense against encroachments and oppression (Isaiah 1:23; Jeremiah 7:6). The widow often typifies weakness and desolation in the Scriptures (see Deuteronomy 10:18; Psalm 146:9). God will take the widow under His protection and see to it that her property is secured. In a country where property was defined by landmarks—stones or similar objects—nothing was easier than to remove these altogether, or alter their position. Scripture amply confirms that the Lord champions the cause of the widow, the orphan, the poor, and the needy.

26 The thoughts of the wicked are an abomination to the LORD: but the words of the pure are pleasant words.

The Ten Commandments, by forbidding coveting, showed that God's Law touched the thought of the heart as well as the outward action. The idea here refers to wicked plans or designs, rather than the secret movements of the mind. The phrase "but the words of the pure are pleasant words" means literally that words of a soothing, comforting tone are not an abomination to the Lord, as are the devices of the wicked; they are pure in a ceremonial sense, as a pure and acceptable offering. The Lord is pleased with plans that have righteous intentions. "Pleasant words" are not sweet nothings; they are the opposite of the "evil plans" of verse 26 (NLT), and thus express the virtuous designs of the just.

These affect not only others, but also oneself, as they act in a healing manner, according to 16:24. On the one hand, the intentions or "thoughts of the wicked" (Heb. *machshabah ra`*, **makh-ash-aw-BAW rah**) are thoughts that will harm other people; these are an abomination to the Lord.

27 He that is greedy of gain troubleth his own house; but he that hateth gifts shall live.

Those who are secure in their circumstances will not succumb to the evil devices of avarice. The "greedy" (Heb. *boseà` batsà*, **bo-SEE-ah baw-TSAH**) is the one who wants a big cut, who is in a hurry to get rich, and who is not particular how it happens. The word "troubleth" (Heb. *àkar*, **aw-KAR**) reminds one of the story of Achan, who, in his greed, appropriated some of the spoil of the banned city Jericho and brought destruction upon himself and his family, when, in punishment of the crime, he and all his family were stoned in the Valley of Achor (Joshua 7:25). So, too, the covetousness of Gehazi caused the infliction of leprosy upon himself and his children (2 Kings 5:27). In Proverbs 15:27, "gifts" (Heb. *mattan*, **mat-TAWN**) could be innocent enough, but they may alter one's values. Hating bribes is the safest path to follow.

28 The heart of the righteous studieth to answer: but the mouth of the wicked poureth out evil things.

Speech is the one thing that many think they have a right to squander. There is probably no more common recklessness than that of the tongue. Yet experience teaches us to be economical with the expense of the tongue. In this verse, we find a contrast between a deliberate speech and a deluge of thoughtless words. The New International Version says that the heart or mind of the righteous "weighs" or "studieth" (Heb. *hagah*, **daw-GAW**), or "considers," "muses," "meditates,"

41

how to answer. The thoughtful discourse of the just is the opposite of the rash, actually "evil" speech of the "wicked" (Heb. *rà*, **rah**). Those who are wise are cautious in how they answer, as opposed to the wicked, who blurt out vicious things. The advice is to say fewer but better things.

29 The LORD is far from the wicked: but he heareth the prayer of the righteous.

The author stresses the importance of approaching God with the right attitudes and conduct. Wickedness puts distance between God and the sinner (Exodus 33:3; Isaiah 59:2). Those who turn their ears away from hearing God's words are inattentive to God's commands, thus making their prayers abominable to God (Psalm 10:1; Proverbs 15:8; 28:9). The distance of God from humans is a symbol of His not hearing their prayers (e.g., Psalm 10:1). The wicked keep a distance from Him; so He is "far" (Heb. *rachaq*, **raw-KHAK**) from them—an idea that signifies He is inaccessible or deaf to their appeals. Of course, a prayer of repentance by the wicked is the exception, for by it they would become the righteous.

30 The light of the eyes rejoiceth the heart: and a good report maketh the bones fat.

Good news is uplifting to hear. The Hebrew *ma'owr`ayim* (**maw-ORE AH-yim**) which means literally "light of the eyes," and in NIV "cheerful look," may indicate the gleam in the eyes of someone who tells good news, as the parallel second clause suggests. The idea of "health to the bones" (NIV) comes from a Hebrew expression found in the KJV "maketh the bones fat," and it is a symbol of health and prosperity. (See also Proverbs 17:22; 25:25.)

31 The ear that heareth the reproof of life abideth among the wise.

A teachable person is willing to become wise. Verse 31 shows how someone who listens to "constructive criticism" (NLT) will feel comfortable among wise people. The development of wisdom requires a willingness to hear and integrate perspectives that may run counter to previously held convictions. This is the implication of the word "reproof," which could mean "censure" but also includes the idea of arguing as well as showing and maintaining the right. This is also in opposition to the "scorner" of verse 12 and to anyone who will not listen to reproof. A listener who hears a rebuke receives it gratefully and obeys it. "Advice is for them that will take it," says one of the old proverbs, and the meaning here is nearly the same. To abide "among the wise" implies that either a person who listens to reproof will thereby be made wise and be esteemed as one of that number; or rather, he or she seeks out and delights in the company and conversation of the wise, by whom he or she may be admonished. On the contrary, fools who hate reproof, avoid and abhor the society of wise men and reprovers.

32 He that refuseth instruction despiseth his own soul: but he that heareth reproof getteth understanding.

Verse 32 emphasizes the reward of teachability (compare with 10:12). The teacher returns to the connection between discipline and understanding, and the neglect of discipline and death. If embracing instruction leads to the preservation of life, he that "refuseth" (Heb. *parà*, **paw-RAH**) neglects or willfully rejects and despises it—throws it all in the way of danger. This willful rejection of wise counsel is tantamount to considering one's "own soul" as vile and worthless, as the word "despise" (Heb. *mâ'ac*, **maw-AS**) signifies. According to the Septuagint (the Greek version of the Old Testament commonly designated by LXX), such a person commits moral suicide because he does not follow the path of life. He is like a sick man who "thrusts away" (Gk. *apotheitai*, **ap-o-THEH-om-ahee**) the wholesome medicine that offers his only hope of cure. In contrast, the person who hears reproof acquires understanding. Discipline is often at odds with youthful inclinations, but accepting discipline is both necessary and important to spiritual development. Being a good disciple demands being a good listener, which in turn implies a willingness to receive rebuke.

33 The fear of the LORD is the instruction of wisdom; and before honour is humility.

The verse takes up the theme of "fear of the LORD" from Proverbs 1:7 and 9:10. Humble submission in faith to the Lord is not only the beginning of wisdom but also its continuance. As an old sage once wrote, "No wisdom, no fear of God; no fear of God, no wisdom. No knowledge, no discernment; no discernment, no knowledge." The last part of Proverbs 15:33, "before honour is humility," has its contrast in 18:12, where pride leads to destruction. Here humility brings honor. It is the overestimation of self that makes us contemptuous in any sense toward others. A person who fears God must be humble, and as the fear of God leads to wisdom, it may be said that humility leads to the honor and glory of being wise and reckoned thusly among the wise (v. 31). A man with a lowly opinion of himself will hearken to the teaching of the wise, will scrupulously obey the Law of God, and will be blessed for doing so. "God resisteth the proud, but giveth grace unto the humble" (Proverbs 3:34; see also James 4:6). To look down as from a superior height

on others is the most mischievous hindrance to progress. God shall honor those who have the humility to accept Him and His guidance.

Sources:

Baltes, A. J., ed. Biblespeech.com. http://biblespeech.com (accessed July 6, 2010).

Clarke, Adam. *Clarke's Commentary, Vol. 2: Job–Malachi.* Nashville, TN: Abingdon, n.d.

Garrett, Duane A. *Proverbs, Ecclesiastes, Song of Songs. New American Commentary, Vol. 14.* Nashville, TN: Broadman, 1993.

Hebrew and Greek Lexicons. Bible Study Tools.com. http://www.biblestudytools.com/lexicons (accessed September 16, 2010).

Kidner, Derek. *Proverbs: An Introduction and Commentary.* Downers Grove, IL: InterVarsity Press, 1964.

Merriam-Webster Online Dictionary. Merriam-Webster, Inc. http://www.merriam-webster.com (accessed July 6, 2010).

Murphy, Roland E. *Proverbs.* Nashville, TN: Thomas Nelson, 1998.

Strong, James. *New Exhaustive Strong's Numbers and Concordance with Expanded Greek-Hebrew Dictionary.* Seattle, WA: Biblesoft, and International Bible Translators, 1994.

Say It Correctly

Abomination. Ab-o-mi-NA-sion.
Achan. AY-kan.
Achor. AY-kor.
Gehazi. Ge-HA-dzi.
Jericho. JE-ri-kō.
Naaman. NAY-a-man.
Septuagint. Sep-TOO-ə-jint.
Sheol. SHE-ōl.

Daily Bible Readings

MONDAY
A Wise Child
(Proverbs 10:1–5)

TUESDAY
Wise Words
(Proverbs 10:18–22)

WEDNESDAY
Wisdom and Wealth
(Proverbs 10:23–28)

THURSDAY
The Wicked and the Foolish
(Proverbs 12:12–16)

FRIDAY
A Righteous Life
(Proverbs 14:27–34)

SATURDAY
The Better Way
(Proverbs 15:15–19)

SUNDAY
Instruction in Wisdom
(Proverbs 15:21–33)

Notes

Teaching Tips

Words You Should Know

A. Unsearchable (Proverbs 25:3) *cheqer* (Heb.)—Incomprehensible; beyond human investigation.

B. Debate (v. 9) *riyb* (Heb.)—To strive or plead; to contend against, argue or make a complaint against.

Teacher Preparation

Unifying Principle—Neighborly Advice. The Scripture teaches the importance of wisdom and honor to promote harmony in relationships.

A. Pray for your students and ask God to bring clarity to this lesson.

B. Study and meditate on the entire text.

C. Complete the companion lesson in the *Precepts For Living Personal Study Guide®*.

D. Prepare a presentation (hard copy or PowerPoint) on *wisdom*. List the meaning of *wisdom* and applications for society today.

O—Open the Lesson

A. Open with prayer, including the Aim for Change.

B. Have your students read the Aim for Change and Keep in Mind verse. Discuss the Unifying Principle.

C. Share your presentation.

D. Then ask, "What godly advice do you follow in your relationships?"

E. Allow volunteers to share their testimonies with the class.

F. Now have a volunteer summarize the In Focus story. Discuss.

P—Present the Scriptures

A. Have volunteers read the Focal Verses.

B. Use The People, Places, and Times; Background; Search the Scriptures; At-A-Glance outline; In Depth; and More Light on the Text to clarify the verses.

E—Explore the Meaning

A. Have volunteers summarize the Discuss the Meaning, Lesson in Our Society, and Make It Happen sections.

B. Connect these sections to the Aim for Change and the Keep in Mind verse.

N—Next Steps for Application

A. Make notes of the lesson's principles under the Follow the Spirit or Remember Your Thoughts sections.

B. Close with prayer and praise God for godly advice.

Worship Guide

For the Superintendent or Teacher
Theme: Wisdom and Discernment
Song: "Leaning on
the Everlasting Arms"
Devotional Reading: 1 Kings 3:5–14
Prayer

Wisdom and Discernment

Bible Background • PROVERBS 25:1–28
Printed Text • PROVERBS 25:1–10 | Devotional Reading • 1 KINGS 3:5–14

Aim for Change

By the end of the lesson, we will: KNOW the wisdom of following godly advice in dealing with others; FEEL what it means to treat others as we desire to be treated; and DO an intentional act that promotes harmony with others.

 In Focus

Frantically, Brenda knocked at her neighbor's door. When Veronica opened the door, Brenda asked, "Can you please take me to work? My car won't start! If I'm late another day, I will lose my job."

Immediately, Veronica grabbed her jacket and rushed to take Brenda to work. Later that day, Veronica saw Brenda at the local store, but Brenda didn't speak. Veronica had always spoken to Brenda, but she didn't receive the same response in return.

After Brenda and Veronica had been neighbors for 12 years, Veronica was accustomed to being ignored by Brenda. However, Veronica always treated Brenda with love and compassion. Several weeks later, Brenda called Veronica to drive her to the hospital. Her brother was ill. The entire trip, Veronica spoke but Brenda barely responded. After they arrived at the hospital, Brenda got out of the car without saying anything.

As Veronica drove home, she prayed for Brenda, her family, and decided that she did not want to be treated disrespectfully by Brenda anymore. Veronica asked God to give her instructions on how to deal with Brenda.

How can Veronica continue to reveal God's love to Brenda when her actions are not reciprocated?

Keep in Mind

"Debate thy cause with thy neighbour himself; and discover not a secret to another" (Proverbs 25:9).

"Debate thy cause with thy neighbour himself; and discover not a secret to another" (Proverbs 25:9).

Focal Verses

KJV **Proverbs 25:1** These are also proverbs of Solomon, which the men of Hezekiah king of Judah copied out.

2 It is the glory of God to conceal a thing: but the honour of kings is to search out a matter.

3 The heaven for height, and the earth for depth, and the heart of kings is unsearchable.

4 Take away the dross from the silver, and there shall come forth a vessel for the finer.

5 Take away the wicked from before the king, and his throne shall be established in righteousness.

6 Put not forth thyself in the presence of the king, and stand not in the place of great men:

7 For better it is that it be said unto thee, Come up hither; than that thou shouldest be put lower in the presence of the prince whom thine eyes have seen.

8 Go not forth hastily to strive, lest thou know not what to do in the end thereof, when thy neighbour hath put thee to shame.

9 Debate thy cause with thy neighbour himself; and discover not a secret to another:

10 Lest he that heareth it put thee to shame, and thine infamy turn not away.

NLT **Proverbs 25:1** These are more proverbs of Solomon, collected by the advisers of King Hezekiah of Judah.

2 It is God's privilege to conceal things and the king's privilege to discover them.

3 No one can discover the height of heaven, the depth of the earth, or all that goes on in the king's mind!

4 Remove the dross from silver, and the sterling will be ready for the silversmith.

5 Remove the wicked from the king's court, and his reign will be made secure by justice.

6 Don't demand an audience with the king or push for a place among the great.

7 It is better to wait for an invitation than to be sent to the end of the line, publicly disgraced! Just because you see something,

8 don't be in a hurry to go to court. You might go down before your neighbors in shameful defeat.

9 So discuss the matter with them privately. Don't tell anyone else,

10 or others may accuse you of gossip. Then you will never regain your good reputation.

The People, Places, and Times

Men of Hezekiah. They were scribes or counselors of Hezekiah that compiled and edited 137 proverbs during the reign of King Hezekiah. The Septuagint describes the scribes or group of assistants to Hezekiah as the "Friends of Hezekiah." The words reveal the traditional wisdom and sayings to elevate the forgotten wisdom of David and Solomon.

Hezekiah. Son and successor of Ahaz, Hezekiah was the 15th king of Judah, the Southern Kingdom, who ruled from around 715 to 686 B.C. He began his 29-year reign at the age of 25. Hezekiah was a patron of respect, who removed idolatrous practices and centers, and resumed observance of Passover and temple worship. He prompted civil and religious reform.

Solomon. He was the third king of Israel, David's son, who reigned for 40 years from around 971 to 931 B.C. Solomon is attributed with 3000 proverbs and 1005 songs. He was David's chosen heir; he built

God's Temple in Jerusalem as well as great works that secured the water supply and defended the city of Jerusalem.

Background

The book of Proverbs is a collection of ancient wisdom that parallels pieces of Egyptian and Mesopotamian wisdom literature, such as *The Precepts of Ptah-Hotep* (c. 2500 B.C.), *The Tale of the Eloquent Peasant* (c. 2000 B.C.), and *The Instruction of Amenemope* (c. 1200 B.C.). Proverbs was primarily written by Solomon with contributions from Agur son of Jakeh and Lemuel, a king who received words of wisdom from his mother about wine, women, and legal rights of the weak and poor. Proverbs gives instruction in wisdom, ways of life in God's world, and the preparation for life. The men of Hezekiah transcribed or copied the proverbs and did not author them. Proverbs was formed over a period of several hundred years (c. 1010–699 B.C.).

During the early part of Solomon's reign, he wrote and gathered the book of Proverbs. Solomon passed on his practical advice through the short, concise sentences that communicate moral truth. Forty-seven times the book conveys information about wisdom, which in Hebrew is *chokmah*, essentially, "the skill of living." The wisdom revealed in the book of Proverbs is practical to promote prosperity, productivity, and responsibility in humanity.

At-A-Glance

1. Wisdom Should Build Relationships (Proverbs 25:1–3)

2. Wisdom Should Purify Relationships (vv. 4–5)

3. Wisdom Should Guide Relationships (vv. 6–7)

4. Wisdom Should Handle Relationships (vv. 8–10)

In Depth

1. Wisdom Should Build Relationships (Proverbs 25:1–3)

In Proverbs 25, we read that Hezekiah's men transcribed Solomon's wisdom. Solomon and Hezekiah were both patrons of wisdom in Israel. They were scholarly kings who lived during a time when governmental power and academic power were closely associated. Proverbs 25 through 29 constitute a book within the book of Proverbs. This section gives insight to relationships with kings, but the information can be used to develop good and equitable relationships. The Scripture gives instruction for leaders and individuals who seek to become leaders.

Proverbs 25:2 refers to the "glory of God," which is God's overwhelming presence, authoritative "privilege" (NLT), and display of who God is. God's glory is the ultimate perfection and transcendence. Although God's glory is incomprehensible, Solomon instructs humanity to study and search God's Word (vv. 2–3). The more believers know God, the more we will reflect God's glory. Although difficult at times, the instruction is to search and study God's Word so that His Word can help us in building relationships.

2. Wisdom Should Purify Relationships (vv. 4–5)

A silversmith must purify silver by removing the iron oxide or "dross" that naturally occurs within the metal. If the iron oxide is not removed, the silver will break when it cools or it will corrode. During the smelting process, no foreign matter must fuse with the ore. The metal must be properly refined to make the final product pure. Like the silversmith, a king must remove or purify the kingdom by removing evil. Disloyal and foolish advisors must be removed. The "dross" that exists within society and a kingdom are evil individuals, conspirators, and liars who seek to create problems, division, and difficulty. An evil advisor can create chaos in the workplace, home, or social environment. When the "dross" is taken out of a kingdom, a relationship, or a community, the result is a relationship based on righteousness and honor. Wisdom purifies relationships.

3. Wisdom Should Guide Relationships (vv. 6–7)

Humility and self-denial are important lessons that are taught by wisdom. The message of verses 6 and 7 is reiterated in Luke 14:7–11. Do not seek a place of honor where you will receive attention. Instead, seek to accomplish the purpose that God has given to you. Solomon instructed individuals not to pursue the best or most prominent places in life. Instead, individuals should purposely take the lowest place. On the other hand, society encourages individuals to strive for the most recognizable or viewed position— the place of recognition and believed honor. In Luke 14, Jesus taught that individuals should not seek social recognition through relationships, appearance, titles, or material possessions. Jesus instructed individuals to seek positions where they can serve and allow God to lift them to places of prominence as God purposes.

4. Wisdom Should Handle Relationships (vv. 8–10)

According to societal standards, differences are handled in the court system. Both parties meet in a courtroom where a judge listens to each and then makes a decision based on the evidence that is presented. A third party settles the differences that created the disagreement.

Solomon instructs believers to discuss their differences instead of rushing to court. He instructs that: (1) we should try to handle complaints and disagreements on a private level instead of going to court; (2) we should not complain to others about our neighbor, friend, or coworker; (3) we should not discuss with others what we have discussed with another person in secret because the result will only create trouble and negatively affect our reputations; and (4) after the disagreement has been discussed, end it privately and we will not endure shame.

Search the Scriptures

1. God's Word is sometimes beyond the simple comprehension of humanity. Discuss the importance of searching and studying God's Word (Proverbs 25:2).

2. What advice did Solomon give to men in the kingdom with self-seeking plans and pride (vv. 6–7)?

Discuss the Meaning

1. Consider ways that we can "search out a matter" and honor God.

2. How can believers purify their lives, relationships, and workplaces today?

50

Lesson in Our Society

When we look at society, we discover that because people do not fully obey the truth revealed in God's Word, their actions do not honor God. If society desires to glorify the true and living God, then its people must study God's Word and apply it to every aspect of their daily living.

Make It Happen

Today's lesson reminds us to live for and glorify God in our relationships. In order to develop good and equitable relationships, Solomon gives godly advice: (1) We should realize that to live righteously, we must study and apply God's Word; (2) Pray for leaders, family, friends, and coworkers who do not know God; (3) By our actions, be an example for others to see Christ; (4) If we have a disagreement with others, attempt to settle it privately; (5) Do not bring attention to the disagreement but follow God's instructions; (6) Reflect on our relationships by recognizing evil doers and deceivers that attempt to create chaos; and (7) Purify our relationships.

Follow the Spirit

What God wants me to do:

_____

_____

_____

_____

Remember Your Thoughts

Special insights I have learned:

_____

_____

_____

_____

More Light on the Text

Proverbs 25:1–10

1 These are also proverbs of Solomon, which the men of Hezekiah king of Judah copied out.

This section of the book contains other proverbs attributed to Solomon that were collected by the men of King Hezekiah (715–687 B.C.). The word "also" connects this portion of the collection with Proverbs 10:1 and 24:23. These scribes or scholars "copied out" the sayings (i.e., transcribed them from one book to another). The fact that "men" transcribed these proverbs, instead of referring to a single scribe, suggests that the Hebrew word *àthaq* (**aw-THAK**) most likely refers to the entire process of "writing," "arranging," and the "collation of texts."

2 It is the glory of God to conceal a thing: but the honour of kings is to search out a matter.

This first saying expresses a contrast between God and earthly rulers in general. One of the great responsibilities of kings or leaders is to make things understandable to people, but God's providence is beyond knowing. And while earthly rulers rightly search out wisdom and proper judgment, God stands as omniscient—He already knows the matter at hand. In this way, God—in His infinite wisdom—truly is mysterious. He is grandiose and unfathomable. Kings search out things, while God reserves the right to conceal what He chooses to remain veiled. According to Deuteronomy 29:29, "The secret things belong unto the LORD our God: but those things which are revealed belong unto us and to our children for ever, that we may do all the words of this law." Such a contrast brings to the forefront the glory of God, that He is far superior to anyone else.

The real point of Proverbs 25:2 is to exalt the superiority of God. The king is a powerful figure whose actions may not need to be explained to his subjects (v. 2), but his success and achievement is measured by what he has searched out, as verse 3 indicates.

3 The heaven for height, and the earth for depth, and the heart of kings is unsearchable.

The verse speaks of the heart of the king as being "unsearchable." Predictability and lack of imagination are fatal for a ruler, since he no longer will be taken seriously. While a king ought to make judicial matters clear to the people (v. 2), many things cannot be made known because, perhaps, of his superior wisdom, or his tendency to act capriciously, or the necessity of maintaining confidentiality. The king must learn to play his cards close to his chest. He must not give much away. Such a king will win greater respect from his subjects. The word translated "unsearchable" in Hebrew is *cheqer* (**KHAY-ker**), which in other passages refers only to God and creation (Job 5:9, 9:10; Psalm 145:3; Isaiah 40:28). God's secret is proof of divine power—these are secrets that humans cannot even guess. What God does not reveal demonstrates who God really is. In contrast, the king is transparent or obvious. He must also ultimately be able to explain ("search out a matter"), and Solomon is praised for his wisdom—a wisdom obtained from God (1 Kings 3:28).

There is another important lesson in Proverbs 25:3. We must abstain from hasty censure of the actions and policies of those in power; the grounds for a policy may be far deeper than anything that meets the eye. If the heart in general is unsearchable, how much more this must be true of leaders, who have not merely their own secrets to keep, but the secrets of nations to keep as well. It reminds us of our limitations in understanding fully all the heartfelt decisions of the king. The verse underscores the fact that the government that wins public confidence is the one that, although it knows and understands when to keep necessary secrets, shows itself dedicated to taking decisions on the basis of careful consideration and analysis of available evidence and relevant facts.

4 Take away the dross from the silver, and there shall come forth a vessel for the finer. 5 Take away the wicked from before the king, and his throne shall be established in righteousness.

In verse 4, the writer employs the imagery of purification of metals as the basis of his analogy in verse 5. The "dross" in verse 4 is analogous to the wicked or scoundrels in verse 5 to show the polluting influence of the wicked when allowed into the corridors of power. Thus, the writer compares the scoundrels in the king's presence to the dross in refining silver. The king must take steps to root out wicked and corrupt officials if he is to lay a solid foundation for a good and just rule. A mark of the wise king or ruler is that he ensures he has surrounded himself with officials and counselors marked by integrity. In Proverbs, one finds numerous examples that contrast the wicked with the righteous. In particular, the wicked represent persons who live outside the confines of a faithful relationship with God and His people. Such persons transgress God's Law with seeming impunity, show injustice toward others, and, overall, exhibit self-centered living. In our day, persons usually are exalted to lofty positions of influence and power based upon academic credentials, social contacts, or outstanding personality traits. However, notice that the writer focuses on the character of those who surround the king. The need for a king to surround himself with honest servants is frequently emphasized (see Psalm 101). This is in agreement with the idea that justice is the foundation of his throne (Proverbs 16:12; 20:28; 29:14).

As the refiner separates the dross from the silver, which mars its beauty and purity, so should the king exclude from his presence and counsels the reckless and the base. Just as it is impossible to have a sterling silver vessel until the silver has been purified, no nation can have a king who is a public blessing until the wicked—all the bad counselors, wicked and interested ministers, and flatterers—are banished from the cabinet and positions of power. When the wise and good are the king's only ministers and advisers, then the throne will be established in righteousness, and his administration be a universal blessing. Any court, pure or vicious, has immense influence on the manners and morals of the community. This is also true of individuals. We should be careful to realize this when seeking advice, choose our company wisely, and be careful whom we allow to speak into our lives.

6 Put not forth thyself in the presence of the king, and stand not in the place of great men: 7 For better it is that it be said unto thee, Come up hither; than that thou shouldest be put lower in the presence of the prince whom thine eyes have seen.

These verses deal with the actions of those in the court of the king or in the presence of someone who is great. Nothing in conduct is unimportant. Fitting and graceful manners should become our routine. Here behavior around our superiors is touched upon and is also taught in Luke 14:7–11. The writer of Proverbs 25:7 warns against self-exaltation, which would bring humiliation: "be put lower" (Heb. *shapel,* **shaw-FALE**). It is wiser to wait to be promoted than to risk demotion by self-promotion. Self-respect is complemented by deference. Promoting yourself while in court may risk public humiliation, but it would be an honor to have everyone in court hear the promotion from the king himself. This is the paradox of Christianity: Humility leads to exaltation, but grasping at more than our due is to lose all and earn condemnation. We must avoid presumption in any of its forms—it is an offense hateful to humankind and God.

8 Go not forth hastily to strive, lest thou know not what to do in the end thereof, when thy neighbour hath put thee to shame.

There are important lessons to learn from Proverbs 25:8. First, disputes are unavoidable. In view of conflict and complicated interests—individual, domestic, social, economic, civic, international—differences and difficulties often arise amongst us. There are always and will be conflicts of opinion—wishes and purposes clash; their divergence may result in dissension, including in Christian congregations. Second, the temptation is to be hasty either in jumping to conclusions or in acting rashly. Using the judicial system to mediate conflicts, including those between neighbors, can be one hastily applied result of struggles. But these actions do no good other than to permanently damage relationships. They erect a barrier between us and our neighbors and make it difficult, if not entirely impossible, to ever again live alongside one another in amity. Instead, we are sowing seeds of bitterness and discord, which will bear fruit throughout our days. We also have to bear in mind that whether we win or lose a case depends on several uncertainties, and even if we have a righteous cause, we may be entirely defeated—a brilliant advocate against us can win over a judge or jury. We may end up impoverished and ashamed. How sad it can be that Christians would need the courts to decide a just and fair outcome in a situation [does not include criminal cases] (cf. 1 Corinthians 6:1–11). We must be mindful that the world will judge us by our failures rather quickly. So, let us stand apart as different—peacemakers who love each other and love God.

9 Debate thy cause with thy neighbour himself; and discover not a secret to another: 10 Lest he that heareth it put thee to shame, and thine infamy turn not away.

Proverbs 25:9 urges the aggrieved party to discuss the conflict with the neighbor. Go at once to the offender and state the complaint in a private, one-on-one manner. It is the Christian, honorable way (Matthew 5:25, 26; 18:15). It is also the way of peace; in most cases, straightforward communication or a very simple apology will set everything right. Together, Proverbs 25:9–10 underline that a person who skips this method—by, for instance, gossiping about the offender's behavior rather than pursuing a peaceful resolution—could undermine the neighbor's good name and might end up with a bad name as a person who is disloyal and untrustworthy. The right thing to do is to keep a quarrel private and settle it in private (cf. Matthew 18:15–17). Proverbs 25:9–10 also show that it is improper to disclose our secrets to another. Personal, domestic, and ecclesiastical contentions are hidden by the wise and the worthy rather than made known to the world. We must not betray confidences, including those obtained from opponents.

In Proverbs 25:10, the writer exposes what is at stake when one goes about with such rash, impetuous behavior. Infamy may remain with a person for a very long time. Instead, settling matters peaceably and privately can prevent escalation in a public arena, where many times things are misconstrued and slander is involved. This can happen, for instance, during a subsequent argument when you reveal someone else's secret—told to you in confidence previously. He hears about your indiscretion and shames you, and you have acquired a bad reputation that is tough to overcome. To put it more directly, do not divulge secrets in order to clear yourself in an argument. It's best not to damage a friendship by involving others in a private quarrel.

Sources:
Baltes, A. J., ed. Biblespeech.com. http://biblespeech.com (accessed July 6, 2010).
Clarke, Adam. *Clarke's Commentary. Vol. 2: Job–Malachi.* Nashville, TN: Abingdon, n.d.
Clifford, Richard J. *Proverbs.* Louisville, KY: Westminster John Knox Press, 1999.
Emerson, Ralph Waldo. "Manners," *Essays: Second Series.* Boston: Phillips, Sampson & Company, 1850. 104.
Garrett, Duane A. *Proverbs, Ecclesiastes, Song of Songs. New American Commentary, Vol. 14.* Nashville, TN: Broadman, 1993.
Hebrew and Greek Lexicons. Bible Study Tools.com. http://www.biblestudytools.com/lexicons (accessed September 16, 2010).
Kidner, Derek. *Proverbs: An Introduction and Commentary.* Downers Grove, IL: InterVarsity Press, 1964.
Merriam-Webster Online Dictionary. Merriam-Webster, Inc. http://www.merriam-webster.com (accessed July 6, 2010).
Murphy, Roland E. *Proverbs.* Nashville, TN: Thomas Nelson Publishers, 1998.

Say It Correctly

Hezekiah. Hez-ay-KIAH.

Daily Bible Readings

MONDAY
The Creator's Hiddenness
(Isaiah 45:9–17)

TUESDAY
Asking for Wisdom
(1 Kings 3:5–14)

WEDNESDAY
Humbly Seeking God
(2 Chronicles 7:12–18)

THURSDAY
Words Fitly Spoken
(Proverbs 25:11–15)

FRIDAY
Wisdom with Neighbors
(Proverbs 25:16–20)

SATURDAY
The Wisdom of Self-Control
(Proverbs 25:21–28)

SUNDAY
Wisdom and Government
(Proverbs 25:1–10)

Notes

Teaching Tips

Words You Should Know

A. Transgression (Proverbs 29:16) *peshà* (Heb.)—Rebellion or sin against God or others; violation of a law.

B. Correct (v. 17) *yacar* (Heb.)—To instruct, chasten, discipline, punish or admonish.

Teacher Preparation

Unifying Principle—The Law and Correction. An ordered life based on God's Word leads to instruction, correction, and order.

A. Pray for your students.

B. Study and meditate on the entire text.

C. Complete the companion lesson in the *Precepts For Living Personal Study Guide®*.

D. Prepare Scripture references about God's unchanging nature.

O—Open the Lesson

A. Open with prayer, including the Aim for Change.

B. After prayer, introduce today's subject of the lesson.

C. Have your students read the Aim for Change and Keep in Mind verse in unison.

D. Discuss the Unifying Principle.

E. Hand out the Scripture references and discuss God's unchanging nature.

F. Then ask, "Where is your level of security with God?"

G. Allow volunteers to share their testimonies.

H. Now have a volunteer summarize the In Focus story. Discuss.

P—Present the Scriptures

A. Have volunteers read the Focal Verses.

B. Now use The People, Places, and Times; Background; Search the Scriptures; At-A-Glance outline; In Depth; and More Light on the Text to clarify the verses.

E—Explore the Meaning

A. Have volunteers summarize the Discuss the Meaning, Lesson in Our Society, and Make It Happen sections.

B. Connect these sections to the Aim for Change and the Keep in Mind verse.

N—Next Steps for Application

A. Take notes of class discussions of the lesson's principles under the Follow the Spirit or Remember Your Thoughts section.

B. Close with prayer and praise God for desiring to live an ordered life.

Worship Guide

For the Superintendent or Teacher
Theme: An Ordered Life
Song: "He Leadeth Me"
Devotional Reading:
Deuteronomy 1:9–17
Prayer

An Ordered Life

Bible Background • PROVERBS 28:1–29:27
Printed Text • PROVERBS 29:16–27 | Devotional Reading • DEUTERONOMY 1:9–17

──────────── **Aim for Change** ────────────

By the end of the lesson, we will: KNOW the relationship between an orderly life and trust in God; FEEL what it means to live an ordered life; and CREATE a strategy, based on godly principles, to live an ordered life.

──────── **In Focus** ────────

The women's choir celebrated their 30th anniversary. Celeste honored God as she glorified Him through song. She was gifted with a beautiful soprano voice, and her joy overflowed as she praised God.

Immediately after the anniversary, Celeste fellowshipped with fellow choir members and friends at the dinner for the choir, which was held in the fellowship hall. Because she had dinner plans later that evening, she didn't eat much.

An hour later, as Celeste walked into a secluded restaurant, she saw Michael sitting at a table in the corner. He stood up and pulled out her chair. Before Celeste had a seat, she leaned over to kiss him. Michael smiled as he said, "Teresa will be at her mother's tonight. Let's make plans to spend the night together."

Celeste quickly responded, "I packed an overnight bag. I hoped your wife would find somewhere else to stay tonight."

Today's lesson teaches that we should change any actions that cause us to step outside of godly principles.

────────── **Keep in Mind** ──────────

"The fear of man bringeth a snare: but whoso putteth his trust in the LORD shall be safe" (Proverbs 29:25).

"The fear of man bringeth a snare: but whoso putteth his trust in the LORD shall be safe" (Proverbs 29:25).

Focal Verses

KJV **Proverbs 29:16** When the wicked are multiplied, transgression increaseth: but the righteous shall see their fall.

17 Correct thy son, and he shall give thee rest; yea, he shall give delight unto thy soul.

18 Where there is no vision, the people perish: but he that keepeth the law, happy is he.

19 A servant will not be corrected by words: for though he understand he will not answer.

20 Seest thou a man that is hasty in his words? there is more hope of a fool than of him.

21 He that delicately bringeth up his servant from a child shall have him become his son at the length.

22 An angry man stirreth up strife, and a furious man aboundeth in transgression.

23 A man's pride shall bring him low: but honour shall uphold the humble in spirit.

24 Whoso is partner with a thief hateth his own soul: he heareth cursing, and bewrayeth it not.

25 The fear of man bringeth a snare: but whoso putteth his trust in the LORD shall be safe.

26 Many seek the ruler's favour; but every man's judgment cometh from the LORD.

27 An unjust man is an abomination to the just: and he that is upright in the way is abomination to the wicked.

NLT **Proverbs 29:16** When the wicked are in authority, sin increases. But the godly will live to see the tyrant's downfall.

17 Discipline your children, and they will give you happiness and peace of mind.

18 When people do not accept divine guidance, they run wild. But whoever obeys the law is happy.

19 For a servant, mere words are not enough—discipline is needed. For the words may be understood, but they are not heeded.

20 There is more hope for a fool than for someone who speaks without thinking.

21 A servant who is pampered from childhood will later become a rebel.

22 A hot-tempered person starts fights and gets into all kinds of sin.

23 Pride ends in humiliation, while humility brings honor.

24 If you assist a thief, you are only hurting yourself. You will be punished if you report the crime, but you will be cursed if you don't.

25 Fearing people is a dangerous trap, but to trust the LORD means safety.

26 Many seek the ruler's favor, but justice comes from the LORD.

27 The godly despise the wicked; the wicked despise the godly.

The People, Places, and Times

Palestine. God allotted this land alongside the Jordan River to Israel as an inheritance. Initially referred to as Canaan, "the Promised Land" was then divided into two kingdoms and designated as "Israel" and "Judah" in 931 B.C. Historically, Greeks have applied the name "Palestine" to the entire southeastern Mediterranean region. West of the Jordan River, Palestine is 6,000 square miles; east of the Jordan, Palestine is 4,000 square feet.

Background

The book of Proverbs reveals two major themes: wisdom and folly. Wisdom is knowledge, understanding, discretion, obedience, and instruction based on God's Word and reverence of God. Folly is everything that contradicts wisdom. The Old Testament provides God's Truth through the Law, which was given by the priest; the wise men or sages gave the Word, which was given by God and wise counsel. Solomon is the sage that provided insight on the perplexities of life (Proverbs 1:6).

When Solomon became king of Israel, God granted his request for understanding (1 Kings 3:9–12). As a result of God's response, Solomon's wisdom was greater than anyone else's. Solomon's counsel was more valuable than the era's notable sages, such as Heman and Chalcol (or Calcol, see 1 Kings 4:31). Because proverbs were not generally written, memorization was an effective way of teaching and learning. The short, concise phrases that comprise Proverbs lend themselves to the best method to reveal and remember a divine truth.

At-A-Glance

1. God Commands Self-Control (Proverbs 29:16–22)

2. God Commands Humility (vv. 23–25)

3. God Is in Control (vv. 26–27)

In Depth

1. God Commands Self-Control (Proverbs 29:16–22)

Proverbs 29:16–22 explained that increased sin leads to increased rebellion. Moral decay has risen because societal moral standards have decayed. As society flourished during biblical times, the transgressions increased as the sinners became bolder. Their confidence increased because there were large numbers of offenders. However, the psalmist David reminds believers, "Wait for the LORD and keep his way," because God will change things according to His time (Psalm 37:34, NIV). The wicked will be cut off and fall; the righteous will witness the downfall of the sinners.

Because children are a blessing, obedient children are a comfort to their parents. The parents can trust the children and rest in the fruits that the children produce through a good education and spiritual foundation. In Proverbs 29:17, Solomon reminds parents that children must be corrected to have peace and happiness. Strict discipline is necessary to correct a child. Wise instruction and discipline are necessary to bring delight instead of shame to a parent's home and reputation.

Proverbs teaches that a moral individual recognizes the immorality that exists within society. Immorality is more pronounced when sin flourishes and moral decay increases. If there is no prophet to share God's commands and God's wisdom, the people are unaware of God's vision. The prophet is God's servant who imparts knowledge, understanding, and faith. Deficiency in hearing the Word of God leads to rebellion. Solomon wrote that the "people perish" (Proverbs 29:18). Therefore, prophetic exhortation is necessary for a viable, godly society. When society heeds the revelation and submits to God's Word, a blessing is pronounced on God's people.

Because continual, thoughtless conversation may lead to sin, Solomon reminds us in verse 20 that wisdom restrains the tongue. Because there is little time spent on thought and reflection when someone speaks hastily, he further reminds believers that rashly spoken words put someone on the level of a hopeless fool. In fact, because the individual believes there is no need for advice from others, hasty speech often reveals self-conceit and pride. Thus, a person who is slow to speak and considers the advice from others reveals control and wisdom.

Solomon then addresses trouble and strife within a neighborhood, workplace, or society that can provoke discord among individuals and ultimately throughout society. He instructed that unnecessary anger leads to sin and creates chaos. Troublemakers do not promote peace; instead, they encourage anger, illicit behavior, and lack of control. Thus, uncontrolled anger leads to sin because bad decisions are made. If a person is easily provoked to anger, he or she is more apt to sin (29:22). There is a difference between righteous indignation—that takes a stand—and uncontrolled, unbridled anger that leads to sin. God, therefore, commands self-control.

2. God Commands Humility (vv. 23–25)

Because people depend on themselves rather than God, Solomon taught that pride can lead people to live independently from God. Pride is evident when we do not trust God. Pharaoh, Nebuchadnezzar, and Herod exemplified this kind of arrogance. Solomon instructed that the prideful will be brought down and the humble will be lifted up (v. 23). Society encourages people to seek high positions where they will be praised, but God is not pleased. He commands humility. Jesus reminds believers that the first will be last and the last will be first (Matthew 19:30). If we are in last place as we follow Jesus, our temporary sacrifice offers eternal reward. The world encourages narcissism, confidence, and arrogance to reign on earth while God encourages humility, meekness, and servanthood to reign as kings with Christ.

Another truth, in Proverbs 29:24, is that if people partner with a thief and do not disclose the truth (become the thief's

"accomplice," NIV), they commit perjury and the result is punishment. A silent witness is guilty before God even though friends, family, and coworkers may not know. Seen and unseen wrongdoing do not please God.

3. God Is in Control (vv. 26–27)

The legal system within society offers temporary relief from injustice. Ultimately, individuals will not be satisfied with a ruler's temporary favor. If believers trust in God with a committed faith, God demands justice. Thus, we must look to God and seek His favor. Ultimately, God controls the rulers that humanity seeks to please because God is sovereign—in control of His universe and never out of control of it.

As believers, then, we must make a choice between the path of righteousness and immorality. We walk uprightly when we obey God's commands and depend upon Him. When we choose to obey God, we have security in the eternal promise of God and not the temporal objects and people in the world.

Search the Scriptures

1. In the family, where does God place the responsibility for discipline (Proverbs 29:17)?

2. Where is the freedom that is associated with the "fear of man" (v. 25)?

Discuss the Meaning

1. Today, in what ways does society experience moral decay?

2. How can God's revelations of wisdom encourage believers and society at large?

Lesson in Our Society

Security is the comfort, protection, and safety that an unchanging God offers through the promise of eternal life. Because the standards of the world constantly change through various styles, designs, and fads, there is no security other than in God.

Therefore, the temporary satisfaction that the world offers cannot compare to the eternal power, love, and security we find in God. Hebrews 13:8 reminds believers that "Jesus Christ [is] the same yesterday, and today, and forever."

Make It Happen

This week, pray that you will increase your trust in God and find more security in your life. Study Scripture on God's unchanging nature. Make a choice to live an ordered life based on godly principles. Today's lesson reminds us to trust in God to have that sense of security. Consider worldly values, which offer a false sense of security, and then reiterate the unchanging nature of God. By believing in His promises, make a wholehearted effort to trust God and lead an ordered life.

Follow the Spirit

What God wants me to do:

_____

_____

_____

_____

Remember Your Thoughts

Special insights I have learned:

_____

_____

_____

_____

More Light on the Text
Proverbs 29:16–27

16 When the wicked are multiplied, transgression increaseth: but the righteous shall see their fall.

This verse is similar in its sense to Proverbs 28:12, 28; and 29:2. The just and the wicked are contrasted, and it is evident that the increase of either group leads to greater power and influence. We see the contrast between the social situations under the control of the just and that of the wicked. The clear implication is that the reign of the just person is beneficial to all, for it ensures the "great glory" of the populace, while the rule of the wicked has the effect of driving people into hiding to get out of the way of injustice (cf. 28:12). The first part of 29:16 affirms that when "the wicked are multiplied" or, literally, when the "wicked thrive" as the Hebrew phrase *rabah rashà* (**raw-BAW raw-SHAW**) suggests, transgression also thrives. The second part of the verse and its first word "but" shows that there will ultimately be a reversal: righteousness will prevail. Although verse 16 does not say how or when, the victory of the just is signaled because the righteous will "see" (Hebrew *ra'ah*, **raw-AH**) "their downfall." No matter how much wickedness spreads in the land, righteousness will live to see it destroyed—an idea that is frequent in the Psalms (cf. Psalm 37:34–36; 54:9).

17 Correct thy son, and he shall give thee rest; yea, he shall give delight unto thy soul.

The numerous references throughout Proverbs to discipline within the home may have affected a societal attitude about family relations during the period that Solomon wrote. There is little doubt a similar situation exists in our times. Discipline or correction is not a popular word; it is sometimes equated or confused with child abuse. However, the writer of Proverbs focuses on discipline in a positive way, expressing the satisfaction and joy that parents will experience in correcting their children and witnessing the wisdom that emerges as a result. This is echoed elsewhere (10:1), as is the need for discipline (19:18; 23:13; 29:15). A disciplined child will cause parents to feel relieved that they have properly handled this aspect of their responsibility. The first part of 29:17 is parallel to the second, but with the second part adding the thought of "delight," which in Hebrew is *màadan* (**mah-ad-AWN**) to that of "rest" (Heb. *nuwach,* **NOO-akh**), or "relieving anxiety," as in Deuteronomy 12:10. The word "delight," used elsewhere for cooking delicacies (Genesis 49:20; Lamentations 4:8), is a metaphor for the joy a responsible son brings; care for aging parents would be a consideration. Used together, "delight" and "rest" suggest the image of a parent taking a deep breath and letting out a sigh of relief and pleasure at a child who has turned out well.

18 Where there is no vision, the people perish: but he that keepeth the law, happy is he.

This popular verse refers to two forms of divine revelation: vision and law. In prophetic literature especially, the Hebrew word *chazown* (**khaw-ZONE**), which translates here as "vision," frequently refers to the vision of the prophet, but it occurs only here in Proverbs. Thus, it often refers to divine communication to prophets (cf. 1 Samuel 3:1) and not to individual or group goals, as "vision" is frequently understood or applied. The word is translated elsewhere as "guidance" in *Today's English Version* and as "revelation" in the New International Version. Whether understood as prophetic vision or revelation, Proverbs 29:18 underscores the significance of leadership that is truly spiritual and godly. If there is no revelation from God, people can expect spiri-

tual and political anarchy. If there is "no revelation" or "no vision, the people perish," or in the NIV, "cast off restraint" (Heb. *parà,* **paw-RAH**). The meaning of "cast off restraint" is reminiscent of Exodus 32:25. A nation's well-being depends on obedience to divine revelation. There is much similarity between Proverbs 11:14, which references the necessity of "counsel" (or "guidance," NIV) in obtaining victory, and this verse. In comparing 11:14 with 29:18, as strategy is necessary for gaining victory, so prophecy is integral to communal flourishing and national well-being. No matter the resources or abilities of a people, without God's guidance and prophetic vision, the results are disastrous. Those who live in the absence of God's prophetic vision experience chaos of many sorts, to the point of societal disorder. In contrast to the first part of 29:18, the second is positive: the one who keeps the law is a happy person. "The law" (Heb. *torah,* **to-RAH**) is not merely the Mosaic Law or the Ten Commandments; the law is the true proclamation of God's Word and will via His representatives.

19 A servant will not be corrected by words: for though he understand he will not answer.

The verse is probably a general observation. It is not sufficient to train servants by words alone. The verse shows that slaves had to be corrected just as sons were (see v. 17). There is no place for justifying disobedience. The second part of verse 19, "For though he understand he will not answer," explains the necessity of correction. The slaves in question were unresponsive, probably a case of silent disobedience. A reluctant slave thoroughly understands the order given, but pays no attention to it, will not trouble himself to execute it, and, therefore, must meet with stern discipline (compare with

29:15; see also 23:13; 26:3). The situation described in 29:19 is well stated by our Lord Jesus Christ in Luke 12:47: "And that servant, which knew his lord's will, and prepared not himself, neither did according to his will, shall be beaten with many stripes." This means that those who know better because they have been instructed properly and still disobey will be punished.

20 Seest thou a man that is hasty in his words? there is more hope of a fool than of him.

The proverb is a strong condemnation of frivolity and rashness of speech. It applies to those who speak hastily without thinking or considering the implications of what they say as this affects the speakers and others. The person who is in a hurry to open his or her mouth may do so with the best of intentions. However, the words may turn out to be unhelpful and ruffle rather than soothe a difficult situation or strained relationship. To such a person the words of James become a sound advice: "Let every man be swift to hear, [and] slow to speak" (James 1:19). As the saying goes, "A fish will not get caught if it keeps its mouth shut." Since the Hebrew word *dabar* (**daw-BAW**), translated here as "word," could mean "action" as well, the proverb may be widely applied. "Hasty," as used in Proverbs 29:20 and elsewhere in the book, has unfortunate references. For example, haste in acquiring wealth (13:11), a hasty temper (14:29), hasty promises (20:25), hasty decisions (21:5), and hasty judgments (25:7–8). Christians must believe the Lord and not make haste.

21 He that delicately bringeth up his servant from a child shall have him become his son at the length.

The Hebrew word *panaq* (**paw-NAK**), which occurs only here in the Old Testament

and is translated as "delicately bringeth up," refers to spoiling a person by over-refinement, luxury, and pampering. To treat a bond servant with great indulgence and lenience is peculiarly unsuitable for Solomon's era and rare to say the least in modern times. Another challenge in the interpretation of the verse is the meaning of the Hebrew word *manown* (**maw-NOHN**), translated as "son" in the King James Version. The Septuagint translates the word as "grief," in which case Proverbs 29:21 simply means that an undisciplined servant causes nothing but grief.

22 An angry man stirreth up strife, and a furious man aboundeth in transgression.

Anger brings strife. Using synonymous parallelism, the parts of verse 22 focus on the "an angry man" and "a furious man." The first such person stirs up dissension, and in so doing, he also causes sin in himself and in others. The Hebrew word *chemah* (**khay-MAW**), translated as "furious," literally means "heat." *Chemah* is also used to refer to the venom of serpents (Psalm 58:4) and the "fiery" effects of wine (Hosea 7:5). A furious person is hotheaded and is the opposite of the one who knows how to restrain temper and tongue. Such a person is to be avoided (Proverbs 22:24, 25). He or she "aboundeth in transgressions" (29:22) and, ultimately, will pay the penalty for the multitude of sins (19:19).

23 A man's pride shall bring him low: but honour shall uphold the humble in spirit.

The same thought, as is in the first part of 29:23, is found in 15:33; 16:18; 25:6; and Luke 14:11. Alongside the condemnation of pride, there is the commendation of humility. In our competitive world of so-called "self-made" men and women, humility is not rated very highly. Instead, it is sometimes seen as a sign of weakness rather than strength of character, but not so with the writer of Proverbs. A humble spirit brings honor and respect. Proverbs 29:23 contrasts consequences: pride leads to abasement, but humility brings exaltation. The humble person does not seek honor, but by his or her life and action unconsciously attains it. As translated by the Septuagint, "Haughtiness brings a man low, but the lowly-minded the Lord upholdeth with glory."

24 Whoso is partner with a thief hateth his own soul: he heareth cursing, and bewrayeth it not.

In the same manner that a person who aids and abets a crime is considered guilty, this verse describes a person who is "partner with a thief" as engaging in spiritual self-hatred. This is explained by the phrase "he heareth cursing, and bewrayeth it not"; or as the *New American Standard Bible* translates it, "He hears the oath but tells nothing." This is in line with the command in Leviticus 5:1 (cf. Judges 17:2). If a theft was committed, the person wronged or the judge pronounced a curse on the thief and on anyone who was privy to the crime and refrained from giving information or refused to speak up. As such, a witness who saw and knew of a crime, and was silent during the formal proceedings, must bear his iniquity; he is not only an accomplice, but he is also a perjurer. One sin leads to another.

25 The fear of man bringeth a snare: but whoso putteth his trust in the LORD shall be safe.

The contrast here is between "the fear of man" and "his trust in" the Lord. Fear here is an inordinate fear of harm or suffering from others, particularly those in position of authority. It is opposed to trust in God, because it arises from a distrust of God's

promises and providence. Such fear becomes a snare, which is an occasion for committing sins, especially when the fearfulness gets to the point of letting others control your life, letting their opinions and attitudes put subtle pressure on you, even hindering you from speaking the truth or doing what is right. Consequently, it brings punishment from God. In contrast, the person who trusts in the Lord—that is, walks in God's ways and completely relies on Him for protection from the schemes and malice of the wicked—shall be safe. That person shall be preserved from all evil, through God's watchful providence. In addition, such persons will be able to say like Peter: "We must obey God rather than men" (Acts 5:29, NIV).

26 Many seek the ruler's favour; but every man's judgment cometh from the LORD.

The contrast here is between seeking the grace of a ruler and finding justice from the Lord. Many try in times of need, by fair or surreptitious means, to curry favor with an important person with something to bestow (comp. 1 Kings 10:24; Psalm 45:12). But we are now reminded that our destiny does not lie in their hands but in the hands of God, who has supreme judgment, though we often ignore His rule. It is a great miscalculation to assume that true justice depends on a human ruler and that supplication must be directed first to her or him. True justice ultimately comes from God, whose approval or disapproval is final and indisputable—not from an earthly official or ruler who may be prejudiced and is certainly fallible.

27 An unjust man is an abomination to the just: and he that is upright in the way is abomination to the wicked.

As the verse shows, virtue and vice are antagonists. An "unjust" person (Heb. *èvel*, **EH-vel**) considers the "upright" or "just" person (Heb. *tsaddiyq*, **tsad-DEEK**) an abomination. The life of one type of person is a reflection on the conduct of the other type of person. The just, or believers, are those who are in covenant relationship with God through their faith in Christ; they exhibit the nature of the Lord, Savior, and Master, Jesus Christ. It is written of Him that in observing the sinners around Him, He "looked round about on them with anger" (Mark 3:5). The psalmist also says that God is "angry with the wicked every day" (Psalm 7:11) and that the Lord "hateth all workers of iniquity" (Psalm 5:5). Therefore, how we feel about the unjust is a reflection of that which is in the heart of God Himself. However, we must be quick to add that we should not harbor personal ill will, or want others to suffer. Rather, we should pray for their salvation; we should wish the soul of the sinful well. However, we fall into a mistake, if not into a sin, when we allow ourselves to find pleasure in witnessing or dwelling on the humiliation or sorrow of the wicked. On the other hand, the hatred of Christians by unbelievers is a well-verified fact—attested by Scripture, history, observation, and probably by experience. The unjust or wicked hate the righteous because their convictions, lifestyle, inclinations, and habits, are those of the good and pure. In addition, the upright are obliged to condemn the unjust, either in private or in public. The Scripture is replete with examples. John the Baptist was beheaded because of his condemnation of Herod (Matthew 14:1–11).

Sources:

Baltes, A. J., ed. Biblespeech.com. http://biblespeech.com (accessed July 6, 2010).

Clifford, Richard J. *Proverbs.* Louisville, KY: Westminster John Knox Press, 1999.

Garrett, Duane A. *Proverbs, Ecclesiastes, Song of Songs. New American Commentary, Vol. 14.* Nashville, TN: Broadman, 1993.

Hebrew and Greek Lexicons. Bible Study Tools.com. http://www.biblestudytools.com/lexicons (accessed September 16, 2010).

Kidner, Derek. *Proverbs: An Introduction and Commentary.* Downers Grove, IL: InterVarsity Press, 1964.

Merriam-Webster Online Dictionary. Merriam-Webster, Inc. http://www.merriam-webster.com (accessed May 4, 2009).

Murphy, Roland E. *Proverbs.* Nashville, TN: Thomas Nelson Publishers, 1998.

The Teacher's Bible Commentary. Nashville, TN: Broadman and Holman Publishers, 1972.

Say It Correctly

Mephibosheth. May-FI-bo-sheth.
Ziba. ZI-ba.

Daily Bible Readings

MONDAY
Impartiality in Judgment
(Deuteronomy 1:9–17)

TUESDAY
The Danger of Pride
(2 Chronicles 32:20–26)

WEDNESDAY
The Wisdom of Justice
(Proverbs 28:1–5)

THURSDAY
Wisdom in Wealth and Poverty
(Proverbs 28:8–16)

FRIDAY
Walking in Wisdom
(Proverbs 28:20–28)

SATURDAY
The Wisdom of the Righteous
(Proverbs 29:2–11)

SUNDAY
Wisdom in Practice
(Proverbs 29:16–27)

Notes

_____

_____

_____

_____

Teaching Tips

Words You Should Know

A. Preacher (Ecclesiastes 1:1, 2, 12) *qoheleth* (Heb.)—A teacher, preacher, or lecturer; the author of Ecclesiastes.

B. Wisdom (9:13, 15, 16, 18) *chokmah* (Heb.)—Biblical wisdom is knowing what is the right thing to do and doing it. Its beginning is the fear of the Lord (Proverbs 1:7).

Teacher Preparation

Unifying Principle—Wisdom. Ecclesiastes teaches that we should *not* ignore the quiet, thoughtful words of the wise.

A. Pray that God will accomplish the Aim for Change in your life and that of your students.

B. Study the entire text.

C. Complete the companion lesson in the *Precepts For Living Personal Study Guide®*.

O—Open the Lesson

A. After taking prayer requests, open with prayer.

B. Ask your students to share *good advice* they have received and who gave the advice.

C. Then ask: "What kind of people do you think have good advice?" Discuss.

D. Have a volunteer summarize the In Focus story. Discuss.

P—Present the Scriptures

A. Summarize the Focal verses. Discuss.

B. Ask: (1) What clues in the book of Ecclesiastes point us to King Solomon as the author of Ecclesiastes; (2) What three books in the Old Testament are considered *wisdom literature?*

C. Discuss the dangers in taking verses out of context, especially from Ecclesiastes.

E—Explore the Meaning

A. Discuss the questions in the Discuss the Meaning and Lesson in Our Society sections.

B. Connect these sections to the Aim for Change.

N—Next Steps for Application

A. Summarize the lesson or write some take-away principles under the Follow the Spirit or Remember Your Thoughts section.

B. Close with prayer.

Worship Guide

For the Superintendent or Teacher
Theme: The Superiority of Wisdom
Song: "I Have Decided
to Follow Jesus"
Devotional Reading: Psalm 33:13–22
Prayer

The Superiority of Wisdom

Bible Background • ECCLESIASTES 9:13–10:20
Printed Text • ECCLESIASTES 9:13–18 | Devotional Reading • PSALM 33:13–22

─────────────── **Aim for Change** ───────────────

By the end of the lesson, we will: DISCUSS the underlying message in the parable of the poor, wise man; TRUST the superiority of wisdom over force; and EXAMINE our attitudes about listening to the thoughtful words of the wise.

─────── 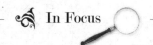 In Focus ───────

OCT
9th

The parents' school council meeting was getting louder and louder. The council president was upset about her daughter getting bad grades in Mr. Washington's class. "I think we ought to get rid of him!" she shouted.

"Did he say why your daughter was getting bad grades?" Ms. Jones asked quietly.

"Oh, he's giving too much homework, and she's not getting it done," the president answered indignantly.

"Well, I make my son do his homework right after school, and he is doing very well in Mr. Washington's class," Ms. Jones quietly interjected.

The other parents weren't saying anything. They knew that the principal and the president were good friends. The principal would probably do whatever the president told her to do.

Do you think the schoolchildren will profit from the principal listening to the powerful parents' school council president? Why is it that people are more likely to listen to an outspoken leader than to the wise words of a person with no power?

─────────────── **Keep in Mind** ───────────────

"Then said I, Wisdom is better than strength: nevertheless the poor man's wisdom is despised, and his words are not heard" (Ecclesiastes 9:16).

"Then said I, Wisdom is better than strength: nevertheless the poor man's wisdom is despised, and his words are not heard" (Ecclesiastes 9:16).

Focal Verses

KJV Ecclesiastes **9:13** This wisdom have I seen also under the sun, and it seemed great unto me:

14 There was a little city, and few men within it; and there came a great king against it, and besieged it, and built great bulwarks against it:

15 Now there was found in it a poor wise man, and he by his wisdom delivered the city; yet no man remembered that same poor man.

16 Then said I, Wisdom is better than strength: nevertheless the poor man's wisdom is despised, and his words are not heard.

17 The words of wise men are heard in quiet more than the cry of him that ruleth among fools.

18 Wisdom is better than weapons of war: but one sinner destroyeth much good.

NLT Ecclesiastes **9:13** Here is another bit of wisdom that has impressed me as I have watched the way our world works.

14 There was a small town with only a few people living in it, and a great king came with his army and besieged it.

15 There was a poor, wise man living there who knew how to save the town, and so it was rescued. But afterward no one thought any more about him.

16 Then I realized that though wisdom is better than strength, those who are wise will be despised if they are poor. What they say will not be appreciated for long.

17 But even so, the quiet words of a wise person are better than the shouts of a foolish king.

18 A wise person can overcome weapons of war, but one sinner can destroy much that is good.

The People, Places, and Times

The Author of Ecclesiastes. The author of Ecclesiastes calls himself *qoheleth,* or "teacher" (KJV calls him the preacher), but he also describes himself as the son of David (1:1) and then in verse 12 the "king over Israel in Jerusalem." All the kings in the line of David were called sons of David, but only Solomon reigned over all of Israel. After Solomon died, the kingdom was divided, and the sons of David ruled only over the kingdom of Judah, which included the tribe of Benjamin.

Ecclesiastes is written from the perspective of an older man who has lived long enough to see that life is not always as simple as we would wish. The lack of a happy ending to the story in today's Scripture passage is just such an example. Nevertheless the author

(qoheleth) has the time that a king at peace would have to consider the meaning of life and this, too, would describe the situation of King Solomon. He also describes himself as having much wisdom (1:16), great opportunities for pleasure (2:3), extensive building programs (2:4–6), unequaled wealth (2:7–8), and as the author of many proverbs (12:9). Again, all these things lead many to conclude that King Solomon is the author of Ecclesiastes.

Wisdom Literature in the Bible. Three Old Testament books are commonly defined as the wisdom literature: Job, Proverbs, and Ecclesiastes (some also include Psalms and Song of Solomon, though these are also regarded as poetic literature). These books contain wise sayings, common sense,

71

observations on life, principles of good governance, and wisdom from the spiritual perspective. The Bible concludes that the fear of the Lord is the beginning of true wisdom (Proverbs 1:7).

Background

We can get into real trouble if we take material out of context from the book of Ecclesiastes. The preacher or teacher looked at things first from an earthly perspective. The key phrase is "under the sun," which we see in the first verse of today's Scripture passage. When we look at things only from an earthly perspective, we can become very cynical. The greedy and the corrupt often seem to come out ahead. But we need to turn to the end of Ecclesiastes to find out the conclusion of the preacher's search for the meaning of life. In verses 11:9 and 12:14 we see that as we enjoy what life can offer us, we must always keep in mind that there is God's judgment in the end. God knows all and sees all, so no one will be able to fool Him.

At-A-Glance

1. The Poor but Wise Man
(Ecclesiastes 9:13–16)

2. The Benefit of Wisdom over Folly
(vv. 17–18)

In Depth

1. The Poor but Wise Man (Ecclesiastes 9:13–16)

Everyone likes a story with a happy ending, but this one does not end that way. We all like to see people give honor to those who are wise and bring about good results. We like to hear that talented people receive rewards, even if they happen to come from circumstances of poverty. But we all know that life is not that way. The book of Ecclesiastes is written from the perspective of an older person who has seen much of life, instead of a starry-eyed young person. If this life on earth is all there is, we cannot count on the "good people" or the wise people to get the rewards. The writer of Ecclesiastes is telling us this parable from the viewpoint of the activities "under the sun," that is, on this earth without eternity in view.

In this story, a powerful army was besieging a small city. The city had walls around it for fortification, as most cities did. The walls were built of thick stone, so an enemy would have to build ramps to go up on top of the city walls. These were called "siege works." The ramps would allow the enemy to enter the city. The writer of Ecclesiastes does not tell us what clever plan the poor but wise man devised. But, whatever it was, the plan was used to defeat the powerful army of the king.

If this story were a fairy tale, it would have a happy ending. The poor but wise man would be honored by everyone. A statue would be erected in his honor. He might even be elected to high office! But that didn't happen. Soon his wisdom that saved the city was forgotten, and he was forgotten as well. He went back to being a "nobody," living in poverty. In fact, in the future, when his wisdom could have continued to profit the little city, no one paid any attention to what he said.

But the writer of Ecclesiastes still says that wisdom is better than strength, even if no one pays any attention to words of wisdom. The wisdom of the poor man is still better than the brute force of the powerful king. In order for this to be true, we need to look at things from an eternal perspective. In heaven, the poor but wise man will finally be rewarded.

Job had similar concerns to that of the writer of Ecclesiastes. He wondered why he was suffering since he had been living a godly life. Many people expect God to bless those who obey God and punish those who do not. But Job wonderfully concludes that this life on earth is not all there is. In Job 19:25–27 (NIV), we read these wonderful words, "I know that my Redeemer lives, and that in the end he will stand upon the earth. And after my skin has been destroyed, yet in my flesh I will see God; I myself will see him with my own eyes—I, and not another. How my heart yearns within me!"

Only with eternity in view can we make sense of the suffering and injustice in this world. When we remember that God will make all things right in the end, it makes sense to pursue wisdom and justice. There may be no happy ending here on earth, but we know that our just and loving God will make all things right.

The preacher and Job were living on the other side of the Cross. But because of Jesus, we can be assured that we shall live on forever and there will be a happy ending.

2. The Benefit of Wisdom over Folly (vv. 17–18)

A wise mentor-teacher once said that, when a classroom of noisy children makes you feel like yelling at them, lower your voice instead. The children will get very quiet as they try to hear what you are saying. This quiet style of administration is advocated in these two verses. A noisy style is often masking a lack of substance. Unfortunately, crowds prefer a flashy dresser, someone who moves and shouts. The preacher explains that those who rule over fools have learned that style counts more than substance.

When we ponder verse 17, we should think about what we expect from our preachers and teachers. Are we ready to listen to quiet words of wisdom or do we expect the big show?

Verse 18 encapsulates wisdom that could end wars in our time, if people really followed these words. Peace negotiators may come with words of wisdom that, if heeded, could prevent wars. But all that is needed to stop negotiations is one rebellious person with a loud mouth or worse yet, with weapons of war. This sinner may stir up a crowd of fools, and soon many people are hurt or even killed.

This situation can also be applied to warring factions of any kind—the gangs in a neighborhood, the faculty of a school, the office we work in, and even church committees! Are we among those who listen to the agitators, or are we willing to listen to quiet words of wisdom and peace?

Search the Scriptures

1. What method of war did the powerful king attempt to use against a small city (Ecclesiastes 9:14)?

2. How did the poor but wise man save the city (v. 15)?

3. What happened to the poor man and his wisdom after he saved the city (vv. 15–16)?

4. How should we respond to quiet words of wisdom (v. 17)?

5. Who or what can destroy the peace brought about by wisdom (v. 18)?

Discuss the Meaning

The writer of Ecclesiastes is viewing a story from the viewpoint of life "under the sun." This is the opposite of viewing things from the perspective of eternity. How do you think God views the poor but wise man? How should our view of eternity affect how we judge the activities we see around us?

73

Lesson in Our Society

Today's Scripture passage describes a political situation. What are some ways that we can encourage those who rule over us to listen to words of wisdom more than to whoever is making the most noise?

Make It Happen

Maybe your class has some quiet members who have some wisdom to share. Give everyone a chance to participate in class discussions.

Follow the Spirit

What God wants me to do:

_____

_____

_____

_____

Remember Your Thoughts

Special insights I have learned:

_____

_____

_____

_____

More Light on the Text

Ecclesiastes 9:13–18

13 This wisdom have I seen also under the sun, and it seemed great unto me:

In most Scripture, the term "wisdom" refers to spiritual understanding and obedience. However, in this instance, it is human reason that is the measure. The first assessment of this observation is that here is a great example of wisdom.

The key to this verse is the phrase "under the sun." The Hebrew for "under the sun" is *tachath shemesh* (**TAKH-ath SHEH-mesh**). This phrase is used 29 times in the book of Ecclesiastes, and it is very important to understanding where the preacher is coming from. This is a metaphor for life on earth without considering whether or not there is an afterlife. What is the meaning of this life? Does it make any sense?

14 There was a little city, and few men within it; and there came a great king against it, and besieged it, and built great bulwarks against it:

The KJV uses the word "bulwarks" in five different places in the Bible and each time it is translated from a different Hebrew word. In this verse, it is translated from the Hebrew *matsowd* (**mah-TSODE**), which can mean a besieging tower, a bulwark, a hold, a munition, a net, or a snare, and we are left to our imaginations as to what sort of military equipment was used against this small town with very few men able to defend it. Since cities in those days were surrounded with heavy stone walls, a number of things were devised to knock down the walls or to gain entrance otherwise. Sometimes a ramp of soil and stones was constructed, which extended partway up the wall. Then the soldiers went up the ramp with a battering ram to knock down the walls. Other times a portable tower was used to come up to the walls and climb over. A walled city had a variety of defenses. They could pour boiling water or boiling oil upon the invaders. They could also hide behind a shield-like portable wall and shoot arrows at their enemies. The exact details of the military machines used against this small city are not necessary for us to understand this text because this is a parable and we will soon see the preacher's point of the story.

15 Now there was found in it a poor wise man, and he by his wisdom delivered the city; yet no man remembered that same poor man.

Again, we are left with no details. What was the advice of this wise but poor man? Scripture gives us a number of examples, such as the wise woman in 2 Samuel 20:14–22. The elderly King David was still mourning the death of his son, Absalom, who had turned the heart of the people away from David. Now David was back in power, but Sheba, who was related to the long dead King Saul, began another uprising against David. Joab, David's chief military leader, chased Sheba and had him surrounded in the city of Abel Beth Maacah. Joab had his men build a siege ramp and go up with a battering ram to knock down the walls. Joab's plan was to destroy the city in which Sheba had taken refuge. But a wise woman appealed to Joab not to destroy a city of Israel, so instead of ruining the entire city, the people cut off the head of Sheba and threw it down and that was the end of the war against this small city in Israel.

In Judges 9:53 another wise woman ended the siege against an entire city. This was a bloody war in which Abimelech had already destroyed the people of the city of Shechem. Some of the people escaped to a tower. Then Abimelech piled branches all around the tower and set them on fire, and over a thousand people died in the fire. When would all this awful war and murder come to an end? Then Abimelech went to another city where the people were once more taking refuge together in a tower. But, as he approached the tower, a wise woman threw a grinding stone down that reached its target—the head of Abimelech—and that was the end of him and of a gruesome war.

We do not know what the wise words of the commoner in the preacher's story were. All we know was that wise words saved the city, but rather than the wise man receiving great honor, he was soon forgotten.

16 Then said I, Wisdom is better than strength: nevertheless the poor man's wisdom is despised, and his words are not heard.

Here is the moral of the story with a rather anticlimactic ending. Although we read in Job of his wonderful faith—that he would see his Redeemer face-to-face, we often find in the Old Testament not such a clear understanding of life after death. If we did not have the further revelation, which tells us that God will someday come and make all things right, could we keep on believing in His justice and love, in spite of some of the injustices we see? As Christians, we are sure of the resurrection of our Savior and we know that we shall one day rise from the dead to live forever with Him. We know that Jesus will make all things right in the end, and so we put our trust in Him when things on earth are unfair. It is this trust that enables us to go on following the wise way. Even if the forces of corruption seem to be winning, we know that wisdom is better than power that is not restrained by goodness.

The problem here is that without a theology of life beyond the grave, wise words may fall on deaf ears. Although King Solomon was the wisest man on earth, he could find no real profit in wisdom, because he had left the spiritual dimension of life aside. He had filled his life with many wives and concubines, and they had turned his heart from God (1 Kings 11:1–3).

17 The words of wise men are heard in quiet more than the cry of him that ruleth among fools.

The Hebrew word for "fools" is *keciyl* (**kes-EEL**), and it can mean silly, stupid, or foolish. This verse suggests that not only did the ruler rule over fools, but that he himself was a fool. One can imagine that this ruler did not want to share his glory with a poor commoner, and so future wise advice for the city was lost. This is a common political situation. The ruler does only what benefits him- or herself, and through a loud and flashy style, people do not notice the ruler's corruption.

The phrase "heard in quiet" in verse 17 refers not to the manner in which the crowd received the words of wisdom, but to the way that they were delivered. In fact, this meaning comes through in other translations of this verse. The wise person is speaking in a gentle but sure voice. Meanwhile, the ruler among the fools shouts and pushes his way to get the attention of the people. In contrast to the foolish ruler of fools, the truly wise person gives advice in a quiet manner. Because he or she is counting on wisdom in words rather than dash and splash, the wise person speaks from a calm spirit within.

18 Wisdom is better than weapons of war: but one sinner destroyeth much good.

We don't know who this sinner is, but it has been suggested that he is the "ruler among fools." If so, we see that he has rejected hearing any more advice from the wise commoner, and so we come to the result that the city will suffer for it.

This verse makes us think of modern-day peace negotiations in many countries. While the negotiator sits down, listens to both sides, and comes up with a solution that is agreeable to all sides, some hotheaded leader is sabotaging the peace process, and thus many people are slaughtered, women are raped, people are starving, and families are torn apart and displaced—all because some leader of one faction wants the fighting to continue. In the meantime, he is not even home in his own country, which is being torn up. He is living in comfort and peace somewhere else.

But if we take this example closer to home, we can also see some church members who like to stir things up, and when they do, the cause of Christ is damaged and believers of all ages are made to stumble.

Sources:

Adeyemo, Tokunboh, ed., et al. *Africa Bible Commentary: A One-Volume Commentary Written by 70 African Scholars.* Nairobi, Kenya: Word Alive Publishers, 2006.

Baltes, A. J., ed. Biblespeech.com. http://biblespeech.com (accessed June 25, 2010).

Bartholomew, Craig G. *Ecclesiastes.* Grand Rapids, MI: Baker Academic, 2009.

Hebrew and Greek Lexicons. Bible Study Tools.com. http://www.biblestudytools.com/lexicons (accessed September 16, 2010).

Merriam-Webster Online Dictionary. Merriam-Webster, Inc. http://www.merriam-webster.com (accessed June 25, 2010).

Miller, Stephen R. "The Book of Ecclesiastes." *Holman Illustrated Bible Dictionary.* Chad Brand, Charles Draper and Archie England, gen. eds. Nashville, TN: Holman Bible Publishers, 2003. 452–455.

Seow, C. L. *Ecclesiastes: A New Translation with Introduction and Commentary.* From *The Anchor Bible.* New York, NY: Doubleday, 1997.

Strong's Concordance with Hebrew and Greek Lexicon. Eliyah.com. http://www.eliyah.com/lexicon.html (accessed June 29, 2010).

Say It Correctly

Abel Beth. A-bel-beth.
Abimelech. A-BIM-e-lek.
Ecclesiastes. E-KLE-se-as-tes.
Maacah. MA-a-kah.
Shechem. SHEK-em.

Daily Bible Readings

MONDAY
Hope in God's Steadfast Love
(Psalm 33:13–22)

TUESDAY
Two Are Better than One
(Ecclesiastes 4:4–12)

WEDNESDAY
Fear God!
(Ecclesiastes 5:1–7)

THURSDAY
Consider the Word of God
(Ecclesiastes 7:1–14)

FRIDAY
Wisdom and Success
(Ecclesiastes 10:5–11)

SATURDAY
Wisdom with Words
(Ecclesiastes 10:12–20)

SUNDAY
Wisdom Is Better than Might
(Ecclesiastes 9:13–18)

Notes

_____

_____

_____

_____

Teaching Tips

Words You Should Know

A. Vanity (Ecclesiastes 11:8, 10; 12:8) *hebel* (Heb.)—Transient, fleeting, and without substance.

B. Judgment (11:9) *mishpat*—The time of giving final account to God.

Teacher Preparation

Unifying Principle—Life Worth Living. Ecclesiastes concludes that the only thing that makes life worth living is to remember and honor our Creator, God, all the days of our lives.

A. Pray for your class and for lesson clarity.

B. Study the entire text, including More Light on the Text and the Daily Bible Readings.

C. Complete the companion lesson in the *Precepts For Living Personal Study Guide®*.

O—Open the Lesson

A. Open with prayer and then review the Aim for Change.

B. Have volunteers share how they think following Jesus Christ will help them manage their aging process and face death.

P—Present the Scriptures

A. Have volunteers read the Focal Verses.

B. Discuss the In Depth commentary according to the At-A-Glance outline and More Light on the Text.

E—Explore the Meaning

A. To answer questions in the Discuss the Meaning, Lesson in Our Society, and Make It Happen sections, divide the class into groups. Assign one or two questions to each group, and have them select a representative to report the responses.

B. Connect these sections to the Aim for Change and the Keep in Mind verse.

N—Next Steps for Application

A. Summarize the main points of today's discussion.

B. Close with prayer.

Worship Guide

For the Superintendent or Teacher
Theme: Wisdom for Aging
Song: "Great Is Thy Faithfulness"
Devotional Reading: Psalm 71:1–12
Prayer

Wisdom for Aging

Bible Background • ECCLESIASTES 11:7–12:14
Printed Text • ECCLESIASTES 11:9–12:7, 13 | Devotional Reading • PSALM 71:1–12

—————— Aim for Change ——————

By the end of the lesson, we will: UNDERSTAND the importance of seeking God early in our lives; REFLECT on the meaning of life as we move toward death; and IDENTIFY ways to honor God with our lives.

——————  In Focus ——————

One of the things that Rev. Smith loved most about being a pastor was the many opportunities he had to talk with older people—people in their 70s, 80s, and 90s. Rev. Smith smiled as he thought about the lessons that could be learned from the lives of these older believers. Mature Christians who have lived seven, eight, or nine decades tend to have learned to distinguish between what is urgent and what is important. They have learned what things need attention and what things need to be overlooked. They have learned to avoid making mountains out of molehills, and they seem never to be in a hurry. They have a wisdom garnered from a sober study of having experienced life at close range. Their years of experience and seasoned perspectives were sometimes amusing, but always informative.

OCT
16th

Rev. Smith's reflection also expressed the mood and concern of Ecclesiastes 11:7–12:8. The question about choice is a sobering one. The days of youth are fleeting. With the passing of each year comes some change in our bodies and in our environment. The aging process and change are inevitable. Like birth, childhood, and youth, the effects of advanced aging, change, and death are an inescapable part of life.

—————— Keep in Mind ——————

"Let us hear the conclusion of the whole matter: Fear God, and keep his commandments: for this is the whole duty of man" (Ecclesiastes 12:13).

"Let us hear the conclusion of the whole matter: Fear God, and keep his commandments: for this is the whole duty of man" (Ecclesiastes 12:13).

Focal Verses

KJV **Ecclesiastes 11:9** Rejoice, O young man, in thy youth; and let thy heart cheer thee in the days of thy youth, and walk in the ways of thine heart, and in the sight of thine eyes: but know thou, that for all these things God will bring thee into judgment.

10 Therefore remove sorrow from thy heart, and put away evil from thy flesh: for childhood and youth are vanity.

12:1 Remember now thy Creator in the days of thy youth, while the evil days come not, nor the years draw nigh, when thou shalt say, I have no pleasure in them;

2 While the sun, or the light, or the moon, or the stars, be not darkened, nor the clouds return after the rain:

3 In the day when the keepers of the house shall tremble, and the strong men shall bow themselves, and the grinders cease because they are few, and those that look out of the windows be darkened,

4 And the doors shall be shut in the streets, when the sound of the grinding is low, and he shall rise up at the voice of the bird, and all the daughters of musick shall be brought low;

5 Also when they shall be afraid of that which is high, and fears shall be in the way, and the almond tree shall flourish, and the grasshopper shall be a burden, and desire shall fail: because man goeth to his long home, and the mourners go about the streets:

6 Or ever the silver cord be loosed, or the golden bowl be broken, or the pitcher be broken at the fountain, or the wheel broken at the cistern.

7 Then shall the dust return to the earth as it was: and the spirit shall return unto God who gave it.

12:13 Let us hear the conclusion of the whole matter: Fear God, and keep his commandments: for this is the whole duty of man.

NLT **Ecclesiastes 11:9** Young man, it's wonderful to be young! Enjoy every minute of it. Do everything you want to do; take it all in. But remember that you must give an account to God for everything you do.

10 So banish grief and pain, but remember that youth, with a whole life before it, still faces the threat of meaninglessness.

12:1 Don't let the excitement of youth cause you to forget your Creator. Honor him in your youth before you grow old and no longer enjoy living.

2 It will be too late then to remember him, when the light of the sun and moon and stars is dim to your old eyes, and there is no silver lining left among the clouds.

3 Your limbs will tremble with age, and your strong legs will grow weak. Your teeth will be too few to do their work, and you will be blind, too.

4 And when your teeth are gone, keep your lips tightly closed when you eat! Even the chirping of birds will wake you up. But you yourself will be deaf and tuneless, with a quavering voice.

5 You will be afraid of heights and of falling, white-haired and withered, dragging along without any sexual desire. You will be standing at death's door. And as you near your everlasting home, the mourners will walk along the streets.

6 Yes, remember your Creator now while you are young, before the silver cord of life snaps and the golden bowl is broken. Don't wait until the water jar is smashed at the spring and the pulley is broken at the well.

7 For then the dust will return to the earth, and the spirit will return to God who gave it.

12:13 Here is my final conclusion: Fear God and obey his commands, for this is the duty of every person.

The People, Places, and Times

The Nature of Life and the Certainty of Death. Some realities about people, places, and times never change. Wise, God-fearing people in every generation have known that life is fragile, brief, and not without urgency. Consequently, the counsel necessary to pursue a meaningful life is relevant for all people, in every place, at all times. To make the most of one's youth, before the difficult days of old age and death arrive, was good counsel during Old Testament times, and it continues to be good counsel for life in the 21st century.

Background

The writer of Ecclesiastes had a deep and abiding desire to make sense out of life. He recognized that, except for death, judgment, and the fleeting days of youth, there were only a few things he could truly depend upon. Nothing seemed to be permanent. The effects of aging were overwhelmingly obvious. He also recognized that God's ways did not always meet his expectations. Consequently, his search for meaning in life was haunted by an anxiety that caused him to view human striving as "vanity" and a "chasing after the wind." In an attempt to find a way out of this dilemma, he resorts to reason. Through reason he concludes, as did the agnostics of his day, that life and human striving are indeed futile. But, unlike the agnostics, he added that life is futile only for those who disregard God.

Life is futile only when God and the acknowledgment of His rule are left out of the picture. Even reason is curtailed when it fails to recognize God, His gifts, and His purposes. While reason is good, it cannot answer all of life's questions and contradictions. The best reasoning will never replace God.

At-A-Glance

1. Rejoice in Life (Ecclesiastes 11:9–10)

2. Honor God (12:1)

3. Live Vigilantly (vv. 2–5)

4. Accept Death as a Normal Part of Life (vv. 6–7)

5. The Duty of Humankind (v. 13)

In Depth

1. Rejoice in Life (Ecclesiastes 11:9–10)

One of the greatest challenges of life is to truly live while we are alive. God wants us to enjoy life. Verse 9 also encourages readers to take their desires seriously and to act upon them: "Rejoice, O young man, in thy youth; and let thy heart cheer thee in the days of thy youth, and walk in the ways of thine heart, and in the sight of thine eyes . . ." (v. 9). The enjoyment of life and the pursuit of one's desires, however, are to be governed and managed by a keen awareness of one's accountability to God: "but know thou, that for all these things God will bring thee into judgment" (from v. 9).

The use of the word *judgment* in verse 9 should be understood in the light of the Olympian athlete who trains diligently, and after giving his or her all in competition, awaits expectantly to receive the appropriate recognition and reward. In biblical thought, judgment is not a moment to be feared; rather, it is a crowning moment to be welcomed by all those who have spent their days celebrating life and pursuing the desires of their heart in ways that honor God.

Verse 10 is a transitional sentence that helps set the stage to consider the brevity of life and the urgency to employ one's youthful years wisely as well.

2. Honor God (12:1)

The motivation to enjoy life and to pursue the heart's desires is sparked, in part, by the brevity of life and fleetingness of youth. Therefore, one's youthful days should be taken seriously, and the opportunities presented during youth should be promptly acted upon out of reverence for God.

This is not to suggest, however, that opportunities vanish with one's aging years. Quite the contrary, just as there are opportunities available to youth, opportunities are also available throughout one's life. What is at stake, however, is the potential impact of the aging process upon one's capacity to maximize life's pleasures.

According to the Ecclesiastical writer, youth is the optimum time to make oneself available to God and thereby maximize responsibly the pleasures God would have us enjoy. "Enjoy life's pleasures while you're young" is often stated with flippancy, but it resonates with the Ecclesiastical perspective. The only caution is that one's involvement in life's pleasures would honor God, our Creator (12:1).

3. Live Vigilantly (vv. 2–5)

The book of Ecclesiastes offers no illusions about the potential effects of the aging process and the certainty of death. If one continues to live, aging and death are imminent and inescapable. Generally speaking, verses 2 through 5 seem to comprise a soliloquy about the effects of aging and the inevitability of death. Exactly how the specific images referenced in these verses are to be interpreted is open for debate. What is clear, however, is the emphasis on the progressive nature of the decay of living things, which eventually leads to death.

Where human life is concerned, the aging process affects, in a variety of ways, one's capacity to function. Ultimately, the aging process leads to death and "man goes to his eternal home and mourners go about the streets" (v. 5, NIV).

The message of verses 2 through 5 is intended to give urgency to the invitation of verse 1 to "remember . . . thy Creator in the days of thy youth." In other words, we are to begin early in life to enjoy life by living vigilantly, "soberly, righteously, and godly, in this present world" (from Titus 2:12).

4. Accept Death as a Normal Part of Life (vv. 6–7)

There is a sense that human death is like the destruction of everyday objects that have ceased to be useful. A severed silver cord, a broken golden bowl, a shattered pitcher, and a broken wheel or pulley— whether used individually or collectively as a vessel suspended by a rope from a pulley over a dried-up abandoned well—are all metaphorical images of death.

Usually, it is understood and accepted that each of these objects used to draw water from a well do not last forever. Moreover, wells sometimes dry up and become useless. This, too, is understandable and accepted as par for the course of life. So also should it be where human death is concerned. Death is a normal part of life.

While its coming may occasion grief, God has ordained its place in the unfolding mystery of His ways. Since God has ordained death, we can honor Him by accepting what He has ordained.

5. The Duty of Humankind (v. 13)

Now we come to the end of the book of Ecclesiastes and the author gives us his conclusion. The "fear of the Lord" is reverential awe of Him. In our efforts to make the Christian faith more palatable to the modern mind, we have soft-pedaled fear of the Lord. We need to remember who God is—the Creator of the universe and all that is in it. He is the one who holds our eternal future in His hands. No matter what else this world holds out to us, we need to remember that God is the Almighty God. The order of the original Hebrew words is "God you shall fear." The conclusion of the book begins with the word "God." The evidence of our wholehearted belief in Him should be obedience to all His commands.

Search the Scriptures

1. "Childhood and youth are _____" (Ecclesiastes 11:10).

2. "Remember now thy _____ in the days of thy _____, while the evil _____ come not, nor the years _____ _____, when thou shalt say, I have no pleasure in them" (Ecclesiastes 12:1).

Discuss the Meaning

1. In what sense are we to understand the statement, "All that cometh is vanity. . . .Vanity of vanities, saith the preacher; all is vanity" (Ecclesiastes 11:8; 12:8)?

2. Discuss the meaning of Ecclesiastes 12:7.

Lesson in Our Society

While we may reflect with gratitude on the blessings of our earlier years, the reality is that the days of our youth pass all too quickly. The existential moment of realization is upon us; youth and vitality do not continue unabated forever. We are challenged to adapt ourselves to the diminishing abilities of increased age. The question is: Can we do so gracefully? Can we stand face-to-face with the aging process and embrace the inevitable approach of death as a time of reunion, renewal, and fulfillment? Those who keep God first and who are confident of His goodness can truly live. They can enjoy and find a way to celebrate all the events of life.

Make It Happen

Spend some time reflecting upon the days of your youth, and thank God for the distance He has brought you. Recommit yourself to Him. Ask Him to give you sufficient grace to manage the diminishing abilities of your own aging. Ask Him to supply you with the resources necessary to enjoy and celebrate life in ways that honor Him.

Follow the Spirit

What God wants me to do:

_____

_____

_____

_____

Remember Your Thoughts

Special insights I have learned:

_____

_____

_____

_____

More Light on the Text
Ecclesiastes 11:9–12:7, 13

9 Rejoice, O young man, in thy youth; and let thy heart cheer thee in the days of thy youth, and walk in the ways of thine heart, and in the sight of thine eyes: but know thou, that for all these things God will bring thee into judgment.

Verse 9 expresses the advice an older person might give to a younger person: "Make the most of your younger years." On the surface, it appears that Solomon is encouraging young men to live a life of folly. The recommendations to, for instance, "walk in the ways of [your] heart" seem like an invitation for young people to go out and do whatever they'd like to do. However, when our wants are attuned to what God wants from us, then what we want to do will be what He wants us to do. Solomon also reminds us that in the end "all these things God will bring. . . into judgment." Someday all our words and works will be weighed by God's eternal evaluation.

10 Therefore remove sorrow from thy heart, and put away evil from thy flesh: for childhood and youth are vanity.

In light of God's future judgment, Solomon advised youth to get rid of grief and avoid sin (or evil). Some teens and young adults are impatient or lack self-control. Others may focus on pleasing themselves and dislike anything that contradicts their way of thinking. Solomon reminds us that youth is fleeting, and although we should enjoy life during our youth, we should live in a way that glorifies God.

12:1 Remember now thy Creator in the days of thy youth, while the evil days come not, nor the years draw nigh, when thou shalt say, I have no pleasure in them;

Since God is our Creator, we'd better follow His Word if we want our lives to run as smoothly as possible. God's manual of operations tells us how to get the maximum benefits out of this life we are living. (In Deuteronomy 8:18 and Psalm 119:55 the word *remember* is another form of saying we should keep God's Word or "law.") The phrase "days of thy youth" in Ecclesiastes 12:1 is literally translated from Hebrew as "days of black hair," meaning before your hair turns gray.

2 While the sun, or the light, or the moon, or the stars, be not darkened, nor the clouds return after the rain:

In verse 2, the deteriorating days of old age are depicted as a cloudy period. Since those dark days inevitably come, the writer urges the readers to remember their Creator "before the sun and the light and the moon and the stars grow dark, and the clouds return after the rain" (v. 2, NIV).

3 In the day when the keepers of the house shall tremble, and the strong men shall bow themselves, and the grinders cease because they are few, and those that look out of the windows be darkened,

Modern people have humorously referred to the five B's of old age: baldness, bifocals, bridges, bulges, and bunions. However, here, we should proceed with care as we seek to examine the correlation between each picture and some failing frailty in an aging person's body. The metaphors in verses 3 through 8 are hard to understand without the help of Bible scholars. But even the scholars are not in agreement about what each word picture means. The "keepers [or guardians] of the house" in this verse may refer to muscular arms that are now weakening and beginning to tremble. The "strong men" may refer to the once-strong legs that are beginning to become feeble (compare Song of Solomon 5:15).

In the era when this text was written, women regularly did the grinding of the grain for bread baking on a grindstone. The reference to "grinders" probably portrays an older person's loss of teeth. The fourth picture in Ecclesiastes 12:3, "those that look out of the windows," may refer to dimming eyesight often associated with old age. Our eyes are like windows in a house that look out on the world.

4 And the doors shall be shut in the streets, when the sound of the grinding is low, and he shall rise up at the voice of the bird, and all the daughters of musick shall be brought low;

The closed doors to the house in verse 4 could present a picture of becoming so hard of hearing that we feel like the world is being shut out, or since in Hebrew the expression refers to "double doors," it might refer to a person's jaws, which don't always express what he or she would like to remember.

"The sound of the grinding is low" indicates that the older person no longer hears sounds as distinctly as in younger years. Paradoxically, even though elderly individuals may not hear what others are talking about, they may wake up extraordinarily early at the mere twittering of a bird outside (which may be the meaning of "rise up at the voice of the bird").

The "daughters of musick" is perhaps a reference to songs. In other words, it's as though a father is the music-maker and the daughter is the song. So the phrase "all the daughters of musick shall be brought low" could indicate a time when an older person may complain of being unable to hear the words of a song.

5 Also when they shall be afraid of that which is high, and fears shall be in the way, and the almond tree shall flourish, and the grasshopper shall be a burden, and desire shall fail: because man goeth to his long home, and the mourners go about the streets:

Verse 5 is difficult for the scholars to translate. The first part undoubtedly refers to the aging individual's increasing fears and difficulty with heights.

The almond tree has pretty pink petals at first, but then it bursts into an all-white color, similar to the change experienced by a white-haired elderly individual. "The grasshopper shall be a burden" is translated in the NIV as "the grasshopper drags himself along," bringing to mind the slow and stiff walk of an elderly person.

The next phrase says that "desire shall fail." The Hebrew word *abiyownah* (**ab-ee-yo-NAW**) may refer to a caperberry, which many considered in the ancient Middle East to be an aphrodisiac or love potion. This is why the King James translators rendered it "desire." The aging person's appetites (whether for sex or food) diminish. In fact, the last part of this verse almost sounds like the pallbearers are parading outside in the street, rehearsing for the funeral!

6 Or ever the silver cord be loosed, or the golden bowl be broken, or the pitcher be broken at the fountain, or the wheel broken at the cistern.

Verse 6 may be painting two pictures: (1) a lamp with oil and (2) a well with water. Lamps during biblical times usually looked like clay dishes with a wick sitting in oil in the dish. The wick would stay lit as long as oil was present. The author may have pictured a "golden [lamp] bowl" hung on a "silver cord" that was broken or smashed. As a result, the lamp became useless. A well (or cistern) during biblical times might have had a "wheel" that held an attached bucket or "pitcher" to a rope that went down into the well to obtain water below. If the bucket were to strike the well's side, it might also become broken. These images refer to the end of life. Just as useful devices and their parts eventually wear out, our lives eventually come to an end.

7 Then shall the dust return to the earth as it was: and the spirit shall return unto God who gave it.

"Dust to dust and ashes to ashes" is the familiar refrain at funerals. In verse 7, the "dust" of our bodies returns to the dust of the earth, and "the spirit" returns to God who gave us breath and life. In Genesis 2:7, God's formation of Adam consisted of a dust body and divine breath (spirit). The primary emphasis on "spirit" (Heb. *ruwach*, **ROO-akh**) here refers to how God as the source of life keeps all of us alive, and perhaps secondly to our composition as humans. Regarding the latter, what this means for Christians is that our physical/material bodies go down to the grave at death, but the immaterial spiritual aspect of us goes to be with God until the final resurrection. Those that do not know God are in a sleep-like state until they are resurrected at the final judgment. The day will come when we all must stand before God. Are you prepared to meet God? You can be ready by believing that Christ died for you and receiving God's gift of eternal life and becoming part of His family.

12:13 Let us hear the conclusion of the whole matter: Fear God, and keep his commandments: for this is the whole duty of man.

Various biblical scholars have speculated on the theme of the book of Ecclesiastes, but in this verse, we have the author's own word on this. *Cowph* (**sofe**), the Hebrew for "conclusion," implies this is more than simply the end—it is the conclusion based on all that is written in Ecclesiastes. Ecclesiastes contains the meditations of a man who has lived to see old age. He has seen much that does not seem to make sense, but in the end he realizes all that really matters is that we fear the Lord and obey Him. The Hebrew word for "fear" is *yare'* (**yah-RAY**). In addition to fear, it means "to revere" or "to dread," so we definitely see that we should tremble when we think about disobeying Almighty God.

The fear of God opens the possibility of a relationship with Him. We see His awesomeness and His holiness. We realize that we are sinful beings unable to enter into His presence, even though we want to more than anything else. We find ourselves being drawn to Him, but how can we come before Him? The writer of Hebrews tells us that because Jesus sacrificed Himself on the Cross, we are able to enter the presence of God (10:19–22). And because of His sacrifice for us, we desire to please Him and obey Him.

The Hebrew for "man" in Ecclesiastes 12:13 is *'adam* (**a-DAWM**), the same word as the name of the first man—Adam. But in this case it simply refers to a human being. Whether male or female, our primary task in life is to bow down in reverence before God and obey Him.

Sources:
Baltes, A. J., ed. Biblespeech.com. http://biblespeech.com (accessed November 4, 2009).
Bible Study Tools.com. Old Testament Hebrew Lexicons. http://www.biblestudytools.com/lexicons/hebrew/kjv (accessed June 10, 2010).
Hebrew and Greek Lexicons. Bible Study Tools.com. http://www.biblestudytools.com/lexicons (accessed September 16, 2010).
Leupold, H. C. *Exposition of Ecclesiastes.* Columbus, OH: The Wartburg Press, 1952.
Seow, C. L. *Ecclesiastes: A New Translation with Introduction and Commentary. The Anchor Bible.* New York, NY: Doubleday, 1997.

Say It Correctly

Ecclesiastes. E-KLE-se-as-tes.

Daily Bible Readings

MONDAY
Do Not Forsake Me
(Psalm 71:1–12)

TUESDAY
Nothing New under the Sun?
(Ecclesiastes 1:1–11)

WEDNESDAY
Nothing To Be Gained?
(Ecclesiastes 2:1–11)

THURSDAY
Toiling for the Wind
(Ecclesiastes 5:10–20)

FRIDAY
Everything Has Its Time
(Ecclesiastes 3:1–8)

SATURDAY
Ignorance of God's Work
(Ecclesiastes 11:1–8)

SUNDAY
Remember Your Creator
(Ecclesiastes 11:9–12:7, 13)

Notes

Teaching Tips

Words You Should Know

A. Sister (Song of Solomon 4:9) *àchowth* (Heb.)—A term of endearment meaning "beloved;" it denotes an intimate relationship.

B. Enclosed (v. 12) *naàl* (Heb.)—Something that is locked, bolted, or shut up.

Teacher Preparation

Unifying Principle—A Kiss Is Still a Kiss. Solomon used poetry to speak of his love for his wife. His example provides a model for couples seeking ways to express their feelings of love and commitment.

A. Read the Focal Verses in the KJV and NLT.

B. Study 1 Corinthians 13 for New Testament standards of love.

C. Prepare a list of classical literature where love is a key theme.

D. Bring in a short poem or short excerpt from your list.

E. Complete the companion lesson in the *Precepts For Living Personal Study Guide*®.

O—Open the Lesson

A. Invite a student to open the class with prayer.

B. Have volunteers read the Aim for Change. Discuss.

C. Read the Keep in Mind verse in unison.

D. Have a volunteer read 1 Corinthians 13:4–8a. Discuss.

E. Share your selected poem and connect it to the Keep in Mind verse.

F. Discuss why Song of Solomon is important for today's couples.

P—Present the Scriptures

A. Have volunteers read the Focal Verses.

B. Now use The People, Places, and Times; Background; Search the Scriptures; At-A-Glance outline; In Depth; and More Light on the Text to clarify the verses.

E—Explore the Meaning

A. Have a student read the In Focus story.

B. Summarize the Discuss the Meaning, Lesson in Our Society, and Make It Happen sections.

N—Next Steps for Application

A. Invite students to use the Remember Your Thoughts section to write a short love poem or letter to a real or imagined spouse.

B. Close with prayer.

OCT
23rd

Worship Guide

For the Superintendent or Teacher
Theme: Tradition and Love
Song: "Great Is Thy Faithfulness"
Devotional Reading: Genesis 2:18–24
Prayer

Tradition and Love

Bible Background • SONG OF SOLOMON 4:8–5:1a
Printed Text • SONG OF SOLOMON 4:8–5:1a | Devotional Reading • GENESIS 2:18–24

Aim for Change

By the end of the lesson, we will: DISCUSS the beauty and wonder of love in a committed relationship; REFLECT on our attitude about love and commitment; and EXPLAIN how to build a relationship that honors a marriage commitment.

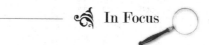 In Focus

Charlene and Rodney, both attorneys, celebrated their seventh wedding anniversary in two different hotels in two different states. They expressed their love via text message, each too busy to place a call. When they finally caught up with each other a week later, celebrating their anniversary was the last thing on their minds. Charlene's major corporate client had just landed in the midst of an environmental crisis while one of Rodney's elite athletic clients was embroiled in a messy federal probe.

When they received a call that one of their best friends had died in a fiery car crash along with his wife and son, the couple was crushed. This friend was the same one who had set Charlene and Rodney up for a blind date nine years ago. He recently reminded them to slow down and refocus their priorities because "tomorrow is not promised." The accident was a wake-up call for the couple, compelling them to finally act on their friend's advice.

Many priorities vie for a couple's attention, but nothing is as important as their devotion to God and each other. Building a relationship that honors a marriage commitment helps couples outsmart the "little foxes" that destroy marriages. The Song of Solomon gives us a godly perspective.

Keep in Mind

"Awake, O north wind; and come, thou south; blow upon my garden, that the spices thereof may flow out. Let my beloved come into his garden, and eat his pleasant fruits" (Song of Solomon 4:16).

"Awake, O north wind; and come, thou south; blow upon my garden, that the spices thereof may flow out. Let my beloved come into his garden, and eat his pleasant fruits" (Song of Solomon 4:16).

Focal Verses

KJV **Song of Solomon 4:8** Come with me from Lebanon, my spouse, with me from Lebanon: look from the top of Amana, from the top of Shenir and Hermon, from the lions' dens, from the mountains of the leopards.

9 Thou hast ravished my heart, my sister, my spouse; thou hast ravished my heart with one of thine eyes, with one chain of thy neck.

10 How fair is thy love, my sister, my spouse! how much better is thy love than wine! and the smell of thine ointments than all spices!

11 Thy lips, O my spouse, drop as the honeycomb: honey and milk are under thy tongue; and the smell of thy garments is like the smell of Lebanon.

12 A garden inclosed is my sister, my spouse; a spring shut up, a fountain sealed.

13 Thy plants are an orchard of pomegranates, with pleasant fruits; camphire, with spikenard,

14 Spikenard and saffron; calamus and cinnamon, with all trees of frankincense; myrrh and aloes, with all the chief spices:

15 A fountain of gardens, a well of living waters, and streams from Lebanon.

16 Awake, O north wind; and come, thou south; blow upon my garden, that the spices thereof may flow out. Let my beloved come into his garden, and eat his pleasant fruits.

5:1a I am come into my garden, my sister, my spouse:

NLT **Song of Solomon 4:8** "Come with me from Lebanon, my bride. Come down from the top of Mount Amana, from Mount Senir and Mount Hermon, where lions have their dens and panthers prowl.

9 You have ravished my heart, my treasure, my bride. I am overcome by one glance of your eyes, by a single bead of your necklace.

10 How sweet is your love, my treasure, my bride! How much better it is than wine! Your perfume is more fragrant than the richest of spices.

11 Your lips, my bride, are as sweet as honey. Yes, honey and cream are under your tongue. The scent of your clothing is like that of the mountains and the cedars of Lebanon.

12 "You are like a private garden, my treasure, my bride! You are like a spring that no one else can drink from, a fountain of my own.

13 You are like a lovely orchard bearing precious fruit, with the rarest of perfumes:

14 nard and saffron, calamus and cinnamon, myrrh and aloes, perfume from every incense tree, and every other lovely spice.

15 You are a garden fountain, a well of living water, as refreshing as the streams from the Lebanon mountains."

16 *Young Woman:* "Awake, north wind! Come, south wind! Blow on my garden and waft its lovely perfume to my lover. Let him come into his garden and eat its choicest fruits."

5:1a *Young Man:* "I am here in my garden, my treasure, my bride!

The People, Places, and Times

Weddings and Marriage. Compatibility and romance were not necessarily essential to marriages in Solomon's day. In biblical times, couples did not meet, date, fall in love, and then marry. Rather, marriage was a vastly different four-step process that had little to do with emotional involvement. First, fathers chose their sons' brides. Indeed, marriage was an arranged contract between two families who sought alliances with each other for various reasons, such as to enhance a social, territorial, or financial position. Second, to seal the contract, the bridegroom's father paid a "bride price" to the bride's family. Third, the couple became betrothed to each other after their parents ratified the contract either verbally (pre-exile) or by signing a covenant (post-exile). The year-long betrothal encompassed the groom-to-be's preparation of the home and the couple's abstinence. Sex between the couple was forbidden, as was sex with other individuals (Deuteronomy 22:13:21; 23–24; 28:2). Fourth, after the successful completion of the betrothal, the couple fulfilled their legal (and social) responsibility to marry. Wedding feasts—elaborate events that often lasted a week—provided ample opportunity for family and friends to applaud the new alliance and celebrate the marriage consummation.

Background

Son of King David and Bathsheba, Solomon was part of the lineage of Jesus. He was the third king of Israel. He reigned in Israel for 40 years. Israel was at peace during much of Solomon's reign. During that time, Solomon became renowned for his unequalled wisdom, vast wealth, and impressive Temple construction project (which took seven years to complete). Of the three, wisdom was Solomon's greatest claim to fame.

Solomon's wisdom was a gift of God, drawing worldwide acclaim (1 Kings 4:34). Some of Solomon's wisdom is contained in the three thousand proverbs—wise sayings—and more than one thousand songs he wrote. While the authorship of the Song of Solomon—also dubbed the "Song of Songs"—has been debated, many scholars attribute it to King Solomon.

By Solomon's day, many men had strayed from God's one-wife design for marriage. Most had multiple wives. Few, however, could attest to having as many as Solomon. He had 700 wives and 300 concubines (1 Kings 11:1–13). Concubines, considered to be secondary wives, held lower social rank than women who bore the title "wife." The foreign women in his life influenced Solomon's worship of foreign gods. However, he may have had a change of heart later in life (Ecclesiastes 12:13).

At-A-Glance

1. Invitation to Love
(Song of Solomon 4:8–9)

2. Love Expressed
(vv. 10–15)

3. Love Cherished
(4:16–5:1a)

In Depth

1. Invitation to Love (Song of Solomon 4:8–9)

Song of Solomon remains a text to which Christians can turn for encouragement as they contemplate love and commitment. Every marriage begins with an invitation to love, the point at which a relationship becomes more serious and leads up to the exchange of vows. In today's text, the groom-to-be issues the invitation to love and awaits his beloved's response. He invited his beloved, "Come with me from Lebanon, my bride. Come down from the top of Mount Amana, from Mount Senir and Hermon, where lions have their dens and panthers prowl" (Song of Solomon 4:8, NLT). Then he utters the words that have enthralled women for centuries: "You have ravished my heart, my treasure, my bride" (from v. 9, NLT).

His words are reminiscent of Adam's when God presented Eve to the world's first bridegroom. He said, "She is part of my own flesh and bone!" (from Genesis 2:23, NLT). Many singles wonder if they will ever find the suitable mate, while couples wonder how to revive a stalled marriage.

Consider the following: No two men or women are exactly alike. That is why there is no "one size fits all" formula to finding or keeping a mate. Also, it is important to acknowledge that many Christians skip to the altar without first asking God, "Is this the one?" Inviting God into the mate selection process has helped many couples make the right decision. Struggling couples can seek God's help, committing to biblical principles—not worldly wisdom—to renew their commitment to each other.

2. Love Expressed (vv. 10–15)

Solomon eloquently enumerates the bride's endearing qualities. By doing so, he reminds us that love needs expression. How can married or dating couples express love verbally? First, mediate on a beloved's good or sweet qualities! Second, extol a spouse's physical attributes. For example, Solomon talked about the sweetness of his bride's lips. Third, consider the beauty, joy, and value that your beloved adds to your life.

Sometimes the root of an inability to express love is one or more of the following

"little foxes": (1) *Past experiences.* These include verbal abuse, childhood sexual or physical abuse, a failed marriage, or even wrong advice. Many husbands believe "real men never share their feelings," while many wives heed, "Girl, do not let that man know how much you love him." Whatever the cause, couples can look to God for healing and wholeness, knowing He designed marriage to be the place for couples to experience satisfying love. (2) *Harsh words.* Sometimes familiarity breeds contempt in marriage as evidenced by how a wife speaks to her husband and vice versa. The apostle James warned, "The tongue is a small thing, but what enormous damage it can do" (from James 3:5, NLT). Couples are reminded: "Don't use foul or abusive language. Let everything you say be good and helpful, so that your words will be an encouragement to those who hear them" (Ephesians 4:29, NLT). (3) *Family and friends.* Marriages do not play out in enclosed gardens out of the presence of other people's eyes, ears, and comments. Nonetheless, while couples need trusted advisors at different seasons of their marriage, they should rely only on individuals who honor confidentiality. These include friends, family members, church leaders, or marriage counselors who seek the couple's best interests.

3. Love Enjoyed (4:16–5:1a)

Solomon's poetic words whet the appetite for building a marriage that honors a marriage commitment. Acknowledging the following makes this an attainable goal: (1) *True love surpasses all else.* After the honeymoon, couples need to continually prioritize as they remember the why of love and execute the how of love. (2) *True love is satisfying.* It quenches emotional and physical thirsts, thus eliminating the need to sip from any other fountain. (3) *True love is physical.*

Solomon celebrated the beauty of sex in the confines of marriage. It is passionate and fulfilling. Marital sex catapults a couple back to the Garden of Eden where love is freely given and received, and where there is the vulnerability characteristic of being "naked and unashamed." (4) *True love is faithful.* A husband needs to know he can trust his wife and vice versa. Infidelity is a sin and a serious breach of one's wedding vows. First Corinthians 13:1–13 offers additional insight into the attributes of true love. (5) *True love is a mix of sweet and bitter herbs.* Only in fairy tales do couples live happily ever after without disagreements, trials, or struggles. Health concerns, financial problems, and other issues impact relationships. The key is to assure that external situations strengthen, not weaken, marriage commitments.

It is important to note that Song of Solomon is applicable for singles, as well. For example, the analogy of the "enclosed garden" reminds singles to reserve intimacy for marriage and to seek other ways to express love to each other. For single women this means: (1) keeping her garden closed; (2) looking beyond physical attributes to a man's heart; and (3) not buying into society's "ticking clock" mantra. For single men this entails: (1) not pressuring a woman to open her garden; (2) looking beyond physical attributes to a woman's heart; and (3) expressing love in non-physical ways.

Search the Scriptures

1. What did Solomon's beloved do to him (Song of Solomon 5:19)?

2. List some of the things Solomon had to say about her (5:10).

Discuss the Meaning

Solomon expressed his feelings for his bride without detailing exactly what occurred in the privacy of their bedroom. What lessons can couples learn from his example? How can couples sidestep questions that are an invasion of marital privacy?

Lesson in Our Society

Social media sites allow users to rekindle "old flames" more easily than ever. In light of Song of Solomon 4:7, what can couples do to avoid the comparison traps that often lead husbands and wives to seek out people they once dated?

Make It Happen

Couples seeking to improve their marriages can take lessons from Solomon who knew how to verbally bless his bride and give romantic gifts. Likewise, dating singles headed for the altar can begin today to build a strong foundation for marriage by using uplifting words. One Scripture worth remembering is Ephesians 4:29. Commit it to memory and live it out—beginning today. If you have been guilty of demeaning your husband or wife, ask for forgiveness.

Follow the Spirit

What God wants me to do:

_____

_____

_____

_____

Remember Your Thoughts

Special insights I have learned:

_____

_____

_____

_____

More Light on the Text

Song of Solomon 4:8–5:1a

Introduction

Until the 19th century, Jewish and Christian communities both interpreted Song of Solomon as an allegory of God's love for His people. Today, the book is recognized for what it really is: love poetry.

The Song of Solomon celebrates erotic love as something that is beautiful—a good gift of God for which we should be thankful. However, the book is also clear that sexual expression carries responsibilities with it, and it must conform to God's law in order to be a blessing. We are repeatedly warned against stirring up or awakening love until the right time (2:7; 3:5; 8:4). Although there is no explicit mention of a marriage ceremony in the book, there can be no doubt that the author only condones sexual intercourse within the bounds of marriage.

In this week's passage, the man speaks passionately about his admiration for the woman. In 4:1–7, he praised her beauty by describing her features from the top of her head to her breasts. In verse 8, his focus shifts slightly to the impact that her beauty has on him.

8 Come with me from Lebanon, my spouse, with me from Lebanon: look from the top of Amana, from the top of Shenir and Hermon, from the lions' dens, from the mountains of the leopards.

The man calls for his lover to come to him from Lebanon, the country to the immediate north of Israel. Shenir (in Hebrew *Sheniyr*, **shen-EER**, also known as Senir), a mountain in this area, is part of a range that extends into Lebanon and includes Mount Amana. Hermon is another name for Shenir. Naming Lebanon and these mountains creates the perception of separation by distance. The mention of lions and leopards paints a picture of danger, but also of mystique, grandeur, and power. It is worth noting that this kind of desolate, mountainous imagery was commonly used in the ancient world in descriptions of goddesses. Although the Jewish author and audience would have rejected the pagan myths of gods and goddesses who engage in sexual relations, the man's words were influenced by that motif. He is saying that his beloved is a goddess to him. She is, at least to this point, "off limits" or inaccessible to him. She does not yet belong to him, so in his mind she might as well be at the top of a distant mountain. He wants her to be close to him.

9 Thou hast ravished my heart, my sister, my spouse; thou hast ravished my heart with one of thine eyes, with one chain of thy neck.

The phrase "ravished my heart" is used twice to describe the impact the woman has on her suitor. The Hebrew verb *labab* (**law-BAB**) comes from the word for "heart" and occurs in an intensified stem that emphasizes the resulting state. It could mean that she leaves him feeling weak or shaken; it may also mean that she energizes and arouses him. The New International Version translates this as "stolen my heart." The New

Living Translation renders it as "captured my heart." Less formal ways to capture the sentiment being expressed could include "I am hopelessly in love with you" (Garrett, 406) or "You drive me crazy!" (Longman, 151).

That the man refers to the woman as "sister" was not unusual to the original audience. This was a common expression of romantic affection in the Ancient Near East. It certainly implies marriage because in his mind they are family.

All that it takes to capture his attention is "one glance of [her] eyes" or one "jewel from her necklace" (NIV). The Hebrew word translated "chain of thy neck" is *ànaq* (**aw-NAWK**), and it refers to a beaded jewel from a necklace. Since goddesses in the Ancient Near East were frequently portrayed nude except for a necklace, this may be another subtle reference to goddess myths.

10 How fair is thy love, my sister, my spouse! how much better is thy love than wine! and the smell of thine ointments than all spices!

Having described the impact the woman has on him in verses 8 and 9, the man now focuses on the sensory experience of her love. A man of fewer words would simply say, "I love everything about you." But that would not do justice to her beauty. The only fitting way to communicate his captivation with her is to use finely crafted metaphors that compare her attributes to the finest and best things known in the ancient world.

Wine has already been used as an analogy for love in this book (1:2; 1:4). A fine wine has both mood-altering power and a sophisticated, refined beauty. The comparison of her love with wine says that her love is elegant and has an intoxicating effect. Her "ointments" are her perfumes. The Hebrew word translated "spices" is *besem* (**BEH-sem**). Also used in verse 14, *besem* was an ingredient in the anointing oil used in the temple (Exodus 25:6) and was given to Solomon by the Queen of Sheba (1 Kings 10:2, 10, 25). Doubtless, it was a valuable, high-end product. By comparing her scent to the most prized fragrances of the day, the man is saying that not only does he prefer her to anyone or anything else, but she is also the gold standard.

11 Thy lips, O my spouse, drop as the honeycomb: honey and milk are under thy tongue; and the smell of thy garments is like the smell of Lebanon.

Honey and honeycomb were highly prized luxury items in the Ancient Near East. Note that when Jacob wanted to pacify the ruler of Egypt, he instructed his sons to take a gift package that included, among other things, honey (Genesis 43:11). "Milk and honey" are common expressions in the Old Testament used to indicate fertility, prosperity, and an abundance of good things. In other words, honey and milk were some of the best things in the ancient world. The appeal of this kind of luxury item is multidimensional: sweetness perfectly balanced with texture and aroma. Such delicacies cannot be properly enjoyed quickly, but must be savored. He is dreaming of long, slow kisses.

At the time of Solomon, Lebanon was renowned for its cedar forests. To say that the smell of her clothes is like the smell of a cedar forest does not necessarily mean that she smells like cedar. However, there is something ideal about the aroma of Lebanon and her aroma is likewise a very fine thing. Note that in the first seven verses of Song of Solomon 4, her hair is compared to a flock of goats and her breasts are compared to gazelles. This kind of metaphor does not indicate resemblance, but a shared standard of excellence or quality.

12 A garden inclosed is my sister, my spouse; a spring shut up, a fountain sealed.

The appeal of the woman is based not only on her excellent physical features, but on her skill in self-presentation, air of nobility, and overpowering charm. Her virtue overpowers and enhances all these charms. She is not readily available for any who want her—or even for her lover at this point in the poem. The fact that she has saved herself for him and has waited for the right time to consummate their love intensifies his desire for her.

The Hebrew word translated "garden" is *gan* (**gan**). Gardens in the Ancient Near East had more in common with our parks than what we typically think of as a "garden." Although they would have contained a variety of herbs, vegetables, fruit trees, and flowering plants (see verses 13 and 14), they were not simply thought of as a place to grow things. Rather, they were regarded as sources of great beauty and pleasure. By using this garden metaphor, the man is building anticipation for the day his lover gives herself fully to him.

Fountains were another source of pleasure to the ancients and a metaphor for sexual pleasure. A garden is a feast to the senses of sight, smell, and taste; a fountain satisfies the eye as well as refreshing the skin and quenching the thirst of the one who partakes of it. Proverbs 5:18–20 describes the wife of his youth as a fountain and exhorts him to be delighted with her breasts.

In Song of Solomon 4:12, the Hebrew word translated "inclosed" is *naàl* (**naw-AL**) and is used to refer to "locked" doors elsewhere in the Old Testament. She is "shut up" and "sealed" so that no one has yet been able to enjoy the pleasure she has to offer. Of course, her virginity is evidence of her moral integrity. But the overriding thought here is that she recognizes it would be a tragedy to throw her pearls before swine. Her sexuality is a valuable commodity—too valuable to be wasted on the wrong man or used at the wrong time.

13 Thy plants are an orchard of pomegranates, with pleasant fruits; camphire, with spikenard, 14 Spikenard and saffron; calamus and cinnamon, with all trees of frankincense; myrrh and aloes, with all the chief spices:

The man extends the garden metaphor to praise the excellence of the woman's love by listing a variety of plants found in her garden. The Hebrew word translated "orchard" is *pardec* (**par-DACE**), a word used only rarely in the Old Testament and a noticeable change from the word *gan* in verse 12. Although we shouldn't read too much into it, *pardec* is the word from which the English word "paradise" is derived.

The list of plants is impressive. Pomegranates are an edible fruit slightly smaller than a grapefruit with a reddish color. Inside its thick skin are roughly 600 arils—seeds covered with juicy pulp. The arils separate from each other and are eaten raw. "Camphire" (Heb. *kopher*, **KO-fer**) is henna, a shrub that bears white flowers. It is still used today to make orange dye for hair, nails, fingers, and toes. "Spikenard" (Heb. *nerd*, **nayrd**) is nard, an aromatic plant native to the Himalays, China, and Japan. It was used to make perfume that was quite costly in ancient times. Mark 14:3 and John 12:3 report that the perfume used to anoint Jesus at Bethany was pure nard, and its cost aggravated certain disciples—most notably Judas Iscariot. "Saffron" is a type of crocus with purple flowers native to Asia, Asia Minor, and the eastern Mediterranean. It produces an oil with a sweet, spicy floral scent. "Calamus" (Heb. *qaneh*, **kaw-NEH**) is an aromatic reed or sweet cane, probably imported from northern India (cf. Jeremiah 6:20). "Cinnamon" can refer to the aromatic bark of a number of trees. "Frankincense" and "myrrh" are fragrant tree gums; along with gold, they were the tribute gifts given to Jesus by the Magi. Calamus, cinnamon, and myrrh were ingredients in the anointing oil used by the temple priests (Exodus 30:23). Cinnamon, myrrh, and aloes are mentioned by the adulteress of Proverbs 7:17 as perfumes for her bed. A large amount of myrrh and aloes was used by Nicodemus in the wrapping and burial of Jesus' body (John 19:39).

Even a brief survey of this list reveals several important facts. First, there is a wide diversity of plants, many of which are not native to Palestine. The chances are low that any one garden would contain all of these items. Clearly, the man is speaking of an ideal "dream" garden—not comparing her to one with which he is familiar. Second, all of the plants mentioned are beautiful; many appeal to more than one sense. Third, this list contains items that were highly prized and extremely valuable. To him, she is beyond comparison. She has no equal. Her love satisfies his every desire, and he could never be satisfied with anyone else.

15 A fountain of gardens, a well of living waters, and streams from Lebanon.

Although fountains and springs have already been mentioned in verse 12, the focus there was on her desirability and inaccessibility. Here the focus of the water imagery is the refreshing and sustaining quality of her love. "Fountain of gardens" refers to a "garden fountain." A well of "living water" is a supply of water that never runs dry. Her appeal is lasting, and the satisfaction she offers her lover will never diminish. Known for its beautiful mountain ranges, Lebanon was a source of mountain streams fed by melting snow. All of these water sources provide fresh, high-quality water—nothing like the cistern water that sustained the inhabitants of ancient Palestine when their springs ran dry.

16 Awake, O north wind; and come, thou south; blow upon my garden, that the spices thereof may flow out. Let my beloved come into his garden, and eat his pleasant fruits.

For the first time in this poem, the woman responds to her lover. The Hebrew word "awake" (`uwr, **oor**) is the word used in 2:7; 3:5, and 8:4 to warn against stirring up or awakening love before the right time. But now the time has come for their love to be consummated. The references to north and south wind are a bit mysterious but may simply indicate that all the gates that had been locked are now open. In any case, "blow upon my garden" clearly suggests physical contact. The purpose clause "that the spices thereof may flow out" indicates that it is time for her beauty to be fully enjoyed—for the spices to be tasted—but only by one man. Whereas she was simply "a garden" in verse 12, she now refers to herself as "his garden"— she belongs to him and is eager for him to exercise his ownership. For a time, it would not have been right to open herself to him. Now, by implication on their wedding day, it is unthinkable that they would withhold themselves from each other.

5:1a I am come into my garden, my sister, my spouse:

The husband's reply to his bride confirms that sexual union has occurred. He echoes her acknowledgment of ownership: "my garden." The language of "come into" speaks to more than just the act of sexual intercourse; it describes a new stage in their relationship. His position is one of great privilege and pleasure, but also of great responsibility. "My garden" reminds us that marital relationships take time, attention, and effort in order to grow and flourish. He is not only taking advantage of the sexual pleasure now available to him; he is committing himself to loving his wife faithfully by attending to her needs for the rest of his life. Although we no longer see this book as an analogy of Christ's love for the church, the attitude of the husband is a reminder that Jesus loved the church, sacrificing Himself for her, faithfully nourishing and cherishing her (Ephesians 5:25–29).

Sources:

Baker's Evangelical Dictionary. Bible Study Tools.com. http://www.biblestudytools.com/dictionaries/bakers-evangelical-dictionary (accessed May 23, 2010).

Baltes, A. J., ed. Biblespeech.com. http://biblespeech.com (accessed November 5, 2009).

Beers, V. Gilbert. *The Victor Handbook of Bible Knowledge*. Wheaton, IL: Victor Books, 1981. 224–25, 228–31.

Elwell, Walter A., ed. *Baker's Evangelical Dictionary of Biblical Theology*. Grand Rapids, MI: Baker Books, 1996.

ESV Study Bible, The. Wheaton, IL: Crossway Bibles, 2008. 1221–22.

Garrett, Duane A. *Proverbs, Ecclesiastes, Song of Songs. New American Commentary, Vol. 14*. Nashville, TN: Thomas Nelson Publishers, 1993. 406.

Longman, Tremper III. *Song of Songs, New International Commentary on the Old Testament*. Grand Rapids, MI: William B. Eerdmans, 2001. 148–59.

NET Bible Study Dictionary. http://www.net.bible.org/dictionary (accessed May 29, 2010).

Say It Correctly

Amana. A-MA-na.
Calamus. KAL-a-mus.
Camphire. KAM-fir.
Hermon. HUR-mon.
Saffron. SAF-run.
Shenir. SHE-ner.
Spikenard. SPIK-nard.

Daily Bible Readings

MONDAY
God Blessed Them
(Genesis 1:26–31)

TUESDAY
One Flesh
(Genesis 2:18–24)

WEDNESDAY
The Consequences of Unfaithfulness
(Jeremiah 3:1–5)

THURSDAY
A Covenant of Love
(Hosea 2:16–23)

FRIDAY
The Source of Love
(1 John 4:7–12)

SATURDAY
The Expectations of Love
(1 Corinthians 13)

SUNDAY
How Sweet Is Love!
(Song of Solomon 4:8–5:1a)

Teaching Tips

Words You Should Know

A. Blessed (Matthew 5:3-11) *makarios* (Gk.)—Fortunate, happy.

B. Kingdom (vv. 3, 10) *basileia* (Gk.)—Royal dominion; God's rule.

Teacher Preparation

Unifying Principle—Seeking True Happiness. People seek happiness in their lives. In the Beatitudes, Jesus lists nine ways that God blesses those who seek first the kingdom of God.

A. Begin by prayerfully reading and studying Matthew 5–7.

B. Start early in the week with your study of the Beatitudes.

C. Complete the companion lesson in the *Precepts For Living Personal Study Guide®*.

O—Open the Lesson

A. Open with prayer, praying for the lesson and using the Aim for Change.

B. Have volunteers quote the Beatitudes from memory. Discuss.

C. Read the In Focus story.

D. Ask some of the students to say whether they are in the fortunate group of Christians who know their blessings and live royally or if they are often unaware of all that God has done for them. Discuss why some Christians experience more joy and gratitude than others.

P—Present the Scriptures

A. Use Words You Should Know; Background; and The People, Places, and Times to help explain the lesson.

B. Discuss each section of the lesson according to the At-A-Glance outline.

C. Have volunteers to answer the Search the Scriptures questions.

E—Explore the Meaning

A. Have volunteers summarize the Discuss the Meaning, Lesson in Our Society, and Make It Happen sections.

B. Connect these sections to the Aim for Change and the Keep in Mind verse.

N—Next Steps for Application

A. Summarize the main points of today's lesson.

B. Close with prayer.

OCT
30th

Worship Guide

For the Superintendent or Teacher
Theme: Living as God's People
Song: "Make Me a Blessing"
Devotional Reading: James 5:7–11
Prayer

Living as God's People

Bible Background • MATTHEW 5:1–12
Printed Text • MATTHEW 5:1–12 | Devotional Reading • JAMES 5:7–11

——— Aim for Change ———

By the end of the lesson, we will: DISCUSS the blessings outlined in the Beatitudes; REFLECT on examples of blessings of God's reign already present on the earth; and IDENTIFY ways to apply the Beatitudes to our daily lives.

——— In Focus ———

When Lydia, our firstborn, was a baby, my husband and I agreed to raise her differently. At Christmastime, we wanted to place the main emphasis on the birth of Christ and not merely on an abundance of gifts received. However, we forgot about the gifts Lydia would receive from her grandmothers, her aunts, and others. On Christmas morning, Lydia, who was now 2, was surrounded by brightly colored packages. She was so excited; she hardly knew which one to open first.

Unfortunately, many Christians open the gift of salvation and stop there. The Sermon on the Mount—particularly the first part of the message, the Beatitudes—reminds believers that when we trust Christ for our salvation and enter into the kingdom of God, He provides His children with an abundance of gifts. He wants Christians to be overwhelmed with delight, like a 2-year-old with too many gifts on Christmas morning!

——— Keep in Mind ———

"Blessed are they which do hunger and thirst after righteousness: for they shall be filled" (Matthew 5:6).

"Blessed are they which do hunger and thirst after righteousness: for they shall be filled" (Matthew 5:6).

Focal Verses

KJV Matthew 5:1 And seeing the multitudes, he went up into a mountain: and when he was set, his disciples came unto him:

2 And he opened his mouth, and taught them, saying,

3 Blessed are the poor in spirit: for theirs is the kingdom of heaven.

4 Blessed are they that mourn: for they shall be comforted.

5 Blessed are the meek: for they shall inherit the earth.

6 Blessed are they which do hunger and thirst after righteousness: for they shall be filled.

7 Blessed are the merciful: for they shall obtain mercy.

8 Blessed are the pure in heart: for they shall see God.

9 Blessed are the peacemakers: for they shall be called the children of God.

10 Blessed are they which are persecuted for righteousness' sake: for theirs is the kingdom of heaven.

11 Blessed are ye, when men shall revile you, and persecute you, and shall say all manner of evil against you falsely, for my sake.

12 Rejoice, and be exceeding glad: for great is your reward in heaven: for so persecuted they the prophets which were before you.

NLT Matthew 5:1 One day as the crowds were gathering, Jesus went up the mountainside with his disciples and sat down to teach them.

2 This is what he taught them:

3 "God blesses those who realize their need for him, for the Kingdom of Heaven is given to them.

4 God blesses those who mourn, for they will be comforted.

5 God blesses those who are gentle and lowly, for the whole earth will belong to them.

6 God blesses those who are hungry and thirsty for justice, for they will receive it in full.

7 God blesses those who are merciful, for they will be shown mercy.

8 God blesses those whose hearts are pure, for they will see God.

9 God blesses those who work for peace, for they will be called the children of God.

10 God blesses those who are persecuted because they live for God, for the Kingdom of Heaven is theirs.

11 "God blesses you when you are mocked and persecuted and lied about because you are my followers.

12 Be happy about it! Be very glad! For a great reward awaits you in heaven. And remember, the ancient prophets were persecuted, too."

The People, Places, and Times

The Mount. Some have speculated that Jesus was near Capernaum at the beginning of His ministry when He delivered the Sermon on the Mount. The writer (Matthew) avoids identifying either a specified time or place. He wanted the attention to be on the sermon and its content, not on the setting.

Mercy. Mercy means to show compassion, kindness, sympathy, or benevolence to someone in need. God does not condone sin or ignore it; instead, He pours out mercy and compassion on the person who is constantly falling short. One who is merciful realizes the misery of an unbeliever and shows pity to the sinner, prays for that individual, loves him, and does whatever he or she can to help.

Background

Matthew 5–7 is known as the Sermon on the Mount and is a collection of Jesus' teachings on spiritual maturity. The Sermon on the Mount can be summarized in one verse: "Be ye therefore perfect, even as your Father which is in heaven is perfect" (Matthew 5:48). Jesus' sermon explained how His followers could be perfect, meaning mature and complete in Christ and all that God intended for His children to be.

The Sermon on the Mount contrasts a new way of following God with the old way taught by the scribes and Pharisees. The religious leaders emphasized strict observance of the letter of the law. Jesus elaborated on the spirit of the law and displayed the heart of God revealed in the law.

Jesus taught His committed followers the proper character, duties, and attitudes of the Christian disciple, as well as the dangers and rewards of following Christ. He wanted His followers to know what it meant to become a part of the kingdom of God (i.e., yield to God as the king and ruler of one's entire life, to live as a citizen of the kingdom).

At-A-Glance

1. Kingdom Children: Taught by Jesus
(Matthew 5:1–2)

2. Kingdom Children: Blessed by God
(vv. 3–6)

3. Kingdom Children: Blessing One
Another (vv. 7–9)

4. Kingdom Children: Under
Persecution (vv. 10–12)

In Depth

1. Kingdom Children: Taught by Jesus (Matthew 5:1–2)

The night before, Jesus had gone up into the mountain and prayed. In the morning, He chose His 12 disciples and then Jesus began this sermon. Other devoted disciples were also part of the crowd on the mountain, along with a multitude of people.

In this sermon, Jesus made God's expectations clear to His apostles and close followers. He also told them what to expect as a result of their allegiance and devotion to God. He preached this sermon to the unbelievers in the crowd as well, encouraging them to join those who were already a part of the kingdom.

2. Kingdom Children: Blessed by God (vv. 3–6)

The beginning of the Sermon on the Mount consists of 10 statements of blessing. These declarations are referred to as "the Beatitudes." The word "blessed" introduces someone who is to be congratulated for something. Many Bible translators use the word "happy" instead of "blessed," but a temporary mental state like happiness is not what is being described here. "Blessed" is a condition of life and describes one who is fortunate or well-off.

Jesus' sermon began by addressing those who are "poor in spirit" (v. 3). He is speaking to the meek who are humbly trusting God, even though their loyalty may result in oppression and material disadvantage. The poor in spirit are individuals who are "empty before God"—humble in heart. Daily, they reach up unfilled hands to the Heavenly Father and receive grace.

This "poor in spirit" group has been promised the "kingdom of heaven." This is not an identifiable place. If you can, imagine each believer surrounded by the presence of God and His precious gifts. This kind of "place" exists wherever Jesus reigns as King; His power and might are evident.

"They that mourn" are the next group Jesus addresses (v. 4). The verb "mourn" denotes loud wailing, such as a lament for the dead or grieving over a severe, painful loss. This sorrow is the recognition of the power of sin and of our helplessness to ward it off and escape—a constant, repentant distress cry. This kind of mourning requires a special kind of comfort; therefore, God Himself addresses this cry. God's comfort flows to a believer in distress. This verse is often used to comfort those grieving over a death or a loss, but the verse is really speaking to those who have suffered because of their loyalty to God.

The next group addressed are the "meek" (v. 5). Meekness is an inward virtue that displays itself when a person is wronged or abused. It is not weakness. A meek person will react not with bitterness, anger, or violence, but instead with mildness, gentleness, and patience.

Jesus is the greatest example of meekness. He totally relied on God to take vengeance on His enemies. He constantly entrusted Himself to the Heavenly Father who promised that He would get what He was due. For people who have this inner attitude, the divine blessing constantly follows them in this life.

The righteous—those living according to God's standards—are the next group addressed in the Beatitudes. Those in God's kingdom hunger and thirst for forgiveness, and God satisfies that need daily. People cannot achieve righteousness through their own effort. Once again, the believer has to turn to God and receive the gift of righteousness. The moment faith in Christ is wrought, the believer is declared righteous.

3. Kingdom Children: Blessing One Another (vv. 7–9)

The next three beatitudes are more active, particularly in regard to our behavior toward others. Christians receive God's mercy in abundance. He forgives His undeserving children for a multitude of sins. Mercy is not merely an emotion ("Oh-h-h, I'm so sorry.") but a practical action ("Here, let me help.").

The phrase "pure in heart" (v. 8) means singleness of heart and refers to a child of God who is honest and has no hidden motives or selfish interests. It denotes one who loves God wholeheartedly and shows it outwardly in sincere service to others.

Those with a pure heart are promised that they shall see God. Viewing God fully will only be realized in heaven, when we shall see Him just as He is. The greatest joy for the Christian in heaven will be to see God. However, the person who is free from sin, cleansed and forgiven, will begin to see God in His true character and will experience His presence here on earth.

"Peacemakers" (v. 9) are rare in our society. We live in a world of people who pour forth violence, conflict, and anger. The absence of selfish ambition and a concern for the good of others is pleasing to God.

The peacemaker is—first of all—at peace with God. When believers are filled with God's sweet peace, peace with others is a natural result. A peacemaker is a reconciler. This includes reconciling others to God, a chief responsibility of all Christians (2 Corinthians 5:19–20).

4. Kingdom Children: Under Persecution (vv. 10–12)

The Beatitudes emphasize rewards in the kingdom of God. Yet, as God's children display the character of God on earth, not everyone is going to encourage the Christian in his or her positive, godly attitudes. Jesus walked this earth as a perfect man, and yet He endured suffering and persecution—and God's children will encounter the same.

The tone of the phrase "they which are persecuted" (v. 10) seems to indicate those who have allowed themselves to be persecuted. They did not flee from persecution but willingly submitted to it when it came to them. And they endured "for righteousness sake." Their whole lives, their character, and their actions stood as a rebuke to the world, and, therefore, the world persecuted them. By taking this kind of stand for God in opposition to the world, they displayed the grace and gifts provided in the kingdom of God.

Jesus says that in the face of this kind of persecution, we are to rejoice. Jesus endured the Cross "for the joy that was set before him" (Hebrews 12:2). "Blessed" are those believers who are persecuted, insulted, and lied about because they dare to take a stand for Christ (Matthew 5:11). Jesus encourages this group to be happy and to be glad. Why? He does so because those who suffer with Christ will experience the comfort that He experienced. They will also receive a future reward. In heaven, a "crown of reward" is waiting for all who have shared in His sufferings.

Jesus also mentions the prophets, the martyrs of the past who gave up their lives for God. When we suffer persecution for Christ's sake, we can have joy because we are part of this great company of believers.

Search the Scriptures

1. "Blessed are the ____ in _____: for theirs is the _____ of _____" (Matthew 5:3).

2. "Blessed are they that _____: for they shall be _____" (v. 4).

Discuss the Meaning

1. What does it mean to be "blessed"?

2. Are all Christians experiencing God's blessings? Why or why not?

Lesson in Our Society

During times of popularity, it's easy to witness and take a stand for Christ. But what about when people ridicule you for your faith? In times of opposition and times of peace, remember all that God has and is. All of that is available to His children.

Make It Happen

Reflect on the idea of blessing as displayed in today's text. How does this compare to the way many people speak of it today? Consider how to expand the way you understand how God shows favor to us.

Follow the Spirit

What God wants me to do:

_____

_____

_____

_____

107

Remember Your Thoughts

Special insights I have learned:

_____

_____

_____

_____

More Light on the Text

Matthew 5:1–12

5:1 And seeing the multitudes, he went up into a mountain: and when he was set, his disciples came unto him: 2 And he opened his mouth, and taught them, saying,

The narrative in verses 1 and 2 serves as an introduction to the passage. Here we learn that Jesus was teaching from a mountain. The word "and" (Greek *de,* **deh,** which can also be translated as "now, moreover, but") that begins this chapter is a conjunction and serves to connect what follows to the previous passage (4:25).

In chapter 4, we read of Christ's ministry of teaching, miracles, and healing throughout the regions of Palestine and Galilee. These events attracted large crowds to Him. When He saw the multitudes, He "went up into a mountain" (5:1). The significance of the mountain here relates to the number of people. The crowd was so great that Jesus needed a higher and broader space where He could address them.

Verse 1 seems to suggest that there were two different types of people in the crowd. The first represented the larger group (mentioned in 4:25), who came from different regions around Jerusalem. The people that made up the second group were Jesus' disciples, among whom were those Jesus had called earlier to follow Him (4:18–22). This smaller group probably sat in a semicircle close to Him, and the rest of the crowd formed a larger semicircle down the slope of the mountain. The word translated as "set" is the Greek word *kathizo* (**kath-ID-zo**), and it means "to sit down," "settle down," or "sojourn." This means that Jesus sat down as He taught the people, which was customary for teachers in Jewish circles (see 13:2; 23:2; Luke 4:20–21).

"And he opened his mouth, and taught them" (Matthew 5:2) is a familiar phrase that is usually used to introduce an important teaching. The phrase may also demonstrate a conscious and deliberate decision on the part of the Teacher to teach, seizing the opportunity afforded Him by the surging crowd to set forth the fundamental ordinances of the kingdom.

To whom does the pronoun in "taught them" refer? At first glance, one might assume that the immediate antecedent is "his disciples" in verse 1. However, at the conclusion of the sermon, one observes that "the people were astonished at his doctrine: For he taught them as one having authority, and not as the scribes" (7:28–29).

3 Blessed are the poor in spirit: for theirs is the kingdom of heaven.

Verse 3 begins the second section consisting of "blessed" sayings, or more correctly, the Beatitudes (vv. 3–12). Each of the verses starts with the word "blessed" (Greek *makarios,* **mak-ar-EE-os**), which also means "fortunate" or "happy." The word "beatitude" is derived from the Latin *beatus* (which means blessed), the equivalent of *makarios.*

Jesus begins His teaching by pronouncing blessings on, or proclaiming God's favor to, the "poor in spirit." As we have already noted, *makarios* may be translated as either "blessed" or "happy." If the former is the case, it means that the "poor in spirit" are blessed because "theirs is the kingdom of heaven." If the latter is the case, then those who are "poor in spirit" (here on earth by implication) will inherit the kingdom of heaven (God).

Although the "poor" in the Old Testament were usually the pious (Psalm 69:29–36; Isaiah 61:1), the phrase "poor in spirit" is not found in the Old Testament. There are two distinct options in trying to understand the precise meaning of this phrase in Matthew 5. It refers to those who cultivate the spirit of humility and self-abasement; or it describes those in need, like the poor, whose poverty is an affliction of the spirit. The phrase does not speak of those who are fainthearted, as some would contend, but speaks of the humble in heart. Thus, it means the humble—those who acknowledge their unworthiness before God and absolute dependence on the Lord. The reward is that the kingdom of heaven belongs to them (as we see in Matthew 3:2 and 4:17); they will partake in the reign of the Messiah and enjoy the blessings He brings. Christ is the perfect example of humility and its rewards, as Paul describes in Philippians 2:6–11.

4 Blessed are they that mourn: for they shall be comforted.

While the humble or "poor in spirit" will inherit the "kingdom of heaven" (Matthew 5:3), those who mourn will be comforted. What makes them mourn? It is their fallen and sinful condition. The beatitude here speaks of the deplorable condition of the world, both then and now. Christ says that He has come to change mourning into joy and "to bestow . . . the oil of gladness instead of mourning, and a garment of praise instead of a spirit of despair" (Isaiah 61:3, NIV). These blessings, yet only partially realized, will be fully consummated at the return of the Messiah (Revelation 7:17).

5 Blessed are the meek: for they shall inherit the earth.

The next group to be rewarded are the "meek." The word "meek" (Greek *praus,* **prah-OOCE**) is difficult to define. The nearest synonym is "gentleness," which is better to exemplify than to merely define. Abraham demonstrated a spirit of meekness when he gave Lot first choice of the land, although the promise was made to him (Genesis 13:8–12). *Praus* refers to mildness of disposition, or gentleness of spirit. Meekness toward God is that disposition of spirit in which we accept His dealings with us as good, and therefore submit without dispute or resistance. In the Old Testament, the meek are those who wholly rely on God rather than their own strength to redress injustice. Thus, meekness toward evil people means knowing that God is using the injuries they inflict to purify His elect and that He will deliver His elect in His time (Isaiah 41:17; Luke 18:1–8).

Gentleness or meekness is the opposite of self-assertiveness and self-interest. It does not refer to weakness or passivity, but stems from trust in God's goodness and control over the situation. A meek person is not occupied with oneself at all. As noted in 1 Peter 3:4, 14–15, meekness can signify absence of pretension, but generally suggests gentleness (Matthew 11:29; James 3:13) and self-control. This is the work of the Holy Spirit, not of the human will (Galatians 5:23). It is a virtue to aspire to, but for the Greeks, it was a vice because of their inability to distinguish it from servitude.

Jesus asserts that the meek, rather than the strong, aggressive, harsh, and tyrannical, will inherit the earth. The verb "inherit" is often used in Scripture, especially in the Old Testament, in relation to the Promised Land (see Deuteronomy 16:20; Isaiah 57:13; 60:21). The word "earth" or "land" in this beatitude has a broader meaning.

6 Blessed are they which do hunger and thirst after righteousness: for they shall be filled.

The next group in the Beatitudes whom Matthew congratulates are those who hunger or long for righteousness. Eating and drinking is used metaphorically in the Old Testament to express the desire to have a relationship with God (Isaiah 55:1–3)—a desire that only God satisfies (Psalm 107:9). Therefore, those who "hunger and thirst for righteousness" are the people who yearn for a deeper, right relationship with the Lord (see Matthew 6:33).

Apart from having a personal relationship with God or living uprightly before Him, which this beatitude tends to address, is there any other sense in which the word "righteousness" can be used? The answer lies in the alternative definition of the term as expressed here in the Greek word *dikaiosune* (**dik-ah-yos-OO-nay**), which means "justification" or "equity," and is from the word *dikaios,* meaning "just." It carries with it the idea of justice—dealing fairly or rightly and equitably with others—with social justice as the undertone. Therefore, this beatitude addresses those who hunger and thirst, not only for personal righteousness (i.e., living uprightly before the Lord), but who also strongly desire that justice be done everywhere and to all humankind.

They yearn for the new kingdom where there is justice, equality, and holiness (2 Peter 3:13); they are not satisfied with the status quo. They desire both personal spiritual growth and change in society. The reward for their yearning is that they will be filled or satisfied. Note that the verb "filled" (Greek *chortazo,* **khor-TAD-zo**) is the same word used in Matthew 14:20, after Jesus fed the 5,000 (cf. Philippians 4:12; Revelation 19:21). They are, therefore, "blessed" and (will be) happy because their desire and curiosity will (most likely) be fulfilled in the actualization of the kingdom.

7 Blessed are the merciful: for they shall obtain mercy.

The simplest way to talk about the beatitude in Matthew 5:7 is in terms of reaping and sowing (i.e., you reap what you sow), but in a positive sense. The word "mercy" contains the idea of both forgiveness and compassion (i.e., showing kindness). Both understandings of mercy are common themes in Matthew's Gospel (in the Lord's Prayer, 6:12–15; in Jesus' teachings and parables, 9:13; 12:7; 18:33–34). The reward for showing mercy is obtaining (i.e., also receiving) mercy, not necessarily from other people or from the immediate recipients, but from the Lord. Although showing mercy to others is not always grounds for God's mercy, it can be its "occasional ground," as someone put it (6:14–15). Mercy is part of God's character and is not dependent on our merciful acts; it is in God's nature and a gift to sinful man.

8 Blessed are the pure in heart: for they shall see God.

"The pure in heart" seems to address genuineness of faith and those who reflect truthfulness and purity of mind without duplicity. This beatitude is a reflection of Psalm 24:3–6, which poses the question of who is able to ascend to the temple and see the Lord. In his answer, the psalmist (most likely David) replies that it is "He that hath clean hands, and a pure heart; who hath not lifted up his soul unto vanity, nor sworn deceitfully" (v. 4). From this psalm, it is apparent that only those who are internally clean (Deuteronomy 10:16; 30:6) and those who relate to God and others with sincerity of mind—as opposed to merely the externally pious—will see God (James 4:8).

The beatitude of Matthew 5:8 speaks of those whose thoughts are pure and free from deceit as opposed to the hypocrites (6:1–18); they will see God. To see God is to experience His presence in an intimate way by having a close relationship with Him. Moses had this experience with the Lord; hence, God spoke "face-to-face" with him in the wilderness—an experience the psalmist desired and, in fact, had (Psalm 63:1–2). Abram (Abraham) had such an intimate relationship with the Lord that God "talked with him" (Genesis 17:3). Isaiah also had this experience, which was terrifying and yet transforming (Isaiah 6:5; cf. Genesis 32:26–30). These were glimpses of the revelation of God's presence, but the complete unveiling of this truth, promise, and blessing to the "pure in heart" (Matthew 5:8) is yet the future.

9 Blessed are the peacemakers: for they shall be called the children of God.

Among those who are blessed are the "peacemakers," not the "peaceful." Their reward is that they will be called the children of God. Isaiah prophesied that the Promised Son would be called "Prince of Peace" (Isaiah 9:6–7). Jesus is the fulfillment of Isaiah's prophecy and the supreme example of a peacemaker. He brings reconciliation between God and people and between one person to another. The Greek word *eirenopoios* (**i-ray-nop-oy-OS**), which is translated "peacemakers," occurs only here in the New Testament, but related words are found in other parts of the New Testament. For example, James 3:18 says that "the fruit of righteousness is sown in peace of them that make peace." In Ephesians and Colossians, Paul attributes peacemaking to God through the blood of His Son (Ephesians 2:13–16; Colossians 1:19–20).

It is interesting that the people Jesus blesses here are neither the peaceful, nor lovers of peace, nor those who only speak of peace, but rather those who work actively to make or bring about peace. With God as their example, they strive to make peace at all costs (sometimes sacrificing their own peace or even their lives) and with all persons, whether friends or foes (Matthew 5:45). By imitating the Lord in peacemaking, the peacemakers demonstrate that they are the true children of God. Hence, Jesus says that God will accept them as His own at the consummation of all things.

10 Blessed are they which are persecuted for righteousness' sake: for theirs is the kingdom of heaven.

The next group consists of those who are persecuted for their righteousness or right deeds, probably referring to the peacemakers and those who fight for justice (v. 6). In a world that is full of hate and prejudice, the peacemakers and those who endeavor to live uprightly in the sight of God are never cherished or welcomed in society. Often, they are persecuted and receive the brunt of society's anger and hatred. Persecution, or oppression, is the mark of discipleship, as Jesus reminded His disciples (John 15:18–25). The promise, or blessing, for the "poor in spirit" (Matthew 5:3) is the same here. Indeed, this beatitude tends to tie together all the other beatitudes, for all the virtues therein can be summed up under the theme of righteousness, or right living.

11 Blessed are ye, when men shall revile you, and persecute you, and shall say all manner of evil against you falsely, for my sake. 12 Rejoice, and be exceeding glad: for great is your reward in heaven: for so persecuted they the prophets which were before you.

Verses 11 and 12 deal with the attitude believers ought to cultivate when they face persecution and oppression because of their faith in Christ. Jesus lists three forms of oppression that the disciples (and all those who believe in Him) would suffer because of their faith and their relationship with the Lord Jesus: revilement, persecution, and slander. The word "revile" (Greek *oneidizo*, **on-i-DID-zo**) means "to defame," "rail at," "taunt," or "reproach." It also means to ridicule somebody because of what that person does, how the person acts or behaves, how the person looks physically, or what the person believes.

The second opposition is "persecution," translated from the Greek word *dioko* (**dee-O-ko**). Persecution would include harassment, molestation, violence, and maltreatment in various forms. The third form of opposition the disciples will suffer is that people "shall say all manner of evil against [them] falsely" (i.e., slander or falsely and maliciously accuse). In the parallel passage, Luke adds that they would be hated and excluded from the synagogue (Luke 6:22–23).

Jesus urges His disciples to rejoice with exceeding gladness even in the face of their tribulations. The first reason is that they will be greatly rewarded for their faith—that their reward will be great in heaven. The second reason is that they are in the same company with the Old Testament prophets before them, who were likewise persecuted.

The beatitude of Matthew 5:11–12 does not imply that Christians, or believers, should seek persecution (though it should not surprise us when it occurs), nor does it permit retreat from it or revenge. Rather, it speaks of steadfast faith in the Lord under any and all circumstances with humility and singleness of heart and continuing reliance on and faithfulness to God, irrespective of what may come our way, good and bad.

Sources:

Baltes, A. J., ed. Biblespeech.com. http://biblespeech.com (accessed July 1, 2010).

Gardner, Richard. "Matthew." *Believers Church Bible Commentary.* Scottsdale, PA: Herald Press, 1991. 95.

Hebrew and Greek Lexicons. Bible Study Tools.com. http://www.biblestudytools.com/lexicons (accessed September 16, 2010).

Say It Correctly

Beatitudes. Be AT-i-toods.

Daily Bible Readings

MONDAY
A Lowly Spirit
(Proverbs 16:16–20)

TUESDAY
Comfort for All Who Mourn
(Isaiah 61:1–7)

WEDNESDAY
The Inheritance of the Meek
(Psalm 37:10–17)

THURSDAY
The Way of Righteousness
(Isaiah 26:7–11)

FRIDAY
Be Merciful
(Luke 6:32–36)

SATURDAY
The Strength of My Heart
(Psalm 73:10–26)

SUNDAY
Blessed by God
(Matthew 5:1–12)

Teaching Tips

Words You Should Know

A. To fulfill (Matthew 5:17) *pleroo* (Gk.)—To accomplish or complete something.

B. Be reconciled (v. 24) *diallasso* (Gk.)—Conciliated; caused the nature of a broken relationship to change.

Teacher Preparation

Unifying Principle—Living in Harmony with Others. Jesus taught that the road to reconciliation is paved with forgiveness.

A. Pray for your students that God will open their hearts to forgiveness.

B. Study the text, including the Devotional Readings.

C. Use a dictionary to research the meaning of "reconciliation."

D. Be prepared to share recent news stories of forgiveness or reconciliation.

E. Complete the companion lesson in the *Precepts For Living Personal Study Guide®*.

O—Open the Lesson

A. Open with prayer.

B. Have volunteers read the Aim for Change and the Keep in Mind verse.

C. Ask, "What does the word *reconciliation* mean to you?" Discuss.

D. Share some of your findings on forgiveness and reconciliation.

E. Ask students to share some of their experiences or testimonies.

P—Present the Scriptures

A. Invite students to read the Focal Verses.

B. Now use The People, Places, and Times; Background; Search the Scriptures; At-A-Glance outline; In Depth; and More Light on the Text to clarify the verses.

E—Explore the Meaning

A. Have a student read the In Focus story.

B. Ask students to summarize how it relates to the Lesson in Our Society and Make It Happen sections.

N—Next Steps for Application

A. Have students rewrite Aim for Change in their own words in the Remember Your Thoughts section.

B. Have students participate in a one-minute silent prayer to prepare their hearts for reconciliation.

C. Close in prayer, thanking God for restored relationships.

NOV
6th

Worship Guide

For the Superintendent or Teacher
Theme: Forgiving as God's People
Song: "I Surrender All"
Devotional Reading: Psalm 32:1–5
Prayer

113

Forgiving as God's People

Bible Background • MATTHEW 5:17–26
Printed Text • MATTHEW 5:17–26 | Devotional Reading • Psalm 32:1–5

Aim for Change

By the end of the lesson, we will: KNOW Jesus' teaching about reconciliation; REFLECT on the joy of forgiving and being forgiven; and SEEK to repair a damaged relationship.

 In Focus

Becari sat in the examination room, anxiously awaiting the cardiologist and the results from a recent battery of tests. He hoped to learn the source of persistent chest and back pains. A nonsmoker and non-drinker, Becari was 40, physically fit, and had no family history of cardiac problems. Despite this, he was advised to see a cardiologist when nothing eased his discomfort. After meeting with the doctor, Becari left relieved that he did not have heart disease. At the same time, he was a bit dismayed at some of the doctor's suggestions to reduce stress, including improving personal relationships. Becari knew that included his estranged father.

Damaged relationships are particularly troublesome, impacting one's mental, physical, and emotional health. Working to resolve issues with family, friends, and coworkers can go a long way in promoting physical and social well-being. Today's lesson teaches us how to forgive as God's people.

Keep in Mind

"Therefore if thou bring thy gift to the altar, and there rememberest that thy brother hath ought against thee; Leave there thy gift before the altar, and go thy way; first be reconciled to thy brother, and then come and offer thy gift" (Matthew 5:23–24).

"Therefore if thou bring thy gift to the altar, and there rememberest that thy brother hath ought against thee; Leave there thy gift before the altar, and go thy way; first be reconciled to thy brother, and then come and offer thy gift" (Matthew 5:23–24).

Focal Verses

KJV **Matthew 5:17** Think not that I am come to destroy the law, or the prophets: I am not come to destroy, but to fulfil.

18 For verily I say unto you, Till heaven and earth pass, one jot or one tittle shall in no wise pass from the law, till all be fulfilled.

19 Whosoever therefore shall break one of these least commandments, and shall teach men so, he shall be called the least in the kingdom of heaven: but whosoever shall do and teach them, the same shall be called great in the kingdom of heaven.

20 For I say unto you, That except your righteousness shall exceed the righteousness of the scribes and Pharisees, ye shall in no case enter into the kingdom of heaven.

21 Ye have heard that it was said by them of old time, Thou shalt not kill; and whosoever shall kill shall be in danger of the judgment:

22 But I say unto you, That whosoever is angry with his brother without a cause shall be in danger of the judgment: and whosoever shall say to his brother, Raca, shall be in danger of the council: but whosoever shall say, Thou fool, shall be in danger of hell fire.

23 Therefore if thou bring thy gift to the altar, and there rememberest that thy brother hath ought against thee;

24 Leave there thy gift before the altar, and go thy way; first be reconciled to thy brother, and then come and offer thy gift.

25 Agree with thine adversary quickly, whiles thou art in the way with him; lest at any time the adversary deliver thee to the judge, and the judge deliver thee to the officer, and thou be cast into prison.

26 Verily I say unto thee, Thou shalt by no means come out thence, till thou hast paid the uttermost farthing.

NLT **Matthew 5:17** Don't misunderstand why I have come. I did not come to abolish the law of Moses or the writings of the prophets. No, I came to fulfill them.

18 I assure you, until heaven and earth disappear, even the smallest detail of God's law will remain until its purpose is achieved.

19 So if you break the smallest commandment and teach others to do the same, you will be the least in the Kingdom of Heaven. But anyone who obeys God's laws and teaches them will be great in the Kingdom of Heaven.

20 "But I warn you—unless you obey God better than the teachers of religious law and the Pharisees do, you can't enter the Kingdom of Heaven at all!

21 "You have heard that the law of Moses says, 'Do not murder. If you commit murder, you are subject to judgment.'

22 But I say, if you are angry with someone, you are subject to judgment! If you call someone an idiot, you are in danger of being brought before the high council. And if you curse someone, you are in danger of the fires of hell.

23 "So if you are standing before the altar in the Temple, offering a sacrifice to God, and you suddenly remember that someone has something against you,

24 leave your sacrifice there beside the altar. Go and be reconciled to that person. Then come and offer your sacrifice to God.

25 Come to terms quickly with your enemy before it is too late and you are dragged into court, handed over to an officer, and thrown in jail.

26 I assure you that you won't be free again until you have paid the last penny."

The People, Places, and Times

Matthew. Matthew, also known as Levi, was the son of Alphaeus (Mark 2:14; Luke 5:27). A tax collector by trade, he worked along the main road leading to Capernaum receiving taxes from farmers and merchants. The Roman government imposed taxes on everything from animals to real estate and income. Also known as "publicans," tax collectors were despised and distrusted, mainly because of the wealth they accumulated doing their jobs. Matthew gave up his lucrative position to follow Christ, later becoming one of the first apostles (Matthew 9:9–13; 10:3).

Matthew's account, which scholars date around A.D. 56–58, spans the very early days of Jesus' ministry through Jesus' ascension. He wrote mostly for Jewish audiences, providing firsthand evidence that Jesus was—and is—the promised Messiah. While he covered many topics later discussed in the Gospels of Mark, Luke, and John, Matthew also included three miracles and 10 parables not included in the other apostles' Gospels.

Background

On the heels of a triumphant victory in the wilderness, Jesus begins His public ministry. His fame spread rapidly, due in part to Jesus' astounding power to heal various diseases. While the "multitudes" followed Jesus to receive healing, they shunned commitment to Him or His teaching.

Disciples, on the other hand, willingly sought a deeper relationship with Jesus. On one occasion, Jesus took to a mountain to speak to His chosen Twelve and the large crowd. His "Sermon on the Mount" expounded on various aspects of harmonious living, including the need for forgiveness and reconciliation.

At-A-Glance

1. Law Fulfilled (Matthew 5:17–18)

2. Hypocrisy Condemned (vv. 19–20)

3. Harmonious Living (vv. 21–26)

In Depth

1. Law Fulfilled (Matthew 5:17–18)

"Think not that I am come to destroy the law, or the prophets: I am not come to destroy, but to fulfil" (v. 17). By uttering these words early on in ministry, Jesus made it clear that His purpose was not to dismantle the Law or the work of Old Testament prophets. Regarding His relationship to the Law, Jesus said, "I assure you, until heaven and earth disappear, even the smallest detail of God's law will remain until its purpose is achieved" (Matthew 5:18, NLT).

Jesus' purpose was to fulfill the Law and establish God's kingdom. That meant living a God-honoring life marked by obedience, self-denial, and love. Before dying, Jesus declared, "'It is finished.' With that, he bowed his head and gave up his spirit" (John 19:30, NIV). Jesus finished the work of fulfilling the Law, but not in ways people expected. For example, the scribes were outraged when Jesus told a sick man, "Take heart, son; your sins are forgiven" (Matthew 9:2, NIV). Knowing the bystanders' emerging criticism, Jesus queried, "Is it easier to say, 'Your sins are forgiven' or 'Get up and walk'? I will prove that I, the Son of Man, have the authority on earth to forgive sins" (from Matthew 9:5–6, NLT). Jesus then turned to the man and said, "'Stand up, take your mat, and go on home!'" (from Matthew 9:6, NLT).

The law exacted punishment for sin, but also provided a system of sacrifices for unintentional and intentional sin (Leviticus 4). The sacrifices of animals, however, could not completely atone for sin and only foreshadowed the atonement of Jesus Christ. For Jesus, fulfilling the Law meant becoming the sacrificial Lamb slain for humankind's sins. "He died for our sins, just as God our Father planned, in order to rescue us from this evil world in which we live" (Galatians 1:4, NLT). Beholding Jesus, John the Baptist exclaimed, "'Look! There is the Lamb of God who takes away the sin of the world!'" (John 1:29, NLT). His was a one-time-only sacrifice that completely fulfilled the Law (Hebrews 10:12).

2. Hypocrisy Condemned (vv. 19–20)

In Jesus' day, the Pharisees and scribes were the epitome of hypocrisy. On one occasion Jesus said, "How terrible it will be for you teachers of religious law and you Pharisees. Hypocrites! For you won't let others enter the Kingdom of Heaven, and you won't go in yourselves" (Matthew 23:13, NLT). Ironically, they accused Him of hypocrisy because Jesus ate with known sinners, offered compassion to tax collectors and harlots, and associated with non-Jews.

Rather than exemplifying hypocrisy, Jesus' life and ministry proved that the Law requires more than outward obedience. It requires a change of heart, evidenced by authentic living free from hypocrisy. This kind of lifestyle promotes reconciliation, allowing us to exist harmoniously with others. Jesus warned, "'Beware of the yeast of the Pharisees and Sadducees'" (Matthew 16:6, NLT). He later helped the disciples understand that "yeast" referred to the false teaching among the Pharisees and Sadducees— a small amount could rise and spread (vv. 7–12, NLT).

3. Harmonious Living (vv. 21–26)

The Sixth Commandment prohibited murder (Exodus 20:13). Strict adherence to the Law taught that the commandment referred to killing a person. Jesus, however, helped listeners understand that the spirit of the Law meant much more. For example, anger is akin to murder and has its own consequences. On another occasion, Jesus explained: "But the things that come out of the mouth come from the heart, and these make a man 'unclean.' For out of the heart come evil thoughts, murder, adultery, sexual immorality, theft, false testimony, slander" (Matthew 15:18–19, NIV).

He also used legal terminology to reinforce the truth that reconciliation is a less costly alternative to continuing to harbor offenses. Albeit, forgiving can be difficult. Biblical examples of people who forgave others in the midst of extreme situations include the apostle Stephen, who prayed for those who stoned him (Acts 7:60), and Jesus, who prayed for His enemies before being crucified. He prayed, "Father, forgive these people, because they don't know what they are doing" (Luke 23:34, NLT). Jesus' words implied that sometimes people do not fully comprehend their offenses. Similarly, individuals today do not always know the depth of their offenses until it is too late.

When we live harmoniously with other people, we can foster reconciliation. As we do, we can experience:

The power of forgiveness. Forgiveness promotes reconciliation on two levels: between God and humankind, and between people. The power of forgiveness allows us to heal past, present, and future emotional wounds. For example, forgiving a childhood offense can empower a person to finally seek and maintain harmonious relationships. Forgiving present offenses circumvents the formation of grudges that divide entire households. Meanwhile, a commitment to forgive future offenses acknowledges the inevitable: someone will probably offend you daily and vice versa.

The peace of forgiveness. Forgiveness promotes inner peace. Psalm 32:3–4 offers a glimpse of the turmoil of unforgiveness, while verses 1 and 2 describe the peace received from being forgiven.

The joy of forgiveness. Forgiveness not only promotes peace, it also sparks joy. That's true whether we are forgiving someone or being forgiven. To experience fullness of joy, dare to be the first to say, "I'm sorry."

Search the Scriptures

1. What is required to enter the kingdom of heaven? Is this salvation by works or something else (Matthew 5:20)?

2. What did Jesus say needs to be accomplished before bringing a gift to God (vv. 23–24)?

Discuss the Meaning

If we expect people to forgive us when we make mistakes or inadvertently hurt others, why it is so difficult for some Christians to repay the same kindness to people who offend them?

Lesson in Our Society

Many lives and much property are lost when workers have chosen violence over anger management. Jesus warned of the consequences of anger in Matthew 5:22, while providing instruction in verses 23 and 24 on how to improve relationships. Based on these verses, how can Christians help serve as peacemakers in the workplace?

Make It Happen

Many people feel forgiveness should be earned. But that is not a scriptural approach. Scripture encourages us to forgive uncondi-

tionally—and repeatedly (Matthew 18:21–23, NLT). Tap into the power of forgiveness. This week, ask God to help you identify harmful habits that block forgiveness. Allow Him to open your eyes to the way in which you extend—and receive forgiveness. Then take every opportunity to grasp or extend forgiveness in a Christ-honoring manner.

Follow the Spirit

What God wants me to do:

_____

_____

_____

_____

Remember Your Thoughts

Special insights I have learned:

_____

_____

_____

_____

More Light on the Text

Matthew 5:17–26

17 Think not that I am come to destroy the law, or the prophets: I am not come to destroy, but to fulfil. 18 For verily I say unto you, Till heaven and earth pass, one jot or one tittle shall in no wise pass from the law, till all be fulfilled.

"The law and the prophets" is a shorthand expression for what we know as the Old Testament. Jesus prepares His listeners for what He is about to say by explaining that His teaching does not destroy, but rather fulfills the Old Testament. The Greek word translated "destroy" is *kataluo* (**kat-al-OO-o**). In other contexts, it means "dissolve, disunite, subvert, demolish." Here it means "do away with, annul, make invalid." To "fulfill" (Gk. *pleroo*, **play-RO-o**) the law and prophets, then, would be to uphold the Laws of the Old Testament, and to bring to fulfillment their Messianic and kingdom prophecies.

The Law and the prophets are the Word of God, and God has made it clear that His Word will not ever fail (Isaiah 40:8; Isaiah 55:10–11). Jesus is in full agreement with the Scriptures and goes to the extent of saying that not even a "jot" or "tittle" will pass away. The Greek word translated "jot" is *iota* (**ee-O-tah**), the name of the smallest letter of the Greek alphabet. The Greek word translated "tittle" is *keraia* (**ker-AH-yah**), and it refers to a projection or hook of a letter. Jesus was saying that not even the smallest letter—or even a small part of a letter—will ever be removed from God's Law (see also Luke 16:17; 21:33). In fact, God's Word will endure until heaven and earth pass away—an event that Jesus Himself asserts is a certainty (Matthew 24:35), but not until everything that is written comes to pass.

19 Whosoever therefore shall break one of these least commandments, and shall teach men so, he shall be called the least in the kingdom of heaven: but whosoever shall do and teach them, the same shall be called great in the kingdom of heaven.

Since Jesus' kingdom does not destroy the Old Testament Law, neither should we. The Greek word translated "break" is *luo* (**LOO-o**) and means literally "loosen, untie." Violations of God's Law are an attack on that Law; they attempt to weaken and destroy it.

Jesus uses a play on the word "least" to make a memorable point: if you break the least commandment, you will be the

least. The Greek word translated "least" is *elachistos* (**el-AKH-is-tos**) and means "smallest in importance." The rabbis of Jesus' time classified the Laws of the Old Testament according to their importance. Jesus uses their terminology to make a point that contradicts their practice: it is a grave error to minimize any of God's commandments.

The consequence for living in deliberate violation of God's Law is being called "least" in the kingdom of heaven. What God wants is not a display of religious behavior that impresses others, but our wholehearted submission to His will. It is impossible to rise to greatness in God's eyes without a firm commitment to total obedience.

20 For I say unto you, That except your righteousness shall exceed the righteousness of the scribes and Pharisees, ye shall in no case enter into the kingdom of heaven.

The scribes and Pharisees were some of the spiritual elite in Jesus' day. The scribes were the expert teachers and interpreters of the Law. The Pharisees were a Jewish religious party whose name comes from the Aramaic word *Pharisaios* (**far-is-AH-yos**), meaning "separated." Among other things, they attempted to distinguish themselves through fastidious obedience to the Law (Philippians 3:4–6). However, they also added human traditions to the Laws of God and modified God's Laws through their interpretations and traditions. Because their lives were so dominated by conformity to their religious rules, they were highly regarded by the Jewish people for their outward appearance of righteousness.

Jesus' statement that our righteousness must exceed that of the Pharisees would have shocked His audience. Most of His hearers would have assumed that if anyone could make it to heaven on the basis of their good works, it would be the Pharisees.

Doubtless they would have thought, "If even the Pharisees aren't good enough, is there any hope for the rest of us?" But Jesus' point is not that we must do more than the Pharisees, but that their righteousness is not true righteousness.

21 Ye have heard that it was said by them of old time, Thou shalt not kill; and whosoever shall kill shall be in danger of the judgment:

Jesus now begins to address specific commandments from God's Law to show just how the scribes and Pharisees have misunderstood and misrepresented them. He starts with the Sixth Commandment, found in Exodus 20:13: "Thou shalt not kill." The Old Testament Law required that anyone guilty of murder (intentional, unjustified homicide) be put to death. Those guilty of unintentional homicide (manslaughter) could avoid the death penalty, but did have to stand before the congregation for judgment to determine whether or not it really was manslaughter (Numbers 35:12). Any conviction required a trial and the testimony of at least two witnesses (35:30). But Jesus reveals that simply abstaining from murder does not count as true righteousness. He lists two common offenses that reveal a murderous heart: anger and ridicule

22 But I say unto you, That whosoever is angry with his brother without a cause shall be in danger of the judgment: and whosoever shall say to his brother, Raca, shall be in danger of the council: but whosoever shall say, Thou fool, shall be in danger of hell fire.

The anger at issue here is clearly unjustified anger, even though the best Greek manuscripts do not include the phrase "without a cause." Jesus Himself was sometimes angry (Matthew 21:12–13; Mark 3:5), but His anger was always justified and was directed at those whose evil was exposed by their hypocrisy

and their exploitation of the vulnerable. In brief, the anger that qualifies as a violation of God's Law is: (1) anger that is unjustly aroused, such as Cain's jealous anger of Abel (Genesis 4:5–6); and (2) anger that is not swiftly resolved, making it likely that we will sin (Ephesians 4:26–27).

Most scholars take the Aramaic term "Raca" to mean "empty-headed, numbskull, fool." The Greek word for "you fool" is *moros* (**mo-ROS**), an adjective used elsewhere in the New Testament to mean "foolish." Any words that communicate to someone that he or she is worthless are a violation of true righteousness, whether or not that violation is punished by a human authority.

23 Therefore if thou bring thy gift to the altar, and there rememberest that thy brother hath ought against thee; 24 Leave there thy gift before the altar, and go thy way; first be reconciled to thy brother, and then come and offer thy gift.

The altar in question here is the temple altar, and the gift is the offering being brought for sacrifice. This teaching underscores the priority of forgiveness in two ways. First, it warns us against the hypocrisy of pretending to be at peace with God when we are at odds with others. If our faith is genuine, God's forgiveness of us in Christ transforms us and makes us willing to pursue reconciliation with others. Secondly, Jesus is saying forgiveness is so important that we need to pursue reconciliation, even in situations when others—not ourselves—are the angry ones. Note that it is not the worshiper himself who is harboring unforgiveness; it is a brother. And Jesus doesn't even discuss whether or not the brother's anger is unjustified. Unforgiveness is so dangerous that we are responsible to make sure we don't tempt our brother to sin by leaving conflicts unresolved. We must do everything in our power to eradicate the poison of resentment from our lives as well as the lives of others. Our faithfulness to do so is far more important than even the most solemn act of worship.

25 Agree with thine adversary quickly, whiles thou art in the way with him; lest at any time the adversary deliver thee to the judge, and the judge deliver thee to the officer, and thou be cast into prison. 26 Verily I say unto thee, Thou shalt by no means come out thence, till thou hast paid the uttermost farthing.

Jesus ends His interpretation of the Sixth Commandment by discussing the urgency and wisdom of forgiveness. The Greek word translated "agree with" is *isthi* (**IS-thee**) and literally means "give yourself wholly to an idea or a person." The Greek word translated "adversary" is *antidikos* (**an-TID-ee-kos**) and refers to an opponent in a lawsuit. Because of the preceding verses, we know that Jesus is not speaking only of legal affairs, but is using a legal situation as an example to make His point. He is speaking about our need to reconcile as quickly as possible in any kind of conflict. Just as in the preceding situation with the brother, who is right and who is wrong is irrelevant.

The word translated "farthing" is *kodrantes* (**kod-RAN-tace**), and it referred to the smallest Roman coin. Unresolved conflict creates situations in which others may seek to get "every last penny" from us. Failure to reconcile quickly can have dramatic, painful, and even permanent consequences. It is a foolish and unnecessary risk to let a matter wait. The best time to attempt reconciliation will always be right now!

Sources:

Baltes, A. J., ed. Biblespeech.com. http://biblespeech.com (accessed May 29, 2010).

Beers, V. Gilbert. *The Victor Handbook of Bible Knowledge.* Wheaton, IL: Victor Books, 1981. 374–76, 389, 390–91.

Brand, Chad, Charles Draper and Archie England, gen. eds. *Holman Illustrated Bible Dictionary.* Nashville, TN: Holman Bible Publishers, 1998. 596.

Doriani, Daniel M. *Matthew. Reformed Expository Commentary, Vol. 1.* Phillipsburg, NJ: P&R Publishing, 2008. 138–49.

ESV Study Bible, The. Wheaton, IL: Crossway Bibles, 2008. 1828–29.

Hebrew and Greek Lexicons. Bible Study Tools.com. http://www.biblestudytools.com/lexicons (accessed September 16, 2010).

Henry, Matthew. *Concise Commentary on the Whole Bible.* Nashville, TN: Thomas Nelson, n.d. 864–66.

Merriam-Webster Online Dictionary. Merriam-Webster, Inc. http://www.merriam-webster.com (accessed May 8, 2010).

Morris, Leon. *The Gospel According to Matthew.* Grand Rapids, MI: William B. Eerdmans, 1992. 106–17.

Say It Correctly

Jot. JAT.
Pharisee. FA-rə-sē.
Raca. Rhak-AH.
Tittle. TI-təl.

Daily Bible Readings

MONDAY
A Covenant of Forgiveness
(Hebrews 10:11–18)

TUESDAY
Rejoicing in God's Forgiveness
(Psalm 32:1–5)

WEDNESDAY
The Prayer of Faith
(James 5:13–18)

THURSDAY
Forgive and Be Forgiven
(Luke 6:37–42)

FRIDAY
How Often Should I Forgive?
(Matthew 18:21–35)

SATURDAY
Forgiveness Begets Love
(Luke 7:40–47)

SUNDAY
First Be Reconciled
(Matthew 5:17–26)

Notes

_____

_____

_____

_____

Teaching Tips

Words You Should Know

A. Neighbor (Matthew 5:43) *plesion* (Gk.)—Any other person; fellow humankind.

B. Perfect (v. 48) *teleios* (Gk.)—A state of being completely mature, complete.

Teacher Preparation

Unifying Principle—Adopting an Attitude of Love. We reflect God's love when we love our enemies, and pray for them.

A. Pray for your students and that God will open their hearts to praying for their enemies.

B. Study the entire lesson.

C. Think about one time when you loved an enemy as yourself. Be prepared to share the experience.

D. Complete the companion lesson in the *Precepts For Living Personal Study Guide*®.

O—Open the Lesson

A. Open with prayer, and ask God to show students a better way of dealing with enemies.

B. Read the Keep in Mind verse aloud.

C. Share your "loving my enemy" story.

D. Invite students to share a time when they succeeded or failed at loving an enemy.

E. Ask: "Why did you fail or succeed?" Discuss.

F. Have students read the Aim for Change in unison. Discuss.

P—Present the Scriptures

A. Invite students to read the Focal Verses.

B. Now use The People, Places, and Times; Background; Search the Scriptures; At-A-Glance outline; In Depth; and More Light on the Text to clarify the verses.

E—Explore the Meaning

A. Have a student summarize the In Focus story and how it relates to the Aim for Change.

B. Ask a volunteer to read the Make It Happen section. Discuss.

C. In relation to loving others, invite students to briefly share the role of "prayer journals" in their lives.

N—Next Steps for Application

A. Have students record the initials of at least one "enemy" they plan to pray for, and a related petition.

B. Close with prayer.

Worship Guide

For the Superintendent or Teacher
Theme: Loving as God's People
Song: "They Will Know We Are Christians by Our Love"
Devotional Reading:
Matthew 22:34–40
Prayer

Loving as God's People

Bible Background • MATTHEW 5:43–48
Printed Text • MATTHEW 5:43–48 | Devotional Reading • Matthew 22:34–40

——— Aim for Change ———

By the end of the lesson, we will: DISCUSS Jesus' teachings concerning loving and praying for our enemies; CONSIDER the relationship between loving our enemies and being a child of God; and DECIDE to pray daily for our enemies,

——— In Focus ———

Sharon reread the e-mail that had popped into her inbox earlier today from her favorite social media site. She could not fathom why Kelly wanted to be one of her "friends." The last time she saw Kelly was the day they both were kicked out of college a decade earlier for hacking into their college's supposedly secure exam portal. Kelly was the culprit, but no one believed that the computer whiz, Sharon, had not enticed her Christian roommate to access the site. It had taken Sharon three years and thousands of dollars to clear her name. More so, the situation had left a bitter taste in Sharon's mouth for so-called Christians who used other people for their personal gain.

Ironically, it was the success of her legal battle that led Sharon to make Jesus her Savior. Back then, she had even gone through the motions of forgiving Kelly, but then she never expected to see her old "roomie" again. Now this. What to do?

Whether our enemies were once friends who wronged us, or people who have persecuted us from the day we met them, God expects us to love them. When we pray daily for our enemies, we can continue to walk in love, just like Jesus.

NOV 13th

——— Keep in Mind ———

"But I [Jesus] say unto you, Love your enemies, bless them that curse you, do good to them that hate you, and pray for them which despitefully use you, and persecute you; That ye may be the children of your Father which is in heaven: for he maketh his sun to rise on the evil and on the good, and sendeth rain on the just and on the unjust" (Matthew 5:44–45).

"But I [Jesus] say unto you, Love your enemies, bless them that curse you, do good to them that hate you, and pray for them which despitefully use you, and persecute you; That ye may be the children of your Father which is in heaven: for he maketh his sun to rise on the evil and on the good, and sendeth rain on the just and on the unjust" (Matthew 5:44–45).

Focal Verses

KJV **Matthew 5:43** Ye have heard that it hath been said, Thou shalt love thy neighbour, and hate thine enemy.

44 But I say unto you, Love your enemies, bless them that curse you, do good to them that hate you, and pray for them which despitefully use you, and persecute you;

45 That ye may be the children of your Father which is in heaven: for he maketh his sun to rise on the evil and on the good, and sendeth rain on the just and on the unjust.

46 For if ye love them which love you, what reward have ye? do not even the publicans the same?

47 And if ye salute your brethren only, what do ye more than others? do not even the publicans so?

48 Be ye therefore perfect, even as your Father which is in heaven is perfect.

NLT **Matthew 5:43** "You have heard that the Law of Moses says, 'Love your neighbor' and hate your enemy.

44 But I say, love your enemies! Pray for those who persecute you!

45 In that way, you will be acting as true children of your Father in heaven. For he gives his sunlight to both the evil and the good, and he sends rain on the just and on the unjust, too.

46 If you love only those who love you, what good is that? Even corrupt tax collectors do that much.

47 If you are kind only to your friends, how are you different from anyone else? Even pagans do that.

48 But you are to be perfect, even as your Father in heaven is perfect."

The People, Places, and Times

Enemies. *Holman's Illustrated Dictionary* defines "enemy" as "adversary or foe; one who dislikes or hates and seeks to harm the person." The Israelites were instructed to treat their neighbors well. They were warned, "Do not nurse hatred in your heart for any of your relatives. Confront your neighbors directly so you will not be held guilty for their crimes" (Leviticus 19:17, NLT). Over time, the Jewish people began using a strict interpretation of "neighbor," limited to only Jews. People of other nations or religions were treated as non-neighbors or enemies.

The Jews' keen hatred of Samaritans, for example, was legendary—so much so that Jesus deliberately cast a Samaritan as a hero in a parable depicting what makes a real neighbor. He told the story on an occasion when He was tested by a teacher of the Law who wanted to know what to do to inherit eternal life. Jesus in turn asked him what the law required. "The man answered, 'You must love the LORD your God with all your heart, all your soul, all your strength, and all your mind.' And, 'Love your neighbor as yourself'" (Luke 10:27, NLT).

Background

Continuing His "Sermon on the Mount" in Matthew 5, Jesus touches on another thorny subject: treatment of one's enemies. As was His practice, Jesus dealt directly with the topic. He openly refuted practices that made people shun, rather than embrace, others. His message was especially needed given the Jews' manner of treatment of their enemies, especially those of different ethnic and social status.

He challenged them to be like their Father in heaven. God pours out blessings on His enemies, giving them plenty of sunshine and rain. Christ's comment here may have been to prevent the elitism the Jews exhibited because they were God's chosen people.

At-A-Glance

1. Unlike the World
(Matthew 5:43, 46–47)

2. Like the Father (vv. 44–45, 48)

In Depth

1. Unlike the World (Matthew 5:43, 46–47)

In His talks with the disciples and the multitudes, Jesus often shared messages that seemed paradoxical to listeners' expectations. In each instance, Jesus shed light on fallacies or sin that hindered people's ability to get along with each other. On one occasion, when asked what the greatest commandment of the Law was, Jesus noted, "'You must love the LORD your God with all your heart, all your soul, all your mind, and all your strength.' The second is equally important: 'Love your neighbor as yourself'" (Mark 12:30–31, NLT).

However for their own purposes, the Jews had twisted this to mean "Love your neighbor and hate your enemy" (from Matthew 5:43). Yet Jesus made it clear that in God's eyes, enemies and friends should be treated equally well. Everyone is to be treated as a neighbor. And to assure that listeners understood, Jesus provided three specific ways to love enemies:

Bless them. Scripture includes 544 forms of the word "bless," and 282 uses of the term "curse." In the Old Testament, *barak* was used quite frequently, and it meant to "fill with benefits" or praise. In the New Testament,

makarios denoted good fortunate, or happiness. Meanwhile, "curse" always referred to ill fortune and separation from either God or community. The act of blessing or cursing was used to show favor or disfavor. The social fallout could be significant. This is why Jesus' instruction was so important. He encouraged fair treatment in all circumstances. "If your enemies are hungry, give them food to eat. If they are thirsty, give them water to drink. You will heap burning coals of shame on their heads, and the LORD will reward you" (Proverbs 25:21–22, NLT).

Do good to them. Jesus' words recall the advice in Proverbs: "Do not rejoice when your enemies fall into trouble. Don't be happy when they stumble" (Proverbs 24:17, NLT).

Pray for them. It is possible that many of Jesus' listeners had already prayed for their enemies. But it is also possible that the nature of those prayers were vindictive, similar to those David prayed for his enemies (see Psalm 109). While Jesus did not give specifics on what to pray, it is clear from His instruction in Matthew 5:44 that it would not be to curse enemies or ask for their harm. Treating enemies as Jesus directed would set listeners apart from their counterparts.

2. Like the Father (vv. 44–45, 48)

"So now we can tell who are children of God and who are children of the Devil. Anyone who does not obey God's commands and does not love other Christians does not belong to God" (1 John 3:10, NLT; the KJV uses "brother" to denote loving anyone other than oneself). The goal of Jesus' teaching was to help listeners understand the need for impartiality in their dealings with others.

More so, He wanted to give them a glimpse of what it would take to love as God's people. The apostle Paul put it this way, "Pay all your debts, except the debt of love for others. You can never finish paying that! If you love your neighbor, you will fulfill all the requirements of God's law" (Romans 13:8, NLT). Paul also wrote, "You must make allowance for each other's faults and forgive the person who offends you. Remember, the Lord forgave you, so you must forgive others. And the most important piece of clothing you must wear is love. Love is what binds us all together in perfect harmony." (Colossians 3:13–14, NLT).

There is no faking it until you make it a provision for loving our enemies. Rather, we must seek to love as God does; for God is love, and love is a fruit of His Spirit (Galatians 5:22). "But anyone who does not love does not know God—for God is love" (1 John 4:8, NLT). Here are some other attributes of God's love, which we need to extend to our enemies:

Faithful. *Chesed* is the Hebrew word that conveys the covenantal love God has for us. He is faithful, displays loving-kindness to us, and expects us to do the same (1 Corinthians 1:9).

Impartial. As Jesus pointed out in Matthew 5:45, God does not withhold some of His blessings from unbelievers. Thus, as children of God we must endeavor to love impartially, regardless of how difficult it may be in some circumstances.

Complete. There is no half-stepping with God. He offers all of Himself to us. Similarly when loving our enemies, we cannot choose when or how to help them.

Permanent. God does not pick and choose which day He will love us. Similarly, we cannot use excuses such as "it's a bad hair day" or "it's Monday" to excuse the way we treat our enemies. "Long ago the LORD said to Israel: 'I have loved you, my people, with an everlasting love. With unfailing love I have drawn you to myself'" (Jeremiah 31:3, NLT).

Never fails. Often people do not reach out to their enemies because they believe it is useless. But the apostle Paul reminds us, "Love never fails" (1 Corinthians 13:8, NIV).

Lesson in Our Society

In the season of Thankgiving and Christmas, few people think to add their enemies to their guest or gift list. In light of today's lesson, how can we bring holiday cheer to those who need it, but may not want it from us?

Make It Happen

A prayer journal is a useful tool for recording petitions. It also helps us to see the faithfulness of God. The answers may not be what we thought they would be, but they are always what we need. Even if you have never used a prayer journal, try it for at least this week. Record your petitions, and include those for your enemies. Then remember to go back and jot down any answers you received, including any internal or external changes you see as a result of your prayer.

Follow the Spirit

What God wants me to do:

_____

_____

_____

_____

Remember Your Thoughts

Special insights I have learned:

_____

_____

_____

_____

More Light on the Text

Matthew 5:43–48

43 Ye have heard that it hath been said, Thou shalt love thy neighbour, and hate thine enemy.

Jesus' audience has heard the commandment "Love thy neighbour," which is found in Leviticus 19:18. However, Jesus' quote of the commandment is different from the Old Testament in two ways: it is missing "as yourself," and in its place is added "and hate thine enemy." It seems most likely that Jesus is using the words of the Jewish teachers of the day, who have twisted God's standard in their interpretation of the law.

The Bible is realistic about the fact that some will ultimately oppose God, and their destruction will be a vindication of God and His people. The Psalms even talk of hating evildoers and idolaters (Psalm 26:5; 31:6) and of God's hatred for evildoers (5:5). But the Scriptures also require God's people to welcome outsiders (Leviticus 19:33–34). And Jesus' own example was to lovingly reach out to hardened "sinners" such as the Samaritan woman and Zacchaeus the tax collector. So the clear mandate for us is to hope, pray, and work for the salvation—not the destruction—of unbelievers. One day we will rejoice in God's victory over His enemies, but right now, we do not know who will be saved in the end. We should never presume that any individual or group is beyond hope. The apostle Paul is proof that even a hardened enemy of Jesus can be dramatically converted through God's grace. The Christian has no justification for hatred of any "neighbour" (Gk. *plesion*, **play-SEE-on**).

44 But I say unto you, Love your enemies, bless them that curse you, do good to them that hate you, and pray for them which despitefully use you, and persecute you;

In Matthew 5:44 and 45, Jesus articulates God's standard of righteousness, which is higher than even what the Old Testament law required. The earliest and best manuscripts of Matthew do not include the phrases "do good to them which hate you," "bless them that curse you," and "(them) which despitefully use you" (v. 44). We can be confident that Jesus did in fact say all of those things because they are recorded in Luke 6:27–28 (KJV), but they almost certainly were not a part of Matthew's original text.

The enemies in question here are not simply people who dislike us. The Greek word for "enemies" is *echthros* (**ech-THROS**), an adjective meaning "hated, hostile" that is used in the New Testament as a noun. The Greek word translated "persecute" is *dioko* (**dee-O-ko**), which means "to make to run or flee, to pursue, to harass, trouble, molest." So the enemies of whom Jesus speaks are those who are actively trying to do us harm, or those who would do us harm if they could.

The Greek word for "love" is *agapao* (**ag-ap-AH-o**). It means "have affection for, cherish." Consider, then, what Jesus is not teaching. He is not teaching nonviolence—the philosophy that we are in the right as long as we do no harm. He is also not teaching self-preservation ("do the least amount of harm necessary to survive"). Instead, He instructs us to intentionally move toward those who want to harm us and desire their well-being.

Although Jesus does not here explain the purpose for such a difficult teaching, we see it clearly and powerfully in His example. When one of the disciples attempted to defend Jesus by force on the night of His arrest and cut off the ear of the high priest's servant, Jesus healed the ear (Luke 22:49–51). And while still on the Cross, He asked the Father to forgive those responsible for His death (23:34). Love for enemies is not a suicide mission, but a rescue mission founded on self-sacrificial love. Christ calls His followers to advance His kingdom by joining Him in this mission of self-sacrifice (1 Peter 2:21–24). In the days of the early church, Stephen and Paul both stand out as examples of this kind of love (Acts 7:60; 1 Corinthians 4:12–13).

45 That ye may be the children of your Father which is in heaven: for he maketh his sun to rise on the evil and on the good, and sendeth rain on the just and on the unjust.

The phrase "may be the children" is literally "may become sons" in the Greek text. "Become" is the common Greek word *ginomai* (**GHIN-om-ahee**), a word with a wide range of meanings, most commonly "to be born or produced." Here Jesus' message is not that we become children of God by loving like God, but that we grow into our identity as God's children as we learn to love. The increasing resemblance with our Heavenly Father proves that we really are His.

God's love for even His enemies is seen in ways so ordinary that they are easy to overlook: the fact that the sun rises and rain falls the world over, regardless of who lives where. The Greek word for "just" is *dikaios* (**DIK-ah-yos**) and means "righteous, upright, and virtuous." The Greek word for "unjust" is the antonym *adikos* (**AD-ee-kos**). Jesus is articulating the concept theologians have termed "common grace": even though God's saving grace is only experienced through faith in Christ, all humanity experiences some undeserved favor. By virtue of our fall into sin, we do not deserve to live. None of us is in fact truly righteous in the strictest sense. But in His kindness, God sustains

the functions of the universe that make it possible for us to live.

46 For if ye love them which love you, what reward have ye? do not even the publicans the same? 47 And if ye salute your brethren only, what do ye more than others? do not even the publicans so?

Jesus now uses rhetorical questions to prove that anything less than God's highest standard is not true righteousness, even if it appears to comply with the letter of the Old Testament law. The Greek word translated "salute" is *aspazomai* (**as-PAD-zom-ahee**) and means "greet, welcome." Both verses say the same thing, although verse 47 focuses more on the external expression of love.

If the Pharisees and scribes were viewed as religious high achievers (cf. Matthew 5:20), "publicans" were at the opposite end of the spectrum. Publicans were tax collectors and were even less popular in Jesus' day than today. Their cooperation with the occupying Romans was viewed as betrayal of their people and nation. Also, tax collectors routinely became rich by overcharging the people. They were "sellouts" to the enemy, and they profited richly from their disloyalty. Note that John the Baptist instructed tax collectors, who wanted to repent, to stop overcharging (Luke 3:12–13). And when Jesus reached out to Zacchaeus, Zacchaeus demonstrated the sincerity of his faith in Christ by offering to repay fourfold anyone he had defrauded (19:8).

Jesus' point with His questions in Matthew 5:46–47 is not that we can earn something from God by loving others well enough, or that God judges human righteousness by comparing us to each other, but that people who pride themselves on their religious perfection aren't actually meeting any higher standard than people widely regarded as scoundrels. The Greek word translated "reward" (*misthos,* **mis-THOS**) means "wages," and it is used in Romans 4:4 to refer to what we expect God to give us in return for living righteously. The religious elite assumed that they were earning points from God through their elaborate rituals and stringent rule keeping, but Jesus is showing us that true righteousness will distinguish itself in an entirely different kind of love than what their religion produced. The shocking truth is that human-powered religion can't make us any more righteous in God's eyes than a hardened sinner.

48 Be ye therefore perfect, even as your Father which is in heaven is perfect.

"Therefore" reminds us to think of what we have already heard so far in the Sermon on the Mount, but especially verses 44 through 47, in order to understand what comes next. What we have heard is that external righteousness, even when it conforms to the Old Testament law, is totally inadequate in God's eyes. The best behavior that religion can produce in us makes us no better than a tax collector—and everybody knows that tax collectors are not viewed as being anywhere near holy enough to be approved by God.

The only right way to live is to pursue perfection and live up to God's standards. The Greek word translated "perfect" is *teleios* (**TEL-i-os**), and it is used in the New Testament to mean "mature, complete" (Colossians 4:12; James 1:4). It is possible to see this definition as a bit of a loophole. After all, "mature" is not the same as "perfect," and mature people make mistakes. But such reasoning misses the point. We are to be as mature as God, so whether *teleios* means perfect or mature really doesn't matter because either way it is a very, very high standard and it is unreachable apart from God's work in our life.

Matthew 5:48 is not telling people outside the kingdom of God how to enter. Jesus is explaining the kingdom way of life to those who strive for full citizenship.

Sources:

Beers, V. Gilbert. *The Victor Handbook of Bible Knowledge.* Wheaton, IL: Victor Books, 1981. 442.

Butler, Bradley S. "Enemy." *Holman Illustrated Bible Dictionary.* Chad Brand, Charles Draper and Archie England, gen. eds. Nashville, TN: Holman Bible Publishers, 1998. 487.

Clendenen, E. Ray. "Blessing and Cursing." *Holman Illustrated Bible Dictionary.* Chad Brand, Charles Draper and Archie England, gen. eds. Nashville, TN: Holman Bible Publishers, 1998. 223–24.

Doriani, Daniel M. *Matthew. Reformed Expository Commentary, Vol. 1.* Phillipsburg, NJ: P&R Publishing, 2008. 186–95.

ESV Study Bible, The. Wheaton, IL: Crossway Bibles, 2008. 1830–31.

Hebrew and Greek Lexicons. Bible Study Tools.com. http://www.biblestudytools.com/lexicons (accessed September 16, 2010).

Henry, Matthew. *Concise Commentary on the Whole Bible.* Nashville, Tennessee: Thomas Nelson, n.d. 866.

Lanier, Daniel. "Love." *Holman Illustrated Bible Dictionary.* Chad Brand, Charles Draper and Archie England, gen. eds. Nashville, TN: Holman Bible Publishers, 1998. 1054–55.

Merriam-Webster Online Dictionary. Merriam-Webster, Inc. http://www.merriam-webster.com (accessed May 8, 2010).

Morris, Leon. *The Gospel According to Matthew.* Grand Rapids, MI: William B. Eerdmans, 1992. 129–34.

Say It Correctly

Despitefully. Di-SPIT-fə-lē.
Persecute. PER-si-kyüt.
Publicans. PE-bli-kəns.

Daily Bible Readings

MONDAY
The Greatest Commandment
(Matthew 22:34–40)

TUESDAY
Loving Your God
(Deuteronomy 6:1–9)

WEDNESDAY
Loving Your Neighbor
(Leviticus 19:13–18)

THURSDAY
Loving the Alien
(Leviticus 19:33–37)

FRIDAY
Loving Your Wife
(Ephesians 5:25–33)

SATURDAY
Loving Your Husband and Children
(Titus 2:1–5)

SUNDAY
Loving Your Enemies
(Matthew 5:43–48)

Notes

_____

_____

_____

_____

Teaching Tips

Words You Should Know

A. Pray (Matthew 6:5–7) *proseucho-mai* (Gk.)—Make earnest supplication; worship of God.

B. Forgive (vv. 12, 14, 15) *aphiemi* (Gk.)—To release from an obligation, debt or guilt.

Teacher Preparation

Unifying Principle—Valuing the Inner and Outer Actions. Jesus taught that it is more important to develop our inner relationship with God through prayer.

A. Pray for your students.

B. Prayerfully study the entire lesson.

C. Complete the companion lesson in the *Precepts For Living Personal Study Guide®*.

D. Materials needed: 3" x 5" index cards, pencils, small receptacle to hold cards (perhaps a shoe box).

O—Open the Lesson

A. After taking requests, ask at least two students to open with prayer.

B. Ask: "Is prayer important today?" Discuss.

C. Summarize and discuss the In Focus story.

P—Present the Scriptures

A. Have one volunteer read the Focal Verses 5 through 9a; have everyone recite the Lord's Prayer together; and another volunteer read verses 14 and 15.

B. Use The People, Places, and Times; Background; Search the Scriptures; At-A-Glance outline; In Depth; and More Light on the Text to clarify the verses.

E—Explore the Meaning

A. After reading section 1, "Our Praying," discuss "repetitious prayers."

B. After reading section 2, "Our Forgiving," have students silently search their hearts for unforgiveness.

N—Next Steps for Application

A. Have students write a prayer request on a 3" x 5" card (no names). Then place the cards in the small receptacle.

B. Have students select a prayer request card (not their own), and each day during the week pray for that request.

C. Close with prayer.

Worship Guide

For the Superintendent or Teacher
Theme: Praying as God's People
Song: "I'm Just One Prayer Away"
Devotional Reading: Isaiah 12
Prayer

Praying as God's People

Bible Background • MATTHEW 6:5–15
Printed Text • MATTHEW 6:5–15 | Devotional Reading • ISAIAH 12

Aim for Change

By the end of the lesson, we will: SUMMARIZE Jesus' teaching about prayer; BECOME CONVINCED that Jesus' model of praying should be our guide; and DECIDE to model our prayers after the Lord's Prayer.

 In Focus

Virginia sat at her desk with her hands folded together, head bowed, and eyes closed. It was the lunch hour, and she had decided to forgo her lunch in favor of prayer. She needed to hear from God. After nine years of employment at the university, it looked as though she was going to be fired.

She had transferred into the position only seven months ago, when her former job had been phased out. Up until now, her work record had been impeccable. Now her new supervisor was telling her that her work was unsatisfactory. "Dear Lord," she prayed. "Please give me the strength to endure whatever comes my way and help me to have the right attitude, especially toward my supervisor. I trust in You and not the situation. Show me what to do, Lord."

Have you ever had something happen to you that was not in your control? Where did you turn? Today we want to examine God's teachings on prayer.

Keep in Mind

NOV 20th

"But thou, when thou prayest, enter into thy closet, and when thou hast shut thy door, pray to thy Father which is in secret; and thy Father which seeth in secret shall reward thee openly" (Matthew 6:6).

"But thou, when thou prayest, enter into thy closet, and when thou hast shut thy door, pray to thy Father which is in secret; and thy Father which seeth in secret shall reward thee openly" (Matthew 6:6).

Focal Verses

KJV **Matthew 6:5** And when thou prayest, thou shalt not be as the hypocrites are: for they love to pray standing in the synagogues and in the corners of the streets, that they may be seen of men. Verily I say unto you, They have their reward.

6 But thou, when thou prayest, enter into thy closet, and when thou hast shut thy door, pray to thy Father which is in secret; and thy Father which seeth in secret shall reward thee openly.

7 But when ye pray, use not vain repetitions, as the heathen do: for they think that they shall be heard for their much speaking.

8 Be not ye therefore like unto them: for your Father knoweth what things ye have need of, before ye ask him.

9 After this manner therefore pray ye: Our Father which art in heaven, Hallowed be thy name.

10 Thy kingdom come, Thy will be done in earth, as it is in heaven.

11 Give us this day our daily bread.

12 And forgive us our debts, as we forgive our debtors.

13 And lead us not into temptation, but deliver us from evil: For thine is the kingdom, and the power, and the glory, for ever. Amen.

14 For if ye forgive men their trespasses, your heavenly Father will also forgive you:

15 But if ye forgive not men their trespasses, neither will your Father forgive your trespasses.

NLT **Matthew 6:5** "And now about prayer. When you pray, don't be like the hypocrites who love to pray publicly on street corners and in the synagogues where everyone can see them. I assure you, that is all the reward they will ever get.

6 But when you pray, go away by yourself, shut the door behind you, and pray to your Father secretly. Then your Father, who knows all secrets, will reward you.

7 "When you pray, don't babble on and on as people of other religions do. They think their prayers are answered only by repeating their words again and again.

8 Don't be like them, because your Father knows exactly what you need even before you ask him!

9 Pray like this: Our Father in heaven, may your name be honored.

10 May your Kingdom come soon. May your will be done here on earth, just as it is in heaven.

11 Give us our food for today,

12 and forgive us our sins, just as we have forgiven those who have sinned against us.

13 And don't let us yield to temptation, but deliver us from the evil one.

14 "If you forgive those who sin against you, your heavenly Father will forgive you.

15 But if you refuse to forgive others, your Father will not forgive your sins."

The People, Places, and Times

Prayer. It is the communication from the heart of a person to the ear of God. Throughout the Old and New Testaments, we find God answering the prayers of those persons who needed Him. The Hebrews, while in Egypt, cried out because of their hard taskmasters, and God sent Moses to deliver them (Exodus 3:1–4:17). David prayed for forgiveness and restoration after being caught in sin, and God heard his prayer (Psalm 51). Elisha prayed for his servant's eyes to be opened to see the army of the Lord, and God made it so (2 Kings 6:17). Peter prayed and Tabitha woke up from the dead (Acts 9:40–41). Both faith (Mark 11:24) and forgiveness (Mark 11:25) are needed in order for prayers to be answered.

Background

Jesus taught that the true righteousness of the kingdom must be applied in life's everyday activities. He cautioned against practicing piety to impress other people. Almsgiving was designed to be a display of mercy, but the Pharisees had distorted the showing of mercy by using it to demonstrate their devotion to religious duties in almsgiving and prayer. Jesus also taught that those who give without fanfare and quietly pray will receive their rewards.

Just as the Pharisees made a public display in giving, so they did in praying. They prayed in public places to be seen and heard by other men. Jesus says they got their reward in the applause of the people. Instead of condemning prayer of this kind, the Lord purified the practice by directing us into a private place to be alone and pray to our Father. Jesus went on to give us an example of how to pray with certain guidelines.

At-A-Glance

1. Our Praying (Matthew 6:5–13)

2. Our Forgiving (vv. 14–15)

In Depth

1. Our Praying (Matthew 6:5–13)

Jesus gave instructions to guide us in our praying. He taught that prayer should be done confidentially. It is not wrong to pray in public, but it is not right to pray in public if you are not in the habit of praying in private. It is not wrong to seek God's help or bless our food. Our Lord prayed privately (Mark 1:35); so did Elisha (2 Kings 4:32–33) and Daniel (Daniel 6:10). We should pray sincerely and not use empty phrases, because God knows what we need before we ask (Matthew 6:7–8). Repetitious requests are done in vain when we babble without a sincere heart's desire to seek and do God's will (6:9–13).

Jesus gave His followers a model prayer known as the Lord's Prayer. We should use this prayer as a pattern; Jesus said to pray "after this manner" (v. 9). The purpose of prayer is to glorify God, and these are the guidelines for prayer: (1) it should involve worship, reverence, and exaltation of our Father; (2) it should concern itself with the work God is engaged in, namely, the establishment of God's kingdom and His will being done on earth; (3) it should be concerned with daily needs; (4) it should contain confession and seek forgiveness; and finally, (5) it should seek protection and deliverance from the evil one.

Notice this model prayer begins with the phrase "Our Father" (v. 9). We put God's concerns first, and then we can bring our own needs. This is the God-appointed way of having our needs met because prayer also prepares us for God's answer.

2. Our Forgiving (vv. 14–15)

We must pray with a forgiving spirit toward others. If you do not forgive repentant offenders, God will not forgive you. Christians must be prepared and willing to forgive the offenses of others; if we do not forgive, our prayers are of no avail. If God would answer the prayers of a person who is unforgiving, then He would be encouraging sin. Forgiveness puts you in right relationship with your brothers and sisters, and with God. It enables you to pray effectively; therefore, forgiveness is an important part of prayer.

The basic concept of prayer is forgiveness. Forgive your brother and be forgiven. To be forgiven is to be released from all guilt and condemnation. We all need forgiveness. Forgiving means we should not be bitter or hostile, seeking revenge, or holding hard feelings against another person. We should not rejoice when others fall on hard times or experience trouble and trials in their lives. "Blessed are the merciful: for they shall obtain mercy" (Matthew 5:7).

Search the Scriptures

1. To whom should we pray (Matthew 6:6)?
2. How is forgiveness connected to prayer (v. 14)?

Discuss the Meaning

1. If God knows what we need, why pray (Matthew 6:8)?
2. What is prayer (v. 9)?

Lesson in Our Society

The Pharisees wanted to be seen praying so that people would see how religious they were. They sought the approval of people. We see the same thing today in our churches and on our televisions. Yet more and more people seek answers through psychics or other mystical leaders because they do not want to spend the time developing a relationship with their Creator. If we really want answers to today's complex issues, we must ask God because He sees the complete picture from beginning to end.

Make It Happen

Prayer is needed more today than ever. This week, set aside a specific time each day for prayer. Psalm 63:1 (KJV) says, "early will I seek thee." Ask the Father to bring to your mind those people who have hurt you or

persecuted you. Then ask Him to help you to forgive those people. If you can contact any of them, do so, and resolve whatever differences you may have. Remember, prayer changes things.

Follow the Spirit

What God wants me to do:

_____

_____

_____

_____

Remember Your Thoughts

Special insights I have learned:

_____

_____

_____

_____

More Light on the Text

Matthew 6:5–15

5 And when thou prayest, thou shalt not be as the hypocrites are: for they love to pray standing in the synagogues and in the corners of the streets, that they may be seen of men. Verily I say unto you, They have their reward. 6 But thou, when thou prayest, enter into thy closet, and when thou hast shut thy door, pray to thy Father which is in secret; and thy Father which seeth in secret shall reward thee openly.

The previous verses in this chapter tell us to do our giving to the needy without seeking a public pat on the back. Verses 5 and 6 apply this same "secrecy" principle to prayer. Jesus declared that praying to impress others makes people hypocrites. He described the hypocrites as those who found conspicuous places to stand and pray in the synagogue and even on the street corners. Their objective was to have everyone see them and admire their devotion and dedication. Instead, we should go into a secret closet and, even though no one else may know what we are doing, God will see, know, and reward us. This is not to say we should avoid praying in public, but we should not pray to show the public how pious and spiritual we are. Even in public, our motivation should be to glorify and seek God and God alone.

7 But when ye pray, use not vain repetitions, as the heathen do: for they think that they shall be heard for their much speaking. 8 Be not ye therefore like unto them: for your Father knoweth what things ye have need of, before ye ask him.

In verse 7, Jesus continued His instructions about prayer. Not only are we to avoid praying in order to be seen by others, but we are to avoid the practice that was common to the Gentiles of using lots of words to try to impress or manipulate God. The Gentiles had so many gods and so many names for them that they would try to list them all to make sure they included the right one. Also, they would try to flatter the gods in order to convince them to answer the prayer. Jesus said, specifically, to not be like them. He assures us that God, our Father, the omniscient One (all-knowing), knows already what we need even before we ask. And God cannot be manipulated. God stands ready to answer our prayers and bless us because of the love He has for us.

Even reciting the Lord's Prayer can become a vain repetition. We can rattle off the words in church without even thinking about the meaning of the words. Whenever we pray, we should remember that we are in the presence of the holy God, the God of the universe. Our thoughts need to be focused on Him.

9 After this manner therefore pray ye: Our Father which art in heaven, Hallowed be thy name.

In verses 9 through 14, He tells us how we should pray in a model prayer that we commonly call the Lord's Prayer. Although the prayer recorded in Luke 11:1–4 is very much like it, it was probably prayed by Jesus at a different time and a different place. According to Luke's Gospel, Jesus gives this prayer in response to a request from one of the disciples (11:1). Matthew does not include this request, but he includes a longer and more developed version of the prayer. It was not intended to replace the corporate prayer in the synagogue, but to give His disciples a model for their own private prayer time. Books have been written analyzing this prayer. It is so rich in meaning and subject to various interpretations. Although it is short, it is a powerful model for the way that we should pray in our own prayer closets. It was not given just for us to memorize and recite in church, but to give us a prayer format. The prayer begins with words of worship, expresses a desire for God's will to be done, thanks God for supplying one's physical needs, and asks forgiveness for sins and help to stand against temptation.

Jesus started by affirming that God is the Father, the one in the heavens. This was typical of many formal Jewish prayers. We know that Jesus referred to God as "*Abba*" (**ab-BAH**), which is an affectionate, familiar term, similar to our current use of the term "dad" or "daddy." It shows the kind of relationship He had with God, the Father. We should seek to have that same kind of closeness and intimacy in our relationship with God.

But in this prayer, God is addressed as "Father," not as "Daddy." The Greek for "Father" is *pater* (**pat-AYR**). This is His title. He is the parent, and then we are reminded that our Father is the God of heaven. He is absolute holiness. He is our Father, the Father of all who have received Jesus Christ as Savior.

Fatherhood is a very sensitive and delicate issue in African American communities. So many forces have conspired, from personal irresponsibility to the lingering effects of slavery to the current evils of racism and other forms of oppression against African American men. The result is that many homes and families are headed by women. There are some negative feelings associated with the term "father" for this reason and others. Some modern theologians are questioning whether we really should address God as Father, since it does evoke such powerfully negative feelings in so many.

It is the wrong strategy to alter, because of horrible experiences, how God has revealed Himself as Father. Instead of regarding Scripture primarily through the lens of negative experience, our perception of "Father" should be transformed by divine revelation. To those who have not experienced the love and security of a father in the home, we look at Psalm 68:5 (NIV) where God says that He is "A father to the fatherless." God extends His arms to those who have not had a father in their lives. God desires and is able to fill this void in a person's life.

For those whose earthly fathers have not been loving role models to their children, the problem is greater. A bad image needs to be replaced with our wonderful Father God. We cannot take away the fact that this is how Jesus addressed God—as *pater*/Father

(*Abba*/Daddy). This picture of the father-son, father-daughter relationship can guide us as we work to repair the damage and heal the pain in African American communities. The seams of our families can be mended and made strong by using God, the perfect, all-loving, all-caring Father, as our model.

After this opening address, the Lord's Prayer contains seven petitions. There are three "Thou" or "Thy" God petitions—things we are praying God will do for His glory. These are followed by four "we" petitions—things we want God to do for His children.

The first "Thou" petition, "Hallowed be thy name" (Matthew 6:9), would more accurately be stated, "Let Thy name be hallowed." This means that God's name should be sanctified, revered, and considered holy. For Jewish people, the name of God was considered so holy it could not be spoken or even written in its entirety. The name of God was treated with reverence because for them it was synonymous with God. For us, the prayer is a request that in all the earth the name of God would speak of God's holiness and kingdom.

This is both a personal request and a missionary request. We are asking that we personally would do nothing that would bring shame to the name of God. We should want to act and speak in such a way that others will give honor to our God instead of saying that if that's what Christians are like, they want no part of such a faith and such a God. In addition, this is a request that people all over would come to worship and honor the Lord our God. We are asking God to help us share the Good News in any way we can—whether by praying, giving, or telling the person next door about salvation in Jesus Christ.

10 Thy kingdom come. Thy will be done in earth, as it is in heaven.

In one respect, this refers to the end times, when there will be fulfillment of all prophecies and expectations. At that time, God's kingdom will prevail, and God will rule and reign on earth as He does in heaven. This is what we look forward to as Christians, and we seek to make it a reality in our daily lives as we wait for the kingdom to come in totality. We are also praying that God will reign as King in our hearts. When Jesus said that His kingdom was near (Matthew 3:2; 4:17; Mark 1:15), He was inviting people to make Him the King of their hearts right then and there. He desires to have complete rule in our lives today as well.

The second half of Matthew 6:10 continues with the desire for the coming of the kingdom, that is, God's ultimate will for the earth and humanity. As we pray these words, we have to consider what we are doing day-to-day to witness to God's kingdom on earth. It is also a prayer for God's will to be done in our individual lives. We can ask this prayer in complete confidence because we know that God loves us and would not do anything in our lives that ultimately would be bad for us. We can pray this in confidence because God has all wisdom. While something we desire may look good to us today, God can see in the future whether it truly will be good.

11 Give us this day our daily bread.

At this point the "we" petitions begin, as we request things from God. Some scholars have debated over whether this means literal bread in terms of our daily physical needs, or whether "daily bread" should be taken in the spiritual sense, or even in the understanding of what will be consumed at the heavenly banquet. The Greek word for "daily" is *epiousios* (**ep-ee-OO-see-os**). It was once thought to be a made-up word, and then one day some archaeologists found it on a fragment of paper—a grocery shopping list with the daily needs written on it. This is a simple request. We are not asking God to set up a large bank account for us. We are simply asking Him to give us what we need for today. Elsewhere in Scripture we are advised to be wise in financial matters, but here we are trusting children just asking Him for what is needful for today.

Many of us pass over this verse quickly because we have never known days without enough to eat, but Christians in many parts of the world are hungry—some do not live very far from us. They have learned what it means to truly have to trust God to provide for their basic needs. When we pray this prayer, we should remember those who are hungry. James 2:15–16 tells us that we need to give food to those who are hungry and not just wish them well.

12 And forgive us our debts, as we forgive our debtors.

Some translations (such as KJV and NIV) use the word "debts," others use "transgressions," and still others (such as NLT) use "sins." The best understanding of this word is perhaps a combination of all three. The Greek word for "debts" is *opheilema* (**of-I-lay-mah**), which literally means failure to pay what is due. All of us have failed to live up to our duties to both God and humankind. It also has the sense of a moral failure or a fault. Sin is a universal disease in all of us.

This verse literally means that we are asking God to forgive us in the same proportion in which we forgive others. That is pretty scary. This means that if we say, "I will never forgive so-and-so for what he has done" or "I will never forget what you did to me," we are actually asking God not to forgive us! Human forgiveness and God's forgiveness are all wrapped up together.

But only as we have experienced the initial forgiveness of God at the Cross are we capable of forgiving others. Here are a few tips from William Barclay on forgiving (*The Gospel of Matthew, Vol. 1*). First, we must try to understand the person that we perceive as hurting us. When we ourselves do wrong, we always seem to have an excuse for ourselves. Others do too. There are probably pains and problems they are facing that we know nothing of.

Secondly, we must learn to forget just as God has forgiven and forgotten our sins. The writer of Hebrews paraphrases Jeremiah 31:34 when he says, "'Their sins and lawless acts I will remember no more'" (Hebrews 10:17, NIV). If the Almighty God can forget our sins, surely we can forget the hurts that others have caused us. Adopting an attitude based on our New Covenant is also very good for the psyche. We cannot be at peace when bitterness is consuming us. When we don't forgive others, we are literally eaten up with such an attitude. Something as simple as a rush hour drive can give us ulcers if we let the other drivers get to us.

Thirdly, we need to love in order to truly forgive. We read in 1 Peter 4:8 (NIV) that "love covers . . . a multitude of sins." Just think of the love-struck teenagers who cannot see anything wrong in each other. Some older married couples need to be challenged to look at each other with such deep love that they are able to forgive each other for their shortcomings. Therefore, all of us in the family of God need this kind of love for each other that forgives the sister with the big mouth, the brother who tends to be tactless, etc. Let's remember how much God has forgiven us and have that same attitude toward others.

13 And lead us not into temptation, but deliver us from evil: For thine is the kingdom, and the power, and the glory, for ever. Amen.

This is a difficult passage to understand, because it implies God actively "leads" us into temptation. The expression is intended as a petition for God's help when we face the inevitable temptations and trials that come in this life. The epistle of James cautions us never to say that God is tempting us (James 1:13–14). Most scholars agree that this means God doesn't allow us to be tempted or tested beyond our ability to persevere. There is a very popular saying inspired by 1 Corinthians 10:13, that especially in times of trial, "God won't put more on you than you can bear."

Then the Lord's Prayer continues with a request to be delivered from evil (Matthew 6:13). The more accurate translation of the Greek word *poneros* (**pon-ay-ROS**) is used here as "evil one." When times of testing come, as they will, then we pray to be delivered from the evil one—Satan. The devil "comes only to steal and kill and destroy" (John 10:10, NIV). These two petitions in Matthew 6:13—to resist temptation and to be rescued from evil—go together.

Some people feel Christians should not undergo trials and temptations. But Jesus said we would have tribulation in the world (John 16:33). We should be of good cheer in the midst of them, however, because we know that He has overcome the world. So when we are tempted, when we suffer, when we are tossed and driven by the storms of life, we pray for the strength to bear it, to come through it, and to be liberated from the evil one.

14 For if ye forgive men their trespasses, your heavenly Father will also forgive you: 15 But if ye forgive not men their trespasses, neither will your Father forgive your trespasses.

Finally, Jesus goes back to the subject of forgiveness in verses 14 and 15. These verses are not part of the Lord's Prayer, but are included to emphasize the importance of forgiveness and the fact that it must go two ways in the life of the Christian.

We sing and pray the Lord's Prayer so often that it can become rote and lose its meaning for us. But when we look at it with fresh eyes, the prayer can come alive again and give us, as Jesus intended, clear instructions on how to pray effectively.

How serious are we in wanting God's kingdom to come and His will to be done? Do we live as kingdom people, aware of who and whose we are? How easy or difficult is it for us to forgive others when they do something wrong to us? How satisfied are we with having just our daily needs met, as opposed to all our wants and desires met? And, in the course of going about our daily lives, how much awareness do we show—in our thoughts, actions, and treatment of others—of the truth of Matthew 6:14–15? These are all questions that arise when we take time to really reflect and meditate on the Lord's Prayer.

Sources:
Barclay, William. *The Gospel of Matthew, Vol. 1 (Chapters 1 to 10).* Rev. ed. Philadelphia, PA: The Westminster Press, 1975. 219–24.
Greek and Hebrew Lexicons. Eliyah.com. http://www.eliyah.com/lexicon.html/greek/kjv (accessed June 1, 2010).

Say It Correctly

Babbling. BAB-ling.
Hypocrites. HIP-o-krits.
Pagans. PAY-gans.

Daily Bible Readings

MONDAY
A Prayer for Deliverance
(Genesis 32:6–12)

TUESDAY
A Prayer for Forgiveness
(Numbers 14:13–19)

WEDNESDAY
A Prayer for God's Blessing
(2 Samuel 7:18–29)

THURSDAY
A Prayer for Healing
(1 Kings 17:17–23)

FRIDAY
A Prayer of Thanksgiving
(Isaiah 12)

SATURDAY
God's Assurance for Prayer
(Jeremiah 29:10–14)

SUNDAY
The Practice of Prayer
(Matthew 6:5–15)

Teaching Tips

November 27
Bible Study Guide 13

Words You Should Know

A. Lay (not) up (Matthew 6:19-21) *thesaurizo* (Gk.)—This word is discussed as background for the text of today's lesson; it is important to know that in the Greek, the verb "lay up" and the noun "treasures" are both rooted in the same word.

B. Take (no) thought (Matthew 6:25, 27, 28, 31, 34) *merimnao* (Gk.)—"Be anxious" in contemporary translations.

Teacher Preparation

Unifying Principle—Putting Worry in Its Place. Jesus taught that depending on God to meet our needs can relieve our worries.

A. Begin your study by reviewing the entire Sermon on the Mount (Matthew 5–7).

B. Read the Keep in Mind verse to determine how it applies to you personally.

C. Prepare to give a testimony.

D. Complete the companion lesson in the *Precepts For Living Personal Study Guide®*.

O—Open the Lesson

A. Open with prayer.

B. Have the students read the Aim for Change in unison. Discuss.

C. Ask a volunteer to read the In Focus story. Discuss.

D. Share testimonies about worrying.

P—Present the Scriptures

A. Assign volunteers to summarize or read the Background and Focal Verses, alternating verse by verse, according to the At-A-Glance outline.

B. Lead the students in answering the Search the Scriptures questions.

C. Highlight salient points from the In Depth commentary.

E—Explore the Meaning

A. Discuss the Discuss the Meaning questions.

B. Now, summarize the Lesson in Our Society and Make It Happen sections.

N—Next Steps for Application

A. Summarize the entire lesson.

B. Remind students to study and meditate on the Daily Bible Readings.

C. Lead the class in closing prayer, thanking God for His tender care for each student present.

Worship Guide

For the Superintendent or Teacher
Theme: Facing Life without Worry
Song: "I'd Rather Have Jesus"
Devotional Reading: Psalm 37:1–8
Prayer

NOV
27th

Facing Life without Worry

Bible Background • MATTHEW 6:25–34
Printed Text • MATTHEW 6:25–34 | Devotional Reading • PSALM 37:1–8

—————————— Aim for Change ——————————

By the end of the lesson, we will: REVIEW Jesus' teaching about God as the great provider; REFLECT on what can and cannot relieve worry and stress; and DECIDE to express reliance on God to meet needs.

—————————— In Focus ——————————

At the conclusion of a sermon about worry, a pastor passed out blank envelopes and sheets of paper to his congregation. Each person in the church that morning was instructed to list all the things that were troubling him or her, no matter how big or small. They were then instructed to place the list in the envelopes and address the envelopes to themselves.

A month later, the pastor mailed the envelopes out to his congregation. With few exceptions, most of the congregation saw their month-old concerns in a whole new light. Though some troubles were ongoing in the lives of the people, the majority of the worries that seemed so enormous at the time the lists were penned had diminished drastically in urgency and intensity. Bills had gotten paid, arguments had been resolved, problems at work had changed, and health problems had been healed. This simple experiment taught the congregation a lesson about the nature of worries that none of them would soon forget.

Job worries, financial problems, health concerns, family issues—every one of these problems is out of our control to some degree. The only thing that is under our control is our response to these difficult issues. Today's lesson is about gaining God's eternal perspective on worry.

—————————— Keep in Mind ——————————

"But seek ye first the kingdom of God, and his righteousness; and all these things shall be added unto you. Take therefore no thought for the morrow: for the morrow shall take thought for the things of itself. Sufficient unto the day is the evil thereof" (Matthew 6:33–34).

"But seek ye first the kingdom of God, and his righteousness; and all these things shall be added unto you. Take therefore no thought for the morrow: for the morrow shall take thought for the things of itself. Sufficient unto the day is the evil thereof" (Matthew 6:33–34).

Focal Verses

KJV **Matthew 6:25** Therefore I say unto you, Take no thought for your life, what ye shall eat, or what ye shall drink; nor yet for your body, what ye shall put on. Is not the life more than meat, and the body than raiment?

26 Behold the fowls of the air: for they sow not, neither do they reap, nor gather into barns; yet your heavenly Father feedeth them. Are ye not much better than they?

27 Which of you by taking thought can add one cubit unto his stature?

28 And why take ye thought for raiment? Consider the lilies of the field, how they grow; they toil not, neither do they spin:

29 And yet I say unto you, That even Solomon in all his glory was not arrayed like one of these.

30 Wherefore, if God so clothe the grass of the field, which to day is, and to morrow is cast into the oven, shall he not much more clothe you, O ye of little faith?

31 Therefore take no thought, saying, What shall we eat? or, What shall we drink? or, Wherewithal shall we be clothed?

32 (For after all these things do the Gentiles seek:) for your heavenly Father knoweth that ye have need of all these things.

33 But seek ye first the kingdom of God, and his righteousness; and all these things shall be added unto you.

34 Take therefore no thought for the morrow: for the morrow shall take thought for the things of itself. Sufficient unto the day is the evil thereof.

NLT **Matthew 6:25** "So I tell you, don't worry about everyday life—whether you have enough food, drink, and clothes. Doesn't life consist of more than food and clothing?

26 Look at the birds. They don't need to plant or harvest or put food in barns because your heavenly Father feeds them. And you are far more valuable to him than they are.

27 Can all your worries add a single moment to your life? Of course not.

28 "And why worry about your clothes? Look at the lilies and how they grow. They don't work or make their clothing,

29 yet Solomon in all his glory was not dressed as beautifully as they are.

30 And if God cares so wonderfully for flowers that are here today and gone tomorrow, won't he more surely care for you? You have so little faith!

31 "So don't worry about having enough food or drink or clothing.

32 Why be like the pagans who are so deeply concerned about these things? Your heavenly Father already knows all your needs,

33 and he will give you all you need from day to day if you live for him and make the Kingdom of God your primary concern.

34 "So don't worry about tomorrow, for tomorrow will bring its own worries. Today's trouble is enough for today."

The People, Places, and Times

Grass. During biblical times, fuel was scarce. Withered plants of all kinds were used for fuel. The term in verse 30 (KJV) that is translated "grass" actually includes all sorts of vegetation not classified as trees, including the beautiful lilies mentioned in verses 28 and 29. Even the magnificent plants that displayed God's care in creation ended up as fuel to be used by the people that He valued and loved.

Solomon. He reigned from approximately 960–922 B.C. and was known as Israel's richest king. When he asked God for wisdom, God also granted him long life, fame, and great riches (1 Kings 3:6–14).

Background

Jesus always used illustrations in His sermon that His listeners could understand. For instance, those who heard this message knew of the wealth of Solomon and could probably visualize how beautifully he was clothed in the richest cloth with elaborate ornamentation. Jesus also used objects that were right in front of Him. As He sat upon the mountain, He may even have picked one of the wildflowers right beside Him as He spoke of the lilies of the field as "one of these" (Matthew 6:29) and gestured toward the birds that flew overhead (v. 26) as He told the people that they were much more important to God than these creatures. Therefore, to fully understand God's Word, we have to dig a little to discover the setting and ideas of the people of the time in which the Scripture was written. We can also look for contemporary illustrations to help listeners understand what God is saying today.

At-A-Glance

1. Examples of God's Care
(Matthew 6:25–31)

2. Anxiety's Antidote (vv. 32–34)

In Depth

1. Examples of God's Care (Matthew 6:25–31)

The promise of God's kingdom resides in our hearts if we are Christians (see 1 Peter 1:3–5). This hope is not like the wistful wishing that accomplishes nothing ("Oh, how I wish I could have a vacation"). It is a "favourable and confident expectation . . . a purifying power" (*Vine's Expository Dictionary*). The kingdom of God resides in us! Heaven is not just a future element; it also has a present-tense impact on our lives as believers.

In this section of today's text, Jesus gives us a simple instruction, followed by three examples that every hearer could easily understand. In Eugene Peterson's paraphrase of Scripture entitled *The Message*, he interprets Jesus' teaching in Matthew 6:25 thusly: "If you decide for God, living a life of God-worship, it follows that you don't fuss about what's on the table at mealtimes or whether the clothes in your closet are in fashion. There is far more to your life than the food you put in your stomach, more to your outer appearance than the clothes you hang on your body."

First, Jesus uses birds to support His argument. They don't plant seeds, harvest, or store crops, yet they are well cared for. It is important to note that the birds are not self-sufficient creatures. Their care comes from the Father. Jesus then simply, pointedly asks, "Are you not of more value than they?" (v. 26, NKJV).

Next, He asks a rhetorical question: "Which of you by taking thought can add one cubit unto his stature?" (v. 27). We can't make ourselves grow any taller, no matter how hard we wish to! Some commentators have interpreted this verse to mean a continuance of life (adding days to our lives) rather than an increase in height. Either way, our most intensive worrying will not add a centimeter to our height or a second to our lives. Those things are out of our control.

Jesus' third examples (vv. 28–30) were the common field lilies and the grass of the field. The common field lilies were simple prolific wildflowers. It is as though He pointed to the dandelions that pepper our landscapes and asked us to consider their growth. (Well, lilies are prettier!) These flowers did not work or weave their own garments, yet they were more beautifully adorned than the wealthiest king that Israel had ever known.

In verse 31, Jesus delivers the punch line: If God takes such good care of some of the simplest of His creation, then He can be trusted to take care of our needs. Food and clothing are some of our most basic necessities. He doesn't promise designer clothing or gourmet cuisine. He promises that He will care for us. We are of much greater value to Him than a flower or bird.

Anxiety robs us of our ability to trust God's care for us. Worry causes us to try to figure out a way to obtain for ourselves that which God has already promised to supply. Worry leaves us hopeless and fearful. Jesus diagnoses the problem for us in this section. The next section of today's study provides His cure for our worries.

2. Anxiety's Antidote (vv. 32–34)

"But seek ye first the kingdom of God, and his righteousness; and all these things shall be added unto you" (v. 33). Carl Henry wrote, "The sons of the Kingdom should therefore live in complete trust that God will supply the necessary provisions for the physical life; they are not to be pressed by anxiety and worry for these things. Ambition is to be directed toward the Kingdom of God and God's righteousness, rather than the acquisition of wealth" (*The Biblical Expositor,* 31).

Jesus gently reminded His hearers that the Father knew their needs (v. 32). Too many people spend their lives chasing after ways to get their needs (and, too often, their wants) met. By focusing on this, they have put the cart before the horse. However, our "ambition" for the things of God as Carl Henry described it, causes temporal things to take their proper position in our hearts. Jesus ends this passage by giving a practical application of how a God-seeking life should function. Trusting God with each day and leaving tomorrow in His hands further limits the possibility for anxiety to rule our lives.

Search the Scriptures

1. What three examples did Jesus give to illustrate the Father's care (Matthew 6:26–30)?

2. What is Jesus' instruction about "tomorrow" (v. 34)?

Discuss the Meaning

What does it mean, in practical terms, to seek God first (Matthew 6:33)?

Lesson in Our Society

We live in an extremely materialistic culture. It is so easy to get locked in to the lie that who you are equals the pile of stuff you can accumulate. Those who do not have the ability to contribute financially (the elderly, the ill, the disabled, and the unwanted unborn) are assigned a lesser value than those who have big earning power. God, on the other hand, values every person, and is not at all impressed by our material possessions.

By learning to seek His kingdom first, you declare to the world around you that you serve a radically different King. Desiring Him above all else will help to set everything else in proper, eternal perspective. It has the added bonus of subduing worry, which can also be a powerful statement to the world around you that your King is completely trustworthy.

Make It Happen

You might want to try the experiment described in the In Focus story, either as individuals or as a group. Make a list of everything that is worrying you today, date it, place it in an envelope, and do not open it for a month. While you are listing your concerns, pray about each one. When you open your envelope a month from now, you will have a fresh perspective (and answered prayer) about today's problems. You can trust God—you are of great value to Him!

Follow the Spirit

What God wants me to do:

_____

_____

_____

_____

Remember Your Thoughts

Special insights I have learned:

_____

_____

_____

_____

More Light on the Text

Matthew 6:25–34

25 Therefore I say unto you, Take no thought for your life, what ye shall eat, or what ye shall drink; nor yet for your body, what ye shall put on. Is not the life more than meat, and the body than raiment?

"Therefore" that begins this section serves as transition from the previous verses (vv.

22–24), which reemphasize the need for total focus and undivided loyalty to the Lord God. Therefore, setting our affection and desire on earthly possessions or occupying ourselves with amassing and hoarding earthly wealth will influence our affection, love, service, and loyalty toward God. It will mean making wealth our master rather than God, or having two masters, which Jesus says is impossible. For if we love money or riches, we cannot love God; and if we love God, then our love for riches will be eliminated.

What will cause someone to love money or have money as his or her "master"? Need! These include primarily the necessities of life—food, clothing, and sustenance. Lack of these necessities can lead one into worry and anxiety, or doing all sorts of things that might lead to evil. Aware of this, Jesus advises His audience against anxiety and worry. He does this by using two negative imperatives (vv. 25, 31) and develops His arguments by offering positive alternatives. Then He concludes with another negative imperative and positive advice (v. 34).

The phrase in verse 25, "I say unto you," underscores the importance of what Jesus has already said and what He is about to say, and the truthfulness and certainty of what He is talking about. The prohibition "Take no thought" translates a Greek verb *mee merimnao* (**may me-rim-NAH-o**), which can be rendered either "do not worry or fret" or "do not be anxious" for your life or about what to eat, drink, or wear. Jesus then follows this statement with a rhetorical question: "Is not the life more than meat, and the body than raiment?" Of course, the answer is yes—life is more than meat (food) and the body more than raiment (clothing). However, the importance and implication of these questions are not realized until verse 33. In support of His argument against an anxious approach to life, Jesus illustrates His point about food by urging His audience to think next about the birds and how they get their food.

26 Behold the fowls of the air: for they sow not, neither do they reap, nor gather into barns; yet your heavenly Father feedeth them. Are ye not much better than they? 27 Which of you by taking thought can add one cubit unto his stature?

The word "behold" in Greek *emblepo* (**em-BLEP-o**), which means "to gaze up or look upon," is used metaphorically here. It means "to look with the mind or to consider," or "to observe closely." What should we consider concerning fowl or birds of the air? When one considers how birds eat, one realizes that birds do not sow or cultivate their food, reap or harvest what they planted; nor do they worry about storing their food in barns. "Yet," says Jesus, "your heavenly father feeds them" (v. 26, NAS). Therefore, we should learn from how the Lord cares for the birds. He will in the same way, or even more than that, care for our needs. Stating His providential authority and care over His creation, the Lord rhetorically questions Job, "Wilt thou hunt the prey for the lion? or fill the appetite of the young lions, When they couch in their dens, and abide in the covert to lie in wait? Who provideth for the raven his food? when his young ones cry unto God, they wander for lack of meat" (Job 38:39–41).

Jesus strengthens this truth again with another rhetorical question: "Are ye not much better than they?" (Matthew 6:26). Of course, the answer is in the affirmative; since man is created in the image of God, humankind is worth more than birds. It is noteworthy to understand clearly that Jesus is neither encouraging laziness nor that the disciples do not need to work and expect "manna to fall from heaven," as the saying goes. Birds do not wait for their food to be

dropped into their beaks. The point here is that they go about their daily search for food without fretting. In His providential plan and care, God provides for birds daily. In the same way, we need to trust the Lord for our daily food (see the Lord's Prayer, Matthew 6:11).

As though the disciples did not get His point, Jesus poses another rhetorical question (v. 27) to drive home the truth about God's care for them. The point is that worrying is useless and profitless, since it cannot "add one cubit" to one's stature. "Cubit" is the Greek word *pechus* (**PAY-khoos**), a measure of length equal to the distance from the joint of the elbow to the tip of the middle finger (approximately 18 inches), but its precise length is uncertain. It is used figuratively here, and many interpreters believe that "cubit" refers to a short span of time. Hence, the NIV translates verse 27 as, "Who of you by worrying can add a single hour to his life?" Indeed, it has been medically proven that anxiety causes stress, which is detrimental to health and can cause stroke, heart failure, and even death. Instead of adding to life, worry shortens life.

28 And why take ye thought for raiment? Consider the lilies of the field, how they grow; they toil not, neither do they spin: 29 And yet I say unto you, That even Solomon in all his glory was not arrayed like one of these.

Christ's second argument against the futility of worries focuses on clothing. He questions the rationale of worrying about clothes—what we should wear—and then directs our attention to the lilies or flowers of the field. He uses the verb "consider" (Gk. *katamanthano*, **kat-am-an-THAN-o**), which literally means "to consider well, to examine" or "note carefully," and carries the same idea as "behold" (v. 26), though with a stronger emphasis in this verse. Here Jesus calls on the listeners to thoroughly consider the flowers of the field and "how they grow." They do nothing ("toil" or "spin") of themselves to grow. The lilies or flowers of the field refer to wild plants in general (Psalm 104:14–16) rather than flowers planted in the garden (see Matthew 6:30 where they are described as "grass of the field"). He then describes the beauty of these grasses by comparing them with the splendor of King Solomon's robes. Their magnificence surpasses that of Solomon (the most decorated king of all time) with no effort of their own. Who gives them their beauty? The answer is obvious—God.

30 Wherefore, if God so clothe the grass of the field, which to day is, and to morrow is cast into the oven, shall he not much more clothe you, O ye of little faith?

Then the argument follows, just as in verse 26 (from the lesser to the greater): if God could "clothe the grass of the field," which has no lasting value, but is destined to be burned for fuel, "shall he not much more clothe you, O ye of little faith?" Again, Jesus is not advocating laziness, although the thought here differs slightly from that of the birds. The birds work without fretting, the flowers do nothing—but become destined for the oven—and yet they are adorned with beauty that is unparalleled and greater than Solomon's. Jesus then rebukes the disciples by calling them *oligopistoi* (plural) from the noun singular *oligopistos* (**ol-ig-OP-is-tos**), which means people of little faith—a term Jesus uses often in the book of Matthew (see 8:26; 14:31; 16:8). *Oligopistos* could mean "lack of trust or trusting too little." Very little affects our faith and trust in the Lord more than anxiety and worry.

31 Therefore take no thought, saying, What shall we eat? or, What shall we drink? or, Wherewithal shall we be clothed? 32 (For after all these things do the Gentiles seek:) for your heavenly Father knoweth that ye have need of all these things.

Jesus reemphasizes the command "do not worry." He does this by using the word *oun* (**oon**), meaning "so" or "therefore." That is, in light of God's providential care, there is no need to fret about food, drink, or clothing. Jesus lists the common questions that go through the minds of those who worry. Such questions are useless and unprofitable because they do not serve any helpful purpose (Matthew 6:27). He continues by saying that worrying too much about all the earthly needs is the mark of the Gentile—"all these things do the Gentiles (pagans) seek" (v. 32). Gentiles here are those who have no relationship with the Lord—those who do not trust in the providential power of God to provide for His own people. It is also useless and indeed foolhardy to fret about food, drink, and clothes since the Lord is always aware of our circumstances and knows what our needs are, including the above-mentioned necessities. Christ's disciples should therefore lead lives that contrast those of the pagans who have no trust in God's fatherly care for them and whose fundamental goals are materialistic.

33 But seek ye first the kingdom of God, and his righteousness; and all these things shall be added unto you.

Rather than fretting and worrying about all our needs, and pursuing earthly materials and possessions as the Gentiles (pagans) do, we are to make the kingdom of God and God's righteousness our preeminent concern. The Lord who knows all our needs (vv. 8, 32) will also give us "all these things" (v. 33). To "seek" or in Greek *epizeteo* (**ep-eed-zay-TEH-o**) means "to desire, to strive for," or "seek after" or "to clamor for"—the same word is used in reference to the Gentiles seeking earthly things. Therefore, when we seek "first" the kingdom of God and His righteousness, we make God our utmost, continuous priority in service and worship. It means that we strive to live in a right relationship with God our Father and allow Him to govern our lives—in all activities of life and in all our relationships with other people. By seeking Him first, we give our absolute allegiance to God, submitting wholeheartedly to His will always. We have the assurance that if we will earnestly pursue His kingdom, hunger and thirst for His righteousness (Matthew 5:6), God will meet our needs because of who He is and because He cares for us (Philippians 4:6; 1 Peter 5:7). After all, He cares for the birds (Matthew 6:26) and the plants (vv. 28, 30), which are of lesser value.

34 Take therefore no thought for the morrow: for the morrow shall take thought for the things of itself. Sufficient unto the day is the evil thereof.

Jesus concludes this section with another negative imperative: "do not worry." In view of the assurance that God will meet the needs of those who commit themselves to His kingdom and righteousness, "take . . . no thought for the morrow" ("do not worry about tomorrow," NIV; "do not be anxious about tomorrow," ESV). The phrase "for the morrow shall take thought for the things of itself" is a way of saying, "Leave tomorrow's

problems for that day" or "allow nature to take its course," as people would say. Focus on today's issues; they are enough for today. Don't add tomorrow's "evil" (Gk. *kakia,* **kak-EE-ah**) or "trouble" to today's. God's grace for today is sufficient for today and should not be wasted on tomorrow's worries. God will provide new grace to meet whatever trouble tomorrow may bring.

Sources:

Baltes, A. J., ed. Biblespeech.com. http://biblespeech.com (accessed July 6, 2010).

Hebrew and Greek Lexicons. Bible Study Tools.com. http://www.biblestudytools.com/lexicons (accessed September 16, 2010).

Ladd, George Eldon. *The Biblical Expositor: The Living Theme of The Great Book.* Carl Henry, ed. Philadelphia, PA: A. J. Holman, 1960. 31.

Merriam-Webster Online Dictionary. Merriam-Webster, Inc. http://www.merriam-webster.com (accessed July 6, 2010).

Peterson, Eugene H. *The Message: The Bible in Contemporary Language.* Colorado Springs, CO: NavPress Publishing Group, 2002. 1755.

Vine, W. E., Merrill F. Unger and William White Jr. *Vine's Expository Dictionary.* Nashville, TN: Thomas Nelson Publishers, 1996. 562–63.

Say It Correctly

Pagans. PAY-gans.

Daily Bible Readings

MONDAY
Do Not Fret
(Psalm 37:1–8)

TUESDAY
The Consequences of Worry
(Matthew 13:18–23)

WEDNESDAY
Guard against Worry
(Luke 21:29–36)

THURSDAY
Do Not Be Afraid
(Matthew 10:24–31)

FRIDAY
The Spirit as Our Resource
(Matthew 10:16–20)

SATURDAY
Give Your Worries to God
(1 Peter 5:6–11)

SUNDAY
Don't Worry about Tomorrow
(Matthew 6:25–34)

Notes

God Establishes a Faithful People

The study this quarter focuses on God's covenant through Abraham. The theological emphasis is on faith. God promised Abraham that through him all the nations of the earth would be blessed. That promise was passed on from generation to generation until it was ultimately fulfilled in Christ. The lessons for this quarter are taken from Genesis, Exodus, Luke, and Galatians.

UNIT 1 • GOD'S COVENANT

"God's Covenant," tells the story of God's promise to Abraham. The first three lessons are studies in Genesis. These narratives from Genesis are appropriate for Advent because they point us to Christ's coming. The fourth lesson (the Christmas lesson) leaps forward from Genesis to Luke and Galatians where we hear on Mary's lips that she will give birth to Christ, the seed of Abraham's promise.

Lesson 1: December 4, 2011
A Blessing for All Nations
Genesis 12:1–9

The Lord instructs Abram to take his family to another country and promises to make him a great name and nation. Abram obeyed the Lord and went toward the Land of Canaan.

Lesson 2: December 11, 2011
A Promise to Abraham
Genesis 15:1–6, 12–18

Because he has no children, Abram questions God's promise. The Lord reassures him that his descendents will be too many to count. Abram also sees a terrifying vision of the journey his descendents will endure, including oppression for 400 years.

Lesson 3: December 18, 2011
The Lord Provides
Genesis 22:1–2, 6–14

Abraham is instructed to offer his only son, Isaac, to the Lord. He proceeds until an angel of the Lord tells him to stop. Abraham proves his faith by being obedient to God.

Lesson 4: December 25, 2011
According to the Promise
Luke 1:46–55

Mary expresses praise and gratitude toward God for what He was going to do for the world through her. In these verses, often referred to as "the Magnificat," Mary sees God as concerned for the poor, oppressed, and lowly.

UNIT 2 • GOD'S PROTECTION

Lessons 5–9 have five lessons. The first four are Joseph's story in Genesis 39–50. We see how God's promise to Abraham is passed on from generation to generation and carried with Abraham's descendants into Egypt. The final lesson of the unit considers the songs of Moses and Miriam in Exodus 15. God delivers Israel and leads them to safety in the desert. God's covenant faithfulness is proven again.

Lesson 5: January 1, 2012
God Watches over Joseph
Genesis 39:7–21a

Potiphar's wife aggressively petitions Joseph for sexual favors. Because of his loyalty to Potiphar and to God, he refuses; consequently, she accuses him of attempted rape and he is imprisoned. God stays with Joseph and he receives grace.

Lesson 6: January 8, 2012
Joseph Finds Favor
Genesis 41:37–45, 50–52

Joseph is appointed to the Pharoah's court and becomes responsible for Egypt's survival strategy for the next 14 years. God's favor rests on him as he is named the wisest man in the land and placed second in command.

Lesson 7: January 15, 2012
God Preserves a Remnant
Genesis 45:3–15

Joseph reveals his identity to his brothers and welcomes them. He tells them that God sent him to Egypt to preserve their family and keep His promise to Abraham. Joseph asks them to bring their father and the rest of the family to Egypt as soon as they can.

Lesson 8: January 22, 2012
Joseph Transmits Abraham's Promise
Genesis 50:15–26

Joseph forgives his brothers and discusses how God can use even evil plans for good. Before he dies, Joseph makes requests as to what should be done with his body when he dies. When he does die at 110, Joseph's family honors his request.

Lesson 9: January 29, 2012
Out of Egypt
Exodus 15:1–3, 19, 22–26

Moses leads the people through the Red Sea and desert. When they complain, Moses puts his faith in God for answers.

UNIT 3 • GOD'S REDEMPTION

"God's Redemption" has four lessons. These lessons from Paul's letter to the Galatians emphasize the New Testament interpretation of the Law, of justification by faith, and of Christ's disciples as heirs of Abraham's promise.

Lesson 10: February 5, 2012
Justified by Faith in Christ
Galatians 2:15–21

Paul teaches that faith in Christ, not obedience to laws, is the way to obtain righteousness. Christ's work is what saves. Therefore, believers should put faith in Christ.

Lesson 11: February 12, 2012
Freed from Law through Christ
Galatians 3:1–14

Paul explains to the Galatians that it is impossible to become perfect with human efforts alone. He reminds them that faith in the work of Christ is how to achieve righteousness.

Lesson 12: February 19, 2012
Heirs to the Promise
Galatians 3:15–18; 4:1–7

Paul explains how God's promise to Abraham was fulfilled in Jesus and how Christ's work benefits all believers.

Lesson 13: February 26, 2012
Fruits of Redemption
Galatians 5:22–6:10

Apostle Paul teaches the Galatians the fruit of the spirit and to relate to other Christians with humility and service.

Faith: Empowered by a Faithful God

by Rosa M. Sailes, Ed.D.

Faith? We all know what faith is. "Faith is the substance of things hoped for, the evidence of things not seen" (Hebrews 11:1). We can say it from memory—and unfortunately, we can say it without really thinking about what it means for our daily walk. We live in a society where people have "faith" in many things. There are people who have great faith that jumping from a bridge supported only by a bungee cord will be both safe and fun. Others believe that despite poor eating habits, no exercise, and a family history of illness, they will be healthy and live well for eternity—right here on earth. Our recent global economic disaster began with people who had such faith in currency that they selfishly focused on making money and living large with no regard to the injustice and poverty others would suffer. These are obvious examples of misguided faith, but how can we know when our faith is rightly placed?

Faith does not waiver. The person whose faith fluctuates with every situation is "double-minded" and "unstable" (James 1:8). We saw this in many of the voters who supported President Barack Obama in 2008. For many of these people, their vote for the first African American president of the nation was cast out of their mistaken thought that Obama was a rock star and the Messiah all in one. In less than two years, many lost sight of the economic realities of 2008. Despite the President's abatement of a worse disaster, voters soon had their faith diverted because of the national struggle with job loss and a failing housing market—a situation that existed before the elections. By the 2010 election, many of these same people had shifted their faith to people who had nothing to offer but egotistical ambition and flashy media sound bites. Our media-rich society, in fact, inundates us with programs and advertisements on TV, radio, the Internet, and various other outlets that suggest we put our faith in "something" they endorse. This begs the question of whether it really matters what that "something" is.

If faith is to be truly faithful, it must be anchored in a strong foundation. There is no stronger foundation than God. Beginning with His command to our first parents in the Garden and subsequently in His covenant with Abraham, God defined and demanded faithfulness. God's promise in Genesis 12:2 to make Abraham a great nation and to bless him, came *after* God's instructions in Genesis 12:1 that Abraham should leave his country and his family and travel to a place God would show him—eventually! God's promise didn't even adhere to Abraham's time frame. The promise of a son—the hope of the great name and the great nation—was put off until Abraham and Sarah were deemed too old for the promise to be possible. Still God was faithful!

Like Abraham, we must anchor our faith in the faithfulness of God. We must trust our God who framed the world simply by His word (Hebrews 11:3). We are required to believe our God who fashioned man with His own hand and placed His own breath in him (Genesis 2:7). We can never doubt that our God, who chose us in Him before the foundation of the world, has blessed us with all spiritual blessings, and predestined us and adopted us that we should be holy and without blame before Him (Ephesians 1:3–5). How can we do anything other than anchor our trust in Him?

It is no wonder then that we talk of our faith with others. The expression of our faith, however, must be more than lip service. The struggles of this world require that we express our faith by holding fast to our anchor in God. When our lives and circumstances cause us to doubt, we must still be able to trust God's promises. In the face of uncertainty, we must continue to believe God for the impossible. In the dawning of despair, we must resist the useless temptation to "create" for ourselves what God has promised. In other words, we must come to understand fully the source of our confidence.

Like Joseph, we must learn to trust God rather than place our hope in the promises of a fellow prisoner who swears to remember our plight and "put in a good word" for us. Joseph eventually realized that his only true hope was a faith anchored in God. It took time in the face of hardship for Joseph's faith to move from childish bragging to faithful trust. Through faith, Joseph became confident that God had gifted him and enabled him to do the great work God had ordained for his life. In the end, Joseph realized that what others meant for evil, God meant for good (Genesis 50:20). Likewise, our response to the faithfulness of God cannot allow self-righteousness or self-confidence to distort our faith. Through our adversities and our joys, our trials and our triumphs, the faithfulness of God hones our faith in Him. God's faithfulness, even in the midst of our crises, anchors our trust more deeply in Him.

Because of our trust, we are called to show our faith through our works or actions (James 2:18). How exactly can we do that today? Are we to be oblivious to our economic circumstances? Can we ignore the fear of violence that is prevalent in our cities? Must we smile regardless of the drama we face? Are we expected to keep moving without a tear in the midst of disaster? Are we to pretend? Are we to sail through life without letting anyone know that life can be harsh, even for those who trust God? Our answer lies in the example of Jesus Christ (1 Peter 2:21).

The writer of Hebrews explains that Jesus is the brightness of God's glory (see Hebrews 1:3). The Greek term for "brightness" means to shine forth, radiate, or reflect. God's splendor is His majesty and excellence. Jesus Christ is the shining forth, the living declaration of the fullness of these qualities of His Father. The Father has all majesty, dominion, and power; the Son is the vibrant demonstration of that glory. If we are to be faithful people, then we, too, are called to shine regardless of—and even in the midst of—our circumstances. Our faithfulness to God must be evident by our representation of God. Then those who see our faithfulness will be encouraged to seek the source of our trust.

Jesus Christ is the "express image" of His Father (Hebrews 1:3). The Greek term for "express image" is *charakter* (**khar-ak-TARE**). This reference is to a finely engraved image that is burned into a substance. God's faithfulness, in the midst of our trials, etches faith in our hearts. God's blessing and mercy in our day-to-day circumstances engraves faith into our inner being. It is through God's faithfulness that our character is developed. Character describes the internal identity of a person, the nature that makes that person who he or she is. Jesus' character is the expressed image of who He is—the Son of God, God incarnate, our Savior and Lord. Our character must be the expressed image of who we are: children of God, saved by grace through faith in Jesus Christ (Ephesians 2:5–6, 8). Our faith is the mark of our character. The fiber and essence of our being compels us to shine as the expressed image of God's love through Christ Jesus.

As the image of the Father, Jesus Christ has come into this world exercising the power of the throne of Grace. Jesus moves in the authority of His divine nature. He bestows upon those who call upon His name enough mercy to come before God's presence with singing and enough grace to enter God's courts with praise (Psalm 100:2, 4). When we walk life's journey in the presence of God's faithfulness, we understand that our hope is anchored in Him. When we focus our attention on Calvary's Cross, we are experiencing the evidence of what we cannot otherwise envision. When the Spirit of the Living God falls fresh upon us, we are empowered to faithfully expect what we cannot see.

It is the sacrifice of Calvary that makes us faithful people of God. Because of the Cross, our faith is grounded in Christ. By Jesus' sacrifice, we have become heirs to the Promise. It is as *faithful heirs* that we engage every relationship and every situation with a deepened sense of humility and trust. Through Jesus Christ, and by the indwelling of the Holy Spirit, we are empowered to bow before God's presence as His faithful people who represent His faithfulness to the world.

_____

Rosa Sailes, Ed.D., is the Director of Editorial at UMI.

God Establishes a Faithful People

by Rukeia Draw-Hood, Ph.D.

Do you remember the nursery rhyme "Father Abraham"? Most of us learned it in early childhood. It goes like this:

Father Abraham had many sons,
Many sons had Father Abraham.
I am one of them and so are you,
So let's all praise the Lord.
Right arm, left arm, right foot, left foot,
Chin up, turn around, sit down!

What fun came about from singing and moving to these lyrics! The enthusiasm over this simple song should continue in our later years, for it contains one of the most profound theological truths in all of Scripture for God's children of every age and era. Here's an opportunity to take an exciting journey as we explore our faith genealogy. We'll discover where we fit in this faith genealogy and what we've inherited.

Four people and three covenants are central to God's establishment of a faithful people. The lives of Abraham, Moses, Joseph, and Mary present diverse circumstances in varied time periods, but share significant commonalities. The events surrounding their calling are designed to try their faith and obedience and set them apart for special services intended by God (Henry, 83). Promise or covenant, faith, and obedience are recurring themes.

Lewis Drummond used *Baker's Dictionary of Theology* to define "covenant" as "a gracious undertaking entered into by God for the benefit and blessing of man, and specifically of those men who by faith receive the promise and commit themselves to the obligations which this undertaking involves" (Drummond, 70). The Abrahamic Covenant, whereby God chose the lineage of Abraham to demonstrate the truth of His Word, is the foundation for additional covenants in the Bible. The Mosaic Covenant marks the beginning of the nation of Israel and their entrance into the Promised Land. The New Covenant supercedes the Mosaic Covenant and is characterized by the internalization of the law, knowledge of God, and forgiveness of sin.

God's establishment of a faithful people began with God's promise to and covenant with Abraham. The Abrahamic Covenant includes the following promises (Genesis 12:2–7; 13:14–17; 15:18–21; 17:2–8):

- nationhood
- a great name
- protection
- blessing for all people
- innumerable offspring
- land

Sounds like a great deal! However, it required that Abraham move his family to a hostile, foreign land. Abraham began his journey to a "promised" land shortly thereafter. Abraham questioned God's promise as he aged and still had no children. God reassured him that his offspring would be as numerous as the stars in the sky and he believed God (Genesis 15:6). Later, Abraham had a child and God tested his faith in a seemingly contradictory request for him to sacrifice his beloved son, Isaac (22:1–2). Abraham was obedient, although not required to complete the act (22:6–14). His rewards followed and the promise was repeated to succeeding generations (26:2–5, 24; 28:10–15; 35:11–13; Hebrews 11:8–19).

In Genesis, we also learn of Joseph whose faithfulness saved the lineage of his forefathers—Jacob, Isaac, and Abraham (Genesis 37). Joseph was favored by his father, Jacob, more than his brothers. He had dreams he shared with his family. His family interpreted those dreams as Joseph indicating he would rule over them. His brothers were envious, and presumably fed up with what they must have perceived as his arrogance, so they plotted to kill him. They decided to sell him into slavery instead. Joseph landed in Egypt where he found favor with Potiphar, a high-ranking government official. He managed Potiphar's household until the official's wife falsely accused him of attempted rape. While Joseph was jailed for this offense, he correctly interpreted the dreams of two government employees. He later interpreted the king's dreams and was given a position as prime minister of Egypt. Joseph appropriately prepared the Egyptian government for an impending famine and was reconciled to his family after they traveled there seeking relief from it. Joseph saved their lives and the covenant continued to be passed down to succeeding generations (Genesis 39–48).

God remembered His covenant with Abraham and was concerned when the people of Is-rael cried out against their oppressors in Egypt (Exodus 2:24–25). Moses was chosen to bring the people of Israel out of slavery and start them on their journey to the Promised Land. As an aged and inarticulate fugitive who made a living as a shepherd, Moses was the obvious choice for the mission, right? Wrong! Moses had significant concerns about his credibility and personal inadequacies. Therefore, God sent Moses' brother, Aaron, along with him.

The Pharoah (king) let the Israelites go, but then changed his mind. When he and his army pursued them, God covered the Egyptians after the Israelites walked safely through the sea (Exodus 14:26–30). After this victory, Moses gave praise. An excerpt reads:

The LORD is my strength and my song;
he has become my salvation.
He is my God, and I will praise him,
my father's God, and I will exalt him
(Exodus 15:2, NIV).

Shortly thereafter, the people of Israel became dissatisfied and disgruntled. Three months after they left Egypt, the Mosaic covenant was initiated. Moses received the Law and the people agreed to abide by it (Exodus 24:3–8). Despite their best efforts, the Israelites continued to violate the law. The chosen people were not necessarily faithful people.

Their struggles proved beneficial in two ways. Their inability to uphold their side of the Mosaic covenant left room for a new and improved covenant to be desired. Their example was evidence to the world that it was necessary! Also, salvation came to non-Jews because of their sin. Therefore, their rejection brought reconciliation to the world (Romans 11:12–15). Drummond quotes Ward as saying, "The entire Bible is the account of God's call and preparation of a people, in order that through them the nations of the earth might be blessed. For this purpose God called the patriarchs and from their children called the nation of Israel into being." When the "fullness of time" had come, God sent his Son, born of a woman to redeem those under the law that they might receive the full rights of sons (Galatians 4:4–5) (*The Word of the Cross*, 71).

The Abrahamic Covenant and the continued failure of Israel to abide by the Mosaic Covenant made way for Jesus and His redemptive work in the world.

This brings us to Mary who gives birth to Jesus—the seed of Abraham (Galatians 3:16). As an unmarried virgin, Mary was confused when the angel delivered the message of her mission. The angel explained that God's power will come over her and the child will be called the holy Son of God (Luke 1:26–38). The Lord blessed her because she believed (v. 45).

The *Magnificat* of Mary is prominent among the proclamations identifying the birth of Jesus as significant (Baylis, 91). The song concludes: "He has helped his servant Israel, remembering to be merciful to Abraham and his descendants forever, even as he said to our fathers" (Luke 1:54–55, NIV).

The fame of this song parallels that of Moses' victory song in Exodus (Exodus 15:1–18). Mary carries the promise in her womb and gives birth to Jesus who is Mediator and High Priest of the New Covenant (Hebrews 7:22–28; 12:24).

According to Paul, Jesus bridges the old and new covenants. Paul affirms that God established a faithful people starting with His promises to Abraham. Then the apostle emphatically states that you and I are seeds of Abraham. Paul says:

"Consider Abraham: 'He believed God, and it was credited to him as righteousness.' Understand, then, that those who believe are children of Abraham. The Scripture foresaw that God would justify the Gentiles by faith, and announced the gospel in advance to Abraham: 'All nations will be blessed through you.' So those who have faith are blessed along with Abraham, the man of faith" (Galatians 3:6–9, NIV).

No one can add or take away from a human covenant and the one between Abraham and God is no different. The promises were spoken to Abraham and his seed (singular), who is Christ. Because of what Jesus did on the Cross with the shedding of blood for the forgiveness of sin, He is the New Covenant (Matthew 26:28; Luke 22:20). You receive the promise through faith in Jesus Christ. If you belong to Christ, then you are Abraham's seed and heirs according to the promise (Galatians 3:15–25).

It is here we discover where we fit into this story of faith. The blessing promised to Abraham was taken to the Gentiles. This happened so that by faith we would be given the promised Holy Spirit to transform our hearts and thereby truly live a life of obedience to God (Ezekiel 11:18–21; Galatians 3:14). The Spirit produces character traits of love, joy, peace, patience, kindness, goodness, faithfulness, gentleness, and self-control in the believer (Galatians 5:22–23). When these traits are developed in us, the intended purpose of the Mosaic Law is fulfilled, which is that we love God and the rest of humanity (Matthew 22:35–40; Galatians 5:13–14).

Sources:

Baylis, Albert H. *From Creation to the Cross.* Grand Rapids, MI: Zondervan, 1996. 91.

"Covenant." *Baker's Dictionary of Theology.* Grand Rapids, MI: Baker Book House, 1960. 142.

Drummond, Lewis A. *The Word of the Cross.* Nashville, TN: Broadman Press, 1992. 70, 71.

Henry, Matthew. *A Commentary on the Whole Bible. Volume 1—Genesis to Deuteronomy.* Old Tappan, NJ: Revell, 1721. 83.

Somerville, Robert. *The Seed of Abraham.* Awareness Ministry.org http://www.awarenessministry.org/seedabrahamchristiansjews.htm (accessed August 29, 2010).

Rukeia Draw-Hood, Ph.D., *received a Master of Arts in Christian Education from Oral Roberts University and a Doctor of Philosophy in Educational Studies from Trinity International University.*

Effective Christianity: Avoiding Shortcuts to Maturity

by Lisa Crayton

Shortcuts work—sometimes. Often, however, the shortest path to accomplishing a goal results in a dream deferred. Countless scholastic objectives, home improvement projects, and weight loss/exercise programs are abandoned each day simply because goal seekers take shortcuts that promise quick-and-easy paths to success. The result? Broken focus and shipwrecked ambitions.

Similarly, spiritual shortcuts that appear to be fast tracks to growth and maturity are usually detours to destruction. While not always easy to detect, these can by identified by their overemphasis of works, self-confidence, personal gain, and/or abilities. These sharply contrast, respectively, with the Bible's teachings about grace, faith, service (to God and mankind), and spiritual gifts. Jesus warned of spiritual shortcuts when he advised, "Enter ye in at the strait gate: for wide is the gate, and broad is the way, that leadeth to destruction, and many there be which go in thereat: Because strait is the gate, and narrow is the way, which leadeth unto life, and few there be that find it" (Matthew 7:13–14). Effective Christians will seek that narrow way, embracing a foolproof covenant with God that overflows to self and others.

An Enduring Covenant

A covenant is a fully enforceable, binding agreement. Like a legal contract, it affords privileges and responsibilities to each party. Knowing contract provisions makes it easier to adhere to them and avoid forfeiture of contractual promises. Ignorance, on the other hand, hinders a party's ability to fulfill contractual obligations, and may result in forfeiture. Whether you're the policyholder or beneficiary, it is necessary for you to understand and adhere to the contracts to which you are a party.

Covenant with God. When it comes to covenant with God, effective Christians can easily understand their rights and responsibilities by turning to a trusted source: the Bible. From it we understand that recognizing one's sin nature is a necessary first step to making peace with God (Romans 5:1). Accepting, by faith, the atoning sacrifice of Jesus is a second. "For by grace are ye saved through faith; and that not of yourselves: it is the gift of God: Not of works, lest any man should boast" (Ephesians 2:8–9). "And [Jesus] is the propitiation for our sins: and not for ours only, but also for the sins of the whole world" (1 John 2:2). Conforming to biblical definitions of godly behavior is a third. "For the grace of God that bringeth salvation hath appeared to all men, Teaching us that, denying ungodliness and worldly lusts, we should live soberly, righteously, and godly, in this present world" (Titus 2:11-12).

It would be impossible to live such a life if not for the example of Jesus Christ. He modeled godly behavior while on earth, and then sent the Holy Spirit to give us the power to do the same. Nonetheless, if a spiritual shortcut exists, it will likely manifest during that third step. And it will be subtly encouraged by friends, family, coworkers, and others who resent the effective Christian's Christlike behavior.

Like the serpent that wooed Eve, those seemingly caring individuals will question, "Did God really say that?" Translated in modern vernacular—"Who says you can't do this or that? Why can't you go (to such a place)? Why must you tithe, attend church regularly, serve others, etc.?" But the biggest temptation usually comes in the form of, "You used to be more fun (caring, sharing, forgiving, etc.) before you were a Christian." That's the one that usually hurts the most, as it questions whether we're self-righteous or spiritual. And, it often compels otherwise effective Christians to water down the Word of God in their lives to become more acceptable to others.

Covenant with self. The cure for that ailment is to acknowledge that our covenant with God spurs self-improvement. No matter how good we think we are before coming to Christ, we're reminded that, "All have sinned, and come short of the glory of God; Being justified freely by his grace through the redemption that is in Christ Jesus" (Romans 3:23–24). But, warns the apostle James, "Be ye doers of the word, and not hearers only, deceiving your own selves" (James 1:22).

Heeding James's admonition, effective Christians actively seek to know the written and Living Word (Jesus). Thus, prayer, Bible reading and study, and regular church attendance become vehicles through which knowledge is gleaned, retained, and acted upon.

Spiritual health is only one aspect of our self-covenant. The other is physical health. As living "temple[s] of God" (1 Corinthians 3:16), effective Christians take care of their bodies by fueling them with proper nutrition, rest, and—yes—exercise. Proper medical care also becomes essential, especially regular annual examinations as one ages.

Covenant with others. Serving others is also an integral right and responsibility of our covenant with God. Leading others to follow Christ, or grow up in Him, also is a great privilege. From sharing the Gospel, to treating our enemies with kindness, to helping those less fortunate, we become instruments of grace, peace, and hope as we reach out to others. More so, embracing a global perspective of the term *neighbor* opens doors for us to be more effective as we adapt to changing societal needs in times of peace and war.

Long-Term Effectiveness

Spiritual effectiveness is a worthy goal, but it won't happen overnight. That's why shortcuts won't work. They'll compel you to focus on short-term achievement garnered by either physical, mental, or emotional power. Admonishing the Galatians' reliance on a similar shortcut, the apostle Paul queried, "Are ye so foolish? having begun in the Spirit, are ye now made perfect by the flesh?" (Galatians 3:3).

Lisa Crayton is an award-winning, internationally published freelance writer and the editor of Spirit-Led Writer, *an online magazine for Christian writers. Lisa is also an ordained, licensed minister.*

Rich Cain
1825–1887

Richard Cain was a Christian who lived out his beliefs, especially in the areas concerning social justice for African Americans. He was born in Virginia to a Cherokee mother and an African American father. When Richard was 6 years old, he and his family moved to Ohio. Because he lived in a "free state," he was able to get an education, which was primarily through the Sunday School.

He was always interested in the ministry, but he had a variety of job experiences. He worked on the steamboats that chugged up and down the Ohio River as one of his first jobs. By 1844, he had entered the Methodist ministry as a pastor. Four years later, he left that denomination because of its segregated worship practices, joined the African Methodist Episcopal church, and served as a deacon and then a pastor in Muscatine, Iowa. He desired an education to better prepare himself for the ministry, so he attended Wilberforce University, the first American college founded by African Americans.

When Pastor Cain was assigned to a church in Brooklyn, New York, he soon became actively involved in supporting the vote for all men. After the Civil War, Pastor Cain was assigned to a church in Charleston, South Carolina, which had been closed due to a slave revolt in 1822. But under his leadership, the congregation grew to be the largest in the state by 1871.

Pastor Cain was both a great speaker and a great writer. In order to spread his strong views, particularly in regard to granting land to the newly freed slaves, he began writing and publishing a newspaper, *The South Carolina Leader,* in 1866. Between his church and his newspaper, he was building a strong political group. First, he served on the South Carolina group that fashioned a new state constitution. Then he went on to be elected as a state senator.

When land for former slaves still was not made available, he purchased land to sell. Unfortunately, that project eventually went bankrupt. After this unsuccessful attempt, he ran for a seat in the United States Congress and won it. His biggest effort was geared toward the passage of the Civil Rights Bill. As a member of Congress, he was able to make several very stirring speeches on its behalf. He went on to found Paul Quinn College in Waco, Texas, and served as its president until 1884. He returned to Washington, D.C., and served as the bishop of the AME conference until he died in 1887.

Source:
Black Americans in Congress––Richard Harvey Cain, Representative from South Carolina. http://baic.house.gov/member-profile.html?intID=2 (accessed September 4, 2010).

Teaching Tips

December 4
Bible Study Guide 1

Words You Should Know

A. Blessing (Genesis 12:2) *berakah* (Heb.)—Prosperity, benediction, benefit, favor, peace, invocation of good.

B. Seed (Genesis 12:7) *zara`* (Heb.)—Offspring, issue, progeny, posterity, family, race.

Teacher Preparation

Unifying Principle—Sharing Good Fortune. Because of their faith in God's promises, Abram and Sarai in their old age risked everything to move their family and all their possessions to a new land.

A. Read and study the entire lesson.

B. Reread the Focal Verses in different translations.

C. Pray for your students and for lesson clarity.

D. Complete the companion lesson in the *Precepts For Living Personal Study Guide*®.

O—Open the Lesson

A. Ask if any students are struggling with difficult life decisions, then include these in the opening prayer.

B. Have students read the Lesson Aim. Explain.

C. Summarize the In Focus story. Discuss.

P—Present the Scriptures

A. Read and explain the Focal Verses using The People, Places, and Times; Background; the At-A-Glance outline; In Depth; Search the Scriptures; and More Light on the Text.

B. Discuss the significance of Abram being called out from his family.

C. Ask students to give examples on how we conduct our lives based on promises made (e.g., promissory note, marriage covenant, and credit card agreement).

E—Explore the Meaning

A. Reexamine how Abram walked in obedience.

B. Review the Lesson in Our Society and Make It Happen sections and then reflect.

N—Next Steps for Application

A. Summarize the lesson.

B. Close with prayer.

Worship Guide

For the Superintendent or Teacher
Theme: A Blessing for All Nations
Theme Song: "The Blessing of Abraham"
Devotional Reading: Hebrews 6:13–20
Prayer

A Blessing for All Nations

Bible Background • GENESIS12:1–9
Printed Text • GENESIS 12:1–9 | Devotional Reading • HEBREWS 6:13–20

—————— Aim for Change ——————

By the end of the lesson, we will: LEARN the story of God's call and promise to Abram; REFLECT on the joy that Abram and Sarai's faith gave to them from obeying the Lord; and DECIDE what we are willing to sacrifice to claim the promises of God.

——————  In Focus ——————

Desmond and his wife, Mary, have been married for 25 years and live a very comfortable life. Desmond is a respected corporate and community leader, and Mary is a district manager for a major retail chain. Both are active and faithful members of their church and within their circle of friends. Lately, they both had been thinking about doing more for God, even in distant lands. One day during Desmond's morning devotion, he felt in his spirit that it was time to leave. When he felt it again as he was shaving, he immediately stopped what he was doing and inquired of the Lord. He knew in his spirit that it was time to move on to a new workplace assignment, which might include moving to another country to make a greater impact for God on the world. At work that morning, he learned that the company was in fact reorganizing. They were expanding operations to compete globally, and he was tapped to run overseas operations.

As we will see with Desmond and Mary, and Abram and Sarai in today's lesson, a decision to follow God's command continues to reap a reward for those who by faith in Jesus Christ become His seed.

—————— Keep in Mind ——————

"And I will make of thee a great nation, and I will bless thee, and make thy name great; and thou shalt be a blessing" (Genesis 12:2).

"And I will make of thee a great nation,
and I will bless thee, and make thy name great;
and thou shalt be a blessing" (Genesis 12:2).

Focal Verses

KJV **Genesis 12:1** Now the LORD had said unto Abram, Get thee out of thy country, and from thy kindred, and from thy father's house, unto a land that I will shew thee:

2 And I will make of thee a great nation, and I will bless thee, and make thy name great; and thou shalt be a blessing:

3 And I will bless them that bless thee, and curse him that curseth thee: and in thee shall all families of the earth be blessed.

4 So Abram departed, as the LORD had spoken unto him: and Lot went with him: and Abram was seventy and five years old when he departed out of Haran.

5 And Abram took Sarai his wife, and Lot his brother's son, and all their substance that they had gathered, and the souls that they had gotten in Haran; and they went forth to go into the land of Canaan; and into the land of Canaan they came.

6 And Abram passed through the land unto the place of Sichem, unto the plain of Moreh. And the Canaanite was then in the land.

7 And the LORD appeared unto Abram, and said, Unto thy seed will I give this land: and there builded he an altar unto the LORD, who appeared unto him.

8 And he removed from thence unto a mountain on the east of Bethel, and pitched his tent, having Bethel on the west, and Hai on the east: and there he builded an altar unto the LORD, and called upon the name of the LORD.

9 And Abram journeyed, going on still toward the south.

NLT **Genesis 12:1** Then the LORD told Abram, "Leave your country, your relatives, and your father's house, and go to the land that I will show you.

2 I will cause you to become the father of a great nation. I will bless you and make you famous, and I will make you a blessing to others.

3 I will bless those who bless you and curse those who curse you. All the families of the earth will be blessed through you."

4 So Abram departed as the LORD had instructed him, and Lot went with him. Abram was seventy-five years old when he left Haran.

5 He took his wife, Sarai, his nephew Lot, and all his wealth—his livestock and all the people who had joined his household at Haran—and finally arrived in Canaan.

6 Traveling through Canaan, they came to a place near Shechem and set up camp beside the oak at Moreh. At that time, the area was inhabited by Canaanites.

7 Then the LORD appeared to Abram and said, "I am going to give this land to your offspring." And Abram built an altar there to commemorate the LORD's visit.

8 After that, Abram traveled southward and set up camp in the hill country between Bethel on the west and Ai on the east. There he built an altar and worshiped the LORD.

9 Then Abram traveled south by stages toward the Negev.

The People, Places, and Times

Abram. The significance of God's call for a nation through Abram was that up to this point there was no distinction between people and races in the manner that we think of today. After the Flood, the people were dispersed at the Tower of Babel (Genesis 11:1–9). The Bible depicts a detailed review of Shem's descendants—Noah's eldest son. It is out of Shem's lineage, through Abram, that God would call out a people unto Himself to be witnesses in the earth of His greatness. They would receive the blessing for serving the one true and living God in the midst of universal idolatry. Ultimately, Abram's seed through 42 generations would bring forth the Messiah who would reconcile the world back to the Father (Matthew 1:1–17). Abram exemplifies the faith necessary to obtain righteousness and access to the promises of God through Jesus Christ.

The Land of Canaan. The Hebrew word for "Canaan" (*Kena`an*, **ken-AH-an**) means low region or lowland. Its name denotes that the country resides west of the Jordan and the Dead Sea, between those waters on the eastern shore of the Mediterranean Sea. Named after Noah's fourth son Ham, the land was given by God to Abram's posterity, the Children of Israel, as promised. In modern geography, Canaan is now Palestine.

Background

In the preceding chapter (Genesis 11:10–32), we learn of Abram's lineage as a descendant of Noah's son Shem. In Genesis 9:26, Noah prophesied over Shem, after he and his brother Japheth covered his nakedness, declaring that he would be blessed and that Canaan would be his servant. Genesis 11 ends with Abram's father, Terah, leading his family's migration from his native land Ur of the Chaldees to make their way to the land of Canaan, but instead the group settles in Haran (Genesis 11:31). It is noted in verse 32, however, that Terah remained in Haran until his death. Geographically, scholars maintain that Haran was perched between Ur and Canaan, so they were in the middle of their intended destination. Terah's name was believed to mean "delay," and as referenced in a review of Israel's history (Joshua 24:2), he was an idol worshiper. We will see why Abram and Sarai's faith and obedience were pivotal to the blessing for all nations as God separates him from his people.

At-A-Glance

1. God's Call for a Blessed Nation (Genesis 12:1–3)

2. Abram's Response to God's Call (vv. 4–6)

3. God's Promise of Generational Blessings (v. 7)

4. Abram's Obedience in Answering God's Call (vv. 8–9)

In Depth

1. God's Call for a Blessed Nation (Genesis 12:1–3)

Abram was the youngest son of Terah. He was a descendant of Noah's son Shem. According to Stephen's account in Acts 7:2–4, the God of glory appeared to Abram while he was in Mesopotamia, which was before he settled in Haran. Therefore, when Abram heard God's call in Genesis 12:1, this was his second encounter with the Lord Jehovah, and it's believed to be not long after his father's death. Abram was told to leave his country and his family, and uproot his home to go to a place the Lord would soon reveal. The Scripture does not indicate that there was a discussion after this command was given, but that Abram moved at God's word. Abram was surrounded by people, including his own family, who were polytheistic (worshiped multiple gods). For him to hear the voice of the true and living God was monumental. Because of his obedience, Abram is forever etched as "the father of faith." With this second encounter, however, God made Abram a promise to bless him and make him a great nation, to make his name great and for him to be a blessing (v. 2). This promise from God was astounding due to Abram's age (v. 4), and as first noted in Genesis 11:30, his wife Sarai was barren. God gave Abram further motivation to adhere to His command with the pronouncement of future blessings. For leaving his father's house, Abram would receive a father's blessing—a namesake. God told Abram His sovereign promise to fulfill His word to make a great nation from him and to make his name great. Abram went from not having any children and with no hope of ever being a father to having the promise of an entire nation coming from his loins.

In Genesis 12:3, God established His relationship and the power of this connection by stating that He would bless those who blessed Abram and curse those who cursed him. God's presence is marked in the lives of those chosen by Him. Verse 3 ends with the most important component of this promise: God commits to blessing all the families of the earth through Abram. Abram's seed birthed three world religions; Judaism, Christianity, and Islam (Ishmael) all lay claim to him as father. However, the ending of this verse points to the coming Christ who would bring salvation and restoration to the world. Abram's seed is the divinely appointed channel through which blessing would come to all humankind by faith in Jesus Christ (Galatians 3:6–7, 14).

2. Abram's Response to God's Call (vv. 4–6)

Abram followed God's spoken command and departed from his familiar surroundings to a place unknown. Abram, after having departed once with his kindred from his native land of Ur, was once again a nomad at the age of 75, leaving Haran. He took with him his wife, all their possessions, his nephew Lot, and his servants. We can imagine how very unsettling it must have been for Abram to be uprooted again and to move everything he owned to answer God's call. However, in spite of the circumstances, Abram walked in obedience and trusted God based on what God had revealed to him. He went forward and began the journey. His father, Terah, stopped short his migration to Canaan (see Genesis 11:31, NIV). When God declares a call on your life, not everyone is privy to see the revelation of God's plan. Therefore, even close relatives may need to be left behind.

In Genesis 12:6, Abram arrives in Canaan and the land is already occupied by the Canaanites. He is yet again a stranger in a strange land. He was put in an uncomfortable position by coming into a land that was promised to him, but was already inhabited, which could have been a reason to give up. But Abram continued to follow God and remain confident that he heard God correctly. Oftentimes, when God gives us a directive, it may not come with full disclosure of the details—like what we have to go through to get to the promise. Just like Jesus, Abram teaches us to keep moving forward by focusing on God's promise (Hebrews 12:2).

3. God's Promise of Generational Blessings (v. 7)

In this instance, rather than just speaking to Abram, God appeared in the form of a theophany—God appeared in human form. Some scholars believe this appearance was Christ in His pre-incarnate state. He showed Abram once again the land He was going to bless Abram with and reinstated His promise to give him seed or offspring. Abram yet again heard a word from the Lord declaring that he would not only receive this land that is already occupied, but that his children would live in it. In response to God's appearance, Abram built an altar unto the Lord. The proper response to God's presence and confirmation of His promise is worship. Abram had God's continued assurance that he would receive that which God had spoken, and by making a personal appearance, it further sealed the guarantee.

4. Abram's Obedience in Answering God's Call (vv. 8–9)

Abram continued to move forward at God's command and thus declared his own allegiance to serve God alone. In spite of the culture around him, which had a god for everything, Abram is the father of a monotheistic religion that is based on a relationship with the true and living God. Abram pitched his tent, and wherever he pitched his tent, he built an altar unto the Lord. He remained in constant contact with Him through worship and prayer as he called on the name of the Lord. Abram lived a disciplined life of worship and walked in obedience by listening for the voice of the Lord God. Abram's faithful response to God's promise to make him a great nation required a close relationship and strict adherence God's instructions. Abram would have been shortsighted if he only thought of the personal impact of this promise, but because the call was greater than he could ever imagine, he was willing to make the sacrifice with his wife by his side.

Search the Scriptures

1. What was God's instruction to Abram (Genesis 12:1)?

2. What was God's promise to Abram (vv. 2–3)?

3. What was Abram's response to God's call (vv. 4–5)?

Discuss the Meaning

How would you respond if God told you to uproot your life and leave behind all you know to follow Him with only a promise of what's to come?

Lesson in Our Society

Today, we are reaping the benefits of the blood, sweat, and tears of our heroes and heroines of the Civil Rights Movement, as well as the ancestors before them who sacrificed so that we might have freedom to be whatever God called us to be. Like Abram, Dr. Martin Luther King did not live to see the fullness of this vision of freedom, but he moved at God's Word and did as he was instructed, walking in love. He trusted God and sacrificed his own personal comfort and gain by believing that God would do what He said. We can continue to honor Dr. King's legacy by showing our willingness to submit to God's plan no matter where it takes us as we serve others and strive to move toward lives of freedom.

Make It Happen

As you reflect on today's lesson, what has God promised in your life that will bless you and others now as well as in generations to come? What are you willing to risk to follow through with God's plan and bring Him glory, even at the risk of your own comfort? Pray and assess your own ambitions, goals, and interests to see if they line up with God's Word. Allow the Holy Spirit to speak to you about anything that needs adjustment.

Follow the Spirit

What God wants me to do:

_____

_____

_____

_____

Remember Your Thoughts

Special insights I have learned:

_____

_____

_____

_____

_____

More Light on the Text

Genesis 12:1–9

1 Now the LORD had said unto Abram, Get thee out of thy country, and from thy kindred, and from thy father's house, unto a land that I will shew thee:

No one enjoys being uprooted, especially when one has been settled in a place for an extended period of time and enjoys a comfortable living. Abram and his family had lived in Ur of Chaldees with his father and brothers. During Abram's time, Ur of Chaldees was a port city that offered wealth and prosperity to its inhabitants, but for some unexplained reason, Terah, Abram's father, moved himself and his extended

family to Haran. It was in Haran that God spoke to Abram. God first called to Abram while he was living in Ur of Chaldees (see Genesis 15:7 and Acts 7:2). Here, God issues an imperative command to *yalak* (**yaw-LAK**), the Hebrew word for "depart, get out." With this command, God indicated three specific areas Abram was to abandon: (1) Abram was to leave the country he had come to call home; (2) he was to leave the safety and security of his extended family; and (3) Abram was to leave his father's home. This was no small command on God's part. Family provided a hedge against misfortune and mishap, but God was asking Abram to trust Him completely to provide for his safety and security. Abram was to venture, by faith, into the desert and to an unnamed location.

2 And I will make of thee a great nation, and I will bless thee, and make thy name great; and thou shalt be a blessing: 3 And I will bless them that bless thee, and curse him that curseth thee: and in thee shall all families of the earth be blessed.

It is hard to overstate the importance of God's call to Abram (and Abram's final obedient response) for the rest of the Gospel story. With the focus on Abram, God enters human history in a new way and begins to work out His own plan for the redemption of humankind. God follows His command to Abram with a series of promised blessings. Note the three times that God obligates Himself to Abram with the phrase "I will (do)," which is *'asah* in the Hebrew (**aw-SAW**). God promises to: (1) give Abram a child from which a nation will come; (2) make Abram's name renowned; (3) bless Abram personally; (4) bless Abram to be a blessing to others; (5) bless nations that bless Abram; (6) curse nations that choose not to be a blessing to Abram; and finally, (7) provide a means for all the nations of

174

the earth to be blessed through Abram. These blessings, taken collectively, become a reversal of the curses pronounced by God at the Tower of Babel (Genesis 11:1–9). At Babel, men came together to build a city so that they could *shem* (**Heb. "shame"**) or "make a name" for themselves. Through Abram, however, God established His own means by which someone would achieve renown and "become a nation," which translates in the Hebrew as *gowy* (**GOO-wee**). What a person tried to accomplish through his or her own efforts, God would do through Abram as a divine gift. However, these promises of blessing were conditional. Abram must trust God with faith, believing that God will do as He has promised. The obedience would see Abram become *barakah* (**ber-aw-KAW**), Hebrew for "the source of blessing" for all humankind. God also wanted Abram to understand that He would be with him, and the nation that would flow from him in a very special way. God will bless those who bless Abram, but God will also "curse," in Hebrew *'arar* (**aw-RAR**), those who chose not to be a blessing to Abram or the nation that was to have its origin in him. History has borne out the reality that God's promise to Abram was not made lightly. At the Red Sea, God destroyed the armies of Egypt because of the way Egypt had treated the Jews. Those nations that flowed from Ham, but found themselves at odds with Israel, were either destroyed or reduced to a minor state by God. These nations included the Canaanites, the Hittites, and Amorites, to name a few.

4 So Abram departed, as the LORD had spoken unto him: and Lot went with him: and Abram was seventy and five years old when he departed out of Haran.

So Abram departed. Until this point, no indication is given that Abram has done anything at all to commend himself to God.

But now he acted. In obedience to God's "spoken" word, which in Hebrew is *dabar* (**daw-BAW**), and implies a command, Abram left Haran.

The writer of Hebrews (11:8ff) informs us that it was on the basis of Abram's belief in God's word that he acted and this belief expressed by action was accounted to Abram for faith. We can appreciate the faith that Abram demonstrated. At 75 years of age, he was relatively old. Additionally, Sarai (his wife) was barren and was incapable of producing a son for Abram. Still, Abram trusted God that he would be blessed personally with prosperity, land, and an heir. Further, Abram trusted God that through him the whole world would also be blessed.

5 And Abram took Sarai his wife, and Lot his brother's son, and all their substance that they had gathered, and the souls that they had gotten in Haran; and they went forth to go into the land of Canaan; and into the land of Canaan they came. 6 And Abram passed through the land unto the place of Sichem, unto the plain of Moreh. And the Canaanite was then in the land.

Lot's father, Haran, was dead. He died while the family resided in Ur of Chaldees. It is likely that Abram took his nephew into his own home after his brother's death because he and his wife were childless. In the ancient culture of that day, families that were childless were considered to be out of favor with the gods. Sarai's barrenness then was, no doubt, a source of shame and embarrassment for Abram. Still, in responding to God's command, Abram takes Sarai and Lot with him. In addition to his nephew and wife, verse 5 records that Abram also took his servants, "substance" or "possessions" (NIV), translated in Hebrew as *rekuwsh* (**rek-OOSH**) and implied material goods as well as animals. They set off for

175

Canaan. When God first called for Abram's father, Terah, to leave Ur of Chaldees and venture to an unnamed land, the patriarch only made it as far as Haran. This time Abram entered Canaan and traveled to Sichem and the plain of "Moreh" (Heb. *Mowreh*, **mo-REH,** meaning "teacher"). Moreh was home to a great oak tree used as a place of worship by the pagan priests of Canaan. It was located near the heart of the land of Canaan and was probably a place where the Canaanite priests came to instruct their people in the worship of their gods. By venturing so deeply into Canaan, Abram was signaling his intent to remain obedient to God's instruction. He would not be returning to the life of comfort and security that he had once known.

7 And the LORD appeared unto Abram, and said, Unto thy seed will I give this land: and there builded he an altar unto the LORD, who appeared unto him.

It took a lot of faith on Abram's part to pack up his family and possessions and cross into the land of Canaan on the basis of a promise from God. To this point, God had not revealed to Abram what land He was going to give the patriarch as a possession for his obedience. Abram had been proceeding purely by faith. However, his faith was rewarded at Moreh when God took on human form and "appeared" (Heb. *ra'ah*, **raw-AW**) to Abram. This type of personal visitation by God is called a "theophany." The purpose of this theophany was for God to confirm the promise He had made earlier to the future patriarch. Abram was to be given land for a possession, and in fact, the land on which he was standing was to be that land. However, God now makes clear that the land will go to Abram's descendants, even though Abram is childless at the time of God's promise. In a repeated expression of his faith

and as an act of worship, after the visitation, Abram erected an "altar" (Heb. *mizbeach*, **miz-BAY-akh**), to the true God upon that site. The altar demonstrated that Abram believed God, even though he did not know at this point in the Scripture it would be 500 years before his family would be in possession of the land.

8 And he removed from thence unto a mountain on the east of Bethel, and pitched his tent, having Bethel on the west, and Hai on the east: and there he builded an altar unto the LORD, and called upon the name of the LORD.

Probably in an act of great wisdom, Abram left Moreh. The altar he had "builded" or "established" (Heb. *banah*, **baw-NAW**) would serve as an indication that Abram was staking a claim to the land on behalf of his God. Now he would need a place within Canaan to call home. After leaving Moreh, Abram journeyed deeper into the southern portion of the land of Canaan and temporarily settled upon a mountain, built another altar, and worshiped his God.

9 And Abram journeyed, going on still toward the south.

There would be no turning back for Abram. After God's visit and the view of the "promised" land from the heights of the mountain, Abram now knew what his future looked like. Abram removed himself from the mountain and headed further south into Canaan. His life would now become the life of a nomad. By stating in verse 9 that Abram "journeyed" (Heb. *naca`*, **naw-SAH**), the writer of Genesis is indicating that Abram continually moved about. Abram's wanderings in the desert of Canaan, awaiting the fulfillment of God's promises, would serve to strengthen the future patriarch's developing trust and faith in God.

Sources:

"Abraham." Christian Answers.net. http://www.christiananswers.net/dictionary/abraham.html (accessed June 25, 2010).

"Genesis." *Scofield Reference Notes.* Bible Study Tools.com. http://www.biblestudytools.com/commentaries/scofieldreferencenotes/genesis/genesis-11.html (accessed June 25, 2010 and June 29, 2010).

"Genesis 12." Net Bible.org. http://www.Net.Bible.org (accessed July 12, 2010).

Hebrew Greek Key Word Study Bible, King James Verion. 2nd ed. Chattanooga, TN: AMG Publishers, 1991. 1648, 1657.

Henry, Matthew. *The Matthew Henry Study Bible, King James Version.* Iowa Falls, IA: World Bible Publishers, 1994. 34–35.

Mays, James L., gen. ed. *Bible Commentary.* San Francisco, CA: HarperCollins, 2000.

Skinner, John. *A Critical and Exegetical Commentary of Genesis.* Edinburgh, UK: Morrison and Gibb Limited, 1980.

Smith's Bible Dictionary. Peabody, MA: Hendrickson Publishers, 1999. 109.

Von Rad, Gerhard. *Genesis: A Commentary.* Philadelphia, PA: Westminster Press, 1972.

Say It Correctly

Canaan. KAY-nuhn.
Haran. HAY-ran, -ruhn.
Moreh. MOH-ray.
Sichem. SHEE-kem.

Daily Bible Readings

MONDAY
Abraham's Story
(Acts 7:1–8)

TUESDAY
A God So Near
(Deuteronomy 4:5–9)

WEDNESDAY
The Lord Heard Our Voice
(Deuteronomy 26:1–11)

THURSDAY
Look to Abraham
(Isaiah 51:1–6)

FRIDAY
Abraham, Our Ancestor?
(Matthew 3:1–10)

SATURDAY
We Have This Hope
(Hebrews 6:13–20)

SUNDAY
God's Call to Bless
(Genesis 12:1–9)

Teaching Tips

Words You Should Know

A. Bowels (Genesis 15:4*) me`ah* (Heb.)— Womb, intestines, the abdomen.

B. Righteousness (v. 6) *tsedaqah* (Heb.)—Rightness, rectitude, virtue, prosperity, piety.

Teacher Preparation

Unifying Principle—Believing the Impossible. Even though he and his wife were beyond the age of childbearing, Abram believed God when he was told that he would have descendants more numerous than the stars.

A. Read and study the entire lesson.

B. Reread the Focal Verses in different translations aloud.

C. Pray for your students and for lesson clarity in class.

D. Bring some 3" x 5" cards to class.

E. Complete the companion lesson in the *Precepts For Living Personal Study Guide®*.

O—Open the Lesson

A. Ask for any prayer requests and ask if they are waiting on God to do something in their lives (self, family, friends, career, etc.).

B. Then have students write out on 3" x 5" cards what they are waiting for and pray with them.

C. Read the Lesson Aim in unison. Discuss.

D. Discuss some of the difficulties in waiting on God.

E. Ask if any students have settled for less than God's best or given up in the midst of the wait.

P—Present the Scriptures

Explain the Focal Verses using The People, Places, and Times; Background; the At-A-Glance outline; In Depth; Search the Scriptures; and More Light on the Text.

E—Explore the Meaning

A. Emphasize the salient points in the Discuss the Meaning, Lesson in Our Society, and Make It Happen sections.

B. Ask students if God has revealed something to them or a family member that impacts future generations.

N—Next Steps for Application

A. Summarize the lesson.

B. Close with prayer.

Worship Guide

For the Superintendent or Teacher
Theme: A Promise to Abraham
Theme Song:
"They That Wait on the Lord"
Devotional Reading:
Hebrews 13:17–22
Prayer

178

A Promise to Abraham

Bible Background • GENESIS 15:1–6, 12–18
Printed Text • GENESIS 15:1–6, 12–18 | Devotional Reading • HEBREWS 13:17–22

—————— Aim for Change ——————

By the end of the lesson, we will: REVIEW God's promise of a child to Abram and Sarai; APPRECIATE God's ability to accomplish what seems impossible; and EXERCISE faith in God's power to manifest present-day promises.

——————— In Focus ———————

Tracey was a beautiful 30-something single who was committed to her relationship with the Lord. In her late 20s, when it came to dating, she decided not to be unequally yoked with an unbeliever. With the lack of available like-minded men, even in her local church, her commitment to God made interactions with men difficult. She gathered once a month with other Christian single women to pray over their situations. However, too often she encountered the same question concerning her marital status: "When will you be getting married?"

Tracey pondered her exchanges at church and when she arrived home, began to talk to the Lord about what was in her heart. "God, You know I have been striving to live a holy life by not compromising my walk with You and by honoring You in my relationships. You know the desire of my heart for a marriage that glorifies You! But when are You going to bless me with a mate?"

Oftentimes, like Tracey, waiting on God causes us to question how or when God will bring the desire of our hearts to pass. In today's lesson, once again Abram received God's promise of a namesake and a nation being birthed through him in old age, but because he had no children at the time, he wondered how those things would happen.

—————— Keep in Mind ——————

"And he believed in the LORD; and he counted it to him for righteousness"
(Genesis 15:6).

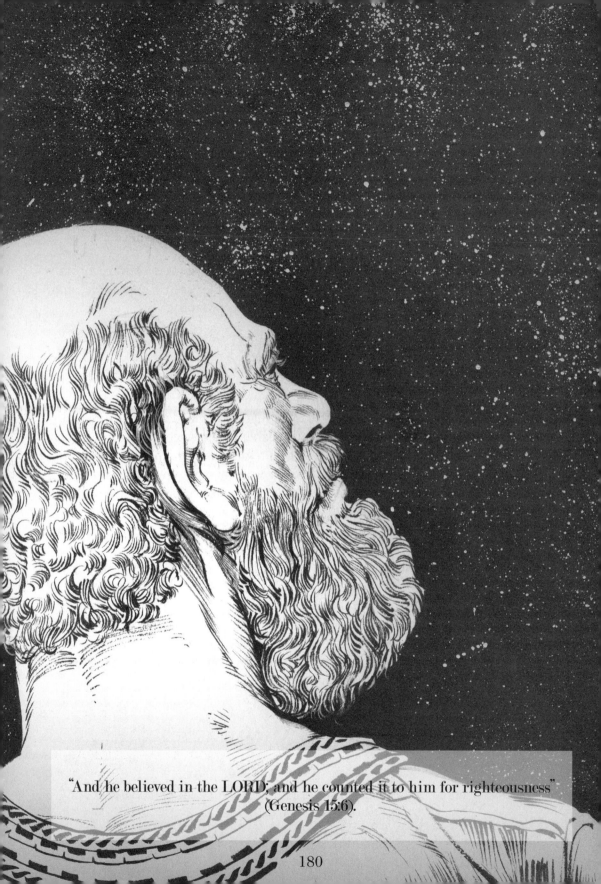

"And he believed in the LORD; and he counted it to him for righteousness" (Genesis 15:6).

Focal Verses

KJV **Genesis 15:1** After these things the word of the LORD came unto Abram in a vision, saying, Fear not, Abram: I am thy shield, and thy exceeding great reward.

2 And Abram said, LORD God, what wilt thou give me, seeing I go childless, and the steward of my house is this Eliezer of Damascus?

3 And Abram said, Behold, to me thou hast given no seed: and, lo, one born in my house is mine heir.

4 And, behold, the word of the LORD came unto him, saying, This shall not be thine heir; but he that shall come forth out of thine own bowels shall be thine heir.

5 And he brought him forth abroad, and said, Look now toward heaven, and tell the stars, if thou be able to number them: and he said unto him, So shall thy seed be.

6 And he believed in the LORD; and he counted it to him for righteousness.

15:12 And when the sun was going down, a deep sleep fell upon Abram; and, lo, an horror of great darkness fell upon him.

13 And he said unto Abram, Know of a surety that thy seed shall be a stranger in a land that is not theirs, and shall serve them; and they shall afflict them four hundred years;

14 And also that nation, whom they shall serve, will I judge: and afterward shall they come out with great substance.

15 And thou shalt go to thy fathers in peace; thou shalt be buried in a good old age.

16 But in the fourth generation they shall come hither again: for the iniquity of the Amorites is not yet full.

17 And it came to pass, that, when the sun went down, and it was dark, behold a smoking furnace, and a burning lamp that passed between those pieces.

18 In the same day the LORD made a covenant with Abram, saying, Unto thy seed have I given this land, from the river of Egypt unto the great river, the river Euphrates:

NLT **Genesis 15:1** Afterward the LORD spoke to Abram in a vision and said to him, "Do not be afraid, Abram, for I will protect you, and your reward will be great."

2 But Abram replied, "O Sovereign LORD, what good are all your blessings when I don't even have a son? Since I don't have a son, Eliezer of Damascus, a servant in my household, will inherit all my wealth.

3 You have given me no children, so one of my servants will have to be my heir."

4 Then the LORD said to him, "No, your servant will not be your heir, for you will have a son of your own to inherit everything I am giving you."

5 Then the LORD brought Abram outside beneath the night sky and told him, "Look up into the heavens and count the stars if you can. Your descendants will be like that—too many to count!"

6 And Abram believed the LORD, and the LORD declared him righteous because of his faith.

15:12 That evening, as the sun was going down, Abram fell into a deep sleep. He saw a terrifying vision of darkness and horror.

13 Then the LORD told Abram, "You can be sure that your descendants will be strangers in a foreign land, and they will be oppressed as slaves for four hundred years.

14 But I will punish the nation that enslaves them, and in the end they will come away with great wealth.

15 (But you will die in peace, at a ripe old age.)

16 After four generations your descendants will return here to this land, when the sin of the Amorites has run its course."

17 As the sun went down and it became dark, Abram saw a smoking firepot and a flaming torch pass between the halves of the carcasses.

18 So the LORD made a covenant with Abram that day and said, "I have given this land to your descendants, all the way from the border of Egypt to the great Euphrates River—"

The People, Places, and Times

Abrahamic Covenant. It was formed in Genesis 12:1–4 and confirmed in Genesis 13:14–17; 15:1–7; 17:1–8. In this covenant agreement, God vowed to multiply the descendants of Abraham, to give them the land of Canaan, and to make them a blessing to the nations. He swore by no greater than Himself to bring it to pass.

Background

In Genesis 12–14, Abram migrated from Canaan to Egypt to Negeb to Hebron, always building an altar unto the Lord for worship. Along the way, he also had some missteps and situations that could have derailed him. but he remained faithful to the Lord his God. In the process, God continued to reinforce His promise of land and a multitude of descendants to Abram (Genesis 13:14–18). However, Abram was still childless. As we move to Genesis 14, Abram rescued his nephew Lot, who is caught in the middle of conflicts between neighboring kingdoms. Afterward, Abram encountered King Melchizedek of Salem and priest of the Most High God—a symbol of Christ (Genesis 14:18–20; Hebrews 7). King Melchizedek brought forth bread and wine (communion) and declared a blessing over Abram, reinforcing the favor and relationship with the Most High God. The king gave thanks for victory over his enemies. Abram, in his gratitude to God for the victory, offered up a 10th or a tithe of everything he gained from the spoils (Genesis 14:20). King Sodom sought to tweak the offering, but Abram refused because he promised God that He would be his only source of blessing and would not give anyone else the credit for his prosperity. Abram once again sincerely honored God over the customs and influences of the world he lived in, vowing to stay singularly focused

on pleasing the Lord first. It is at this point that we begin today's lesson.

At-A-Glance

1. God Reinforces His Promise to Abram (Genesis 15:1–3)

2. God Unveils Details of His Promise to Abram (vv. 4–6)

3. God Foretells Abram and His Seed's Future (15:12–16)

4. God Ratifies His Covenant with Abram (vv. 17–18)

In Depth

1. God Reinforces His Promise to Abram (Genesis 15:1–3)

After representing Abram with honor before kings and defeating his enemies, God came to Abram in a vision with words of comfort: "Fear not, Abram: I am thy shield, and thy exceeding great reward" (Genesis 15:1). The Lord reinforced that He would give Abram safety and security and that he would not want for anything, because everything he needed was to be found in the self-existent, eternal, and almighty God. Because Abram declared that God was his source of blessing, God Himself was all the reward and protection Abram would ever need.

In verses 2 and 3, Abram responded to God's declaration of blessing by acknowledging God's sovereign Lordship. Yet he humbly asked how God was going to bring this promise to pass seeing that Abram had yet to have a son of his own. Moreover, Abram stressed to the Lord that thus far the next in his line was his servant, Eliezer, of Damascus. Abram expressed great concern, because due to his and Sarai's advanced age a slave born in his house would be the heir. In this era, it was a disgrace for a husband and wife not to produce children (especially sons) because children marked fruitfulness and continuation of the family lineage and property. It was a custom of the region that a childless couple would leave their land and earthly possessions to a servant who was born in their house. Then that servant would become their namesake. This greatly disturbed Abram, and he expressed his concern to God.

2. God Unveils Details of His Promise to Abram (vv. 4–6)

In past references to His promise, God showed Abram the land Abram would possess, told Abram that his seed would be great, that He (God) would make Abram's name great, that Abram's descendants would be too numerous to count, and that all the nations of the world would be blessed because of Abram (Genesis 12:2; 13:16). As Abram expressed his concern to the Lord about how and when this would come to pass and reminded God of being aged and childless, God offered Abram more affirming and confirming details. God assured him that Eliezer would not be his heir, but that Abram's heir would come from his "own bowels" (Genesis 15:4). God displayed His life-giving power in seemingly dead situations and did not withdraw His plan because of Abram and Sarai's age. With humans, it's impossible, but with God all things are possible and there is nothing too hard for the Lord. God brought Abram outside and by using the stars in the sky, He gave Abram another visual of how vast Abram's descendants would be. The common eye cannot count the number of stars in the sky or the amount of dust of the earth. Yet, this is how innumerable Abram's offspring would be, and God assured Abram that it would come from his own loins.

After receiving yet another visual of God's promise and confirmation that a son would come through his blood, Abram believed God, which forever placed him in right standing with the Lord (v. 6) and in the Faith Hall of Fame (Hebrews 11:8, 11).

3. God Foretells Abram and His Seed's Future (15:12–16)

To solidify His promise, God reminded Abram of what God had already done and what He said He was going to do. Thus, God began the process for establishing His covenant with Abram (Genesis 15:7–10). He caused Abram to go into a deep sleep (v. 12). In this state, the deep sleep became an intense concentration on the awesome power of God's holy presence. The Lord gave Abram a preview of events in his descendants' futures, including the migration to Egypt—first in peace, then as slaves. God even specified the amount of time (400 years) for their captivity (v. 13). Although Abram's seed would be afflicted, God assured him that his descendants would benefit from God's promise to him. God would also deal with their enemies, and they would continue to receive the blessing of reward. He promised to give Abram and his descendants land and to make them great. Most notably, they would walk away from slavery with great substance. God then gave Abram the personal prophecy that Abram would live in peace the rest of his days because God would provide divine protection for him and all connected to him in his lifetime. He would live a rich and fruitful life and would die at "a good old age" (v. 15) because of his faithfulness.

4. God Ratifies His Covenant with Abram (vv. 17–18)

God ratified His covenant with Abram through this sacrifice, thus giving Abram the confirmation he desired. According to

Matthew Henry's commentary, "The *smoking furnace* [in verse 17] signified the affliction of his seed in Egypt. The *burning lamp* denotes comfort in this affliction, the surety of God's word to be with them, and God's deliverance for his people as well as the destruction of their enemies. The passing between the pieces of the animal sacrifice [Genesis 15:9–10], signified God confirming His covenant and that God's covenants with man are made by sacrifice: no agreement, no atonement. The consumed pieces completed and testified of God's acceptance of this agreement and His pledge to honor His word" (40–41).

God further guaranteed the demarcation of the Promised Land where Abram's seed would dwell and take ownership (v. 18). Although God had given His promise before concerning the land, this time He reinforced the covenant with specific details. The Lord does not forget what He says He will do.

Search the Scriptures

1. What was Abram's concern regarding God's promise (Genesis 15:2–3)?
2. What is Abram's response to God (v. 6)?

Discuss the Meaning

1. How can we apply Abram's kind of faith in God in today's world?
2. Why is it often hard to wait on the Lord to bring to pass the things we are believing Him for?

Lesson in Our Society

God is so perfect and precise in everything He does. He knows exactly when to release what we need and when we need it. There are single adults who are so discouraged during their season of singleness that they either make wrong choices—thus disobeying God—or they live with discontentment and bitterness, which displeases God. They neglect to be fruitful for the kingdom.

No matter what you are waiting on God to do in your life, you must remain faithful to God's Word and trust that His promises are true. Isaiah 1:19 (NKJV) says, "If you are willing and obedient, you shall eat the good of the land."

Make It Happen

Whatever you are waiting on God to do for you, whatever the breakthrough you seek, don't give up for He who has promised is faithful. Decide today that you are going to believe God in spite of the circumstances.

Follow the Spirit

What God wants me to do:

_____

_____

_____

_____

Remember Your Thoughts

Special insights I have learned:

_____

_____

_____

_____

More Light on The Text

Genesis 15:1–6, 12–18

1 After these things the word of the LORD came unto Abram in a vision, saying, Fear not, Abram: I am thy shield, and thy exceeding great reward.

Yahweh (God) spoke directly to Abram by way of a "vision." The Hebrew word for "vision" is *machazeh* (**makh-az-EH**), and it is used to signify a state of ecstasy, in the sense of an overwhelming feeling and visual scene given from the Lord. In verse 1, Yahweh made two statements of extreme importance. First, He stated, "I am thy shield." Abram lived a relatively blessed and prosperous life. God was continuously with Abram, even when he was completely unaware of it. This care from the Lord extended also into times of conflict. Abram, with 318 trained men from his house, defeated five kings and their armies with the intention of retrieving Lot, his nephew (Genesis 14:14–16). Secondly, in Genesis 15:1, Yahweh proclaimed, "And thy exceeding great reward." From this statement, we can understand God's awareness of Abram's activities. Abram declined the king of Sodom's offer of a reward and God knew this. Yahweh's statement that He Himself is Abram's great reward reiterated His approval of Abram's decision.

2 And Abram said, LORD God, what wilt thou give me, seeing I go childless, and the steward of my house is this Eliezer of Damascus?

Abram's response to God was immediately directed toward his passion for an heir. One can assume he was thinking back to Yahweh's original command and promise for him to leave his father's household in order for a nation to be built through him (Genesis 12:1–3). Abram had a wife and was wealthy, but lacked the one thing he desired greatly, an heir to the family—a son to call his own. As James McKeown stated in *Genesis: The Two Horizons Old Testament Commentary,* "Abram does not indicate any concern about the future greatness of his offspring, but he relates passionately to the problems facing him as a wealthy person with no heir" (90). Instead of having a son to point toward, the next responsible male among Abram's house was a man from

Damascus named Eliezer. The Hebrew word for "steward" is *mesheq* (**MEH-shek**), and it can be translated to mean "to hold," or to indicate a "son of possession."

3 And Abram said, Behold, to me thou hast given no seed: and, lo, one born in my house is mine heir.

Without a biological son, a male born within Abram's house, Eliezer of Damascus was the next logical option, and this disappointed Abram, who continued to justify his reasoning and actions to Yahweh. Although he was aware of God's promise for an heir, his impatience affected his faith, and as a result, rather than express his belief in God's promise, he chose to point out that Eliezer was his heir by default. The Hebrew word for "seed" is *zara`* (**zaw-RAH**). The word is understood to indicate a descendant born through sexual relations, not of adoption.

In *Genesis: Fair Beginnings, Then Foul,* Daniel Berrigan states: "Faith that comes easily, departs just as easily. But the faith that is tested, stands firm. Here the testing takes the form of delay; the promise is tardy in coming true. And for the first time, Abram addresses God directly" (129). God is always patient with us, even when we lose patience with Him. The truth of the matter is that God's timing is always perfect, and the exercising of patience will always strengthen our faith in Him.

4 And, behold, the word of the LORD came unto him, saying, This shall not be thine heir; but he that shall come forth out of thine own bowels shall be thine heir.

"The word of the LORD" came to Abram (v. 4). Whether this was continuous with Yahweh's last message or not, wasn't made clear. Sometimes when we wish to have it, God chooses to withhold His voice or a response to our prayers. One thing is for sure, eventually

Yahweh will respond. Yahweh makes it clear that Eliezer "shall not be" the heir to Abram. John Walton explains: "Yahweh's response is to assure Abram that the family he has been speaking about will not simply come about through a legal transaction. The heir will be his biological son" (420).

5 And he brought him forth abroad, and said, Look now toward heaven, and tell the stars, if thou be able to number them: and he said unto him, So shall thy seed be.

Yahweh continued His conversation with Abram, providing him with an astonishing visual for his eyes. In verse 5, He told Abram to count the stars in heaven "if thou be able to number them." The purpose of this statement and visual was to show Abram the magnitude of Yahweh's blessing. The task to count the stars in heaven is not only overwhelming, but ultimately impossible for any human to accomplish. Likewise, one cannot place a value on any blessing of God, nor can one attempt to fulfill it on his or her own. This imagery by Yahweh is given against the backdrop of Abram's wife, Sarai, who was elderly and barren. God was showing Abram that his actions alone could not bring about a satisfactory heir. His actions were futile in terms of achieving this. Only God had the ability to provide a miracle that would fulfill His promise of a biological heir to Abram. In addition, Abram's descendants would be innumerable.

6 And he believed in the LORD; and he counted it to him for righteousness.

Through God's voice and the visual provided to him that night, Abram "believed" the Lord. The KJV renders the word "believed" in a causative sense, indicating that the interaction with God was so influential that it had no course but to convince Abram of its validity and truth. Thus, he believed

with his whole being. Yahweh was pleased by this, and Abram was declared righteous. The Hebrew word for "righteousness" is *tsedaqah* (**tsed-aw-KAW**). The word is also used to signify a "righteous person," "integrity," and "faithfulness." Although our actions and lifestyles have value to God, Abram's righteousness was not attached to a deed. Like many who have been born and passed on, Abram did things against the will of God. Nonetheless, his righteousness was linked to his faith in God. This principle is displayed in the New Testament, as well (Romans 4:3; Galatians 3:6; James 2:23).

15:12 And when the sun was going down, a deep sleep fell upon Abram; and, lo, an horror of great darkness fell upon him.

Genesis 15:12 brings us to the second vision given to Abram. The first vision was probably given at night, since Yahweh told Abram to count the stars. This second vision was given during the evening, when the sun hadn't set. Verses 1 through 6 focused on Yahweh's promise of a son to Abram, and verses 12 through 18 deals with Yahweh's promise of consecrated land.

Abram began to experience fatigue and drifted into a deep sleep. The Scriptures don't make known whether God Himself brought this on or not, but more than likely, this could have been the case. If we recall, in Genesis 2:21, Yahweh put Adam into a "deep sleep" in order to take a rib from his body, creating Eve (woman) from it. The Hebrew word for "sleep" is *tardemah* (**tar-day-MAW**) and can also mean a "trance." Once in this state, Abram experienced horror from the darkness that surrounded him. In this state of fear, Abram was attentive to what God was telling him. The full presence of God can place a person in a state of fear or a perceived horror. The darkness we sense could be none other than the sin within ourselves

186

that becomes apparent, once pure light and perfection are in front of us.

13 And he said unto Abram, Know of a surety that thy seed shall be a stranger in a land that is not their's, and shall serve them; and they shall afflict them four hundred years;

Yahweh provided Abram with a prophetic word about his future descendants, which was given in absolute terms. The seed of Abram would live through more than 400 years of bondage and oppression (Exodus 12:40). One wonders how Abram may have reacted to this news. To have the birth of his son withheld and then told that his future descendants would experience centuries of slavery would have been difficult to bear. God's children, in both the Old and New Testaments, must experience times of testing, pain, and suffering. This is part of the life of God's people, and at times, the only action we can take is to have faith in our loving God. As McKeown pointed out, "Genesis shows that there are periods of darkness even for the most faithful of God's servants and times when they feel inadequate to change the situation" (94).

14 And also that nation, whom they shall serve, will I judge: and afterward shall they come out with great substance.

God sent reassurance to Abram. God would ultimately judge the nation that would oppress Abram's descendants. Yahweh showed His sovereignty over not only Abram and his descendants, but that of the nations throughout the world, as well. Egypt was the nation that would eventually oppress Israel, and it was God who defeated them and their worthless deities with His plagues (Exodus 7–11). The 430 years of persecution would end, and Yahweh would bless them with freedom and material goods.

15 And thou shalt go to thy fathers in peace; thou shalt be buried in a good old age.

God suddenly changed the focus of the vision. He promised Abram a life that would conclude in peace and end with him "in a good old age." The future patriarch was told he would not live long enough to see the establishing of this nation of descendants, nor the beginning of their enslavement, but understanding and solace must manifest in his faith that God would take care of everything.

16 But in the fourth generation they shall come hither again: for the iniquity of the Amorites is not yet full.

This prophetic verse alluded to Israel's conquest of Canaan. Israel didn't initially receive the land that was promised to them. As Israel (Abram's descendants) left Egypt in freedom, their constant disobedience brought upon them punishment from Yahweh. They were to bear their guilt, as each year represented a day that they spied out the land. Thus, they would wander in the wilderness for 40 years, until the disobedient generations died completely.

The term "Amorites" (Heb. *'Emoriy*, **em-o-REE**) is designated normally to a specific people group, but in this context, it is used in reference to a collection of nations. The fourth generation of Abram's descendants would return to the land after their 40-year punishment, ridding the land of its alien inhabitants.

17 And it came to pass, that, when the sun went down, and it was dark, behold a smoking furnace, and a burning lamp that passed between those pieces.

On the surface, this verse seems odd and out of place. After careful inspection, one can see the covenantal symbolism Yahweh was showing Abram. By this time, the sun was completely set, and there was total darkness. The objects that were extremely noticeable were connected to fire and light. The smoking furnace and burning lamp were symbols relating to the covenant that was being established. This imagery is also connected to the ceremony Abram conducted in Genesis 15:7–10, where he cuts the sacrificial animals in half. We can also view a reference to such a covenant in Jeremiah 34:18.

18 In the same day the LORD made a covenant with Abram, saying, Unto thy seed have I given this land, from the river of Egypt unto the great river, the river Euphrates:

Yahweh made a final confirmation of His promise to Abram. What was expressed through prophetic visions of imagery was finalized on that day. This covenantal promise was repeated throughout the generations, including those who would actually be the fulfillment of that promise (Genesis 17:8; Joshua 21:43).

Sources:
Aalders, G. Charles. *Bible Student's Commentary: Genesis, Volume 1.* Grand Rapids, MI: Zondervan, 1981.
Berrigan, Daniel. *Genesis: Fair Beginnings, Then Foul.* Lanham, MD: Rowman & Littlefield Publishers, 2006. 129.
"Genesis." *Scofield Reference Notes.* Bible Study Tools.com. http://www.biblestudytools.com/commentaries/scofield-reference-notes/genesis/genesis-15.html#Ge15_18 (accessed June 25 & June 30, 2010).
Hebrew Greek Key Word Study Bible King James Version. 2nd ed. Chattanooga, TN: AMG Publishers, 1991. 1648.
Henry, Matthew. *The Matthew Henry Study Bible, King James Version.* Iowa Falls, IA: World Bible Publishers, 1994. 40–41.
McKeown, James. *Genesis: The Two Horizons Old Testament Commentary.* Grand Rapids, MI: William B. Eerdmans, 2008. 90, 94.
Walton, John H. *Genesis: The NIV Application Commentary.* Grand Rapids, MI: Zondervan, 2001. 420–23.

Say It Correctly

Amorites. AM-uh-rahyt.
Masheq. MEH-shek.
Tardemah. Tar-day-MAW.
Zara. ZAH-rah.

Daily Bible Readings

MONDAY
The Faith of Abraham
(Hebrews 11:8–16)

TUESDAY
Abraham's Faith Tested
(Hebrews 11:17–22)

WEDNESDAY
Righteousness by Faith
(Romans 4:9–15)

THURSDAY
Strong in Faith
(Romans 4:16–25)

FRIDAY
An Everlasting Covenant
(Psalm 105:4–11)

SATURDAY
The Eternal Covenant
(Hebrews 13:17–21)

SUNDAY
A Covenant with God
(Genesis 15:1–6, 12–18)

Teaching Tips

Words You Should Know

A. Tempt (Genesis 22:1) *nacah* (Heb.)—To test, prove, put to the proof, to qualify.

B. Know (v. 12) *yada'* (Heb.)—To ascertain by seeing, be assuredly aware, with certainty.

Teacher Preparation

Unifying Principle—Passing the Test. Abraham was unquestioning in his faith and devotion to God, who eventually rescinded His demand to kill Isaac.

A. Prayerfully read and study the entire lesson for today.

B. Continue to pray over the 3" x 5" cards from last week.

C. Complete the companion lesson in the *Precepts For Living Personal Study Guide®*.

O—Open the Lesson

A. Take prayer requests, and then open with prayer.

B. Then ask students what they would do if, after receiving from God what they have waited for, they were then asked to give it up. Discuss.

C. Review The People, Places, and Times and Background sections.

D. Discuss why tests are necessary in the natural and spiritual realms.

E. Tie in the In Focus story.

P—Present the Scriptures

Explain the Focal Verses using The People, Places, and Times; Background; the At-A-Glance outline; In Depth; Search the Scriptures; and More Light on the Text.

E—Explore the Meaning

A. Emphasize the salient points in the Discuss the Meaning, Lesson in Our Society, and Make It Happen sections.

B. Discuss why faith is not a one-time event, but an ongoing journey that requires tests along the way.

C. Ask students to recount God's faithfulness in the past.

N—Next Steps for Application

A. Instruct students to help others live their dreams and be blessed.

B. Close with prayer, asking God to build up the students' faith.

Worship Guide

For the Superintendent or Teacher
Theme: The Lord Provides
Theme Song: "The Lord Will
Make a Way"
Devotional Reading:
Philippians 4:15–20
Prayer

The Lord Provides

Bible Background • GENESIS 22:1–14
Printed Text • GENESIS 22:1–2, 6–14 | Devotional Reading • PHILIPPIANS 4:15–20

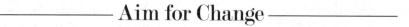

Aim for Change

By the end of the lesson, we will: LEARN of Abraham's willingness to sacrifice his only son to please God; IMAGINE the unquestioning faith Abraham exhibited; and COMMIT to increasing faith in God and obedience to Him.

In Focus

Michael was a sports agent and a man of great integrity. Not only did he honor his wife, but he chose not to take on clients that did not follow a Christian lifestyle. He recently took on his friend, Wayne, as a new business partner and wanted to test his loyalty to see if he shared his vision and integrity. Michael contacted a friend of his, who worked for a world-renowned athlete, and asked him to introduce Wayne at a networking function. Although highly sought after, Michael didn't agree with this athlete's lifestyle.

Michael already briefed the athlete on the test. The athlete started making hints to the possibility of making a change in his representation. However, Wayne knew that because of this athlete's reputation, he would not be a good fit for his firm. Wayne began to talk about how much he admired Michael's integrity, how he honored God in his business and his hopes to learn from him.

The athlete called Michael to the side and said, "Your boy is on the up and up. He's good people." Michael was excited to know that Wayne had passed the test.

In this week's lesson, Abraham was put to the ultimate test of loyalty and faith in God; he is commanded to give up the son he waited so long for.

Keep in Mind

"And he said, Lay not thine hand upon the lad, neither do thou any thing unto him: for now I know that thou fearest God, seeing thou hast not withheld thy son, thine only son from me" (Genesis 22:12).

"And he said, Lay not thine hand upon the lad, neither do thou any thing unto him: for now I know that thou fearest God, seeing thou hast not withheld thy son, thine only son from me" (Genesis 22:12).

Focal Verses

KJV **Genesis 22:1** And it came to pass after these things, that God did tempt Abraham, and said unto him, Abraham: and he said, Behold, here I am.

2 And he said, Take now thy son, thine only son Isaac, whom thou lovest, and get thee into the land of Moriah; and offer him there for a burnt offering upon one of the mountains which I will tell thee of.

22:6 And Abraham took the wood of the burnt offering, and laid it upon Isaac his son; and he took the fire in his hand, and a knife; and they went both of them together.

7 And Isaac spake unto Abraham his father, and said, My father: and he said, Here am I, my son. And he said, Behold the fire and the wood: but where is the lamb for a burnt offering?

8 And Abraham said, My son, God will provide himself a lamb for a burnt offering: so they went both of them together.

9 And they came to the place which God had told him of; and Abraham built an altar there, and laid the wood in order, and bound Isaac his son, and laid him on the altar upon the wood.

10 And Abraham stretched forth his hand, and took the knife to slay his son.

11 And the angel of the LORD called unto him out of heaven, and said, Abraham, Abraham: and he said, Here am I.

12 And he said, Lay not thine hand upon the lad, neither do thou any thing unto him: for now I know that thou fearest God, seeing thou hast not withheld thy son, thine only son from me.

13 And Abraham lifted up his eyes, and looked, and behold behind him a ram caught in a thicket by his horns: and Abraham went and took the ram, and offered him up for a burnt offering in the stead of his son.

14 And Abraham called the name of that place Jehovah-jireh: as it is said to this day, In the mount of the LORD it shall be seen.

NLT **Genesis 22:1** Later on God tested Abraham's faith and obedience. "Abraham!" God called.

"Yes," he replied. "Here I am."

2 "Take your son, your only son—yes, Isaac, whom you love so much—and go to the land of Moriah. Sacrifice him there as a burnt offering on one of the mountains, which I will point out to you."

22:6 Abraham placed the wood for the burnt offering on Isaac's shoulders, while he himself carried the knife and the fire. As the two of them went on together,

7 Isaac said, "Father?"

"Yes, my son," Abraham replied.

"We have the wood and the fire," said the boy, "but where is the lamb for the sacrifice?"

8 "God will provide a lamb, my son," Abraham answered. And they both went on together.

9 When they arrived at the place where God had told Abraham to go, he built an altar and placed the wood on it. Then he tied Isaac up and laid him on the altar over the wood.

10 And Abraham took the knife and lifted it up to kill his son as a sacrifice to the LORD.

11 At that moment the angel of the LORD shouted to him from heaven, "Abraham! Abraham!"

"Yes," he answered. "I'm listening."

12 "Lay down the knife," the angel said. "Do not hurt the boy in any way, for now I know that you truly fear God. You have not withheld even your beloved son from me."

13 Then Abraham looked up and saw a ram caught by its horns in a bush. So he took the ram and sacrificed it as a burnt offering on the altar in place of his son.

14 Abraham named the place "The LORD Will Provide." This name has now become a proverb: "On the mountain of the LORD it will be provided."

The People, Places, and Times

Isaac. He was the promised son of Abraham and Sarah. His name means "laughter." In their old age, God brought joy and fulfillment to them. Abraham and Sarah received their namesake who would go on to inherit the land promised to the patriarch and continue the blessing of Abraham through his son Jacob. Isaac was the only biblical patriarch whose name was not changed, and the only one who did not leave Canaan.

Burnt Offering. A sacrifice which is set afire and is entirely burned, ascending up to God. A burnt offering signified the total surrender of a worshiper's heart and life to God.

Background

God appeared to Abram and Sarai on two more occasions prior to the birth of the promised child as outlined in Scripture. The Lord appeared to reinforce His covenant to make a great nation from them by giving them a son, He changed their names to Abraham (meaning "father of multitudes") and Sarah (which means "princess"), and He gave them a sign of His covenant by instilling circumcision of all males (Genesis 17). Then an angel of the Lord appeared to tell Abraham and Sarah that in due season, approximately one year later, the child would come. At the age of 100 and 90 respectively, Abraham and Sarah became the proud parents of Isaac. The impossible had happened, and a child was conceived in their old age (Genesis 17:19–21). At long last, God's promise had come to pass, and although Abraham already had a son (Ishmael) born to him from Sarah's maidservant Hagar, he was not the promise. Sarah told Abraham to send Hagar and Ishmael away from their household because he was not to share in Isaac's inheritance. Abraham was distressed and hurt deeply to have

to send Ishmael away because he loved him, but at Sarah's word, which was in agreement with God's command, Abraham sent them away. However, God heard Abraham's heart and concern for Ishmael and because he, too, was Abraham's seed, God promised to make a nation of him also (Genesis 21:8–20). Abraham was obedient to God and remained a loyal friend throughout the years of waiting on the fulfillment of his promise.

At-A-Glance

1. God's Command for a Sacrifice (Genesis 22:1–2)

2. Abraham's Sojourn of Faith (vv. 6–8)

3. Abraham's Willingness to Obey God (vv. 9–10)

4. God Keeps His Promise and Provides (vv. 11–14)

In Depth

God's Command for a Sacrifice (Genesis 22:1–2)

At the close of the previous chapter, Genesis 21:22–34, Abraham made a covenant with King Abimelech of Gerar, who had an interest in striking a political alliance with Abraham because he could see that God was with him. Upon making an agreement of peace and to dig a well, Abraham staked his claim by planting a grove in Beer-sheba and named it in the Lord's honor as an outward sign in a pagan and idolatrous world that he served the everlasting God (Genesis 21:22). Genesis 22 opens with, "And it came to pass after these things, that God did tempt Abraham." Even after making an outward sign of his dedication in the previous chapter, God put Abraham to the test to prove his loyalty. God called on him to take his and Sarah's only son, Isaac, whom he loved, and offer him up as a burnt offering, and God would tell him exactly where to go to do this. It may appear strange that God would tell Abraham to take the son that he and Sarah waited so long for and offer him up as a sacrifice when God clearly did not want His people to act like the other nations around who offered up child sacrifices (Leviticus 18:21; Deuteronomy 18:10). God's command for Abraham to offer Isaac as a sacrifice gave us a picture of God's release of His own Son Jesus for the redemption of the world. Abraham had a love relationship with the Lord and once again he listened to the Lord, presented himself ready to obey, and upon instruction, he got up and moved at God's word. Out of His love for us, Jesus also presented Himself ready and moved at the Father's command to be the propitiation (sacrifice) for our sins (1 John 4:10).

Abraham's Sojourn of Faith (vv. 6–8)

Abraham and Isaac traveled to the destination God had designated, leaving behind those who journeyed with them. Isaac carried the wood for the burnt offering, and Abraham carried fire (a small, lit log, perhaps) and the knife. What an ominous responsibility it must have been for Abraham to carry the very instruments he would use to kill his son. Isaac unknowingly was carrying the wood that he would lie upon and in doing so, would lay down his life out of love and obedience to his father and his God. This is quite a picture prefiguring Jesus carrying the Cross to Calvary for our sins, out of love and obedience. As they walked along, Isaac made an observation, noticing the wood and fire for the burnt offering, and questioning his father on where the lamb was. It has been widely believed and portrayed in children's Bible stories and films that Isaac was a small child. However, traditional Jewish sources maintain that he was an adult or at least over the age of 12, which is considered to be an adult in Jewish custom (*The Jewish Study Bible*, 44–46). In light of Isaac's perceived age, it makes this story even more powerful because his father was now a very old man, and Isaac could have refused to go with him or turned back when he didn't see the lamb. Abraham replied to Isaac's question by prudently stating that God would provide a lamb for the burnt offering (Genesis 22:8, NLT). Abraham did not lie to his son by not telling him what God commanded or what his pending fate involved. He trusted God, did not give cause for alarm, and was unwavering in his faith that somehow God was going to take care of His request. The father and son continued on this journey of faith and sacrifice together.

Abraham's Willingness to Obey God (vv. 9–10)

Abraham already committed in his heart to follow through with what the Lord God commanded, and Isaac was willing to obey his father's command. Abraham methodically built an altar, placed the wood his son carried and everything else in order, and bound up his son. He stretched forth his hand and with the stroke of the knife, he was prepared to offer his son to the Lord as a burnt offering. One can only imagine the pain in their eyes as they continued to believe God, but moved forward with this sacrifice. After years of waiting and the promise to make him the father of many nations, his seed was lying on the altar prepared to die.

God Keeps His Promise and Provides (vv. 11–14)

God continued to prove Himself faithful, even in the midst of this test. Abraham demonstrated unyielding loyalty to God by raising his hand to strike his son with what would be a deadly blow. But an angel of the Lord stopped Abraham; calling out to Abraham from heaven, the angel immediately halted the sacrifice and told him not to kill or hurt Isaac in any way. Abraham's obedience revealed that he feared and revered God with his whole heart. A sacrifice was still needed to bring to pass what Abraham spoke of in verse 8: "God will provide himself a lamb for a burnt offering." Abraham saw a ram in nearby bushes and offered it up to God with thanksgiving instead of his son. Then in verse 14, Abraham formally named the place of this sacrifice Jehovah-jireh, in honor of God's provision (in NLT, the place is called "The LORD Will Provide"). This sacrifice reflects the fact that Jesus was our substitution, taking on the sins of the world. Mount Moriah, the place of this sacrifice, would later be the site of the temple built by Solomon (2 Chronicles 3:1), and Mount Calvary, where Christ was eventually crucified, was not far off.

Search the Scriptures

1. Where did God tell Abraham to take his son and what did He tell him to do there (Genesis 22:2)?

2. What was Abraham's response when Isaac asked him where the lamb for sacrifice was (v. 8)?

Discuss the Meaning

It's easy to love God at church where it's safe or when things are going our way, but how might God call on us today to prove or demonstrate our love and devotion for Him?

Lesson in Our Society

As Christians, we will all at critical points in our lives face decisions that demonstrate where we stand and what is truly in our hearts. There are brothers and sisters around the world who have laid down their lives or did not partake in or condone some activity because of their relationship with the Lord. The God and Father of our Lord and Savior Jesus Christ gave His very best, and we must resolve as the Body of Christ to do the same for Him. We must take a stand to ensure that we represent the Lord well and that our loyalty to God is not merely lip service, but when the moment of decision comes, He would be pleased with our choices.

Make It Happen

God has blessed and has repeatedly proven Himself to be faithful. It is easy for us to take God's goodness for granted and forget the Giver of the gifts and blessings. Examine how you can love the Lord more passionately, determine to walk in obedience to His Word, and remain in faith even through the storms of life. If God calls on you to let go of something or someone, trust that He would never call you to do so without having something greater in mind.

Follow the Spirit

What God wants me to do:

_____

_____

_____

_____

_____

Remember Your Thoughts:

Special insights I have learned:

_____

_____

_____

_____

More Light on the Text

Genesis 22:1–2, 6–14

1 And it came to pass after these things, that God did tempt Abraham, and said unto him, Abraham: and he said, Behold, here I am.

Abram, in obedience to God's word, packed up his family and left Haran for Canaan. Living the life of a nomad, he met with God face-to-face, witnessed the increase of his fortune, the change of his name, and the miraculous birth of his son and heir, Isaac. Now God calls to him again. Abraham did not hesitate to answer God's voice, hinting at the fact that he had grown quite familiar with it during his sojourn in the "promised" land. What Abraham didn't realize is that God has called to him in order to "tempt" (Hebrew *nacah*, **naw-SAW**), or "test" the patriarch's faith.

2 And he said, Take now thy son, thine only son Isaac, whom thou lovest, and get thee into the land of Moriah; and offer him there for a burnt offering upon one of the mountains which I will tell thee of.

God's test for Abraham consisted of three parts. Abraham was to "take" hold of (Heb. *laqach*, **la-KAKH**), or fetch his son and future heir. The fact that God knew what He was asking of Abraham was evident by God identifying Isaac as the object of Abraham's love. Secondly, with Isaac in hand, Abraham

was to "go" (Heb. *yalak*, **yaw-LAK**); God was instructing Abraham to lead Isaac away or cause him to walk away with him into a land called Moriah. Today, the location of Moriah is uncertain but is believed by most to be the place where the Holy City of Jerusalem now resides. Thirdly, Abraham was to "offer" (Heb. *`alah*, **aw-LAW**) back to God his and Sarah's only son. Abraham understood that it would be necessary for Isaac to die because he was to be offered as a burnt sacrifice, a practice that required the slaughter of the animal.

22:6 And Abraham took the wood of the burnt offering, and laid it upon Isaac his son; and he took the fire in his hand, and a knife; and they went both of them together.

In verse 6, there is a sense of anticipation as Abraham and Isaac walk together, father and son. Abraham's love for Isaac is apparent as he entrusts the less dangerous "wood" (Heb. *`ets*, **ates**) to Isaac while Abraham carries the more dangerous knife and fire. The writer of Genesis chose not to disclose the thoughts that must have been going through Abraham's mind. But there is a solemn reality that Abraham knew exactly what he intended to do. So that he could have the privacy required, Abraham had ordered earlier for his servants to remain behind while he and Isaac walked alone (v. 5). The future patriarch was going to be obedient to God's command, and any potential interference to the plan was now neutralized.

7 And Isaac spake unto Abraham his father, and said, My father: and he said, Here am I, my son. And he said, Behold the fire and the wood: but where is the lamb for a burnt offering?

It was Isaac's voice that broke the silence as the two trekked up the mountain. There is a sense of endearment and pride as Isaac calls Abraham "my father" (Heb. *'ab,* **ab**). He was devoted to his aged father and his question betrayed an innocence, trust, and intelligence on the part of the young man. Obviously he had participated in this sort of activity with his father before and knew the elements that were required for a successful sacrifice. For Isaac the most obvious element, the lamb, was missing.

8 And Abraham said, My son, God will provide himself a lamb for a burnt offering: so they went both of them together.

Abraham's answer to his son is both revealing and ambiguous. He doesn't openly tell Isaac what God has told him that he is to do to his son. Yet the answer is also revealing of the deep faith that Abraham now possesses. When departing from the servants now waiting at the bottom of the mountain, Abraham informed them that he and Isaac would soon return after worshiping on the mountain. Abraham knew that God intended for him to slay Isaac and offer him as a sacrifice. Abraham's faith was revealed in his belief that God could return life to the slain and burnt body of his beloved son or "provide" (Hebrew *ra'ah,* **raw-AW**), some other means to help him through his ordeal. Yet he didn't share any of his thinking with his son as "together" (Heb. *yachad,* **yaw-KHAD**), they silently continued their journey up Mount Moriah. *Yachad* gives the sense that they walked in unity and of one accord.

9 And they came to the place which God had told him of; and Abraham built an altar there, and laid the wood in order, and bound Isaac his son, and laid him on the altar upon the wood. 10 And Abraham stretched forth his hand, and took the knife to slay his son.

God guided Abraham to a place on Mount Moriah. Many scholars today associate that particular place with the site where Solomon would later build his temple to God. The site is also the present-day location of the Dome of the Rock, one of the holiest places on the earth for Muslims. Once at the location that God had desired, Abraham established or "built" (Heb. *banah,* **baw-NAW**), an altar and worshiped his living God. The fact that Abraham would worship God in the midst of this trial, spoke to the depth of his love and trust of God. Abraham probably did not understand why God had asked him to sacrifice Isaac. The sacrifice of children was a common practice among the nations that surrounded Abraham, but was not a thing that Abraham's God had ever encouraged or indicated that He desired, until now. The birth of Isaac had been miraculous and Abraham knew that God intended for Isaac to be the means by which He would fulfill the covenant promises to which God had bound Himself. So the "slaying" (Heb. *shachat,* **shaw-KHAT**) of Isaac must have seemed illogical to Abraham. Still, the sacrifice of Isaac was what God wanted, and Abraham would be obedient to God no matter the cost to himself.

After building the altar and worshiping God, Abraham arranged the wood on the altar, "bound" (Heb. *`aqad,* **a-KAD**) his son, and laid him upon the wood. The Scriptures seem to hint that Isaac lived in total submission and obedience to his father as he did not protest, resist, or object in any way to his father's actions. Finally, with everything in place for the sacrifice, Abraham lifted the knife high above his head and set about to plunge it into his son.

11 And the angel of the LORD called unto him out of heaven, and said, Abraham, Abraham: and he said, Here am I. 12 And he said, Lay not thine hand upon the lad, neither do thou any thing unto him: for now I know that thou fearest God, seeing thou hast not withheld thy son, thine only son from me.

Only when there was no doubt about Abraham's willingness to give Isaac back to God as a sacrifice did God call out to him from above. Abraham responded to God in what had become his usual manner, "Here am I," indicating not so much location as state of being. It is not hard to imagine that Abraham was in a continual state of prayer from the moment he began his trek up the mountain with Isaac. At this point God responded to his prayers and in a fashion that must have brought great relief to Abraham. Abraham had passed God's test of obedience. God understood that Isaac was the most important thing in Abraham's life. Isaac was to be the source of Abraham's legacy, and it is easy to imagine that the patriarch would have done anything to protect him. However, in his willingness to plunge the knife into his son, Abraham's reverence for God demonstrated in a very practical sense that Isaac held second place. God is to have pre-eminence in all things. This was the lesson God sought to teach Abraham. It seems Isaac had passed his test, as well. He helped his father to understand that his life had come from God and that he would not resist if Abraham, by God's instruction, needed to give his life back to God.

13 And Abraham lifted up his eyes, and looked, and behold behind him a ram caught in a thicket by his horns: and Abraham went and took the ram, and offered him up for a burnt offering in the stead of his son.

Abraham had been so intent in offering Isaac that he was unaware of events around him. It was probably the sound of God calling to him that roused Abraham from his deep concentration and caused him to look up. One can sense his surprise as he saw a ram "caught in a thicket." The "ram" (Heb. *'ayil*, **AH-yil**), was the confirmation from God to Abraham that his faith had been justified and the test was over. In verse 8, when asked by Isaac about the location of the sacrificial lamb, Abraham responded that God would provide it. However, God provided a much stronger, less gentle ram. It was this ram that Abraham subdued and offered to God as a burnt offering in place of Isaac.

14 And Abraham called the name of that place Jehovah-jireh: as it is said to this day, In the mount of the LORD it shall be seen.

So that the events of that day would not be lost to future generations of Abraham's posterity, Abraham named the site Jehovah Jireh (**yeh-ho-VAH yir-EH**), which means "God will provide." In so naming the site, Abraham placed the focus of the events on God and not on himself. Though the test was for obedience, Abraham wanted Isaac to remember that God was merciful, gracious, and able to provide anything that was necessary to carry out His instructions.

Sources:
Berlin, Adele, and Marc Brettler, eds. *The Jewish Study Bible.* New York, NY: Oxford University Press, 2004. 44–46.
"Genesis 22." Net Bible.org. http://www.Net.Bible.org (accessed July 25, 2010).
Hebrew Greek Key Word Study Bible, King James Version. 2nd ed. Chattanooga, TN: AMG Publishers, 1991. 33, 1637, 1644–45.
Henry, Matthew. *The Matthew Henry Study Bible, King James Version.* Iowa Falls, IA: World Bible Publishers, 1994. 60.
Mays, James L., gen. ed. *Bible Commentary.* San Francisco, CA: HarperCollins, 2000.
Skinner, John. *A Critical and Exegetical Commentary of Genesis.* Edinburgh, UK: Morrison and Gibb Limited, 1980.
Von Rad, Gerhard. *Genesis: A Commentary.* Philadelphia, PA: Westminster Press, 1972.

Say It Correctly

Canaan. KAY-nuhn.
Haran. HAY-ran, -ruhn.
Moriah. Muh-RI-uh.

Daily Bible Readings

MONDAY
All Your Needs
(Philippians 4:15–20)

TUESDAY
Born through the Promise
(Galatians 4:21–28)

WEDNESDAY
Not Withholding His Only Son
(Genesis 22:15–19)

THURSDAY
Faith Completed by Works
(James 2:14–24)

FRIDAY
Concern for Our Descendants
(Joshua 22:21–29)

SATURDAY
Righteousness and Justice
(Proverbs 21:1–5)

SUNDAY
The Challenge to Commitment
(Genesis 22:1–2, 6–14)

Notes

_____

_____

_____

_____

Teaching Tips

December 25
Bible Study Guide 4

Words You Should Know

A. Magnify (Luke 1:46) *megaluno* (Gk.)—Root word for "*Magnificat,*" Mary's song of praise, which is the first word of Mary's song in the Latin Vulgate scriptural text, and it means "glorify."

B. Soul (v. 46) *psuche* (Gk.)—The seat of feelings, emotion, desire, and affection.

Teacher Preparation

Unifying Principle—Celebrating Promises Fulfilled. Because Abraham was faithful to God and God was faithful to the promise to give Abraham many descendants, God acknowledged Mary's faithfulness to Him by choosing her to be mother of the Savior.

A. Read today's lesson text. Then read the Old Testament verses on which Mary based her words of praise—Deuteronomy 10:21; Psalm 103:17; and Psalm 111:1–9.

B. Review material concerning the promised Messiah, including the prophecies of Isaiah.

C. Complete the companion lesson in the *Precepts For Living Personal Study Guide®*.

O—Open the Lesson

A. Open in prayer, incorporating the thoughts from the Aim for Change.

B. Read today's In Focus story. Talk about ways to look for God's faithfulness in our lives, in spite of difficult circumstances.

P—Present the Scriptures

A. Compare Mary's song of praise with other songs of praise, such as Hannah's Song (1 Samuel 2:1–10), Moses' Song (Exodus 15:1–18) and Miriam's Song (Exodus 15:21).

B. Discuss the Hebrews' expectation concerning a Messiah and how Mary's Song affirms the fulfillment of God's promise through her.

E—Explore the Meaning

Have volunteers summarize the Discuss the Meaning, Lesson in Our Society, and Make It Happen sections.

N—Next Steps for Application

A. Summarize the lesson.

B. Close with prayer and praise God for the victory He's won in our lives and for who He is.

Worship Guide

For the Superintendent or Teacher
Theme: According to the Promise
Theme Song: "Hark the Herald Angels Sing"
Devotional Reading:
2 Corinthians 1:18–22
Prayer

According to the Promise

Bible Background • LUKE 1:26–56; GALATIANS 3:6–18
Printed Text • LUKE 1:46–55 | Devotional Reading • 2 CORINTHIANS 1:18–22

**DEC
25th**

―――――――――― Aim for Change ――――――――――

By the end of the lesson, we will: REVIEW Mary's song praising God's faithfulness; APPRECIATE the faithfulness of God's people from generation to generation; and EXAMINE areas in our lives where our faithfulness to God can be strengthened.

―――――――― 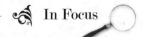 In Focus ――――――――

It was Christmas morning, and it was Teddy's turn to have the children. Karen felt so alone. Life just had not worked out the way she had thought it would. She walked into church and Sister Brenda gave her a great big hug.

"Where're the kids?" Brenda asked.

"Their father has them," Karen answered, as the tears streamed down her face.

"Come, sit by me," said Sister Brenda, as her arms enfolded Karen.

Sister Brenda allowed Karen to freely cry out of her pain and disappointments. She did not try to console her with words; just her touch seemed to comfort Karen.

Karen remembered how her family had once been whole—intact. She vowed that her children would never have to live and deal with the problems of a dysfunctional home as she did. She vowed that she would do all she could to honor God with her marriage. She did all she could, but problems still came into the marriage and ripped it apart. No matter what she did or did not do, her husband still chose to leave the marriage. Now, on Christmas Day, her precious little ones were spending time with their dad, instead of with the two of them together. Karen's heart seemed to break in two.

God was still caring for Karen and loving her, even in a very rough situation. God is always faithful. Sometimes we just have to ask God to help us see things from His perspective.

―――――――――― Keep in Mind ――――――――――

"And Mary said, My soul doth magnify the Lord,
And my spirit hath rejoiced in God my Saviour" (Luke 1:46–47).

"And Mary said, My soul doth magnify the Lord,
And my spirit hath rejoiced in God my Saviour" (Luke 1:46–47).

Focal Verses

KJV **Luke 1:46** And Mary said, My soul doth magnify the Lord,

47 And my spirit hath rejoiced in God my Saviour.

48 For he hath regarded the low estate of his handmaiden: for, behold, from henceforth all generations shall call me blessed.

49 For he that is mighty hath done to me great things; and holy is his name.

50 And his mercy is on them that fear him from generation to generation.

51 He hath shewed strength with his arm; he hath scattered the proud in the imagination of their hearts.

52 He hath put down the mighty from their seats, and exalted them of low degree.

53 He hath filled the hungry with good things; and the rich he hath sent empty away.

54 He hath helped his servant Israel, in remembrance of his mercy;

55 As he spake to our fathers, to Abraham, and to his seed for ever.

NLT **Luke 1:46** *The Magnificat: Mary's Song of Praise* Mary responded, "Oh, how I praise the Lord.

47 How I rejoice in God my Savior!

48 For he took notice of his lowly servant girl, and now generation after generation will call me blessed.

49 For he, the Mighty One, is holy, and he has done great things for me.

50 His mercy goes on from generation to generation, to all who fear him.

51 His mighty arm does tremendous things! How he scatters the proud and haughty ones!

52 He has taken princes from their thrones and exalted the lowly.

53 He has satisfied the hungry with good things and sent the rich away with empty hands.

54 And how he has helped his servant Israel! He has not forgotten his promise to be merciful.

55 For he promised our ancestors— Abraham and his children—to be merciful to them forever."

The People, Places, and Times

Angels. Angels are created beings whose primary purpose is to serve God and worship Him. Some angels are used specifically to bring messages to people from God. These angels appear like human beings and are never described as having wings. They are never described as children or women. The angels with wings are the cherubim and seraphim. The cherubim and seraphim never leave the immediate presence of God and are continually worshiping Him. Since angels are created, they have a beginning. They are not all-knowing or present everywhere as God is. They do not marry.

Background

Mary sang the beautiful words of today's Scripture passage while she was visiting Elizabeth, her relative. Elizabeth and her husband, Zechariah, were an elderly, childless couple. They had prayed many years for a child until they reached the age where they no longer expected God to answer this request. Both Elizabeth and Zechariah were of the tribe of Aaron, so

Zechariah was in rotation for serving at the Temple in Jerusalem.

After Luke's introduction to his Gospel record, he plunges right into the story of the birth of John the Baptist. It was Zechariah's turn to serve at the Temple, a great privilege for a godly Jew. As he went in to burn incense, suddenly the angel Gabriel was standing beside the incense altar (Luke 1:11). Zechariah had the same reaction that all who have ever been visited by an angel had—he was afraid.

After telling him not to be afraid, Gabriel told Zechariah that God was answering his and Elizabeth's prayers for a child, a very special child that they were to name "John" (v. 13). Unfortunately, Zechariah found this hard to believe, and so he became speechless until after the birth of John, their baby. John grew up to be the prophet we know as John the Baptist (or Baptizer).

Word must have traveled, in spite of the lack of modern communication devices, because Mary heard that her elderly relative was now pregnant. Mary was on the other end of the age spectrum, probably only around 15 years old, the age when women of those days usually got married. Gabriel had also visited Mary to tell her that she would be pregnant in the most miraculous way ever (vv. 26–38). Mary was going to give birth to the Son of God and this would be a virgin birth.

Shortly after Gabriel's announcement to Mary, she hurried to see Elizabeth (about an 80-mile hike). As soon as she walked in the door and Elizabeth heard her, baby John in her womb leaped in praise at the presence of the Baby who was growing within Mary. At this time, Elizabeth was already six months pregnant, while Mary's pregnancy had just begun. After Elizabeth had finished praising God for the com-

ing Savior, Mary began singing a song of praise to God that reminds us very much of Hannah's song of praise when she became pregnant with baby Samuel in answer to her prayers. The similarity of Mary's prayer to others in the Bible makes us think that Mary studied Scripture and meditated upon it even in an era when women had little access to formal education.

At-A-Glance

1. God's Personal Blessings on Mary
(Luke 1:46–49)

2. God's Blessings on His People
(vv. 50–53)

3. God's Faithfulness in Sending
the Messiah (vv. 54–55)

In Depth

1. God's Personal Blessings on Mary (Luke 1:46–49)

This stanza of Mary's song sings of how blessed she is. From a worldly perspective, this would seem to be the opposite of Mary's situation. Mary came from Nazareth, a town that was so poor that many of its few inhabitants lived in caves. She was engaged to a very godly man with a respectable job, but now she was pregnant—and not by him. Where are the blessings in such a situation?

First, she rejoices because God is her Savior. Every Christian, regardless of his or her situation, should remember that the greatest blessing is to have God as Savior. Then, thinking upon the news from angel Gabriel, Mary praises God for choosing her for this blessing, in spite of her humble status—she is poor and a woman, two things that in that era assigned one to an automatic inferior status.

But Mary does not see her lowly status as a disadvantage in the sight of the Lord. God delights in blessing the ones who are of a very humble socio-economic status, but who put all of their trust in the Lord.

2. God's Blessings on His People (vv. 50–53)

Mary has trust in the Lord showing mercy to His people, because she knows that Scripture details how God had blessed His people in the past. This is more than simple optimism. This is hope based upon knowledge of how God has worked in the past. Based upon how He has blessed His people, Mary knows that He will continue to do so in the future.

As we look closely at the things that Mary sings about concerning how God acts, we see that when Jesus came to the earth, He brought about a moral revolution. He is using His mighty arm to sweep aside the proud. Pride has no place in the Christian, because our standard is Jesus Christ. When we see ourselves compared to Him, we realize how far we are from how God desires us to be.

Then we see a social revolution. Jesus brings an end to the labels and titles that people think elevate them. In the sight of our Lord, the lowest person is just as important as the person with money and power.

Next, there is an economic revolution. Just think about the first Christians in Acts 2:44–45. No one went hungry in that first Christian community, because the rich sold their riches so the poor could have the basic necessities of life. Probably that ideal community existed for only a short time, but no Christians should go hungry while others have an abundance. We live in a very materialistic and greedy society, but Christians should have a different set of values than that of the world.

3. God's Faithfulness in Sending the Messiah (vv. 54–55)

Mary acknowledges that all these great and revolutionary changes in us can only come about through the coming of the Messiah that God had promised to send. Mary is thinking about God's promises to Abraham, Father of her people; but God promised Mother Eve back in Genesis 3:15 that He would send a Savior that we all so much need (see also Genesis 4:25). God is always faithful to keep His promises, even if we have to wait!

Search the Scriptures

1. What specific blessings does Mary thank God for (Luke 1:46–49)?

2. What sort of people does God bless (vv. 50–53)?

3. What attributes of God did Mary recite (vv. 50–55)?

4. How did God treat the descendants of Abraham (vv. 54–55)?

Discuss the Meaning

When Jesus was born, He brought blessings for individuals and for certain groups of people. What sort of people does Jesus favor? Why do you think He reaches out to those who fear Him, and to the poor, the humble, and the hungry? Compare these categories of people to the ones who are blessed in the Beatitudes (Matthew 5:3–12).

Lesson in Our Society

Mary's song highlights the different set of values that emerged from the birth of Jesus. God is concerned for the people who are on the bottom of society. In what ways can Christians as individuals bring about some of the things that Jesus came for? How can churches model His values?

Make It Happen

Some people are facing a difficult Christmas. Look around you and see if you can find someone to help before the day is over.

Follow the Spirit

What God wants me to do:

_____

_____

_____

_____

Remember Your Thoughts

Special insights I have learned:

_____

_____

_____

_____

More Light on the Text

Luke 1:46–55

Introduction

Verses 46 through 55 constitute what is generally known as "the *Magnificat*" or "Mary's song." The song can be divided into three strophes (stanzas). The first strophe, verses 46 through 49, speaks of God's grace or favor on Mary. The second strophe, verses 50 through 53, talks about what God has done in the life of the people of Israel. The third strophe, verses 54 and 55, is about God's faithfulness in keeping His promise to Abraham by sending the Messiah.

46 And Mary said, My soul doth magnify the Lord, 47 And my spirit hath rejoiced in God my Saviour.

We first notice that Mary praises the Lord after Elizabeth, by the Holy Spirit, has revealed to her the mind of God concerning her, confirming what the angel had told her earlier. Overwhelmed with joy and gratitude, and in acceptance of the promise of God, Mary reacts spontaneously and glorifies God. The statement "My soul doth magnify the Lord, And my spirit hath rejoiced in God my Saviour" indicates a total involvement of the whole of self (emotional and spiritual) in the praise of God. The use of both "soul" and "spirit" underlies this fact. The word "soul" is a translation of the Greek word *psuche* (**psoo-KHAY**), which generally means self or inmost being. It is the center of and makes up the whole being. The soul is the seat of feelings, emotion, desire, and affection. The word "magnify" in Greek is *megaluno* (**meg-al-OO-no**), and it means to make great, to extol, or to esteem highly. "Spirit" in Greek is *pneuma* (**PNYOO-mah**), and oftentimes it is synonymous with "soul." Here, "spirit" speaks of the rational, or mental, disposition—the core of the inner being. Mary employs the totality of her being (the soul and spirit) to glorify God in grateful worship of God her "Saviour" (v. 47).

48 For he hath regarded the low estate of his handmaiden: for behold, from henceforth all generations shall call me blessed. 49 For he that is mighty hath done to me great things; and holy is his name.

In verse 48, Mary gives the reason for her rejoicing and gratitude—God "hath regarded the low estate of his handmaiden." This means that God looked upon her with respect, that God showed favor to her, an otherwise insignificant person. Mary calls herself God's "handmaiden" (Gk. *doule*,

206

DOO-lay), which means female slave. This is the lowest position one can get in Jewish custom. Women and slaves were regarded as the lowest class in the Jewish community of the day. They were relegated to the background, to the place of dishonor. To be both (woman and slave) makes her place even worse; the society has no regard for her. In contrast, God has regard for her. He has looked upon Mary with favor, and has given her a place of honor. The magnitude and extent of her elevation is brought to bear in the person who made it possible, the "mighty" and the "holy" (v. 49).

Here, Mary brings out what systematic theologians call the immutable (i.e., unchangeable) and the incommunicable attributes of God—His omnipotence (all-powerfulness) and holiness. The incommunicable attributes of God are those characteristics that are not true of us human beings and which we lack sufficient words to define. We are not omnipotent (all-powerful) and we can never be. We are not holy and we can never be holy as God is holy. But here we see God, who is so mighty and holy, yet He is able to look upon and have regard for Mary, who is of the lowest class. Her low estate is not only because of her person, but also because of her heritage—Nazareth. Nazareth was one of the most insignificant and despised villages in Galilee.

When the apostle Philip told Nathanael, "'We have found him of whom Moses in the Law and also the prophets wrote, Jesus of Nazareth, the son of Joseph,' Nathanael replied, 'Can anything good come out of Nazareth?'" (John 1:45–46, ESV). In spite of these seeming "disadvantages," God is able to exalt and honor Mary. She has been tremendously blessed of God, she says. For "all (every) generations shall call me blessed," which means every generation will acknowledge her as one blessed and most fortunate woman among all women (Luke 1:48; cf. vv. 28, 42). As the mother of the Messiah, Mary is uniquely blessed.

We have seen that the first strophe deals with God's blessing to Mary. She next sings about what God has done in the life of the people of Israel (vv. 50–53).

50 And his mercy is on them that fear him from generation to generation.

Mary brings to bear the merciful attributes of God, His consistency, and His faithfulness. In verse 50, she celebrates God's mercy on all those who "fear" (Gk. *phobeo*, **fob-EH-o**) Him, meaning those who venerate or reverence Him. The fear of God is verifiable by the people's obedience and keeping of God's Law. God's mercy is accorded specifically to the people of Israel in keeping with God's promises, which started with Abraham (Genesis 17:7; 18:18; 22:17). This mercy is demonstrated in the display of God's strength and power (Luke 1:51–53).

51 He hath shewed strength with his arm; he hath scattered the proud in the imagination of their hearts. 52 He hath put down the mighty from their seats, and exalted them of low degree. 53 He hath filled the hungry with good things; and the rich he hath sent empty away.

Here are two pairs of contrasting parallels that are the direct results of God's mighty act in the coming of the Messiah. This one act results in the reversal of the human principles of living or thought. By His show of strength, God has completely altered the human view of life in general. The "proud" (Gk. *huperephanos*, **hoop-er-AY-fan-os**), the haughty, or those who exalt themselves, are scattered (v. 51). The verb "scattered" (Gk. *diaskorpizo*, **dee-as-kor-PID-zo**) is figuratively used here and has either a military or an agricultural idea in view. In its military sense, the strong, proud army, which relies on its own strength without God, is brought to nothing and is driven and dispersed by a stronger force. In its agricultural sense, "scattered" refers to the winnowing process, where the chaff is separated from the wheat and is blown away (or abroad in the air) by the wind.

Not only are the proud scattered, like chaff, or put in disarray, like an egotistical army, but God has also "put down the mighty from their seats" (v. 52). Here the mighty are synonymous with the proud. They are the "powers that be," the oppressors of the poor, the self-exalted who look down on and tyrannize others. The mighty are deprived of their self-exalted positions, while those who are truly humble ("them of low degree"), the insignificant, are exalted.

In verse 53, the next pair of parallelism starts with the insignificant, "the hungry," which is synonymous with "them of low degree," and associated with poverty. The hungry here describes those who realize their need for God and aspire for spiritual food, those who "fear him" (v. 50). They are fed— "filled . . . with good things" (v. 53)—and are shown mercy (v. 50). On the contrary, those who are "rich," proud, and self-sufficient without God are sent "empty away" (v. 53). This is revolutionary indeed; it describes the purpose of Christ's coming into the world (to change the human view and principles of living). Christ spells out this principle in His Sermon on the Mount, generally known as the "Beatitudes" (esp. Matthew 5:3–6), and teaches the same to His disciples (Matthew 23:12; Luke 11:1–4; 18:14). Mary insinuates God's transformation of society, whereby the proud and powerful are brought low, while the lowly are brought up. Not only does Mary represent the humble who have been exalted, but Nazareth as well, which signifies the revolutionary aspect of God's act through the coming of the Messiah.

Historically, the Old Testament is full of examples of the "proud" and "mighty" whom God, by His infinite power and design, brought down. Examples include Pharaoh (Exodus 15:1–11), Haman (Esther 6:6–14), and Nebuchadnezzar (Daniel 4:24–37). The Scriptures include "all proud" and haughty people (Psalm 33:10; 1 Peter 5:5; James 4:6). Likewise, there are abundant examples of the humble exalted by God: Joseph (Genesis 41:16), David (1 Samuel 18; 2 Samuel 7), Mordecai (Esther 6:6–14), and Daniel (Daniel 1:8–21). The Bible includes all the humble (James 4:6; 1 Peter 5:3–6; cf. Matthew 23:12).

54 He hath helped his servant Israel, in remembrance of his mercy; 55 As he spake to our fathers, to Abraham, and to his seed for ever.

The third strophe of Mary's hymn reveals God's faithfulness in fulfilling His promises to Abraham by sending the Messiah. Here, Mary celebrates God's mercy to Israel. Just as He promised Abraham and his descendants, God has kept His promise in keeping His word to Israel and helping them partake in this promise, not forgetting His promise but remembering His mercy. This act of mercy is an old promise (covenant) God made to Abraham and to all his generations after him. It is a living covenant to all humankind that is fulfilled in the incarnation of Jesus Christ—the Son of God.

Through this hymn of praise, Mary reveals the excellent nature of God: His divine power and authority over all things both spiritual and human (Luke 1:49, 51); His holiness (v. 49); His mercy and justice (v. 50); and His faithfulness and trustworthiness in fulfilling His promises (vv. 54–55). Through the incarnation of Christ, we realize the omnipotence, holiness, mercy and justice, and faithfulness of God.

Sources:
Baltes, A. J., ed. Biblespeech.com. http://www.biblespeech.com (accessed August 11, 2010).
Cox, Steven L. "Angel." *Holman Illustrated Bible Dictionary.* Nashville, TN: Holman Reference, 2003. 66–67.

Say It Correctly

Anakims. AN-uh-kims.
Chaldees. KAL-dees.
Debir. DEE-buhr.
Eleazar. El-ee-AY-zuhr.
Negev. NEG-ev.
Seir. SEE-uhr.

Daily Bible Readings

MONDAY
God Is Faithful
(2 Corinthians 1:18–22)

TUESDAY
A Faithful Heart
(Nehemiah 9:6–10)

WEDNESDAY
Descendants of Abraham
(Galatians 3:6–12)

THURSDAY
Inheritance through the Promise
(Galatians 3:13–18)

FRIDAY
Jesus' Birth Foretold
(Luke 1:26–38)

SATURDAY
Elizabeth's Blessing
(Luke 1:39–45)

SUNDAY
Mary's Song of Praise
(Luke 1:46–55)

Teaching Tips

Words You Should Know

A. Mock (Genesis 39:14) *tsachaq* (Heb.)—To laugh and make fun of.

B. Hebrew Servant (v. 17) `ebed (Heb.)—Proper name for some sort of a servant, slave, or attendant.

Teacher Preparation

Unifying Principle—A Life of Integrity. Potiphar's complete faith in Joseph's integrity, Joseph's faith in and loyalty to God, and Joseph's loyalty to Potiphar led Joseph to decline [reject] his mistress's sexual demands.

A. Pray for your students and that God will bring clarity to this lesson.

B. Study and meditate on the entire text.

C. Bring in news clippings on sexual misconduct in our society.

D. Complete the companion lesson in the *Precepts For Living Personal Study Guide®*.

O—Open the Lesson

A. Open with prayer.

B. Introduce today's lesson and the Aim for Change.

C. Pick a volunteer to read the In Focus story aloud.

D. Talk about the news clippings.

P—Present the Scriptures

A. Have volunteers read the Focal Verses.

B. Use The People, Places, and Times; Background; Search the Scriptures; At-A-Glance outline; In Depth; and More Light on the Text to clarify the verses.

E—Explore the Meaning

A. Allow students to share in open dialogue the Discuss the Meaning, Lesson in Our Society, and Make It Happen sections.

B. Clarify.

N—Next Steps for Application

A. Summarize the lesson.

B. Close with prayer.

Worship Guide

For the Superintendent or Teacher
Theme: God Watches over Joseph
Theme Song: "Blessed Be the Name of the Lord"
Devotional Reading:
1 Corinthians 10:1–13
Prayer

God Watches over Joseph

Bible Background • GENESIS 39:1–23
Printed Text • GENESIS 39:7–21a | Devotional Reading • 1 CORINTHIANS 10:1–13

Aim for Change

By the end of the lesson, we will: EXAMINE Joseph's loyalty and faithfulness to Potiphar; REFLECT on how loyalty influences decisions and behavior; and COMMIT to faithfulness and loyalty in our relationship with God.

JAN
1st

In Focus

Alma accidentally dropped the punch bowl on the kitchen floor. She watched the glass scatter across the tile. Kneeling down to pick up the pieces, her mind reflected on how her life used to resemble these broken pieces. Just two years ago, she worked for a well-known brokerage firm. Her company terminated her employment after she refused to falsify documents in an ongoing court battle. She was excluded from numerous professional activities and her reputation was smeared. Yet, through it all, God collected the pieces of her broken life and sustained her during that difficult time.

Just like shattered glass, when we make the decision to live right for God, we may feel crushed and fragmented. God promises to stand alongside us in our commitment to serve Him faithfully with integrity. In today's lesson, Joseph found God to be faithful in his time of need.

Keep in Mind

"There is none greater in this house than I; neither hath he kept back any thing from me but thee, because thou art his wife: how then can I do this great wickedness, and sin against God?" (Genesis 39:9).

"There is none greater in this house than I; neither hath he kept back any thing from me but thee, because thou art his wife: how then can I do this great wickedness, and sin against God?" (Genesis 39:9).

Focal Verses

KJV **Genesis 39:7** And it came to pass after these things, that his master's wife cast her eyes upon Joseph; and she said, Lie with me.

8 But he refused, and said unto his master's wife, Behold, my master wotteth not what is with me in the house, and he hath committed all that he hath to my hand;

9 There is none greater in this house than I; neither hath he kept back any thing from me but thee, because thou art his wife: how then can I do this great wickedness, and sin against God?

10 And it came to pass, as she spake to Joseph day by day, that he hearkened not unto her, to lie by her, or to be with her.

11 And it came to pass about this time, that Joseph went into the house to do his business; and there was none of the men of the house there within.

12 And she caught him by his garment, saying, Lie with me: and he left his garment in her hand, and fled, and got him out.

13 And it came to pass, when she saw that he had left his garment in her hand, and was fled forth,

14 That she called unto the men of her house, and spake unto them, saying, See, he hath brought in an Hebrew unto us to mock us; he came in unto me to lie with me, and I cried with a loud voice:

15 And it came to pass, when he heard that I lifted up my voice and cried, that he left his garment with me, and fled, and got him out.

16 And she laid up his garment by her, until his lord came home.

17 And she spake unto him according to these words, saying, The Hebrew servant, which thou hast brought unto us, came in unto me to mock me:

NLT **Genesis 39:7** And about this time, Potiphar's wife began to desire him and invited him to sleep with her.

8 But Joseph refused. "Look," he told her, "my master trusts me with everything in his entire household.

9 No one here has more authority than I do! He has held back nothing from me except you, because you are his wife. How could I ever do such a wicked thing? It would be a great sin against God."

10 She kept putting pressure on him day after day, but he refused to sleep with her, and he kept out of her way as much as possible.

11 One day, however, no one else was around when he was doing his work inside the house.

12 She came and grabbed him by his shirt, demanding, "Sleep with me!" Joseph tore himself away, but as he did, his shirt came off. She was left holding it as he ran from the house.

13 When she saw that she had his shirt and that he had fled,

14 she began screaming. Soon all the men around the place came running. "My husband has brought this Hebrew slave here to insult us!" she sobbed. "He tried to rape me, but I screamed.

15 When he heard my loud cries, he ran and left his shirt behind with me."

16 She kept the shirt with her, and when her husband came home that night,

17 she told him her story. "That Hebrew slave you've had around here tried to make a fool of me," she said.

18 "I was saved only by my screams. He ran out, leaving his shirt behind!"

KJV cont.

18 And it came to pass, as I lifted up my voice and cried, that he left his garment with me, and fled out.

19 And it came to pass, when his master heard the words of his wife, which she spake unto him, saying, After this manner did thy servant to me; that his wrath was kindled.

20 And Joseph's master took him, and put him into the prison, a place where the king's prisoners were bound: and he was there in the prison.

21a But the LORD was with Joseph.

NLT cont.

Joseph Put in Prison

19 After hearing his wife's story, Potiphar was furious!

20 He took Joseph and threw him into the prison where the king's prisoners were held.

21a But the LORD was with Joseph there, too.

The People, Places, and Times

Joseph. Joseph is the beloved son of Jacob and the firstborn son of his father's favorite wife, Rachel. The richly ornamented coat worn by Joseph was given to him by his father. This gesture of kindness served as confirmation of paternal favor. The eldest son, Reuben, had forfeited his birthright as heir when he committed incest (Genesis 35:22; 49:3–4; 1 Chronicles 5:1–2). Simeon and Levi, next in line, were ruled out because of their violence at Shechem (Genesis 49:5–7). The fourth son, Judah, was the next heir. However, Joseph, the 11th in order, is believed by some scholars to be the recipient of the birthright.

Background

In Genesis 37, readers are left wondering about the fate of Joseph. In chapter 39, the story picks up and we learn Joseph has been sold by Ishmaelites to an Egyptian named Potiphar, an official of Pharaoh (Genesis 37:28; 39:1). Joseph lives in Potiphar's house and is appointed to a position of authority. In his younger days, Joseph was a very self-confident young man. He knew God's plan for his life, and before coming to work for Potiphar, he had boasted about ruling over others. Joseph's buoyancy became unbearable when he revealed to his brothers his dreams of dominion over them. Out of anguish and jealousy, his brothers plotted to kill him. Subsequently, when Joseph was sent to check on his brothers and the flocks near Shechem, his brothers sold him to a caravan of traders going down to Egypt. His brothers then took his robe, dipped it in goat's blood, and brought it to their father, who concluded Joseph had been killed by wild animals. But Joseph was alive; in fact, the caravan of traders took him to Egypt, where his life changed dramatically again. In today's lesson, Joseph finds himself serving a member of the personal staff of Pharaoh, the king of Egypt. This extremely rich officer's name is Potiphar.

At-A-Glance

1. Refusing to Give In
(Genesis 39:7–12)

2. Refusing to Give Up (vv. 13–21a)

In Depth

1. Refusing to Give In (Genesis 39:7–12)

The position of Potiphar's wife has given this text special attention. She remains unnamed and has a role of grand consequence and tremendous freedom. She utilizes her liberty with authority as she confronts Joseph. Her power is displayed boldly as she commands Joseph, "Lie with me" (Genesis 39:7). In her statement, she relinquishes all preludes to intimacy and gets right down to business. Her attitude is one of control rather than love; she is the master's wife, a woman who demands, not seduces. Joseph refuses her orders and responds to her with equal authority. Joseph turns down an invitation to engage in sexual immorality. In doing so, he gives a testimony of faithful service to both God and Potiphar.

How often do we seize the occasion to turn from sin when it is tugging at our coattails? Joseph reiterates to Potiphar's wife that he has been given power over her husband's household. He has authority over and access to all things except her. In his rhetorical question, "How then can I do this great wickedness, and sin against God?" (Genesis 39:9), Joseph declares that such an act of adultery is not without great consequences. This is more than a sin against another man; this act involves disobedience against the Lord. In order to remain true to God, he must also remain true to his master, Potiphar.

Potiphar's wife does not accept Joseph's replies. She is relentless and continues her onslaught of sexual advances. Nevertheless, Joseph repeatedly denies her sexual overtures. He avoids her at all cost. Finally, on one occasion while working alone in the house, Joseph encounters her again, and she grabs his cloak and demands that he sleep with her. Joseph runs out of the house leaving his cloak behind.

What are we willing to leave behind and give up for the sake of our Christian integrity? So many Christians fail in the area of sexual temptation. Too often, we compromise our Christian values for the sake of self-gratification. Instead of running from temptation, we start walking toward it. We fail, also, to realize that infidelity does not happen in a vacuum; this sin hurts other people, rips apart families, destroys our testimony and reputation, and strips us of our integrity. Sometimes we have to do like Joseph and literally run from sin!

2. Refusing to Give Up (vv. 13–21a)

With Joseph's garment in her hand and Joseph in her power, Potiphar's wife conjures up a story of lies and deception. She accuses Joseph of attempted rape. She not only fabricates a story of sexual assault, but she also slanders the integrity of Potiphar's household. Her remark, "This Hebrew has been brought to us to make sport of us!" (Genesis 39:14, NIV), suggests that Joseph has a condescending attitude toward her, his master Potiphar, and his entire household.

She accuses her husband of doing wrong by bringing this foreigner into their midst. She shifts the focus from herself and makes Joseph and her husband the culprits. By blaming her husband, Potiphar's wife raises the stakes. When she recounts the lie to her husband, she strategically uses the words, "That Hebrew slave that you brought us..." (Genesis 39:17, NIV), emphasizing that her husband hired Joseph and brought his supposedly wicked influence into their home. Her assertion is clever; the blame is now on Potiphar's shoulders. He is literally forced to make a hasty decision. She shrewdly implies that Potiphar's integrity is in question. How could a man of his stature make such a horrible miscalculation of another man's character? No doubt, Potiphar could not take the word of a Hebrew slave over the allegations of his wife. He had to act quickly to evade dishonor. Fueled with anger and guilt, Potiphar rectifies the situation by throwing Joseph in prison.

Joseph is placed into another pit and launched into another tribulation. Again, he is not given the opportunity to tell his side of the story or argue against any evidence found against him. He is plunged into his master's prison. Joseph is a victim of a false accusation. Although he is silenced and thrown into jail, God is with him. Potiphar gave up on him, yet Joseph knew God would not forget him. Joseph did not forget God's promises to him. Joseph refused to give up and remained faithful. He sustained harsh mistreatment and injustice. Truly, the favor of the Lord was with him for his punishment could have been death instead of prison.

Sometimes our decision to remain loyal to God places us on the receiving end of someone else's scorn and anger. Nevertheless, God honors our allegiance to Him. Our commitment to live in accordance with God's Word will orchestrate our choices, navigate our paths, and dictate our behavior. The Lord was with Joseph, and He is with us when we stand on the principles of His Word. Do not give up and compromise what we know is the right thing to do. Do not surrender the opportunity to experience a deeper, richer, and enduring relationship with Jesus Christ. Don't give up doing what is right!

Search the Scriptures

1. What did Potiphar's wife do with Joseph's garment (Genesis 39:16)?

2. How did Potiphar react when he heard his wife's words (v. 19)?

Discuss the Meaning

Why do you think the Lord allows Christians to endure temptations that have the potential to jeopardize our integrity?

Lesson in Our Society

Sexual immorality has become commonplace in our society and is present in the church. Some secular psychologists claim that some people suffer from an "unfaithful gene." Others argue that the church is too rigid, irrational, and old-fashioned in its stand on sexual abstinence. Despite these ridiculous claims, the Bible is still right. Do you think the church is too rigid or conservative in teachings on sexual purity and integrity?

Make It Happen

Peer pressure, loneliness, and a desire to be needed are some reasons why Christians get involved in sexual misconduct. Many individuals want to share their struggles and are afraid of being judged. Over the next week, ask the Lord to lay on your heart someone who is struggling with faithfulness and integrity. Pray and ask the Lord what you can do to help. Follow the Lord's instruction as He guides you in approaching this individual.

Follow the Spirit

What God wants me to do:

_____

_____

_____

_____

Remember Your Thoughts

Special insights I have learned:

_____

_____

_____

_____

More Light on the Text

Genesis 39:7–21a

7 And it came to pass after these things, that his master's wife cast her eyes upon Joseph; and she said, Lie with me.

"After these things" is a statement affirming that God blessed Joseph, even as he was taken into slavery by the Ishmaelites, and sold to Potiphar, an officer in Pharoah's army.

At 17, Joseph's life was destined for greatness and prophetic fulfillment, although he had little understanding of his ultimate purpose. All Joseph knew was that his brothers hated him, they stole the coat that their father had given him, and he was thrown into a pit, where he was eventually sold to the Midianites (see Genesis 37:25–28). The Midianites were actually descendants of Joseph, through Abraham and his concubine Keturah (see Genesis 25:1–2). From there, Joseph became the property of Potiphar and served him. Potiphar had enough sense and insight to recognize that there was something different about this foreigner. Every task he assigned Joseph was successfully completed. Because of his integrity, Joseph was promoted quickly to oversee all the work and people in Potiphar's house.

Even though Joseph was far away from his family, God never left him. He showed the young man loyalty, and blessed the work of his hands. As God showed loyalty to Joseph, Joseph was loyal to Potiphar. Thus, God blessed Potiphar for Joseph's sake. No matter what situation young Joseph encountered on his journey to greatness, it was evident that God was with him. The favor of Joseph's life was not only appealing to Potiphar, but also to Potiphar's wife. Perhaps because Moses did not find it necessary to identify her, we are not given "Mrs. Potiphar's" first name. She was just a tool to be used by God to get Joseph into the place of greatness. She is only recognized as a woman who seemed to have an insatiable appetite for sex outside of marriage as she approached Joseph with a horrible proposition: "Lie with me."

With success also come tests or temptations for believers. It was only after Potiphar had promoted Joseph, and the favor and authority of God were evident in his life, that the wife wanted to sleep with him.

8 But he refused and said unto his master's wife, Behold my master wotteth not what is with me in the house, and he had committed all that he hath to my hand:

The text is rather ambivalent on why "Mrs. Potiphar" wanted Joseph in her bed. Did she not already have everything she could have wanted from her husband? Did not her husband meet her sexual needs? What could Joseph have given to Mrs. Potiphar that her husband could not provide? Did she need to be reminded of her marital obligations by this Hebrew? Whatever the reason, Joseph wanted no part of the role of paramour. He refused her advances. The word "refused" in verse 8 comes from the Hebrew word *ma'en* (**maw-ANE**) and the idea is to be unwilling to participate in any wrong or sinful activity. The text does not go in detail as to how Joseph was able to rebuff Potiphar's wife. There is no reference that he learned his morality or integrity from his father Jacob, or his brothers (see Genesis 34 and 38).Yet, Joseph had the ability to see beyond the immediate "pleasures of sin" (see Hebrews 11:25), to a full, surrendered life.

9 There is none greater in this house than I; neither hath he kept back any thing from me but thee, because thou art his wife: how then can I do this great wickedness, and sin against God?

Because of his loyalty and integrity, Joseph had won the trust and confidence of his superior and God. He dared not cross the line, no matter how strong the temptation that came his way. Therefore, Joseph reminded Poitphar's wife of two obvious points: (1) Despite his promotion and influence, he would not violate Potiphar's trust. He had authority over the servants and other employees, but not over Potiphar's wife; and (2) Joseph would not sin against his God.

The word "sin" in Hebrew is *chatta'ah* (**khat-taw-AW**) and it means to miss the way, forfeit, and abandon righteousness. Another meaning is to be off target and get lost. Joseph had already been abandoned by his brothers and was "lost" in Egypt, away from all his familiar surroundings. To yield to the sexual desires of Potiphar's wife would have taken him farther away from the God who sustained him. It is difficult for many of us to comprehend that when we fall into temptation and sin, we really are violating our relationship with God. We should consider the bigger picture when we are faced with temptation and recognize that when we sin, our failure is against God, who gives us the ability to say no.

10 And it came to pass, as she spoke to Joseph day by day, that he hearkened not unto her, to lie by her, or to be with her.

If there was one characteristic that marked Potiphar's wife, it was her relentless pursuit of Joseph. She would not take no for an answer, and his explanation as to why he does not want to be with her apparently increases her resolve to undermine his integrity. Potiphar's wife is like a dripping faucet that cannot be shut off. Sooner or later, she was determined to have her way with Joseph. But Joseph showed Potiphar's wife a servant of God who would not compromise his convictions or relationship with God. Joseph endured her barrage of sexual advances "day by day" and "hearkened not unto her." The Hebrew word for "hearken" is *shama`* (**shaw-MAH**), and one of its meanings is to give undivided listening attention to another, or perceive a message with the intention of obeying. Potiphar's wife "kept putting pressure on him" (v. 10, NLT), with her incessant sexual advances, but Joseph did not relent. In the process, his integrity and faith strengthened.

11 And it came to pass about this time, that Joseph went into the house to do his business; and there was none of the men of the house there within. 12 And she caught him by his garment, saying lie with me: and he left his garment in her hand, and fled, and got him out.

With the phrases "day by day" (v. 10) and "it came to pass about this time" (v. 11), Moses conveyed a time lapse between Potiphar's wife's first and subsequent approaches of Joseph. Perhaps she had developed a strategy to get Joseph into her bed, and she needed some time before its details unfolded. Or she may have temporarily backed away from Joseph to give him the idea that she had gotten the message. But Potiphar's wife was brazen, determined to get her prized possession if it took her one day, month, or year (see Proverbs 7:10). The idea of "brazen" is something harsh, loud, and marked by contemptuous boldness, with defiance or impudence. Indeed, Potiphar's wife was bold! She waited for the opportune time, and as Joseph worked in the house alone, she struck again. This time, she grabbed his tunic garment, perhaps given to him by Potiphar, and pulled him close. "Lie with me," she said again (Genesis 39:12).

Joseph had two choices: (1) yield to her demand, and hope no one found out; or (2) leave his garment in her hands, and run out of the house with all his might. Joseph chose the latter. He may have left his garment with her, but he left with his integrity in the hands of God.

13 And it came to pass, when she saw that he had left his garment in her hand, and was fled forth, 14 That she called unto the men of her house, and spake unto them, saying, see he hath brought in an Hebrew unto us to mock us; he came in unto me to lie with me, and I cried with a loud voice: 15 And it came to pass, when he heard that I lifted up my voice and cried, that he left his garment with me, and fled, and got him out. 16 And she laid up his garment by her, until his lord came home.

Potiphar's wife was angry with Joseph. Not only had he rebuffed her sexual advances, but he also ran away. How insulted she must have been! Wasn't she attractive to the young man? Didn't he find her enticing and alluring? As a servant, shouldn't he have done what she told him to do? For the second time in his young life, another of Joseph's garments was used against him. The accusation was damning. Joseph left the garment to flee from an aggressive woman. Now the garment would be used to seal his fate.

Potiphar's wife had all the evidence she needed. She called all of her husband's servants into the house and showed them Joseph's garment. She also planned to use the servants and instigated that Potiphar brought Joseph into the house to mock,

not just Potiphar's wife, but everyone else, including the servants. The word "mock" in Hebrew is *tsachaq* (**tsaw-KHAK**) and means "to laugh; to make a toy of." She was enraged that a mere servant, a mere Hebrew, would do such a thing. She made sure that the servants would turn against "[this] Hebrew" by including them in her scheme (vv. 14–15).

John MacArthur says that Potiphar's wife used the term "Hebrew servant" as "a pejorative, intended to heap scorn upon someone whom she considered definitely unworthy of any respect" (*MacArthur Study Bible*, 73). Potiphar's wife repeated her story to the servants to instill within them contempt and anger. By the time Potiphar arrived home, everyone would be able to convey to him just how vile and wicked Joseph was. ("We thought he was a man of integrity, but he tried to sleep with your wife. Look, here is his garment to prove that he was in your wife's bedroom.")

17 And she spake unto him according to these words, saying, The Hebrew servant, which thou hast brought unto us, came in unto me to mock me: 18 And it came to pass, as I lifted up my voice and cried, that he left his garment with me, and fled out. 19 And it came to pass, when his master heard the words of his wife, which she spake unto him, saying after this manner did they servant to me; that his wrath was kindled.

Whether Potiphar's wife's sole purpose for plotting against Joseph was to get him out of the house, as her resentment of a foreigner was palpable, or she was really attracted to him and was angered by his rebuffs, is uncertain. When Potiphar arrived home, his wife blamed him for bringing Joseph to the home, and she accused Joseph of sexual advances. She also indicated that Joseph was nothing more than a foreigner that Potiphar had given special privileges and authority, which should have gone to the Egyptians. What a mockery! She also planted the seed in her husband that she was a victim and had nothing to do with the attempted adultery or rape. She made it seem like it was a scheme cooked up by Joseph, the foreigner that Potiphar had brought to their home.

There are always two sides to every story, but Potiphar's wife was so convincing in spinning her web of deceit that Potiphar didn't bother to ask for more specific details of the incident. All he knew was that his wife had been illicitly approached, and it kindled his wrath and anger against Joseph. Certainly, he would believe his wife before a servant.

In verse 19, the word "wrath" comes from the Hebrew word 'aph (**af**) and expresses the idea of an intense, boiling anger where the nose and eyes are dilated, breathing becomes more pronounced, and the emotional tone of the voice is raised significantly. It would appear that once the incident was conveyed to Potiphar, he was "boiling mad" and perhaps, ready to bring physical judgment onto Joseph. Solomon affirms, "Jealousy is a husband's fury; Therefore he will not spare in the day of vengeance. He will accept no recompense, Nor will he be appeased though you give him many gifts" (Proverbs 6:34–35, NKJV). The servant that Potiphar trusted had become his enemy.

20 And Joseph's master took him, and put him into the prison, a place where the king's prisoners were bound: and he was there in the prison. 21a But the Lord was with Joseph.

Potiphar did not bother to ask Joseph what happened, or why he thought he could get away with having sexual intercourse with his wife, especially in his house. Instead, he consigned Joseph to a prison that is reserved for the royal servants of the king. Moses does not infer whether Potiphar may have been reluctant to turn Joseph over to the prison, nor does he identify the other prisoners, at least at this time. Still, Moses made this point clear: "But the LORD was with Joseph" (Genesis 39:21a).

Though Joseph was wrongfully accused, and his integrity tested by a wanton and brazen woman, he could rest assured that, no matter the outcome, God was with him. At the time, Joseph may have felt God was a million miles away, and there was no hope for him in prison. But he received special grace and favor to resist sexual temptation, and remain truthful to Potiphar and his God, because Jehovah Jireh was truly Joseph's provider, and He demonstrated His nearness to the young Hebrew, in prison, too.

Sources:

Berlin, Adele, and Marc Brettler, eds. *The Jewish Study Bible.* New York, NY: Oxford University Press, 2004. 78–79.

Bruce, F. F. et al., eds. *Zondervan Bible Commentary.* Grand Rapids, MI: Zondervan Publishing, 2008. 50.

Elwell, Walter A., and Philip W. Comfort. *Tyndale Bible Dictionary.* Wheaton, IL: Tyndale House Publishers, 2001. 736.

Hayford, Jack W., Litt.D. et al., eds. *The New Spirit-Filled Life Bible, NKJV.* Nashville, TN: Thomas Nelson Publishers, 2002. 57–58.

Life Application Study Bible (NLT). Wheaton, IL: Tyndale House, 1996.

MacArthur, John. *The MacArthur Study Bible, NKJV.* Nashville, TN: Thomas NelsonPublishers, 1997. 72–73.

Mattingly, Gerald L. "Midan, Midianites." *The Harper Collins Bible Dictionary.* Paul J. Achtemeir et al., eds. San Francisco, CA: HarperCollins Publishers, 1996. 682–83.

The New Interpreters Bible, Vol. I. Nashville, TN: Abingdon Press, 2002. 607–12.

The New Strong's Exhaustive Concordance of the Bible. Nashville, TN: Thomas Nelson Publishers, 1990.

"Potiphar." *The Harper Collins Bible Dictionary.* Paul J. Achtemeir et al., eds. San Francisco, CA: HarperCollins Publishers, 1996. 867–68.

Say It Correctly

Garment. GAR-mint.
Hearkened. HAR-kined.
Hebrew. HEE-broo.
Joseph. JOH-sif, -suhf.
Potiphar. POT-uh-fahr.

Daily Bible Reading

MONDAY
A Man Sent Ahead
(Psalm 105:16–22)

TUESDAY
Joseph's Story
(Acts 7:9–16)

WEDNESDAY
Facing Temptation
(Luke 22:39–46)

THURSDAY
Enduring Temptation
(1 Corinthians 10:1–13)

FRIDAY
Choosing the Way of Faithfulness
(Psalm 119:25–32)

SATURDAY
A Responsible Servant
(Genesis 39:1–6)

SUNDAY
Guided by a Loving Lord
(Genesis 39:7–21a)

Teaching Tips

Words You Should Know

A. Manasseh (Genesis 41:50–51) *Menashsheh* (Heb.)—Grandson of Jacob; the firstborn son of Joseph and his Egyptian wife, Asenath; the name means "causing to forget."

B. Ephraim.(v. 52) *'Ephrayim* (Heb.)—Joseph's younger son, born of Joseph and Asenath before the seven years of famine in Egypt; He was the ancestor of an Israelite tribe, and his name came to designate the Northern Kingdom of Israel.

Teacher Preparation

Unifying Principle—Real Success. Because Joseph performed so well for the Egyptian king, Pharaoh had faith in Joseph's abilities, elevated him to the second position in all of Egypt, and gave him responsibility for ruling the day-to-day activities of the kingdom.

A. Pray for your students and that God will bring clarity to this lesson.

B. Study and meditate on the entire text.

C. Research and bring in biographies of people who have accomplished great success (e.g., Rev. Dr. Martin Luther King and people in the local community, too).

D. Complete the companion lesson in the *Precepts For Living Personal Study Guide®*.

O—Open the Lesson

A. Open with prayer.

B. Introduce today's lesson and the Aim for Change.

C. Have a volunteer read the In Focus story aloud.

D. Share and discuss the biographies.

P—Present the Scriptures

A. Have volunteers read the Focal Verses.

B. Use The People, Places, and Times; Background; Search the Scriptures; At-A-Glance outline; In Depth; and More Light on the Text to clarify the verses.

E—Explore the Meaning

A. Allow students to share in open dialogue the Discuss the Meaning, Lesson in Our Society, and Make It Happen sections together.

B. Clarify.

N—Next Steps for Application

A. Summarize the lesson.

B. Close with prayer.

Worship Guide

For the Superintendent or Teacher
Theme: Joseph Finds Favor
Theme Song: "Thank You Lord"
Devotional Reading: Genesis 49:22–26
Prayer

Joseph Finds Favor

Bible Background • GENESIS 41:1–52
Printed Text • GENESIS 41:37–45, 50–52 | Devotional Reading • GENESIS 49:22–26

—————————— **Aim for Change** ——————————

By the end of the lesson, we will: STUDY how Joseph's faithfulness is rewarded; EXPLORE how superior performance can lead to honor; and COMMIT to responsible actions and superior performance.

—————————— 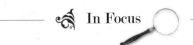 **In Focus** ——————————

"My counting mail days are over!" Jeff said, as he sat in the swivel chair in his new office.

For quite some time, Jeff took night classes while working in the mailroom. He studied hard to pass the bar exam. On his first attempt, he passed the test and landed a position in a prestigious law firm. Jeff never complained about working in the mailroom. He was diligent, working hard in the mailroom and studying regularly for class. He knew it was only God's favor that landed him this new position!

The favor of God requires commitment to faithful and responsible service at our jobs, in school, church, and in our relationships with others. In this lesson, we will see how Joseph's faith in God opened doors of opportunity and provided great rewards for his superior performance.

—————————— **Keep in Mind** ——————————

"And Pharaoh said unto his servants, Can we find such a one as this is,
a man in whom the Spirit of God is?" (Genesis 41:38).

"And Pharaoh said unto his servants, Can we find such a one as this is, a man in whom the Spirit of God is?" (Genesis 41:38).

Focal Verses

KJV Genesis 41:37 And the thing was good in the eyes of Pharaoh, and in the eyes of all his servants.

38 And Pharaoh said unto his servants, Can we find such a one as this is, a man in whom the Spirit of God is?

39 And Pharaoh said unto Joseph, Forasmuch as God hath shewed thee all this, there is none so discreet and wise as thou art:

40 Thou shalt be over my house, and according unto thy word shall all my people be ruled: only in the throne will I be greater than thou.

41 And Pharaoh said unto Joseph, See, I have set thee over all the land of Egypt.

42 And Pharaoh took off his ring from his hand, and put it upon Joseph's hand, and arrayed him in vestures of fine linen, and put a gold chain about his neck;

43 And he made him to ride in the second chariot which he had; and they cried before him, Bow the knee: and he made him ruler over all the land of Egypt.

44 And Pharaoh said unto Joseph, I am Pharaoh, and without thee shall no man lift up his hand or foot in all the land of Egypt.

45 And Pharaoh called Joseph's name Zaphnath-paaneah; and he gave him to wife Asenath the daughter of Poti-pherah priest of On. And Joseph went out over all the land of Egypt.

41:50 And unto Joseph were born two sons before the years of famine came, which Asenath the daughter of Poti-pherah priest of On bare unto him.

51 And Joseph called the name of the firstborn Manasseh: For God, said he, hath made me forget all my toil, and all my father's house.

NLT Genesis 41:37 Joseph's suggestions were well received by Pharaoh and his advisers.

38 As they discussed who should be appointed for the job, Pharaoh said, "Who could do it better than Joseph? For he is a man who is obviously filled with the spirit of God."

39 Turning to Joseph, Pharaoh said, "Since God has revealed the meaning of the dreams to you, you are the wisest man in the land!

40 I hereby appoint you to direct this project. You will manage my household and organize all my people. Only I will have a rank higher than yours."

41 And Pharaoh said to Joseph, "I hereby put you in charge of the entire land of Egypt."

42 Then Pharaoh placed his own signet ring on Joseph's finger as a symbol of his authority. He dressed him in beautiful clothing and placed the royal gold chain about his neck.

43 Pharaoh also gave Joseph the chariot of his second-in-command, and wherever he went the command was shouted, "Kneel down!" So Joseph was put in charge of all Egypt.

44 And Pharaoh said to Joseph, "I am the king, but no one will move a hand or a foot in the entire land of Egypt without your approval."

45 Pharaoh renamed him Zaphenath-paneah and gave him a wife—a young woman named Asenath, the daughter of Potiphera, priest of Heliopolis. So Joseph took charge of the entire land of Egypt.

41:50 During this time, before the arrival of the first of the famine years, two sons were born to Joseph and his wife, Asenath, the daughter of Potiphera, priest of Heliopolis.

KJV cont.

52 And the name of the second called he Ephraim: For God hath caused me to be fruitful in the land of my affliction.

NLT cont.

51 Joseph named his older son Manasseh, for he said, "God has made me forget all my troubles and the family of my father."

52 Joseph named his second son Ephraim, for he said, "God has made me fruitful in this land of my suffering."

The People, Places, and Times

Zaphenath-Paaneah. The name given to Joseph by Pharaoh when Joseph assumed his governmental responsibilities in Egypt (Genesis 41:45). The name most likely means "says the god, he will live."

Potipherah. Priest of On whose daughter, Asenath, was given to Joseph as his wife by Pharaoh (Genesis 41:45, 50). Potipherah is believed to be the high-ranking priest of a sun-god cult in On (or Heliopolis). His name, which means, "he whom Re [the sun god] has given," does not appear in Egyptian records until the tenth century B.C.

Background

While Joseph languishes in prison, Pharaoh of Egypt has two disturbing dreams. In the first dream, the setting is the Nile, Egypt's lifeline. The first dream depicts seven lean and fat cows that come out to the Nile and begin to graze. After that, seven hideous and scrawny cows appear and eat the fat ones. In the second dream, seven plump and choice ears of grain grow on one stalk; then seven ears of grain, skinny and parched by the hot desert wind, blossom on that stalk and consume the hearty grain. The dreams imitate each other, and Pharaoh is extremely troubled by these imaginings. The strange makeup of the dreams appears to point to a very gloomy future, a disturbance that Pharaoh cannot control or change. Pharaoh beckons experts to give meaning to the dreams, but none of them provide a suitable analysis.

Eventually, these events activate the cupbearer's memory. The cupbearer, a former inmate of Joseph, recalls how Joseph interpreted his and the baker's dreams with meticulousness and accuracy. Pharaoh wastes no time bringing Joseph out of the dungeon. Joseph is cleaned up, shaven, bathed, given fresh clothes, and brought to Phraoah. Joseph is pulled out of a dark, dingy dungeon to stand at the feet of a great ruler! Before Joseph interprets Pharaoh's dreams, he announces that it is not he that provides the interpretation but God. Pharaoh retells the dreams to Joseph with a slight variation and assumes the explanation will be negative. Joseph points out that the dreams contain both literal and figurative elements. The number seven symbolizes the number of years, the healthy cows and grain represent the years of plenty, and the unhealthy cows and grain represent the years of severe food shortage. Joseph's interpretation demonstrates that God speaks through chosen vessels (Joseph), and what is said should not be taken lightly.

Joseph does more than interpret Pharaoh's dreams. He gives Pharaoh instructions on what he should do to avoid catastrophic damage to the country. He urges Pharaoh to implement a plan to address these events. Phroah has to make a wise decision and select a man who is judicious and intelligent, someone who can strategically develop a plan of action that enables Egypt to tackle the food crisis in a way that brings the maximum possible safety to all. No doubt, shrewd administrators should also be selected for the job. However, Joseph is confident that God has prepared him for any responsibility that will unfold. Joseph proposes a plan that requires enough food (20 percent of the crop) each year to be stored during the years of prosperity in order to provide a reserve for the years of food crisis. The plan would be implemented by Joseph, yet would be under the authority of Pharaoh.

Little did Joseph know that his ability to interpret dreams would alter his life forever. Joseph, a man once sold into slavery and sentenced to prison, is now catapulted to Pharaoh's palace. Joseph, a man once overconfident in his own human frailties, now stands at the feet of an Egyptian Pharaoh. He is a man now humbled by life circumstances and is on the brink of becoming the second most powerful man in Egypt.

At-A-Glance

1. The Favor of God (Genesis 41:37–45)

2. The Fruitfulness of God (vv. 50–52)

In Depth

1. The Favor of God (Genesis 41:37–45)

Pharaoh concludes that Joseph's ability to interpret his dreams serves as evidence that the hand of God rested upon him. There is no way mere human understanding could accomplish this feat; only a divinely inspired revelation could provide such an analysis. Pharaoh decides to make Joseph the prime minister in charge of the palace and the country (v. 40). He is second in command

only to Pharaoh, with full range of authority (vv. 41, 43). No one has authority to rebel or lift a hand against Joseph. With such authority given to him, Joseph is marked as a wise and discerning man. Pharaoh's position is elevated as well, for it takes an astute leader to recognize wisdom in someone else (v. 44).

Verses 41 through 44 illustrate an act of installation. Joseph is promoted and formally given symbols that designate his new status. Pharaoh gives Joseph his signet ring, gold chain, and garments of royalty. These items signify his prominent new role. Joseph rides in a royal chariot throughout the city while the Egyptians cry out to him, bending their knees in honor of him and acknowledging his role as ruler of Egypt. Pharaoh renames Joseph and calls him Zaphenath-paaneah, which means "God speaks and lives." Pharaoh also gives Joseph a wife from a noble family. Joseph is now established as a man of great esteem, status, and success.

It is important to recognize that Joseph did not run after fame. He did not bribe his way to the top or manipulate his circumstances. He relied on God and remained obedient to the Lord. Even after experiencing hardship, Joseph endured and waited on the Lord. When it came time for him to stand before Pharaoh, Joseph performed honorably. He did not blame the cupbearer or anyone else for his time in prison. He spoke with confidence and wisdom. He won the heart and favor of Pharaoh, an Egyptian ruler, who neither knew nor served his God. We should see from this study that the Lord has the supernatural ability to work in the lives of those inside and outside the faith community. When we are faithful to our Lord, God can elevate us to positions where we have favor even with those who do not know Jesus. In the positions God calls us to serve, we have the ability to make enormous contributions that will impact our society for the good. In order for God to use us, however, we must commit to acting responsibly.

This story reminds us of how God works through a humbled heart. Joseph was pulled up from the lowest rungs to lead a people from the highest levels of authority. God worked through the lives of an Egyptian Pharaoh and Hebrew servant. Joseph had no idea that he would be crowned prime minister of Egypt. It is amazing what God can do through our lives when we commit to serving Him faithfully.

2. The Fruitfulness of God (vv. 50–52)

Thirty years old and 13 years after his enslavement, Joseph is carrying out the economic program in Egypt. The fruitfulness of the land mirrors Joseph and Asenath's life together. They have two sons, Ephraim and Manasseh. Joseph names them in recognition of God's involvement in his life: Manasseh, because God has enabled Joseph's slavery in Canaan and Egypt to be forgotten; and Ephraim, because God has brought Joseph prosperity in the very land in which he has experienced so much misfortune. These names reveal Joseph's life experience of seeing God's preserving and prospering activity in the midst of great personal hardship.

Search the Scriptures

1. What items did Pharaoh give Joseph to signify his new status in Egypt (Genesis 41:42)?

2. What names did Joseph give his children and why (vv. 51–52)?

Discuss the Meaning

Why do you think God allows us to endure trials, tribulation, and hardship prior to elevating us to positions of status and authority?

Lesson in Our Society

Some Christians want quick esteem and instant stardom. We have heard stories of risen and fallen stars, individuals who have plummeted from the height of their success because they lacked the ability to handle the pressure and responsibility. We have also heard stories where God's supposed "favor" has been used to manipulate others for deceitful gain. The church must teach that the favor of God involves commitment and faithfulness to Jesus, and compels superior performance and responsible moral and work ethics.

Make It Happen

Ask God to reveal to you where His favor reigns in your life. Pray and ask God if you are honoring Him with your actions in this area. Listen closely to what He says and commit to changing whatever He tells you to modify.

Follow the Spirit

What God wants me to do:

_____

_____

_____

_____

Remember Your Thoughts

Special insights I have learned:

_____

_____

_____

_____

More Light on the Text
Genesis 41:37–45, 50–52

37 And the thing was good in the eyes of Pharaoh, and in the eyes of all of his servants. 38 And Pharaoh said unto his servants, Can we find such a one as this is, a man in whom the Spirit of God is?

The Pharaoh of Egypt had two dreams that disturbed him for two reasons: (1) the dreams were strange; and (2) there was no one among his wise men to interpret either one. John MacArthur states that *oneiromancy*, the science of interpreting dreams, often flourished in the ancient Near East because dreams were thought to determine the future (*MacArthur Study Bible*, 74). In both Egypt and Babylon, professional dream interpreters were part of the false religious system that was prevalent in both nations. In the meantime, Joseph spent more than two years in prison for a crime that he did not commit. But once again, we see the providential hand of God that was with him. No one was able to interpret Pharaoh's dreams or clarify the visions—until Joseph was allowed access to Pharaoh.

While in prison, Joseph met two of Pharaoh's closest aides, the chief baker and the chief butler, who were also in prison. Each had a dream they did not understand, but God gave Joseph spiritual insight to communicate to both men. The butler's dream was that Pharaoh would restore him to a position of honor, while he would hang the chief baker (see Genesis 40).

Pharaoh's full counselors and advisors had no idea how to interpret his dreams. Suddenly, the chief cupbearer had an epiphany. He remembered, "A Hebrew youth was there with us, a servant of the chief steward; and when we told him our dreams, he interpreted them for us, telling each of the meaning. . . . And as he interpreted for us, so it came to pass: I was restored to my post" (Genesis 41:12–13, JSB). Pharaoh immediately called for Joseph to come out of prison, and he had his hair cut and clothing changed, to resemble an Egyptian, rather than a Hebrew. Egyptians were clean-shaven. Adele Berlin and Marc Brettler suggest that Joseph's clothes were "changed . . . as a sign of elevation to the next level of his faith journey with the Lord" (*Jewish Study Bible*, 81).

As he stood before the Pharaoh, the first admonition that Joseph gave him before sharing the dreams' interpretations was that the answer to Pharaoh's dreams was not "in [him]; God will give Pharaoh an answer of peace" (Genesis 41:16, NKJV). Pharaoh shared the dreams, and the basic interpretation involved a famine that would overtake Egypt for 14 years. Joseph not only enumerated the interpretation to Pharaoh, but also the means to survive it. Brettler and Berlin state that Joseph gave Pharaoh foresight and prudence to survive the catastrophe (*ibid.*).

MacArthur says that Joseph appended to the interpretation a long-term strategy for establishing reserved food to meet the needs of the people, and gave Pharaoh the qualifications of the person who could help them survive the famine (*MacArthur Study Bible*, 75). Coincidentally, famines had ravaged Egypt before, but this time a divine dream given to Pharaoh by God, and interpreted by Joseph, helped provide serious and sustained advanced planning in Egypt (see Genesis 41:16–36).

Pharaoh was given the strategic plan and vision that would save his land and people, and he was impressed with Joseph. In fact, Moses used the word "good" to affirm Pharaoh's appreciation (v. 37). The Hebrew word for "good" is *yatab* (**yaw-TAB**), and it means to be pleasing, cheerful, and glad. Bruce says that Pharaoh was immediately convinced, and readily perceived, that Joseph was the man to get the job done, and worked out the good plan that was given to him (50–52). MacArthur says the reason Pharaoh was impressed with Joseph was that the young Hebrew spoke God-given revelation and insight, with his focus on the Lord as the Conveyer of the dreams, and the One through whom the plan would be fulfilled (*MacArthur Study Bible*, 75). Pharaoh declared to his royal court that indeed Joseph must be the one because he had the "Spirit of God" (Genesis 41:38). Truly, Egyptian culture affirmed that they had no knowledge of the Holy Spirit, nor the work of the Third Person of the Trinity. Pharaoh only declared that God was in control of the plans.

39 And Pharaoh said unto Joseph, forasmuch as God hath showed thee all this, there is none so discreet and wise as thou art: 40 Thou shalt be over my house, and according unto thy word shall all my people be ruled; only in the throne will I be greater than thou. 41 And Pharaoh said unto Joseph, See, I have set thee over all the land of Egypt.

Once Joseph had interpreted the dreams and divine plans to Pharaoh, Pharaoh immediately honored the young man with favor. Pharaoh recognized that Joseph's wisdom and understanding came from God (v. 39). Therefore, he avowed that the young Hebrew would be rewarded handsomely for his discernment and wisdom.

The word "favor" comes from the Hebrew word *ratsown* (**raw-TSONE**) and the idea is pleasurable, delightful, to be pleased with, or be favorable toward something or someone. Joseph's was a unique "rags to riches" story. In a short period of his life, he went from the pit to the palace, from obscurity to influence, all because of the favor and blessings of God. We must keep in mind that we needn't try to selfishly promote ourselves. God is the

One who gives us favor with our superiors, relatives, and others. If we are faithful and committed to the Lord, He will bless us as well (see Psalm 75:6–7). The first area where Joseph would have tremendous influence would be in the house of Pharaoh. The word "house" carries the idea of palace or royal court. Just as he was influential over Potiphar's house (see Genesis 39:4), so, too, would Joseph reign over Pharaoh's palace (Genesis 41:40). In fact, Pharaoh declared that Joseph's reign and responsibility would be so vast that the only person with greater responsibility and power than Joseph would be Pharaoh himself. All of Pharaoh's people would submit to Joseph's authority and commands. Thus, Joseph becomes the prime minister of Egypt.

42 And Pharaoh took off his ring from his hand, and put it upon Joseph's hand, and arrayed him in vestures of fine linen, and put a gold chain about his neck; 43 And he made him to ride in the second chariot which he had; and they cried before him, Bow the knee: and he made him ruler over all the land of Egypt. 44 And Pharaoh said unto Joseph, I am Pharaoh, and without thee shall no man lift up his hand or foot in all the land of Egypt.

Pharaoh gave Joseph various symbols of authority that came along with his new responsibility. First, Pharaoh took off his own signet ring that indicated the royal seal of the kingdom. Joseph now had the right to transact all affairs of state on behalf of Pharaoh. Next, Pharaoh dressed Joseph in "vestures of fine linen" (v. 42). The word "vestures" is *beged* (**BEHG-ed**) in Hebrew and it means a wardrobe that is fit for royalty. Joseph looked the part of an Egyptian ruler as Pharaoh gave him some of the most expensive silk clothing in the land. Berlin and Brettler say this was Joseph's fifth and final change of clothing and acknowledged him as regal in the eyes of the people (*Jewish Study Bible*, 82). Third, Pharaoh put a gold chain around Joseph's neck as another symbol of royal power and authority. Finally, Joseph was given royal transportation in the "chariot of his second-in-command" (v. 43, JSB), the official chariot that affirmed, with Pharoah's blessing, he governed the whole kingdom. To complete Joseph's transformation from the young Hebrew in prison to the new Egyptian prime minister, the people cried out as he rode by, "Bow the knee" (v. 43). The Hebrew translation for this phrase *'abrek* (**ab-RAKE**), or as *John Gill's Exposition of the Bible* indicates, "tender father," suggests that the people would make way for him as the man in charge.

Pharaoh addressed the kingdom and made it known to all of his court and people that no one would be able to do anything in all of Egypt without first consulting with Joseph. In the same manner, Pharaoh also made it clear to Joseph that he was still accountable to him (v. 44).

Bruce suggests that the various symbols of office indicated in the story attest to the genuine Egyptian background of Joseph's story (50–52). Zodhiates says that Joseph's service in the house of Potiphar and his prison term were divinely ordained preparations that gave him the wisdom to direct the most populous nation in the ancient Near East (62–63). John MacArthur affirms that the dreams revealed by God, which manifested themselves in Joseph being established as a royal leader in Egypt, were proof that God would preserve His own people in the midst of the famine (*MacArthur Study Bible*, 75).

Joseph might never have imagined he would go from the prison to the palace and be recognized as one of the most powerful men in the world. But the favor of God was aptly bestowed upon him because he was faithful to the Lord, even while he languished in prison.

45 And Pharaoh called Joseph's name Zaphnath-paaneah; and he gave him to wife Asenath the daughter of Potipherah priest of On. And Joseph went out over all the land of Egypt. 50 And unto Joseph were born two sons before the years of the famine came, which Asenath the daughter of Potipherah priest of On bare unto him. 51 And Joseph called the name of the firstborn Manasseh: For God, said he, hath made me forget all my toil, and all my father's house. 52 And the name of the second called he Ephraim: for God hath caused me to be fruitful in the land of my affliction.

Pharaoh completed the transformation of his new prime minister. He altered his Hebrew name, from Joseph to Zaphnath-Paaneah. The Coptic language states that the name may mean "a revealer of secrets," or "a man in whom secrets are revealed." MacArthur states that Joseph's new name probably meant "the Nourisher of the Two Lands, the Living One," or "for God speaks, and He lives."

Then Pharaoh gave Joseph an Egyptian wife named Asenath. Her name meant "one who belongs to the goddess Neith." Moses affirms that she was the daughter of "Potiphera, a priest of On" (v. 45). The name Potiphera in Egyptian means "he whom Ra has given." Potiphera was probably a very important figure in an Egyptian cult. On was one of the four great Egyptian cities called Heliopolis and was the place where they worshiped the sun god Ra. The priests of On often engaged in widely varied commercial, political, and cultic responsibilities. Thus, Joseph was enveloped in Egyptian culture, but never lost his faith and commitment to Jehovah God.

Jewish tradition came to interpret Asenath as a prototype of Judaism conversion. Her powerful story is told at length in an important Hellenistic novella *Joseph and Asenath*. Joseph was now an "Egyptian" ruler and the prime minister of Pharaoh's entire kingdom. He settled in Egypt and began a family before the famine engulfed the land. He had two sons, born to Asenath. The first was named Manasseh (*Menashsheh*, **men-ash-SHEH**), and the English translation of the Hebrew means "cause to forget" or "forgetful." The second son was called *Ephraim,* and from the Hebrew, the English word would be "double fruit" or "fruitful." Joseph's experience was tragic, from the time he left his father's home, until his ascendancy to prime minister. From a human perspective, the young man did not want to remember all he endured. His son Manasseh would affirm that Joseph had "turned the corner" on his oppression and difficulties ("toil," v. 51), because he had put his trust in the Lord.

Consequently, his son Ephraim would always remind Joseph, that only through God's grace and favor, Joseph had been promoted in Egypt and received increase (was "fruitful") and influence as a result of his faithfulness to the Lord. Even in "the land of [his] affliction," Joseph recognized the centrality of God's compassion and grace. Separation from his father and all that he held dear had not diminished Joseph's perspective that he was still in the hands of God.

Sources:

Achtemeir, Paul J. et al., eds. *The Harper Collins Bible Dictionary.* San Francisco, CA: HarperCollins Publishers, 1996. 82, 544–45, 868.

Berlin, Adele, and Marc Brettler, eds. *The Jewish Study Bible.* New York, NY: Oxford University Press, 2004. 81–83.

Bruce, F. F. et al., eds. *Zondervan Bible Commentary.* Grand Rapids, MI: Zondervan Publishing, 2008. 50–52.

Elwell, Walter A., and Philip W. Comfort. *Tyndale Bible Dictionary.* Wheaton, IL: Tyndale House Publishers, 2001. 736–37.

"Genesis 41." *John Gill's Exposition of the Bible.* Bible Study Tools. com. http://www.biblestudytools.com/commentaries/gills-exposition-of-the-bible/genesis-41-43.html (accessed December 12, 2010).

MacArthur, John. *The MacArthur Study Bible.* Nashville, TN: Thomas Nelson Publishers, 1997. 74–76.

The New Interpreters Bible, Vol. I. Nashville, TN: Abingdon Press, 2002. 617–24.

The New Strong's Exhaustive Concordance of the Bible. Nashville, TN: Thomas Nelson Publishers, 1990.

Zodhiates, Spiros. *The Hebrew-Greek Key Word Study Bible, KJV.* Chattanooga, TN: AMG Publishers, 1991. 62–63.

Say It Correctly

Asenath. AS-uh-nath.
Ephraim. EE-fray-im.
Manasseh. Muh-NAS-uh.
Pharaoh. FAIR-oh.
Vestures. VES-chers.

Daily Bible Readings

MONDAY
Interpretations Belong to God
(Genesis 40:1–8)

TUESDAY
Restored to Office
(Genesis 40:9–15)

WEDNESDAY
The Predictions Come True
(Genesis 40:16–23)

THURSDAY
The Interpreter Remembered
(Genesis 41:1–13)

FRIDAY
Pharaoh's Dreams
(Genesis 41:14–24)

SATURDAY
The Dreams Interpreted
(Genesis 41:25–36)

SUNDAY
A Discerning and Wise Leader
(Genesis 41:37–45, 50–52)

Notes

_____

_____

_____

Teaching Tips

Words You Should Know

A. Earing (Genesis 45:6) *chariysh* (Heb.) —Plowing; plowing time.

B. Nourish (v. 11) *kuwl* (Heb.)—Feed, attend to, contain, sustain, endure.

Teacher Preparation

Unifying Principle—Sharing Blessings. Jacob and Joseph were both faithful to God, and God remained faithful to His promise to Abraham by putting Joseph in a position to save the entire family from starvation during the famine.

A. Pray for the students in your class, asking God to open their hearts to today's discussion and lesson.

B. Study and meditate on the entire text in *Precepts For Living*®.

C. Complete the companion lesson in the *Precepts For Living Personal Study Guide*®.

O—Open the Lesson

A. Open with prayer, including the Aim for Change.

B. After prayer, introduce today's subject of the lesson.

C. Have your students read the Aim for Change and Keep in Mind verse in unison. Discuss.

D. Ask, "Have you ever wondered why something negative happened to you?"

E. Allow volunteers to share their testimonies. Discuss.

F. Have a volunteer summarize the In Focus story. Discuss.

P—Present the Scriptures

A. Have volunteers read the Focal Verses aloud to the class.

B. Then use The People, Places, and Times; Background; Search the Scriptures; At-A-Glance outline; In Depth; and More Light on the Text to clarify the verses.

E—Explore the Meaning

A. Have volunteers summarize the Discuss the Meaning, Lesson in Our Society, and Make It Happen sections.

B. Connect these sections to the Aim for Change and the Keep in Mind verse.

N—Next Steps for Application

A. Summarize the lesson.

B. Close with prayer and praise God for the victory He's won in their lives and for who He is.

Worship Guide

For the Superintendent or Teacher
Theme: God Preserves a Remnant
Theme Song: "Victory Is Mine"
Devotional Reading: Psalm 81:1–10
Prayer

God Preserves a Remnant

Bible Background • GENESIS 42:1–38; 45:1–28
Printed Text • GENESIS 45:3–15 | Devotional Reading • PSALM 81:1–10

Aim for Change

By the end of the lesson, we will: KNOW the story of Joseph reuniting with his brothers; FEEL protected and supported by people in the Faith Community; and PROTECT and support other members of our Faith Community.

 In Focus

As a teenager, Joni Eareckson Tada loved life. She enjoyed riding horses and loved to swim. One summer in 1967, she was swimming with some friends; Joni dove into a lake not knowing how shallow it really was. She broke her neck, paralyzing her body from the neck down. Since then, Joni has written 14 books, has recorded several musical albums, and is an active advocate for disabled people.

JAN 15th

Then in January 1996, 9-year-old Amber Hagerman was riding her bicycle and a neighbor saw a man pull Amber off her bike, throw her into the front seat of his pickup truck, and drive away at a high speed. Four days later, Amber's body was found in a drainage ditch four miles away. A suggestion was made that Dallas radio stations should repeat news bulletins about abducted children just like they do for severe weather warnings. "The Dallas Amber Plan" was started in July 1997 to help safely recover missing children that police believe have been abducted. In 2001, the National Center for Missing and Exploited Children started a campaign to establish fully automated AMBER Alert systems nationwide.

In the above accounts, what Satan meant for evil, God worked for good. In today's lesson, God did the same for Joseph and his family.

Keep in Mind

"So now it was not you that sent me hither, but God: and he hath made me a father to Pharaoh, and lord of all his house, and a ruler throughout all the land of Egypt" (Genesis 45:8).

"So now it was not you that sent me hither, but God: and he hath made me a father to Pharaoh, and lord of all his house, and a ruler throughout all the land of Egypt" (Genesis 45:8).

Focal Verses

KJV **Genesis 45:3** And Joseph said unto his brethren, I am Joseph; doth my father yet live? And his brethren could not answer him; for they were troubled at his presence.

4 And Joseph said unto his brethren, Come near to me, I pray you. And they came near. And he said, I am Joseph your brother, whom ye sold into Egypt.

5 Now therefore be not grieved, nor angry with yourselves, that ye sold me hither: for God did send me before you to preserve life.

6 For these two years hath the famine been in the land: and yet there are five years, in the which there shall neither be earing nor harvest.

7 And God sent me before you to preserve you a posterity in the earth, and to save your lives by a great deliverance.

8 So now it was not you that sent me hither, but God: and he hath made me a father to Pharaoh, and lord of all his house, and a ruler throughout all the land of Egypt.

9 Haste ye, and go up to my father, and say unto him, Thus saith thy son Joseph, God hath made me lord of all Egypt: come down unto me, tarry not:

10 And thou shalt dwell in the land of Goshen, and thou shalt be near unto me, thou, and thy children, and thy children's children, and thy flocks, and thy herds, and all that thou hast:

11 And there will I nourish thee; for yet there are five years of famine; lest thou, and thy household, and all that thou hast, come to poverty.

12 And, behold, your eyes see, and the eyes of my brother Benjamin, that it is my mouth that speaketh unto you.

13 And ye shall tell my father of all my glory in Egypt, and of all that ye have seen;

NLT **Genesis 45:3** "I am Joseph!" he said to his brothers. "Is my father still alive?" But his brothers were speechless! They were stunned to realize that Joseph was standing there in front of them.

4 "Come over here," he said. So they came closer. And he said again, "I am Joseph, your brother whom you sold into Egypt.

5 But don't be angry with yourselves that you did this to me, for God did it. He sent me here ahead of you to preserve your lives.

6 These two years of famine will grow to seven, during which there will be neither plowing nor harvest.

7 God has sent me here to keep you and your families alive so that you will become a great nation.

8 Yes, it was God who sent me here, not you! And he has made me a counselor to Pharaoh—manager of his entire household and ruler over all Egypt.

9 "Hurry, return to my father and tell him, 'This is what your son Joseph says: God has made me master over all the land of Egypt. Come down to me right away!

10 You will live in the land of Goshen so you can be near me with all your children and grandchildren, your flocks and herds, and all that you have.

11 I will take care of you there, for there are still five years of famine ahead of us. Otherwise you and your household will come to utter poverty.'"

12 Then Joseph said, "You can see for yourselves, and so can my brother Benjamin, that I really am Joseph!

13 Tell my father how I am honored here in Egypt. Tell him about everything you have seen, and bring him to me quickly."

14 Weeping with joy, he embraced Benjamin, and Benjamin also began to weep.

KJV cont.

and ye shall haste and bring down my father hither.

14 And he fell upon his brother Benjamin's neck, and wept; and Benjamin wept upon his neck.

15 Moreover he kissed all his brethren, and wept upon them: and after that his brethren talked with him.

NLT cont.

15 Then Joseph kissed each of his brothers and wept over them, and then they began talking freely with him.

The People, Places, and Times

Goshen. This Semitic place name most likely refers to the delta region of Lower Egypt in the area of the Wadi Tumelat (from the eastern arm of the Nile River to the Great Bitter Lake). Egyptian texts from the Hyksos period refer to Semites in this region, and it is an area with excellent pasturage for herds. Also arguing in favor of its location in Egypt proper is the use of the phrase "in the district of Rameses" (Genesis 47:11, NIV). "So Joseph assigned the best land of Egypt—the region of Rameses—to his father and his brothers, just as Pharaoh had commanded" (Genesis 47:11, NLT).

Background

Joseph was a man who honored God, in every situation he found himself; whether it was suffering or success, he honored the one true and living God. Potiphar's wife tried to tempt him, but because Joseph wanted to honor his Master, he would not yield (Genesis 39:9). Although God had given him the ability to interpret dreams, Joseph always gave God the credit for being able to do so (Genesis 40:8). Even when he was before Pharaoh, he honored God, his Maker. Joseph boldly told Pharaoh there would be a specific number of years of plenty and famine would surely follow (Genesis 41:14–36). When

Joseph named his own son, Manasseh (which means "to forget"), he was stating that God helped him to forget his sorrow. In today's lesson, Joseph told his brothers who he was and acknowledged that God was responsible for him being in Egypt. After Jacob died, Joseph reassured his brothers that God had ordered his steps, and He did it for the good of all. He further assured them they should not be afraid of him because he was not God (Genesis 50:15–21).

At-A-Glance

1. Joseph Makes Himself Known
(Genesis 45:3–8)

2. A Family Reunited (vv. 9–15)

In Depth

1. Joseph Makes Himself Known (Genesis 45:3–8)

In today's lesson, after having held back his emotions as best he could for quite a while, Joseph told his brothers who he really was: "I am Joseph" (v. 3). His brothers did not know him as Joseph. They knew him by his Egyptian name, Zaphnath-paaneah. His Hebrew name had been lost and seemingly forgotten in Egypt. Now he boldly states, "I

238

am Joseph." So they wouldn't be confused about who he really was, he gave them more details: "I am Joseph, your brother" (v. 4). In knowing exactly who he was, this would likely humble them as they remembered what they had done. In addition, they might also be hopeful that Joseph might be compassionate toward them.

But now that they knew who Joseph really was, they were afraid and stood in disbelief or amazement, unable to move or speak. Joseph saw their concern and tried to ease their minds. He called out to them, beckoning them closer and assuring them that they didn't have reason to fear. This was reflective of Christ when He manifests Himself. He urges His people to come near to Him as He draws near to them.

A shift was under way in Joseph's character development. At first, when he no longer held back his identity, he was quite emotional. Then he spoke quietly to his brothers and became calm in his demeanor as he offered more details about himself and the depth of his true nature.

Joseph began to assure them of God's sovereignty. He understood and wanted them to understand that whatever they tried to do for evil, God meant it for good and a lot of good came out of it. He did not want them to grieve or be angry with themselves for selling him (v. 5). Instead of having a vindictive attitude toward them, he was giving recognition to who God is, what God had done, and what He was going to do. God had a perfect plan in mind and was about to use the brothers' sinful acts to preserve a remnant of His chosen people.

In verses 7 and 8, Joseph's statements weren't meant to make light of sin or sinners, but rather to illuminate how God does things. This was not to give an excuse for sinning, but rather to appreciate and celebrate the almighty power of God in those things we could refer to as "misfortune." God is in divine control.

Joseph further explained how long the famine would last, reflecting that it had already been occurring for the past two years. He reassured them that he was in a position to help his family in their dire circumstances. He emphasized that they weren't the ones who sent him ahead to Egypt, but an all-knowing God had done this (v. 8). God not only sent Joseph, but God made him "a father" to Pharaoh, "lord of all his house, and a ruler throughout all the land of Egypt" (v. 8).

2. A Family Reunited (vv. 9–15)

Again, in an effort to make his brothers feel more confident and secure, Joseph promised to take care of his father and all his family during the next years of the famine. He urged his brothers to hurry back to Canaan (the Promised Land) to get this news to their father Jacob and let him know about Joseph's authority in Egypt. Joseph was well and had enough power to help them all. "I will nourish thee," promised Joseph (v. 11). He was delighted to be in the position to help his father and his family. He was excited for his father to know where God had placed him, and he was eager to relieve his father of the stress of the famine.

Benjamin, one of Joseph's brothers, was approximately 1-year-old when Joseph was separated from his family and was too young to have had any involvement in the other brothers' maltreatment—too young, as well, to have known Joseph before he was sent away. But Joseph remembered him, and he hugged Benjamin. They began to weep on each other's neck (v. 14). Then Joseph hugged and wept with all of them, and everyone "talked freely" (v. 15). Joseph's words and actions made his brothers realize that he was not holding a grudge and was genuinely affectionate toward them. Knowing what God had done for all of them and would do in the future, Joseph was compassionate toward the brothers who had hurt him so much. He did not let past experiences with his brothers defeat the purpose of all that the Lord allowed him to go through. Instead, Joseph was warm toward them, and they were able to reciprocate these feelings.

Search the Scriptures

1. When Joseph announced himself to his brothers, and asked if his father was alive, why couldn't his brothers answer him (Genesis 45:3)?

2. Why did God send Joseph to Egypt ahead of his brothers (v. 5)?

Discuss the Meaning

Consider this: Satan's plan was to use Pontius Pilate, Judas Iscariot, the mob in the streets, and the cruel Roman soldiers to end the plan God had for Jesus Christ. How did these men's actions actually fulfill God's divine plan of salvation for humankind through His only Son, Jesus Christ? Compare and contrast this example from the New Testament with the actions of Joseph's brothers, before and after they encountered him in Egypt.

Lesson in Our Society

Tragedy is happening all around us and the first question is, why? In recent years, Chicago's public schools have suffered the loss of too many students due to gang and gun violence. God is speaking through these circumstances to show people who He is. It may appear as though the enemy is having

his way, but we can be assured that God's plan is being fulfilled for His perfect purpose.

Make It Happen

Living in our world can prove to be disappointing at times. When we come to church, we should expect to be treated differently. Joseph's brothers didn't know what to expect after finding out who Joseph was, the position he held, and remembering what they had done to him. Joseph relieved them of their worries by embracing them and being very kind. As we interact with our brothers and sisters in Christ, let us try to adopt Joseph's attitude toward others, especially family members. Let us remember to be kind and warm to others always.

Follow the Spirit

What God wants me to do:

_____

_____

_____

_____

Remember Your Thoughts

Special insights I have learned:

_____

_____

_____

_____

More Light on the Text
Genesis 45:3–15
Introduction

True to God's word, Egypt knew seven good years of prosperity and plenty (Genesis 41:46ff), just as Joseph had said when he interpreted Pharaoh's dreams. As the good years ended and the seven years of famine began, all of the lands around Egypt experienced the famine, but initially Egypt did not. When the people began to feel the effects of the famine, they pleaded with the Pharaoh to feed them. He directed them to do whatever Joseph instructed (vv. 53–57). Among the persons seeking food from the storehouses under Joseph's rule were 10 of his brothers (Genesis 42:1ff). He recognized them, but they did not recognize him. More humble in his position now, Joseph showed his brothers favor without revealing his identity and lavishly provided for his family. Each time the brothers returned to restock grain, they were laden with gifts from an anonymous donor (Genesis 43:1–44:34).

3 And Joseph said unto his brethren, I am Joseph; doth my father yet live? And his brethren could not answer him; for they were troubled at his presence.

Revealing who he was, Joseph immediately inquired of his father's condition and whether he was still alive. Even though the brothers had told him earlier that his father was indeed alive, they had said this when they knew Joseph as an Egyptian official (Genesis 44:20). Perhaps Joseph was asking this of them again with a son's emphatic love and longing for his father. Whatever his reasons, at first Joseph's brothers could not "answer" (Heb. `anah, **aw-NAH**), meaning "respond, speak" to him because they were "troubled" (Heb. bahal, **baw-HAL**), meaning "disturbed, alarmed, terrified"—most likely they were shocked by Joseph's "presence" (Heb. paniym, **paw-NEEM**), meaning "face" and position. They surely remembered the occasion years ago when they had hated Joseph so and had conspired to kill him.

4 And Joseph said unto his brethren, Come near to me, I pray you. And they came near. And he said, I am Joseph your brother, whom ye sold into Egypt.

But Joseph, overjoyed to see them, called out to them, "Come near" (Heb. nagash, **naw-GASH**), meaning "approach" him to get a closer look at the brother they had indeed "sold" (Heb. makar, **maw-KAR**) to the Midianites when he was only a teenager. The phrase "whom ye sold into Egypt" was not meant to remind them of their foolish indiscretion and diabolical plot, but rather to impress upon them the truth of his identity.

5 Now therefore be not grieved, nor angry with yourselves, that ye sold me hither: for God did send me before you to preserve life.

In a gracious turn of events, the same Joseph who had been left to die and eventually sold into slavery encouraged his brothers not to be "grieved" (Heb. `atsab, **aw-TSAB**), meaning "hurt, vexed" by his revelation and not to be "angry" (Heb. charah, **khaw-RAH**), meaning "kindled, incensed" against themselves for past actions. Joseph assured the brothers that God had used those very events to send him ahead of them to Egypt "to preserve life" (Heb. michyah, **mikh-YAH**), meaning "provide sustenance" for them now that a famine was upon the region. Although his brothers' actions had not been a dream, Joseph the dreamer was using his interpretive skill to present God's redemptive plan for Israel!

6 For these two years hath the famine been in the land: and yet there are five years, in the which there shall neither be earing nor harvest. 7 And God sent me before you to preserve you a posterity in the earth, and to save your lives by a great deliverance.

For the first two years of the famine, Joseph had kept his identity a secret. He now told his brothers that the ensuing five years would produce no "earing" (Heb. *chariysh*, **khaw-REESH**), meaning no "plowing time" and no harvest, assuring them that God, not their angry jealousy, had placed him in position for a "posterity" (Heb. *she'eriyth*, **sheh-ay-REETH**), meaning "remainder, remnant," or portion, during the seven good years. Because Joseph had been established as overseer, their lives were going to be preserved as an act of great deliverance from an all-consuming famine then upon the land and most likely the result of a severe drought.

8 So now it was not you that sent me hither, but God: and he hath made me a father to Pharaoh, and lord of all his house, and a ruler throughout all the land of Egypt.

Joseph assured his brothers of God's providential hand in the situation. God had established him as "a father" (another title for a viceroy or official spiritual advisor), a "lord" (Heb. *'adown*, **aw-DONE**), meaning "firm, strong, master" over Pharaoh's immediate household, and "ruler" (Heb. *mashal*, **maw-SHAL**), meaning "someone with dominion" over all inhabitants of the land during the famine.

9 Haste ye, and go up to my father, and say unto him, Thus saith thy son Joseph, God hath made me lord of all Egypt: come down unto me, tarry not: 10 And thou shalt dwell in the land of Goshen, and thou shalt be near unto me, thou, and thy children, and thy
children's children, and thy flocks, and thy herds, and all that thou hast:

Joseph then charged his brothers to hasten and return to their father with the good news of his life, appointment, and favor. Joseph sent his brothers away with a message of hope and celebration. He invited his brothers and father to come and dwell in the land of Goshen (**GO-shen**), a Hebrew word for a place whose name means "drawing near," a region in northern Egypt east of the lower Nile, where they could be near him and enjoy all the rights, privileges, and protection suitable to his kin. (The Children of Israel lived there from the time of Joseph to the time of Moses.) Joseph's invitation extended to his brothers' "children" (Heb. *ben*, **bane**), meaning "son, grandson, child, member of a group"; their "flocks" (Heb. *tso'n*, **tsone**), meaning "small cattle and flocks"; and also to their "herds" (Heb. *baqar*, **baw-KAWR**) meaning "large cattle and oxen."

11 And there will I nourish thee; for yet there are five years of famine; lest thou, and thy household, and all that thou hast, come to poverty.

It would be while they were in Goshen—or more importantly, in this region near Joseph—that he would directly "nourish" (Heb. *kuwl*, **kool**), meaning "sustain, maintain, contain" all of his brothers' and father's households, and thereby prevent them from being overcome by "poverty" (Heb. *yarash*, **yaw-RASH,** meaning "impoverished, disinherited").

12 And, behold, your eyes see, and the eyes of my brother Benjamin, that it is my mouth that speaketh unto you.

Perhaps because the encounter was truly incredible, Joseph appealed to his brothers to verify his identity, especially Benjamin. He and Benjamin barely knew each other, but Joseph knew that Benjamin was his only full brother and he had seen that his brothers were treating Benjamin very similarly to the way they had treated him (Genesis 44:3–5, 12, 30–33). Joseph urgently needed his brothers to understand that it was he, Joseph, who "speaketh" to them (Heb. *dabar*, **daw-BAR**), meaning "declared, promised, warned." He knew them, had been aware of what they were doing all along, and still cared about them.

13 And ye shall tell my father of all my glory in Egypt, and of all that ye have seen; and ye shall haste and bring down my father hither. 14 And he fell upon his brother Benjamin's neck, and wept; and Benjamin wept upon his neck. 15 Moreover he kissed all his brethren, and wept upon them: and after that his brethren talked with him.

What concerned Joseph at this point was his father, Jacob. Joseph entreated his brothers to inform their father that he (Joseph) was doing quite well in Egypt—he was highly esteemed. In order to get Jacob to come quickly, Joseph insisted that his brothers tell Jacob of all of Joseph's "glory" (Heb. *kabowd*, **kaw-BODE**), which means "abundance, riches, splendor." In other words, in a midst of a famine, God had seen to it that Joseph (Jacob's 11th son) was flourishing. God had made the impossible, possible.

Then Joseph could no longer contain himself. He had experienced several encounters in Egypt with his brothers not knowing who they were dealing with while Joseph had known precisely who they were (Genesis 42–44). He had chosen to reveal the truth of his identity, and then he had graciously offered his forgiveness and his help. He wept with joy and embraced Benjamin. Joseph did not let his honored position hinder his pure tears of joy and his expectations upon seeing his family again—a family that he probably thought that he would never see again. This was a heart-wrenching moment. Not only did Joseph weep over his baby brother, but he wept over the brothers who had sold him into slavery and had plotted to kill him. When these brothers saw Joseph's genuine, forgiving spirit—that he was not going to take revenge against them—their guard came down and they began to freely talk to him. Joseph sent his brothers back to Canaan for their father and the whole family so that they could live in Egypt and survive the famine. What Satan had meant for evil, God indeed worked for good. God used Joseph's personal suffering to bless Joseph's family for generations to come. It was a time of healing and restoration that only a loving and merciful God could bring to what had been an extremely dysfunctional family.

Sources:

"AMBER Alert: Frequently Asked Questions." U.S. Department of Justice, Office of Justice Programs. http://www.amberalert. gov/faqs.htm (accessed December 2, 2010).

Henry, Matthew. "Commentary on Genesis 45." Blue Letter Bible. org. http://www.blueletterbible.org/commentaries/Henry/ (accessed December 11, 2010).

Joni Eareckson Tada Story. http://joniearecksontadastory. com/joni-story-page-1/ (accessed August 28, 2010).

Life Application Study Bible (New Living Translation). Wheaton, IL: Tyndale House, 1996. 81–82.

Merriam-Webster Online Dictionary. Merriam-Webster, Inc. http:// www.merriam-webster.com (accessed August 13, 2010).

The Origin of the Amber Plan. Mid Ohio AMBER Alert.org. http://www.midohioamberalert.org/origin_Amber. htm (accessed August 28, 2010).

Youngblood, Ronald F., ed. *Nelson's New Illustrated Bible Dictionary.* Nashville, TN: Thomas Nelson, 1995. 704–05.

Say It Correctly

Canaan. KAY-nuhn.
Genesis. JEN-uh-sis.
Midianites. MID-ee-uh-nites.
Pharaoh. FAIR-oh.

Daily Bible Readings

MONDAY
A Famine in Canaan
(Genesis 42:1–5)

TUESDAY
Joseph Recognized His Brothers
(Genesis 42:6–17)

WEDNESDAY
Paying the Penalty
(Genesis 42:18–25)

THURSDAY
Hold Me Accountable
(Genesis 43:1–14)

FRIDAY
Benjamin Detained in Egypt
(Genesis 44:1–13)

SATURDAY
A Father's Suffering
(Genesis 44:24–34)

SUNDAY
A Brother Revealed
(Genesis 45:3–15)

Notes

Teaching Tips

Words You Should Know

A. Requite (Genesis 50:15) *shuwb* (Heb.)—Return again, turn back, turn away, restore.

B. Sent (v. 16) *tsavah* (**tsaw-VAW**) (Heb.)—Charged or commanded by another with a verbal communication.

Teacher Preparation

Unifying Principle—The Power of Forgiveness. Even though some people commit acts of faithlessness, they may be overcome by acts of others' faithfulness. Because Jacob and Joseph were both faithful to God, Joseph was able to forgive his brothers' treachery from so many years before.

A. Pray for your students.

B. Read and meditate on the entire lesson for today.

C. Reread the Focal Verses in two or more translations (NLT, ESV, NIV, etc.).

D. Complete the companion lesson in the *Precepts For Living Personal Study Guide®*.

O—Open the Lesson

A. Open with prayer, including the Aim for Change.

B. After prayer, have a volunteer read the In Focus story.

C. Then tie in the In Focus story with the Aim for Change and Keep in Mind verse.

D. Allow volunteers to share their testimonies with the class.

P—Present the Scriptures

A. Have volunteers read the Focal Verses.

B. Now use The People, Places, and Times; Background; Search the Scriptures; At-A-Glance outline; In Depth; and More Light on the Text to clarify the verses.

E—Explore the Meaning

A. Have volunteers summarize the Discuss the Meaning, Lesson in Our Society, and Make It Happen sections.

B. Connect these sections to the Aim for Change and the Keep in Mind verse.

N—Next Steps for Application

A. Summarize the lesson.

B. Close with prayer.

Worship Guide

For the Superintendent or Teacher
Theme: Joseph
Transmits Abraham's Promise
Theme Song: "We've Come
This Far by Faith"
Devotional Reading:
Deuteronomy 7:6–11
Prayer

Joseph Transmits Abraham's Promise

Bible Background • GENESIS 50:1–26
Printed Text • GENESIS 50:15–26 | Devotional Reading • DEUTERONOMY 7:6–11

Aim for Change

By the end of the lesson, we will: KNOW how Joseph forgave his brothers; FEEL thankful for forgiveness; and FORGIVE those who need to be forgiven in our lives.

In Focus

James Earl Potts walked from the corner store. Several years before, there had been a disturbance in the neighborhood, so the police circled the area looking for the man who fit the description of the criminal. James Earl had been with his family all day until he decided to go for his evening stroll to the store. His mother, Miss Allie B, became concerned because of the length of time he had been gone. So she sent his brothers to look for him. They found him sitting in the back of a police car because he had been arrested.

An elderly man was sure James Earl committed the crime, so he testified in court. He was convicted and sent to prison for 15 years. While in prison, he witnessed to other men about Jesus. DNA results later proved another man was guilty, and James Earl was released and returned to his family.

James Earl remained faithful to God while in prison by leading others to Christ, and God remained faithful to him. As he headed home a free man, he recalled how Jesus demonstrated forgiveness on the Cross, and therefore James Earl could implement forgiveness on earth.

Today's In Focus story and lesson help to remind us of God's faithfulness and how we should hold on to our faith, just as we see here in James Earl and in Joseph's life.

Keep in Mind

"But as for you, ye thought evil against me; but God meant it unto good, to bring to pass, as it is this day, to save much people alive" (Genesis 50:20).

"But as for you, ye thought evil against me; but God meant it unto good, to bring to pass, as it is this day, to save much people alive" (Genesis 50:20).

Focal Verses

KJV **Genesis 50:15** And when Joseph's brethren saw that their father was dead, they said, Joseph will peradventure hate us, and will certainly requite us all the evil which we did unto him.

16 And they sent a messenger unto Joseph, saying, Thy father did command before he died, saying,

17 So shall ye say unto Joseph, Forgive, I pray thee now, the trespass of thy brethren, and their sin; for they did unto thee evil: and now, we pray thee, forgive the trespass of the servants of the God of thy father. And Joseph wept when they spake unto him.

18 And his brethren also went and fell down before his face; and they said, Behold, we be thy servants.

19 And Joseph said unto them, Fear not: for am I in the place of God?

20 But as for you, ye thought evil against me; but God meant it unto good, to bring to pass, as it is this day, to save much people alive.

21 Now therefore fear ye not: I will nourish you, and your little ones. And he comforted them, and spake kindly unto them.

22 And Joseph dwelt in Egypt, he, and his father's house: and Joseph lived an hundred and ten years.

23 And Joseph saw Ephraim's children of the third generation: the children also of Machir the son of Manasseh were brought up upon Joseph's knees.

24 And Joseph said unto his brethren, I die: and God will surely visit you, and bring you out of this land unto the land which he sware to Abraham, to Isaac, and to Jacob.

25 And Joseph took an oath of the children of Israel, saying, God will surely visit you, and ye shall carry up my bones from hence.

26 So Joseph died, being an hundred and ten years old: and they embalmed him, and he was put in a coffin in Egypt.

NLT **Genesis 50:15** But now that their father was dead, Joseph's brothers became afraid. "Now Joseph will pay us back for all the evil we did to him," they said.

16 So they sent this message to Joseph: "Before your father died, he instructed us

17 to say to you: 'Forgive your brothers for the great evil they did to you.' So we, the servants of the God of your father, beg you to forgive us." When Joseph received the message, he broke down and wept.

18 Then his brothers came and bowed low before him. "We are your slaves," they said.

19 But Joseph told them, "Don't be afraid of me. Am I God, to judge and punish you?

20 As far as I am concerned, God turned into good what you meant for evil. He brought me to the high position I have today so I could save the lives of many people.

21 No, don't be afraid. Indeed, I myself will take care of you and your families." And he spoke very kindly to them, reassuring them.

22 So Joseph and his brothers and their families continued to live in Egypt. Joseph was 110 years old when he died.

23 He lived to see three generations of descendants of his son Ephraim and the children of Manasseh's son Makir, who were treated as if they were his own.

24 "Soon I will die," Joseph told his brothers, "but God will surely come for you, to lead you out of this land of Egypt. He will bring you back to the land he vowed to give to the descendants of Abraham, Isaac, and Jacob."

25 Then Joseph made the sons of Israel swear an oath, and he said, "When God comes to lead you back to Canaan, you must take my body back with you."

26 So Joseph died at the age of 110. They embalmed him, and his body was placed in a coffin in Egypt.

The People, Places, and Times

Canaan. God had strategically located His people in this land so that all the major powers—Egypt, Assyria, and Babylon—had to come in contact with Abraham's seed in order to transact any type of business or interact with others. Somewhat arid, Canaan was dependent on God sending the rain to survive. God was faithful to His people in this place.

Abraham. He was the father of a multitude, son of Terah, and named before his older brothers Nahor and Haran because he was the heir of the promises (Genesis 11:27). Until the age of 70, Abram sojourned among his kindred in his native country of Chaldea. He then, with his father and his family and household, left the city of Ur and went some 300 miles north to Haran, where he stayed 15 years. The cause of his migration was a call from God (Acts 7:2–4). There is no mention of this first call in the Old Testament; it is implied, however, in Genesis 12. While they were at Haran, Terah died at the age of 205. Abram then received a second and more definite call, accompanied by a promise from God (Genesis 12:1–2). It was then that he departed, taking his nephew Lot with him, "not knowing whither he went" (Hebrews 11:8). He trusted God. At the time of his migration to Canaan, Abram had a large household of probably a thousand people.

Background

The Lord calls Abraham out of Ur (Genesis 12:1–3) and makes promises to him. Included in those promises was that Abraham's seed would be a stranger in a land that wasn't theirs (Genesis 15:13). After being afflicted for many years, Joseph earns a reputation of being one who could interpret dreams. One day, the Pharaoh of Egypt has a dream that no one can interpret; Joseph is called on to interpret Pharaoh's dream. Afterward, Pharaoh implemented Joseph's recommendation that he find a discreet, wise overseer of Egypt and selected Joseph for the role (Genesis 41:25–57). As foretold, a severe famine came throughout the region. However, because God had prepared Egypt through Joseph, all countries came there to buy corn as supervised by Joseph (v. 57). Jacob's sons—Joseph's brothers—were impacted by the famine and came to Egypt to have their needs met. Joseph recognized his brothers, although they did not recognize him, and he used this as an opportunity to demonstrate forgiveness.

At-A-Glance

1. Joseph Reassures His Brothers
(Genesis 50:15–21)

2. The Death of Joseph (vv. 22–26)

In Depth

1. Joseph Reassures His Brothers (Genesis 50:15–21)

Now Jacob, father of Joseph and his brothers, was dead. Joseph's brothers were feeling guilty for what they had done to him. They worried that Joseph may have felt a surge of bad memories about his youth, and they became suspicious that he would seek revenge on them. But Joseph's actions did not exemplify this at all. He was sincere in his motives and showed them nothing less. Still, his brothers were sure Joseph would hate them for what they had done.

In response to their fears, these brothers humbled themselves, confessed their wrongdoing, and begged Joseph to forgive them. At first, they sent a message to Joseph and then they went in person, stressing that Jacob told them to ask Joseph to forgive his brothers. Joseph reassured them he indeed forgave them because of what God had done in him. He knew that, despite the trauma of his youth, God remained faithful to him and that whatever situation he found himself in, God always brought him out.

The brothers even went so far as to say they would be his servants (his "slaves," v. 18, NLT). They were really trying to mend the relationship. Joseph felt sad and began to weep. This moment was bittersweet. He was sad because they still felt the need to suspect his motives even after a lengthy period of his support of them in Egypt, and he was moved because he saw their efforts at submission.

Joseph assured them there was no need to be afraid. He also asked, "Am I God, to judge and punish you?" (v. 19, NLT), which focused their attention on the true, ultimate source of forgiveness of sin. Joseph reminded his brothers that they were intending to do evil against him, but God used their cruelty to bring about good to people who were not even full-blood relations. By comforting them, he demonstrated there was no need to be afraid. Joseph's attitude helped them to release their fears.

2. The Death of Joseph (vv. 22–26)

Joseph lived to be 110 years old. He had honored his father and was given many days on this earth. Joseph was given the privilege of seeing his great-grandchildren from both his sons. This was indeed a blessing within itself. God blessed Joseph for his faithfulness.

Joseph knew his death was approaching and there were some things he wanted those who were still living to know. He had his brothers make a promise to him. First, he assured them that even though he was about to die, they would still return to Canaan in due time. These words were intended to

give them hope and assurance. Joseph had already done a great deal for them and now he was dying. Undoubtedly, their thoughts turned to questions of what would become of them after Joseph, who had nourished them and taken good care of them, was gone. Joseph probably sensed their apprehension and tried to offer them comfort.

He went on to say, "God will surely visit you" (v. 24). Joseph was passing on, but God's care of them would make up for his absence. Although Joseph had been taking care of them, now they could see that it had been God's doing all along. Through Joseph, God provided comfort for them, and they would continue to live comfortably. Joseph further encouraged them, letting them know that God would bring them back to the land of Abraham, Isaac, and Jacob.

Joseph made them promise to bury him in Canaan instead of Egypt where he would die. They honored his request. He was put in a coffin in Egypt, but he wasn't buried until his children had received their inheritance in Canaan.

Search the Scriptures

1. Who had intended to harm Joseph (Genesis 50:15)?

2. Who had a temporary burial in Egypt (v. 26)?

Discuss the Meaning

Faith and forgiveness work together. The same faith to live our lives also gives us the strength to forgive. Joseph had faith in God about the promise. He had faith in the promise God had given to Abraham and was able to forgive his brothers because he knew they would see the Promised Land. Abraham believed God, and Joseph believed God as demonstrated by the request to have his body buried in the land God had promised his great-grandfather, Abraham.

Lesson in Our Society

Our nation is in a state of emergency—the economy is declining rapidly. People are struggling with the aftermath of losing their jobs, homes, families, and the security they once felt they had. The hopes of retirement funds, savings accounts, and any type of financial security are vanishing right before our eyes. These are examples of wind, rain, and the flood in our present-day life. We must hold on to our faith that God has given us. God will remain faithful to us and make good on the promises He has made to us.

Make It Happen

"Therefore everyone who hears these words of Mine and acts on them, may be compared to a wise man who built his house on the rock. And the rain fell, and the floods came, and when winds blew and slammed against that house; and yet it did not fall, for it had been founded on the rock. Everyone who hears these words of Mine and does not act on them, will be like a foolish man who built his house on the sand. The rain fell, and the floods came, and the winds blew and slammed against that house; and it fell, and great was its fall" (Matthew 7:24–27, NASB). Build your house upon the Rock: Jesus.

Joseph's faith in God allowed him to endure the trials he went through. God remained faithful to Joseph and he did not fall. His example encourages us to continue to hold on to our faith because God will remain faithful to us. In addition, we must make sure we adhere to our responsibility to minister to those who are not building on solid foundations and encourage those who are building.

Follow the Spirit

What God wants me to do:

_____

_____

_____

_____

Remember Your Thoughts

Special insights I have learned:

_____

_____

_____

_____

More Light on the Text

Genesis 50:15–26

15 And when Joseph's brethren saw that their father was dead they said, Joseph will peradventure hate us, and will certainly requite us all the evil which we did unto him.

Israel's patriarch Jacob lived 147 years, 17 of them in the land of Goshen (Genesis 47:27–28), a fertile region in the eastern delta of the Nile River in Egypt. It is here that Jacob and his family settled once they came into the land. He was finally able to spend the remainder of his life with Joseph, his favorite son (Genesis 37:3). Before Jacob died, he blessed all of his sons, emphasizing the promise and provision that would follow God's people throughout their history (Genesis 49:28).

Joseph, his 11 brothers, and a large entourage of Egyptians ("the senior members of Pharaoh's court, and all of Egypt's dignitaries," Genesis 50:7, JSB), traveled to Canaan to bury Jacob in the cave of Machpelah, the same burial site of Abraham, Sarah, Isaac, Rebekah, and Leah. When the family returned to Egypt, the realization of Jacob's death finally set in with the brothers (Genesis 49:30). What would their relationship with Joseph be now that Jacob's powerful influence was gone? Would Joseph finally exact revenge on them for the way they had treated him?

Joseph was an important figure in Egypt, and he had already demonstrated his authority over his brothers (see Genesis 42–45:3). Now that Jacob was gone, the brothers surmised that Joseph would not only hate them, but he would also "requite [us] all the evil" they had done to him (Genesis 50:15). The Hebrew word for "requite" is *shuwb* (**shoob**), and the idea is to turn back, restore, or give back to another. To a large extent, the brothers were saying, "Joseph is going to treat us as we have treated him."

Bruce suggests that one of the reasons why the brothers may have been fearful and intimidated by Joseph was the long memory for vengeance that was often prevalent in the Ancient Near East (Genesis 27:41). Certainly, an Old Testament concept of "an eye for an eye, and a tooth for a tooth" (Exodus 21:24; Leviticus 24:19–20; Deuteronomy 19:21) teaches that revenge is appropriate and just, especially in civil matters. But Jesus came to teach us a higher law called love. We may feel that our cause is just and right in retaliating against another, but does that satisfy the purposes and plans of Christ?

16 And they sent a messenger unto Joseph, saying, Thy father did command before he died, saying, 17 So shall ye say unto Joseph, Forgive, I pray thee now, the trespass of thy brethren, and their sin; for they did unto thee evil: and now, we pray thee, forgive the trespass of the servants of the God of thy father. And Joseph wept when they spake unto him.

Joseph's brothers demonstrated their true character. They lied and essentially "forged" their dead father's words to try to appease Joseph: "Forgive, I pray thee now, the trespass of thy brethren, and their sin" (Genesis 50:17). The problem with this picture is that there is no record where Jacob requested forgiveness for his sons. After all, wouldn't he have appealed to Joseph directly to forgive his brothers if this was truly Jacob's concern? Secondly, the Talmud suggests that it is permissible for a person to modify a statement in the interest of peace. It would appear that the brothers chose the latter strategy. They lied because they felt it would appeal to Joseph's character, and as Joseph was still mourning the death of Jacob, the last thing he would consider was revenge against his own brothers.

Third, the Scripture says that the brothers "sent a messenger" on their behalf to speak with Joseph (v. 16). The Hebrew word for "sent" is *tsavah* (**tsaw-VAW**), and the idea is that they charged or commanded another with a verbal communication. Perhaps the brothers found a low-level courier from Joseph's household who would share the supposed "words of Jacob" and thus, play on his emotions. The text says that Joseph wept after he had received the message; in *New Jerome Biblical Commentary*, Roland Murphy suggests that Joseph's tears were those of exasperation (42–43). Despite Joseph's concerns and care for their entire family during their stay in Egypt, his brothers still did not understand him. Joseph was no longer the little lad who had been thrown into the pit in Dothan (Genesis 37:17–24). He was now the progenitor of Israel. Would the 11 brothers ever learn?

18 And his brethren also went and fell down before his face; and they said, Behold, we be thy servants. 19 And Joseph said unto them, Fear not: for am I in the place of God?

After their return to Egypt, Joseph's brothers finally mustered enough courage to face him. Without a word, they "flung themselves before Joseph" and announced, "We are prepared to be your slaves" (v. 18, JSB). Ironically, at 17 years old, Joseph had told them that one day they would bow before him (Genesis 37:6–10). In fact, Joseph's foretelling of his dream was one of the catalysts that started his long sojourn in Egypt, his reunion with Jacob and the family, and his role as Egypt's prime minister.

Joseph must have had an "A-ha" moment as he saw his brothers show obeisance toward him. But his attitude and disposition quickly changed. He realized that no matter what wrong the brothers had done to him, he had no true power or authority to settle the score—that power belonged only to God.

We are often like those who want to see justice prevail over the wicked and evildoers of our society, especially if they have harmed those we love. But we are reminded by King Solomon that those who dig a hole for others will fall into the same hole that is dug (see Proverbs 26:27; 28:10). The apostle Paul writes to the church of Rome, about an important principle that supersedes our need and desire for retaliation: "Vengeance is mine; I will repay, saith the Lord" (Romans 12:19).

Joseph looked at all that had taken place between him and his brothers from a more eternal point of view, and he chose to separate himself from the human passion of revenge. He would let God take care of the matter. Besides, as they had sold Joseph into slavery, the brothers were now enslaved by their own fears and trepidation. Joseph didn't need to add more anxiety.

20 But as for you, ye thought evil against me; but God meant it unto good, to bring to pass, as it is this day, to save much people alive. 21 Now therefore, fear ye not: I will nourish you, and your little ones. And he comforted them, and spake kindly unto them.

Joseph continued his oratory as he declared the most important characteristic of God: His Sovereignty. "Ye thought evil against me; but God meant it unto good…" (Genesis 50:20). God does as He pleases, and can use the most tragic and illogical circumstances in our lives for His divine purpose. The apostle Paul says, "All things work together for good to them that love God, to them who are called according to his purpose" (Romans 8:28).

Joseph recounted that, because of their jealousy, the brothers' sole intention was to rid themselves of him, not realizing—or caring—how much sadness it would bring upon their father and evil into their own lives. But despite their actions, God used them as tools to get Joseph into the right place, at the right season, and for the right purpose. Berlin suggests that through God's sovereignty of allowing Joseph to be sold into slavery, put in prison, and assist Pharaoh, Joseph was the instrument that helped Israel survive the worldwide famine.

God's sovereignty is not capricious or unstable. He rules over people's affairs and can use whosoever He wills to fulfill His purpose. What Joseph's brothers thought to be evil against him was actually "good" in the plans of God. In Genesis 50:20, the word "good" comes from the Hebrew word *towb* (**tobe**), and one of its important meanings is moral goodness as opposed to moral evil. Joseph's life in Egypt had a twofold good purpose: "to save many people," and to "nourish" his brothers and their families so they would truly understand the providence of God. Indeed, Joseph would show true forgiveness, a side of God they could not comprehend.

22 And Joseph dwelt in Egypt, he and his father's house: and Joseph lived a hundred and ten years. 23 And Joseph saw Ephraim's children of the third generation: the children also of Machir the son of Manasseh were brought up upon Joseph's knees.

Joseph lived in Egypt approximately 93 years of his life. During that period, he went from a dreamer to a provider, from an obscure young man to the prime minister, and to the one who gave Pharaoh the plan to save Egypt and Israel during the famine. By the time he was 110, Joseph was an old man. Moses suggests that Joseph lived "well" (Heb. *chayah*, **chah-YAH**) because he had a right relationship with God: "The LORD was with him; and whatever he did, the LORD made it to prosper" (Genesis 39:23, NKJV). Brown suggests that at 110 years old, Joseph had an ideal lifespan in view of ancient Near East customs. Bruce says that Joseph's lifespan, though shorter than Jacob's, was long enough for him to see the third generation of his son Ephraim's children (57–60). Additionally, Joseph adopted his other son Manasseh's grandchildren (Machir) as his own ("brought up upon Joseph's knees" Genesis 50:23; also see 30:3). These "sons" would eventually make up the tribe of Manasseh (see Numbers 32:39–40).

24 And Joseph said unto his brethren, I die: and God will surely visit you, and bring you out of this land unto the land which He sware to Abraham, to Isaac, and to Jacob. 25 And Joseph took an oath to the children of Israel, saying, God will surely visit you, and ye shall carry up my bones from hence.

Like Jacob before him, Joseph acknowledged to his brothers that his life had come to an end. But he gave them assurances of a divine visitation from God. In verses 24 and 25, Joseph declared in the Hebrew *paqad* (**paw-KAD**), meaning "God will surely visit you," "God will take notice of you," and "God has taken notice of you" (of the brothers' sojourn in Egypt). The Hebrew words are the same, but the tense in both verses is different, indicating that God not only has monitored their circumstances during the life of Jacob and Joseph, but He also would continue to watch over them long after Joseph was gone. In fact, Joseph was confident that God would take care of Israel until the set time that He brought them out of Egypt into the land of Canaan where the patriarchs Abraham, Isaac, and Jacob rested. They would not remain in Egypt forever. God had a plan for His people, and it seems that Joseph had an inkling of that plan. Joseph charged his brothers that, when God brought the people out of Egypt (through the hands and work of Moses), they must take his bones with them to the place of his birth.

26 So Joseph died, being an hundred and ten years old: and they embalmed him, and he was put in a coffin in Egypt.

Joseph's bones would eventually be buried in Shechem (Joshua 24:32), the same city where Jacob had first sent his favorite son to find the 10 brothers and where his journey to Egypt began. The irony is that at the hands of God, Joseph's life would come to a complete circle. Even though Joseph was embalmed, and put in a coffin tomb fitting for Egyptian royalty, his final resting place would be with the patriarchs, and more specifically, his father, Jacob.

Sources:

Achtemeir, Paul J. et al., eds. *The Harper Collins Bible Dictionary.* San Francisco, CA: HarperCollins Publishers, 1996. 477–79, 544–45.

Baltes, A. J., ed. Biblespeech.com. http://www.biblespeech.com (accessed August 11, 2010).

Berlin, Adele, and Marc Brettler. *The Jewish Study Bible.* New York, NY: Oxford University Press, 2004. 99–101.

Brown, Raymond E., Joseph A. Fitzmyer, and Roland E. Murphy, eds. *Genesis: New Jerome Biblical Commentary.* Englewood Cliffs, NJ: Prentice Hall, 1990. 42–43.

Bruce, F. F. et al., eds. *Zondervan Bible Commentary.* Grand Rapids, MI: Zondervan Publishing, 2008. 57–60.

Henry, Matthew. "Commentary on Genesis 50." Blue Letter Bible. org. http://www.blueletterbible.org/commentaries/Henry/ (accessed September 1, 2010).

Hitchcock, Roswell D. "Abraham." *Hitchcock's Bible Names Dictionary.* Bible Study Tools.com. http://www.biblestudytools.com/dictionaries/hitchcocks-bible-names/ (accessed September 2, 2010).

MacArthur, John. *The MacArthur Study Bible.* Nashville, TN: Thomas Nelson, 1997. 88–90.

Say It Correctly

Egypt. EE-jipt.
Ephraim. EE-fray-im.
Machir. MA-kihr.
Requite. Ri-QUITE.

Daily Bible Readings

MONDAY
A Divine Confirmation
(Genesis 46:1–7)

TUESDAY
Settled in a New Land
(Genesis 46:28–47:6)

WEDNESDAY
A Father's Heritage
(Genesis 48:8–16)

THURSDAY
A Father's Blessing
(Genesis 49:22–26)

FRIDAY
A Father's Final Wish
(Genesis 49:29–50:6)

SATURDAY
A Child's Final Duty
(Genesis 50:7–14)

SUNDAY
Reconciliation in the Family
(Genesis 50:15–26)

Teaching Tips

Words You Should Know

A. Triumphed (Exodus 15:1) *ga'ah* (Heb.)—Rose up or was exalted in victory.

B. Salvation (v. 2) *yeshuw'ah* (Heb.)—Deliverance, victory, or help.

Teacher Preparation

Unifying Principle—Following a Trusted Leader. The Bible teaches that we can trust God during times of trials and suffering; He is faithful and is a trusted Leader.

A. Pray for your students and for understanding of the lesson.

B. Research and study the entire 15th chapter of Exodus.

C. Be prepared to discuss some of the struggles and trials people are suffering in the community and world.

D. Complete the companion lesson in the *Precepts For Living Personal Study Guide®*.

O—Open the Lesson

A. Open with prayer, including the Aim for Change.

B. Have your students read the Aim for Change and Keep in Mind verse inunison.

C. Share your presentation.

D. Ask, "What struggles are you or someone you know going through?" Discuss.

E. Ask a volunteer to summarize the In Focus story. Discuss.

P—Present the Scriptures

A. Have volunteers read the Focal Verses.

B. Now use The People, Places, and Times; Background; Search the Scriptures; At-A-Glance outline; In Depth; and More Light on the Text to clarify the verses.

E—Explore the Meaning

A. Divide the class into three groups to answer questions in the Discuss the Meaning and Lesson in Our Society sections, and then discuss the Make It Happen section. Tell the students to select a representative to report their responses to the rest of the class.

B. Connect these sections to the Aim for Change and the Keep in Mind verse.

N—Next Steps for Application

A. Summarize the lesson.

B. Close with prayer.

Worship Guide

For the Superintendent or Teacher
Theme: Out of Egypt
Theme Song: "'Tis So Sweet
to Trust in Jesus"
Devotional Reading:
Psalm 77:11–20
Prayer

Out of Egypt

Bible Background • EXODUS 1:8–14; 15:1–27
Printed Text • EXODUS 15:1–3, 19, 22–26 | Devotional Reading • PSALM 77:11–20

— Aim for Change —

By the end of the lesson, we will: REVIEW the story of the Israelites' journey of faith through the Red Sea and wilderness; FEEL confidence to trust God during trying times; and REMAIN faithful when times and situations are difficult.

 ## In Focus

Keisha and Gary had been married for 10 years. Keisha was now 40 years old and Gary was 47. They both came from large families and wanted children. At every family gathering, Keisha's sisters would bring up the subject of Keisha and Gary not having any children. It was very painful. Their families had no idea how many times they had gotten their hopes up only to be told Keisha was not pregnant. It was very disappointing and a struggle for both of them. However, Gary knew he was the reason Keisha could not have a baby.

On many occasions, Gary told Keisha to go find someone who could give her a baby. Keisha knew that she was not going to commit adultery because she loved God and her husband. She was willing to trust God and continue to serve Him in the children's ministry at the church. Then one day, much to Keisha and Gary's surprise, a pregnant teenager at church talked to them about adopting her baby. Gary later acknowledged he had failed to trust God even though Keisha had never lost faith.

JAN 29th

We all will face difficult times and situations, but we can trust God. In today's lesson, Moses had faith in God and the Israelites trusted him to lead them safely across the Red Sea.

— Keep in Mind —

"For the horse of Pharaoh went in with his chariots and with his horsemen into the sea, and the LORD brought again the waters of the sea upon them; but the children of Israel went on dry land in the midst of the sea" (Exodus 15:19).

Focal Verses

KJV **Exodus 15:1** Then sang Moses and the children of Israel this song unto the LORD, and spake, saying, I will sing unto the LORD, for he hath triumphed gloriously: the horse and his rider hath he thrown into the sea.

2 The LORD is my strength and song, and he is become my salvation: he is my God, and I will prepare him a habitation; my father's God, and I will exalt him.

3 The LORD is a man of war: the LORD is his name.

15:19 For the horse of Pharaoh went in with his chariots and with his horsemen into the sea, and the LORD brought again the waters of the sea upon them; but the children of Israel went on dry land in the midst of the sea.

15:22 So Moses brought Israel from the Red sea, and they went out into the wilderness of Shur; and they went three days in the wilderness, and found no water.

23 And when they came to Marah, they could not drink of the waters of Marah, for they were bitter: therefore the name of it was called Marah.

24 And the people murmured against Moses, saying, What shall we drink?

25 And he cried unto the LORD; and the LORD shewed him a tree, which when he had cast into the waters, the waters were made sweet: there he made for them a statute and an ordinance, and there he proved them,

26 And said, If thou wilt diligently hearken to the voice of the LORD thy God, and wilt do that which is right in his sight, and wilt give ear to his commandments, and keep all his statutes, I will put none of these diseases upon thee, which I have brought upon the Egyptians: for I am the LORD that healeth thee.

NLT **Exodus 15:1** Then Moses and the people of Israel sang this song to the LORD: "I will sing to the LORD, for he has triumphed gloriously; he has thrown both horse and rider into the sea.

2 The LORD is my strength and my song; he has become my victory. He is my God, and I will praise him; he is my father's God, and I will exalt him!

3 The LORD is a warrior; yes, the LORD is his name!

15:19 When Pharaoh's horses, chariots, and charioteers rushed into the sea, the LORD brought the water crashing down on them. But the people of Israel had walked through on dry land!

15:22 Then Moses led the people of Israel away from the Red Sea, and they moved out into the Shur Desert. They traveled in this desert for three days without water.

23 When they came to Marah, they finally found water. But the people couldn't drink it because it was bitter. (That is why the place was called Marah, which means "bitter.")

24 Then the people turned against Moses. "What are we going to drink?" they demanded.

25 So Moses cried out to the LORD for help, and the LORD showed him a branch. Moses took the branch and threw it into the water. This made the water good to drink. It was there at Marah that the LORD laid before them the following conditions to test their faithfulness to him:

26 "If you will listen carefully to the voice of the LORD your God and do what is right in his sight, obeying his commands and laws, then I will not make you suffer the diseases I sent on the Egyptians; for I am the LORD who heals you."

The People, Places, and Times

Egypt. Ancient Egypt was located in the northeastern part of Africa, at the eastern part of the Mediterranean Sea. It has a great valley through which the Nile River pours its waters. Egypt is the home to the earliest civilization. It was a long, narrow ribbon of fertile land, 750 miles long, surrounded by uninhabitable desert. Egypt's common name in the Bible is Mizraim. It was an important cultural and political influence on ancient Israel.

Egypt played a dual role as both a place of refuge and a place of oppression in Israel's history. Abraham seeks refuge there because "there was a famine in the land" (Genesis 12:10). In the days of Isaac, another famine nearly drove him to Egypt (Genesis 26:2). Joseph was enslaved in Egypt, and eventually ended up in prison on false charges. It became a place of hope and refuge as Joseph was elevated from slave to second in command of Egypt. Joseph eventually was the person who provided food and refuge for his family. His father Jacob and all his family came from Canaan to live in Egypt and settle there. They ended their days in Egypt (Genesis 39:1–50:26).

Over 100 years later, "Now a new king arose over Egypt, who did not know Joseph" (Exodus 1:8, NRSV). This Pharaoh tried to kill all newborn Israelite boys and enslaved the Israelite people. God heard their cries and raised up a leader named Moses to lead them out of Egypt. God remembered His covenant with Abraham, Isaac, and Jacob.

Moses. Moses was born to an Israelite mother, who put him into the Nile River in a basket (Exodus 2:2–3). He was rescued from the Nile River by the king's daughter. She raised him in the king's palace and Moses received the same quality education as the king's other children. As he grew into adulthood, Moses had compassion for his people. One day he witnessed an Egyptian beating a slave, so he intervened and murdered the Egyptian (Exodus 2:11ff). Moses fled Egypt to avoid being executed by the king. He settled in Midian and married a shepherd's daughter. Moses' wife had a son and he worked as a shepherd until the age of 80.

Moses heard the call of God in the midst of a burning bush and answered the call (Exodus 3:1ff). He expressed doubts the people would accept his call by God to lead them out of Egypt. However, God promised to be with him and sent Aaron, his brother, to speak for Moses to the Israelites and Pharaoh. The Israelites' situation grew worse and Pharaoh treated them more harshly (Exodus 5:1ff). They complained to Moses. Moses complained to God. God promised that after Pharaoh experienced His powerful hand upon him, he would let the Children of Israel go. God sent 10 plagues on the Egyptians (Exodus 7:14–11:10). At the same time, God instituted the first Passover and not one Israelite was harmed during the plagues. Eventually Pharaoh let the people go. Over two million Israelites fled Egypt and God guided them by cloud by day and fire by night. As Moses led them through the wilderness, the Egyptian army was in pursuit to stop the Israelites.

Background

God had promised Moses that He would be with him as he led the Israelites out of Egypt to a land flowing with milk and honey. Moses trusted God and obeyed. He led the people through the wilderness as the Egyptian army tried one last time to recapture them per the orders of Pharaoh. The Israelites were extremely frightened that they were going to die in the wilderness at the hands of Pharaoh's army. However in spite of the danger, Moses was fearless, knowing God was going to somehow deliver them from the threat of the approaching army. His God had proved in the past He was much more powerful than horses and chariots. "Moses said to the people, 'Do not be afraid, stand firm, and see the deliverance that the Lord will accomplish for you today; for the Egyptians whom you see today you shall never see again. The Lord will fight for you, and you have only to keep still'" (Exodus 14:13–14, NRSV).

At-A-Glance

1. The Victory Song
(Exodus 15:1–3, 19)

2. The Faith Test (vv. 22–26)

In Depth

1. The Victory Song (Exodus 15:1–3, 19)

God had promised to deliver the Israelites out of slavery. "For he is faithful that promised" (Hebrews 10:23). Exodus 14 records that God did deliver the Israelites and lead them safely across the Red Sea as Moses stretched his hand out over the water. They walked on dry land to safety. But their enemies drowned when Moses once again stretched his hand out over the water. Moses and the people were in awe of the power of God.

After they had landed on dry ground, Moses composed the song presented in Exodus 15 and he sang it with the men of Israel. Miriam, who was skilled in music, used a timbrel and led the women in singing and dancing (Exodus 15:20–21). Singing was a significant part of religious worship. This song is the first one recorded in Scripture.

Moses had reasons to sing because God had used him to save the people from slavery. Israel had reason to sing as the chosen people of God who were being redeemed from bondage. Moreover, they were brought safely through the Red Sea and were now on dry land. Their enemies had been destroyed. God had triumphed over Pharaoh and all Egyptians, just as Christ has over Satan and sin through His sacrifice on the Cross. We should sing praises to God for the great things He has done.

The Israelites declared, "The LORD is my strength and song, and he is become my salvation" (Exodus 15:2). They were weak, but God gave them strength. When they experienced sorrow, God became their comfort. Sin and death were threatening them, but God was and would be their salvation. However, it was a temporary salvation because Jesus had to come and offer Himself so they and we could have eternal salvation. It was all being done for their ancestors and for their descendants, whom He loved and whom He chose (Deuteronomy 4:37). He is a warrior who always overcomes and defeats the enemy (Exodus 15:3)! God never fails to fulfill His promises! God gave the Israelites courage, strengthened their faith, and removed their fear of the enemy. In the midst of our trials, He will do the same for us.

The words in verse 19 indicate the conclusion of the song. It simply reiterates the purpose of the song, which was to give praise and express gratitude to God. The more we repeat something, the more likely we are to remember it. We should constantly recall and offer praises to God for His great power in saving and delivering us.

2. The Faith Test (vv. 22–26)

After crossing over to dry ground, the Israelites refreshed themselves, enjoyed taking the spoils of the enemy, and sat singing praises to God. Moses gave them marching orders because they had remained too long on the shores of the Red Sea. He did not want them to get too comfortable. They had a long journey ahead of them and Moses wanted to reach the Promised Land.

After marching for three days in the wilderness of Shur, the people and animals were thirsty (Exodus 15:22). There was no water in the hot, sandy desert. This was set up by God to see how the people would respond to adversity. Sometimes the trials and suffering we face are tests of our faith. We cannot always understand why these things are happening to us, but we can choose how we respond.

The Israelites reached Marah, and the water was bitter so they could not drink it. Immediately the people began to murmur against Moses, saying, "What shall we drink?" (Exodus 15:24). Instead of trusting God to provide for them, they complained. How quickly we sometimes forget about the power of God and His promises. Hardships and trials should not cause us to doubt God's faithfulness. If we recall God's works on our behalf in the past, we would have faith to trust Him with our present struggles. He is trustworthy.

The people complained to Moses and Moses cried out to the Lord (Exodus 15:25). Moses knew the power of God and trusted in His faithfulness to make good on the promises to him and the people. God promised He would bring the Israelites into a land flowing with milk and honey (Exodus 3:17). God showed Moses a tree and directed him to cast it into the water (Exodus 15:25). The water immediately became pure and sweet, enabling the people to drink it. God had performed another miracle. This was just a test of Israel's faithfulness and obedience.

God wanted the people to obey Him, even when they were experiencing difficulties. They were to listen and obey all of God's commands whether moral, ceremonial, or judicial (Exodus 15:26). If the Israelites obeyed God, He would not put on them any of the plagues of Egypt. He promised to keep them safe and take care of them wherever they went. God would heal their bodies by preserving them from diseases and curing them, if and when needed. Healing would also come spiritually because God would pardon their iniquities, which is sometimes signified by healing (Psalm 103:3; Malachi 4:2). If they disobeyed, there would be consequences like the plagues God sent on Egypt (Deuteronomy 28:27).

Search the Scriptures

1. Why did Moses create a song (Exodus 15:1)?

2. How did God test Israel's faithfulness (vv. 22–26)?

Discuss the Meaning

As we endure daily struggles and trials, we can trust in God. God has proven He is trustworthy because every promise He has made has been fulfilled throughout the generations. How has God proven to you that He is trustworthy?

Lesson in Our Society

Many people have lost their jobs due to the bad economy. The high unemployment rates in our communities have led to home foreclosures, cars being repossessed, and families breaking up. Some people have lost their health insurance as well and are relying on emergency rooms during illnesses. How can the church be an encouragement to the unemployed who are struggling to survive? What steps can the unemployed take to remain faithful to God in the midst of their trials?

Make It Happen

Moses had faith in God, so the Israelites followed him into the Red Sea where God saved them from the Egyptians and from drowning. God is trustworthy, no matter the circumstances we face. This week as you face struggles, pray to the Lord, praise Him for His past faithfulness and ability to help now, and sing songs that encourage and uplift your spirit. Moreover, you have to keep serving God and never doubt He is working on your behalf.

Follow the Spirit

What God wants me to do:

_____

_____

_____

_____

Remember Your Thoughts

Special insights I have learned:

_____

_____

_____

_____

More Light on the Text

Exodus 15:1–3, 19, 22–26

1 Then sang Moses and the children of Israel this song unto the LORD, and spake, saying, I will sing unto the LORD, for he hath triumphed gloriously: the horse and his rider hath he thrown into the sea.

There is nothing like a song of praise or a handclap of praise, as we so often say and do in our contemporary churches. To make sure our praise is about and toward God, reflection is the key. Notice the first word in verse 1: "then." A simple yet powerful little word, it conveys the idea of immediacy. The Israelites had experienced a great deliverance from the land of Egypt by the strong hand of the Lord. Then they found themselves with their backs against the wall—literally, the Red Sea. When despair set in, God showed out once more: He took them through the Red Sea on dry land and covered their enemies with the waters they were surely fearful of drowning in themselves (see Exodus 14:10–12).

The text says that after they were delivered from the sea, God's people sang unto the Lord. Praise is first and foremost upward. There is nothing wrong with quality and harmony; however, the goal of praise is to glorify, contemplate, and then respond to the power and majesty of God. The Israelites sang about not what they felt God could do; rather, their praise was a testimony reflecting on their personal experiences. An all-sufficient God (El Shaddai) demonstrated He is bigger than any problem that could get in the way of His promise to "deliver them to the promised land." "Triumphed" and "gloriously" are translated in Hebrew as *ga'ah* (**gaw-AW**), which means "high, exalted, and successful." And rightfully so, because the Hebrew word used for "LORD" is the most common in the Bible and simply means "The Self-Existent One" (YHWH). The Lord can do what He does because of Who He is, and He is like none other that we know.

This song (v. 1) begins with the Lord as the focus before turning to what He did—vanquish their enemies before their very eyes. Using a metaphorical analogy, Moses pictures the defeated hordes of Egypt that were on horseback, in hot pursuit of the

Israelites. In the ancient world, horses often symbolized power, swiftness, and those that employed their use were the powerful kings and men of great wealth (*The Pulpit Commentary*, 2004). The picture cannot be plainer—God conquers all. God is the One who has all power and is over all other powers, real and assumed.

2 The LORD is my strength and song, And he is become my salvation: He is my God, and I will prepare him a habitation; my father's God, and I will exalt him. 3 The LORD is a man of war: the LORD is his name.

The text does not say whether this song of praise was an individual or corporate composition. The grammatical structure suggests the former. Nevertheless, the personalization of the song supports the notion. God's acts of deliverance led all to believe, at least for now, the Lord's display of power in delivering them from their greatest fears. This was validation that God was their source of strength and the reason for their praise.

The particular Hebrew word used here for "strength" *is `oz* (**oze**). It is rarely used to describe humans, and it refers to the unwavering ability of deity to do that which only deity can accomplish. Nevertheless, strength is an attribute God chooses to bestow on people who have a relationship with Him. Moses and the Israelites contend God has become their strength, and thereby, God has become their salvation. The Hebrew word for "salvation" (*yeshûwâh*, **yesh-OO-aw**) means "deliverance," and this is significant. Israel came to understand and believe that deliverance is not only what God does, but deliverance is an attribute of God. Therefore, the Lord not only saves; God has also become their salvation and the subject of their song of praise, as well.

Now, as Moses concludes, he must respond to God, prepare a place in his heart for Him, "a habitation" as verse 2 says. Other translations such as NLT use the phrase "I will exalt him... I will praise him," instead of "prepare a place for a habitation" as found in the KJV. A word study of the Hebrew translation of "habitation," *naveh* (**naw-VEH**), suggests "keep at home" or "beautify by acknowledgement of the worth of the object."

In a study of the Scriptures, often when you see the word *naveh* or other words for "praise," the verses before and after normally are definitive statements of the attributes of God. Hence, to praise or prepare of place of habitation, is to know Him. The children sing to God because He is the God of history, "My father's God" as verse 2 says, and therefore they exalt Him. Moreover, they sing to Him because they have experienced God as Protector. He is a Warrior fighting on their behalf—"the LORD is his name" (v. 3). Moses felt that there was nothing remotely compared to Yahweh. God is the Self-Existing One (YHWH).

Beginning with verse 9, over the next 16 verses Moses recounts the intended desires of God's enemies and the outcome for all that oppose Him or have a relationship with Him (vv. 11, 13, 16–18). Moses recalls in graphic detail, precisely and metaphorically, how God defeated not just the enemies of those who call on His name, but more poignantly and fundamentally, the bases of all these enemies' actions. Specifically, there was a difference in fates between those who had a relationship with God—those He has chosen to bless (vv. 16b–19)—and those who opposed Him (vv. 7, 16a). How does God accomplish all this, you ask? As the song says, "Thy right hand, O LORD, is become glorious in power: thy right hand, O LORD, hath dashed in pieces the enemy (v. 6), and "Thou in thy mercy hast led forth the people which thou hast redeemed: thou hast guided them in thy strength unto thy holy habitation" (v. 13).

15:19 For the horse of Pharaoh went in with his chariots and with his horsemen into the sea, and the LORD brought again the waters of the sea upon them; but the children of Israel went on dry land in the midst of the sea.

It is as though Moses had to reiterate why God is worthy of praise. The destruction of evil and deliverance from evil are symbiotic—one cannot take place unless the other is a reality. The Egyptians recognized that God might be at work (see Exodus 14:25). However, many Egyptians may have thought the sea parting was a natural phenomenon; after all, the ground was dry as far as they could see in their pursuit of Israelites. God often challenges conventional wisdom; consider the rationale the disciples had for the man born blind (John 9).

Surely, in pursuing the Israelites into the sea, the Egyptians were not convinced of God's act of deliverance. They did not comprehend that parting the Red Sea would lead to their destruction and Israel's deliverance. One cannot help but reflect on the Cross of Calvary—the judgment and payment for sin. The Egyptians were thinking of conquest, bringing Moses and those he was leading back under their domination. The Israelites were thinking, fearfully most assuredly—go with God, or die (Exodus 14:10). However, their fears were unfounded. In the last half of Exodus 15:19, Moses reiterates, in brief, that the parted waters and dry ground which provided deliverance were the very same waters that destroyed Pharaoh's army (vv. 26–30).

15:22 So Moses brought Israel from the Red sea, and they went out into the wilderness of Shur; and they went three days in the wilderness, and found no water. 23 And when they came to Marah, they could not drink of the waters of Marah, for they were bitter: therefore the name of it was called Marah. 24 And the people murmured against Moses, saying, What shall we drink?

Since singing the song and offering praises, one would expect after witnessing miracle after miracle that the Israelites' faith would be unwavering. They have seen God's mighty hand at work against Pharaoh in Egypt and they have experienced a great deliverance (see Joshua 4:19–24). Now they are challenged to put their faith to the test, albeit in the wilderness, a place that was unknown to many of them. Seemingly, they forgot God's ability to provide. This text gives a picture of daily living with God, trusting Him for all things day by day.

Taking care of personal needs and watering flocks and herds was a constant drain on water supplies. We can do without many things; water is not one of them. The text implies that as they were traveling, they were looking for water and found none. Then, when they finally got to an oasis called Marah, expectations were that there would be water and there was, but the water was bitter—undrinkable. The word "Marah" means "bitter." Even today, the waters of Marah are undrinkable.

God would "lead them the way" (Exodus 13:21), so He led them to Marah. In other words, God designed this place of challenge—this moment of need. What do the people do? They murmur against Moses (Exodus 15:24). Slyly the people make their complaint a question: "What shall we drink?" The record confirms that when God does not do what people expect, they will blame the people God uses to lead them (Exodus 16–17; Numbers 16:11).

Of course, we know murmuring directed at God's leaders is really a subtle way of expressing dissatisfaction with God—rebellion in every sense of the word. That is, we don't trust God even though God has proven He is trustworthy. Numbers 14:11 makes it plain: "And the LORD said unto Moses, How long will this people provoke me? and how long will it be ere they believe me, for all the signs which I have shewed among them?" Moses' response models what every good leader needs to know when the people complain—look to God.

25 And he cried unto the LORD; and the LORD shewed him a tree, which when he had cast into the waters, the waters were made sweet: there he made for them a statute and an ordinance, and there he proved them, 26 And said, If thou wilt diligently hearken to the voice of the LORD thy God, and wilt do that which is right in his sight, and wilt give ear to his commandments, and keep all his statutes, I will put none of these diseases upon thee, which I have brought upon the Egyptians: for I am the LORD that healeth thee.

The Hebrew word for "cried" is *tsa`aq* (**tsaw-AK**), and it means "called out for help under great distress." Imagine Moses' fears! He was God's appointed leader, and the people did have a real need—a need that Moses felt he could not meet. It should be noted that even improper murmuring and complaining can reflect legitimate concerns. The text does affirm the people's murmuring; nonetheless, God does decide, in response to Moses' cry, to meet their need. God directed Moses to a tree and apparently instructed him to throw the tree in the water. The waters were made sweet and distinctly drinkable.

The emphasis of the last half of verses 25 and 26, about rules and laws, is seemingly a departure from the themes of testing and trusting. A closer look resolutely affirms that these verses continue building on the notion that faith is tested and God can be trusted. The end of verse 25 says God "proved them." The word "proved" in Hebrew is *nac ah* (**naw-SAW**), and it means "tested." Remember, it was God who led the Israelites to this place of bitter waters, but it was the Israelites who questioned God's provision, ignoring the overwhelming evidence that God is trustworthy and faithful to His promises.

Verse 26 opens with a conditional particle, the all-important "if." There is the possibility we can hear and not really be paying attention. The phrase "diligently hearken" is one Hebrew word *shama`* (**shaw-MAW**), and it means "to listen effectually," "having a goal, to hear and follow through on that which is heard."

God is calling for a relationship evidenced by our desire and willingness to hear and obey His voice. In essence, "Listen to His voice, do what is right in His eyes, heed His commandments, and keep all His statutes." The words "do" and "keep" in verse 26 provide great insight to what God required of Israel. "Do" in Hebrew is *`asah* (**aw-SAW**), and it can mean "to make come about, to accomplish." The root word for "keep" in Hebrew is *shamar* (**shaw-MAR**) and literally means "to watch," contextually meaning "to observe, be circumspect." God expects those in a covenantal relationship with Him to keep their eyes on Him via His revealed Word—His laws, statutes, and precepts as well as His working in the midst. Nothing has changed from that day to this day. The good news is that listening to the voice of God has always had benefits.

Remember the "big if." God tells the Israelites that if they listen, He has a blessing for them; what happened to the Egyptians would not happen to them. The wording leaves unclear the "diseases" to which God is referring in verse 26. If diseases refer to all forms of sicknesses, as the word can mean, then the verse would imply that if Israel followed God, they would never get sick. Keep reading throughout the Bible and you would find that the testimony in such a reading would be far from an experiential reality, even among God's people. Better to gain an understanding of what the word means from the context. Specifically, the verse says they would not experience the diseases of Egypt. Deuteronomy 7:15; 28:27, 58–60 provide insight. In these verses and their immediate context, particular reference is made to the plagues of Egypt. God is saying, "Follow Me and the judgments of Egypt will not follow you." The concession is made as some scholars note there were particular illnesses indicative of Egypt, and these are also in view. Even so, the point made is the same: "What happened in and to the Egyptians will not happen to you, if you obey Me."

With a climactic ending statement in Exodus 15:26, God says, "I will put none of these diseases upon thee, which I have brought upon the Egyptians: for I am the LORD that healeth thee." The Israelites were not going to be spared because of their goodness or worth; they are spared because of abilities that only God has, in this case to heal. The Hebrew word for "heal" is *rapha'* (**raw-FAW**), and it means "to heal, repair, restore," and is sometimes translated as "physician." The healing can be some form of physical or emotional illness, or national illnesses and personal illnesses manifested as sins. We know that God can heal physical ailments. We also know that the healing of

the "nations" comes by way of the Cross; with His stripes we are healed (Isaiah 53:5). God affirmed in Exodus 15:26 that the future of the nation rested in His divine providence and grace to sustain the Israelites from beginning to end.

Sources:

American Tract Society Bible Dictionary. Studylight.com. http://www.studylight.org/dic/ats/view.cgi?number=T674 (accessed May 12, 2010).

Baker's Evangelical Dictionary of Biblical Theology. Studylight.com. http://www.studylight.org/dic/bed/view.cgi?number=T219 (accessed May 12, 2010).

The Commentary Critical and Explanatory on the Whole Bible. Studylight.com. http://www.studylight.org/com/jfb/view.cgi?book=ex&chapter=015 (accessed May 20, 2010).

The Geneva Study Bible. Crosswalk.com. http://www.biblestudytools.com/commentaries/geneva-study-bible/exodus/exodus-15.html (accessed May 15, 2010).

Holman Illustrated Bible Dictionary. Studylight.com. http://www.studylight.org/dic/hbd/view.cgi?number=T1742 (accessed May 12, 2010).

John Wesley Explanatory Notes on the Bible. Studylight.com. http://www.studylight.org/com/wen/view.cgi?book=ex&chapter=015 (accessed May 16, 2010).

Life Application Bible—New Revised Standard Version. Wheaton, IL: Tyndale House Publishers, 1989. 118–20.

Miller, Stephen M. *The Complete Guide to the Bible.* Urichsville, OH: Barbour Publishing, 2007. 27–30.

The New John Gill Exposition of the Entire Bible. Studylight.com. http://www.studylight.org/com/geb/view.cgi?book=ex&chapter=015 (accessed May 16, 2010). Scofield, C. I., ed. *The New Scofield Study Bible—King James Version.* New York, NY: Oxford University Press, 1967. 71–90.

Spence-Jones, H. D. Maurice, ed. *The Pulpit Commentary—Vol. 1: Genesis.* New York, NY: Funk & Wagnalls, 1890, 2004.

Say It Correctly

Aaron. AIR-uhn.
Marah. MAY-rah.
Miriam. MIR-ee-uhm.
Shur. SHUHR.

Daily Bible Readings

MONDAY
A Mighty Redemption
(Psalm 77:11–20)

TUESDAY
A Strong People
(Exodus 1:1–7)

WEDNESDAY
A New King
(Exodus 1:8–14)

THURSDAY
A Treacherous Plan
(Exodus 1:15–22)

FRIDAY
A Divine Intervention
(Exodus 15:4–10)

SATURDAY
An Unsurpassable God
(Exodus 15:11–18)

SUNDAY
A New Ordinance
(Exodus 15:1–3, 19, 22–26)

Notes

Teaching Tips

Words You Should Know

A. Nature (Galatians 2:15) *phusis* (Gk.)— The way of feeling and acting which has become "normal."

B. Transgressor (2:18) *parabates* (Gk.) —A person who violates a command or law; someone who goes beyond a boundary or limit.

Teacher Preparation

Unifying Principle—Seeking Something to Believe In. Having faith in someone else is the greatest gift one can make to another. If we place our faith in anything other than Christ, Paul stated that Jesus died in vain.

A. Begin with prayer for your students and lesson clarity.

B. Read the entire book of Galatians.

C. Complete the companion lesson in the *Precepts For Living Personal Study Guide*®.

O—Open the Lesson

A. Invite one of the students to open the class with prayer.

B. Ask a volunteer to read the In Focus section aloud.

C. Invite the class to share their insights from the story.

P—Present the Scriptures

A. Ask for volunteers to read the Focal Verses aloud.

B. Invite the students to discuss the relationship between the Focal Verses, the In Focus section, and their own life experiences with each other.

C. Answer the questions in the Search the Scriptures section.

E—Explore the Meaning

A. Ask volunteers to read the Discuss the Meaning section.

B. Answer the questions as a group.

N—Next Steps for Application

A. Read the Lesson in Our Society section. Emphasize that some people might try to place conditions on what they must do to be incorporated into the people of God and the importance of knowing God's Word concerning the issue.

B. Read the Make It Happen section and ask the students to evaluate their beliefs and practices in light of the Bible lesson.

C. End the class with a prayer that includes the Lesson Aim.

Worship Guide

For the Superintendent or Teacher
Theme: Justified by Faith in Christ
Theme Song: "Just as I Am"
Devotional Reading: Luke 18:9–14
Prayer

Justified by Faith in Christ

Bible Background • GALATIANS 1:1–2:21
Printed Text • GALATIANS 2:15–21 | Devotional Reading • LUKE 18:9–14

———— Aim for Change ————

By the end of the lesson, we will: KNOW Paul's argument against salvation by works; APPRECIATE Christ's saving work on the earth; and DEEPEN our faith in Jesus.

——  In Focus ——

Cedric was happy that his younger brother had finally accepted Christ and found a church home. Eric called Cedric to invite him to his baptism and fellowship into the church congregation.

Cedric, who had been a Christian since he was a young boy, was overjoyed. However, his joy was tempered with caution when Eric also revealed that as part of his initiation into that congregation, he would have to hyphenate his last name and add the pastor's last name. He was also required to wear an armband at all times to identify him as a member of that community.

Cedric asked Eric to reconsider joining any congregation that would put conditions on his membership. He prayed with Eric before ending their phone conversation, thanking God for Eric's new life in Christ, and asking God to show Eric that salvation is free and not something he can earn.

FEB 5th

If anything is added to what we need to do to be saved, it is wrong, because our salvation comes by faith alone. Today, we will investigate what Paul had to say about that.

—————— Keep in Mind ——————

"For I through the law am dead to the law, that I might live unto God.
I am crucified with Christ: nevertheless I live; yet not I, but Christ liveth in me:
and the life which I now live in the flesh I live by the faith of the Son of God,
who loved me, and gave himself for me" (Galatians 2:19–20).

"For I through the law am dead to the law, that I might live unto God. I am crucified with Christ: nevertheless I live; yet not I, but Christ liveth in me: and the life which I now live in the flesh I live by the faith of the Son of God, who loved me, and gave himself for me" (Galatians 2:19–20).

Focal Verses

KJV Galatians 2:15 We who are Jews by nature, and not sinners of the Gentiles,

16 Knowing that a man is not justified by the works of the law, but by the faith of Jesus Christ, even we have believed in Jesus Christ, that we might be justified by the faith of Christ, and not by the works of the law: for by the works of the law shall no flesh be justified.

17 But if, while we seek to be justified by Christ, we ourselves also are found sinners, is therefore Christ the minister of sin? God forbid.

18 For if I build again the things which I destroyed, I make myself a transgressor.

19 For I through the law am dead to the law, that I might live unto God.

20 I am crucified with Christ: nevertheless I live; yet not I, but Christ liveth in me: and the life which I now live in the flesh I live by the faith of the Son of God, who loved me, and gave himself for me.

21 I do not frustrate the grace of God: for if righteousness come by the law, then Christ is dead in vain.

NLT Galatians 2:15 You and I are Jews by birth, not 'sinners' like the Gentiles.

16 And yet we Jewish Christians know that we become right with God, not by doing what the law commands, but by faith in Jesus Christ. So we have believed in Christ Jesus, that we might be accepted by God because of our faith in Christ—and not because we have obeyed the law. For no one will ever be saved by obeying the law."

17 But what if we seek to be made right with God through faith in Christ and then find out that we are still sinners? Has Christ led us into sin? Of course not!

18 Rather, I make myself guilty if I rebuild the old system I already tore down.

19 For when I tried to keep the law, I realized I could never earn God's approval. So I died to the law so that I might live for God. I have been crucified with Christ.

20 I myself no longer live, but Christ lives in me. So I live my life in this earthly body by trusting in the Son of God, who loved me and gave himself for me.

21 I am not one of those who treats the grace of God as meaningless. For if we could be saved by keeping the law, then there was no need for Christ to die.

The People, Places, and Times

Paul. Paul was originally named Saul after Israel's first king. He was born in a very religious Jewish family in Tarsus, a city which was located in what is modern-day Turkey. But soon the family moved to Jerusalem where he was educated as a Pharisee. The Pharisees were very devoted to the Law, and Paul could see that Christianity was opposed to what Pharisees believed. So Paul

became a "missionary" Pharisee, beginning in Jerusalem by rounding up Christians and having them put in prison or even killed. (He was a part of those who saw to it that Stephen was stoned for his faith in Jesus Christ.)

Paul was dramatically converted while he was on the road to Damascus, where he planned to ferret out more Christians and have them put in jail. But it was on this road that Jesus Christ spoke to him from heaven and Paul was temporarily blinded, but completely convinced that the only way to salvation was through faith in Jesus Christ.

Shortly after his conversion, Paul concentrated on missionary work to the Gentiles. It was at this time that he was called Paul instead of Saul. Paul was a Gentile name, whereas Saul was a Jewish name. Paul was determined to tear down any barriers for the conversion of Gentiles (non-Jews) to Christ.

So when Jews, who may have been converted to Christianity or may really just have been sham Christians who came along and tried to convince Gentile Christians that they had to be circumcised and obey the whole Law in order to be saved, Paul was filled with holy anger and jealousy for the Gospel. Salvation is by grace through faith alone. No works are required for salvation. It is enough that Jesus died on the Cross for us and rose again! To say that anything else is needed is to belittle the Cross.

Galatians. Galatia was a region in the Roman Empire, also located in what is now part of Turkey. The book of Acts records ministry visits from Paul to Antioch in Pisidia, Iconium, Lystra, and Derbe. So when the people in these cities that Paul had led to Christ were being led astray, Paul, as their spiritual father, was rightly concerned.

Jewish Christians or Christian Jews. Members of a separate group within the Jewish community that continued to adhere to Jewish practices and observances, such as circumcision, attending synagogue, and dietary restrictions that included, among other things, separation from Gentiles during meals. However, they also believed in Jesus' resurrection and His status as the Messiah. Additionally, Jewish Christians observed new rituals such as baptism and Communion. The Law and its observance are central to Jewish piety, and the Jewish Christians expected the Gentiles who became Christians to observe the Law, as well.

Background

Paul returned to Jerusalem after 14 years to meet with the Jerusalem leaders and to present to the leaders the Gospel that he preached to the Gentiles. Titus, an uncircumcised Gentile, accompanied Paul to Jerusalem, and a group separate from the leaders tried to force Titus to be circumcised as proof of his inclusion in the covenant. Paul refused, and the Jerusalem leaders backed him up, affirming his mission to the Gentiles.

Upon leaving the conference in Jerusalem, Paul traveled to Antioch, a Christian community with a large Gentile affiliation. Peter (or Cephas), who had been entrusted with preaching the Gospel to the Jews outside Jerusalem, visited the church at Antioch, sharing meals with the members, even though Jewish law prohibited eating with non-Jews. Shortly after their arrival, another group of Jewish Christians joined them. Their appearance caused Peter to reverse his earlier actions and separate himself from eating with the Gentiles. The Jewish Christians of the church at Antioch did likewise. Even Barnabas, Paul's companion in the mission field, conformed. This led to a big showdown between Paul and Peter, and an impassioned speech to the Galatians by Paul that they are saved by faith through Christ, not the Law. This crisis led to the meeting in Jerusalem found in Acts 15:1–35.

At-A-Glance

1. Justification by Faith Alone
(Galatians 2:15–16)

2. We Live by Faith (vv. 17–21)

In Depth

1. Justification by Faith Alone (Galatians 2:15–16)

In verses 11 through 14 of Galatians 2, Paul recalls a confrontation he had with Peter. As a fellow Jew, Peter's behavior in Antioch toward Gentile Christians was equivalent to treating them as second-class citizens in the church. In essence, the actions of Peter and the other Jewish Christians said to the Gentiles that they had to become Jewish in order to be accepted into the community. Paul argues before his fellow Jewish Christians that they should know better than to require the Gentiles to observe the Law as mandatory for salvation. He further argues that if Jewish Christians know that they, who were born Jews, are saved not by works of the Law but by faith in Christ, how can they demand that the Gentiles obey the Law in order to be saved?

The Law was given to the Jewish people as a means of identifying themselves as the people of God and was not meant to provide a means of salvation, but it was often interpreted that way. Almost all of the Old Testament prophets condemned this view. God has always accepted people based upon their trust in Him.

Most scholars divide the Law into three areas. The first is the moral law, which is the Ten Commandments and which is also spelled out in more detail. Jesus helped people to see that it was not meant to be just an outward set of rules, but was to be an attitude of the heart described as love for God and love for others. The civil law went into detail on how to live out the moral law in the context in which the Jewish people lived. The ceremonial law had to do with regulations for sacrifices and for the priestly system.

No one would deny that Christians should be following the Ten Commandments, but Paul makes it clear that obeying them does not qualify us for salvation. The civil law was limited to Israel's monarchy, and the ceremonial law was completed with the death and resurrection of Jesus Christ. We no longer need to sacrifice animals to atone for our sins. Our sins have been paid for, once and for all, in Jesus' death on the Cross. And circumcision was meant to be the unique physical symbol that the Jewish people were God's chosen people. This has been replaced with Christian baptism, and the celebration of the Jewish Passover meal has been replaced with the Lord's Supper.

2. We Live by Faith (vv. 17–21)

Paul continued his defense that no human being can be justified before God by works of the Law. He argued that he had already died to the Law when he was saved. Since he now shares in Christ's death and resurrection, the Law-free Gospel he shared with the Galatians is sufficient for their salvation. For him to preach otherwise would be the same as returning to the works of the Law. He continued that because Jesus loved him, He died to save him, and to return to the works of the Law would make Jesus' death pointless. Paul wanted the Gentiles to understand that he, a devout Jew, understood that faith in Christ was the only way he could be justified before God.

Search the Scriptures

1. How does Paul say that a man or woman is justified (Galatians 2:16)?

2. If righteousness comes by the Law, what then does Paul say is in vain (v. 21)?

Discuss the Meaning

Paul says that we are justified by the faith of Jesus Christ, not by the works of the Law. What do you think it means to be justified, that is, living in right covenant relationship with God (Galatians 2:16)?

Lesson in Our Society

How many of us have ever heard the words, "If you loved me you would . . . ?" You can fill in the blank. We have all probably heard it at one time, but some of us have even been tempted to fall for that line. We have done or said something to prove our love, fidelity, etc., only to be hurt, disappointed, or betrayed. The Galatians were in a similar situation. Unidentified Jewish Christians were challenging these Gentile Christians to prove the authenticity of their conversion by being circumcised. The Galatians wanted to demonstrate that their faith in Jesus was real, even if that meant giving in to the demands of the Jewish Christians.

What would you do if you were in the Galatians' situation? Have you ever been asked to choose between being accepted in God's family by faith in Christ alone, and doing something to make it "more legitimate"?

Make It Happen

Imagine that you, your parents, and the generations before them maintained a certain tradition all your life. One day someone you greatly respect tells your family to stop observing this long-standing tradition. This is similar to what life was like for the Jewish Christians. They were taught that salvation for the Israelites was received by keeping the Law. Furthermore, they would suffer if they did not keep the Law. Now Paul was teaching them that they could still be saved without observing the Jewish Law. Do you think it was hard for the Jewish Christians? Would it be hard for you to let go of the tradition you observed all your life? Think about your faith. Are there any practices or beliefs that you maintain because your family or pastor

taught you that was the right way, but it is contrary to God's Word?

Follow the Spirit

What God wants me to do:

_____

_____

_____

_____

Remember Your Thoughts

Special insights I have learned:

_____

_____

_____

More Light on the Text
Galatians 2:15–21
Introduction

Paul's message to the Galatians explained that they did not have to become Jewish in order to be Christian. Just as observing the Law did not put the Jewish Christians in right relationship with God, neither would observing the Law put the Galatians in right relationship with God. Rather, both Jewish and Gentile Christians were put right or "justified" by putting their trust in Jesus Christ.

15 We who are Jews by nature, and not sinners of the Gentiles,

Paul set straight his Jewish Christian brothers and sisters, who did not treat the Gentile converts as equals. He taught that the Gentiles had as much right to the covenant of

God as those who were Jewish by birth. African Americans know of such discrimination in the church. In the eighteenth and nineteenth centuries, Blacks were allowed to worship with Whites in the same building but were excluded from worshiping alongside Whites. Instead, they were often relegated to worshiping in the balcony. Some were even physically restrained when they attempted to join Whites in the pews. Consequently, many Blacks withdrew and formed their own churches and denominations, rather than subject themselves to mistreatment.

16 Knowing that a man is not justified by the works of the law, but by the faith of Jesus Christ, even we have believed in Jesus Christ, that we might be justified by the faith of Christ, and not by the works of the law: for by the works of the law shall no flesh be justified.

The terms translated as "justified" or "righteous" are from the Greek word *dikaios* (**DIK-ah-yos**), which means to be acquitted, or found blameless. In the Bible, it also means being in right covenant relationship with God. Paul argued that the Gentile converts were in right covenant relationship with God by their faith in Jesus Christ, not by observing the Jewish Law. The same is true for Jewish believers.

The word "works," from the Greek word *ergon* (**ER-gon**), refers to the deeds or practices exhibited in obedience to the Law—including circumcision, dietary restrictions, and Sabbath observances—that set the Jewish people apart from the Gentiles. Many religions today still observe certain practices, such as not eating pork or beef, as stipulated by similar rules and regulations. Poor diets have greatly contributed to the many illnesses and diseases that affect our community. We should be better stewards of the gift from God of our earthly bodies. However, it is one thing for Christians to restrict certain foods to maintain a healthy lifestyle and quite another for purposes trying to earn God's favor.

The Greek for the word "law" *nomos* (**NOM-os**) stands for the revelation or instruction received by Moses from God that is found in the first five books of the Bible; it details how the Children of Israel were to demonstrate their covenant relationship with God. African Americans can certainly appreciate the importance of the Law to the Jewish people. It was a reminder that they were once slaves in Egypt and that God delivered them.

The Law was central to Jewish piety. The Jews believed that faithful observance of the Law would bring them blessings, and infidelity would bring disaster upon them. It is no wonder the Jewish Christians struggled with relinquishing observance of the Law as a means of justification in addition to their faith in Christ. The Greek word for "faith" is *pistis* (**PIS-tis**), which means to trust, have confidence, faith, or belief in something or someone.

17 But if, while we seek to be justified by Christ, we ourselves also are found sinners, is therefore Christ the minister of sin? God forbid.

The Jewish Christians were justified by believing in Christ, which made them equal to their Gentile counterparts in God's sight. They both had to come to God in the same way. Paul did not mean that Christ made the Jews sinners, rather, both Jews and Gentiles were sinners saved by God's grace through faith in Christ.

18 For if I build again the things which I destroyed, I make myself a transgressor.

Paul taught the Galatians that believing in Christ could save them. Thus submitting to Jewish circumcision would undo all that he taught them about being accepted as Christians without observing the Law. If Paul was to now say that salvation required faith and works of the Law, it would be like tearing down a building and then rebuilding it—making him wrong for destroying it in the first place.

19 For I through the law am dead to the law, that I might live unto God. 20 I am crucified with Christ: nevertheless I live; yet not I, but Christ liveth in me: and the life which I now live in the flesh I live by the faith of the Son of God, who loved me, and gave himself for me.

Paul's reference to the "flesh," (Gk. *sarx*, **sarx**), has several meanings. In this verse, Paul was referring to his physical limitations as a human being. To preach a Gospel that includes circumcision for the Galatians would be a violation of faith in Christ. Paul figuratively died to the Law when he was saved, that he might have life in God through Christ. He could not then preach that the Galatians must follow the Law when he could no longer do the same. Three days after his conversion on the road to Damascus, Paul was baptized (Acts 9:7–19), at which time he role-played what happens to all Christians when they are saved—he died and rose with Christ, whom God raised from the dead. Because of his faith in Christ, who loved him and gave his life for him, Paul now had new life in Christ who lived in him.

Galatians 2:19–20 are the key verses for this week's Scripture passage, and verse 20 is especially important in our understanding and appropriation in order to live a victorious Christian life. We read that the two thieves were crucified with Christ (Matthew 27:44; Mark 15:27; John 19:32), and here Paul uses the same words to say that he is crucified with Christ. When we put our trust in Jesus Christ, we are united with Him so closely that we, along with our sins, are nailed to the Cross. Our old way of life is crucified, and we rise again with Him unto new life. In Romans 6:6, the words can be paraphrased to read "the person we formerly were was crucified with him" (Bruce, 144). Just as death is the final barrier to life, so our salvation separates us from our former way of life.

We might expect Paul to say here that now he lives in Christ, but instead he says that Christ lives in him. So completely do we reckon ourselves dead to sin, that the "I" no longer exists; it is only Christ who lives through us. We are now living the resurrection life of Christ.

21 I do not frustrate the grace of God: for if righteousness come by the law, then Christ is dead in vain.

Paul concludes this passage by stating his final argument to those who want Gentiles to become Jews by law in order to become Christians: If they can be in right relationship with God by observing the Law, then Christ's death on the Cross was meaningless. Indeed, if there were any other way for us to obtain salvation, then Jesus would not have had to die on the Cross. Instead, God's grace is sufficient for salvation.

Sources:

Baltes, A. J., ed. Biblespeech.com. http://www.biblespeech.com (accessed August 11, 2010).

Barclay, William. *The Letters to the Galatians and Ephesians. Translated, with Introductions and Interpretations.* Philadelphia, PA: Westminster Press, 1956.

Browning, Daniel C. "Law, Ten Commandments, Torah." *Holman Illustrated Bible Dictionary.* Chad Brand, Charles Draper, Archie England, eds. Nashville, TN: Holman Bible Publishers, 2003. 1609–10.

Bruce, F. F. *The Epistle to the Galatians: A Commentary on the Greek Text. The New International Greek Testament Commentary.* Grand

Rapids, MI: William B. Eerdmans Publishing Company, 1982.
144.

Quarles, Charles L. "Paul." *Holman Illustrated Bible Dictionary*. Chad
Brand, Charles Draper, Archie England, eds. Nashville, TN:
Holman Bible Publishers, 2003. 1254–61.

Strong, James. *New Exhaustive Strong's Numbers and Concordance with
Expanded Greek-Hebrew Dictionary*. Seattle, WA: Biblesoft, and
International Bible Translators, 1994.

Say It Correctly

Antioch. AN-te-ock.

Circumcise. SIR-cum-size.

Crucified. CRU-ce-fide.

Galatians. Ga-LA-shuns.

Transgressor. Trans-GRES-or.

Daily Bible Reading

MONDAY
Our Only Source of Righteousness
(Isaiah 45:20–25)

TUESDAY
Righteousness through Faith
(Romans 3:21–26)

WEDNESDAY
A Prayer for Mercy
(Luke 18:9–14)

THURSDAY
Challenged by a Different Gospel
(Galatians 1:1–10)

FRIDAY
Called through God's Grace
(Galatians 1:11–24)

SATURDAY
Sent to the Gentiles
(Galatians 2:6–10)

SUNDAY
Justified by Faith
(Galatians 2:15–21)

Notes

Teaching Tips

Words You Should Know

A. Curse (Galatians 3:10, 13) *katara* (Gk.)—The act of denouncing.

B. Faith (v. 14) *pistis* (Heb.)—A strong conviction that Jesus is the Messiah and the One through whom we can by faith obtain eternal salvation.

Teacher Preparation

Unifying Principle—The Place of Ultimate Trust. We have to put our trust in Jesus Christ who sacrificed His life on our behalf. The Law cannot save us, only faith in Christ.

A. Pray for your class and for understanding about the lesson.

B. Study the entire text.

C. Bring news clippings about people who have broken the law and the consequences they face.

D. Complete the companion lesson in the *Precepts For Living Personal Study Guide®*.

O—Open the Lesson

A. Open with prayer, including the Aim for Change.

B. Have your students read the Aim for Change and Keep in Mind verse in unison.

C. Share your news clips. Discuss.

D. Ask, "Have you ever broken a rule? What happened?" Discuss.

E. Now, have a volunteer summarize the In Focus story. Discuss.

P—Present the Scriptures

A. Have a volunteer read the Focal Verses aloud.

B. Use The People, Places, and Times; Background; Search the Scriptures; At-A-Glance outline; In Depth; and More Light on the Text to clarify the verses.

E—Explore the Meaning

A. Divide the class into three groups to answer questions in the Discuss the Meaning and Lesson in Our Society sections, and then discuss Make It Happen. Tell the students to select a representative to report their responses to the rest of the class.

B. Connect these sections to the Aim for Change and the Keep in Mind verse.

N—Next Steps for Application

A. Write some take-away principles under the Follow the Spirit section.

B. Close with prayer.

Worship Guide

For the Superintendent or Teacher
Theme: Freed from Law through Christ
Theme Song: "My Hope Is Built"
Devotional Reading: Matthew 19:16–23
Prayer

Freed from Law through Christ

Bible Background • GALATIANS 3:1–14
Printed Text • GALATIONS 3:1–14 | Devotional Reading • MATTHEW 19:16–23

―――――――――― **Aim for Change** ――――――――――

By the end of the lesson, we will: UNDERSTAND Paul's contrast of faith in law versus faith in Jesus; FEEL loyalty to Christ; and DEMONSTRATE faith in Christ daily.

――――――――――  **In Focus** ――――――――――

Pastor Shepherd had been at his new church for a year. He put a strong emphasis on community outreach. The pastor and members held many community events in the church fellowship hall. Pastor Shepherd noticed that whenever the church held an event, Ursula was always volunteering to help with setting up, cleaning, and cooking as well as anything else she could do. Ursula told him she had been a member of the church for five years and always worked hard for the Lord. Pastor Shepherd was concerned about Ursula because she seemed to be overworking herself. However, she never attended Bible study.

Pastor Shepherd met with Ursula to discuss his concerns. She expressed that she thought working in the church, helping her neighbors, and living a "good life" was all God required for her to go to heaven. No one in the church had ever explained to her the true meaning of faith and salvation. After he explained it to Ursula, she wanted to accept Christ, so he led her in the "sinner's prayer."

Some people assume following rules and regulations is all that is required for salvation. In today's lesson, Paul explains we must have faith in Jesus Christ as our Savior; there is no other way to achieve righteousness.

FEB 12th

―――――――――― **Keep in Mind** ――――――――――

"That the blessing of Abraham might come on the Gentiles through Jesus Christ; that we might receive the promise of the Spirit through faith" (Galatians 3:14).

"That the blessing of Abraham might come on the Gentiles through Jesus Christ; that we might receive the promise of the Spirit through faith" (Galatians 3:14).

Focal Verses

KJV **Galatians 3:1** O foolish Galatians, who hath bewitched you, that ye should not obey the truth, before whose eyes Jesus Christ hath been evidently set forth, crucified among you?

2 This only would I learn of you, Received ye the Spirit by the works of the law, or by the hearing of faith?

3 Are ye so foolish? having begun in the Spirit, are ye now made perfect by the flesh?

4 Have ye suffered so many things in vain? if it be yet in vain.

5 He therefore that ministereth to you the Spirit, and worketh miracles among you, doeth he it by the works of the law, or by the hearing of faith?

6 Even as Abraham believed God, and it was accounted to him for righteousness.

7 Know ye therefore that they which are of faith, the same are the children of Abraham.

8 And the scripture, foreseeing that God would justify the heathen through faith, preached before the gospel unto Abraham, saying, In thee shall all nations be blessed.

9 So then they which be of faith are blessed with faithful Abraham.

10 For as many as are of the works of the law are under the curse: for it is written, Cursed is every one that continueth not in all things which are written in the book of the law to do them.

11 But that no man is justified by the law in the sight of God, it is evident: for, The just shall live by faith.

12 And the law is not of faith: but, The man that doeth them shall live in them.

13 Christ hath redeemed us from the curse of the law, being made a curse for us: for it is written, Cursed is every one that hangeth on a tree:

NLT **Galatians 3:1** Oh, foolish Galatians! What magician has cast an evil spell on you? For you used to see the meaning of Jesus Christ's death as clearly as though I had shown you a signboard with a picture of Christ dying on the cross.

2 Let me ask you this one question: Did you receive the Holy Spirit by keeping the law? Of course not, for the Holy Spirit came upon you only after you believed the message you heard about Christ.

3 Have you lost your senses? After starting your Christian lives in the Spirit, why are you now trying to become perfect by your own human effort?

4 You have suffered so much for the Good News. Surely it was not in vain, was it? Are you now going to just throw it all away?

5 I ask you again, does God give you the Holy Spirit and work miracles among you because you obey the law of Moses? Of course not! It is because you believe the message you heard about Christ.

6 In the same way, "Abraham believed God, so God declared him righteous because of his faith."

7 The real children of Abraham, then, are all those who put their faith in God.

8 What's more, the Scriptures looked forward to this time when God would accept the Gentiles, too, on the basis of their faith. God promised this good news to Abraham long ago when he said, "All nations will be blessed through you."

9 And so it is: All who put their faith in Christ share the same blessing Abraham received because of his faith.

10 But those who depend on the law to make them right with God are under his curse, for the Scriptures say, "Cursed is everyone who does not observe and obey all

281

KJV cont.

14 That the blessing of Abraham might come on the Gentiles through Jesus Christ; that we might receive the promise of the Spirit through faith.

The People, Places, and Times

Galatia. Galatia was situated in the central region of the peninsula of Asia Minor, with the provinces of Asia on the West, Cappadocia on the East, Pamphylia and Cilicia on the South, and Bithynia and Pontus on the North. It became a Roman province under Augustus, reaching from the borders of Asia and Bythnia to the neighbor of Iconium, Lystra, and Derbe. Galatia had fertile soil and a flourishing trade. It was composed of many colonies from various nations, with a large number of Jews. The Galatians had little religion of their own, and easily adopted the superstitions and mythology of the Greeks. This included nature worship.

Paul visited Galatia on both his first missionary journey (Acts 13:51; 14:8, 20) and on his third (Acts 18:23). During his visits, Paul shared the Gospel message and many Galatians converted to Christianity. On his second missionary journey, Paul passed through the area of Phrygia and Galatia, but was forbidden by the Holy Spirit to preach there (Acts 16:6).

Judaizers. Judaizers were Jewish Christians who believed that ceremonial practices of the Old Testament were still in effect for the New Testament church. They insisted that Gentile converts to Christianity abide by the ceremonial rite of circumcision. Also, they argued that Paul was not an authentic apostle and that out of a desire to make the Gospel more appealing to Gentiles, he had removed from the Gospel certain legal requirements.

NLT cont.

these commands that are written in God's Book of the Law."

11 Consequently, it is clear that no one can ever be right with God by trying to keep the law. For the Scriptures say, "It is through faith that a righteous person has life."

12 How different from this way of faith is the way of law, which says, "If you wish to find life by obeying the law, you must obey all of its commands."

13 But Christ has rescued us from the curse pronounced by the law. When he was hung on the cross, he took upon himself the curse for our wrongdoing. For it is written in the Scriptures, "Cursed is everyone who is hung on a tree."

14 Through the work of Christ Jesus, God has blessed the Gentiles with the same blessing he promised to Abraham, and we Christians receive the promised Holy Spirit through faith.

The Gentile Christians had been persuaded by certain teachers to follow a false Gospel (Galatians 1:6). The teachers told the Gentile Christians if they wanted to share in Abraham's blessing, they must be circumcised, offer sacrifices, eat kosher foods, and submit themselves to Old Testament Law. This contradicted Paul's message so the false teachers also claimed that Paul did not have the proper authority to preach the Gospel.

Background

The letter of Paul to the Galatians was written to refute the Judaizers and to call Christians to faith and freedom in Christ. It was written to the churches in southern Galatia that were founded on Paul's first missionary journey, including Iconium, Lystra, and Derbe. The date of the letter is around A.D. 49, prior to the Jerusalem council in A.D. 50.

In this letter, Paul rebukes the Gentile Christians for alienating themselves from him and the truth. He vindicates his authority and his teachings as an apostle by showing he received them from Christ Himself. He also presents the doctrine of Christianity, justification by faith, with its relationship to the Law on the one hand and to holy living on the other. Paul spoke to the Galatians in reference to their faith in the Law versus faith in Jesus.

At-A-Glance

1. The Gift of the Spirit Is by Faith (Galatians 3:1–5)

2. Abraham's Covenant of Faith (vv. 6–9)

3. Freed from the Curse of the Law by Faith (vv. 10–14)

In Depth

1. The Gift of the Spirit Is by Faith (Galatians 3:1–5)

In Galatians 3:1, Paul asked, "O foolish Galatians, who hath bewitched you, that ye should not obey the truth, before whose eyes Jesus Christ hath been openly set forth, crucified among you?" The Galatians had become so intrigued by the false teachings, it was as though they were under a magical spell. Magic was common during that time. Some people did not realize that the mysterious powers came from Satan. This was in direct contradiction to the power of God manifested through the Holy Spirit. Paul wanted to know how they could be so foolish to renounce the Gospel of Christ and turn back to the Law, after having heard, received, and suffered so much for the Gospel.

The Galatians knew they had not received the Holy Spirit by obeying the Jewish laws, but by faith. But they were now trying to complete their salvation by means of the flesh. Flesh refers to human efforts. The Judaizers were emphasizing the need for circumcision and following other Old Testament laws for true salvation. Paul called it foolishness. We grow spiritually through the Spirit's work in us, not by obeying rules. The power of the Spirit is needed for sanctification (consecration, the act of being set apart).

In verse 5, Paul asked, "He, therefore, that ministereth to you the Spirit, and worketh miracles among you, doeth he it by the works of the Law, or by the hearing of faith?" The Galatians knew the answer to this question was faith. Paul was trying to get them to recognize the foolishness of believing works could draw them closer to God. The Holy Spirit came when they believed by faith in Jesus Christ. The Galatians knew only by faith could they grow closer to God and manifest the power of the Holy Spirit in daily living.

2. Abraham's Covenant of Faith (vv. 6–9)

At least 600 years before God gave Moses the Jewish laws, Abraham founded the Jewish nation. Paul reminded the people, "Even as Abraham believed God, and it was accounted to him for righteousness. Know ye therefore that they which are of faith, the same are the children of Abraham" (Galatians 3:6–7). The real children of God are those who put their faith in God, not the Law. Abraham was saved by his faith (Genesis 15:6). Therefore, all nations will be blessed through Abraham if they believe by faith (Galatians 3:8).

The true design of God from the beginning was for salvation to be offered to all nations, including Gentiles. Jesus commissioned the apostles to go evangelize the entire world. "But ye shall receive power, after that the Holy Spirit is come upon you: and ye shall be witnesses unto me both in Jerusalem, and in all Judea, and in Samaria, and unto the uttermost part of the earth" (Acts 1:8). Faith is the sole requirement for salvation for all people. We are not bound by the Law; we are justified "by faith" (Galatians 3:11).

3. Freed from the Curse of the Law by Faith (vv. 10–14)

Whoever subjects themselves to the Law is cursed. "Cursed is every one that continueth not in all things which are written in the book of the law to do them" (Galatians 3:10). Paul quoted Deuteronomy 27:26 to prove that the Law only condemns. We are condemned if we even break one of the Mosaic Laws. Therefore, everyone is condemned to death because no one can keep all of the laws. The Law was temporary "guardian" to condemn sins, preparing the way for Christ. Once Christ comes, the new age of faith breaks in and we do not need a guardian.

We cannot fix our lives on our own. We need God to help us because we are often motivated to submit to the flesh instead of the spirit. "Every time we desire to do good, evil is always present" (Romans 7:21, paraphrased). Only God can save and empower us to live holy lives. Paul quoted Habakkuk 2:4 in saying, "The just shall live by faith" (Galatians 3:11). The Galatians were tricked under the penalty of God's curse to keep the whole Law. The only person able to keep the whole Law was Jesus. It's only by trusting in Christ's redemption of humanity that we be freed from the condemnation of sin and given the power to change.

Christ became the curse for us in the condemnation, sufferings, and death that He endured for us. He became a curse for us. "For it is written, Cursed is every one that hangeth on a tree" (Galatians 3:13; see also Deuteronomy 21:23). If a person was found guilty of a capital offense, his body was hung from a tree. The person was considered under God's curse. Moreover, it represented God had condemned them and hanging on the tree symbolized divine judgment and rejection. Christ accepted the full punishment of our sins, thus becoming a curse for us. Christians have been made free from the curse of the Law. However, Paul affirmed we are justified apart from the Law, but not free to break the Law. The Gospel confirms the Law (Romans 3:31).

The promise of blessings made to Abraham comes to the Gentiles who believe (Galatians 3:14). These promises made to Abraham were conditional based on faith. Therefore, these conditions could not be altered by the giving of the Law, four centuries later. The Galatians needed to reconsider their relationship with Christ. If we base our salvation on works, it is not salvation. We all are made righteous through faith in Jesus Christ (Romans 3:22–24). We all have sinned and are in need of redemption. We are justified freely by the grace of our Lord and Savior, Jesus Christ.

Search the Scriptures

1. Why did Paul call the Galatians "foolish" (Galatians 3:1–5)?

2. Who is under the curse (v. 10)?

3. How did Christ redeem us from the curse of the Law (v. 13)?

Discuss the Meaning

In some religions, there is a strong emphasis on the strict adherence to the letter of the Law just like the Judaizers taught. How can one effectively witness to them and prove that salvation is by faith alone?

Lesson in Our Society

What would happen if you took a random poll on the streets and asked, "How does one get into heaven?" You probably would get many different responses. Some people may say, "Do good for others," "Follow the Golden Rule," "Pray and go to church," "Don't break the Ten Commandments," etc. Many people lack understanding about salvation. Some people are trying to work their way into heaven. How can "justified by faith" be explained to others in the simplest way?

Make It Happen

Jesus wants us to be loyal to Him alone. If we have faith and believe Christ sacrificed Himself on the Cross on our behalf, we are saved. We are to demonstrate our faith in Christ by living holy lives. The only way to conquer the impulses of the flesh is to walk in the Spirit, be led by the Spirit, bear the fruit of the Spirit, and keep connected to the Spirit (Galatians 5:16, 18, 22, 25, paraphrased). How? First, pray and ask God to forgive you of all sins. Secondly, seek God for direction in your life. Thirdly, memorize Scriptures that empower you to overcome temptations. Fourth, you have to yield to the power of the Holy Spirit and act accordingly. God will always guide you in the right direction. This is faith in action!

Follow the Spirit

What God wants me to do:

_____

_____

_____

_____

Remember Your Thoughts

Special insights I have learned:

_____

_____

_____

_____

More Light on the Text

Galatians 3:1–14

1 O foolish Galatians, who hath bewitched you, that ye should not obey the truth, before whose eyes Jesus Christ hath been evidently set forth, crucified among you?

Paul uses rhetorical questions and reasoning to convince the Galatians of their foolishness. He asked who had put a spell on them to make them depart from the Gospel as they heard it from him. He knew the answer already, but he wanted them to face their waywardness. The word "bewitched" (Gk. *baskaino*, **bas-KAH-ee-no**) means to be put under a spell with the stare from one with an "evil eye." In preaching the Gospel, Paul emphasized the importance of Jesus' crucifixion and resurrection before the Galatians.

2 This only would I learn of you, Received ye the Spirit by the works of the law, or by the hearing of faith?

The Galatians enjoyed the life of the Spirit since the profession of their faith and baptism. Paul continued his interrogation of the churches of Galatia. He asked them if they had received the Spirit by observing the Law or by believing the Gospel. Once again, Paul already knew their response.

3 Are ye so foolish? having begun in the Spirit, are ye now made perfect by the flesh?

The word "flesh" (Gk. *sarx,* **sarks**) appears again in this passage with a different meaning. On the one hand, Paul was referring here to an earthly life in disobedience to God, as opposed to a spiritual life with God by faith in Christ. On the other hand, Paul was referring literally to circumcision, which involved the cutting of flesh. The flesh of circumcision had become an obstacle that could lead the Galatians away from a life begun in the Spirit.

Paul appealed to their rational mind with his next rhetorical question. He asked the Galatians if they were justified by faith in Jesus Christ, what was the benefit of being circumcised? It is as though Paul is asking, "Are you so foolish as to pay for something that you have already been freely given?" The Galatians already had what the Jewish Christians had, minus the obstacles.

4 Have ye suffered so many things in vain? if it be yet in vain.

Paul does not identify the source of the Galatians' suffering. It could have come from at least three sources: (1) Family. Sometimes Gentiles who converted to Judaism or Christianity were estranged from their family and friends. (2) Paul's opponents. The pressure on the Galatians to be circumcised must have placed a strain on the churches.

(3) Government. There were occasional persecutions of Christians by the Roman government. Whatever the source, Paul told the Galatians that if they were circumcised, their belief in Christ would be in vain.

5 He therefore that ministereth to you the Spirit, and worketh miracles among you, doeth he it by the works of the law, or by the hearing of faith?

God's gift of the Holy Spirit to every Christian was evident in the churches of Galatia. Miracles abounded in this Gentile Christian community because of God's grace. Paul's diatribe was an attempt to force the Galatians to recognize that they received the Spirit because of their faith, and not by observing the Law.

6 Even as Abraham believed God, and it was accounted to him for righteousness.

This is an almost exact quotation from Genesis 15:6. Paul uses this quote to introduce his argument from the Scriptures. The Greek word for "accounted" is the verb *logizomai* (**log-ID-zom-ahee**), meaning to be considered, to look upon as or to charge to someone's account. Paul is clearly indicating that Abraham did not perform some duty or keep any laws to be considered righteous. Abraham was considered righteous because he believed God. The Greek word for "believed" is *pisteuo* (**pist-YOO-o**), which means to believe or have faith in. God gives Abraham a "stamp of approval" on his "faith account" because Abraham was righteous—he believed what God promised.

7 Know ye therefore that they which are of faith, the same are the children of Abraham.

Verse 7 builds upon the truth of verse 6. Therefore, we should understand the verse to mean that Abraham was justified by faith:

"Therefore, be sure that it is those who are of faith who are sons of Abraham" (NASB). This was an obvious counter to the Judaizers who claimed that circumcision and obedience to the Law made one a son of Abraham.

8 And the scripture, foreseeing that God would justify the heathen through faith, preached before the gospel unto Abraham, saying, In thee shall all nations be blessed.

Here Paul makes two points. One, the Scriptures looked into the future and saw that God was going to save the Gentiles through faith. Two, God "preached before the gospel" (Gk. *proeuaggelizomai*, **pro-yoo-ang-ghel-ID-zom-ahee**) to Abraham, meaning He "announced the Good News in advance" of the Gospel of God's saving grace through faith in Jesus Christ.

It is apparent that this "pre-preaching" or revelation of the Gospel took place as a part of Abraham's call in Genesis 15:1–6. The content of the Good News that was announced in advance was that all nations—including Gentiles—would be blessed. Although the Genesis passage does not identify the nature of the blessing, Paul views the blessing as being concerned with the message of God's saving grace through faith in Jesus Christ.

9 So then they which be of faith are blessed with faithful Abraham.

Paul wants his Gentile readers to know that they have no need to jump through the Judaizers' legalistic hoops. God provided for their salvation when He entered into covenant with Abraham. Thus, Paul's closing statement (which in the Greek emphasizes the results that follow a previous action): "So then," as a result of what God has planned and is currently bringing to pass, "they which be of faith," as opposed to the circumcised who rely on the works of the law, "are blessed with faithful Abraham."

10 For as many as are of the works of the law are under the curse: for it is written, Cursed is every one that continueth not in all things which are written in the book of the law to do them.

In verse 10, Paul quotes Deuteronomy 27:26 as a reminder to the Galatians that only Jesus Christ can save them from their sins. Nor can the Law save us. On the other hand, the Law condemns. When we break any part of God's Law, the Law condemns us. In fact, there is nothing that the Law can do to reverse this condemnation. However, Jesus Christ paid our sin penalty in full when He conquered sin, death, and Satan on that cruel Cross at Calvary and arose from the dead. However, we must accept the gift of our salvation (Colossians 1:20–23). Then we become a part of the "whosoever believeth in him [Jesus Christ] should not perish, but have everlasting life" (John 3:16).

Without the great salvation that Jesus offers, we are under the curse that sin brings. The word "curse" in Greek is *katara* (**kat-AR-ah**), meaning "an execration, imprecation, curse." Paul adds, "For it is written, Cursed is every one that continueth not in all things which are written in the book of the law to do them." In the Greek, "cursed" here is *epikataratos* (**ep-ee-kat-AR-at-os**), meaning "exposed to divine vengeance, lying under God's curse." Thus, trying to be right with God by our own works or merits will not keep us from being exposed to God's divine vengeance. We will still be eternally separate from God—lost. Accepting Jesus as Lord and Savior, then, is the only way of salvation. Without the salvation that Jesus offers, we will be under the punishment of the Law, eternal separation from a Holy (set apart from sin) God. Thus, Paul wanted the Galatians to know and understand that they were no longer under the Law in terms of their salvation, but they were under grace (God's favor) that He gave them when He sent His one and only Son to die for them.

11 But that no man is justified by the law in the sight of God, it is evident: for, The just shall live by faith. 12 And the law is not of faith: but, The man that doeth them shall live in them.

In verse 11, Paul explains, "No man is justified by the law in the sight of God." The word "justified" in Greek is *dikaioo* (**dik-ah-YO-o**), meaning "to render righteous." Therefore, there is nothing that a human being can do to save him- or herself but accept Jesus Christ as personal Savior—accept God's provision for salvation. In addition, Paul explains, "The just shall live by faith. And the Law is not of faith." The word "faith" in Greek is *pistis* (**PIS-tis**), and means "the conviction that God exists and is the creator and ruler of all things, the provider and bestower of eternal salvation through Christ" (*New Exhaustive Strong's Numbers and Concordance with Expanded Greek-Hebrew Dictionary*).

Thus, those whose sins are covered by the blood of Jesus must live daily by trusting in Him and His provisions.

13 Christ hath redeemed us from the curse of the law, being made a curse for us: for it is written, Cursed is every one that hangeth on a tree:

In summation, the apostle Paul reminds the Galatians, "Christ hath redeemed us from the curse of the law." The word "redeemed" in Greek is *exagorazo* (**ex-ag-or-AD-zo**), and means "by payment of a price to recover from the power of another, to ransom,

buy off" (*New Exhaustive Strong's Numbers and Concordance with Expanded Greek-Hebrew Dictionary*). In essence, it was Jesus Christ who purchased our salvation with His shed blood. He paid the ultimate price—He gave His life. Again, He became a curse for us when He died a heinous death on the Cross.

14 That the blessing of Abraham might come on the Gentiles through Jesus Christ; that we might receive the promise of the Spirit through faith.

In conclusion, even Gentiles have access to this wonderful salvation through Jesus Christ. God chose to use Abraham and His lineage to bestow the blessing on all those who will accept Jesus Christ as Savior. Fully divine and fully human, He is sent because God so loved the world (John 3:16). What have you done with Jesus?

Sources:
Abbott, John C. S., and Jacob Abbott. *Illustrated New Testament.* Studylight.org. http://www.studylight.org/com/ain/view.cgi?book=ga&chapter=003 (accessed May 25, 2010).
American Tract Society Bible Dictionary. Studylight.org. http://studylight.org/dic/ats/view.cgi?number=T829 (accessed May 25, 2010).
Baker's Evangelical Dictionary of Bible Theology. Studylight.org. http://www.studylight.org/dic/bed/view.cgi?number=T285 (accessed May 25, 2010).
Clarke, Adam. *Adam Clarke's Commentary.* Studylight.org.http://www.studylight.org/com/acc/view.cgi?book=ga&chapter=003 (accessed May 25, 2010).
Enns, Paul. *The Moody Handbook of Theology.* Chicago, IL: Moody Press. 1989. 110.
Life Application Study Bible. Wheaton, IL: Tyndale House Publishers, 1996.
Scofield, C. I., ed. *The New Scofield Study Bible—King James Version.* New York, NY: Oxford University Press, 1967. 1264–71.
Strong, James. *New Exhaustive Strong's Numbers and Concordance with Expanded Greek-Hebrew Dictionary.* Seattle, WA: Biblesoft, and International Bible Translators, 1994. 2003.

Say It Correctly

Bithynian. Bi-THYN-ee-an.
Cappadocia. Ka-puh-DOH-shee-uh.
Cilicia. Suh-LI-see-uh.
Derbe. DUHR-bee.
Pamphylia. Pam-FIL-ee-uh.

Daily Bible Readings

MONDAY
Blessing All Nations
(Genesis 18:16–21)

TUESDAY
Keep the Law and Live
(Leviticus 18:1–5)

WEDNESDAY
The Curse of Sin
(Deuteronomy 27:15–26)

THURSDAY
The Righteous Live by Their Faith
(Habakkuk 2:1–5)

FRIDAY
Faith and Salvation
(Hebrews 10:32–39)

SATURDAY
What Do I Still Lack?
(Matthew 19:16–26)

SUNDAY
The Blessing for All
(Galatians 3:1–14)

Notes

_____

_____

_____

_____

Teaching Tips

Words You Should Know

A. Covenant (Galatians 3:15, 17) *diatheke* (Gk.)—A promise, contract, or a will.

B. Redeem (4:5) *exagorazo* (Gk.)—To buy something from someone in order to establish ownership.

Teacher Preparation

Unifying Principle—Understanding Values. Paul states that Gentiles received God's blessing as heirs of Abraham, but had to accept the promise for themselves by maturing in their faith in Jesus Christ.

A. Pray for your students and the lesson.

B. Read this week's lesson from several versions of the Bible.

C. Read the entire lesson at least twice this week. Take notes as needed.

D. Complete the companion lesson in the *Precepts For Living Personal Study Guide®*.

O—Open the Lesson

A. Open the class with a prayer focusing on the Keep in Mind verse.

B. After prayer, introduce today's subject of the lesson.

C. Have your students read the Aim for Change and Keep in Mind verse in unison. Discuss.

D. Now, have a volunteer summarize the In Focus story. Discuss.

P—Present the Scriptures

A. Based on the students' reading from the last two weeks, ask them to discuss what they think is the central theme of Galatians.

B. Explain the Focal Verses using The People, Places, and Times; Background; the At-A-Glance outline; In Depth; Search the Scriptures; and More Light on the Text.

E—Explore the Meaning

A. Emphasize the salient points in the Discuss the Meaning, Lesson in Our Society, and Make It Happen sections.

B. Connect these sections to the Aim for Change and discuss.

N—Next Steps for Application

A. Challenge your students to reflect on today's lesson and what it means to be "Heirs to the Promise."

B. Close with prayer.

Worship Guide

For the Superintendent or Teacher
Theme: Heirs to the Promise
Theme Song: "The Only Hope"
Devotional Reading: Romans 4:1–8
Prayer

Heirs to the Promise

Bible Background • GALATIANS 3:15–29; 4:1–5:1
Printed Text • GALATIANS 3:15–18; 4:1–7 | Devotional Reading • ROMANS 4:1–8

—————————— Aim for Change ——————————

By the end of the lesson, we will: KNOW Paul's statements about being heirs of Abraham through faith; FEEL secure through faith in Jesus; and PURSUE a relationship with God that will lead to growth in faith.

————————  In Focus ————————

Annie's dad left her mom when she and her two brothers were just toddlers. All three of them were now in their 50s. But because she never experienced the love of a father, Annie still felt like something was missing in her life. Even in her marriage, she bent over backwards to please her husband. She was so afraid of losing him, just like she had lost her father. Sadly, one day, he walked out of her life and never returned.

Sometimes, her inability to truly feel secure in the love of an earthly father or husband led Annie to difficulties in trusting God, her heavenly Father. But she finally saw that although two important men in her life had deserted her, her heavenly Father would never let her go. She began to rest in the thought that she was His daughter.

When Annie accepted Jesus Christ as her Savior, she began such an intimate relationship with the Holy God of the universe, that she can now call Him her dear Father. How do you think this should affect her Christian walk?

———————— Keep in Mind ————————

FEB 19th

"Wherefore thou art no more a servant, but a son; and if a son, then an heir of God through Christ" (Galatians 4:7).

"Wherefore thou art no more a servant, but a son; and if a son, then an heir of God through Christ" (Galatians 4:7).

Focal Verses

KJV **Galatians 3:15** Brethren, I speak after the manner of men; Though it be but a man's covenant, yet if it be confirmed, no man disannulleth, or addeth thereto.

16 Now to Abraham and his seed were the promises made. He saith not, And to seeds, as of many; but as of one, And to thy seed, which is Christ.

17 And this I say, that the covenant, that was confirmed before of God in Christ, the law, which was four hundred and thirty years after, cannot disannul, that it should make the promise of none effect.

18 For if the inheritance be of the law, it is no more of promise: but God gave it to Abraham by promise.

4:1 Now I say, That the heir, as long as he is a child, differeth nothing from a servant, though he be lord of all;

2 But is under tutors and governors until the time appointed of the father.

3 Even so we, when we were children, were in bondage under the elements of the world:

4 But when the fulness of the time was come, God sent forth his Son, made of a woman, made under the law,

5 To redeem them that were under the law, that we might receive the adoption of sons.

6 And because ye are sons, God hath sent forth the Spirit of his Son into your hearts, crying, Abba, Father.

7 Wherefore thou art no more a servant, but a son; and if a son, then an heir of God through Christ.

NLT **Galatians 3:15** Dear brothers and sisters, here's an example from everyday life. Just as no one can set aside or amend an irrevocable agreement, so it is in this case.

16 God gave the promise to Abraham and his child. And notice that it doesn't say the promise was to his children, as if it meant many descendants. But the promise was to his child—and that, of course, means Christ.

17 This is what I am trying to say: The agreement God made with Abraham could not be canceled 430 years later when God gave the law to Moses. God would be breaking his promise.

18 For if the inheritance could be received only by keeping the law, then it would not be the result of accepting God's promise. But God gave it to Abraham as a promise.

4:1 Think of it this way. If a father dies and leaves great wealth for his young children, those children are not much better off than slaves until they grow up, even though they actually own everything their father had.

2 They have to obey their guardians until they reach whatever age their father set.

3 And that's the way it was with us before Christ came. We were slaves to the spiritual powers of this world.

4 But when the right time came, God sent his Son, born of a woman, subject to the law.

5 God sent him to buy freedom for us who were slaves to the law, so that he could adopt us as his very own children.

6 And because you Gentiles have become his children, God has sent the Spirit of his Son into your hearts, and now you can call God your dear Father.

7 Now you are no longer a slave but God's own child. And since you are his child, everything he has belongs to you.

The People, Places, and Times

Promise. The Bible contains many promises by God to His people. Significant among God's promises is His promise to bless Abraham with a son, who would become a great nation, and that all the nations of the earth would be blessed in Abraham. God also promised Abraham that his descendants would be too many to count. God's promise to Abraham is in the background as God delivered the Children of Israel from Egyptian slavery and made a covenant with them. Israel descended from Abraham through Isaac. God's presence was continually with the Israelites, who trusted in God's future salvation because of His promise to Abraham.

Slavery. Slavery was an integral part of Greco-Roman civilization. Slaves accounted for one-fifth of the population. People became slaves through various circumstances, including breeding, wars, piracy, debt, and birth to a slave mother. Slaves were the property of their owners and had no legal rights. Slaves functioned broadly within the society from civil service to hard labor. Household slaves were entrusted with the care of the home and child rearing. School-age children were under the moral guidance of "pedagogues," or custodians, who also looked after the children's general well-being but were not the children's teachers.

A benevolent master might grant a slave freedom in his will. The slave was freed upon the death of the master. A friend, relative, or other benefactor might also purchase a slave's freedom. "Redemption" means "the act of buying back," as in a purchase from slavery.

Background

Paul was a very highly educated man. He taught under the supervision of Gamaliel, the most highly respected rabbi (Jewish teacher) of his day. Paul also was familiar with Greek and Roman thought, so he could argue points from both the Jewish point of view and the Gentile point of view. In today's Scripture passages, he makes use of both styles of defense.

At-A-Glance

1. The Law and the Promise
(Galatians 3:15–18)

2. Relationship to God Based upon the
Law (Galatians 4:1–3)

3. Slavery and Adoption (4:4–7)

In Depth

1. The Law and the Promise (Galatians 3:15–18)

We first read of God's promise to Abraham in Genesis 12:1–7. God called Abraham to leave his homeland, his relatives, and even his elderly father. God made some wonderful promises to him, but Abraham saw almost none of them fulfilled in his lifetime. God promised that He would make Abraham's descendants into a great nation, that He would make his name famous, and that He would bless Abraham, bless everyone that blessed the Jewish people, and curse those who hurt the Jewish people. In fact, everyone on earth would be blessed through Abraham and his seed.

Paul points out that in Genesis 12:7 and elsewhere in Scripture (God repeated His promise over and over to Abraham and to his descendants) the word for "seed" is singular. We might substitute the word "descendant" for "seed" to grasp the meaning. God promised to bless everyone in the world through one of Abraham's descendants, in particular, Jesus!

So God's promise to Abraham was fulfilled in Jesus. God made the promise to Abraham and Abraham believed God. God's promise to Abraham was given to him based on his faith alone.

Four hundred and thirty years later, God gave the Law to Moses. Moses and all the Israelites were the descendants of Abraham. God gave the promise to Abraham based upon his faith alone, not by obedience to the Law. We are quite sure of this, because the Law had not yet been given. Do you think that if the Israelites did not obey the Law, that God would not keep His promise to send Jesus? We are so blessed that God kept His promise in spite of the fact that His people were unable to keep the Law.

2. Relationship to God Based upon the Law (Galatians 4:1–3)

From the time the Law was instituted (the first five books of the Old Testament), people sought to have a right relationship with God based upon their obedience to the Law. Day after day, person after person, people failed to live up to the standards of perfection.

Paul explains that this time was like the time period in which a rich man's son is growing up. Although he will someday inherit the company his father owns, as long as he is a child, he cannot spend any of the company's money. He may get an allowance, but he cannot dip into the company accounts that he will someday inherit. In fact, his allowance may be no bigger than the servants that work in his home.

If we, as Christians, are struggling to live up to legalistic standards, we are not living like true children of God. Paul is inviting us to take hold of our inheritance as grown children of our heavenly Father.

3. Slavery and Adoption (4:4–7)

The status of children in early Christianity was only a little better than that of slaves. Although freeborn male children would someday inherit their father's property, including the slaves, the children held a subordinate position in the household. Earlier, Paul had described the Jewish people as children under the guardianship of the Law. However, when God's appointed hour had come, He sent Jesus into the world to redeem them from under the Law and adopt them as children. Adoption was a common practice in the Greco-Roman world. A person could be adopted as an adult, as well as a child. The adoptive parent gave the adopted person a new life with a new family name and status. The adopted person received all the rights and privileges of a natural born child, including the family inheritance.

The Galatians, in their faith, were in a new relationship with God. Through Christ Jesus, Gentiles were adopted into God's household with the full rights of natural-born children with the Holy Spirit as God's witness. As children of God, they were no longer under the slave custodian, but instead as God's children, heirs of God through Christ Jesus.

If we are living in a legalistic kind of limbo, we are missing out on all of our rights as full-grown children of God. Instead of a bunch of laws, we have the Holy Spirit in our hearts. Therefore, our motivation for our behavior is a mature desire to please our heavenly Father. We are not slaves; we are royal heirs! We have much we inherit here on earth and even more in heaven to come when we will receive our full inheritance as children of God.

Search the Scriptures

1. What was promised to Abraham concerning his seed (Galatians 3:15–18)?

2. When is an heir the same as a slave or a servant (Galatians 4:1–3)?

Discuss the Meaning

The goal of almost all religions is to make a way to having a relationship with God. But the chief difference between biblical Christianity and all other ways is that other religions say that you must live in such a way as to qualify for that relationship. In other words, your actions, words, and thoughts must be good enough. For this to work, either God must not be holy enough to have high standards, or a person must live a perfect life. Neither position is tenable. To aim to have our good deeds outweigh our bad deeds is just not good enough for our holy God. But despite our sinfulness, God loves us and that is why God had to make a way for us. In light of the Scripture passages for this week, discuss what God did to make it possible for us to call Him Father. Discuss what we have to do to make that happen.

Lesson in Our Society

When I was an adolescent, I began to hear whispers about one of my cousins not being my "real" cousin. Those whispers were fueled by the revelation that my uncle was not my cousin's biological father. Learning this so-called truth about my cousin did not change our relationship, nor did my uncle love my cousin any less than his natural-born child. My cousin carries our family name and is my uncle's heir. All of us who have been born again are adopted children of God. Jesus is the seed of Abraham and Davidic heir and true Son of God, who makes it possible for us to be members of God's family.

Make It Happen

How does it make you feel to know that no matter what the circumstances were surrounding your birth, through Christ Jesus, you have been adopted into God's family and made one with Christ by grace through faith? All your debts are paid, and you now have all the rights of a natural-born child. You share an equal inheritance with all God's children. That is good news! Thank God for all He has done for you!

Follow the Spirit

What God wants me to do:

_____

_____

_____

_____

Remember Your Thoughts

Special insights I have learned:

_____

_____

_____

_____

More Light on the Text

Galatians 3:15–18; 4:1–7

15 Brethren, I speak after the manner of men; Though it be but a man's covenant, yet if it be confirmed, no man disannulleth, or addeth thereto.

When Paul uses the word "covenant" here (Greek *diatheke*, **dee-ath-AY-kay**), he is thinking more of the current legal term as used by the Greeks, not the Old Testament word for covenant. That is the reason he uses the phrase, "after the manner of men." And so "covenant" is closest to meaning "a will." Under Greek law, even the person who made out the will could not change it once it was signed and placed in the record. And just as today, once a person dies, a will cannot be annulled or added to. In the verses that follow, Paul uses the argument that if a will made by mere humans cannot be changed, we can be sure that a covenant made by the holy God can never, ever be broken.

16 Now to Abraham and his seed were the promises made. He saith not, And to seeds, as of many; but as of one, And to thy seed, which is Christ.

Now Paul is talking about the covenant that God made with Abraham. All the Jewish people are the descendants (seed) of Abraham, but in some passages in the Old Testament, the Hebrew for "seed" can be viewed either as one group or one individual. In a very real sense, "all people," Jews or Gentiles that put their faith in Jesus Christ, are blessed. But this blessing comes through just one of Abraham's descendants, and that is Jesus (Genesis 17:7–8; Matthew 1:1).

17 And this I say, that the covenant, that was confirmed before of God in Christ, the law, which was four hundred and thirty years after, cannot disannul, that it should make the promise of none effect.

Now we see the legal point that Paul is making. God made His unconditional covenant of faith and faith alone with Abraham 430 years before He made the Covenant of the Law with Abraham on the top of Mt. Sinai. "The law" is translated from the Greek *nomos* (**NOM-os**), which refers to laws that are imposed and regulated. In this case, it is referring specifically to laws contained from Exodus through Deuteronomy—including

the moral law (the Ten Commandments), and levitical and civil laws. But Paul is reasoning that the Law cannot take precedence over God's covenant of grace with Abraham. We read the wonderful words concerning Abraham, "He believed in the LORD; and he counted it to him for righteousness" (Genesis 15:6). The Covenant of the Law was conditional; its promises were only valid to those who kept the Law perfectly, which no one could. It was a fortunate thing that the Abrahamic Covenant of Promise was not invalidated by the giving of the Law.

We think of the many people in many religions who are seeking a right relationship with God through meticulous keeping of laws. What great frustration! It is just impossible to achieve a right relationship with God through our own efforts. It is only by God's grace that we can come to Him. And the good news is that He is lovingly holding out His arms to welcome us into His family.

18 For if the inheritance be of the law, it is no more of promise: but God gave it to Abraham by promise.

The giving of the Law on Mt. Sinai cannot negate our inheritance from Father Abraham. Our inheritance is based upon our faith in the promises of God. From the beginning of the human race, the only way to a right relationship with God has been by grace through faith. (To understand God's purpose in giving the Law, we can read Galatians 3:19 to the end of the chapter.) This verse and many other New Testament Scriptures make us think of the old fun song, "Father Abraham Had Many Sons." So whether or not we share the same DNA as Abraham, we become his descendants as we put our faith in God, just as he did. We can claim to be sons and daughters of this Jewish patriarch.

4:1 Now I say, That the heir, as long as he is a child, differeth nothing from a servant, though he be lord of all;

Many organizations have developed rites of passages to mark the passage from childhood into adulthood. In observant Jewish families, fathers would take their sons to the temple on the first Sabbath after their 12th birthday. On this day, the boy became a son of the Law. Nowadays, both boys and girls in Jewish families prepare for their *bar mitzvahs* and *bas* (or *bat*) *mitzvahs* with much studying of the Torah and the Hebrew language. A performance will be expected of them.

Romans had other markers; Greeks had other markers still. In the United States there are certain legal milestones, such as 18 years old to vote and perhaps 15 or 16 years old to obtain a driver's license. Educators today realize that a child does not change magically from a child to an adult all in one day, but that developmental stages occur in general progression in many areas and not exactly at the same rate in each individual. One child may be mature enough to drive a car at age 15, but another might not be until age 21.

2 But is under tutors and governors until the time appointed of the father.

We can imagine the spoiled child of a rich man. He pouts and complains because he is compelled to obey the rules of his parents. He thinks he can handle large sums of money, but his father knows how truly immature he is. The aim of the tutors, the governors, and governesses, the father and the mother is to teach him those things he needs to learn, so that when he comes into his inheritance, he will be able to handle it. But the picture here is of a Roman child whose rich father has died. The father has included in his will names of surrogate parents for the child

and at what stage or stages he will begin to manage his own property. Up until that time, the financial guardian will handle the child's estate. Some heirs today may even have to wait until they are 30 years old to take complete charge of their fortunes.

3 Even so we, when we were children, were in bondage under the elements of the world:

Most scholars think that the childhood that Paul is referring to here is the bondage to the Mosaic Law. Others think that perhaps he is including Galatians with a pagan background who were in bondage to various false gods. The Greek word for "elements" is *stoicheion* (**stoy-KHI-on**), and it means something very rudimentary or basic, such as the ABCs. The Law of Moses helps us to see that we are in bondage to sin (Galatians 3:19–29), but in the other case the bondage was to the sin of worshiping false gods. Whether in our backgrounds we were striving to keep the rules and regulations or we were totally confused and following some false religion; in either case, we were locked up and missing the freedom that comes with a deep relationship with our Lord. Even new believers are often stuck on the ABCs of legalism. True freedom comes with a mature relationship with Jesus Christ.

4 But when the fulness of the time was come, God sent forth his Son, made of a woman, made under the law,

At the right time, God sent His Son to redeem all humanity. The same God who made the promise to Abraham now sends His Son in fulfillment of the promise. The Greek word *exapostello* (**ex-ap-os-TEL-lo**) means "sent forth" with a commission. Christ was sent with the commission to fulfill the Father's promise of salvation through faith.

That Christ was God's "Son, made of a woman" indicates His full divinity as well as

His full humanity without sin. Therefore, the Savior could be born under the Law and yet not subjected to its bondage. Thus, He identifies with the experience of those under the Law; yet He is without sin.

5 To redeem them that were under the law, that we might receive the adoption of sons.

Christ came under the Law to redeem those under the Law. The word "redeem" (Gk. *exagorazo*, **ex-ag-or-AD-zo**) was used to denote buying a slave out of the slave market into freedom. Those under the Law were, like the rest of humanity, slaves to sin and not children of God. Slaves usually were not capable of purchasing their own freedom. When Christ made redemption from the slavery of sin possible for those under the Law, the result was a dramatic transformation into adopted children of God.

6 And because ye are sons, God hath sent forth the Spirit of his Son into your hearts, crying, Abba, Father.

As God's children, we receive the Spirit of Christ into our hearts, bearing witness of our filial relationship to God. This is a continuous witness, reassuring us of our new relationship to God. Out of respect, the Jews would not call God by the name of Father. It was therefore a very surprising idea, which derives from Christ (see Mark 14:36) that we should address God as Father, using the very intimate and affectionate Aramaic term "*Abba*" (more like "dear Father" than "Daddy"). The term acknowledges the protective power, care, and concern that God, the Father shows for us—His children.

7 Wherefore thou art no more a servant, but a son; and if a son, then an heir of God through Christ.

With our new status as children of God comes the end of slavery to sin under the Law. We can be children and still be excluded from any inheritance by a will. Such is not the situation of God's children. We are not just children of God in the abstract, nominal sense without any privileges attached. To us belong the full privileges of being His heirs. An "heir" (Gk. *kleronomos*, **klay-ron-OM-os**) is one who receives an inheritance without having to work for it. That is what believers have as "Abraham's seed, and heirs according to the promise" (Galatians 3:29).

Sources:

Baltes, A. J., ed. Biblespeech.com. http://www.biblespeech.com (accessed August 11, 2010).

Barclay, William. *The Letters to the Galatians and Ephesians. Translated, with Introductions and Interpretations.* Philadephia, PA: Westminster Press, 1956.

Bruce, F. F. *The Epistle to the Galatians: A Commentary on the Greek Text. The New International Greek Testament Commentary.* Grand Rapids, MI: William B. Eerdmans Publishing Company, 1982.

Buttrick, George A., ed. "Promise." *The Interpreters' Dictionary of the Bible. Vol. 3.* Nashville, TN: Abingdon Press, 1962. 893–94.

Strong, James. *Strong's Exhaustive Concordance of the Bible.* McLean, VA: MacDonald Publishing Company, n.d.

Say It Correctly

Differeth. DIF-er-eth.
Disannulleth. Dis-a-NULL-eth.
Greco-Roman. GRE-co-RO-man.
Pedagogues. PED-a-gogs.

Daily Bible Readings

MONDAY
Ancestor to a Multitude of Nations
(Genesis 17:1–8)

TUESDAY
The Promise Is for You
(Acts 2:32–39)

WEDNESDAY
The Gift of Righteousness
(Romans 4:1–8)

THURSDAY
Now That Faith Has Come
(Galatians 3:19–29)

FRIDAY
Until Christ Is Formed in You
(Galatians 4:12–20)

SATURDAY
Stand Firm in Christ's Freedom
(Galatians 4:28–5:1)

SUNDAY
Heirs to the Promise
(Galatians 3:15–18; 4:1–7)

Notes

_____

_____

_____

_____

Teaching Tips

Words You Should Know

A. Longsuffering (Galatians 5:22) *makrothumia* (Gk.)—The patience and self-restraint of people who could quickly/easily avenge themselves against wrongdoers.

B. Mocked (6:7) *mukterizo* (Gk.)—Turned up one's nose at someone as a gesture of ridicule, scorn, or contempt.

Teacher Preparation

Unifying Principle—Bearing One Another's Burden. Paul said that whenever possible, we should work for the good of all, especially for those in the family of faith.

A. Pray that students will come to know more fully what it means to live by the Spirit.

B. Study the entire lesson.

C. Read aloud and meditate on the Devotional Readings.

D. Complete the companion lesson in the *Precepts For Living Personal Study Guide®*.

O—Open the Lesson

A. Open with prayer.

B. Have volunteers share what they believe to be the meaning of Christian freedom. Clarify.

C. Read and discuss the In Focus section.

P—Present the Scriptures

A. Ask two or three volunteers to read the Focal Verses.

B. Based on the information in the Background; In Depth; The People, Places, and Times; and More Light on the Text sections, discuss the role of the Holy Spirit in the believer's life.

E—Explore the Meaning

A. Use some of the Discuss the Meaning questions to initiate discussion of ways in which believers can maximize the availability of the Spirit to produce the fruit of the Spirit in their lives.

B. Ask the students to share personal experiences of their own awareness of the Spirit's presence.

N—Next Steps for Application

A. Read the Make It Happen assignment. Challenge the students to select a day next week to put it into practice.

B. Close with prayer.

Worship Guide

For the Superintendent or Teacher
Theme: Fruits of Redemption
Theme Song: "Spirit of the Living God"
Devotional Reading: 2 Peter 1:3–8
Prayer

FEB 26th

Fruits of Redemption

Bible Background • GALATIANS 5:2–6:18
Printed Text • GALATIANS 5:22–6:10 | Devotional Reading • 2 PETER 1:3–8

Aim for Change

By the end of the lesson, we will: HEAR Paul's teaching on faithfulness and sharing others' burdens; FEEL compassion and a sense of duty to others; and SUPPORT one another in the faith through service.

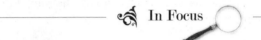 ## In Focus

Following his participation in a drug addiction rehab center and his acceptance of Jesus Christ, a young husband and father of two small children made rapid progress toward getting his life together. He was fortunate to have the support of a loving and caring wife and church family. These support systems, coupled with his desire to make something of his life, resulted in his finishing trade school, landing a good job and staying clean—drug free for four years. However, one day, his wife called me indicating that he was at home with her and wanted to talk with me. Sensing the distress in her voice, I responded immediately.

He confessed that he had "fallen back." He said, "I messed up. I've done drugs twice during the past two weeks."

The tragedy is that this is not an isolated situation. The lust of the flesh renders all believers vulnerable to using their Christian freedom to indulge the sinful nature. Those who refuse to walk in the Spirit will fulfill the lust of the flesh. The good news is that those who allow themselves to "be led of the Spirit" will produce the fruit of the Spirit (Galatians 5:18, 22–23).

God's will is that we walk in the Spirit!

Keep in Mind

"But the fruit of the Spirit is love, joy, peace, longsuffering, gentleness, goodness, faith" (Galatians 5:22).

"But the fruit of the Spirit is love, joy, peace, longsuffering, gentleness, goodness, faith" (Galatians 5:22).

Focal Verses

KJV **Galatians 5:22** But the fruit of the Spirit is love, joy, peace, longsuffering, gentleness, goodness, faith,

23 Meekness, temperance: against such there is no law.

24 And they that are Christ's have crucified the flesh with the affections and lusts.

25 If we live in the Spirit, let us also walk in the Spirit.

26 Let us not be desirous of vain glory, provoking one another, envying one another.

6:1 Brethren, if a man be overtaken in a fault, ye which are spiritual, restore such a one in the spirit of meekness; considering thyself, lest thou also be tempted.

2 Bear ye one another's burdens, and so fulfil the law of Christ.

3 For if a man think himself to be something, when he is nothing, he deceiveth himself.

4 But let every man prove his own work, and then shall he have rejoicing in himself alone, and not in another.

5 For every man shall bear his own burden.

6 Let him that is taught in the word communicate unto him that teacheth in all good things.

7 Be not deceived; God is not mocked: for whatsoever a man soweth, that shall he also reap.

8 For he that soweth to his flesh shall of the flesh reap corruption; but he that soweth to the Spirit shall of the Spirit reap life everlasting.

9 And let us not be weary in well doing: for in due season we shall reap, if we faint not.

10 As we have therefore opportunity, let us do good unto all men, especially unto them who are of the household of faith.

The People, Places, and Times

Walking in the Spirit. The apostle Paul challenged the believers of his day to learn what every believer today would do well to remember: The key to making progress in

NLT **Galatians 5:22** But when the Holy Spirit controls our lives, he will produce this kind of fruit in us: love, joy, peace, patience, kindness, goodness, faithfulness,

23 gentleness, and self-control. Here there is no conflict with the law.

24 Those who belong to Christ Jesus have nailed the passions and desires of their sinful nature to his cross and crucified them there.

25 If we are living now by the Holy Spirit, let us follow the Holy Spirit's leading in every part of our lives.

26 Let us not become conceited, or irritate one another, or be jealous of one another.

We Reap What We Sow

6:1 Dear brothers and sisters, if another Christian is overcome by some sin, you who are godly should gently and humbly help that person back onto the right path. And be careful not to fall into the same temptation yourself.

2 Share each other's troubles and problems, and in this way obey the law of Christ.

3 If you think you are too important to help someone in need, you are only fooling yourself. You are really a nobody.

4 Be sure to do what you should, for then you will enjoy the personal satisfaction of having done your work well, and you won't need to compare yourself to anyone else.

5 For we are each responsible for our own conduct.

6 Those who are taught the word of God should help their teachers by paying them.

7 Don't be misled. Remember that you can't ignore God and get away with it. You will always reap what you sow!

8 Those who live only to satisfy their own sinful desires will harvest the consequences of decay and death. But those who live to please the Spirit will harvest everlasting life from the Spirit.

9 So don't get tired of doing what is good. Don't get discouraged and give up, for we will reap a harvest of blessing at the appropriate time.

the realm of Christian freedom is to keep walking in the Spirit.

Paul is very much aware of the Galatians' need for a power that the Law could not give. The history of the Jewish people consistently revealed that there are some things the Law cannot do (Romans 7:7–12; 8:3). Rules and regulations can command, but they cannot empower one *to do* what is commanded. Rules and regulations serve as a guide or a road map, but they *cannot motivate and enable* one to follow the direction and guidance given.

If the Galatians were to live free from sin's power to control their lives—if they were to fulfill the Law—it would be because they surrendered themselves to the enabling power of the Holy Spirit. Only those who have surrendered and who *continually surrender* themselves to the complete control of the Spirit are empowered to walk according to the Spirit's orders. It is the power of the Holy Spirit that guides and strengthens believers to live righteously and gain victory in their warfare against the desires of the flesh (sinful nature).

Background

Paul had just finished telling the Galatians about their freedom in Christ. They were instructed to use their freedom to make doing God's will and lovingly serving others their highest aim. Paul was not, however, unaware of the inner struggle that such freedom would bring. The desires of the sinful nature are always present to dissuade believers from fulfilling the call of God and living ethical and righteous lives.

Christian freedom requires believers to make choices. There is always the choice to serve the will of God or the desires of the sinful nature. The power to do God's will flows into the hearts of those who are now walking and who make a choice to keep walking in the Spirit.

NLT cont.

10 Whenever we have the opportunity, we should do good to everyone, especially to our Christian brothers and sisters.

At-A-Glance

1. The Way of the Spirit Produces the Fruit of the Spirit (Galatians 5:22–26)

2. Believers Are To Rally Around One Another in the Spirit of Meekness (Galatians 6:1–5)

3. Believers Are To Persevere in Doing Good (vv. 6–10)

In Depth

1. The Way of the Spirit Produces the Fruit of the Spirit (Galatians 5:22–26)

After listing certain manifestations of the sinful nature (the flesh), Paul now mentions some of the manifestations of the Spirit. His listing of the fruit of the Spirit is not meant to be exhaustive, but rather illustrative of the kinds of qualities and behaviors produced by the Spirit.

First, it is worthy to note that Paul's list begins with love, the one quality necessary to create the atmosphere needed for the proper functioning of all the other qualities (see 1 Corinthians 13). Moreover, ending the list with temperance (i.e., self-control) is a clear indication of our Spirit-led ability to control the desires of the sinful nature.

Leon Morris offers a helpful comment about the phrase "fruit (singular) of the Spirit" in Galatians 5:22. Morris suggests that this is not a reference to a "series of fruits" to be distributed among believers "so that one believer has one (and) another (believer has) another. Rather, he is referring to a cluster, such that all these qualities are to be manifested in each believer" (Morris, 173). If Morris is right, then every believer, through the Spirit's grace, has access to all the fruit of the Spirit. Therefore, while the works of the sinful nature lead to destruction, the fruit of the Spirit offers the believer the power to grow in the things of the Spirit.

Given the warfare between the sinful nature and the Spirit, what is the believer's responsibility? What should the believer do to gain victory over the desires of the sinful nature and to grow in the things of the Spirit? To this question, Paul gives three specific responses. First, believers are not to undo what they have already done. What the believer has nailed to the Cross through repentance and faith is not to be removed. They that are Christ's have crucified the flesh; let the flesh remain dead! Do not bring the flesh to life again by choosing to fulfill its desires.

Second, since the Holy Spirit is the source of the believer's life in Christ, the believer is to allow the Spirit to dominate and control his or her behavior. In other words, "If we live in the Spirit, let us also walk in the Spirit" (Galatians 5:25).

Third, the believer must "not be desirous of vain glory" (v. 26). This, Paul adds, will disrupt Christian fellowship and create envy within our hearts. The implication is that the desire for vainglory (being conceited) works against the Spirit's desires for God's glory.

2. Believers Are To Rally Around One Another in the Spirit of Meekness (Galatians 6:1–5)

In these verses, Paul continues to outline the responsibility and expected behavior of those who follow the Spirit's leading. Believers are to be led by the Spirit, avoid arrogance and self-deception, and rally 'round one another in the spirit of meekness, especially when another believer has been "overtaken in a fault" (Galatians 6:1a).

Paul is not naive. He recognizes that there will be occasional instances when a believer will be guilty of missing the mark and yielding to the desires of the sinful nature. In these instances, God's plan is to involve the body of believers in the Spirit's redemptive and restorative process. This plan has no place for judging, self-deception, or arrogance. Rather, "the spirit of meekness" (Galatians 6:1a) is to characterize the congregation. Each believer is to keep in mind that they, too, are vulnerable to the desires of the sinful nature (v. 1b).

In addition, believers are to "bear. . . one another's burdens" (v. 2). No believer should view himself or herself as being superior to another believer (vv. 3–5). Paul makes the point that the fruit of the Spirit is to find expression not only through the lives of individual believers, but also through the collective life of the congregation.

3. Believers Are To Persevere in Doing Good (vv. 6–10)

In verses 6 through 10, Paul reminds believers to persevere in "doing good." They are to remember those who teach them spiritual truths and persevere in the things of the Spirit. In contrast, he clearly states that to give place to the desires of the sinful nature has both current and eternal consequences. The consequence of pursuing the things of the Spirit is "life everlasting" (v. 8b). The consequence of yielding to the desires of the sinful nature is "corruption" (v. 8a).

Therefore, since God cannot be mocked (scornfully disregarded), believers would do well to remember that they will reap the good they have sown if they do not grow weary or give up (v. 9). In light of God's approval and external rewards, we are admonished to take advantage of opportunities to do good, especially for fellow believers in Christ.

Search the Scriptures

1. How many of the fruit of the Spirit can you name (Galatians 5:22–23)?

2. "If a man be overtaken in a fault," what should believers do (Galatians 6:1)?

3. Why do you think that Paul makes it clear that "God is not mocked" (v. 7)?

Discuss the Meaning

1. What is meant by the proverbial phrase "God is not mocked"?

2. What does it mean to "be led of the Spirit"?

3. What does it mean to "prove" one's "own work"?

Lesson in Our Society

Every believer who desires to do the will of God has access to the Spirit's guiding and empowering resources. However, to do so, we must continue to walk in the Spirit. Believers have no reason to grow weary and give up. The rewards that follow those who, by the Spirit's enabling, keep choosing to do good are everlastingly beneficial. Moreover, those believers who dare to remember, and who in remembering take to heart the truth that in love Christ died for us will find themselves increasingly compelled and constrained (2 Corinthians 5:14) to keep choosing to fulfill the desires of the Spirit by living righteously and walking in love. If we want to have a distinctive witness to the world around us, we have to live in the Spirit's power.

Make It Happen

During this week, set aside a day or two to give yourself to prayer and fasting, asking God to make you more aware of the presence and leading of His Spirit. In ad-dition to your praying and fasting, set some priorities for the week so that the pressures of your schedule will not deafen you to the Spirit's voice.

Follow the Spirit

What God wants me to do:

_____

_____

_____

_____

Remember Your Thoughts

Special insights I have learned:

_____

_____

_____

_____

More Light on the Text

Galatians 5:22–6:10

22 But the fruit of the Spirit is love, joy, peace, longsuffering, gentleness, goodness, faith, 23 meekness, temperance: against such there is no law. 24 And they that are Christ's have crucified the flesh with the affections and lusts.

Paul identifies the kind of qualities that will be evident in those believers who are walking in the Spirit. Paul contrasts the "fruit (singular) of the Spirit" with the aforementioned "works (plural) of the flesh (sinful nature)." The singular form of the Greek word *karpos* (**kar-POS**), meaning "fruit," is indicative of the fact that the Spirit is capable of producing this fruit in every believer. *They are not fruits, but fruit.*

307

The Spirit produces character and righteous behavior that is an outgrowth of the changed heart of the believer, thus making obedience to the Law obsolete. Those who walk in the Spirit put to death the sinful nature and its desires and allow the Spirit of God to lead them and produce fruit that does not need legislation.

In other words, those who have identified themselves with Christ and belong to Christ "have crucified" or put to death everything that is in opposition to Christ and are thus free to produce through their behavior the fruit of the Spirit.

25 If we live in the Spirit, let us also walk in the Spirit.

This is a concise summary of what Paul has already said. It is a statement of what is true since "we live in the Spirit." It is also a statement that reflects the logical consequence of the reality of living in the Spirit: "let us also walk in the Spirit." Since we live in the Spirit, let us line up with the Spirit. Believers who claim to live in the Spirit must also allow their profession to find expression in behavior that is the result of the Spirit's control.

26 Let us not be desirous of vain glory, provoking one another, envying one another.

This verse seems to suggest that Paul does not want his readers to become overconfident concerning their position in Christ. To be in Christ and to be led by the Spirit does mean that such a person will always reflect the spirit and attitude of Christ. Sometimes good behavior is carried out in ways that provoke and stir up jealousy in others. This is certainly the case when the good works are done in ways that call attention to oneself.

This is the concern that Paul telescopes in his use of the word "provoking" (Gk. *prokaleomai*, **prok-al-EH-om-ahee**). To illustrate the

meaning of this word, F. F. Bruce cites, "Philo's story of Demosthenes who, when challenged to a slanging match" used this word to decline the challenge "because, as he said, the winner would come off worse than the loser" (Bruce, 257). It is reasonable to think that Paul saw the Galatians disputing among themselves from this vantage point. Those who were right in their comments about salvation may have conducted themselves in ways that provoked others or that stirred up envy. Consequently, those who were right conducted themselves worse than those who were wrong. The implication is that believers have an obligation to manage right conduct in ways that do not tempt others to do wrong.

The spirit that seeks to prove one's "rightness" at the expense of another's spiritual well-being borders on "vain glory." This does not speak well of the Holy Spirit's leading. Therefore, "let us not be desirous of vain glory" (KJV), and "let us not become conceited, provoking and envying each other" (NIV).

6:1 Brethren, if a man be overtaken in a fault, ye which are spiritual, restore such a one in the spirit of meekness; considering thyself, lest thou also be tempted.

Paul's use of the word "overtaken" (Gk. *prolambano*, **pro-lam-BAN-o**) literally means to be entrapped, taken, caught by surprise, or to take a false step. This gives the meaning that the man "overtaken in a fault" was not intentionally doing wrong. Rather, he suddenly became aware, or it was brought to his attention that what he was doing was wrong.

Paul counsels that believers are to handle such situations in a spirit of meekness and with a view toward restoration. In other words, do not satisfy the lust of the flesh by using the situation as occasion for gossip or for viewing oneself as superior to the one at fault. The antidote to such sinful behavior is to "consider thyself, lest thou also be tempted," or to "watch yourself, or you also may be tempted" (NIV).

2 Bear ye one another's burdens, and so fulfil the law of Christ.

Those who are led by the Spirit are called here to be willing and available to help carry one another's loads. The sense of the Greek makes this behavior a style of living in Christian fellowship with other believers. The verb "to bear" is from the Greek word *bastazo* (**bas-TAH-zo**), meaning to take up, carry, or endure. It can also mean to suffer or undergo.

The Greek word for "burdens" is *baros* (**BAR-os**), meaning weight or heaviness. Paul says we are to carry one another's burden. In this verse, he is referring to hardships. We are to support one another by helping to bear the weight of hardship.

Bearing one another's burdens is not an occasional act. Rather, it is a way of living and behaving in the Christian community. By so behaving, we, like Christ, will have fulfilled the Law.

3 For if a man think himself to be something, when he is nothing, he deceiveth himself.

One of the expressions of the Spirit-led life is a proper and legitimate estimate of oneself. When one connects verse 2 with verse 3, the message is clear. Those who think too highly of themselves are unlikely candidates for bearing another's burdens.

4 But let every man prove his own work, and then shall he have rejoicing in himself alone, and not in another.

Each person should evaluate his or her own behavior. Those who are led by the Spirit have no need to compare themselves with other believers. Proving one's own work, or testing and evaluating one's own actions in the light of God's Word, gives a basis for self-evaluation. In fact, rejoicing because one thinks that he or she is better than someone else is in opposition to our life in Christ. It is not the way of the Spirit. Given this interpretation of verse 4, verse 5 is a logical restatement.

5 For every man shall bear his own burden.

This might appear to contradict verse 2 where Paul says we should share each other's burdens. Here, Paul says bear your own burden. The difference is apparent in the Greek. The Greek word for "burden" here is *phortion* (**for-TEE-on**). It is different from the word used in verse 2. The meaning is better conveyed by the use of the word "load," which refers to everyone pulling their own weight in relationship to their responsibilities. In other words, you should do your job and not expect someone else to do it for you. This is so that the work of ministry is shouldered by everyone and not by a few; we each have a responsibility to carry part of the load (burden). This personal responsibility is quite different from helping someone who is burdened down with problems. Nowhere in Scripture is laziness a virtue. Our Christian responsibility is to carry our own weight and help bear the misfortunes of others.

6 Let him that is taught in the word communicate unto him that teacheth in all good things.

In verse 6, Paul transitions from bearing burdens to sharing blessings. He admonishes those who hear God's Word to share all good things with their pastors and teachers. The word translated as "communicate" comes from the Greek word *koinoneo* (**koy-no-NEH-o**), which means to enter into fellowship with, to share with, or to partner with another. The phrase "all good things" does not mean that people are to give all they have to their ministers, but that they should support them liberally and share with them the good things of this life, according to their need.

7 Be not deceived; God is not mocked: for whatsoever a man soweth, that shall he also reap. 8 For he that soweth to his flesh shall of the flesh reap corruption; but he that soweth to the Spirit shall of the Spirit reap life everlasting.

Using the metaphor of a farmer who sows and reaps the harvest, Paul says that what a believer sows determines what he or she will harvest. Put another way, our choices will determine our consequences. Whether we choose to live in the Spirit or to live in the flesh (sinful nature), the respective consequences will follow.

9 And let us not be weary in well doing: for in due season we shall reap, if we faint not.

Believers are encouraged to sow to the Spirit, and refuse to become discouraged. This explains the need for Paul's note of encouragement in verse 9. The Greek word for "weary" is *ekkakeo* (**ek-kak-EH-o**) meaning to lose heart or become tired. The word for "faint" in the Greek is *ekluo* (**ek-LOO-o**), meaning to weaken or give up. Paul encourages the Galatians not to get tired and give up for there is a reward after all is said and done.

10 As we have therefore opportunity, let us do good unto all men, especially unto them who are of the household of faith.

The word "opportunity" is translated from the Greek word *kairos* (kahee-ROS), which means "time" or "season." In the terms of sowing and reaping, we now have a seasonal opportunity to do that what is good and beneficial for others, especially to our brothers and sisters in the family of God.

Sources:
Baltes, A. J., ed. Biblespeech.com. http://www.biblespeech.com (accessed August 11, 2010).
Bruce, F. F. *The Epistle to the Galatians: A Commentary on the Greek Text. The New International Greek Testament Commentary.* Grand Rapids, MI: William B. Eerdmans Publishing Company, 1982. 257.
Morris, Leon. *Galatians: Paul's Charter of Christian Freedom.* Downers Grove, IL: InterVarsity Press, 1996. 173.

Say It Correctly

Corinthians. Kuh-RIN-thee-uhns.
Galatians. Ga-LA-shuns.

Daily Bible Reading

MONDAY
Renewed by the Holy Spirit
(Titus 3:1–7)

TUESDAY
Chosen To Be Obedient
(1 Peter 1:1–5)

WEDNESDAY
Supporting Your Faith
(2 Peter 1:3–8)

THURSDAY
Faith Working through Love
(Galatians 5:2–6)

FRIDAY
Called to Freedom
(Galatians 5:7–15)

SATURDAY
The Works of the Flesh
(Galatians 5:16–21)

SUNDAY
Living by the Spirit
(Galatians 5:22–6:10)

Notes

_____

_____

_____

_____

God's Creative Word

The spring quarter is an in-depth study of John's gospel through the theological lens of creation. Creation is more than God's one time action of bringing the world into existence; it involves God's ongoing action of reconciling and re-creating now and in eternity. God's creating Word was, is, and shall be making all things good.

UNIT 1 • THE WORD WAS IN THE BEGINNING

"The Word Was in the Beginning" has six lessons. The first two stress the creative power of God's Word and the many nuances of understanding in the meaning behind the Word. Lesson 3 looks at the power of Jesus' words to change water into wine, to clear the Temple, to address the longing of the human heart, and to heal. Lesson 4 looks at the power of the Word for salvation. On Palm and Easter Sunday, we look at the death and resurrection of Jesus as recorded in John.

Lesson 1: March 4, 2012
Wisdom's Part in Creation
Proverbs 8:22–35

The personification of Wisdom in this Scripture describes its importance before Creation.

Wisdom is a gift from God that must be accepted by humans. Scripture tells us that God delights in wisdom and our ability to seek and use it in our lives.

Lesson 2: March 11, 2012
The Word Became Flesh
John 1:1–14

Jesus, who was fully human and fully involved in human society, was also personally divine from the beginning and was God's agent in the world, creating and redeeming.

Lesson 3: March 18, 2012
The Wedding at Cana
John 2:1–12

John depicts how Jesus performs a miracle at a special event—a wedding. His strong words with His mother at this wedding tell us that He had not arrived at His final destination: the Cross and Resurrection.

Lesson 4: March 25, 2012
God's Word Saves
John 3:11–21

During Nicodemus' nighttime discussion with Jesus, Nicodemus learns that belief in Jesus gives everyone eternal life. Also, he learned how God's love for the world is the impetus (drive) for why God sent Jesus.

Lesson 5: April 1, 2012
Jesus Testifies to the Truth
John 18:28–37

John agrees with the Synoptic Gospels that Pilate's first question to Jesus was: "Are you the king of the Jews?" Pilate tries to establish that Jesus is a rebel with military might. Jesus refutes this thought because He came to "testify to the truth" (John 18:37, NIV).

Lesson 6: April 8, 2012
(Resurrection Sunday)
The Living Word
John 20:1–10, 19–20

The disciples were afraid and locked themselves in a room. They did not expect a resurrection. When Jesus appeared to them, they greatly rejoiced.

UNIT 2 • THE WORD IS HERE AND NOW

These three lessons (7–9) offer a study in the power of Jesus' words as He lived among us as a human being. Jesus' words have the power not only to purify the Temple, but to restore human life and to heal, as well.

Lesson 7: April 15, 2012
Cleansing the Temple
John 2:13–22

The Jewish people had to buy animals for their sacrifices in the temple. Jesus turns over the tables of the money changers in the temple because they should not have been in the temple cheating those who came to buy and worship.

Lesson 8: April 22, 2012
Woman of Samaria
John 4:7–15, 23–26, 28–30

The dual meaning of water and the dual boundaries that Jesus crosses are expressed in this story. The "living water" refers to fresh drinking water or life-giving water (v. 10). Jesus crosses two cultural boundaries in this story: the boundary between Jews and Samaritans and between men and women.

Lesson 9: April 29, 2012
Healing the Blind Man
John 9:1–17

The healing power of clay made with spittle was a popular form of healing in the Greco-Roman world. John also writes how a person can have sight but not see, and how a blind man received his sight and the gift to see truth.

UNIT 3 • THE WORD WILL BE

There are four lessons in this unit. They look at some of the "I am" statements of Jesus. They also give us a sense of the divinity of Jesus and of His eternal power to promise us life, security, resurrection, and the way of God.

Lesson 10: May 6, 2012
The Bread of Life
John 6:22–35

The phrase "I am" forms a distinctive self-revelation of Jesus in the Gospel of John.

Jesus tells the people in this passage that He is the "bread of life" (v. 35). He promised His followers that if they would come to Him, they would never be hungry or thirsty.

Lesson 11: May 13, 2012
The Good Shepherd
John 10:7–18

John writes about the two "I am" passages in this text: gate and shepherd. Jesus is the Good Shepherd that all of His people will follow.

Lesson 12: May 20, 2012
The Resurrection and the Life
John 11:17–27

John's use of the "I am" statements of Jesus is seen again in verse 25 when Jesus assures Martha that He is "the resurrection and the life." Jesus affirms Martha's belief in Him as the Messiah.

Lesson 13: May 27, 2012
The Way, the Truth, and the Life
John 14:1–14

This passage is the beginning of a "farewell" address Jesus gives to the disciples. He gives comfort to His disciples and reminds Thomas and the others that He is the "the way and the truth, and the life" (v. 6, NIV).

Engaging the Theme

GOD'S CREATIVE WORD

"In the beginning was the Word,
and the Word was with God, and
the Word was God"
(John 1:1).

The Books of the Bible
(God's Creative Word)

The Old Testament

THE LAW	HISTORY	POETRY	PROPHECY
(The Pentateuch)	Joshua	Job	Isaiah
(The Torah)	Judges	Psalms	Jeremiah
Genesis	Ruth	Proverbs	Lamentations
Exodus	1 Samuel	Ecclesiastes	Ezekiel
Leviticus	2 Samuel	Song of Solomon	Daniel
Numbers	1 Kings	(Song of Songs)	Hosea
Deuteronomy	2 Kings		Joel
	1 Chronicles		Amos
	2 Chronicles		Obadiah
	Ezra		Jonah
	Nehemiah		Micah
	Esther		Nahum
			Habakkuk
			Zephaniah
			Haggai
			Zechariah
			Malachi

The New Testament

THE GOSPELS	PAUL'S LETTERS	A LETTER TO JEWISH CHRISTIANS	PROPHECY
Matthew	Romans	**TO JEWISH**	Revelation
Mark	1 Corinthians	**CHRISTIANS**	
Luke	2 Corinthians	Hebrews	
John	Galatians		
	Ephesians	**LETTERS TO THE**	
HISTORY OF THE	Philippians	**ENTIRE CHURCH**	
CHURCH	Colossians	James	
Acts	1 Thessalonians	1 Peter	
	2 Thessalonians	2 Peter	
	1 Timothy	1 John	
	2 Timothy	2 John	
	Titus	3 John	
	Philemon	Jude	

WHAT KING DAVID FELT ABOUT GOD'S WORD

"The law of the LORD

is perfect,

converting the soul:

the testimony of the **LORD**

is sure,

making wise the simple.

The statutes of the LORD

are right,

rejoicing the heart:

the commandment of the **LORD**

is pure,

enlightening the eyes"

(Psalm 19:7–8, emphasis added).

Madam C. J. Walker

1867–1919

Sarah Breedlove's parents were former slaves who sharecropped in the Louisiana Delta. By the time she was 7 years old, they both had died, so she was shifted from one family to the next until she went to live with her sister Louvina and Louvina's husband, Willie Powell. Willie began abusing her, so she ran away and married Moses McWilliams when she was just 14 years old.

After a few years, Sarah gave birth to Lelia, her only child. Then just a few years later, her husband died. Sarah was almost penniless, so she took her little girl and moved to St. Louis where her four brothers were working as barbers. She worked hard during the days as a laundrywoman, so she could provide for her and her daughter, and her daughter's education. She joined the St. Paul African Methodist Episcopal Church, where she sang in the choir. She was greatly influenced by some of the Christian women who were members of that church.

At this time, she developed a scalp ailment that caused her to start losing her hair. Sarah began experimenting with various ingredients to create products specifically for the hair of African American women. When her brother died, she moved to Denver, Colorado. When she arrived, she had only $2.00 in her pocket, so she worked as a cook in the daytime and then worked on developing her hair product business in the evenings. In Denver, she met and married Charles Joseph ("C. J.") Walker and began calling herself and her company Madam C. J. Walker. Mr. Walker was a newspaperman with a talent for marketing. He started placing advertisements for her hair products in African American newspapers throughout the United States. Madam C. J. Walker had a great vision for the growth of her company and Mr. Walker disagreed with her, so they divorced. However, he stayed on as a sales agent. One of his ideas was door-to-door marketing, which was very good for the growth of the business.

By 1906, the company had grown greatly so she brought on her daughter, who had just graduated from college. Lelia ran the business from the office, while Madam Walker traveled throughout the country, Latin America, and the Caribbean, marketing her products and developing new ones. She also started up a college to train women in how to use and sell the products. By 1910, she had 1,000 sales agents, and she moved the company to Indianapolis, Indiana. The company continued growing until Madam C. J. Walker was worth a million dollars. After all the suffering, poverty, and hardship she had gone through, she became the first woman, Black or White, who became a millionaire based upon her own achievements.

Sources:

About.com: Inventors. Madame C. J. Walker (1867–1919). http://inventors.about.com/od/wstartinventors/a/Madame Walker.htm (accessed September 9,2010).

Black Inventor Online Museum – Madam C. J. Walker. http://www.blackinventor.com/pages/madamewalker.html (accessed September 9, 2010).

Teaching Tips

Words You Should Know

A. Hypostatize (Hy-POST–a-tize)—To think of a concept, abstraction, etc., as having a real, objective existence.

B. Metaphor—A figure of speech in which a word or phrase is likened to something, but is not to be taken literally.

Teacher Preparation

Unifying Principle—Wise Up! The writer of Proverbs speaks of wisdom having a divine origin, being present as God created all things, and having a role with God in creation.

A. To become familiar with the comparisons and contrasts of wisdom and folly, read Proverbs 7 and 8.

B. Study the Words You Should Know section.

C. Review the questions in the Discuss the Meaning section and consider possible answers.

D. Complete the companion lesson in the *Precepts For Living Personal Study Guide®*.

O—Open the Lesson

A. After taking prayer requests, lead the class in prayer.

B. Have a volunteer read the In Focus story aloud. Discuss.

C. Discuss the Lesson Aim after reading it aloud.

D. Read the Keep in Mind verse together, and then encourage the class to commit the verse to memory during the week.

P—Present the Scriptures

A. Discuss the Focal Verses according to the At-A-Glance outline and More Light on the Text.

B. Reflect on the availability of God's wisdom to believers.

E—Explore the Meaning

A. Divide the class into groups to answer the Search the Scriptures questions.

B. Read and discuss each Discuss the Meaning question.

C. Review the Lesson in Our Society section. Ask the students to share personal experiences concerning God's wisdom in their lives.

N—Next Steps for Application

A. Challenge students to complete the Make It Happen assignment.

B. Close in prayer, thanking God for the availability of His wisdom to believers.

Worship Guide

For the Superintendent or Teacher
Theme: Wisdom's Part in Creation
Theme Song: "Take Thou Our Minds, Dear Lord"
Devotional Reading: Psalm 8
Prayer

Wisdom's Part in Creation

Bible Background • PROVERBS 8
Printed Text • PROVERBS 8:22–35 | Devotional Reading • PSALM 8

Aim for Change

By the end of the lesson, we will: EXPLAIN what God's wisdom is; REFLECT on God's wisdom in our lives; and PRAY for wisdom in our everyday life experiences.

In Focus

Christ, family, and friendship were the most important things in life for Diane, a successful high school principal. She and her best friend, Asia, had gone to high school and college together. Asia had dropped out of college and ran off with her "dream man" without marrying him. It had been a shock because Asia had been president of the College Christian Fellowship. Shortly after that, they had lost touch.

One Thursday night, Diane received a call from Asia.

"Asia, is it really you?" Diana cried. "It's been 20 years."

"Girl, it's me!" said Asia. "I'm in town. I'd like to swing by your house later."

When Diane opened the door, Asia's face stole her breath away. Asia was scarecrow thin, and her eyes reflected a life of drug abuse and pain.

Suddenly, Diane realized that at some point in her life, Asia had chosen a life quite different from the one they had shared as young girls in Bible study. The folly of a life consumed by narcotics had blinded Asia and robbed her of the ability to make wise decisions.

In Proverbs, we learn that God's wisdom is available to everyone who desires a deeper relationship with Christ. Do you have a desire to respond to God's wisdom?

Keep in Mind

"Hear instruction, and be wise, and refuse it not" (Proverbs 8:33).

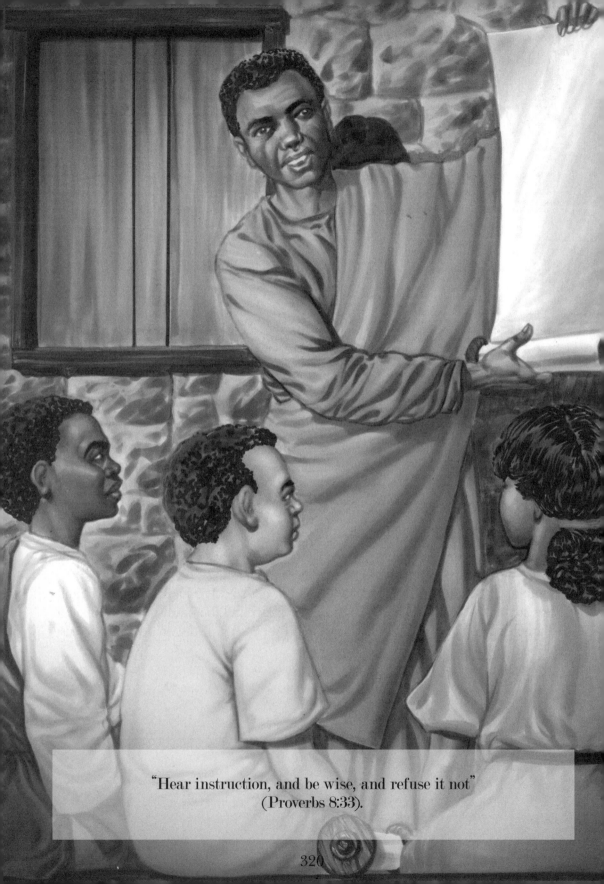

"Hear instruction, and be wise, and refuse it not"
(Proverbs 8:33).

Focal Verses

KJV **Proverbs 8:22** The LORD possessed me in the beginning of his way, before his works of old.

23 I was set up from everlasting, from the beginning, or ever the earth was.

24 When there were no depths, I was brought forth; when there were no fountains abounding with water.

25 Before the mountains were settled, before the hills was I brought forth:

26 While as yet he had not made the earth, nor the fields, nor the highest part of the dust of the world.

27 When he prepared the heavens, I was there: when he set a compass upon the face of the depth:

28 When he established the clouds above: when he strengthened the fountains of the deep:

29 When he gave to the sea his decree, that the waters should not pass his commandment: when he appointed the foundations of the earth:

30 Then I was by him, as one brought up with him: and I was daily his delight, rejoicing always before him;

31 Rejoicing in the habitable part of his earth; and my delights were with the sons of men.

32 Now therefore hearken unto me, O ye children: for blessed are they that keep my ways.

33 Hear instruction, and be wise, and refuse it not.

34 Blessed is the man that heareth me, watching daily at my gates, waiting at the posts of my doors.

35 For whoso findeth me findeth life, and shall obtain favour of the LORD.

NLT **Proverbs 8:22** "The LORD formed me from the beginning, before he created anything else.

23 I was appointed in ages past, at the very first, before the earth began.

24 I was born before the oceans were created, before the springs bubbled forth their waters.

25 Before the mountains and the hills were formed, I was born—

26 before he had made the earth and fields and the first handfuls of soil.

27 "I was there when he established the heavens, when he drew the horizon on the oceans.

28 I was there when he set the clouds above, when he established the deep fountains of the earth.

29 I was there when he set the limits of the seas, so they would not spread beyond their boundaries. And when he marked off the earth's foundations,

30 I was the architect at his side. I was his constant delight, rejoicing always in his presence.

31 And how happy I was with what he created—his wide world and all the human family!

32 "And so, my children, listen to me, for happy are all who follow my ways.

33 Listen to my counsel and be wise. Don't ignore it.

34 "Happy are those who listen to me, watching for me daily at my gates, waiting for me outside my home!

35 For whoever finds me finds life and wins approval from the LORD.

The People, Places, and Times

Wisdom Literature. The "wise men" of ancient times regularly employed figures of speech as they sought to disciple others in the way of wisdom. Biblical wisdom literature can be divided into three different types: The first is *mashal* (**maw-SHAL**), a Hebrew word usually translated as "proverb." The second is the riddle (see Judges 14:14), and the last is the parable (see 1 Kings 20:39–40; 2 Samuel 12:1–6).

The *mashal* is the most prominent type of wisdom literature in Proverbs. Personification (i.e., giving a thing or a concept human qualities) is a favorite figure of speech used by the wise men. In some places in Proverbs, wisdom is personified to the extent that it is almost presented as a real, tangible being. With these vivid word pictures, God reveals the availability of His wisdom to us.

Background

The book of Proverbs was written as instructional material, to be used as a sort of "how-to" manual for life. As such, the book of Proverbs consists of succinct statements about life and human nature. Similes, metaphors, and other figures of speech are used generously to help give the reader a memorable word picture of a particular truth. In today's passage, wisdom is portrayed as "Lady Wisdom," giving us a unique, down-to-earth perspective on an intangible commodity. And, as we will see, wisdom is fulfilled in the person of Jesus Christ. He is wisdom.

At-A-Glance

1. Wisdom's Story (Proverbs 8:22–31)

2. Wisdom's Invitation (vv. 32–35)

In Depth

1. Wisdom's Story (Proverbs 8:22–31)

In this passage, wisdom is personified. Some have called this a "hypostatization"— thinking of a concept, abstraction, etc., as having real, objective existence. But it seems more appropriate to think of this passage merely as a metaphor, that is, a personification of an attribute of God, but not an actual being in any way.

In Proverbs 8, we see wisdom existing eternally. A sweeping panorama of creation is covered in verses 24 through 29, following the order of God's work listed in Genesis. Wisdom was with God before there was anything created. Wisdom was with God before there were oceans and rivers, before there were mountains and hills. Wisdom was there when God created the heavens and when He "set a compass" (v. 27) or "marked out the horizon" (NIV). What an indescribably beautiful picture! The everlasting wisdom of God, an intrinsic fiber of His nature and character that was with Him as He created the world, is available to us! When God set the world into motion, wisdom was there. Wisdom was there when God set the boundaries for the oceans, when He set the stars in motion. Wisdom was there when He placed the clouds in the sky (v. 28). Wisdom is like a skilled artisan, rejoicing in the Master's presence and His creation (vv. 30–31). Wisdom flowed from God's character, and His wonderful, perfect creation was the result. And God desires to give wisdom to those who seek Him. What an incredible thought!

God's creative wisdom is available for the asking. In fact, wisdom "delights" in those who choose her (v. 31). Through wisdom, God set the creation in motion; likewise, through wisdom He orders our lives. He is aware of every detail of our lives and delights in giving us the wisdom to know Him more.

As we know Him more, we begin to walk in wisdom. It's a circular principle, but one that God longs for us to take hold of. The more we know Him, the more wisdom we receive. The more wisdom we receive, the more we seek Him.

2. Wisdom's Invitation (vv. 32–35)

So the plea goes out to all people: "Listen to me; blessed are those who keep my ways" (v. 32, NIV). Receive instruction—don't refuse it. Proverbs 19:20 (NIV) says, "Listen to advice and accept instruction, and in the end you will be wise." Only fools reject instruction that will improve their lives. Respond to God's wisdom! He has made it available to us for our good. We will be blessed when we choose to live by God's wisdom.

What kind of blessings can we expect from living a wise life? Peace with God is certainly high on the list. A good reputation is also a benefit. Wisdom affects every area of our lives. If we conduct our interpersonal relationships with wisdom, we will have meaningful friendships and strong family ties. If we practice our business policies with wisdom, we will enjoy the blessing of a reputable business. If we live our Christian lives with wisdom, we will draw others to Christ. The blessings of wisdom may not always be tangible, but they far outweigh the material blessings that we often desire. Wisdom is worth it.

Wisdom does have another aspect, however. It is not only something that God possesses and something that God gives. We also see wisdom in Jesus. In the New Testament, Jesus is viewed as the ultimate fulfillment of the Old Testament. Proverbs 8:22 tells us that wisdom was with God in the beginning before any of His "works of old." Does this have a familiar ring to it? John 1:1 says, "In the beginning was the Word, and the Word was with God, and the Word was

God." Proverbs speaks of wisdom's eternal existence in a way that parallels John's words about Christ. In the Incarnation, Jesus is the complete demonstration of all that is divine, including wisdom.

Proverbs 8:23 says that wisdom was "appointed" (NIV) or "set up" (KJV) from eternity—before the beginning! Jesus is the Anointed One, the Everlasting God! He was with God in the beginning, before time began. He has always been and always will be. In fact, without Him, "nothing was made that has been made" (John 1:3, NIV). He is and was first. He is and was supreme. He was "rejoicing always before him; Rejoicing in the habitable part" (Proverbs 8:30–31). Jesus, Wisdom Himself, rejoices over those who choose Him.

When we choose Jesus, we avail ourselves of a tremendous, infinite amount of wisdom. Christ is "the power of God, and the wisdom of God" (1 Corinthians 1:24). He has "made unto us wisdom, and righteousness, and sanctification, and redemption" (v. 30). Hallelujah! What a treasure! When we seek Jesus, we gain wisdom. He is our all in all.

Search the Scriptures

1. Describe some of the word pictures used in Proverbs 8:22–26.

2. What role did wisdom play at the time of the Creation (vv. 27–30)?

3. What is the believer's responsibility toward wisdom (vv. 32–33)?

Discuss the Meaning

1. Discuss opportunities that present-day Christians have to extend wisdom's invitation to those around them.

2. Discuss the availability of wisdom. How does God reveal His wisdom to us? How do we gain the wisdom that is available to us?

3. Discuss the imagery of wisdom in Proverbs 8. How does the use of such

imagery help us to understand God's ways and His Word? How is Jesus the fulfillment of all wisdom?

Lesson in Our Society

Wisdom is a scarce commodity in today's world. Watching the evening news is like seeing the "folly" of Proverbs 7 in action. Everywhere we look, people are making bad choices, trying to live life by their own rules. God's Word calls us to a very different life—a life of godly wisdom. Wisdom involves knowing God's will and His Word; then having the ability to apply this knowledge. In short, we must walk in the Spirit. Without a Spirit-led personal relationship with Jesus, we will never truly be able to live a wisdom-filled life. Jesus is wisdom. He is our treasure worth seeking. He extends His gift of wisdom to all who would receive it.

Make It Happen

How would your life be different if you sought God's wisdom on a regular basis? This week, try an experiment. Make a conscious effort to gain godly wisdom before you make a decision or tackle a problem.

Follow the Spirit

What God wants me to do:

_____

_____

_____

_____

Remember Your Thoughts

Special insights I have learned:

_____

_____

_____

_____

More Light on the Text

Proverbs 8:22–35

22 The LORD possessed me in the beginning of his way, before his works of old. 23 I was set up from everlasting, from the beginning, or ever the earth was.

The Hebrew word for "possessed" is *qanah* (**kaw-NAW**), meaning to acquire or create. The Hebrew word for "everlasting" is `*owlam* (**o-LAWM**) meaning "long duration," "antiquity," or "futurity." Wisdom begins to document her credibility in verses 22 and 23. She testifies that she was present with the Lord before and during the Creation (v. 23), before she gave her generous invitation to humankind (vv. 4–5). Therefore, she indeed deserved the respect that was given to an elder. Her words were words of authority, much like God gave to the prophet Ezekiel to speak to the Israelites: "But when I speak to you, I will open your mouth and you shall say to them, 'This is what the Sovereign LORD says.' Whoever will listen let them listen, and whoever will refuse let them refuse; for they are a rebellious house" (Ezekiel 3:27, NIV).

24 When there were no depths, I was brought forth; when there were no fountains abounding with water. 25 Before the mountains were settled, before the hills was I brought forth: 26 While as yet he had not made the earth, nor the fields, nor the highest part of the dust of the world.

Wisdom proclaims that she was the agent of Creation. Proverbs 8:24 points out that wisdom was established before the creation of the "depths" (Heb. *tâhowm, tâhom*, **teh-HOME**), meaning the "deep" or "oceans." The Hebrew word for the phrase "brought forth" is *chiyl* (**kheel**), meaning "travailed" or "was born." While wisdom still proclaims her existence before time began, her dialogue in these verses can be likened to that of childbirth.

27 When he prepared the heavens, I was there: when he set a compass upon the face of the depth: 28 When he established the clouds above: when he strengthened the fountains of the deep: 29 When he gave to the sea his decree, that the waters should not pass his commandment: when he appointed the foundations of the earth:

Wisdom was present with God when He "prepared the 'heavens'" (Heb. *shamayim*, **shaw-MAH-yim**, meaning, "the sky, atmosphere, visible universe abode—where the stars dwell); "strengthened the fountains of the deep," "gave to the sea his 'decree'" (Heb. *choq*, **khoke**, meaning, "prescribed limit" or "boundary"), and "appointed the 'foundations' of the earth" (Heb. *mowcad*, **mo-SAWD**).

In verse 27 the Hebrew word for the phrase "set a compass" is *cheshmown* (**skhesh-MONE**), meaning to cut out, decree, or inscribe. In verse 28 the Hebrew word for "established" is *'amats* (**aw-MATS**), meaning to be alert, of good courage, steadfastly minded, or strong. The Hebrew word for "strengthened" is *`azaz* (**aw-ZAZ**), meaning to be strong.

In these verses, Solomon carries us back to the beginning of time to remind us of Wisdom's presence at the time of Creation. This dialogue is one that demands respect because it emphasizes our Creator's omnipotence as He establishes the boundaries of the heavens and earth.

30 Then I was by him, as one brought up with him: and I was daily his delight, rejoicing always before him; 31 Rejoicing in the habitable part of his earth; and my delights were with the sons of men.

Lady Wisdom's role paralleled the role of the preexistent "Word" (Greek *logos*, **LOG-os**) of John 1:1–3. She brought joy to God and rejoiced in the Creation: "I was daily his delight, rejoicing always before him" (Proverbs 8:30). The Hebrew word for "rejoicing" is *sachaq* (**saw-KHAK**), meaning to laugh or play. The Hebrew word for "delight" is *sha`shua`* (**shah-SHOO-ah**), meaning "enjoyment." And "God saw that it was good" (Genesis 1:10, 12, 18, 21, 25).

The Hebrew word in Proverbs 8:30 translated as "brought up" is *'amown* (**a-MONE**). It means "architect," "master workman," or "skilled workman." The picture is that of wisdom, the faithful master artisan, standing at God's side as He created the universe. "How many are your works, LORD! In wisdom you made them all; the earth is full of your creatures" (Psalm 104:24, NIV).

Wisdom was ecstatic, as she was able to enjoy the "handiwork" of God (Psalm 19:1, NKJV). This implies a wonderful gathering of wisdom and humankind—do we dare envision a party? We celebrate God's creation in many ways. Each time we enjoy a ride through the countryside and see the bursting forth of the springtime flowers, view snowcapped mountains, or enjoy a picnic on a bright sunny day, we share wisdom's pleasure and joy in Creation. As we look at God's creation, we should praise our Creator: "Oh that men would praise the LORD for his goodness, and for his wonderful works to the children of men!" (Psalm 107:8).

32 Now therefore hearken unto me, O ye children: for blessed are they that keep my ways. 33 Hear instruction, and be wise, and refuse it not.

Wisdom delights in those who listen to her, and in these verses she addresses those who keep her ways as her children. The Hebrew word for "children" is *ben* (**bane**), which means "sons" in the widest sense, not excluding daughters. These are the family heirs. Lady Wisdom pleads with her children to obey her so that they might be blessed. This pleading is in light of the previous verses that presented the wisdom of God participating in all of creation. If His wisdom had such an important part to play in how the worlds were designed, surely the wisdom of God will show us the right paths to take in our lowly human lives. Frozen water rises to the top of a pond, allowing cold-blooded creatures to continue living underneath the water. Imagine if this were upside down! It is just as foolish an idea for us not to follow God's wisdom. Blessings come into our lives when we do the right things. The Hebrew word for "blessed" is *'esher* (**EH-sher**), and it means "happy." If we think about the paths of sin—not one leads to happiness. Think of greed, adultery, drugs, etc. How does one feel at the end of a life pursuing such things? Only the wise path will bring us true happiness.

34 Blessed is the man that heareth me, watching daily at my gates, waiting at the posts of my doors. Following the path of wisdom is not just a one-time commitment. How can we watch daily at the gates of wisdom and wait at the posts of her doors? We read in Psalm 1 that the one who delights in the Word of God and meditates upon it day and night will prosper. This is not talking about material prosperity primarily, but is pointing out that we need to read our Bibles

daily and continuously keep our thoughts on the things we have read. That way we will know what is the wise way to walk.

35 For whoso findeth me findeth life, and shall obtain favour of the LORD.

The Hebrew word for "life" is *chay* (**KHAH-ee**), and it means to be alive in a physical sense. Although we see hints in the Old Testament of eternal life, this idea was not yet fully developed. When Jesus came, our understanding of life after death became clear. We read in John 3:36 that those who believe in Jesus Christ, the Son of God, have everlasting or eternal life. And those who do not believe in Him do not have eternal life in heaven, but God's wrath is on them. The book of Proverbs focuses on wisdom, wisdom that comes from God, but this wisdom is incomplete until we receive Jesus Christ, who rightly claims that He is life.

Sources:

Adeyemo, Tokunboh, et al., eds. *Africa Bible Commentary: A One-Volume Commentary Written by 70 African Scholars.* Nairobi, Kenya: Word Alive Publishers, 2006. 758–59.

Kidner, Derek. *The Proverbs: An Introduction & Commentary. The Tyndale Old Testament Commentaries.* Downers Grove, IL: Inter-Varsity Press, 1964.

Old Testament Hebrew Lexicon. Bible Study Tools.com. http://www.biblestudytools.com/lexicons/hebrew (accessed January 7, 2011).

Passage Lookup. Bible Gateway.com. http://www.bible gateway.com/passage (accessed January 7, 2011).

Strong's Exhaustive Concordance of the Bible. McLean, VA: MacDonald Publishing Company. n.d.

Say It Correctly

Hypostatize. Hy-POST–a-tize.
Metaphor. MET-a-for.

Daily Bible Readings

MONDAY
The Call of Wisdom
(Proverbs 8:1–11)

TUESDAY
The Gifts of Wisdom
(Proverbs 8:12–21)

WEDNESDAY
Before the Foundation of the World
(Ephesians 1:3–10)

THURSDAY
The Handiwork of God
(Psalm 8)

FRIDAY
The Firstborn of all Creation
(Colossians 1:15–19)

SATURDAY
Creation Awaits Glory
(Romans 8:18–25)

SUNDAY
Find Wisdom, Find Life
(Proverbs 8:22–35)

Notes

_____

_____

_____

_____

Teaching Tips

Words You Should Know

A. Word (John 1:1, 14) *logos* (Gk.)—The Word; denotes the expression of thought, not the mere name of an object. In John 1:1 and 1:14, Jesus is called "the Word."

B. Witness (v. 7) *martus* or *marturia* (Gk.)—Someone who has seen or heard or knows.

Teacher Preparation

Unifying Principle—From the Beginning. Jesus, who was fully human and fully involved in human society, was also personally divine from the beginning, and was God's agent in the world, creating and redeeming.

A. Read the entire lesson.

B. Then prayerfully read John 1, asking God to give you insight into His Word.

C. Pay special attention to the Lesson Aim and the questions under Discuss the Meaning.

D. Complete the companion lesson in the *Precepts For Living Personal Study Guide®*.

O—Open the Lesson

A. Ask a student to lead the class in prayer by using the Lesson Aim as a guide.

B. Discuss the In Focus; Background; and The People, Places, and Times to provide insight on today's lesson.

P—Present the Scriptures

A. Review the Lesson Aim.

B. Ask for volunteers to read the Focal Verses aloud. Discuss according to the At-A-Glance outline and More Light on the Text.

E—Explore the Meaning

A. Ask the students how the In Focus story relates to today's lesson.

B. Direct the students to the Lesson in Our Society section. Discuss how they can share Christ with others.

N—Next Steps for Application

A. Read the Make It Happen exercise and challenge the students to commit to completing it in the coming week.

B. Summarize the lesson.

C. Close with prayer.

Worship Guide

For the Superintendent or Teacher
Theme: The Word Became Flesh
Theme Song: "O Come, O Come, Emmanuel"
Devotional Reading: Isaiah 40:21–26
Prayer

The Word Became Flesh

Bible Background • JOHN 1:1–14
Printed Text • JOHN 1:1–14 | Devotional Reading • ISAIAH 40:21–26

Aim for Change

By the end of the lesson, we will: KNOW the importance of the divinity and humanity of Jesus; TRUST in a Savior who is eternal and shares the divine nature with God; and IMAGINE and SHARE how Jesus is the Light in our lives and in the world.

In Focus

For the past 16 years, Greg had been a member of a group that did not believe that Jesus was the Son of God; they did not believe that Jesus was truly God and truly man. Greg tried and tried to be good enough to be in the number that would go to heaven. However, he often slipped. It may have been in small ways, but he knew he was slipping and was not good enough to be in that number.

Then Greg began looking into the Bible for himself. He desperately wanted to have a right relationship with God. He looked at John 1:1 where he saw that the Word was God and then at verse 14 where it said that the Word was made flesh. He wondered to himself: Who else could that be but Jesus? Then it hit him—the Bible was saying that Jesus is God! This is not what those in the group had told him about Jesus.

But the clincher was when he read in verse 12 that all he had to do to have that elusive relationship with God was to believe and receive Jesus! Right then and there, that's what Greg did.

Today's Scripture passage contains some very important theology—theology that can get us into a right relationship with God!

Keep in Mind

"And the Word was made flesh, and dwelt among us, (and we beheld his glory, the glory as of the only begotten of the Father,) full of grace and truth" (John 1:14).

"And the Word was made flesh, and dwelt among us, (and we beheld his glory, the glory as of the only begotten of the Father,) full of grace and truth" (John 1:14).

Focal Verses

KJV **John 1:1** In the beginning was the Word, and the Word was with God, and the Word was God.

2 The same was in the beginning with God.

3 All things were made by him; and without him was not any thing made that was made.

4 In him was life; and the life was the light of men.

5 And the light shineth in darkness; and the darkness comprehended it not.

6 There was a man sent from God, whose name was John.

7 The same came for a witness, to bear witness of the Light, that all men through him might believe.

8 He was not that Light, but was sent to bear witness of that Light.

9 That was the true Light, which lighteth every man that cometh into the world.

10 He was in the world, and the world was made by him, and the world knew him not.

11 He came unto his own, and his own received him not.

12 But as many as received him, to them gave he power to become the sons of God, even to them that believe on his name:

13 Which were born, not of blood, nor of the will of the flesh, nor of the will of man, but of God.

14 And the Word was made flesh, and dwelt among us, (and we beheld his glory, the glory as of the only begotten of the Father,) full of grace and truth.

NLT **John 1:1** In the beginning the Word already existed. He was with God, and he was God.

2 He was in the beginning with God.

3 He created everything there is. Nothing exists that he didn't make.

4 Life itself was in him, and this life gives light to everyone.

5 The light shines through the darkness, and the darkness can never extinguish it.

6 God sent John the Baptist

7 to tell everyone about the light so that everyone might believe because of his testimony.

8 John himself was not the light; he was only a witness to the light.

9 The one who is the true light, who gives light to everyone, was going to come into the world.

10 But although the world was made through him, the world didn't recognize him when he came.

11 Even in his own land and among his own people, he was not accepted.

12 But to all who believed him and accepted him, he gave the right to become children of God.

13 They are reborn! This is not a physical birth resulting from human passion or plan—this rebirth comes from God.

14 So the Word became human and lived here on earth among us. He was full of unfailing love and faithfulness. And we have seen his glory, the glory of the only Son of the Father.

The People, Places, and Times

Gnosticism. Many of the early Gentile believers had been exposed to varying strains of Gnosticism (an early heresy) and did not believe in the humanity of Jesus. As people from diverse backgrounds became part of the church, it became necessary for the apostles to correct errors in doctrine as well as encourage the existing believers. In the Gospel of John, the writer seems to be addressing a mixed audience of believers and unbelievers, Jews, and Greeks.

Background

The author of the book of John identifies himself as "the disciple whom Jesus loved" (John 13:23; 19:26; 21:7, 20, NIV). Most scholars agree that the apostle John is the author of this book. John was well-known in the early church and was intimately familiar with Jewish life. He would have been an eyewitness to many of the events recorded in the Gospel of John.

Dating of the Gospel of John is a matter of debate, with dates ranging from A.D. 50 to 95 or later. However, most scholars accept the later date of A.D. 95. Although we may not know the exact date of the writing, we do know that the first century church was thriving. Even amid the threats of persecution and heresy, the church continued to grow.

John wrote to encourage the believers, most of whom were Jewish. He affirms their Jewishness as well as their faith in Jesus Christ, contrasting them with the Pharisees, who claimed to be the true or real Jews.

At-A-Glance

1. Jesus Is the Word (John 1:1–3)

2. Jesus Is the Light (vv. 4–9)

3. Jesus Reveals God's Character (vv. 10–14)

In Depth

1. Jesus Is the Word (John 1:1–3)

The first 14 verses of the book of John summarize the whole Gospel. In these verses,

we are introduced to Jesus—who He is, what He does, and the role He plays in the eternal plan of God for the world.

John began his book with the words "In the beginning." He then introduced Jesus as the "Word." The word used here is *logos*. The Greeks understood *logos* to mean not only the written or spoken word, but also the thought or reasoning in the mind. John's Greek readers would have understood the nuances of *logos*, realizing that John was presenting Jesus as the power that controlled all things.

The Jewish believers used the word *logos* to refer to God and would have connected this concept to the wisdom personified in the Old Testament (see Proverbs 8). In tandem with wisdom was ability; in this case, God's wisdom was used to create the universe. Jesus is that wisdom personified. All of these concepts are bound up in the word *logos*.

As believers today, when we read John 1:1–3, we may not realize all the nuances that the author intended. But what we must learn from verse 1 is clear: Jesus was, is, and always will be. He is God. He is the Creator and the Source of all life. The entirety of our Christian faith rests upon accepting these truths.

Through Jesus, all things were created. The Bible says, "Without him nothing was made that has been made" (John 1:3, NIV). To understand the creation, we must know the Creator.

2. Jesus Is the Light (vv. 4–9)

In this passage, John spoke of Jesus as "the Light." Jesus is Life itself, and that Life is our Light (v. 4). When we receive this life that Jesus offers, our spiritual darkness is replaced by light. As we walk in the light, we learn to comprehend the things of God. We become more like our Creator.

However, many people live in deep darkness. In the Bible, darkness usually connotes sin, guilt, or misery. Even though Jesus is the light and came to dispel darkness, many people refuse to accept the light of salvation. While here on earth, Jesus preached to a mostly Jewish audience. They were not only blinded by their sin, but they were hindered by their religion and preconceived ideas.

It's the same today. People are so thoroughly entrenched in their sin and ignorance that they are blind to the light. Their pride is more important to them than anything else, and they loathe admitting that they could be wrong. It is our joy as believers to shine the light of Jesus to those around us.

God can use anyone and anything to pierce through the darkness. In Jesus' time, God sent John the Baptist to testify, or bear witness, to the revelation of Jesus (vv. 6–7). John the Baptist did not seek for people to believe in him, but he pointed the way to Jesus. In this day and age, God uses His written Word and the power of the Holy Spirit to testify to the Light. He also uses believers who are willing and available. Every believer should view himself or herself as a testimony to the truth of salvation through Jesus Christ.

3. Jesus Reveals God's Character (vv. 10–14)

Although Jesus created the world (Colossians 1:16), the world did not recognize Him as Savior (John 1:10). Verse 11 says, "He came unto his own, and his own received him not." Jesus came to the Jews first, but most of them rejected Him as their Messiah.

His gift of salvation is offered freely to all, but unless one accepts that salvation, the darkness will continue to obscure the light. When we do receive Jesus, God gives us the right to become His children (v. 12). What an amazing statement! We have the right to become God's children. It's not because of anything we have done to deserve it, but because God's grace makes it possible for us to choose to believe and receive Jesus. We are not children in the physical sense; we are spiritual children of our Father, God. When we receive Christ, we are adopted into the family of God (see 1 John 3:1). We are considered heirs of God (Galatians 3:29), eligible to receive all of His promised blessings.

We cannot become God's children by any other means than through salvation in Jesus Christ. John 1:13 makes this clear: God's children are not born in the natural way of conception and birth. We are born of God spiritually. He chose us. God chose to send His Son, Jesus, to the earth to take on the form of human flesh. John first introduced us to Jesus as the eternally existing Word of God. Now he reveals another facet of *logos*— Jesus. The One who has always existed, the One who is God, has become a human being (v. 14).

Although He had always been omnipresent, Jesus had now come to be one of us. He came to live with us, to feel our pain, to experience our joy, and to know our sorrow. He experienced human life fully. John and the other disciples knew Him intimately as Teacher and Friend. They ate with Him, talked with Him, laughed with Him, and cried with Him.

Verse 14 says, "The Word . . . dwelt among us." John's Jewish readers would have understood the word "dwelling" to be connected to the word for "tabernacle." In Old Testament times, the tabernacle was where God's glory dwelled. The disciples watched Him perform miracles, and they knew Him as the Messiah.

As modern-day believers, we can't physically touch Jesus. He is no longer here in the flesh. Yet we can see His glory. We can testify to the miracles He has worked in our lives and the lives of others. We can bear witness to the power of salvation. And, amazingly enough, we can become like Him. In fact, we should strive to become like Him. We are frail humans, but when we receive the *logos*, we will begin to reflect the likeness of Him who is the Living Word.

Search the Scriptures

1. "In the beginning was the _____, and the _____ was with God, and the _____ was God" (John 1:1).

2. "In him was _____; and the _____ was the _____ of men" (v. 4).

3. "Yet to all who _____ him, to those who _____ in his name, he gave the _____ to become children of God" (v. 12, NIV).

4. "The Word became _____ and made his _____ among us. We have seen his glory, the glory of the _____ and only _____, who came from the Father, full of _____ and _____" (v. 14, NIV).

Discuss the Meaning

1. Who is the "Word" (John 1:1)?
2. What is the "light of men" (v. 4)?

Lesson in Our Society

Jesus came into this world in the form of human flesh, yet those around Him did not acknowledge Him for who He is: God. They chose to continue living in darkness rather than receiving the Light.

Things aren't so different in our world today. In modern society, especially in America and other modern societies, many people have become accustomed to a fast-paced, hectic lifestyle. They are easily distracted, often bored, or generally dissatisfied with life.

Jesus came to give meaningful, real life to all who will receive Him. He is the living revelation of God, who expressed God's truth in a way we can understand. It is our task to share this light with others.

Make It Happen

This week, ask God to reveal Himself to you in a new way. Spend time praying, reading the Word, and meditating on what you have read. Let God's Word permeate your spirit so that you might know God more deeply. Rejoice in the fact that God has revealed Himself to you through Jesus, the Word made flesh, and that He will continue to do so.

Follow the Spirit

What God wants me to do:

_____

_____

_____

_____

Remember Your Thoughts

Special insights I have learned:

_____

_____

_____

_____

More Light on the Text
John 1:1–14

1 In the beginning was the Word, and the Word was with God, and the Word was God.

John begins his Gospel with a clear reference to Genesis 1:1. The book of Genesis opens with an affirmation of the nature and character of God, the Creator and Sustainer of the universe. The purpose of the statement in Genesis is threefold: (1) to identify the Creator, (2) to explain the origin of the world, and (3) to tie the work of God in the past to the work of God in the future. Likewise, John is clearly identifying Jesus, the Living Word made flesh, as God the Creator (John 1:3) and affirming Him as the only source of life and redemption. This Gospel from its very start is heralding the deity of Jesus Christ. John is not referring here to a particular time in the past; rather, he is affirming the preexistence of Jesus.

"Word" here is expressed using the Greek word *logos* (**LOG-os**), which has several meanings. Ordinarily, *logos* refers to a spoken word, with an emphasis on the meaning conveyed, not just the sounds produced. But here, *logos* is used as an expression of communication with God. It is more than everyday speech; it is the creative power of God (see Psalm 33:6). John is clearly asserting that the Divine Word is the source of creation and of all that is visible and invisible in the world. John leaves no question as to the nature, character, and glory of the Word—the "Word was God" (John 1:1). John is saying that the Word is deity—one with God in nature, character, and glory.

2 The same was in the beginning with God. 3 All things were made by him; and without him was not any thing made that was made.

John begins the second verse by reiterating the divine, preexistent nature of the Word. He proceeds to explain the role of the Word in the beginning. The word "made" (Gk. *ginomai*, **GHIN-oh-mahee**) means "came into being, happened, or became." John is communicating the idea that this creative work happened out of nothing, that the Word did not rely on preexisting material to create the universe (Colossians 1:16; Hebrews 1:2).

John also begins to give us a hint as to the name of the Word by referring to the Word as "him." The Word is more than just an expression of the personality of God; it is the person of Jesus Christ. So John is saying that the Word, which was preexistent with God, was in complete fellowship with God, possessed all the divine nature and characteristics of deity, and created everything.

4 In him was life; and the life was the light of men.

"Life" in Greek is *zoe* (**dzo-AY**) and is used throughout the Bible to refer to both physical and spiritual life. It is frequently qualified with the word "eternal." Jesus was the embodiment of the fullness and quality of life that God offers to those who believe (John 14:6; cp. 10:10). The life that Jesus was to offer would be the light of all humanity.

5 And the light shineth in darkness; and the darkness comprehended it not.

Here, John uses the metaphors of "light" (Gk. *phos*, **foce**, meaning "to manifest") and "darkness" (Gk. *skotia*, **skot-EE-ah**, meaning "dimness" or "obscurity") to illustrate the differences between a life of grace, mercy, and forgiveness and a life of sin and death. The word "comprehended" (Gk. *katalambano*, **kat-al-am-BAN-o**) has two possible meanings. One meaning is "understood, perceived, or learned" and communicates the fact that those who live in the darkness do not receive the light because of a lack of understanding—they don't get it. Another meaning is the idea "lay hold of or seized" and communicates the fact that the darkness (perhaps Satan or more generally sinful humanity) will never have the ultimate victory over the light of Jesus.

John is saying that some who see the light will be unable to understand and receive it because Satan has blinded them (2 Corinthians 4:4). But John says that no matter how dark the darkness of evil seems in the world, no matter how the global circumstances seem to indicate that the darkness of evil is winning, the darkness cannot overcome the light that comes from the life of Christ.

6 There was a man sent from God, whose name was John. 7 The same came for a witness, to bear witness of the Light, that all men through him might believe.

The apostle John goes on to talk about John the Baptist. The ministry of John the Baptist is prominent in the Gospel of John. Here, the apostle John is affirming the prophetic ministry of John the Baptist. Jesus echoed this assertion when He said that John the Baptist was the last of the great Old Testament prophets, who came in the spirit of Elijah (Matthew 11:9–10; Mark 9:13). John the Baptist had a unique call and ministry to be a witness of Jesus, the Light (cp. Matthew 4:4; John 1:4).

In verse 7, the word "witness" (Gk. *marturia*, **mar-too-REE-ah**) means to affirm by testimony what one has seen, heard, experienced, or known. Therefore, John the Baptist had the prophetic duty of preparing the way for Jesus by preaching the testimonies of God.

The goal of John the Baptist was the same as the goal of John the apostle: to bring humanity to a place of faith in Jesus as Lord and Savior. The author is careful to specify that John the Baptist was not the genuine light, but that he came to "bear witness" (Gk. *martureo*, **mar-too-REH-o**), to testify of, or report on the One to come. John the Baptist testified to the world of the nature and character of Jesus so that "all men through him might believe."

8 He was not that Light, but was sent to bear witness of that Light. 9 That was the true Light, which lighteth every man that cometh into the world.

The apostle John makes it clear that John the Baptist was not the Light. He was only to bear witness of the Light. Like the moon that does not shine its own light, but only reflects the light of the sun, so John the Baptist reflects the Light of Jesus Christ, the Son of God. Jesus would be the true Light that would light every person. The word "true" (Gk. *alethinos*, **al-ay-thee-NOS**) refers to that which is sincere or genuine. The apostle John is saying that John the Baptist pointed others to the light to come, and that Jesus Christ was the authentic Light.

10 He was in the world, and the world was made by him, and the world knew him not. 11 He came unto his own, and his own received him not.

Here, the Greek word for "world" is *kosmos* (**KOS-mos**). It can refer to the universe (both things and people), the inhabitants of the earth (i.e., humanity), and the evil world system alienated from God. Gnostics believed that the flesh and the material world were evil. The apostle John may have been refuting this heresy by making the statement that Jesus "was in the world." In other words, Jesus was not alienated from the material world and its inhabitants; this was the world that He had created (cp. John 1:3).

Even though Jesus was in the world that He had made, the world "knew him not" (v. 10). The Greek word for "knew" is *ginosko* (**ghin-OCE-ko**) and refers to more than just head knowledge. It means "recognized or perceived" and carries the idea of knowing something intimately. John is conveying the real problem with humanity: The world should recognize its Creator. This recognition should motivate humanity to have a relationship with Jesus, but the world does not recognize Him, nor desire to have an intimate relationship with Him.

The rejection of Jesus by the world comes to a head in verse 11. There are two different meanings for the word "own" in this passage. First, He came to His "own" (Gk. *idios*, **ID-ee-os**), meaning "property" or "possessions" (i.e., homeland). Second, His "own" received Him not; the word is masculine in the Greek and refers to His own people, the Jews. For hundreds of years, the Jews had waited for the Messiah; now, when He came, they refused to receive Him as such.

The world belonged to Christ by virtue of His having created it, but the world did not know Him, would not enter into a relationship with Him, and refused to receive Him because they did not recognize Him for who He was. What a scathing commentary on the sinful condition of humanity!

12 But as many as received him, to them gave he power to become the sons of God, even to them that believe on his name:

But there is still hope for sinful humanity. Regardless of how bleak the situation may seem for humanity, God provides hope in the person of Jesus. There will be many who receive Jesus as Savior and Lord and recognize Him for who He is as the Creator of the universe. The word "received" (Gk. *paralambano*, **par-al-am-BAN-o**) means "took what was one's own, took to one's self, or

made one's own." As used here, "received" is more than psychologically accepting or making some emotional assent to Jesus. Therefore, to receive Jesus means to take hold of everything that Jesus is (Lord, Savior, Creator, Redeemer, etc.) and make Him one's own so that His presence affects a person's goals, aims, plans, and desires.

Those who receive Jesus and allow Him to affect their goals, aims, and plans are given the "power to become the sons of God." The Greek word for "power" is *exousia* (**ex-oo-SEE-ah**) and is best translated as "power of authority (influence)" or "power to act." What John is saying is that whoever receives Jesus is given the power and authority to act in a way consistent with being a child of God, and that this power gives us access to all of the privileges that come through God's grace. This power is used when we become children of God. God's power must be at work in our lives in order for us to live and act in a way consistent with being a child of God (cp. John 1:13).

In verse 12, John goes on to say that the privileges of being children of God are bestowed on those who "believe" on (Gk. *pisteuo*, **pist-YOO-o**) or have faith in His name. "Belief" here is more than simply something that happens in the mind. To believe on Jesus Christ means to place complete confidence in the nature, person, and character of Jesus Christ so that He influences the total being (goals, aims, plans, and desires). When you "received [Jesus]" and "believe on his name," John says, you entrusted Him with your life. Then this trust should lead to some sort of action, whereby you take hold of Jesus for yourself in order to be part of the family of God.

13 Which were born, not of blood, nor of the will of the flesh, nor of the will of man, but of God.

In this verse, Johns tells us that this new birth did not come about "of blood" (Gk. *haima*, **HAH-ee-mah**), referring to the blood of humans or animals. Nor was it a result of "the will of the flesh" (Gk. *sarx*), meaning "carnal nature" or "passions." Rather, the new birth was a result of something supernatural (cf. John 3:5–6).

14 And the Word was made flesh, and dwelt among us, (and we beheld his glory, the glory as of the only begotten of the Father,) full of grace and truth.

John 1:14 is one of the key verses in the New Testament that explains the Incarnation. "Incarnation" is defined as that act of grace whereby Christ took our human nature into union with His divine Person, becoming man. The Word was made flesh. Here, John refers to verse 1 and brings our attention back to the divine Word, or *logos*. The Word, who is God, who created the universe and provided light to all humanity, became flesh. The word "made" here (Gk. *ginomai*, **GHIN-oh-mahee**) is the same word used in John 1:3 and means "came into being." John is not saying that Jesus was some created, lesser god; he is affirming that Jesus existed in eternity past and took on a physical body through the Incarnation.

The Divine Word not only took on a physical body, but also dwelt among us. The word "dwelt" (Gk. *skenoo*, **skay-NO-o**) refers to abiding or living in a tabernacle (or tent). One cannot escape John's allusion to the Old Testament tabernacle, which was built as a temporary and mobile dwelling for God (see Exodus 36–40). The original tabernacle was a temporary meeting place. It had provisional status, anticipating the construction of the Temple in Jerusalem. In the Incarnation, when the Word was made flesh, humanity did not receive a temporary tabernacle; rather, God Himself in Jesus came to live among us. We can even say that Jesus is the Temple.

The idea John is trying to communicate here is that the "glory" (Gk. *doxa*, **DOX-ah**, meaning "perfection, honor, and praise") that we see in the incarnate Word is the glory of the Father in heaven. This is the strongest assertion of the deity of Christ that could be made. "Begotten" is the Greek word *monogenes* (**mon-og-en-ACE**) and means "unique, or one of a kind." While we can claim to be children of God in a general sense by receiving and believing in Christ, Jesus is the one and only unique Son of God.

And what is it that we see when we behold His glory? A revelation of God's preeminence and dignity, through Jesus, will reveal that He is "full of grace and truth." God's grace is a demonstration of His love. The word "grace" (Gk. *charis*, **KHAR-ece**) is defined as "favor" or "that which affords pleasure." "Truth" (Gk. *aletheia*, **al-AY-thi-a**) can be defined as "that which conforms to reality." Jesus is the one and only Son of God, and He conforms to the full reality of God in nature, character, and purpose (cp. Colossians 2:9). The truth as it relates to the nature and character of Jesus Christ dispels any heresies that may rise concerning His divine character.

Sources:

Keener, Craig S. *The IVP Bible Background Commentary: New Testament.* Downers Grove, IL.: InterVarsity Press, 1993. 261.

New Testament Greek Lexicon. Bible Study Tools.com. http://www.biblestudytools.com/lexicons/greek (accessed January 7, 2011).

Passage Lookup. Bible Gateway.com. http://www.biblegateway.com/passage (accessed January 7, 2011).

Tenney, Merrill C. *Expositor's Bible Commentary (John and Acts).* Electronic edition. Edited by Frank E. Gaebelein. Grand Rapids, MI: Zondervan Publishing, 1992.

Vincent, Marvin R. *Vincent's Word Studies, Vol. 2: The Writings of John.* Electronic edition. Hiawatha, IA: Parsons Technology, 1998.

Say It Correctly

Dualistic. Du-al-IST-ic.
Emanation. Em-a-NA-shun.
Preexistence. Pre-ex-IST-ens.
Incarnation. In-car-NA-shun.

Daily Bible Readings

MONDAY
The Beginning of the Year
(Exodus 12:1–8)

TUESDAY
The Beginning of Wisdom
(Psalm 111)

WEDNESDAY
In the Beginning, God
(Genesis 1:1–5)

THURSDAY
From the Foundations of the Earth
(Isaiah 40:21–26)

FRIDAY
The Beginning of the Gospel
(Mark 1:1–8)

SATURDAY
Beginning from Jerusalem
(Luke 24:44–49)

SUNDAY
In the Beginning, the Word
(John 1:1–14)

Notes

_____

_____

_____

_____

Teaching Tips

March 18
Bible Study Guide 3

Words You Should Know

A. Firkins (John 2:6) *metretes* (Gk.)—A measure of capacity for liquids (each firkin equals about 10 gallons).

B. Purifying (v. 6) *katharismos* (Gk.)— The process of ritual cleansing, either legal or ceremonial, to purge from the pollution of sin and guilt.

Teacher Preparation

Unifying Principle—The Good Stuff. Jesus' first miracle during the wedding at Cana revealed His power.

A. Study and meditate on the entire text.

B. Pray for your students using the Aim for Change as a guide.

C. Complete the companion lesson in the *Precepts For Living Personal Study Guide®*.

D. Bring index cards to class.

Open the Lesson

A. Before class, write the word "miracle" on the board.

B. Lead the class in prayer.

C. Assign someone to read the In Focus story. Discuss and focus on the Aim for Change.

D. Pass out the index cards and ask the students to write their definitions of "miracle" on them.

E. Then ask volunteers to read their definitions. Clarify from The People, Places, and Times and More Light on the Text.

P—Present the Scriptures

A. Discuss the Background information.

B. Then ask three volunteers to read the Focal Verses.

C. Divide the class into four groups and assign each group a section of In Depth commentary. Ask them to read and discuss. Each group should select a group spokesperson to share the highlights with the class.

D. Ask the corresponding Search the Scriptures questions.

E—Explore the Meaning

A. Direct the students to the Discuss the Meaning questions. Discuss.

B. Now read the Lesson in Our Society. Discuss.

N—Next Steps for Application

A. Share the Make It Happen suggestion.

B. Encourage students to read the Daily Bible Readings.

C. Have a closing prayer.

Worship Guide

For the Superintendent or Teacher
Theme: The Wedding at Cana
Theme Song: "I Know Whom I Have Believed"
Devotional Reading: John 17:1–5
Prayer

The Wedding at Cana

Bible Background • JOHN 2:1–12
Printed Text • JOHN 2:1–12 | Devotional Reading • JOHN 17:1–5

———————— Aim for Change ————————

By the end of the lesson, we will: DISCUSS Jesus' response to Mary; REFLECT on Jesus' transforming power in our lives; and SHARE with others why the power of Jesus is necessary in our lives.

In Focus

Eddie's love of the party life was getting out of hand. He reached a critical point one day when he left work for lunch and returned to the office drunk. He was fired on the spot.

When Eddie finally went home, his wife told him that their marriage was over. Walking the streets with no job, no home, and no family, Eddie knew his life had hit rock bottom. He looked up to the sky and cried out, "Dear God, please help me!"

After a while, Eddie passed a little storefront church and something inside him compelled him to go in. The pastor made his way to Eddie and sat down with him. Eddie broke down and tearfully poured out the whole sad story. The pastor told Eddie that in spite of all the mistakes he had made, God still loved him. That day Eddie accepted Christ as His Lord and Savior, and from that moment on he never took another drink. Within a month, he found a new job. A short time later, he and his wife were reunited.

Eddie told his wife that he was sure God performed a miracle in his life. He said, "He changed my life from hopelessness to happiness and our marriage from failure to fantastic. If Jesus can change me, surely He can change anything." This lesson is about the miracles that only God can do.

—————————— Keep in Mind ——————————

"This beginning of miracles did Jesus in Cana of Galilee, and manifested forth his glory; and his disciples believed on him" (John 2:11).

"This beginning of miracles did Jesus in Cana of Galilee, and manifested forth his glory; and his disciples believed on him" (John 2:11).

Focal Verses

KJV John 2:1 And the third day there was a marriage in Cana of Galilee; and the mother of Jesus was there:

2 And both Jesus was called, and his disciples, to the marriage.

3 And when they wanted wine, the mother of Jesus saith unto him, They have no wine.

4 Jesus saith unto her, Woman, what have I to do with thee? mine hour is not yet come.

5 His mother saith unto the servants, Whatsoever he saith unto you, do it.

6 And there were set there six waterpots of stone, after the manner of the purifying of the Jews, containing two or three firkins apiece.

7 Jesus saith unto them, Fill the waterpots with water. And they filled them up to the brim.

8 And he saith unto them, Draw out now, and bear unto the governor of the feast. And they bare it.

9 When the ruler of the feast had tasted the water that was made wine, and knew not whence it was: (but the servants which drew the water knew;) the governor of the feast called the bridegroom,

10 And saith unto him, Every man at the beginning doth set forth good wine; and when men have well drunk, then that which is worse: but thou hast kept the good wine until now.

11 This beginning of miracles did Jesus in Cana of Galilee, and manifested forth his glory; and his disciples believed on him.

12 After this he went down to Capernaum, he, and his mother, and his brethren, and his disciples: and they continued there not many days.

NLT John 2:1 The next day Jesus' mother was a guest at a wedding celebration in the village of Cana in Galilee.

2 Jesus and his disciples were also invited to the celebration.

3 The wine supply ran out during the festivities, so Jesus' mother spoke to him about the problem. "They have no more wine," she told him.

4 "How does that concern you and me?" Jesus asked. "My time has not yet come."

5 But his mother told the servants, "Do whatever he tells you."

6 Six stone waterpots were standing there; they were used for Jewish ceremonial purposes and held twenty to thirty gallons each.

7 Jesus told the servants, "Fill the jars with water." When the jars had been filled to the brim,

8 he said, "Dip some out and take it to the master of ceremonies." So they followed his instructions.

9 When the master of ceremonies tasted the water that was now wine, not knowing where it had come from (though, of course, the servants knew), he called the bridegroom over.

10 "Usually a host serves the best wine first," he said. "Then, when everyone is full and doesn't care, he brings out the less expensive wines. But you have kept the best until now!"

11 This miraculous sign at Cana in Galilee was Jesus' first display of his glory. And his disciples believed in him.

12 After the wedding he went to Capernaum for a few days with his mother, his brothers, and his disciples.

The People, Places, and Times

Miracle. There are three Greek words used by the Gospel writers to describe our Lord's miracles. *Dunamis* emphasizes God's mighty power to perform supernatural events. *Teras* means "wonder," and it emphasizes the extraordinary character of the Lord's miracles. *Semeion* means "sign." A sign points to something beyond itself. This word indicates that Jesus' miracles are meant to teach spiritual truth.

Background

God has drawn a veil over most of Jesus' life before He began His public ministry. Both Matthew and Luke record Jesus' birth and some of the incidents surrounding His birth and early childhood (Matthew 1:18–2:23; Luke 2:1–40). The next and last glimpse we get of our Lord before His ministry is the pre-teen Jesus visiting the temple in Jerusalem (Luke 2:41–52). There has been a great deal of speculation about the next 18 years of Jesus' life, but Scripture does not reveal anything about those years.

Then suddenly around A.D. 27, John the Baptist explodes out of the Judean wilderness proclaiming the advent of the Messiah and the arrival of the kingdom of God. One day, as John is baptizing along the Jordan River, Jesus shows up. He presents Himself to John for baptism (Matthew 3:13). John realizes who Jesus is and tries to decline the honor. Jesus convinces him that this is all part of God's plan, and John baptizes Him. As Jesus makes His way out of the water, the heavens open and the Holy Spirit descends upon Jesus in the form of a dove. Then the voice of God calls out from heaven, "This is my Son, whom I love; with him I am well pleased" (Matthew 3:17, NIV).

Forty days later, Jesus returns full of the Holy Spirit from His wilderness encounter with Satan. He passes the area where John is baptizing, and when John sees Him, he declares, "Look, the Lamb of God, who takes away the sin of the world!" (John 1:29, NIV). The next day John is talking with two of his disciples, and again he sees Jesus passing. Pointing Jesus out to the disciples, he exclaims, "Look, the Lamb of God!" (v. 36, NIV). The disciples, Andrew and Philip, leave John and immediately begin to follow Jesus. Later, Andrew brings his brother Peter to the Lord and Philip brings his brother Nathaniel (vv. 40–51).

The preparation for Jesus' ministry is now complete. The Lord showed His submission to God at His baptism. He demonstrated His sinlessness and suitability to be our eternal sacrifice when He overcame Satan in the wilderness. Finally, He called His first disciples. The question now is where and how He will begin His ministry.

At-A-Glance

1. The Merry Occasion (John 2:1–2)

2. The Modest Obedience (vv. 3–5)

3. The Miraculous Occurrence (vv. 6–11)

4. The Move to Capernaum (v. 12)

In Depth

1. The Merry Occasion (John 2:1–2)

Cana of Galilee was located just south of Nazareth where Jesus grew up. The bridegroom may have been related to or maybe a close friend of Mary, Jesus' mother. The language of the passage suggests that Mary had some official function at the wedding, while Jesus and His disciples were invited guests. "Jesus' mother was there, and Jesus and his disciples had also been invited to the wedding" (from John 2:1–2, NIV).

Weddings were major events in those days. In small villages, such as Cana, where the people worked hard without much time for recreation, weddings were even more special. The entire village may have participated in the celebration of the couple's union. The actual wedding usually took place on a Wednesday if the bride was a virgin and on Thursday if she was a widow. The phrase "the third day" in verse 1 refers to the succession of incidents recorded in John 1:29 and 1:35.

The series of events began with a celebration at the home of the bride. The bridal party escorted the maiden from her parents' home and then to the home prepared for her by her husband. As the wedding party made its way through the streets, neighbors and townspeople saluted the bride. Many people joined the entourage until it grew into a parade. When the procession arrived at the bride's new home, the couple exchanged vows. Then the bride and groom were crowned with garlands and the legal marriage document was signed. After the prescribed washing of hands and prayers, the marriage supper began with the cups being filled.

Marriage is the very first institution established by God (Genesis 2:24). The Old Testament repeatedly portrays the intimate relationship between God and Israel as a marriage (see Isaiah 62:5; Jeremiah 3:14; Hosea 1:2 and 3:1). In the New Testament, Christ is often referred to as the bridegroom (Matthew 9:15; John 3:29). The apostle Paul portrays the relationship between Christ and His church as that of a husband and wife (2 Corinthians 11:2; Ephesians 5:25–27). The gathering of Christ and His church in

heaven at the end of the age is described as a "wedding supper" (Revelation 19:9, NIV). When we consider the high esteem God has for marriage, it is highly appropriate that Christ would inaugurate the messianic age with a sign at a wedding.

2. The Modest Obedience (vv. 3–5)

Jewish wedding celebrations often lasted an entire week. The bridegroom's family had the sacred responsibility of providing food and beverages for all their guests for as long as the celebration lasted. But, in the midst of this celebration, the unthinkable happened. The wine ran out. This was a matter of grave concern. It would be considered an insult to all those present and cause the family to become socially marginalized. Mary realized the situation was desperate and immediately turned to Jesus for help. She said, "They have no more wine," (John 2:3, NIV).

Mary's urgent request that Jesus do something does not necessarily indicate she expected a miracle. Her husband, Joseph, who is not mentioned again after the temple incident (Luke 2:41–51), had probably been dead for a long time. Over the years, Mary had become accustomed to depending on her eldest son in emergencies, and this situation certainly qualified as an emergency. Mary's absolute confidence in Jesus implies that He had seldom—if ever—disappointed her.

Our Lord's response to His mother seems flippant on the face of it, but Jesus is not being callous or disrespectful. The term "woman" (John 2:4) was one of endearment. Jesus used the same word when He lovingly entrusted His mother to John's care from the Cross: "Woman, behold thy son" (from John 19:26). It is probably better translated as "Dear woman" (from John 2:4, NIV). When the Lord inquires of His mother, "Why do you involve me?" (from John 2:4, NIV), it marks the turning point in His relationship with her and His family. From that moment on, the business of His Father would take precedence over the concerns of His mother (see Luke 2:49–51).

The phrase "my time has not yet come" (John 2:4, NIV) is an idea that will be repeated throughout John's narrative (compare John 4:21, 23; 5:25; 7:30; 8:20; 12:23). Jesus lived His earthly life according to a heavenly clock. His time on earth was always in His Father's hands. The "hour" Jesus refers to (John 2:4) is the final hour of His earthly ministry when He would be manifested as the Christ and share in the glory of God (John 17:1).

Mary may or may not have understood what Jesus meant by His response, but she trusted Him to do what was right. She understood that Jesus was much more than just her Son. He was the Son of God. So the mother humbly submitted herself to the Son and instructed the servants, "Do whatever he tells you" (John 2:5, NIV).

3. The Miraculous Occurrence (vv. 6–11)

Outside the reception room were six large stone pots that contained water used for the ceremonial cleansing of hands. According to Jewish tradition, the primary sources of impurity were contact with dead creatures of any kind, genital flows, and certain skin diseases (Leviticus 11). Any impure object or person gave off a secondary degree of impurity to whatever or whomever it came into contact with. Since ultimately everything touches everything else, maintaining ritual purity was a continual battle.

Therefore, whenever new guests arrive at a wedding feast, water from the pots is poured over their hands in a cleansing ritual. Eating with unclean hands was also considered defilement, so water was poured over the hands of the diners before each meal.

Each of the water pots had a capacity of two or three firkins of water (John 2:6). A firkin is about 10 gallons, so each pot held about 20 to 30 gallons. Jesus commands the servants to fill all the pots with water, and they obediently fill each pot to the brim (v. 7). Filling the pots to the brim eliminates the possibility of anything else being added to the pots other than water. Next, Jesus tells the servants, "Now draw some out and take it to the master of the banquet" (v. 8, NIV). Again, the servants do as they are instructed.

John does not explain how or when the water in the pots becomes wine. He simply states the facts: "And the master of the banquet tasted the water that had been turned into wine" (from v. 9, NIV). When the banquet master tasted the wine, he was shocked. He called for the bridegroom, took him aside, and said, "Everyone brings out the choice wine first and then the cheaper wine after the guests have had too much to drink; but you have saved the best till now" (v. 10, NIV). Both the bridegroom and the banquet master were at a loss to explain the source of the new wine, but the servants knew. So it was that Jesus "chose the foolish things of the world to shame the wise; God chose the weak things to shame the strong" (1 Corinthians 1:27, NIV).

Traditionally, the "choice" (John 2:10, NIV) or "good" (v. 10, KJV) wine was wine that had not lost its sugar content in the fermentation process. Cheaper fermented wine had to be diluted with much more water to ensure that the revelers did not violate the law against drunkenness (see Deuteronomy 21:20–21; Isaiah 28:7). In either case, Jewish law mandated mixing all wine with water. The mixture ranged from three to 10 parts water to one part wine. The ratio of water to wine depended on the amount of alcohol in the wine.

The phrase "when men have well drunk" (John 2:10) means "become drunk" or "become satisfied" (without reference to drunkenness). The phrase must be translated according to its context. In this case, it is illogical to think that Jesus contributed gallons of wine to an already drunken party.

Our Lord is no mere magician performing magical feats to impress the crowds. He is the Son of God. He affects miracles to help His people and glorify His Father. The significance of Jesus' first miracle lies in the result produced. He transforms what would have been a disaster for the host into a joyous and praiseful moment.

The supernatural event portrayed the opening of the new age of grace through the new wine of the Gospel and manifested Jesus' glory as the Son of God. The miracle caused Jesus' disciples to put their faith in Him (v. 11).

Miracles are not merely superhuman feats. They are divine acts of love and power. John refers to Jesus' miracles as signs. These signs always point past the event to the source of the event, Jesus Christ. The signs are recorded so that we may believe in the power and person of Jesus Christ and attain eternal life by believing (1 John 5:13).

4. The Move to Capernaum (v. 12)

Jesus did not stay around to receive public acclaim for this miracle. Instead He moved on to Capernaum, which was His headquarters for most of His ministry.

Search the Scriptures

1. In what Israelite village and on what occasion did Jesus perform His first miracle (John 2:1)?

2. Who brought it to Jesus' attention that the wedding supper had run out of wine for the guests (v. 4)?

3. Who were the four disciples who accompanied Jesus to the wedding (John 1:40–51)?

Discuss the Meaning

1. Can Jesus' miracle of turning water into wine be interpreted as approval of drinking alcoholic beverages? Why or why not?

2. What does Jesus' miracle at the marriage say about His regard for marriage?

Lesson in Our Society

It is appropriate that Jesus chose a wedding ceremony to perform His first miracle. Marriage is the first institution established by God and signifies the beginning of a new way of life. God desires a lifelong commitment of the marriage partners.

In America, about half of all marriages end in divorce. Many people forego the act of marriage altogether and just "shack up." Those who live together without marriage simply walk away from each other when times get hard. The law now grants the same status to "common-law" unions as it does to marriages while making it much easier to get divorced.

Is it possible that our lack of true commitment to our most intimate partners contributes to the breakdown we are experiencing in our society? Should couples be required to undergo counseling before marriage and before being granted a divorce?

Make It Happen

The Gospel of Christ changes people from the inside out. Can you think of any ways God has changed you? This week, make a list of sinful ways or imperfections that God has changed in you. Then make a second list of sinful ways or imperfections you want God to change in you. Be prepared to share your first list with the class next week. Make your second list a matter of prayer and determine to use God's power in you to bring about change.

Follow the Spirit
What God wants me to do:

_____

_____

_____

_____

Remember Your Thoughts
Special insights I have learned:

_____

_____

_____

_____

More Light on the Text
John 2:1–12

1 And the third day there was a marriage in Cana of Galilee; and the mother of Jesus was there: 2 And both Jesus was called, and his disciples, to the marriage.

"The third day" is not the third day of the week. The phrase continues a three-day sequence of time beginning at 1:35 ("Again the next day"), picked up at 1:43 ("The day following"), and ending here.

The "marriage" (Gk. *gamos*, **GAM-os**) or marriage festival included a series of entertainments and usually was spoken of in the plural. The marriage feast was a very important part of the marriage ceremony. Although Scripture does not provide much information about the actual ceremony, historical findings point to a very public event. The Gospels record only this instance of Jesus participating in a marriage feast, but He referred to various aspects of weddings in His teachings (Matthew 22:1–10; 25:1–13; Mark 2:19–20; Luke 14:8).

The marriage took place in a village called Cana of Galilee, so named to distinguish it from another village in Syria with the same name. The exact location of Cana ("place of reeds") is unknown, but many authorities place it near Capernaum about 12 miles north of Nazareth where Jesus was raised. The village is quite significant in Jesus' ministry. Not only did He perform the opening miracle of His ministry here, but later He healed a nobleman's son (John 4:46–54). The village was also the hometown of Nathaniel, one of Jesus' first apostles.

Marriage feasts in ancient Israel generally lasted for a whole week. The guests sat around a great bowl or bowls on the floor. The marriage meal usually consisted of stewed lamb with rice or barley. The servants poured water over the hands of the guests before the meal began. This procedure was repeated at the end of the meal. The guests used pieces of bread as table napkins to wipe their fingers. After the guests dried their hands, the bread was thrown on the ground to be eaten by pet dogs or tossed outside to be picked up by stray dogs (Matthew 15:27; Mark 7:28).

After the meal, guests retired to pillows situated around the walls, where they sat cross-legged and exchanged gossip, listened to entertainment, or engaged in riddles and jokes. Light was supplied by a small lamp or two, or if the night was chilly, by a smoldering fire of weeds kindled in the middle of the room. Sometimes there was a brazier for the fire, but the fire was often kindled in a hole in the floor.

Mary, the mother of Jesus, is known as the "Virgin Mary," although the Gospel writers never refer to her by that term. The Gospel accounts provide only a small amount of information regarding Mary's personal history, but Luke gives her genealogy. She was of the tribe of Judah and the lineage of David (Psalm 132:11; Luke 1:32). She was related by marriage to Elisabeth, the mother of John the Baptist (Luke 1:36).

Because the wedding feast at Cana takes place shortly after Jesus' return from His 40-day wilderness encounter, Jesus would have only four disciples at this time (Andrew, Peter, Philip, and Nathaniel).

3 And when they wanted wine, the mother of Jesus saith unto him, They have no wine.

Here the verb "wanted" (Gk. *hustereo,* **hoos-ter-EH-o**) means "fell short, suffered need, gave out or failed." Thus, a better translation is "when the wine was gone" (NIV). Marriage festivals generally lasted for at least a week. For some reason, perhaps because a larger number of guests than expected showed up, the celebration ran out of wine. This was a potentially embarrassing situation for the hosts of the wedding feast.

Mary, whom John never mentions by name in his narrative, takes the problem to Jesus. Her request is further evidence of her official capacity at the wedding. Mary's request could not be based on any supposition that Jesus would perform a miracle because there is no evidence of Him ever acting miraculously before this time. So why the appeal to Jesus? Partly because during the years since Joseph's death, Mary had probably grown accustomed to depending on her eldest son for help and hoped He would somehow meet the difficulty. Her request was both a testimony of her personal confidence in Him and a realization of the gravity of the situation that threatened the newlyweds.

4 Jesus saith unto her, Woman, what have I to do with thee? mine hour is not yet come.

These words in our language seem harsh and rude, but the term rendered "woman" was a respectful term of endearment (see John 19:26) and is probably better understood as "dear woman." The language Jesus used was a mild rebuke. Jesus' gentle rebuke, literally, "What is this to Me?" rejects Mary's interference. He intended to meet the need in His own way.

In every case, the phrase "mine hour" (John 2:4) refers to a time of personal crisis for the Lord, generally His Passion. Here He speaks of His messianic manifestation as shown in verse 11 but not fully realized until His suffering on Calvary.

5 His mother saith unto the servants, Whatsoever he saith unto you, do it.

Mary evidently understood from Jesus' demeanor, if not His words, that He intended to help in this situation. The family was probably too poor to have actual "servants," so the word here (Gk. *diakonos,* **dee-AK-on-os**) apparently refers to hired attendants for the wedding.

6 And there were set there six waterpots of stone, after the manner of the purifying of the Jews, containing two or three firkins apiece. 7 Jesus saith unto them, Fill the waterpots with water. And they filled them up to the brim.

In Jewish thought, purity was obtained by cleansings and purifications that worshipers were commanded to perform as part of their religious duties. Most of the ceremonial purifications had both ethical and practical applications. The six stone waterpots were used to supply water for the ceremonial cleansing at Jewish feasts (see Mark 7:3–4). Jews were ceremonially unclean if they did not wash both before and after meals. The family probably borrowed some of the pots from neighbors and friends to accommodate all the guests. Each water pot held "two or three firkins" (John 2:6). This translates into about 20 to 30 gallons of water. The water was stored in pots to protect it from contamination, and then it was poured over the hands of the guests.

Following Jesus' instructions, the servants filled each pot to the brim, which eliminated any possibility of anything other than pure water being added. The combined capacity of the water pots was, on average, about 150 gallons. Thus, if each serving cup held a half pint of wine, there would be enough for 2,400 servings—more than enough to meet the need.

8 And he saith unto them, Draw out now, and bear unto the governor of the feast. And they bare it. 9 When the ruler of the feast had tasted the water that was made wine, and knew not whence it was: (but the servants which drew the water knew;) the governor of the feast called the bridegroom, 10 And saith unto him, Every man at the beginning doth set forth good wine; and when men have well drunk, then that which is worse: but thou hast kept the good wine until now.

The "governor" (Gk. *architriklinos*, **ar-khee-TREE-klee-nos**) of the marriage banquet was the "superintendent" whose duty it was to arrange the tables and food. He functioned in the capacity of a headwaiter. The text does not say how or when the water became wine. The servants drew the liquid from the pots and gave it to the governor of the feast. When the governor of the feast tasted the water, it had become wine!

It is probably best at this point to stop and explore the controversy of the wine. The question is whether the wine Jesus supplied for the marriage feast was fermented or unfermented. In Greek, the word for "wine,"

oinos (**OY-nos**), is a generic term that can be used for wine or unfermented juice. The context of a given passage determines which meaning the author intends. Many believe that the wine that was served earlier and the wine Jesus provided were both fermented.

The governor of the feast described the wine provided by Jesus as "good." It is significant that John uses the Greek word *kalos* (**kal-OS**) instead of *agathos* (**ag-ath-OS**). The latter is a qualitative term that refers to the taste of the wine. The former is a more moralistic term and refers to both the quality and character of a person or object. The phrase "when men have well drunk" does seem to imply that the celebrants were drunk. The Greek word *methusko* (**meth-OOS-ko**) means "to make or become drunk." The proponents of the "intoxicating drinks" view say this is proof positive that *oinos* cannot be taken as referring to juice.

In either case, Jewish religious law insisted that all wine be mixed with at least three parts water or it would not be blessed and would defile the drinker. It is also vital to recognize that supplying wine at the wedding is not an endorsement of drunkenness but a miraculous sign that resolved a major crisis at a wedding feast with many guests.

11 This beginning of miracles did Jesus in Cana of Galilee, and manifested forth his glory; and his disciples believed on him. 12 After this he went down to Capernaum, he, and his mother, and his brethren, and his disciples: and they continued there not many days.

The primary purpose of the miracle was to reveal Christ's glory in such a way as to cause people to believe in Christ as God's Holy and righteous Son. In verse 11, the primary meaning of "glory" (Gk. *doxa*, **DOX-ah**) is "favorable thought or opinion," and thus in a secondary sense refers to reputation, praise, honor, and splendor. However, because these qualities are dependent on human opinion, this is not the glory we render to God or Christ. God's glory embraces all that is excellent within the divine nature and finds its perfect revelation in and through Jesus Christ (John 1:14; Hebrews 1:3).

The belief prompted by the sign was not the complete faith Jesus desired, but it was a step above the disciples' initial belief, which was only conjectural. The disciples had seen the miracle with their own eyes and were able to draw their own conclusions that a superior being was in their midst. Jesus proved all His claims through His acts of mercy and power.

Sources:
New Testament Greek Lexicon. Bible Study Tools.com. http://www.biblestudytools.com/lexicons/greek (accessed January 7, 2011).
Passage Lookup. Bible Gateway.com. http://www.bible-gateway.com/passage (accessed January 7, 2011).
Strong's Exhaustive Concordance of the Bible. McLean, VA: MacDonald Publishing Company. n.d.

Say It Correctly

Geneology. Je-ne-OL-o-gy.
Lineage. Li-nē-ij also Li-nij
Messianic. Mes-e-AN-ik.
Manifestation. Man-i-fes-TA-shun.

Daily Bible Readings

MONDAY
Glorify Your Son
(John 17:1–5)

TUESDAY
Glory That Comes from God
(John 5:39–47)

WEDNESDAY
Glory That Belongs to God
(John 7:10–18)

THURSDAY
God Glorifies the Son
(John 8:48–59)

FRIDAY
Loving Human Glory
(John 12:36b–43)

SATURDAY
Glory for the Sake of Unity
(John 17:20–24)

SUNDAY
Glory Revealed
(John 2:1–12)

Teaching Tips

Words You Should Know

Begotten (John 3:16, 18) *monogenes* (Gk.)—The one who is born; brought forth.

Teacher Preparation

Unifying Principle—A New Life. The writer of John gives assurance that, regardless of our choices, God loves us and sent Jesus so the world might be restored to a right relationship with God.

A. Pray for your students.

B. Prayerfully study the entire text and meditate on the lesson.

C. Complete the companion lesson in the *Precepts For Living Personal Study Guide®*.

O—Open the Lesson

A. Open the class with prayer.

B. Introduce the subject of the lesson, Aim for Change, and Keep in Mind verse.

C. Have a volunteer tell the In Focus story and tie it in with today's discussion.

P—Present the Scriptures

A. Assign three students to read the Focal Verses according to the At-A-Glance outline, another to read the Background section, and another to read The People, Places, and Times. Discuss.

B. Review the Search the Scriptures questions. Discuss.

E—Explore the Meaning

A. Use the Discuss the Meaning questions to help the students think through and apply the truths they have learned today.

B. Use the Lesson in Our Society section to help the students grasp the wider implications of these truths.

N—Next Steps for Application

A. Review the Make It Happen section.

B. Assign the Daily Bible Readings as homework for the next week.

C. Take requests and close with prayer.

Worship Guide

For the Superintendent or Teacher
Theme: God's Word Saves
Theme Song: "Born Again"
Devotional Reading: Matthew 5:13–16
Prayer

God's Word Saves

Bible Background • JOHN 3:11–21; Numbers 21:4–8
Printed Text • JOHN 3:11–21 | Devotional Reading • MATTHEW 5:13–16

MAR 25th

─────────── **Aim for Change** ───────────

By the end of the lesson, we will: KNOW why God gave Jesus to the world; REJOICE for the love of Jesus in the world; and LIST ways we can and do share the love of God.

 **In Focus**

Brother Williams is a gifted Christian who serves on his church's Board of Trustees. However, this was not always the case. He is a recovering alcoholic who used to beat his wife and children. After years of tolerating her husband's behavior, Mrs. Williams had finally had enough. One weekend Mr. Williams arrived home drunk as usual and found his wife, children, and all their possessions gone.

Mr. Williams was miserable without his family. One of his coworkers noticed his downward spiral and invited him out to lunch. Mr. Williams confessed to being unable to turn his life around and did not know where he could find help.

His coworker told him about the life-changing relationship he had with Jesus. Then he asked Mr. Williams if he would like to become a new person in Christ. Right there in the restaurant Brother Williams gave his life to Christ. He no longer drinks; he and his family are reunited and happy.

Brother Williams did not just turn over a "new leaf." He actually became a new person in Christ. In today's lesson, Jesus explains to a religious scholar named Nicodemus what it means to be born again.

─────────── **Keep in Mind** ───────────

"For God so loved the world, that he gave his only begotten Son, that whosoever believeth in him should not perish, but have everlasting life" (John 3:16).

"For God so loved the world, that he gave his only begotten Son, that whosoever believeth in him should not perish, but have everlasting life" (John 3:16).

Focal Verses

KJV John **3:11** Verily, verily, I say unto thee, We speak that we do know, and testify that we have seen; and ye receive not our witness.

12 If I have told you earthly things, and ye believe not, how shall ye believe, if I tell you of heavenly things?

13 And no man hath ascended up to heaven, but he that came down from heaven, even the Son of man which is in heaven.

14 And as Moses lifted up the serpent in the wilderness, even so must the Son of man be lifted up:

15 That whosoever believeth in him should not perish, but have eternal life.

16 For God so loved the world, that he gave his only begotten Son, that whosoever believeth in him should not perish, but have everlasting life.

17 For God sent not his Son into the world to condemn the world; but that the world through him might be saved.

18 He that believeth on him is not condemned: but he that believeth not is condemned already, because he hath not believed in the name of the only begotten Son of God.

19 And this is the condemnation, that light is come into the world, and men loved darkness rather than light, because their deeds were evil.

20 For every one that doeth evil hateth the light, neither cometh to the light, lest his deeds should be reproved.

21 But he that doeth truth cometh to the light, that his deeds may be made manifest, that they are wrought in God.

NLT John **3:11** "I assure you, I am telling you what we know and have seen, and yet you won't believe us.

12 But if you don't even believe me when I tell you about things that happen here on earth, how can you possibly believe if I tell you what is going on in heaven?

13 For only I, the Son of Man, have come to earth and will return to heaven again.

14 And as Moses lifted up the bronze snake on a pole in the wilderness, so I, the Son of Man, must be lifted up on a pole,

15 so that everyone who believes in me will have eternal life.

16 "For God so loved the world that he gave his only Son, so that everyone who believes in him will not perish but have eternal life.

17 God did not send his Son into the world to condemn it, but to save it.

18 "There is no judgment awaiting those who trust him. But those who do not trust him have already been judged for not believing in the only Son of God.

19 Their judgment is based on this fact: The light from heaven came into the world, but they loved the darkness more than the light, for their actions were evil.

20 They hate the light because they want to sin in the darkness. They stay away from the light for fear their sins will be exposed and they will be punished.

21 But those who do what is right come to the light gladly, so everyone can see that they are doing what God wants."

The People, Places, and Times

The Pharisees. The Pharisees were members of a Jewish religious sect. They were very concerned with obedience to the Law, and they included their own extensive interpretations of the Law, which were not part of the Old Testament. Because of their emphasis on a legalistic interpretation of Scripture, they came into conflict with Jesus, who pointed to God's concern for love for Him and love for neighbors as being more important than things such as tithing the herbs that grow in our gardens.

Background

Jesus was deep into conversation with Nicodemus one evening. Nicodemus was a respected religious scholar, a Pharisee, and a member of the Jewish ruling council. John does not tell us why Nicodemus came to see Jesus at night. It is possible that he came then because the Pharisees opposed Jesus, and Nicodemus wanted to check out Jesus for himself. Nicodemus seems to be approaching Jesus with a proud attitude. Although he called Jesus "Rabbi" and "teacher" (John 3:2), that seems to be all that he was able to admit.

Jesus had some astonishing news for him. No doubt Nicodemus knew that Gentiles had to be born again to come into God's family, but he thought that he was already a member of the family, since he was a very religious Jew. A post on Facebook that has been going around says something to the effect that just as being born in a garage does not make one a car, so being born in a Christian family, country, etc., does not make one a Christian. Even going to church does not make one a Christian. Jesus stated very clearly that everyone needs to be born again to become a member of God's kingdom.

It seems that Nicodemus made no commitment to Jesus that night, but mulled these things over in his mind. But later on, we find that Nicodemus is ready to step forward and become a believer as he joins Joseph of Arimathea in asking for the body of Jesus as He hung dead on the Cross (John 19:38–42).

At-A-Glance

1. Jesus Speaks of Heavenly Things
(John 3:11–13)

2. Jesus Will Be Lifted Up (vv. 14–15)

3. Jesus Showed God's Love (v. 16)

4. Jesus Brings Both Love and Judgment
(vv. 17–21)

In Depth

1. Jesus Speaks of Heavenly Things (John 3:11–13)

Jesus mildly rebuked Nicodemus for doubt. He assured the Pharisee that "we speak [what] we do know, and testify [to what] we have seen" (v. 11). Then Jesus asked Nicodemus a rhetorical question: "If I have told you earthly things, and ye believe not, how shall ye believe, if I tell you of heavenly things?" (v. 12). If Nicodemus could not accept the basic teaching of redemption, he would never be able to understand the deeper mysteries of God. Jesus used the earthly metaphors of birth and wind to explain heavenly things. Nicodemus probably understood the spiritual truths that Jesus was talking about, but he did not want to believe at this time.

To prove His point, Jesus made an astounding statement: "And no man hath ascended up to heaven, but he that came down from heaven, even the Son of man which is in heaven" (v. 13). Jesus is saying that no human has been to heaven except the Son of man who came down from heaven.

2. Jesus Will Be Lifted Up (vv. 14–15)

Here, Jesus is openly declaring that He came down from heaven to reveal heavenly truths (v. 14). To clarify His identity and explain the meaning of His coming down from heaven, Jesus referred to an incident that Nicodemus was certainly aware of. Shortly before the Israelites entered the Promised Land, they again complained about their situation. The Lord sent venomous snakes among them that bit the people, and many died. Then the Israelites repented of their sin, so God commanded Moses to fashion a bronze serpent and put it on a pole. Anyone who looked up to the serpent would be saved by this simple act of faith (see Numbers 21:4–9). In that same way, Jesus came down from heaven to be lifted up on a pole (cross). Whoever will look to the Cross and accept Jesus' sacrifice as an act of faith will be saved.

3. Jesus Showed God's Love (v. 16)

Nicodemus had spent his life studying and strictly trying to observe the minutest details of the law. Now Jesus was telling him that entrance into God's kingdom was not earned through works. Jesus' explanation of God's loving-kindness is the most well-known and cherished verse in all of Scripture: "For God so loved the world, that he gave his only begotten Son, that whosoever believeth in him should not perish, but have everlasting life" (John 3:16).

This verse reveals God's heart and His purpose. God's love is so wide that it embraces all persons in "the world." It is so long that it reaches out to "whosoever." The depth of His love is shown by what He was willing to sacrifice on our behalf—His "only begotten Son." His love grants us "everlasting life" in heaven in exchange for believing in Jesus Christ, the Son of God, and His sacrifice for us.

4. Jesus Brings Both Love and Judgment (vv. 17–21)

The story of Jesus' conversation with Nicodemus explains that Jesus did not leave heaven and come to earth to condemn lost souls. He came to save the world. However, those who fail to accept the person and work of Christ condemn themselves. It is often difficult for unbelievers to accept the teachings of Christ. The ways of God are impossible to grasp unless the Holy Spirit reveals them. Taking the first step to spiritual rebirth must be based on faith.

Search the Scriptures

1. Why is Jesus uniquely qualified to speak of spiritual things (John 3:11–13)?

2. What is the one requirement for receiving eternal life (vv. 15–16)?

3. Why are people condemned who do not believe in Jesus (vv. 18–21)?

Discuss the Meaning

1. Jesus compared His ministry to the serpent that Moses raised up for Israelites during their desert wanderings. What is the spiritual relationship between Jesus' ministry and the events of Numbers 21?

2. Jesus said that "the Son of Man [must] be lifted up: That whosoever believeth in him should not perish, but have eternal life" (John 3:14b–15). Describe the importance of our faith in Jesus Christ.

Lesson in Our Society

According to several surveys, most citizens consider America to be a Christian nation. Many Americans profess a kind of belief in God and His Son Jesus Christ. Yet this nation is one of the most morally corrupt nations on earth. How do we reconcile our belief in God and Christ with our deeds? Many people think that belief is nothing more than intellectual agreement. How can true believers demonstrate to the masses that true belief means to place one's complete trust and confidence in Christ and to give Him absolute control over our present plans and eternal destiny?

Make It Happen

We must come to God in faith, especially when we have questions or uncertainties. Hebrews 11:6 says, "But without faith it is impossible to please him: for he that cometh to God must believe that he is, and that he is a rewarder of them that diligently seek him." This week, seek out the answers to some questions that you may have as you study God's Word. Remember that God rewards those who seek Him.

Follow the Spirit

What God wants me to do:

_____

_____

_____

_____

Remember Your Thoughts

Special insights I have learned:

_____

_____

_____

_____

More Light on the Text

John 3:11–21

11 Verily, verily, I say unto thee, We speak that we do know, and testify that we have seen; and ye receive not our witness.

Nicodemus, who was a prominent Pharisee, a member of the Sanhedrin Council, a doctor of the Jewish law, and a spiritual leader, lacked an understanding of what Jesus was teaching him. However, Jesus makes it clear that He and His followers know the truth through firsthand experience (John 7:16; 8:38; 1 John 1:3). Yet, Nicodemus and the Jewish authorities refused to believe them.

12 If I have told you earthly things, and ye believe not, how shall ye believe, if I tell you of heavenly things?

What was Jesus referring to when He talked about "earthly things" (Gk. *epigeios*, **ep-IG-i-os**), meaning the things that occur on earth? It is likely that Jesus is speaking of His analogies related to birth, wind, and water. The phrase "heavenly things" (Gk. *epouranios*, **ep-oo-RAN-ee-os**) refers to things that exist or take place in heaven.

The word "believe" (Gk. *pisteuo*, **pist-YOO-o**) means to think or be persuaded that something is true; to place confidence, conviction, and trust in something or someone. This word is used in John 3:12, 15, and 16 to identify a critical requirement. If Nicodemus would not believe, trust, or rely on Jesus' explanation of mere earthly things, how could he believe in the truth about heavenly things associated with the kingdom of God?

13 And no man hath ascended up to heaven, but he that came down from heaven, even the Son of man which is in heaven.

Jesus is uniquely qualified to reveal the truth about heavenly things because He alone "came down from heaven," has "ascended up to heaven," and "is in heaven" (see John 6:38; 16:28; Ephesians 4:10).

The phrase "Son of man" appears in the Old Testament primarily to specify a member of humanity (cf. Psalm 8:4). It was also used to refer to the prophet in the book of Ezekiel. Later, in the apocalyptic book of Daniel, one sees a new development in the use of the phrase. The "Son of man" takes on the character of a divine agent who will carry out judgment and deliverance (see Daniel 7:13).

In the New Testament, John the Baptist testified that Jesus is the Son of God (John 1:34). Also, he stated that this "Son" was the Word become flesh (v. 14). Moreover, this Word was in the beginning with God, and was God (v. 1). Therefore, Jesus is the Word of God, who became flesh and dwelt in the world as a man, the "Son of man." The Word of God is the Son of God who became the Son of man, our Lord Jesus Christ.

14 And as Moses lifted up the serpent in the wilderness, even so must the Son of man be lifted up: 15 That whosoever believeth in him should not perish, but have eternal life.

In the wilderness, when the Israelites murmured against God, God sent fiery (poisonous) serpents among the people to bite them, and many Israelites died. When the people repented, the Lord told Moses to make a bronze serpent and set it upon a pole. Then, if anyone who was bitten would look at that bronze serpent, they would live (Numbers 21). Our just and merciful God provided a means of salvation for a disobedient people, so that they might survive divine judgment.

In John 3:14, the phrase "lifted up" is translated from the Greek word *hupsoo* (**hoop-SO-o**), which means lifted up on high or exalted; both definitions apply in this verse. Jesus was lifted up on the Cross of Calvary to become the source of salvation for all who will look to Him in faith (John 12:32). In addition, Jesus Christ should be exalted as Savior and Lord in the heart and life of every believer (2 Peter 3:18), and He will ultimately be exalted in all the earth (Philippians 2:8–11). The One who suffered death for us is the source of life for all who believe.

16 For God so loved the world, that he gave his only begotten Son, that whosoever believeth in him should not perish, but have everlasting life.

John 3:16 is one of the most beloved verses in all of Scripture. However, in this study, we must also remember that it is found in the context of a conversation between Jesus and Nicodemus.

Out of the darkness of night, under the shadow of uncertainty, Nicodemus came to Jesus, the Light of the world. It is in John 3:16 that Nicodemus (and each of us) finds the answer: God takes away our sins and grants us new birth or "everlasting life" because of His unconditional love for us, which is manifested by the sacrifice of His Son and our Savior, Jesus Christ.

17 For God sent not his Son into the world to condemn the world; but that the world through him might be saved.

God sent Jesus into a world that already was condemned, so condemnation was not His purpose in coming. Elsewhere in Scripture, we read that Jesus came to judge the world. The judge can declare a person innocent or guilty, and this is the power and authority that Jesus, as the second member of the Trinity, has. So Jesus came to our world when we were already condemned because of our sin. And the purpose of His coming was to save us from this condemnation. The Greek for "condemnation" is *krino* (**KREE-no**). In some passages, this word is neutral; it simply means to judge, but in this passage and others, it means to condemn.

18 He that believeth on him is not condemned: but he that believeth not is condemned already, because he hath not believed in the name of the only begotten Son of God.

When Jesus came we were already in need of a Savior, but it is our choice. Do we believe in our Savior, or do we not? If we believe, our condemnation is erased simply because of our faith in Him. If we do not believe, we remain in our sins and we are condemned.

19 And this is the condemnation, that light is come into the world, and men loved darkness rather than light, because their deeds were evil. 20 For every one that doeth evil hateth the light, neither cometh to the light, lest his deeds should be reproved. 21 But he that doeth truth cometh to the light, that his deeds may be made manifest, that they are wrought in God.

We read in John 1:4–9 that Jesus is the true Light, the only light that can bring light to any one of us. But think of all the dark places of this world—such as some bars, clubs, etc.—the lights are kept very low so people can do shameful things. If people prefer that no one see the things they are doing, they want to stay where it is figuratively, if not actually, dark. Their pride keeps them from coming to Jesus; they do not want to change.

But Jesus desires that we come to Him with all our sinful baggage and let Him wash us clean. Then there is a change in our lives, and we want people to see the change. We want people to see the good things we are doing, not because of self-pride, but because we want to give the glory to God, who is doing these things through us.

The Greek makes it clear that this is not simply the contrast of doing bad things versus doing good things. The Greek for "evil" is *poneros* (**pon-ay-ROS**). This refers to many worthless deeds. The Greek for "doeth truth" is *aletheia* (**al-AY-thi-a**). This does not mean good deeds in contrast with evil deeds; it means living by the truth that is in Christ Jesus.

Sources:

Carson, D. A. *The Gospel According to John*. Grand Rapids, MI: William B. Eerdmans Publishing Company, 1991.

New Testament Greek Lexicon. Bible Study Tools.com. http://www.biblestudytools.com/lexicons/greek (accessed January 8, 2011).

Passage Lookup. Bible Gateway.com. http://www.bible-gateway.com/passage (accessed January 8, 2011).

Strong's Exhaustive Concordance of the Bible. McLean, VA: MacDonald Publishing Company. n.d.

Say It Correctly

Apocalytptic. A-poc-a-LIP-tik.

Daily Bible Readings

MONDAY
The Light of the World
(Matthew 5:13–16)

TUESDAY
Lovers of Darkness
(Job 24:13–17)

WEDNESDAY
Loving Evil More than Good
(Psalm 52)

THURSDAY
Look and Live
(Numbers 21:4–9)

FRIDAY
Wrongly Worshiping the Symbol
(2 Kings 18:1–7a)

SATURDAY
Light for the Way
(Nehemiah 9:9–15)

SUNDAY
Whoever Believes in Him
(John 3:11–21)

Notes

_____

_____

_____

_____

Teaching Tips

Words You Should Know

A. Passover (John 18:28) *pecach* (Heb.)—A Jewish celebration commemorating their exodus from bondage in Egypt.

B. Defilement (v. 28) *chalal* (Heb.)—Unclean. No Hebrew, especially a priest could partake of the Passover Feast and be unclean. To be in a Gentile's presence or building rendered that person unclean.

Teacher Preparation

Unifying Principle—Truth Prevails. The truth of God's love is made clear through His sacrifice of His life for us.

A. Pray for your students and that God will bring clarity to this lesson.

B. Study and meditate on the entire text.

C. Complete the companion lesson in the *Precepts For Living Personal Study Guide®*.

O—Open the Lesson

A. Open with prayer, including the Aim for Change.

B. After prayer, introduce today's subject of the lesson.

C. Have your students read the Aim for Change and Keep in Mind verse in unison. Discuss.

D. Ask the question, "Have you ever been persecuted for telling the truth?"

E. Share testimonies.

P—Present the Scriptures

A. Have volunteers read the Focal Verses.

B. Now use The People, Places, and Times; Background; Search the Scriptures; At-A-Glance outline; In Depth; and More Light on the Text to clarify the verses.

E—Explore the Meaning

A. Have volunteers summarize the Discuss the Meaning, Lesson in Our Society, and Make It Happen sections.

B. Connect these sections to the Aim for Change and the Keep in Mind verse.

N—Next Steps for Application

A. Summarize the lesson or write some takeaway principles under the Follow the Spirit or Remember Your Thoughts section.

B. Close with prayer and praise God for the victory He's won in their lives and for who He is.

Worship Guide

For the Superintendent or Teacher
Theme: Jesus Testifies to the Truth
Theme Song: "Jesus Paid It All"
Devotional Reading: John 8:28–38
Prayer

Jesus Testifies to the Truth

Bible Background • John 18–19
Printed Text • John 18:28–37 | Devotional Reading • John 8:28–38

—————— Aim for Change ——————

By the end of the lesson, we will: KNOW the meaning of God's love for all; FEEL that we share the truth in Christ; and WITNESS with others how faith impacts our day-to-day behavior.

**APR
1st**

————————  In Focus ————————

"Do you solemnly swear to tell the whole truth and nothing but the truth, so help you God?"

The court clerk's words echoed in Rodney's mind. His thoughts raced over the events of the past few weeks. How had he ended up in this hearing? He and his friends only meant to have some fun. No one was supposed to get hurt.

As his thoughts tumbled over each other, he knew he couldn't go against the code of the streets. That could endanger him. After all, he knew what happened to those who ratted on their friends.

Then Rodney remembered Mrs. Miller's Sunday School class. Oh, how he loved getting up on Sunday morning and walking around the corner to the little sanctified church! How many years had it been since he had gone to church?

Mrs. Miller taught her class that God sees everything we do. She said even God knows what we are thinking. As Rodney began to recall those lessons from long ago, he thought about one lesson in particular. His childhood teacher taught that it is best to tell the truth, even if it hurts.

That Sunday School lesson from days gone by began to make sense. As he raised his head, he replied, "Yes, I do swear to tell the whole truth."

In today's lesson, we learn how Jesus testifies to the truth, and we should follow His lead.

———————— Keep in Mind ————————

"Pilate therefore said unto him, Art thou a king then? Jesus answered, Thou sayest that I am a king. To this end was I born, and for this cause came I into the world, that I should bear witness unto the truth. Every one that is of the truth heareth my voice" (John 18:37).

"Pilate therefore said unto him, Art thou a king then? Jesus answered, Thou sayest that I am a king. To this end was I born, and for this cause came I into the world, that I should bear witness unto the truth. Every one that is of the truth heareth my voice" (John 18:37).

Focal Verses

KJV **John 18:28** Then led they Jesus from Caiaphas unto the hall of judgment: and it was early; and they themselves went not into the judgment hall, lest they should be defiled; but that they might eat the passover.

29 Pilate then went out unto them, and said, What accusation bring ye against this man?

30 They answered and said unto him, If he were not a malefactor, we would not have delivered him up unto thee.

31 Then said Pilate unto them, Take ye him, and judge him according to your law. The Jews therefore said unto him, It is not lawful for us to put any man to death:

32 That the saying of Jesus might be fulfilled, which he spake, signifying what death he should die.

33 Then Pilate entered into the judgment hall again, and called Jesus, and said unto him, Art thou the King of the Jews?

34 Jesus answered him, Sayest thou this thing of thyself, or did others tell it thee of me?

35 Pilate answered, Am I a Jew? Thine own nation and the chief priests have delivered thee unto me: what hast thou done?

36 Jesus answered, My kingdom is not of this world: if my kingdom were of this world, then would my servants fight, that I should not be delivered to the Jews: but now is my kingdom not from hence.

37 Pilate therefore said unto him, Art thou a king then? Jesus answered, Thou sayest that I am a king. To this end was I born, and for this cause came I into the world, that I should bear witness unto the truth. Every one that is of the truth heareth my voice.

NLT **John 18:28** Jesus' trial before Caiaphas ended in the early hours of the morning. Then he was taken to the headquarters of the Roman governor. His accusers didn't go in themselves because it would defile them, and they wouldn't be allowed to celebrate the Passover feast.

29 So Pilate, the governor, went out to them and asked, "What is your charge against this man?"

30 "We wouldn't have handed him over to you if he weren't a criminal!" they retorted.

31 "Then take him away and judge him by your own laws," Pilate told them. "Only the Romans are permitted to execute someone," the Jewish leaders replied.

32 This fulfilled Jesus' prediction about the way he would die.

33 Then Pilate went back inside and called for Jesus to be brought to him. "Are you the King of the Jews?" he asked him.

34 Jesus replied, "Is this your own question, or did others tell you about me?"

35 "Am I a Jew?" Pilate asked. "Your own people and their leading priests brought you here. Why? What have you done?"

36 Then Jesus answered, "I am not an earthly king. If I were, my followers would have fought when I was arrested by the Jewish leaders. But my Kingdom is not of this world."

37 Pilate replied, "You are a king then?" "You say that I am a king, and you are right," Jesus said. "I was born for that purpose. And I came to bring truth to the world. All who love the truth recognize that what I say is true."

The People, Places, and Times

The Passover. Following 400 years of bondage in Egypt, the descendants of Abraham were instructed by Moses to place the blood of a lamb upon the door posts and lintel ("the horizontal beam forming the top of a door" [Wycliffe, 1043]) of their homes. This blood permitted the death angel to pass over the homes of the Hebrew nation, causing Pharaoh to relent and release them from slavery.

The Children of Israel were commanded to keep the Passover throughout their generations forever (Exodus 12:24). The Levitical Law laid out specific requirements, particularly for priests, to prepare for the Feast of Passover. No one who was unclean or defiled could partake in the Passover Feast. Among the ways a Jew could be defiled was to enter a Gentile dwelling or come in contact with an unclean person.

Background

Pilate's Judgment. Jerusalem was occupied by the Roman Empire during the days of Jesus. Pontius Pilate served as the Roman Governor of Judea. Caiaphas, the High Priest, sought a death sentence from Pilate. Pilate, however, did not want the responsibility of sentencing Jesus to death. Instead, he relied on public opinion and bartered for the life of Jesus with Barabbas.

When the mob chose Barabbas to be released according to custom, Pilate claimed to have found no fault in Him. However, Pilate released Jesus to be crucified (Luke 23:22–25).

At-A-Glance

1. Defiled and Unclean (John 18:28)

2. Make Up Your Mind (vv. 29–31)

3. Thought You Knew (v. 32)

4. The Kingship of Christ (vv. 33–37)

In Depth

1. Defiled and Unclean (John 18:28)

Jesus had been questioned in the palace of the High Priest, Caiaphas. There He was ridiculed, challenged, and struck. While there, His disciple Peter denied Him three times. From the palace, Jesus was taken to Pilate's judgment hall. The envoy of priests would not enter the hall of judgment or they would have been defiled. Instead, they stood outside yelling their accusations against Jesus to Pilate.

Consider the irony of the priests' position. They would not walk into the Hall of Judgment because entering the Gentile building would make them unclean. However, they sought to take the life of the Passover Lamb in the person of Jesus Christ. No wonder Jesus referred to them as hypocrites.

2. Make Up Your Mind (vv. 29–31)

According to Roman law, the Jews needed a legitimate complaint against Jesus in order to press charges against Him. The same is true in today's courts of law. A person cannot be indicted for a crime unless proper charges have been filed.

Pilate asked the priests, "What accusation bring ye against this man?" (v. 29). In their arrogance, the priests replied, "If he were not a malefactor, we would not have delivered him up unto thee" (v. 30). In other words, "We would not have brought Jesus to you if He wasn't guilty of a punishable crime." Attempting to avoid sentencing Jesus, Pilate suggested that they try Him by their own law. This met with opposition from the priests because they were prevented by the Mosaic Law from giving anyone the death sentence. They wanted Jesus to die, but sought to make Pilate a pawn who would administer the death penalty in their stead. This would let them off the hook.

3. Thought You Knew (v. 32)

One of God's characteristics is that He is omniscient; He knows all things. Jesus had already shared His coming demise with His disciples (Matthew 20:17–19; John 3:14). Isaiah the prophet spoke of our Savior's suffering in Isaiah 53:5, "But he was wounded for our transgressions, he was bruised for our iniquities: the chastisement of our peace was upon him; and with his stripes we are healed." Jesus knew the price that must be paid for humankind's sin. He was willing to die, even the death of the Cross (Philippians 2:8).

4. The Kingship of Christ (vv. 33–37)

Pilate was looking for a way out of the predicament the Jews had put him in. He was well aware of Jesus being tried before the High Priest. In fact, when Pilate thought Jesus could be tried in another jurisdiction, he sent Jesus to Herod (Luke 23:7).

After all this, Pilate finds Jesus back in his court. Frustrated, he asks Jesus, "Are you the King of the Jews?" (John 18:33, NLT). This line of questioning was an attempt to establish a rebellion that as the governor he would be able to crush. If he could establish that Jesus posed a military threat to the Roman Empire, his problem would be solved.

Instead, Jesus let Pilate know that His kingdom is not of this world. If it were, His followers would have fought the Jews who arrested Him and they wouldn't be having this conversation. Rather, His kingdom is God's and not Caesar's, and ultimately the reign of God will extend to the ends of the earth—but not yet. His kingdom is the true kingdom. Those who understand the truth of Jesus' words are of that kingdom—His kingdom. The apostle Paul explained it in this way: "For the preaching of the cross is to them that perish foolishness; but unto us which are saved it is the power of God" (1 Corinthians 1:18). Jesus said, "My sheep hear my voice, and I know them, and they follow me" (John 10:27, ESV).

The confrontation with Jesus left Pontius Pilate defenseless. How could he rule against a power that he couldn't put a finger on? How could he provide justice when he was not part of the kingdom Jesus spoke of? Yet he was fulfilling God's plan for His Son without even realizing it.

Search the Scriptures

1. What time of year is the Feast of the Passover (John 18:28)?

2. How did Pilate play into the hands of those who brought accusations against Jesus (vv. 31, 35, 39)?

Discuss the Meaning

Pilate and the religious leaders were unable to hear the voice of truth. Are there similar examples in the church today where we are not hearing the voice of Jesus?

Lesson in Our Society

Many churches have outreach activities with their communities such as food banks, support groups, bill assistance, housing, and the list goes on. What other practical ways can the church be an expression of truth to the world around us?

Make It Happen

Share some of the insights you have received from today's lesson with someone you may not normally approach. Pray that the Holy Spirit will minister to him or her, enabling him or her to hear the truth and be made free.

Follow the Spirit

What God wants me to do:

_____

_____

_____

_____

Remember Your Thoughts

Special insights I have learned:

_____

_____

_____

_____

More Light on the Text

John 18:28–37

28 Then led they Jesus from Caiaphas unto the hall of judgment: and it was early; and they themselves went not into the judgment hall, lest they should be defiled; but that they might eat the Passover.

The verse begins with "then" (Gk. *oun*, **oon,** meaning "consequently"), showing the connection between the Sanhedrin appearance (see Matthew 26:57–68; Mark

14:53–65) and now the appearance before Pilate. The Jewish leaders brought Jesus from the high priest, Caiaphas, to Pilate, the man representing Rome in Judea, to have the governor validate their verdict, authorize, and then immediately carry out the execution of Jesus.

It was "early" in the morning (Gk. *proia,* **pro-EE-ah**). The Jewish leaders did not want to enter the building where the governor was, lest they should become ceremonially defiled before the Passover (see Exodus 12:18–19). Pilate's residence was a place from which leavened bread had not been removed. It was the house of an uncircumcised man (see Matthew 8:8; Acts 11:3). The Passover festival probably is meant here. It lasted seven days.

It is sad to see that on the one hand, the priests were so concerned about ceremonial cleansing in order to be accepted before God; and on the other hand, they were plotting to kill Jesus the Son of God. Their preoccupation with the fulfillment of ritual observances and their view of faithfulness blinded them from seeing the true Messiah; they wanted to be rid of Jesus. Empty ritual can hinder true relationship with God and other people (cp. 1 Samuel 15:20–23).

29 Pilate then went out unto them, and said, What accusation bring ye against this man?

Pilate was governor of Judea from A.D. 20 to A.D. 36. He did not seem to have had good dispositions toward the Jewish people (see Luke 13:1). Here, he was willing to accommodate the scruples of the Jewish leaders, so he came out to meet them. He initiated an informal inquiry, asking about the accusations against Jesus: "What is your charge against this man?" (John 18:29, NLT). Pilate was simply observing due form in asking for a formal charge or "accusation" (Gk. *kategoria,* **kat-ay-gor-EE-ah**), meaning "the act of speaking against someone"; a charge of wrongdoing.

30 They answered and said unto him, If he were not a malefactor, we would not have delivered him up unto thee.

The leaders did not answer Pilate's question directly. They did not point out a precise crime done by Jesus. Instead, they spoke of Him as someone who was always doing evil. The Greek word *kakopoios* (**kak-op-oy-OS**), translated "malefactor," is a periphrasis in the imperfect tense and represents an action as continued, repeated, or habitual. Thus, the Jewish leaders said that Jesus was someone who habitually did wrong or had the habit of doing evil. So there was no need to point to a precise crime. If He was not a malefactor, they would not have handed Him over to Pilate.

31 Then said Pilate unto them, Take ye him, and judge him according to your law. The Jews therefore said unto him, It is not lawful for us to put any man to death:

Since they were not able to produce clear charges that would be accepted by Roman law, Pilate told them to take Jesus and judge Him according to their own law. He refused to be their executioner. He knew that the Jewish leaders were jealous of Jesus (see Matthew 27:18). The accusation of blasphemy could not stand up to Roman laws. The Jewish leaders' reply was that they were not allowed to put anyone to death. In John 18:31, the expression "to put . . . to death" (Gk. *apokteino*, **ap-ok-TI-no**) is an aorist infinitive in the active form. It means that, at this point in time, they were not authorized to kill in any way whatever. While Jews would have carried out an execution by stoning, they knew the Romans practiced crucifixion. Only a Roman official could allow death by crucifixion (this may be deduced from verse

32). The leaders wanted the death of Jesus by crucifixion (see 19:15; Deuteronomy 21:23; cp. John 3:14; 8:28; 12:32–34), instead of by stoning (see John 8:1–11, 59; 10:31; cp. Acts 7:54–8:2), probably so that He would be seen as a curse. Crucifixion was a way for the leaders of the Jews to dishonor Jesus. But God used it to take away the sins of the world (cp. Genesis 50:19–20; Romans 8:28; Galatians 3:13–14).

32 That the saying of Jesus might be fulfilled, which he spake, signifying what death he should die.

This is the fulfillment of one of Jesus' prophecies (see John 3:14; 8:28; 12:32–34; 18:9; cp. Deuteronomy 21:23; Galatians 3:13–14). The Jewish leaders' determination to secure a crucifixion fulfills the divine purpose (John 3:14; 19:36–37). The Gospel of John points out again and again the conformity of the life of Jesus with the affirmations of the Scriptures, on which the Jewish leaders prided themselves—in rejecting Jesus they were in fact witnessing for Him (see John 5:39–40).

33 Then Pilate entered into the judgment hall again, and called Jesus, and said unto him, Art thou the King of the Jews?

Having talked to the Jewish leaders, the governor went back into the building and continued his interrogation of Jesus. The expression "judgment hall" (Gk. *praitorion*, **prahee-TO-ree-on**) is the official residence of the governor including his offices, courts, etc. The Jewish leaders told Pilate that Jesus was trying to get people to riot and to stop paying taxes to the emperor, and worse, He claimed to be king (see Luke 23:2–5). Thus, Pilate asked Jesus: "Are You the King of the Jews?" (23:3, NKJV). His question has an emphatic tone expressing surprise and incredulity (cp. John 19:2–3). Jesus never used the title "king"; others attributed it to Him (John 1:49; 6:15). This title seems to be the substance of the accusations that were brought against Him (see John 18:30, 35; Matthew 27:11; Mark 15:2; Luke 23:3).

34 Jesus answered him, Sayest thou this thing of thyself, or did others tell it thee of me?

Jesus, not intimidated by Pilate, asked him whether his declaration was "of thyself" (Gk. *apo heautou*, **apo heh-ow-TOO**, meaning "of your own accord") or was told this by others. Jesus refused to be the king of the Jews in the political sense given to Pilate by His accusers. In his willingness to act without more information, other than what he had received from the leaders of the Jews, Pilate was placing himself in a precarious situation from which he would not be able to escape.

35 Pilate answered, Am I a Jew? Thine own nation and the chief priests have delivered thee unto me: what hast thou done?

The governor replied to Him sarcastically, "Am I a Jew?" The accusations came from the chief priests and their followers. The accusers of Jesus understood Jesus' messianic kingdom in a political sense. They told Pilate that Jesus was in effect a political leader and, therefore, a danger to the Roman authority (see Luke 23:3; it was on the basis of this accusation that Jesus was condemned; cp. Acts 17:7). Pilate was anxious to find out if the accusation was true and if there was any criminal activity involved from the Roman's standpoint. He asked Jesus, "What have you done?" (John 18:35, NLT). He wanted Jesus to say something in His own defense.

36 Jesus answered, My kingdom is not of this world: if my kingdom were of this world, then would my servants fight, that I should not be delivered to the Jews: but now is my kingdom not from hence.

Jesus told him that there is a sense in which He is the head of a kingdom, but His kingdom is not of this world. It is not a kingdom as the world understands kingdoms. If His kingdom were of this world, His servants would support him at this very moment. They would fight to free Him. In the Greek, the tense of the verb "would fight" (*agonizomai*, **ag-o-NID-zom-ahee**) is the imperfect expressing a past action as continued. It means "they would now be fighting so that I would not be handed over to you." Jesus is saying here that His authority is not derived from or dependent upon political organization. He does not mean that His kingdom has no political concerns or that its righteousness is not to be applied to the political sphere (cp. Matthew 5–7, the Sermon on the Mount).

37 Pilate therefore said unto him, Art thou a king then? Jesus answered, Thou sayest that I am a king. To this end was I born, and for this cause came I into the world, that I should bear witness unto the truth. Every one that is of the truth heareth my voice.

From Jesus' words, Pilate made a deduction with a note of irony: "Art thou a king then?" The Greek word *oukoun* (**ook-OON**) implies an inference "so then...?" Jesus said to Pilate, "You say that I am a king" (v. 37, NLT). He went on to explain to Pilate the true nature of His kingdom. The eschatological kingdom inaugurated by Jesus in this world at this hour does not emerge by violence associated with political revolution. People are brought into His kingdom by new birth (John 3:3; Colossians 1:13). According to the will of the Father who sent the Son, His kingdom is realized by accepting the truth of God that is manifested in Jesus, the incarnated Word (see John 1:1;

3:11, 32; 8:13–14, 46; 14:6). His kingdom is a kingdom of truth. As stated in John 18:37, His mission is to "bear witness" (Gk. *martureo*, **mar-too-REH-o**), or testify to the truth, to point people to the real "truth" (Gk. *aletheia*, **al-AY-thi-a**), meaning here divine truth. To be "of the truth" is to depend on, to be in harmony with the truth (see also John 3:21), to submit with joy to its influence (7:17) as being from God (8:47).

People who accept the One sent from God are in the truth (John 3:21; 6:42; 17:2). Jesus is the perfect expression of the Father for humankind. He showed it by His deeds and His words (1:18; 17:8, 14). He introduces the believer to the fellowship with the Father (1:4; 3:16; 17:3).

Sources:

Bauer, Walter. *A Greek-English Lexicon of the New Testament and Other Early Christian Literature (BACD)*. Chicago, IL: University of Chicago Press, 1979.

Bonnet, Louis. *Evangile Selon Jean. Bible Annotée NT2*. St-Légier, Suisse, 1983.

Bruce, F. F. *The Gospel of John*. Grand Rapids, MI: W. B. Eerdmans Publishing Company, 1983.

The Holy Bible. Contemporary English Version (CEV). New York, NY: American Bible Society, 1995.

New Testament Greek Lexicon. Bible Study Tools.com. http://www.biblestudytools.com/hebrew/dictionary. (accessed May 13, 2010).

Old Testament Hebrew Lexicon. Bible Study Tools.com. http://www.biblestudytools.com/hebrew/dictionary. (accessed May 13, 2010).

Passage Lookup. Bible Gateway.com. http://www.bible-gateway.com/passage (accessed May 26, 2010).

Pfeiffer, Charles F., Howard F. Vos, and John Rea, eds. *Wycliffe Bible Dictionary*. Peabody, MA: Hendrickson Publishers, 1998. 1043.

"Pilate." *Merriam-Webster Dictionary Online*. http://www.merriam-webster.com/dictionary/pilate (accessed September 30, 2010).

Rochedieu, Charles. *Les Trésors du Nouveau Testament*. Saint-Légier, Suisse: Editions Emmaüs, 1972.

Strong's Concordance with Hebrew and Greek Lexicon. Eliyah.com. http://www.eliyah.com/lexicon.html (accessed September 30, 2010).

Thompson, Frank Charles. *Thompson Chain-Reference Bible*. Indianapolis, IN: B. B. Kirkbride Bible Co., 1982.

Say It Correctly

Barabbas. Buh-RAB-uhs, Bahr-AB-uhs.
Caiaphas. KAH-ee-af-as.
Levitical. Li-VI-ti-kəl.

Daily Bible Readings

MONDAY
Lead by Truth and Light
(Psalm 43)

TUESDAY
Walking in God's Truth
(Psalm 86:8–13)

WEDNESDAY
Arrest of Jesus
(John 18:1–11)

THURSDAY
Denial of Jesus
(John 18:12–18)

FRIDAY
Questioning of Jesus
(John 18:19–24)

SATURDAY
What Is Truth?
(John 8:31–38)

SUNDAY
"Are You the King?"
(John 18:28–37)

Teaching Tips

Words You Should Know

A. Sepulchre (John 20:1–4, 6, 8) *mnemeion* (Gk.)—A grave or tomb. Jesus was buried in a sepulchre, which was a room carved out of a rocky hill.

B. Resurrection *anastasis* (Gk.)—The act of having life restored after death.

Teacher Preparation

Unifying Principle—Dawn of a New Day. Is there life after death? Jesus' followers were confused when His body was missing, but when Jesus appeared to them, they greatly rejoiced.

A. Pray for your students, asking God to open their hearts to this lesson.

B. Read and study the entire lesson, paying attention to the disciples' reaction to the empty tomb.

C. Complete the companion lesson in the *Precepts For Living Personal Study Guide®*.

O—Open the Lesson

A. Before the class arrives, write the words *sin*, *death*, and *resurrection* on the board.

B. After taking prayer requests, lead the class in prayer.

C. Share a testimony about a personal loss due to death and your hope because of Christ's triumph.

D. Discuss sin, death, and resurrection.

E. Ask volunteers to read the In Focus story. Discuss.

F. Summarize The People, Places, and Times and the Background sections.

P—Present the Scriptures

A. Ask volunteers to summarize the Focal Verses.

B. Discuss according to the corresponding In Depth section and More Light on the Text.

E—Explore the Meaning

A. Discuss the Discuss the Meaning section.

B. Summarize the lesson.

N—Next Steps for Application

A. Have volunteers discuss the Lesson in Our Society and Make It Happen sections.

B. As a review, tell the students to complete the Search the Scriptures questions during the week.

C. End the class in prayer.

Worship Guide

For the Superintendent or Teacher
Theme: The Living Word
Theme Song: "Moment by Moment"
Devotional Reading: Psalm 31:1–5
Prayer

The Living Word

Bible Background • JOHN 20:1–23
Printed Text • JOHN 20:1–10, 19–20 | Devotional Reading • PSALM 31:1–5

———————— Aim for Change ————————

By the end of the lesson, we will: DESCRIBE the disciples' response to Jesus' death and resurrection; APPRECIATE the beginning of a new life in Christ; and INVITE someone to Sunday School or Bible study to learn more about Christ.

————————  In Focus ————————

Kim wanted her girls to look special for Easter. Early Sunday morning their hair was all done and their new dresses were all laid out for church. Kim fell into bed exhausted. She woke up with the sun shining into her room. It was so late! Would she be able to make it to church on time?

No time for breakfast, she thought, as she hastily rushed the girls out of bed. No time for Sunday School. They would really have to hurry if they were going to make it even to the last half of the church service!

As Kim and her girls squeezed into the overflow room at church, Kim was feeling cranky and sweaty—not at all in the mood for worshiping the Resurrected Savior, who lives within our hearts today.

Kim vowed to place more time on preparing for worship next Easter. Let's worship our Resurrected Lord with all our hearts. Let's remember that He is alive within us every moment of every day.

——————— Keep in Mind ———————

"And when he had so said, he shewed unto them his hands and his side. Then were the disciples glad, when they saw the LORD" (John 20:20).

"And when he had so said, he shewed unto them his hands and his side.
Then were the disciples glad, when they saw the LORD" (John 20:20).

Focal Verses

KJV John 20:1 The first day of the week cometh Mary Magdalene early, when it was yet dark, unto the sepulchre, and seeth the stone taken away from the sepulchre.

2 Then she runneth, and cometh to Simon Peter, and to the other disciple, whom Jesus loved, and saith unto them, They have taken away the LORD out of the sepulchre, and we know not where they have laid him.

3 Peter therefore went forth, and that other disciple, and came to the sepulchre.

4 So they ran both together: and the other disciple did outrun Peter, and came first to the sepulchre.

5 And he stooping down, and looking in, saw the linen clothes lying; yet went he not in.

6 Then cometh Simon Peter following him, and went into the sepulchre, and seeth the linen clothes lie,

7 And the napkin, that was about his head, not lying with the linen clothes, but wrapped together in a place by itself.

8 Then went in also that other disciple, which came first to the sepulchre, and he saw, and believed.

9 For as yet they knew not the scripture, that he must rise again from the dead.

10 Then the disciples went away again unto their own home.

20:19 Then the same day at evening, being the first day of the week, when the doors were shut where the disciples were assembled for fear of the Jews, came Jesus and stood in the midst, and saith unto them, Peace be unto you.

20 And when he had so said, he shewed unto them his hands and his side. Then were the disciples glad, when they saw the LORD.

NLT John 20:1 Early Sunday morning, while it was still dark, Mary Magdalene came to the tomb and found that the stone had been rolled away from the entrance.

2 She ran and found Simon Peter and the other disciple, the one whom Jesus loved. She said, "They have taken the Lord's body out of the tomb, and I don't know where they have put him!"

3 Peter and the other disciple ran to the tomb to see.

4 The other disciple outran Peter and got there first.

5 He stooped and looked in and saw the linen cloth lying there, but he didn't go in.

6 Then Simon Peter arrived and went inside. He also noticed the linen wrappings lying there,

7 while the cloth that had covered Jesus' head was folded up and lying to the side.

8 Then the other disciple also went in, and he saw and believed—

9 for until then they hadn't realized that the Scriptures said he would rise from the dead.

10 Then they went home.

20:19 That evening, on the first day of the week, the disciples were meeting behind locked doors because they were afraid of the Jewish leaders. Suddenly, Jesus was standing there among them! "Peace be with you," he said.

20 As he spoke, he held out his hands for them to see, and he showed them his side. They were filled with joy when they saw their Lord!

The People, Places, and Times

Mary Magdalene. She was first introduced to us by Luke, the physician (Luke 8:2–3), as one of the women from whom Jesus cast demons. Mary had been delivered from seven demons and apparently spent her days joining the other women who devoted themselves to ministering to Jesus.

Simon Peter. He served as the head of the band of disciples. The other disciples recognized Peter's authority after the Lord entrusted him with the keys of the kingdom. It is not surprising, therefore, that Mary and John would defer to his leadership upon seeing the empty tomb.

Background

For three years, Jesus walked the earth teaching His disciples and demonstrating before the Jewish religious authorities that He was their long-awaited Messiah. Finally, in an ultimate show of rejection and contempt, the religious authorities conspired with the Roman government and the Jewish populace to kill the Lord. The Roman form of capital punishment was chosen, and Jesus was hung on a cross until He died. After all were certain of Jesus' death, Joseph of Arimathea and Nicodemus were permitted to take His body down from the cross and lay it in Joseph's unused tomb. On the first day of the week, Mary Magdalene was returning to the tomb to tend to the body of the Lord when she discovered that the stone covering the tomb's opening had been rolled away and the body was no longer there.

The wealthy people of this time had tombs carved out of the rocky hills. The tomb was usually prepared in advance of death, because the carving was arduous and time-consuming. Usually a small room with a low ceiling was carved out with a slab that served as a bed for the body. Tombs that have been discovered in this area and from this period usually had large round flat stones that served as doors, often with a slanted groove in which the stone was rolled. It was easy to roll the stone down the groove to cover the mouth of the tomb, but very difficult to roll it back up the groove to open the tomb.

At-A-Glance

1. Mary Magdalene at the Tomb
(John 20:1–3)

2. Peter and John at the Tomb
(vv. 4–10)

3. Jesus Appears to His Disciples
(vv. 19–20)

In Depth

1. Mary Magdalene at the Tomb (John 20:1–3)

After Roman soldiers were certain that Jesus was dead and intervention was made with Pontius Pilate, loving hands were permitted to lower Him from the cross, wrap His body in strips of cloth with spices and ointment, and place it in a borrowed tomb. The tomb belonged to Joseph of Arimathea's family (Matthew 27:59). On the first day of the week, Mary Magdalene arrived at the tomb only to discover that its stone covering had been rolled away and the body of Jesus was gone. She promptly returned to the city where she informed John and Peter of her discovery.

2. Peter and John at the Tomb (vv. 4–10)

The two disciples began running toward the site where they knew that Jesus had been buried. Because he was younger, John outran Peter and arrived at the tomb first, but out of respect for Peter's position as the leader of the disciples, he did not enter. Rather, John waited until Peter arrived and then followed him into the grave.

Peter didn't hesitate before entering the Lord's tomb. The same eagerness and impulsiveness that characterized his life before the Lord's death remained. Once inside, Peter could observe that the burial cloth (napkin), which had been used to cover the Lord's face, was neatly folded together in a place separate from the other grave clothes. John, after following Peter into the cave, was also able to observe the burial cloth. Scripture does not record Peter's response to what he observed. However, John saw, and because of what he saw, he believed.

The physical evidence of the empty grave clothes bolstered John's faith, and he was able to believe what he did not understand. In time, Peter would believe as well. Perhaps his exposure to the empty tomb and John's faith helped him.

3. Jesus Appears to His Disciples (vv. 19–20)

It was now the evening of Resurrection Day. In spite of the appearance of the Risen Lord to Mary and the evidence of the folded cloth, the disciples were very much afraid. If the authorities would kill the Lord, what would they do to His followers? So they gathered together and locked the doors, probably in the same room where they had eaten the Last Supper with the Lord. We can imagine them trying to sort out the strange things that had happened that day.

Then suddenly Jesus appeared—without the doors opening—and was suddenly visible among with them. The appearance may have occurred among 10 of the disciples—Judas had committed suicide, and for some reason, Thomas was not there. (Although others who followed Jesus were considered His disciples, the original 12 apostles had a unique role.) Jesus' first words to them were,

"Peace be unto you" (John 20:19). Maybe the men were expecting some sort of reprimand. After all, they had all run away when Jesus was captured in the Garden of Gethsemane. Instead, Jesus offered a lovely greeting, with no recriminations.

We know from Luke 24:37 that the disciples thought they were seeing a ghost, but Jesus proved to them that He was their Lord in the flesh, although a resurrected kind of flesh. Jesus showed them His hands and His side to prove that He was indeed the same Jesus who had died on the Cross for them. At this, they believed and were overjoyed.

Search the Scriptures

1. When did Mary Magdalene go to the tomb where Jesus was buried (John 20:1)?

2. Where was the napkin that had covered the Lord's face (v. 7)?

3. What was John's response upon entering the tomb and seeing the napkin (v. 8)?

4. What were the two responses of the disciples upon seeing their Risen Lord (vv. 19–20)?

Discuss the Meaning

1. Why do you think Mary was returning to the tomb before daybreak? Do you think she was alone?

2. Why do you suppose Mary did not enter the tomb with the disciples?

3. What is the significance of the fact that the burial clothes were still present in the tomb?

Lesson in Our Society

Movies, DVDs, and books have all conspired to condition our response to the notion of death. We see it as a terrible realm inhabited by demons, zombies, and the like. However, when we lose a loved one to death, our response to that realm as Christians should be completely different. If we are sure that they have trusted in Christ, our fear gives way to a hope that they have gone to a place of light, rest, and peace in the presence of our Lord. How does our relationship with God change the way we view death? Which would you prefer to have: the popularity and wealth of this world or the assurance that when you die, you will go to live with Jesus?

Make It Happen

Jesus, by living a life pleasing to God, broke the bonds of death over those who believe in Him. God confirmed this by raising Jesus from the dead. Write a poem or song celebrating the victory of Christ over death.

Follow the Spirit

What God wants me to do:

_____

_____

_____

_____

Remember Your Thoughts

Special insights I have learned:

_____

_____

_____

_____

More Light on the Text

John 20:1–10, 19–20

1 The first day of the week cometh Mary Magdalene early, when it was yet dark, unto the sepulchre, and seeth the stone taken away from the sepulchre.

Mary Magdalene's association with Jesus most likely begins when He cures her and other women of demon possession (Luke 8:2), sometime during the second year of His ministry. Prior to that time, the Scriptures have no mention of her. Her name indicates that she either came from or was a resident of the town of Magdala, situated on the western shore of the Sea of Galilee. The identification of Mary Magdalene as a prostitute is widely believed, especially by American Catholics and those in many western European countries where homes for unwed mothers routinely are named "Magdalene" homes. This notion is, however, unfounded and bears no scriptural evidence to support it.

There is, however, plenty of evidence to show that from the time of her deliverance, at the hands of Jesus, all of the Gospel writers acknowledge Mary Magdalene as a constant presence in the life and ministry of Jesus. Her miraculous cure by Jesus brought Him her untiring faith and devotion. She appears to have been a woman of substantial means, as it seems she ministered to the needs of Jesus and the other disciples with her own money (Luke 8:1–3). Interestingly, the account of the sepulchre visitation differs ever so slightly between the Gospel writers. Matthew reports that Mary Magdalene was accompanied by the "other Mary" (Matthew 28:1). Mark records the presence of three women: Mary Magdalene; Mary, the mother of James; and Salome (Mark 16:1). Luke records the greatest number of women. He writes, "It was Mary Magdalene and Joanna, and Mary the mother of James, and other women that were with them" (from Luke 24:10). John only mentions Mary Magdalene's visit at the tomb. The fact that her name always appears first when listed with a group of women indicates that she was obviously a leader in the female circle of disciples (Matthew 27:56; Mark 16:1; Luke 24:10). The only exception is at the foot of the cross when Jesus' female family members' names are listed first (John 19:25).

Faithful to Jesus, even after His death, John presents her rising early and going to Jesus' tomb to anoint His body with precious ointments and spices, as was the custom of the day. Both Mark (15:47) and Luke (23:55) record that Mary and the other women had watched Jesus' burial and the sealing of the tomb. While we are not surprised that Mary could locate the tomb in the darkness of the early morning hours, it is not clear how Mary expected to remove the huge stone placed at the entrance of the tomb. Perhaps she expected the Roman soldiers, who were guarding the tomb, to roll the stone for her. In any case, when Mary Magdalene arrives at the burial site, the giant stone has already been removed.

2 Then she runneth, and cometh to Simon Peter, and to the other disciple, whom Jesus loved, and saith unto them, They have taken away the LORD out of the sepulchre, and we know not where they have laid him. 3 Peter therefore went forth, and that other disciple, and came to the sepulchre.

At this point in John's narrative, Mary Magdalene runs to tell Peter and the other disciples that Jesus' body is missing. John does not tell us that Mary has yet to enter the interior of the tomb. In John's account, Mary does not enter the tomb until after she notifies the men (John 20:11–12). Matthew's account tells of a "great earthquake" and has the angel rolling back the stone, making the announcement to the women, and inviting them inside the tomb to see for themselves

(28:2–6). The narratives of both Mark and Luke indicate that the women enter the tomb and encounter an angel who announces that Jesus has risen. John's different presentation does not imply any disharmony in the Gospels. Instead, it suggests a contrasting view of the account's significant points. We must also remember that of the four Gospel writers, John is the only writer who was actually an eyewitness to this event. It is quite possible that he prioritized the notification of Peter and himself and simply chose to leave out details that occurred before his arrival at the tomb. This is logical in light of the fact that his Gospel is written after the other three; he knows they have already included this detail. The fact that Mary announces that the body is missing implies she has indeed entered the sepulchre.

Interesting, too, is the fact that John does not name the other disciple, the one "whom Jesus loved" (John 20:2). There is no doubt that it can only be the writer of the Gospel, John, the brother of James. John never identifies himself in his own Gospel, choosing instead to refer to himself only as the son of Zebedee or, as he does in this account, the one Jesus loved.

4 So they ran both together: and the other disciple did outrun Peter, and came first to the sepulchre.

Only John's Gospel records that "the other disciple" outran Peter to the sepulchre. Again, this does not indicate disharmony; rather, it reflects a writer's privilege of highlighting certain details. Here, John, who also happens to be a central character, is relating the sense of excitement he surely must have felt at that time. He was younger than Peter and certainly would have been able to outdistance the older man as they raced to the tomb.

5 And he stooping down, and looking in, saw the linen clothes lying; yet went he not in.

Although John arrives at the sepulchre before Peter, he does not go in. Some have argued that perhaps John was afraid to enter the tomb alone. A more likely reason is that he simply defers to the older apostle. It is probably out of respect for Peter's position as leader of the apostles that John allows Peter to enter the tomb first.

6 Then cometh Simon Peter following him, and went into the sepulchre, and seeth the linen clothes lie, 7 And the napkin, that was about his head, not lying with the linen clothes, but wrapped together in a place by itself.

John seems to emphasize the supernatural implications concerning the burial linens. The folded up cloth would not indicate grave robbers, who would have just hurriedly cast it aside. Also, since Jesus was no longer dead and had conquered death by His Resurrection, He no longer needed burial clothing. The linen grave clothes were for the dead; those who had not risen and could not, and had not, conquered death. Only the Son of God could win and seal the victory over sin and death, therefore securing our own salvation.

8 Then went in also that other disciple, which came first to the sepulchre, and he saw, and believed.

John's Gospel alone records that upon seeing the empty grave and the discarded grave clothes, he "believed." This is understandable since the writer, better than anyone else, would know this to be a fact. It is interesting to note that in Luke's account, upon seeing the discarded burial clothing, Peter "wonder[ed] in himself at that which was come to pass" (Luke 24:12). While Peter, the elder statesman, puzzles over the occurrence, the younger disciple believes. John uses the Greek word for "believed," *pisteuo* (**pist-YOO-o**), which means one who had faith or conviction.

9 For as yet they knew not the scripture, that he must rise again from the dead. 10 Then the disciples went away again unto their own home.

Verse 9 offers a fuller explanation for Peter's puzzlement and John's subsequent belief by emphasizing how unexpected these events were for both he and Peter. Although the two of them were closer to Jesus than any of the other apostles, these events still take these men by surprise. Only a few days earlier, Jesus spoke to His disciples and asked them if they understood what He meant when He said, "A little while, and ye shall not see me: and again, a little while, and ye shall see me?" (John 16:19). The apostles were unsure of what Jesus meant. That He would defy the laws of nature and physically be raised from the dead had not occurred to them. Therefore, in John 20:10, they simply went to their homes again, pondering all that they had seen and heard.

20:19 Then the same day at evening, being the first day of the week, when the doors were shut where the disciples were assembled for fear of the Jews, came Jesus and stood in the midst, and saith unto them, Peace be unto you.

John emphasizes that this was the first day of the week. The Resurrection changed everything—even the day that was considered the first day of the week and the day on which Christians have chosen to worship.

Jesus greeted them with the beautiful words, "Peace be unto you." The Hebrew word for "peace" is *shalowm* (**shaw-LOME**) and is used by Jews today. But the Jews of the New Testament spoke Aramaic, and the New Testament was written in Greek. The Greek word for "peace" is *eirene* (**i-RAY-nay**) and includes the wish for prosperity, peace, quietness, and rest. When Jesus uttered "It is finished" while He hung on the Cross, He was indicating that the work of atonement was completed; but now that God has raised Him from the dead, He is indicating that our reconciliation with God is complete and we have peace with God and with one another. He is also setting His disciples at ease; this appearance must have been a pleasantly shocking surprise.

20 And when he had so said, he shewed unto them his hands and his side. Then were the disciples glad, when they saw the LORD.

Jesus had promised His disciples that He would turn their sadness into joy. He knew that for the few days between the Crucifixion and the Resurrection, the disciples would feel like orphans (John 14:18) and they would grieve, but He promised to turn their grief into gladness (16:20–22). The Greek for "glad" is *chairo* (**KHAH-ee-ro**) and it means to rejoice and to be glad.

Sources:

Carson, D. A. *The Gospel According to John.* Grand Rapids, MI: William B. Eerdmans Publishing Company, 1991.

New Testament Greek Lexicon. Bible Study Tools.com. http://www.biblestudytools.com/lexicons/greek (accessed January 8, 2011).

Old Testament Hebrew Lexicon. Bible Study Tools.com. http://www.biblestudytools.com/lexicons/hebrew (accessed January 7, 2011).

Passage Lookup. Bible Gateway.com. http://www.bible-gateway.com/passage (accessed January 7, 2011).

Strong's Exhaustive Concordance of the Bible. McLean, VA: MacDonald Publishing Company. n.d.

Say It Correctly

Recriminations. Re-KRIM-i-NA-shuns.
Sepulchre. SEP-ul-ker.
Populace. POP-u-lus.

Daily Bible Readings

MONDAY
To Save Sinners like Me
(1 Timothy 1:12–17)

TUESDAY
Judgment of Jesus
(John 19:4–16)

WEDNESDAY
"We Have a Law"
(Leviticus 24:10–16)

THURSDAY
Crucifixion of Jesus
(John 19:17–25)

FRIDAY
"Father, into Your Hands"
(Psalm 31:1–5)

SATURDAY
Burial of Jesus
(John 19:38–42)

SUNDAY
Resurrection of Jesus
(John 20:1–10, 19–20)

Teaching Tips

Words You Should Know

A. Passover (John 2:13) *pascha* (Gk.)—"A celebration in memory of the day on which the Israelites' fathers, who were preparing to leave Egypt, were told by God to sprinkle their doorposts with lamb's blood, so that the destroying angel, seeing the blood, could pass over their dwellings" (Strong, 1996).

B. Scourge (v. 15) *phragellion* (Gk.)—A whip.

Teacher Preparation

Unifying Principle—Restoration and Re-creation. Many people stray from their central purpose in life and need restoration. Jesus' action in cleansing the Temple was intended to restore God's central place in worship and in the lives of the people.

A. Pray for your students and lesson clarity.

B. Study and meditate on the entire lesson.

C. Complete the companion lesson in the *Precepts For Living Personal Study Guide®*.

O—Open the Lesson

A. After taking prayer requests, lead the class in prayer.

B. Share a testimony about a time when God cleansed your life—restored you.

C. Ask volunteers to read the In Focus story. Discuss.

D. Summarize The People, Places, and Times and the Background sections.

P—Present the Scriptures

A. Ask volunteers to summarize the Focal Verses.

B. Discuss according to the corresponding In Depth section and More Light on the Text.

E—Explore the Meaning

A. Discuss the Search the Scriptures and Discuss the Meaning sections.

B. Summarize Lesson in Our Society. Discuss.

N—Next Steps for Application

A. Discuss the Make It Happen section.

B. Summarize the lesson.

C. End the class with prayer.

Worship Guide

For the Superintendent or Teacher
Theme: Cleansing the Temple
Theme Song:
"Give Me a Clean Heart"
Devotional Reading: Psalm 122
Prayer

Cleansing the Temple

Bible Background • JOHN 2:13–22
Printed Text • JOHN 2:13–22 | Devotional Reading • PSALM 122

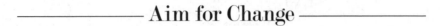 Aim for Change

By the end of the lesson, we will: DESCRIBE how Jesus' cleansing the Temple represents restoration in our lives; DESIRE a fresh revelation of God in the church; and CREATE a list of ways that we see God's power in our daily lives.

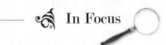 In Focus

Max could not recall when he began to lose his zeal for the Lord and the sacred things of God. He had been saved in his '20s and now at the age of 45, he felt that he was just going through the motions. Even attending church on Sundays had become routine and halfhearted. Often the services would be spirit-filled as other congregants praised and lifted up the name of Jesus, but he just felt numb—hollow inside. Max knew that his demanding management job at a Fortune 500 company often had him making some ethically questionable decisions, yet he always cooperated because he had to be a "team player." Still, each time he made an unethical choice, something in him died; his spirit seemed to cringe. It was as though the Holy Spirit was asking him, "Who is your Master?"

APR 15th

Late one night, Max earnestly went to God in prayer, asking Him to forgive his sins, cleanse his life, and make him whole again.

Today's lesson deals with Jesus cleansing the Temple of everything that was not of God—everything that hindered true worship of the Living God. Like with the Temple, sometimes God has to help us clean up our lives as He brings restoration.

Keep in Mind

"And said unto them that sold doves, Take these things hence; make not my Father's house an house of merchandise" (John 2:16).

"And said unto them that sold doves, Take these things hence;
make not my Father's house an house of merchandise" (John 2:16).

Focal Verses

KJV **John 2:13** And the Jews' passover was at hand, and Jesus went up to Jerusalem,

14 And found in the temple those that sold oxen and sheep and doves, and the changers of money sitting:

15 And when he had made a scourge of small cords, he drove them all out of the temple, and the sheep, and the oxen; and poured out the changers' money, and overthrew the tables;

16 And said unto them that sold doves, Take these things hence; make not my Father's house an house of merchandise.

17 And his disciples remembered that it was written, The zeal of thine house hath eaten me up.

18 Then answered the Jews and said unto him, What sign shewest thou unto us, seeing that thou doest these things?

19 Jesus answered and said unto them, Destroy this temple, and in three days I will raise it up.

20 Then said the Jews, Forty and six years was this temple in building, and wilt thou rear it up in three days?

21 But he spake of the temple of his body.

22 When therefore he was risen from the dead, his disciples remembered that he had said this unto them; and they believed the scripture, and the word which Jesus had said.

NLT **John 2:13** It was time for the annual Passover celebration, and Jesus went to Jerusalem.

14 In the Temple area he saw merchants selling cattle, sheep, and doves for sacrifices; and he saw money changers behind their counters.

15 Jesus made a whip from some ropes and chased them all out of the Temple. He drove out the sheep and oxen, scattered the money changers' coins over the floor, and turned over their tables.

16 Then, going over to the people who sold doves, he told them, "Get these things out of here. Don't turn my Father's house into a marketplace!"

17 Then his disciples remembered this prophecy from the Scriptures: "Passion for God's house burns within me."

18 "What right do you have to do these things?" the Jewish leaders demanded. "If you have this authority from God, show us a miraculous sign to prove it."

19 "All right," Jesus replied. "Destroy this temple, and in three days I will raise it up."

20 "What!" they exclaimed. "It took forty-six years to build this Temple, and you can do it in three days?"

21 But by "this temple," Jesus meant his body.

22 After he was raised from the dead, the disciples remembered that he had said this. And they believed both Jesus and the Scriptures.

The People, Places, and Times

Herod's Temple

The Temple. Located in Jerusalem, the Temple was the religious and political seat of Palestine, on a hill overlooking the city. During their festivals, Jewish families from all over the world traveled there for the grand celebrations. "(King) Solomon had built the first Temple on this same site almost 1,000 years earlier (959 B.C.), but his Temple had been destroyed by the Babylonians, who took many of the Jews into captivity (2 Kings 2:5). The Temple was rebuilt in 515 B.C., and Herod the Great had enlarged and remodeled it" (*The Life Application Study Bible*, 1622). According to Strong, the temple embraces "the entire aggregate of buildings, balconies, porticos, courts (that is that of the men of Israel, that of the women, and that of the priests), belonging to the temple; the latter designates the sacred edifice properly so called, consisting of two parts, the 'sanctuary' or 'Holy Place' (which no one except the priests was allowed to enter), and the 'Holy of Holies' or 'the most holy place' (which was entered only on the great day of atonement by the high priest alone). Also there were the courts where Jesus or the apostles taught or encountered adversaries, and the like, 'in the temple'; also the courts of the temple, of the Gentiles, out of which Jesus drove the buyers and sellers and the money changers, court of the women" (1996).

Background

The apostle John, the son of Zebedee and brother of James, is the author of the Gospel of John. He and his brother were called "Sons of Thunder." John wrote to prove that Jesus Christ is not just a man, but is indeed the eternal Son of the Living God, and all who believe on Him will have everlasting life (reign with Him forever and ever in His kingdom). In other words, Jesus is fully God and fully man. In addition, because Jesus offers the gift of eternal life to all who believe on Him, He is also the Light of the world. He is the Word—the long-awaited Messiah. John not only reveals Jesus to us in both power and magnificence, he also shows us Jesus' power over everything created as well as His love for all humanity.

At-A-Glance

1. Jesus Shows That the Temple Is Sacred (John 2:13–18)

2. Jesus Reveals Another Meaning of the Temple (vv. 19–22)

In Depth

1. Jesus Shows That the Temple Is Sacred (John 2:13–18)

In the outer courts of the Temple—the Court of the Gentiles—the animal merchants and moneychangers were allowed to set up booths to do business. Since there were thousands of out-of-town visitors who came to celebrate the Passover, business was booming. The religious leaders gave these merchants and moneychangers permission to carry out their trades so that the leaders could make money for the Temple's upkeep. However, they did not consider the fact that because there were so many people doing business, it interfered with the worship of the true and living God—the main purpose for visiting the Temple. This is one of the reasons that Jesus was angry.

In addition, because the Temple's tax had to be paid in the local currency, many of the foreigners who came to the Passover celebration had to have their money converted. The moneychangers, however, cheated or exploited the people by charging exorbitant exchange rates. Therefore, their business interfered with worship, and they were cheating the people at the place of worship. Adding to these infractions was the fact that after the cattle, sheep, oxen, and doves that foreigners brought for the sacrifices were rejected for imperfections, the animal merchants sold new ones at inflated prices. This was also big business. Thus, Jesus was angry at the exploitation and greedy practices of these merchants and moneychangers. When He saw their blatant disrespect for the Temple and for those worshiping there, Jesus drove out the sheep and oxen, and "scattered the moneychangers' coins over the floor, and turned over their tables" (v. 15, NLT). He even told the people selling the doves to get their merchandise out of the Temple and admonished them not to turn His "Father's house into a marketplace!" (v. 16). Jesus knew that turning the area into a marketplace was misusing God's Temple; they had insulted Almighty God—His Father. When the disciples saw how Jesus responded to such disrespect, they remembered the prophecy from the Scriptures: "Passion for God's house burns within me (Jesus)" (v. 17, NLT). Of course, the Jewish leaders' beliefs were in fundamental conflict with Jesus, and they demanded to know by what authority He carried out these acts. They insisted that Jesus show them a miraculous sign to prove that His authority was from God (v. 18).

2. Jesus Reveals Another Meaning of the Temple (vv. 19–22)

Again, the religious leaders were not on the same page as Jesus. Here, Jesus speaks of His body as a temple, and the leaders thought He was still talking about the Temple where He had disrupted business— where He had driven out the merchants and moneychangers. They thought He was speaking of the Temple that Zerubbabel had built over 500 years earlier and Herod the Great had begun enlarging and enhancing. Herod's efforts with the Temple were still under way, even though the remodeling project had started 46 years prior (*Life Application Study Bible*, 1623). Therefore, the religious leaders thought that Jesus was telling them this earthly temple could be torn down and rebuilt in three days.

Knowing how long it took to build the Temple, they were startled. However, Jesus was telling them that His body, God's temple, would be crucified and resurrected in three days. Jesus' words would, of course, mean more to the disciples after Jesus' resurrection. These words would prove that indeed He is the Messiah—the Son of the Living God!

Search the Scriptures

1. Why was Jesus so angry with the merchants and moneychangers (John 2:15–16)?

2. What did Jesus mean when He said, "Destroy this temple, and in three days I will raise it up" (v. 19, NLT)?

Discuss the Meaning

Some people have interpreted John 2:13–22 to mean that there is to be no selling of any kind in the church. Is this the principle that you drew from the text? Why? Why not?

Lesson in Our Society

God's House is for worshiping the true and living God. It is never to be taken for anything other than that. It is a sacred place where congregants assemble to praise, lift up the name of Jesus, and hear from His inerrant Word. However, sometimes congregants do not respect the sanctuary and forget that they are entering the Holy God's presence. Some may even throw paper on the floor and leave their bulletins on the seats after the service. You take the lead in respecting God's House!

Make It Happen

Pray that God's House will always be respected as a house of worship and prayer, where seekers and believers can collectively come and share with God. Pray that His

Word will always go forth with authority and power, and those who do not know Him as Lord and Savior will find Him.

Follow the Spirit

What God wants me to do:

_____

_____

_____

_____

Remember Your Thoughts

Special insights I have learned:

_____

_____

_____

_____

More Light on the Text

John 2:13–22

13 And the Jews' passover was at hand, and Jesus went up to Jerusalem, 14 And found in the temple those that sold oxen and sheep and doves, and the changers of money sitting:

The "Passover" was "the festival instituted by God for Israel at the time of the Exodus in order to commemorate the night when Yahweh spared all the firstborn of the Israelites but struck dead all those of the Egyptians (Exodus 12:1–30, 43–49)" (Wycliffe, 1283). It was a time when thousands came from all over the world to participate in the celebration of what God had done to save His people by delivering them from slavery. In the Greek, "Passover" is *pascha*

(PAS-**khah**), supplementing the definition that "the paschal feast, the feast of the Passover, extends from the 14th to the 20th day of the month Nisan" (Strong, 1996). Nisan is the first month of the Jewish sacred calendar (Nehemiah 2:1; Esther 3:7), called "Abib" in the Pentateuch (The Books of the Law—Genesis, Exodus, Leviticus, Numbers, and Deuteronomy). Nisan "corresponds to our March-April" (Wycliffe, 1210). It was during this time that Jesus went up to Jerusalem, went to the Temple, and found the animal merchants and moneychangers doing the big business of exploiting worshipers.

One principle that can be drawn from this study is that God's House—the sanctuary—should always be a place of worship of the true and living God. Therefore, God's people should never be guilty of exploiting or participating in overcharging anyone, even though as happened in our lesson today, the Temple tax had to be paid—the church has bills to pay. The church must remain beyond reproach. She represents a Holy (set apart from sin) God. Therefore, her witness must be untarnished.

15 And when he had made a scourge of small cords, he drove them all out of the temple, and the sheep, and the oxen; and poured out the changers' money, and overthrew the tables; 16 And said unto them that sold doves, Take these things hence; make not my Father's house an house of merchandise.

Here we see the righteous anger of Jesus. His ire was so aroused by what He saw in His Father's House that "he made a scourge of small cords" (John 2:15). The word "scourge" in Greek is *phragellion* (**frag-EL-le-on**) and means "whip." In dealing with these defilers of the Temple, Jesus meant business as well, and He made a whip to get the job done. Not only did He drive out the merchants and moneychangers, but He did the same with the sheep and oxen and then overturned the tables. After He spoke, "Make not my Father's house an house of merchandise" (v. 16), there was no doubt as to where He stood on the matter and how distasteful He found their actions to be. After all, God's House is where worshipers go to commune with Him.

From this passage, we learn that there are times when the church must stand on what is right—God's principles. If something is not right in God's House, then the church must, with the whole armor of God, set God's House in order.

17 And his disciples remembered that it was written, The zeal of thine house hath eaten me up.

Jesus' disciples then remembered what was written about Jesus. The word "zeal" in the Greek is *zelos* (**DZAY-los**), meaning "ardour in embracing, pursuing, defending anything" (Strong, 1996). In other words, Jesus saw the wrong being done and would not stand still and let it continue. He set out to correct the matter, pursuing and defending. He was consumed with righting the situation. Therefore, He took action. He did not wait for someone else to right the wrong.

18 Then answered the Jews and said unto him, What sign shewest thou unto us, seeing that thou doest these things?

The religious leaders were expecting Jesus to show them a sign to prove His authority to rid the Temple of the merchants and moneychangers as well as their merchandise. The word "sign" in Greek is *semeion* (**say-MI-on**), and means "of miracles and wonders by which God authenticates the men sent by him, or by which men prove that the cause they are pleading is God's" (Strong, 1996). In other words, these religious leaders were in charge of the Temple and they would

not just accept Jesus' word that He was who He said He was. They wanted to see a miracle to prove that He was sent by God. They wanted Him to demonstrate that He received His authority from God.

19 Jesus answered and said unto them, Destroy this temple, and in three days I will raise it up.

However, Jesus stopped talking about the Temple that had been enlarged and remodeled for 46 years (20 B.C.) by Herod the Great and still was not finished; He started speaking of another "temple"—His body. The word "temple" in Greek is *naos* (**nah-OS**), which means "used of the temple at Jerusalem, but only of the sacred edifice (or sanctuary) itself, consisting of the Holy place and the Holy of Holies (in classical Greek it is used of the sanctuary or cell of the temple, where the image of gold was placed which is distinguished from the whole enclosure)" (Strong, 1996). Jesus applies this word to Himself; He shifts attention to something else that was sacred—His body that would be sacrificed for the sins of humanity. He predicts His crucifixion on that cruel Cross at Calvary. Three days He would be in the grave, but He would rise again on the third day. Death could not and would not keep Him in the grave!

20 Then said the Jews, Forty and six years was this temple in building, and wilt thou rear it up in three days?

The Jewish leaders could not believe Jesus' words. They misunderstood Him. They reminded Him that the Temple out of which He drove the merchants and moneychangers had taken 46 years to build and remodel, so they asked if He was saying that He could "rear it up in three days." The word "rear" in Greek is *egeiro* (**eg-I-ro**),

389

meaning "to raise up, construct, erect." They wanted to know if Jesus meant that He could erect the Temple in three days. Of course, if they truly recognized Him as the Son of the Living God, they would not have asked that question. However, they were in spiritual darkness.

21 But he spake of the temple of his body. 22 When therefore he was risen from the dead, his disciples remembered that he had said this unto them; and they believed the scripture, and the word which Jesus had said.

Again, Jesus was speaking of His own body as "the temple" (v. 21). Yet, even the disciples—who still did not fully appreciate who Jesus was—remembered after He was risen from the dead that He had told them about rising again. The word "remembered" in Greek is *mnaomai* (**MNAH-om-ahee**) and means "to be recalled or to return to one's mind, to remind one's self of" (Strong, 1996). Jesus was true to His Word. He did rise again, just as He said He would.

Sources:
E-Bible Teacher.com. http://www.ebibleteacher.com/images.html (accessed October 15, 2010).
Life Application Study Bible, New Living Translation. Wheaton, IL: Tyndale House Publishers, 1996. 1622–23.
Merriam-Webster Online Dictionary. http://www.merriam-webster.com (accessed October 14, 2010).
New Testament Greek Lexicon. Bible Study Tools.com. http://www.biblestudytools.com/lexicons/hebrew (accessed January 8, 2011).
Passage Lookup. Bible Gateway.com. http://www.bible-gateway.com/passage (accessed January 7, 2011).
Pfeiffer, Charles F., Howard F. Vos, and John Rea, eds. *Wycliffe Bible Dictionary.* Peabody, MA: Hendrickson, 1998. 1210, 1672–78.
Strong, James. *The Exhaustive Concordance of the Bible.* electronic ed. Woodside Bible Fellowship: Ontario, 1996 (accessed October 13, 2010).

Say It Correctly

Herod. HER-od.
Nisan. NI-san.

Daily Bible Readings

MONDAY
Building the Temple
(1 Chronicles 28:1–10)

TUESDAY
The Lord Has Chosen Zion
(Psalm 132:1–14)

WEDNESDAY
Keeping the Passover
(2 Chronicles 30:1–9)

THURSDAY
The House of the Lord
(Psalm 122)

FRIDAY
My Father's House
(Luke 2:41–51)

SATURDAY
Zeal for God's House
(Psalm 69:6–15)

SUNDAY
Cleansing the Temple
(John 2:13–22)

Teaching Tips

Words You Should Know

A. Living water (John 4:10–11) *zao* (Gr.)—Living water has vital power in itself and exerts the same upon the soul; represents the Holy Spirit in this text.

B. Messias (v. 25) *Messias* (Gr.)— The Greek form of Messiah, meaning "anointed"; a name of Christ.

Teacher Preparation

Unifying Principle—Turning Life Around. The Bible teaches that God's love and the gift of salvation is for all people, even though cultural standards did not consider this appropriate. Jesus turned the Samaritan woman's life around by breaking barriers and sharing His love with her. As Christians, we are called to do the same.

A. Pray that God will bring lesson clarity.

B. Study and meditate on the entire text.

C. Complete the companion lesson in the *Precepts For Living Personal Study Guide®*.

O—Open the Lesson

A. Open with prayer, including the Aim for Change.

B. Introduce today's subject of the lesson.

C. Read the Aim for Change and Keep in Mind in unison. Discuss.

D. Discuss cultural boundaries and discrimination.

E. Allow volunteers to share their testimonies of personal discrimination.

F. Then have a volunteer summarize the In Focus story. Discuss.

P—Present the Scriptures

A. Have volunteers read the Focal Verses.

B. Now use The People, Places, and Times; Background; Search the Scriptures; At-A-Glance outline; In Depth; and More Light on the Text to clarify the verses.

E—Explore the Meaning

A. Summarize the Discuss the Meaning, Lesson in Our Society, and Make It Happen sections.

B. Connect these sections to the Aim for Change and the Keep in Mind verse.

APR 22nd

N—Next Steps for Application

A. Summarize the lesson.

B. Close with prayer.

Worship Guide

For the Superintendent or Teacher
Theme: Woman of Samaria
Theme Song: "I Am Somebody"
Devotional Reading:
Revelation 22:10–17
Prayer

Woman of Samaria

Bible Background • JOHN 4:1–42
Printed Text • JOHN 4:7–15, 23–26, 28–30 | Devotional Reading • REVELATION 22:10–17

Aim for Change

By the end of the lesson, we will: DISCUSS who and what is acceptable based on societal norms; BE EMPOWERED to know that we can change because of Jesus; and SHARE how our perception of others influences our actions toward them.

In Focus

Terrell, Marcus, and Randis were excited about their youth camp's trip to a local swim club. The boys' camp leader paid a fee for the campers to spend the day at the club and made the proper arrangements with the facility.

Once the youth campers arrived, the three boys put on their swim trunks and dove into the pool. The sparkling water was refreshing in the summer heat. The boys and the other kids had a grand time doing cannonballs and splashing around in the water. But some of the club members were not amused and complained to the manager. The boys' skin color was part of these complaints.

When it was time for the group to leave, the club's manager pulled the youth leader aside and told him they could no longer visit the club. The youth pastor asked why, and the club manager told him that the members had a problem with the boys' "disruptive" behavior and were concerned that the presence of Blacks would change the "atmosphere" of the club. The youth leader stared at the manager in disbelief.

Life is full of unfair discrimination, but God does not discriminate. In today's lesson, we will see how Jesus accepts all people, regardless of societal standards, and welcomes them into the kingdom of heaven.

Keep in Mind

"But whosoever drinketh of the water that I shall give him shall never thirst; but the water that I shall give him shall be in him a well of water springing up into everlasting life" (John 4:14).

"But whosoever drinketh of the water that I shall give him shall never thirst;
but the water that I shall give him shall be in him a well of water
springing up into everlasting life" (John 4:14).

Focal Verses

KJV **John 4:7** There cometh a woman of Samaria to draw water: Jesus saith unto her, Give me to drink.

8 (For his disciples were gone away unto the city to buy meat.)

9 Then saith the woman of Samaria unto him, How is it that thou, being a Jew, askest drink of me, which am a woman of Samaria? For the Jews have no dealings with the Samaritans.

10 Jesus answered and said unto her, If thou knewest the gift of God, and who it is that saith to thee, Give me to drink; thou wouldest have asked of him, and he would have given thee living water.

11 The woman saith unto him, Sir, thou hast nothing to draw with, and the well is deep: from whence then hast thou that living water?

12 Art thou greater than our father Jacob, which gave us the well, and drank thereof himself, and his children, and his cattle?

13 Jesus answered and said unto her, Whosoever drinketh of this water shall thirst again:

14 But whosoever drinketh of the water that I shall give him shall never thirst; but the water that I shall give him shall be in him a well of water springing up into everlasting life.

15 The woman saith unto him, Sir, give me this water, that I thirst not, neither come hither to draw.

4:23 But the hour cometh, and now is, when the true worshippers shall worship the Father in spirit and in truth: for the Father seeketh such to worship him.

24 God is a Spirit: and they that worship him must worship him in spirit and in truth.

25 The woman saith unto him, I know that

NLT **John 4:7** Soon a Samaritan woman came to draw water, and Jesus said to her, "Please give me a drink."

8 He was alone at the time because his disciples had gone into the village to buy some food.

9 The woman was surprised, for Jews refuse to have anything to do with Samaritans. She said to Jesus, "You are a Jew, and I am a Samaritan woman. Why are you asking me for a drink?"

10 Jesus replied, "If you only knew the gift God has for you and who I am, you would ask me, and I would give you living water."

11 "But sir, you don't have a rope or a bucket," she said, "and this is a very deep well. Where would you get this living water?

12 And besides, are you greater than our ancestor Jacob who gave us this well? How can you offer better water than he and his sons and his cattle enjoyed?"

13 Jesus replied, "People soon become thirsty again after drinking this water.

14 But the water I give them takes away thirst altogether. It becomes a perpetual spring within them, giving them eternal life."

15 "Please, sir," the woman said, "give me some of that water! Then I'll never be thirsty again, and I won't have to come here to haul water."

4:23 But the time is coming and is already here when true worshipers will worship the Father in spirit and in truth. The Father is looking for anyone who will worship him that way.

24 For God is Spirit, so those who worship him must worship in spirit and in truth."

25 The woman said, "I know the Messiah will come—the one who is called Christ. When he comes, he will explain everything to us."

KJV Cont.

Messias cometh, which is called Christ: when he is come, he will tell us all things.

26 Jesus saith unto her, I that speak unto thee am he.

4:28 The woman then left her waterpot, and went her way into the city, and saith to the men,

29 Come, see a man, which told me all things that ever I did: is not this the Christ?

30 Then they went out of the city, and came unto him.

NLT Cont.

26 Then Jesus told her, "I am the Messiah!"

4:28 The woman left her water jar beside the well and went back to the village and told everyone,

29 "Come and meet a man who told me everything I ever did! Can this be the Messiah?"

30 So the people came streaming from the village to see him.

The People, Places, and Times

Samaria. This country is located north of the Dead Sea and west of the Jordan River. The land is inhospitable for use and difficult for travel, full of mountains, deep cracks in the earth, and valleys. During Bible times, mountain passes connected Samaria with other countries, which made them accessible. The well where Jesus met the "woman of Samaria" was located in a town called Sychar, which was near a plot of ground that Jacob had given to his son, Joseph (John 4:5–7). Therefore, the well is often referred to as "Jacob's Well."

During this time, Samaritans and Jews hated one another. Because of this strained relationship, it was not common or safe to see a Jew traveling through Samaria. In this passage, Christ is traveling from Judea to Galilee, and He has taken the road leading directly through Samaria. Being a Jew, Jesus was vulnerable to mistreatment and even violence from the Samaritan people, making this story even more significant because Jesus befriended a Samaritan woman and showed her love and kindness. Typically, a man of Jesus' heritage would have been on high alert while traveling through Samaria, but Jesus extinguished the fires of hatred with the healing waters of love.

Background

Jesus had been traveling and preaching for many days. Like most travelers during this time, He was poor and journeyed on foot. He then became fatigued, which reveals that He was truly human. Because sin, toil, and strife are part of human existence, Christ became weary because He submitted Himself to our human condition. The roads through Samaria were accessible, but the country was full of hills and mountains, which required great energy and strength to climb. On this trip, Jesus was headed to Galilee. He decided to leave Judea and return to Galilee because the Pharisees had heard that Jesus was baptizing more disciples than John, even though they were actually His disciples (John 4:1–3).

At-A-Glance

1. Living Water (John 4:7–15)

2. The Messiah Revealed (vv. 23–26)

3. Telling Others (vv. 28–30)

In Depth

1. Living Water (John 4:7–15)

At the beginning of this story, we find Jesus in a rather unique circumstance: He's alone. He was becoming a celebrity primarily by performing miracles. People followed Him wherever He went, and His disciples constantly surrounded Him. On this rare occasion, the disciples had gone into town to buy food, and Jesus was left alone.

Being tired from His journey, Jesus sat by a well. A Samaritan woman approached to fill her water jar. Jesus asked her for a drink of water. Surprised and confused, the Samaritan woman questioned Jesus. She didn't understand why He would ask her that, let alone even acknowledge her existence. She knew the cultural rules of her time. There were three reasons why she was shocked by Jesus' actions: (1) Jewish men did not initiate conversation with unknown women; (2) Jewish teachers did not host public discussions with women; and (3) Jews and Samaritans hated each other and did not converse.

Regardless of societal standards, Jesus continued to engage in conversation with the woman, revealing her sinfulness and need for a Savior (vv. 16–18). Throughout the discussion, it is obvious that the woman was knowledgeable. She asked Jesus questions based on her knowledge of culture, history, and religious beliefs. She knew the history of the land, the cultural drama between the Jews and Samaritans, and the prophecy of a coming Messiah. She was eager, or "thirsty," to learn more and hung on Jesus' every word (v. 15).

2. The Messiah Revealed (vv. 23–26)

At this point, Jesus continued to tell the woman that the time has come where true worshipers will worship the Father in truth and spirit. Interestingly, she knew what He was telling her. She told Him that she had heard the Messiah was coming. Up until this point in the conversation, the woman did not seem quite in sync with Jesus. He had been talking about living water, and she had been talking about H_2O (the water we drink). He was breaking barriers, while she was abiding by them.

During this entire time, Jesus had been talking about Himself. The Samaritan woman was oblivious to this fact until Jesus finally revealed His identity to her. "Then Jesus declared, 'I who speak to you am he'" (John 4:26, NIV). What a shock it must have been when the Samaritan woman realized to whom she was speaking!

3. Telling Others (vv. 28–30)

Amazed by what she heard, the Samaritan left her water jar and went to tell others about Jesus. It is significant to note that she left her water jar. Perhaps her excitement simply made her forget. It is plausible that she did not want to lug the heavy vessel with her because she wanted to hurry and bring others to see the Christ before He left. Once she reached the town, the Samaritan woman told people what Jesus had told her. She suggested that He might very well be the Christ. Just like the Samaritan woman, others had heard the prophecy of a coming Messiah, and now they had the chance to see Him. The Samaritan woman's words about Jesus being the Christ sparked the interest of others.

Because of her excitement, people left what they were doing and headed to see Jesus. How authentic the woman's amazement and faith must have been! She, a woman of questionable reputation, convinced an entire town of Samaritans to stop their work, leave their businesses, and put their livelihoods on hold to see a Jewish man who might be the Messiah. Her faith and joy were contagious, and she broke down more cultural barriers. Christ had changed her life in a significant way.

Search the Scriptures

1. Where were Jesus' disciples (John 4:7)?
2. How did the Samaritan woman respond to Jesus' request for water (v. 9)?
3. How does Jesus reveal His identity to the Samaritan woman (vv. 25–26)?

Discuss the Meaning

1. What was the significance of Jesus asking the Samaritan woman for a drink of water (John 4:7–9)?
2. What did Jesus mean by "living water" (vv. 10, 13–14)?
3. Based on the Samaritan woman's reaction to her conversation with Jesus, what sort of impact did He have on her (vv. 28–30)?

Lesson in Our Society

African Americans know how societal norms can promote discrimination and unbiblical principles. People have been inflicting these kinds of boundaries since the beginning of time, and it all comes down to a selfish struggle for power. Skin color, religious beliefs, health, age, gender, and financial worth are just a few of the futile reasons people have turned on each other. In the United States, African Americans have the unique opportunity to show forgiveness and share Christ's love with others, in spite of this country's history of slavery and abuse. People of faith must overcome cultural barriers in order to grow as Christians and share the message of salvation.

Make It Happen

Jesus revealed to the Samaritan woman (and to us) that His love extends beyond societal boundaries to all people. He loves everyone, regardless of gender, nationality, and social class. Therefore, as Christians, we must follow Christ's example and reach out to everyone, including societal outcasts, in order to share Christ's love with others. Challenge yourself to extend a loving hand and share the message of Jesus Christ to someone who has a difficult time because of societal or cultural factors.

Follow the Spirit

What God wants me to do:

_____

_____

_____

_____

Remember Your Thoughts

Special insights I have learned:

_____

_____

_____

_____

More Light on the Text

John 4:7–15, 23–26, 28–30

7 There cometh a woman of Samaria to draw water: Jesus saith unto her, Give me to drink. 8 (For his disciples were gone away unto the city to buy meat.)

While the disciples were in the town of Sychar to buy some food, a Samaritan woman came to draw water from the well. Jesus did something astonishing. He started a conversation with a woman He had never met before (see v. 9). In verse 8, the particle "for" (Gk. *gar*, **gar**) shows why Jesus asked a service of the woman that no one else could have done for Him, because the disciples had gone away into the city. Jesus' request was simple and sincere. He was tired and thirsty (v. 6). He used a personal need as a point of contact with the woman (cp. Luke 5:1–3).

9 Then saith the woman of Samaria unto him, How is it that thou, being a Jew, askest drink of me, which am a woman of Samaria? For the Jews have no dealings with the Samaritans.

Essentially, the woman said to Jesus, "How is it that you, 'being' (Gk. *on*, **oan**) a Jew would ask for a drink from me, a Samaritan woman?" Jesus' request to the woman of Samaria presents two difficulties for her: She was a woman and a Samaritan. The custom in many areas during the time of Jesus and as reinforced by the rabbinic laws was that a man was not allowed to talk to a woman in public places. Secondly, over the course of the Jews' history, they did not associate with Samaritans. The reasons dated from the annexation of the Northern Kingdom of Israel by the Assyrians in 722–721 B.C. (2 Kings 17:24–41; Ezra 4:1–5; cp. Luke 9:52; Acts 1:8; 8:5–25). The Samaritans were the progeny of Israelites who intermarried with them after the deportation to Assyria and pagans brought from the East by the king of Assyria.

Surprised and curious, the woman could not understand how He dared to ask her for water. The Greek verb *sugcravomai* (**soong-KRAH-om-ahee**) translated as "have dealings with," "make use of," or "to associate with on friendly terms." The relationship between the two nations was not friendly.

10 Jesus answered and said unto her, If thou knewest the gift of God, and who it is that saith to thee, Give me to drink; thou wouldest have asked of him, and he would have given thee living water.

Having caught her full attention and stimulated her curiosity, Jesus replied metaphorically to make her think more deeply. She needed to ponder the answer to these questions: Who is Jesus? What is the gift of God? What does "living water" mean? Jesus was progressively revealing Himself to the woman as He did with Nicodemus (see John 3). Basically, Jesus said to her, "If you knew the gift of God who is telling you to give Me a drink, He would have given spring (flowing) water."

The Greek *dorea* (**do-reh-AH**) rendered by "gift" is always applied to a divine gift in Acts and the Epistles (Acts 2:38; 8:20; 10:45). Here it refers to the Holy Spirit (see John 7:38–39). The "spring water" or "living water" is used metaphorically to refer to the Holy Spirit (see John 7:38–39; in Jeremiah, spring water is opposed to stagnant cistern water; see Jeremiah 2:13; cp. 17:13).

11 The woman saith unto him, Sir, thou hast nothing to draw with, and the well is deep: from whence then hast thou that living water? 12 Art thou greater than our father Jacob, which gave us the well, and drank thereof himself, and his children, and his cattle?

The Samaritan woman interpreted the metaphor literally. She knew about the living water in the well near her. This well belonged to her and her people. Thus, it was absurd to her that Jesus, without a bucket, would offer to give her water from a deep well. Such an exploit would outrank what Jacob did in digging the well. It is interesting to notice that in John 4:12 she called Jacob "our father" or "ancestor" since Jews considered him the founder of their nation. The Samaritans also considered Jacob their ancestor. The implied answer to the woman's question is "no" (Greek *me,* **may**) or "never." What she meant was that Jesus could not do what He was saying. She could not conceive that Jesus was greater than Jacob.

13 Jesus answered and said unto her, Whosoever drinketh of this water shall thirst again: 14 But whosoever drinketh of the water that I shall give him shall never thirst; but the water that I shall give him shall be in him a well of water springing up into everlasting life.

Jesus contrasted water that quenched thirst temporarily with water that quenched thirst permanently. The latter is superior because it leads to eternal life. Jesus was trying to get to the woman's fundamental longing, which was spiritual thirst, so He was speaking of the Holy Spirit (see John 7:38–39). He was telling her that at the Holy Spirit's coming, holy places such as the well of Jacob would lose their meaning. Religious and ethnic identities based on holy sites would give way to a new identity whose source would be in the Holy Spirit (see John 4:21, 23; cp. Acts 7:47–48).

In John 4:14, the verbs "shall give" (Gk. *didomi,* **DID-o-mee**) and "springing up" (Gk. *hallomai,* **HAL-lom-ahee**) are future tense. Jesus was saying to the woman: "Everyone (now) who drinks this water will thirst (future tense), whoever (in the future) drinks the water I will give, will never be thirsty again." The water Jesus would give would spring up for all eternity.

15 The woman saith unto him, Sir, give me this water, that I thirst not, neither come hither to draw.

The woman misunderstood Jesus' words. She was still hearing "water" in merely physical terms. She was thinking of some magical source of water that would keep her from the need of laborious drawing from a well. She asked Jesus to give her the water He was speaking of so that she would not keep coming to this place to "draw" (Gk. *antleo,* **ant-leh-o**), meaning "pump out water." The Greek verb *erchomai* (**ER-khom-ahee**) is the verb "come," as in "keep coming day by day," referring to a repeated action in the present.

4:23 But the hour cometh, and now is, when the true worshippers shall worship the Father in spirit and in truth: for the Father seeketh such to worship him.

The true question about worship is not "where" but "how." The time of "true" (Gk. *alethinos,* **al-ay-thee-NOS**) or "genuine" worship is now at hand because the Messiah is now at hand. "The true worshippers" genuinely understand that Jesus is the truth of God (John 3:21; 14:6; Acts 4:12). The Father wants people of this kind as His worshipers. They are to worship in spirit and in truth. To worship in spirit is to worship in a new way revealed by God to humanity in Jesus. To worship in truth is to worship God through Jesus. True worship is offered through Jesus by the means of the Holy Spirit. True worship is in contrast with religious formalism such as that of the Pharisees. The Father is seeking true worshipers because its authentic nature requires that worship be spiritual.

24 God is a Spirit: and they that worship him must worship him in spirit and in truth.

By this affirmation of the essence of God ("God is a Spirit"), Jesus justified what He had said about genuine worship in John 4:23. Worship must be in harmony with the nature of the one being worshiped. We cannot relate to God satisfactorily in physical terms since He is Spirit. He is invisible and intangible. For God to be known, He must reveal

Himself to us. He did so in the Scriptures. His fuller revelation is now at hand in Jesus (see John 1:18). True and satisfactory worship is worship offered in and through Jesus.

25 The woman saith unto him, I know that Messias cometh, which is called Christ: when he is come, he will tell us all things.

The Samaritans had a messianic anticipation based on the Pentateuch (Deuteronomy 18:15–18). They were waiting for the Messiah they called *Taheb* (meaning the "converter" or "restorer"), a second Moses who would reveal the truth, restore true belief, and renew true worship. They did not expect the Messiah to be the King born of David. The Samaritan woman was beginning to understand part of what Jesus was telling her. She was waiting with nostalgia for the coming of the Messiah who "will tell us all *things*" (John 4:25). The verb "tell" (Gk. *anaggello*, **an-ang-EL-lo**) means "to report" (such as in Acts 14:27; 15:4; 2 Corinthians 7:7), but it is generally rendered as "announce," "proclaim," or "teach." All these meanings can be understood in the Messiah's ministry.

26 Jesus saith unto her, I that speak unto thee am he.

Jesus revealed to the concerned woman that she was speaking with the Messiah in person. "I am . . . he" (Gk. *ego eimi*, **eg-Oi-MEE**, cp. John 6:20; 8:24, 58; Exodus 3:14–15). Jesus had never before expressed His messianic title so clearly. The situation here was different from when He was among Jews. Many Jews had false messianic hope. They were expecting a political figure to deliver them from their enemies, the Romans (see John 6:14–15; 18:36). It was dangerous for Jesus to declare openly that He was the Messiah (cp. Matthew 16:20; Mark 8:30; Luke 9:21).

4:28 The woman then left her waterpot, and went her way into the city, and saith to the men, 29 Come, see a man, which told me all things that ever I did: is not this the Christ?

Leaving her water jar, the woman hurried back to town to share her discovery with her people. She said, "Come" (Gk. *deute*, **DYOO-teh**), and she pointed out two things about Jesus:

1. He told her "all (the) things" she ever did (Gk. *pas*, meaning "everything," see John 4:10–19; cp. 1:48).

2. He might be the Messiah. Her first impression of Jesus was that He was a prophet (John 4:19). As their conversation continued, she wondered if He was indeed the long-awaited Messiah.

30 Then they went out of the city, and came unto him.

Just as Jesus caught her attention by awakening her curiosity, she was able to get people to listen to her. They were impressed by her words and decided to see for themselves. Despite the woman's likely unpopular lifestyle, the people went out to see Jesus. In the Greek, "went out" (*exerchomai*, **ex-ER-khom-ahee**) and "came" (*erchomai*), meaning "came from one place to another"), express how the people hastened to leave town and go to see Jesus. One can easily picture the Samaritans coming out of the town like a stream and going toward Jesus.

Sources:
Bauer, Walter. *A Greek-English Lexicon of the New Testament and Other Early Christian Literature (BACD)*. Chicago, IL: University of Chicago Press, 1979.
Bonnet, Louis. *Evangile Selon Jean. Bible Annotée NT2*. St-Légier, Suisse, 1983.
Bruce, F. F. *The Gospel of John*. Grand Rapids, MI: W. B. Eerdmans Publishing Company, 1983.
"Dictionary and Word Search for *'Living Water'* in the KJV." Blue Letter Bible.org., 1996–2010. http://www.blueletterbible.org/search/translationResults.cfm?Criteria=living+water&t=KJV (accessed July 30, 2010).

"Dictionary and Word Search for "Messias" (Strong's 3323)." Blue Letter Bible.org., 1996–2010. http://www.blueletter-bible.org/lang/lexicon/lexicon.cfm?Strongs=G3323&t=KJV (accessed July 30, 2010).

Henry, Matthew. *Matthew Henry's Concise Commentary on the Whole Bible.* Nashville, TN: Thomas Nelson, 1997. 986–87.

The Holy Bible. Contemporary English Version (CEV). New York: American Bible Society, 1995.

New Testament Greek Lexicon. Bible Study Tools.com. http://www.biblestudytools.com/lexicons/greek (accessed January 9, 2011).

Packer, J. I., Merrill C. Tenney, and William White Jr. *Nelson's Illustrated Encyclopedia of Bible Facts.* Nashville, TN: Thomas Nelson, 1995. 191–93.

Passage Lookup. Bible Gateway.com. http://www.bible-gateway.com/passage (accessed January 9, 2011).

Rochedieu, Charles. *Les Trésors du Nouveau Testament.* Saint-Légier, Suisse: Editions Emmaüs, 1972.

Yancey, Philip, and Tim Stafford. The Student Bible: New International Version. Grand Rapids, MI: Zondervan, 986. 931–932.

Say It Correctly

Judea. Joo-DEE-ah.
Samaria. Suh-MAIR-ee-ah.

Daily Bible Readings

MONDAY
Planted by Streams of Water
(Psalm 1)

TUESDAY
Longing for God
(Psalm 42)

WEDNESDAY
The Water of Life
(Revelation 22:10–17)

THURSDAY
The Samaritans' Heresy
(2 Kings 17:26–34)

FRIDAY
Worshiping What You Do Not Know
(John 4:16–22)

SATURDAY
Fields Ripe for Harvest
(John 4:35–42)

SUNDAY
"Come and See"
(John 4:7–15, 23–26, 28–30)

Notes

_____

_____

_____

_____

Teaching Tips

Words You Should Know

A. Sin (John 9:2) *hamartano* (Gk.)—To wander from the law of God; violate God's law.

B. Should be made manifest (v. 3) *phaneroo* (Gk.)—Made visible or known what has been hidden or unknown.

Teacher Preparation

Unifying Principle—What Comes First? People's critical personal needs often outweigh the rules and regulations made by other human beings. Jesus put the blind man's need to see before the Jewish rules about Sabbath observance.

A. Pray that God will bring lesson clarity.

B. Study and meditate on the entire text.

C. Complete the companion lesson in the *Precepts For Living Personal Study Guide*®.

O—Open the Lesson

A. Open with prayer, including the Aim for Change.

B. Introduce today's subject.

C. Read the Aim for Change and Keep in Mind verse in unison. Discuss.

D. Discuss how rules and regulations may sometimes interfere with human needs.

E. Allow volunteers to share their testimonies of how naysayers caused them to miss out on a personal blessing.

F. Use the In Focus story to segue into today's lesson.

P—Present the Scriptures

A. Have volunteers read the Focal Verses.

B. Now use The People, Places, and Times; Background; Search the Scriptures; At-A-Glance outline; In Depth; and More Light on the Text to clarify the verses.

E—Explore the Meaning

A. Summarize the Discuss the Meaning, Lesson in Our Society, and Make It Happen sections.

B. Connect these sections to the Aim for Change and the Keep in Mind verse.

N—Next Steps for Application

A. Summarize the lesson.

B. Close with prayer.

Worship Guide

For the Superintendent or Teacher
Theme: Healing the Blind Man
Theme Song:
"O To Be Kept by Jesus!"
Devotional Reading: Isaiah 29:17–21
Prayer

Healing the Blind Man

Bible Background • JOHN 9
Printed Text • JOHN 9:1–17 | Devotional Reading • ISAIAH 29:17–21

Aim for Change

By the end of the lesson, we will: KNOW that traditions should not be used to ignore human suffering or needs; REFLECT on a situation where we felt discriminated against or ostracized; and PARTICIPATE in activities that help people in need.

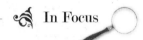
In Focus

"Stefan? Is that you?" The voice came from across the plaza. "It's Rico. Man, I haven't seen you since high school."

"Rico! How's it going?" said Stefan. "Last I heard, you were doing time in jail."

"Best thing that could have happened to me," said Rico. "The prison chaplain led me to the Lord."

"Really? I didn't see that coming."

"Yeah, me neither. I got out early for good behavior, and now I'm going to seminary to become a pastor."

APRIL 29th

"Well, no offense, but do you really think a church is going to hire someone with a record like yours? They're looking for positive role models, not drug dealers. And you know these prison conversions aren't always legit."

"That's harsh, man," said Rico. "All I can say is look at what I was before, and look at what I am now. I used to push drugs, and now I'm pushing the Gospel. How could that happen without Jesus?"

Legalistic religion can make people judgmental, but true faith in Jesus results in a supernaturally transformed life.

Keep in Mind

"Therefore said some of the Pharisees, This man is not of God, because he keepeth not the sabbath day. Others said, How can a man that is a sinner do such miracles? And there was a division among them" (John 9:16).

"Therefore said some of the Pharisees, This man is not of God, because he keepeth not the sabbath day. Others said, How can a man that is a sinner do such miracles? And there was a division among them" (John 9:16).

Focal Verses

KJV **John 9:1** And as Jesus passed by, he saw a man which was blind from his birth.

2 And his disciples asked him, saying, Master, who did sin, this man, or his parents, that he was born blind?

3 Jesus answered, Neither hath this man sinned, nor his parents: but that the works of God should be made manifest in him.

4 I must work the works of him that sent me, while it is day: the night cometh, when no man can work.

5 As long as I am in the world, I am the light of the world.

6 When he had thus spoken, he spat on the ground, and made clay of the spittle, and he anointed the eyes of the blind man with the clay,

7 And said unto him, Go, wash in the pool of Siloam, (which is by interpretation, Sent.) He went his way therefore, and washed, and came seeing.

8 The neighbours therefore, and they which before had seen him that he was blind, said, Is not this he that sat and begged?

9 Some said, This is he: others said, He is like him: but he said, I am he.

10 Therefore said they unto him, How were thine eyes opened?

11 He answered and said, A man that is called Jesus made clay, and anointed mine eyes, and said unto me, Go to the pool of Siloam, and wash: and I went and washed, and I received sight.

12 Then said they unto him, Where is he? He said, I know not.

13 They brought to the Pharisees him that aforetime was blind.

NLT **John 9:1** As Jesus was walking along, he saw a man who had been blind from birth.

2 "Teacher," his disciples asked him, "why was this man born blind? Was it a result of his own sins or those of his parents?"

3 "It was not because of his sins or his parents' sins," Jesus answered. "He was born blind so the power of God could be seen in him.

4 All of us must quickly carry out the tasks assigned us by the one who sent me, because there is little time left before the night falls and all work comes to an end.

5 But while I am still here in the world, I am the light of the world."

6 Then he spit on the ground, made mud with the saliva, and smoothed the mud over the blind man's eyes.

7 He told him, "Go and wash in the pool of Siloam" (Siloam means Sent). So the man went and washed, and came back seeing!

8 His neighbors and others who knew him as a blind beggar asked each other, "Is this the same man—that beggar?"

9 Some said he was, and others said, "No, but he surely looks like him!"

And the beggar kept saying, "I am the same man!"

10 They asked, "Who healed you? What happened?"

11 He told them, "The man they call Jesus made mud and smoothed it over my eyes and told me, 'Go to the pool of Siloam and wash off the mud.' I went and washed, and now I can see!"

12 "Where is he now?" they asked.

"I don't know," he replied.

13 Then they took the man to the Pharisees.

KJV Cont.

14 And it was the sabbath day when Jesus made the clay, and opened his eyes.

15 Then again the Pharisees also asked him how he had received his sight. He said unto them, He put clay upon mine eyes, and I washed, and do see.

16 Therefore said some of the Pharisees, This man is not of God, because he keepeth not the sabbath day. Others said, How can a man that is a sinner do such miracles? And there was a division among them.

17 They say unto the blind man again, What sayest thou of him, that he hath opened thine eyes? He said, He is a prophet.

NLT Cont.

14 Now as it happened, Jesus had healed the man on a Sabbath.

15 The Pharisees asked the man all about it. So he told them, "He smoothed the mud over my eyes, and when it was washed away, I could see!"

16 Some of the Pharisees said, "This man Jesus is not from God, for he is working on the Sabbath." Others said, "But how could an ordinary sinner do such miraculous signs?" So there was a deep division of opinion among them.

17 Then the Pharisees once again questioned the man who had been blind and demanded, "This man who opened your eyes—who do you say he is?"

The man replied, "I think he must be a prophet."

The People, Places, and Times

Pharisees. The Pharisees were a group of orthodox Jews who prided themselves on strict faithfulness to their rigid interpretations of the Law of Moses. Jesus' emphasis on the proper interpretation and spirit of the law and the hypocrisy of self-righteousness led to many clashes with them.

Siloam. The pool of Siloam was a spring-fed pool located in the southeastern corner of Jerusalem. The Gospel writer points out that the Hebrew word *Siloam* means "sent," probably referring originally to the outflow of water from the spring, but in this context serving as a symbol connected to Christ's messianic ministry as well. Jesus was the Messiah sent by God, and He sent the blind man to be healed.

Background

In the first-century world, blindness was a severe hardship. Usually, it meant that blind people had to support themselves by begging. Some scholars report that mud made from spittle was a common treatment for eye problems in Jewish medicine of the time (Vincent, 182). Modern medical science suggests that, for that remedy to work, it would take a miracle.

At-A-Glance

1. Jesus and the Disciples: A Doctrine or a Person? (John 9:1–7)

2. The Healed Blind Man: A New Creation (vv. 8–12)

3. The Pharisees: The Poison of Legalism (vv. 13–17)

In Depth

1. Jesus and the Disciples: A Doctrine or a Person? (John 9:1–7)

As long as people have talked about theology, they have debated the problem of evil. Why does a loving God allow people to suffer? Why do bad things happen to good people? These are deeply troubling concerns, but sometimes doctrinal debates about them cause us to miss the point.

That seems to be what happened with Jesus' disciples. John begins the story: "And as Jesus passed by, he saw a man which was blind from his birth. And his disciples asked him, saying, Master, who did sin, this man, or his parents, that he was born blind?" (John 9:1–2).

When the disciples saw the man who had been born blind, their minds jumped to an old theological argument. Many people (going all the way back to Job's friends) believe that suffering is a punishment for sin or lack of faith. Among the many problems with this belief, it doesn't explain how a person could suffer from blindness since the moment he was born. Some might argue that the man's parents had sinned or that the man had somehow sinned before birth. The disciples were curious about Jesus' opinion.

Jesus, however, didn't see a theological problem. "He saw a man" (v. 1). Even if we were able to completely understand all the theological issues, it doesn't change the fact that people are suffering. When our neighbors are in pain or need, God asks us to help and comfort them, not to figure out why they are suffering. They are not puzzles; they are people.

Jesus answered the disciples' question by showing that their way of thinking was flawed: "It was neither that this man sinned, nor his parents; but it was so that the works of God might be displayed in him" (v. 3, NASB). As Job realized, suffering should not be seen as a punishment for sin but as an opportunity for us to see the goodness of God against a background of contrast.

Jesus said that since He is "the light of the world," He must do the works that God does (vv. 4–5). By using the word "we," He shows that the same is true of us (compare Matthew 5:14). Jesus was about to do something that had never been done before.

Jesus spat on the ground, made mud, applied it to the blind man's eyes, and told him to wash it off in the Pool of Siloam. When the blind man came back, he could see.

2. The Blind Man Healed: A New Creation (vv. 8–12)

Not surprisingly, the sight of the man who had until recently been a blind beggar created a stir in the neighborhood. Some of the neighbors tentatively recognized him; others thought he was a different person who happened to look the same.

The neighbors' question—"Isn't this the same man who used to sit and beg?" (John 9:8, NIV)—shows how greatly Jesus' miracle affected the man's life. The man used to sit and beg, but after Jesus healed him, he could walk and run on his own and would be able to earn his own living. By giving the man the ability to see, Jesus transformed his entire life.

This miraculous healing is one of many fulfillments of prophecies foretelling that the Messiah would give sight to the blind. God declares through Isaiah, "I will keep you and will make you to be a covenant for the people and a light for the Gentiles, to open eyes that are blind, to free captives from prison and to release from the dungeon those who sit in darkness" (Isaiah 42:6–7, NIV; compare Isaiah 35:5; Matthew 11:2–6). Miracles, like this one, point directly to Jesus' identity as God's promised Servant.

Blind eyes being opened is also used throughout Scripture as a metaphor for spiritual insight or visions that people could only have received from God (Numbers 22:31; 2 Kings 6:17; Luke 24:31).

The healed man is eager to claim his identity as the former blind beggar: "I am the man" (John 9:9, NIV). When his neighbors pressed him for details of this extraordinary event, he replied with a simple, matter-of-fact retelling of his story, centered on Jesus. Later, he summarized his experience in a brilliant, pithy statement: "One thing I do know. I was blind but now I see!" (John 9:25, NIV).

3. The Pharisees: The Poison of Legalism (vv. 13–17)

Not all the witnesses of this remarkable event were enthusiastic. The neighbors brought the healed man before the Pharisees, religious authorities who (perhaps they expected) would be interested to see a real-life miracle. Instead, the Pharisees grilled the man with questions, observing that Jesus healed him on the Sabbath (vv. 13–14).

According to the Pharisees' interpretation of Moses' Law, activities such as making clay or washing your eyes were considered work that was unlawful on the day of rest (Vincent, 184). Some of them reasoned, "This man is not from God, for he does not keep the Sabbath" (v. 16, NIV).

This is a clear case of legalism. The law—or worse, someone's interpretation of it—is set as a measure for judging a person's standing with God. While the law itself is not a bad thing, God never intended it to be the foundation of our relationship with Him. The law points out our sinfulness, but it has no power to keep us from sinning or make us live better. For those things, we need faith in Christ alone. "The law was our schoolmaster to bring us unto Christ, that we might be justified by faith" (Galatians 3:24).

Some of the Pharisees pointed out the flaw in the legalistic logic: "How can a man that is a sinner do such miracles?" (John 9:16). This led to a disagreement and a quarrel. In the end, all the Pharisees missed the point. They were judging people based on their own inflexible understanding of the law, rather than allowing for any compassion toward their neighbors or understanding of the fact that God doesn't always work the way we expect.

Though he lacked specifics, the healed man knew what he thought about Jesus: "He is a prophet" (v. 17). The healed man's insistence that Jesus could represent God without following the Pharisees' legalistic understanding of the law led them to verbally harass him and ultimately throw him out of the synagogue (vv. 27, 34). This is a sad instance of what has been called "spiritual abuse": using religious beliefs as a pretext for authoritarianism, abuse, manipulation, and other hurtful behavior (Provender).

Jesus rebuked the Pharisees, saying that insistence on one's self-righteousness is the real form of blindness. Jesus' miraculous healing, His acceptance of the blind man, and His refusal to work within the system of legalism show that the Pharisees' approach missed the point. The point is to allow God to transform us supernaturally into something new. It is similar to what Paul said, "Neither circumcision nor uncircumcision means anything; what counts is a new creation" (Galatians 6:15, NIV).

Search the Scriptures

1. What answer did Jesus give to the disciples' question about the cause of the beggar's blindness?

2. How did the Pharisees understand the law? How should we understand the purpose of the Sabbath?

Discuss the Meaning

1. According to Jesus, should we view suffering as a punishment for someone's sin or lack of faith? What is a better response to seeing someone in pain or need?

2. The Pharisees' legalism caused them to condemn the healed man and Jesus. According to Scripture, what is wrong with their attitude? What biblical arguments can you think of that show why legalism is contrary to the Gospel of Jesus?

Lesson in Our Society

In this story, the Pharisees show several characteristics of what modern researchers call "spiritual abuse," such as legalism, judgmentalism, authoritarianism, rejection, and placing doctrine above people. If you're not familiar with the topic of spiritual abuse, study a list of its characteristics. Have you seen spiritually abusive or legalistic behaviors in religious groups in your experience? How can you avoid these in your own church or ministry? What facts about Jesus might you point to if you needed to encourage someone who had suffered this kind of abuse in His name?

Make It Happen

Examine your own approach to people in need. Is it theoretical like the disciples, judgmental like the Pharisees, or compassionate like Jesus? If there are any people or groups of people you've been avoiding unintentionally or on purpose, take the initiative to offer them some tangible help or encouragement in Jesus' name.

Follow the Spirit

What God wants me to do:

_____

_____

_____

_____

Remember Your Thoughts

Special insights I have learned:

_____

_____

_____

_____

More Light on the Text

John 9:1–17

1 And as Jesus passed by, he saw a man which was blind from his birth.

Jesus saw a blind man as He was walking along in the city of Jerusalem or probably outside the temple (see John 8:59; cp. Acts 3:2). The man had been blind from birth. His case was desperate (compare [cp.] John 5:5–6). Jesus is all-powerful (cp. Luke 1:37). He is able to help even in a hopeless situation.

2 And his disciples asked him, saying, Master, who did sin, this man, or his parents, that he was born blind?

For the disciples, and for the Jews of the time of Jesus, personal suffering of this nature was supposedly due to personal sin. Here, since the suffering began at birth, the problem was in identifying who was responsible: either this man sinned in the

409

womb, or his parents had committed a sin before the man's birth (cp. Ezekiel 18:4; Exodus 20:5).

The Greek conjunction *hina* (**HIN-ah**), translated "that" or "as a result," indicates a consecutive (result) clause declaring the end of some sequence of events. To people of Bible times, the man's blindness was a consequence of his sin or the sin of his "parents" (Gk. *goneus,* **gon-YOOCE**). While the Bible allows a general relationship between suffering and sin due to the Fall, it refuses to permit the principle to be individualized in every case (cp. Genesis 3; Romans 5; Job). A person's suffering is not always due to a particular sin he or she committed. Sometimes, of course, it may be, as when suffering results from alcoholism or sexual promiscuity.

3 Jesus answered, Neither hath this man sinned, nor his parents: but that the works of God should be made manifest in him.

Jesus told the disciples that this man's blindness was not due to his sin or the sin of his parents. It occurred so that the work of God might be displayed in his life (cp. Exodus 4:11; 2 Corinthians 12:9). It is not to be understood that God made this man blind (or allowed it) in order to use him to reveal His glory (see James 1:12–18). As in all seemingly hopeless cases, the man's blindness allows the works of God to be revealed. The man's story is a sign revealing the glory of Jesus sent by God. One of the marks of the coming of the messianic age is the receiving of sight by the blind (Isaiah 29:18; 35:5).

4 I must work the works of him that sent me, while it is day: the night cometh, when no man can work. 5 As long as I am in the world, I am the light of the world.

Jesus pointed out to the disciples an urgency to be reckoned with (cp. John 4:34; Matthew 24:36–51). Jesus used a short parable about day and night to talk primarily about His ministry and later the ministry of the disciples. He compared His ministry to light shining in darkness (see John 1:9; 3:19; 8:12), with limits just as the light of the day. His life is compared to one day of labor, and it will finish with the night of His death (5:17; Luke 13:32). Thus, He must take advantage of the hours of the day in order to finish the job before the coming of the night (see John 11:9–10). He was talking about His imminent death. This is an explicit connection to Jesus' earlier claim (John 8:12). As the Light of the world, Jesus offers salvation to all human beings. After His death, His disciples will be called to be His witnesses (John 4:34–38; 11:7, 15; Acts 1:8).

6 When he had thus spoken, he spat on the ground, and made clay of the spittle, and he anointed the eyes of the blind man with the clay,

Jesus proceeded to heal the blind man using a mudpack made from saliva. No reason is given for using a mudpack instead of just saying a word as in previous healings (see John 4:50, 53). It may be that the man needed to be involved in the healing process by an act of obedience to Jesus. Jesus probably used the mudpack, not as medicine, to stimulate the man's faith (cp. 2 Kings 5:13).

7 And said unto him, Go, wash in the pool of Siloam, (which is by interpretation, Sent.) He went his way therefore, and washed, and came seeing.

Jesus sent the man to the pool called "Siloam" (Gk. *hermeneuo,* **her-mayn-YOO-o,** in Hebrew *shalach,* **shaw-LAKH**), meaning "explained," "interpreted," or "sent" (cp. 2 Kings 20:20; 2 Chronicles 32:30). Water flowed from the spring at Gihon into a pool in the city of Jerusalem. Jesus sent the man, and He Himself was sent by the Father. In John 9:7, having obeyed the command to go and wash in Siloam, the man "came (back) seeing" (Gk. *erchomai blepo,* **ER-khom-ahee BLEP-o**), meaning "he came away seeing or able to see." Healing was the reward of his obedience (cp. 1 Samuel 15:22–23). It is not that the water of Siloam had a curative virtue; it is his faith leading him to where he had been sent (cp. Luke 17:14, 19).

8 The neighbours therefore, and they which before had seen him that he was blind, said, Is not this he that sat and begged? 9 Some said, This is he: others said, He is like him: but he said, I am he. 10 Therefore said they unto him, How were thine eyes opened?

As a result, of the miracle the man's neighbors started discussing his identity. They were used to seeing him when he was a beggar (cp. Acts 3:2), but they were seeing a different person. They were not sure he was the same person who used to be a blind beggar. They explored different opinions. The man assured them that he was the same person. He used the same self-identifying expression used by Jesus: "I am he" (cp. John 6:20; 8:24, 28, 58). He was asked to tell them what happened to him.

11 He answered and said, A man that is called Jesus made clay, and anointed mine eyes, and said unto me, Go to the pool of Siloam, and wash: and I went and washed, and I received sight.

The how of a miracle is always difficult to explain, but the man stuck to the facts. He explained very simply how the miracle happened and who did it. The man who healed him was called Jesus.

12 Then said they unto him, Where is he? He said, I know not.

They asked the man where Jesus was. In F. F. Bruce's view, "The question 'Where is he?' suggests that those who questioned the man would have liked to question Jesus too, to see if the two accounts tallied" (Bruce, 211). Since the man could not see when Jesus made mud and smeared his eyes with it, when he went back home after his healing, he could not really know where Jesus was.

13 They brought to the Pharisees him that aforetime was blind.

They took the man to the Pharisees "aforetime" (Gk. *pote,* **pot-EH**), meaning at some time or "once." They "brought" (Gk. *ago,* **AG-o,** "to lead to a court of justice" or "to a magistrate" in this context) him to the Pharisees, probably because the miracle was so out of the ordinary and religious issues related to the Sabbath were involved (see v. 14). The Pharisees as religious authorities would know how to handle the situation.

14 And it was the sabbath day when Jesus made the clay, and opened his eyes.

The day on which the healing occurred was the Sabbath day. At this point, the reader is told that the healing of the man, who was born blind, had happened on the Sabbath. "One of the categories of work specifically forbidden on the sabbath in the traditional interpretation of the law was kneading, and the making of mud or clay with such simple ingredients as earth and saliva was construed as a form of kneading" (Bruce, 212). For the Pharisees, the healing of this man violated the laws of the Sabbath. The making of clay constituted work and caused the worker to be a Sabbath-breaker.

15 Then again the Pharisees also asked him how he had received his sight. He said unto them, He put clay upon mine eyes, and I washed, and do see.

The Pharisees asked the man "again" (Gk. *palin*, **PAL-in**), meaning "anew," to explain how he was healed. They repeated the same question as the neighbors' in verse 10: "How can you see?" It was important for them to find out a basis for an accusation of the breaking of the law (see v. 16). The man explained the healing very simply and briefly using three verbs: "put" (Gk. *epitithemi*, **ep-ee-TITH-ay-mee**), meaning "to lay on" or "put upon"; "wash" (Gk. *nipto*, **NIP-to**), meaning "to wash oneself," "to bathe"; and "see" (Gk. *blepo*, **BLEP-o**). Basically, the man told them, "He put clay upon my eyes, I washed myself, and now I see."

16 Therefore said some of the Pharisees, This man is not of God, because he keepeth not the sabbath day. Others said, How can a man that is a sinner do such miracles? And there was a division among them.

The man's account of what happened was so persuasive that some of the Pharisees were clearly impressed (cp. John 3:2). They said, "How can a man that is a sinner do such miracles?" Others, however, accused Jesus of breaking the Sabbath instituted by God and of being a false prophet trying to lead the people away from God (cp. Deuteronomy 13:3–5). So, they were divided (see John 7:43; 10:19).

17 They say unto the blind man again, What sayest thou of him, that he hath opened thine eyes? He said, He is a prophet.

They asked for the man's opinion of Jesus. His opinion did not count much among the hostile Pharisees (see vv. 22, 34). They probably just wanted to get some words out of the man that would allow them to make an accusation against Jesus and even the man. The man said that Jesus was a prophet maybe "in the succession of Elijah and Elisha … [or] perhaps he simply used 'prophet' as a synonym for 'man of God'" (Bruce, 214). It may also have been that it was the highest category the man could think of at this point (see John 4:19; 6:14).

Sources:

Bauer, Walter. *A Greek-English Lexicon of the New Testament and Other Early Christian Literature (BACD)*. Chicago, IL: University of Chicago Press, 1979.

Bonnet, Louis. *Evangile Selon Jean. Bible Annotée NT2*. Saint-Légier, Suisse, 1983.

Bruce, F. F. *The Gospel of John*. Grand Rapids, MI: W. B. Eerdmans Publishing Company, 1983. 211–12, 214.

The Holy Bible. Contemporary English Version (CEV). New York, NY: American Bible Society, 1995.

Merriam-Webster Online Dictionary. http://www.merriam-webster.com (accessed October 4, 2010).

New Testament Greek Lexicon. Bible Study Tools.com. http://www.biblestudytools.com/lexicons/greek (accessed January 9, 2011).

Passage Lookup. Bible Gateway.com. http://www.biblegateway.com/passage (accessed January 9, 2011).

Provender: A Clearinghouse of Sources on Spiritual Abuse and Cult-like Practices in Churches and Groups. http://pureprovender. blogspot.com (accessed July 26, 2010).

Rochedieu, Charles. *Les Trésors du Nouveau Testament*. Saint-Légier, Suisse: Editions Emmaüs, 1972.

Vincent, Marvin R. *Word Studies in the New Testament. Vol. 2*. Grand Rapids, MI: W. B. Eerdmans Publishing Company, 1957. 182, 184.

Say It Correctly

Pharisees. FAIR-uh-sees.
Sabbath. SAB-uhth.

Daily Bible Readings

MONDAY
Hope for the Future
(Isaiah 29:17–21)

TUESDAY
Separating Light from Darkness
(Genesis 1:14–19)

WEDNESDAY
Light for the Journey
(Exodus 13:17–22)

THURSDAY
The Blind Questioning Blindness
(John 9:18–23)

FRIDAY
Teaching the Unteachable
(John 9:24–34)

SATURDAY
Seeing but Not Seeing
(John 9:35–41)

SUNDAY
The Light of the World
(John 9:1–17)

Notes

_____

_____

_____

_____

Teaching Tips

Words You Should Know

A. Labour (John 6:27) *ergazomai* (Gr.)—To work, to do, to commit.

B. Believe (vv. 29, 30) *pisteuo* (Gr.)—To accept as true, to place confidence in, to rely on.

Teacher Preparation

Unifying Principle—Nourishment for Life. Many people are hungering for what will make their lives complete. Jesus promised His followers that if they would come to Him, they would never be hungry or thirsty again.

A. Pray and ask for God's guidance.

B. Study and meditate on the entire lesson.

C. Be ready to share your own testimony of hungering and thirsting for God.

D. Complete the companion lesson in the *Precepts For Living Personal Study Guide*®.

O—Open the Lesson

A. Open with prayer and then introduce the subject of the lesson.

B. Use the In Focus story to segue into your own testimony.

C. Share testimonies.

P—Present the Scriptures

A. Ask another two volunteers to read The People, Places, and Times and Background sections. Discuss.

B. Discuss the Focal Verses according to the At-A-Glance outline and More Light on the Text.

C. Discuss the Search the Scriptures section.

E—Explore the Meaning

A. Have the class answer the question in the Discuss the Meaning section, using examples from their own experiences.

B. Discuss Lesson in Our Society and ask the question, "Do Christians ever lose their focus on Jesus, and what can they do to get back on track?"

N—Next Steps for Application

A. Read the Make It Happen section and ask the class to pray about at least three people with whom they can share the Bread of Life—Jesus.

B. Close with a prayer.

Worship Guide

For the Superintendent or Teacher
Theme: The Bread of Life
Theme Song: "I Surrender All"
Devotional Reading: Psalm 107:1–9
Prayer

The Bread of Life

Bible Background • JOHN 6
Printed Text • JOHN 6:22–35 | Devotional Reading • PSALM 107:1–9

—————— Aim for Change ——————

By the end of the lesson, we will: EXPLAIN why Jesus is the Bread of Life; TRUST that Jesus is our Bread of Life; and LIST the ways that we can share the Bread of Life with others.

—————— In Focus ——————

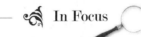

"An education, a career, a house, a car, a husband, and children––that's the winning combination for the perfectly complete life," said Donna, admiring her mirrored reflection while sporting her cap and gown.

"Honey, there's nothing wrong with those things, but what about Jesus? Any room in that plan for Him?" asked her father.

"Oh, Daddy, of course I'll make room for Him at some point. I'm only 21. I have time."

After graduating from law school at the top of her class and passing the bar with ease, Donna landed a position at a prestigious law firm where she made partner in less than three years. She bought a house in the best neighborhood and had two luxury cars by age 30. At 35, Donna married Richard, a fellow lawyer, and two years later, with the first of what they expected would be three children on the way, they opened their own law firm.

Then the walls of Donna's perfectly complete life began to crumble. After Donna and Richard had to devote more time to their youngest daughter, who was born with a life-threatening disease, their practice folded. When the recession hit, they lost the house.

Many people, like Donna, are seeking that which perishes, but Jesus tells us that He offers the Bread of Life.

MAY 6th

—————— Keep in Mind ——————

"And Jesus said unto them, I am the bread of life: he that cometh to me shall never hunger; and he that believeth on me shall never thirst" (John 6:35).

"And Jesus said unto them, I am the bread of life: he that cometh to me shall never hunger; and he that believeth on me shall never thirst" (John 6:35).

Focal Verses

KJV **John 6:22** The day following, when the people which stood on the other side of the sea saw that there was none other boat there, save that one whereinto his disciples were entered, and that Jesus went not with his disciples into the boat, but that his disciples were gone away alone;

23 (Howbeit there came other boats from Tiberias nigh unto the place where they did eat bread, after that the Lord had given thanks:)

24 When the people therefore saw that Jesus was not there, neither his disciples, they also took shipping, and came to Capernaum, seeking for Jesus.

25 And when they had found him on the other side of the sea, they said unto him, Rabbi, when camest thou hither?

26 Jesus answered them and said, Verily, verily, I say unto you, Ye seek me, not because ye saw the miracles, but because ye did eat of the loaves, and were filled.

27 Labour not for the meat which perisheth, but for that meat which endureth unto everlasting life, which the Son of man shall give unto you: for him hath God the Father sealed.

28 Then said they unto him, What shall we do, that we might work the works of God?

29 Jesus answered and said unto them, This is the work of God, that ye believe on him whom he hath sent.

30 They said therefore unto him, What sign shewest thou then, that we may see, and believe thee? What dost thou work?

31 Our fathers did eat manna in the desert; as it is written, He gave them bread from heaven to eat.

32 Then Jesus said unto them, Verily, verily, I say unto you, Moses gave you not that

NLT **John 6:22** The next morning, back across the lake, crowds began gathering on the shore, waiting to see Jesus. For they knew that he and his disciples had come over together and that the disciples had gone off in their boat, leaving him behind.

23 Several boats from Tiberias landed near the place where the Lord had blessed the bread and the people had eaten.

24 When the crowd saw that Jesus wasn't there, nor his disciples, they got into the boats and went across to Capernaum to look for him.

25 When they arrived and found him, they asked, "Teacher, how did you get here?"

26 Jesus replied, "The truth is, you want to be with me because I fed you, not because you saw the miraculous sign.

27 But you shouldn't be so concerned about perishable things like food. Spend your energy seeking the eternal life that I, the Son of Man, can give you. For God the Father has sent me for that very purpose."

28 They replied, "What does God want us to do?"

29 Jesus told them, "This is what God wants you to do: Believe in the one he has sent."

30 They replied, "You must show us a miraculous sign if you want us to believe in you. What will you do for us?

31 After all, our ancestors ate manna while they journeyed through the wilderness! As the Scriptures say, 'Moses gave them bread from heaven to eat.'"

32 Jesus said, "I assure you, Moses didn't give them bread from heaven. My Father did. And now he offers you the true bread from heaven.

KJV Cont.

bread from heaven; but my Father giveth you the true bread from heaven.

33 For the bread of God is he which cometh down from heaven, and giveth life unto the world.

34 Then said they unto him, Lord, evermore give us this bread.

35 And Jesus said unto them, I am the bread of life: he that cometh to me shall never hunger; and he that believeth on me shall never thirst.

NLT Cont.

33 The true bread of God is the one who comes down from heaven and gives life to the world."

34 "Sir," they said, "give us that bread every day of our lives."

35 Jesus replied, "I am the bread of life. No one who comes to me will ever be hungry again. Those who believe in me will never thirst."

The People, Places, and Times

Capernaum. Located on the northwestern shore of the Sea of Galilee, Capernaum, a city in the Galilean province, was a central location for Jesus' earthly ministry. Jesus lived in Nazareth until He came to Galilee and was baptized by John the Baptist (Mark 1:9). After John the Baptist was imprisoned, Jesus returned to Galilee and resided in Capernaum (Matthew 4:12–16). Here, on the shore of the Sea of Galilee, the Lord called His first disciples—Peter, Andrew, James, and John (Matthew 4:18–22). Peter's home in Capernaum became the residence for Jesus and the apostles when they were not traveling (Mark 1:29; Luke 4:38). The Lord often preached in the synagogue in Capernaum (Mark 1:21; John 6:52–59) and performed many miracles in the city. These miracles included the healing of the centurion's servant (Matthew 8:5–13), the healing of the man with palsy (Mark 2:1–12), and the casting out of a demon in a man in the synagogue (Luke 4:31–36). After having performed so many miracles in Capernaum and the people still had not repented, Jesus said, "And you people of Capernaum, will you be honored in heaven? No, you will go down to the place of the dead. For if the miracles I did for you had been done in wicked Sodom, it would still be here today. I tell you, even Sodom will be better off on judgment day than you" (Matthew 11:23–24, NLT).

Bread. Bread was considered a staple in the ancient world. It was either baked in a loaf or round cake form. Barley bread usually was baked in the round form and was broken into pieces when eaten. It was barley bread that was used in the miraculous feeding of the 5,000 (John 6:9), indicating the crowd consisted of mostly poor people. In the Roman Empire, those with money could afford to make bread from wheat, but barley bread was relegated to the poor. The Romans had such a disdain for barley bread that soldiers regarded having to eat it as a punishment.

Background

In today's lesson, the day before coming to Capernaum, Jesus and His disciples had been on the other side of the Sea of Galilee. At this time in Jesus' earthly ministry, He was often surrounded by huge crowds, who were intrigued by the miracles He performed. The particular crowd in John 6 presented the occasion for another miracle—the feeding of the 5,000 with five loaves and two fish (John 6:1–13). The enthusiastic crowd wanted to make Jesus king in that moment.

The king they had in mind was one who would free them from Roman domination, restoring their national glory. They did not understand, even as Jesus compassionately satisfied their physical hunger, His deeper purpose was to show that He is the Messiah. He had come to make the way for eternal salvation. Consequently, Jesus slipped from the crowd and went to the hills to pray. In the night, the disciples boarded their boat and attempted to cross the sea, but they were embattled by a storm. Jesus came walking on the water to aid them, and when He entered the boat, the storm ceased (Matthew 14:22–35). The crowd that had dispersed earlier did not witness this miracle.

At-A-Glance

1. The Search for Jesus (John 6:22–25)

2. The Perishable Food (vv. 26–31)

3. The Bread of Life (vv. 32–35)

In Depth

1. The Search for Jesus (John 6:22–25)

Some of the crowd of the previous day had lingered in the night near the shore of the Sea of Galilee, fully expecting the next morning to see Jesus and witness more miracles. The crowd was very excited to have been fed the day before, so much so, that they wanted to make Jesus their king (John 6:14). The people expected Jesus to deliver them from Roman rule, just as they believed Moses had delivered their ancestors. You can imagine that as they desperately searched for Jesus, excitement was again welling up in their hearts, only to be dashed by the realization that He was not there. They were,

of course, disheartened by the prospect of not seeing Jesus, but also, on a very practical note, they would not get a meal, to which Jesus alludes later in the text. The people saw the disciples board the only boat the night before, and they remembered that Jesus had not left with them, but had gone to the mountains. By the time the people realized Jesus must have somehow left that side of the sea, boats from Tiberias had docked. So they took the boats across the sea to resume their search in Capernaum, the city known as Jesus' town (Matthew 9:1, Amplified Bible). Because Jesus could often be found teaching in the synagogue, the people knew where to find Him (see John 6:59). At the lakeshore, they addressed Him as Rabbi—a title of respect for Jewish teachers—and asked when He had arrived there. Though their inquiry seemed simple, their question also led to others: By what means had He arrived there since no one saw Him get on the boat with His disciples? Had they missed a miracle?

2. The Perishable Food (vv. 26–31)

Jesus, being a searcher of hearts (1 Chronicles 28:9; Jeremiah 17:10; Romans 8:27), knows every motivation. For this reason, He did not answer the questions the people asked, but instead addressed their true motive: "The truth is, you want to be with me because I fed you, not because you saw the miraculous sign" (John 6:26, NLT). Because many in the crowd were severely poor, the meal Jesus provided may have been the first in a long while in which they ate until full. In addition to the quantity of food, perhaps the quality was better than that to which they were accustomed. Barley bread was usually harsh on the stomach, but because Jesus had a hand in this meal, the quality was better. For example, Matthew Henry commented that just as the water Jesus turned into wine at the wedding in Cana was better than the wine initially served (John 2:9, 10), the food He provided here was "more than usually pleasant" (*Complete Commentary on the Whole Bible*). For this reason, the people diligently sought Jesus with the hope of having another good meal. However, Jesus told them not to be consumed with laboring for perishable food, or the things of this world, but rather focus on eternal life, the gift the Father had ordained Him to give. It is not that their physical needs were unimportant, but they needed to "seek first the kingdom of God and His righteousness" and trust that "all these things shall be added to you" (Matthew 6:33, NKJV). The people then wanted to know how they could do God's work and what tasks they must perform. Their question reflects their understanding that to please God was to do acts of the Law, but the Law could not save (Romans 8:3). Jesus told them the only work God wanted was for them to "believe in the one he has sent" (John 6:29, NIV).

3. The Bread of Life (vv. 32–35)

Jesus explained Himself yet again. The people were mistaken in believing Moses had given their ancestors manna. In fact, God had provided it for them. Manna was a precursor to the true Bread God was now giving them. It was of greater value than any food their ancestors received, because it more than sustains the body; this Bread provides eternal life, not just for the Jews but also for the whole world. However, the people were still focused on physical things. When they asked Jesus to give them this bread every day, they were talking about actual food. They had not perceived that Jesus spoke of the One whom God had sent to redeem them. Jesus is the Bread of Life who would make eternal life possible by fulfilling His messianic purpose. Anyone who would believe in Him would never hunger and thirst again. Manna sustained physically, but Jesus sustains spiritually, making the way for eternal redemption.

Search the Scriptures

1. How were the people able to reach Capernaum (John 6:23–24)?

2. What was the real reason the people were searching for Jesus (v. 26)?

3. Who is the Bead of Life, and what does He offer (vv. 33, 35)?

Discuss the Meaning

What are some very concrete ways we as Christians can illustrate in our lives that we believe Jesus is the Bread of Life and that knowing this is more important than any material gain?

Lesson in Our Society

There are certain things we need in order to function well in society: food, clothes, shelter, and an income. In and of themselves, these things are not bad. However, letting our pursuit of them consume our lives is the problem. Christians need these things too, but we must live with the understanding that Jesus, not material things, makes our lives complete. Make Him your focus always.

Make It Happen

In recent years, many people have lost much of their material wealth and their lives have spiraled out of control, as a result. It is a good time to witness to them, but make sure your life reflects your belief that Jesus is the Bread of Life. This week, be in constant prayer as you examine your life to ensure you are trusting in the Lord. Then also pray about to whom you can witness and the best way to witness to them.

Follow the Spirit

What God wants me to do:

_____

_____

_____

_____

Remember Your Thoughts

Special insights I have learned:

_____

_____

_____

_____

More Light on the Text

John 6:22–35

22 The day following, when the people which stood on the other side of the sea saw that there was none other boat there, save that one whereinto his disciples were entered, and that Jesus went not with his disciples into the boat, but that his disciples were gone away alone; 23 (Howbeit there came other boats from Tiberias nigh unto the place where they did eat bread, after that the Lord had given thanks:)

"The day following" in verse 22 refers to the miracle of the feeding of the 5,000 the day prior, which happened on the Tiberias side of the Sea of Galilee. Jesus had crossed over from Capernaum with the disciples in one boat. The crowd apparently did not miss this detail because when the disciples left in the same boat, they knew Jesus had not gone with them. In Matthew 14:22 and Mark 6:45,

it was Jesus who directed or "constrained" the disciples to return to the other side.

In the first century, boats were not nearly as prolific as they are today, and every arrival and departure was a memorable event. Now, via John's inserted parenthetical clarification, the crowd witnessed "other boats" returning to Tiberias, but Jesus was not on any of them either. The reference at the end of John 6:23 to Jesus having "given thanks" uses the Greek *eucharisteo* (**yoo-khar-is-TEH-o**), which is the same word used at the Last Supper (Matthew 26:27; Mark 14:23; Luke 22:17), and which captures the flavor and theme of the entire chapter, especially the verses following the lesson that speak specifically of Jesus' body and blood.

24 When the people therefore saw that Jesus was not there, neither his disciples, they also took shipping, and came to Capernaum, seeking for Jesus. 25 And when they had found him on the other side of the sea, they said unto him, Rabbi, when camest thou hither?

Not to be deterred, the crowd got into boats (not everyone; perhaps many) and went looking for Jesus. To their great surprise, because they had been carefully watching the coming and going of boats, Jesus was already on the Capernaum side. Even though they had just witnessed a major feeding miracle, they did not assume Jesus had crossed miraculously. In their thinking, He would have had to walk most of the night to get there by foot or found a boat they did not know about. What they did not even conceive of was that He had walked across the water to meet the disciples in the middle of the lake and then rode the rest of the way with them. This was another miracle—important to the context and symbolic of Jesus' ability to be present in any situation.

The collective account in the Gospels tells the whole story (Matthew 14:22–26; Mark 6:45–51; John 6:16–21). The disciples had been rowing across at dusk when the water typically was its choppiest. They seemed to have encountered a strong headwind and made little progress. They were only halfway, about 3.5 miles, when Jesus suddenly appeared. They knew the shore was nowhere near, so they assumed He had to be a ghost. The writer has crossed the Sea of Galilee in a boat, which took at least 30 minutes under the power of a diesel engine. Tenney captures the moment: "Jesus calmed their fears by speaking to them. When they recognized his voice, they were willing to take him into the boat" (Tenney, 73). Jesus had just proven His power over matter by feeding the 5,000, and now He proved His power over nature. He was eminently qualified for the teaching He was about to deliver. The version of the incident in Matthew captures the story of Peter walking on water (Matthew 14:28–31).

26 Jesus answered them and said, Verily, verily, I say unto you, Ye seek me, not because ye saw the miracles, but because ye did eat of the loaves, and were filled. 27 Labour not for the meat which perisheth, but for that meat which endureth unto everlasting life, which the Son of man shall give unto you: for him hath God the Father sealed.

When the crowd caught up with Jesus back on the Capernaum side, He began to teach them again, as was His custom and as He had done the entire day before. Jesus' message was similar to a previous word He had given to the Samaritan woman (John 4:7–15). Physical water only temporarily satisfies, but spiritual water gives eternal life. Likewise, physical food only temporarily satisfies (and also spoils), but spiritual food gives eternal life.

In verse 27, "labour" in the Greek is *ergazomai* (**er-GAD-zom-ahee**) and is the normal use, as in business, working for a goal or reward. In the next verse, the crowd zeroes in on the meaning. What the Father "sealed," which in the Greek is *sphragizo* (**sfrag-ID-zo**), the Father gave divine approval to (see also John 3:33). This event also is indicated but by a different word ("pleased") at Jesus' baptism (Matthew 3:17; see also John 1:32–34). *Sphragizo* is used for God's approval and safekeeping of the saints (2 Corinthians 1:22; Ephesians 1:13; 4:30).

28 Then said they unto him, What shall we do, that we might work the works of God? 29 Jesus answered and said unto them, This is the work of God, that ye believe on him whom he hath sent.

"Labour" in verse 27 and "work" here come from the same Greek word (*ergazomai*), but the phrase "works of God" in verse 28 uses the noun for "work," which is *ergon* (**ER-gon**), while *ergazomai* is a verb. Thus, it is a straightforward question, which Jesus answers just as directly. One can believe in biblical facts, concepts, and ethics about Jesus but still not have faith in Him. For many, the "work of God" is the hardest work of all because it requires belief—suspending disbelief, stifling mistrust, and ignoring fear. It is a courageous prayer of confidence, from a humble heart—not as easy as it sounds or everyone would believe. Verse 29 contains the Gospel message in a sentence. Jesus also may have referenced Malachi 3:1.

30 They said therefore unto him, What sign shewest thou then, that we may see, and believe thee? What dost thou work? 31 Our fathers did eat manna in the desert; as it is written, He gave them bread from heaven to eat.

This is quite an amazing question by the same crowd that just the day before had witnessed the miraculous feeding of more than 5,000 people. Yet the very next day they were asking for a sign, ironically pointing to the miraculous feeding of the Israelites in the desert as an example of what they wanted to see. It is as though they were saying, "Feeding this crowd was nothing compared to the crowd Moses fed, and food for one day is nothing compared to food for 40 years." What the crowd seemed to have forgotten was that in spite of the daily miracle in the desert, the Israelites quickly abandoned their faith. Their memory had been no better than that of the crowd Jesus faced. David Ball notes, "The crowd's misunderstanding of Jesus' sign becomes the basis for his explanation of the true understanding of the miracle" (Ball, 1996).

In John 6:31, "manna" in the Greek is *manna* (**MAN-nah**), and it refers specifically to the manna given to the Israelites in the desert, which also was kept in the Ark of the Covenant (see also "bread of God" and "food of God" in Leviticus 21:6, 8, 17). "Bread from heaven" in the Greek is *artos ouranos* (**AR-tos oo-ran-OS**), which as a phrase clearly has original language alliteration. Psalm 78:23–25 refers to the wilderness manna, calling it the corn of heaven and food of angels, raining down from the open doors of heaven. This manna from heaven in the wilderness prefigured the Bread of Life from heaven, which was Jesus.

32 Then Jesus said unto them, Verily, verily, I say unto you, Moses gave you not that bread from heaven; but my Father giveth you the true bread from heaven. 33 For the bread of God is he which cometh down from heaven, and giveth life unto the world.

In John 6:32, "true" in the Greek is *alethinos* (**a-lay-thee-NOS**), which means genuine or original; also veracious or sincere. Jesus reminded the people that Moses' bread was merely ordinary bread that had been provided miraculously; besides, it had not come from Moses but from God, who used Moses as His agent. The Israelites hadn't even been able to save it until the next day. And the next day they were hungry again. Jesus' bread was not like that (see also Deuteronomy 8:3). Both the bread from heaven and Jesus' true bread from heaven were gifts from God (see John 3:16), provided for all, and the permanent answer to their true hunger. Physical bread is needed to sustain physical life, but only spiritual bread can sustain spiritual life. As David Thomas wrote, "Men want bread, not theories of bread."

34 Then said they unto him, Lord, evermore give us this bread.

The response by the crowd was uncannily similar to the response of the Samaritan woman (John 4:15). Once the Samaritan woman heard about Jesus' living water, she wanted some. Likewise, once the crowd heard about Jesus' spiritual bread, and they wanted some.

35 And Jesus said unto them, I am the bread of life: he that cometh to me shall never hunger; and he that believeth on me shall never thirst.

The book of John uniquely contains six of these "I AM" statements by Jesus. Tenney writes, "Each represents a particular relationship of Jesus to the spiritual needs of men" (Tenney, 76). In order, the *bread of life* is spiritual food (John 6:35, 48, 51); the *light of the world* is for sight in spiritual darkness (John 8:12); the *door of the sheep* is for safety in a dangerous world (10:7–11); the *resurrection* is for power over death and eternal life (11:25); the *way, truth, and life* is for clarity and guidance in spiritual confusion (14:6); and the *true vine* is for spiritual nourishment (15:1). The bottom line in each instance of Jesus' messages is that He is the answer for their human needs. According to Tenney, "He desired that men should receive him not simply for what he might *give* them, but for what he might *be* to them" (Tenney, 76, emphasis added). Belief is a core theme of the sixth chapter (see also vv. 36, 40, 64, 69).

The conditions for receiving the Bread of Life are simple—no payment or work is needed; only the "work" of trust and belief. In the Gospel of John, Jesus stated six times that He was *the bread from heaven* and four times that He was *the bread of life*. He also repeatedly explained that eating regular bread still resulted in death, but eating spiritual bread resulted in eternal life.

Sources:
Alcock, Joan P. *Food in the Ancient World: Food through History.* Westport, CT: Greenwood Press, 2006. 33.
Ball, David M. *'I Am' in John's Gospel: Literary Function, Background & Theological Implications.* Sheffield, England: Sheffield Academic Press, 1996. 237.
Barrett, C. K. *The Gospel according to St. John: An Introduction with Commentary and Notes on the Greek Text.* 2nd ed. Philadelphia, PA: Westminster Press, 1978. 282.
Bruce, F. F. *The Gospel of John: Introduction, Exposition and Notes.* Grand Rapids, MI: William B. Eerdmans Publishing Company, 1983. 149–53.
Henry, Matthew. *Complete Commentary on the Whole Bible.* Bible Study Tools.com. http://www.biblestudytools.com/commentaries/matthew-henry-complete/john6.html (accessed January 10, 2011).
Lindars, Barnabas. *Behind the Fourth Gospel.* London, England: SPCK, 1971. 137.
Merriam-Webster Online Dictionary. http://www.merriam-webster.com/dictionary (accessed October 6, 2010).
Old and New Testament Concordances, Lexicons, Dictionaries, Commentaries, Images, and Bible Versions. Blue Letter Bible.org. http://www.blueletterbible.org/ (accessed July 10, 2010).
Strong's Concordance with Hebrew and Greek Lexicon. Eliyah.com. http://www.eliyah.com/lexicon.html (accessed October 4, 2010).
Tenney, Merrill C. *John, Acts. The Expositor's Bible Commentary, vol. 9.* Edited by Frank E. Gaebelein. Grand Rapids, MI: Zondervan, 1981. 70–78.

Say It Correctly

Capernaum. Kuh-PUHR-nee-uhm.
Galilee. GAL-uh-lee.
Manna. MAN-uh.
Sodom. SOD-uhm.
Tiberias. Ti-BIHR-ee-uhs.

Daily Bible Readings

MONDAY
Feeding the Hungry
(John 6:1–15)

TUESDAY
Walking on Water
(John 6:16–21)

WEDNESDAY
Giving Eternal Life
(John 6:36–40)

THURSDAY
Offering Living Bread
(John 6:41–51)

FRIDAY
The Life-Giving Spirit
(John 6:60–65)

SATURDAY
To Whom Can We Go?
(John 6:66–71)

SUNDAY
The True Bread of Heaven
(John 6:22–35)

Teaching Tips

Words You Should Know

A. Door (John 10:7) *thura* (Gk.)—A portal, gate, or entrance.

B. Shepherd (v. 11) *poimen* (Gk.)—A shepherd or pastor; used in this instance to illustrate Jesus' ownership and commitment to those who follow Him.

Teacher Preparation

Unifying Principle—Following Good Leaders. Jesus was a strong leader of people and was willing to give up His life to save them from spiritual harm.

A. Pray for lesson clarity.

B. Study the entire lesson.

C. Complete the companion lesson in the *Precepts For Living Personal Study Guide®*.

O—Open the Lesson

A. After taking prayer requests, open with prayer.

B. Read the subject of the lesson and the Keep in Mind verse in unison. Discuss.

C. Have a volunteer read the In Focus story. Discuss.

D. Ask students to share a time when they were aware of God's protection in their lives.

P—Present the Scriptures

A. Ask volunteers to read The People, Places, and Times and the Background sections. Discuss.

B. Divide the students into three groups. Reflecting on the At-A-Glance outline, assign each group an In Depth section to read silently and discuss within the groups.

C. Ask for one volunteer from each group to share the group's insights with the class.

E—Explore the Meaning

A. Do the Discuss the Meaning section.

B. Ask volunteers to: (1) explain the difference between the "shepherd" and the "hired hand," and (2) tell which one they would prefer to be and why.

C. Discuss the significance of the terms *thieves* and *robbers*.

N—Next Steps for Application

A. Read and discuss the Lesson in Our Society and Make It Happen sections.

B. Remind the students to read the Daily Bible Readings to prepare for next week's lesson.

C. End the class with prayer.

MAY 13th

Worship Guide

For the Superintendent or Teacher
Theme: The Good Shepherd
Theme Song:
"I Gave My Life for Thee"
Devotional Reading: Psalm 28
Prayer

The Good Shepherd

Bible Background • JOHN 10:1–18
Printed Text • JOHN 10:7–18 | Devotional Reading • PSALM 28

—————— Aim for Change ——————

By the end of the lesson, we will: DISCUSS why good leadership is important; TRUST and REJOICE that Jesus is the Good Shepherd; and DESCRIBE the characteristics of a good shepherd that we follow in others.

—————  In Focus —————

All eyes were on Kevin as he stood behind the microphone trembling. Kevin was the choir director for a world-renowned, inspirational gospel choir. But he had finally gotten up the nerve to tell his fellow choir members the truth.

"I've been deceiving all of you for quite some time now," Kevin began. He told about how he had almost died one night about a year ago when he overdosed on cocaine before a big gospel concert. Kevin began to cry as he recounted the fornication and debauchery that he had fallen into because of his drug abuse. He admitted that for the past several years, most of the time when the choir was performing, he was high on drugs. He ended his testimony by saying, "I was under God's protection through all those dangers, seen and unseen. I truly repented of my sins, and I admitted myself into a substance abuse program. I have been drug free for over nine months now, and I am thankful to God for His hedge of protection."

That night, Kevin's testimony had a greater effect on his fellow choir members than any of the millions of records they had sold.

Today's lesson reveals Christ as the Good Shepherd who invests great amounts of time to redeem His sheep and provide sustenance for all our needs.

————— Keep in Mind —————

"And when he putteth forth his own sheep, he goeth before them, and the sheep follow him: for they know his voice" (John 10:4).

"And when he putteth forth his own sheep, he goeth before them,
and the sheep follow him: for they know his voice" (John 10:4).

Focal Verses

KJV **John 10:7** Then said Jesus unto them again, Verily, verily, I say unto you, I am the door of the sheep.

8 All that ever came before me are thieves and robbers: but the sheep did not hear them.

9 I am the door: by me if any man enter in, he shall be saved, and shall go in and out, and find pasture.

10 The thief cometh not, but for to steal, and to kill, and to destroy: I am come that they might have life, and that they might have it more abundantly.

11 I am the good shepherd: the good shepherd giveth his life for the sheep.

12 But he that is an hireling, and not the shepherd, whose own the sheep are not, seeth the wolf coming, and leaveth the sheep, and fleeth: and the wolf catcheth them, and scattereth the sheep.

13 The hireling fleeth, because he is a hireling, and careth not for the sheep.

14 I am the good shepherd, and know my sheep, and am known of mine.

15 As the Father knoweth me, even so know I the Father: and I lay down my life for the sheep.

16 And other sheep I have, which are not of this fold: them also I must bring, and they shall hear my voice; and there shall be one fold, and one shepherd.

17 Therefore doth my Father love me, because I lay down my life, that I might take it again.

18 No man taketh it from me, but I lay it down of myself. I have power to lay it down, and I have power to take it again. This commandment have I received of my Father.

NLT **John 10:7** so he explained it to them. "I assure you, I am the gate for the sheep," he said.

8 "All others who came before me were thieves and robbers. But the true sheep did not listen to them.

9 Yes, I am the gate. Those who come in through me will be saved. Wherever they go, they will find green pastures.

10 The thief's purpose is to steal and kill and destroy. My purpose is to give life in all its fullness.

11 "I am the good shepherd. The good shepherd lays down his life for the sheep.

12 A hired hand will run when he sees a wolf coming. He will leave the sheep because they aren't his and he isn't their shepherd. And so the wolf attacks them and scatters the flock.

13 The hired hand runs away because he is merely hired and has no real concern for the sheep.

14 "I am the good shepherd; I know my own sheep, and they know me,

15 just as my Father knows me and I know the Father. And I lay down my life for the sheep.

16 I have other sheep, too, that are not in this sheepfold. I must bring them also, and they will listen to my voice; and there will be one flock with one shepherd.

17 "The Father loves me because I lay down my life that I may have it back again.

18 No one can take my life from me. I lay down my life voluntarily. For I have the right to lay it down when I want to and also the power to take it again. For my Father has given me this command."

The People, Places, and Times

The Shepherd. Jesus pointed out that the most important trait of the good shepherd is that he lays down his life for the sheep. A shepherd's life could at times be dangerous. Wild animals were common in the countryside of Judea, and oftentimes the shepherd had to risk life and limb to save his sheep.

The Sheepfold. In biblical times, a communal sheepfold held everyone's sheep at night. A strong door protected the sheepfold, and only the guardian of the door had a key.

Background

Jesus described Himself as both the "good shepherd" and the "door" (John 10:7, 9, 14). As a good shepherd, He owned His sheep and was not a hired hand. As owner, the shepherd was on intimate terms with his sheep; that is, he knew their names and personalities. He invested great amounts of time in the sheep. Unlike the hired hand, the owner will give his life, if necessary, to save his sheep from wolves or other predators.

Jesus also described Himself as the "door" through which one must come to become one of His sheep. There was normally only one entrance into the sheep pen, which reduced the likelihood of unwanted persons entering and harming the sheep.

The door is the main entrance. Jesus explained that anyone who tried to get in any other way besides going through the gate (door) would be a thief—that person would be up to no good. In this passage, Jesus compares Himself to a shepherd who enters the gate; Jesus went on to say that only the shepherd enters through the gate. Only the shepherd has the right to enter the sheepfold and call his own sheep out to follow him.

When the shepherd arrived, he would call his own sheep by name. Because sheep recognize the voice of their shepherd, they follow him out to pasture. Just as a sheep would respond to the voice of the shepherd calling its name, when the Good Shepherd Jesus came, all believers recognized His voice and followed Him.

At-A-Glance

1. Jesus Is the Devoted and Dedicated Shepherd (John 10:7–14)

2. Jesus Knows His Sheep (vv. 15–16)

3. Jesus Is the Good Shepherd (vv. 17–18)

In Depth

1. Jesus Is the Devoted and Dedicated Shepherd (John 10:7–14)

These verses consist of a series of four "I am" statements. These statements reveal who Jesus is in relationship to those that follow Him. There are four characteristics that set this good shepherd apart from the thief or robber: (1) He approaches directly—He enters at the gate; (2) He has God's authority—the gatekeeper allows Him to enter; (3) He is trustworthy and meets real needs—the sheep recognize His voice and follow Him; and (4) He has sacrificial love—He is willing to lay down His life for the sheep.

At the same time, there is also a vast difference between the good shepherd, the thief, and the hired hand. The thief comes to steal, kill, and destroy the sheep. The hired hand protects the sheep, but does the job only for money and quickly flees when danger comes. In contrast, the "good" shepherd is committed to the sheep. Jesus is not merely doing a job; He is committed to loving us and even laying down His life for us.

2. Jesus Knows His Sheep (vv. 15–16)

Jesus' followers know Him to be their Messiah—they love and trust Him. Such knowledge and trust between Jesus and His followers is compared to the relationship between Jesus and the Father. Thus, Jesus is the Good Shepherd, not only because of His relationship with the sheep, but also because of His relationship with God the Father.

In verse 16, Jesus tells the Pharisees that He has other sheep. By using this metaphor, Jesus is letting the Pharisees know that He came to save Gentiles as well as Jews. This is an insight into Jesus' worldwide mission: to die for sinful people all over the world. The new Gentile believers and the Jewish believers would form one flock and have one Shepherd.

3. Jesus Is the Good Shepherd (vv. 17-18)

Here, Jesus abandons the sheep metaphor and speaks directly about His relationship with God. Jesus laid down His life of His own accord, and of His own accord He would also take it up again in resurrection. Jesus was living out God's commission (John 3:16). When Jesus said He laid down His life voluntarily and that He had the power to take it up again, He was claiming His authority to control His own death and resurrection.

Jesus, the Good Shepherd, has the best interests of His sheep in mind at all times. He is on constant guard to keep His sheep upright and in the fold. He is prepared to meet every need and even to give His life to rescue the sheep from danger. As the Good Shepherd, He protects us from danger and provides for our sustenance. Like the Pharisees of Jesus'

day, we need to be reminded that it was Jesus' choice to give up His life; it was not taken from Him. It is because of His sacrifice that we can have eternal life. The Son's authority to lay down His life and take it up again did not originate with Himself; it came from the Father.

Search the Scriptures

1. What was Jesus' promise to those who enter through the door (John 10:9)?

2. Why did the "hireling" leave sheep in the face of trouble (v. 13)?

3. How did Jesus plan to save the other sheep (v. 16)?

Discuss the Meaning

1. Why did Jesus refer to Himself as the "door" (John 10:9)?

2. Who were Jesus' other sheep (v. 16)?

3. How can we identify God's protective voice amidst all the perilous voices?

Lesson in Our Society

We live in a society where people make daily decisions to live by pleasure principles rather than God's principles. Such pleasure principles lead to acts of adultery, stealing, debauchery, deceitfulness, and so on. Jesus died to rescue us from these pitfalls. God commands us to live for Him and in Him.

As the Good Shepherd, Jesus cares for us and protects us from evil. Yet many of us are living outside of the door of His will. What changes are you willing to make in order to know the voice of the Good Shepherd?

Make It Happen

People seek protection from those things that pose a threat to their well-being. Think about your own life. Into what category do you fall? Have you followed the voice of the Good Shepherd, Jesus Christ, our Lord and Savior, for protection? If you have, thank God for opening your ears, your heart, and your eyes so that you recognize the voice of the Good Shepherd. Or are you a hired hand, a thief, or a robber? If you are a leader, do you only care about yourself? If so, ask God to strengthen you so that you might know the voice of the Shepherd and follow Him when He calls.

Follow the Spirit

What God wants me to do:

_____

_____

_____

_____

Remember Your Thoughts

Special insights I have learned:

_____

_____

_____

_____

More Light on the Text

John 10:7–18

7 Then said Jesus unto them again, Verily, verily, I say unto you, I am the door of the sheep.

In the first six verses of this chapter, Jesus has spoken to the Pharisees' situation figuratively. He realized His audience would certainly understand the inferences to be drawn from the illustration of the shepherd/sheep relationship; unfortunately, they missed the spiritual lesson Jesus was trying to teach. So Jesus shifts metaphors and declares,

"I am the door of the sheep." Again, Jesus' hearers would be familiar with the figure of a shepherd as a "door" (Gk. *thura*, **THOO-rah**) of the sheep. Since shepherds habitually lie down across the entrance of the sheepfold with their bodies forming a barrier to thieves and wild beasts, they speak of themselves as the door to let the flock in or out and to protect the flock from intruders. Through the door, the flock goes in and out to graze and to rest. If attacked or frightened, the sheep can retreat into the security of the fold.

Several times in the Gospel of John, Jesus describes Himself using the phrase "I am" (Gk. *ego eimi*, **eg-O i-MEE**; cf. John 6:35; 8:12, 58; 9:5). Christ's usage of *ego eimi* in this manner leaves no question about His claim to deity. In fact, to a perceptive Jew who understood the term *ego eimi* as used in Exodus 3:14, Jesus was making Himself equal to God (cf. John 10:33).

8 All that ever came before me are thieves and robbers: but the sheep did not hear them.

This verse is not a reference to Old Testament prophets, but to all messianic pretenders and religious charlatans, like many of the Pharisees and chief priests of the time. Here, Jesus describes them as "thieves" (Gk. *kleptes*, **KLEP-tace**) who divest the unwary of their precious possessions, and "robbers" (Gk. *lestes*, **lace-TACE**) who plunder brazenly by violence. They were the type that did not care about the spiritual good of the people, but only about themselves. As a result, the sheep (i.e., those who are faithful) would not heed their voice.

9 I am the door: by me if any man enter in, he shall be saved, and shall go in and out, and find pasture.

Christ claims to be *the* door, not just *a* door. Jesus is explicitly identifying Himself here as the means to salvation (cf. Psalm 118:19–21). As the Shepherd, Jesus provides safety and sustenance for His flock. He is the only way of salvation. Through Him, believers find "pasture" (Gk. *nome*, **nom-AY**) or provision for all of their daily needs.

10 The thief cometh not, but for to steal, and to kill, and to destroy: I am come that they might have life, and that they might have it more abundantly.

The thief's motive is diametrically opposed to that of the shepherd. His interest is selfish. He steals the sheep in order to kill them and feed himself, thus destroying part of the flock. In this description, we see a veiled glimpse into the character of the Pharisees and religious authorities who opposed Jesus. In contrast, Christ is the Life-Giver and Life-Sustainer. His interest is the welfare of the sheep. He enables the sheep to have full and secure lives. Conversely, the thief takes life, but Christ gives life abundantly.

11 I am the good shepherd: the good shepherd giveth his life for the sheep.

The adjective "good" (Gk. *kalos*, **kal-OS**) carries the meaning of being a true or a model shepherd. Here, Jesus is referring to the model of a shepherd found in Ezekiel 34:11–16. According to Ezekiel, the good shepherd gathers, feeds, and protects the sheep. A strong bond exists between sheep and shepherd. It was not unusual for Palestinian shepherds to risk their lives for their flocks. Wild beasts, lions, jackals, wolves, and bears were on the prowl. In his experience as a shepherd, David's fights with

a lion and a bear over the life of his flock convinced him that God was also able to give Goliath into his hands (1 Samuel 17:34–37). When Jesus says in John 10:11, "I am the good shepherd" (i.e., the true Shepherd), He is expressing the manner in which He carries out His mission of salvation.

12 But he that is an hireling, and not the shepherd, whose own the sheep are not, seeth the wolf coming, and leaveth the sheep, and fleeth: and the wolf catcheth them, and scattereth the sheep.

A "hireling" (Gk. *misthotos*, **mis-tho-TOS**), or hired servant, denotes someone who both has no real interest in his duty and is unfaithful in the discharge of it. As a wage earner, a hireling's interest is in the money he makes and in self-preservation. He has no real commitment to the sheep. Therefore, if a wolf shows up, he runs to save his own life, leaving the sheep to fend for themselves. The result is devastating for the sheep. His carelessness exposes the flock to fatal danger. As is the case today, Israel (the Old Testament church) had many false religious leaders, selfish kings, and imitation messiahs; as a result, the flock of God suffered constantly from their abuse.

13 The hireling fleeth, because he is a hireling, and careth not for the sheep. 14 I am the good shepherd, and know my sheep, and am known of mine.

The "hireling" (Gk. *misthotos*) is just that—a hired hand. The image of the hired hand is reflective of Israel's selfish kings and false prophets found in the Old Testament (Ezekiel 34:5–6; Jeremiah 23:1–3; Zechariah 11:15, 17). Both here and in the Old Testament passages, the hired hand's main concern is for himself. The sheep are only a means to an end.

By contrast, the "good" (Gk. *kalos*, **kal-OS**, meaning "noble" or "true") shepherd cares for the sheep—so much so that he is willing to lay down his life for them. It is important to note that there is a bond of intimacy between the shepherd and his sheep, as indicated by the phrase in John 10:14, "I . . . know" (Gk. *ginosko*, **ghin-OCE-ko**). The use of the Greek word *ginosko* implies Christ's ownership and watchful oversight of the sheep. The reciprocal point that the sheep know their shepherd identifies the sheep's response to Christ's love and intimate care. Moreover, the use of *ginosko* indicates that this knowledge is of high value to the shepherd.

15 As the Father knoweth me, even so know I the Father: and I lay down my life for the sheep.

The deep mutual knowledge between Christ (the Shepherd) and His sheep is likened to the relationship between the Father and the Son. God the Father and Jesus, His Son, "know" one another (v. 15, NLT); they have a uniquely intimate relationship. The connection between the sheep and the shepherd who knows his sheep and lays down his life for them shows unity of purpose between the Father and the Son. Jesus is more than the Good Shepherd; He is the fulfillment of God's promises to God's people. Christ voluntarily laid down His life for us. His death was not an unfortunate accident, but part of the planned purpose of God.

16 And other sheep I have, which are not of this fold: them also I must bring, and they shall hear my voice; and there shall be one fold, and one shepherd.

Jesus was addressing His immediate audience—those already in the fold, the Israelites who believed. But the phrase "other sheep" (Gk. *allos probaton*, **AL-los PROB-at-on**) is a direct reference to the Jews and Gentiles who had not yet come to believe. Therefore, they were still outside of Jesus' protection. The fold, then, is a metaphor for God's covenant people—the church—and none other than the Shepherd Jesus will gather His sheep together into one fold. As they hear His voice, His people from among Jews and Gentiles will come and be formed into one body of Christ as one flock with one Shepherd. There is one people of God, comprised of believers inside and outside of ethnic Israel.

17 Therefore doth my Father love me, because I lay down my life, that I might take it again.

Jesus reaffirms the love the Father has for Him and picks up again on the theme of His death and resurrection. He will voluntarily lay down His life for the salvation of the world. The Father's "love" (Gk. *agapao*, **ag-ap-AH-o**) is linked with the Son's willingness to lay down His life for the world. The mutual love of the Father and Son come together in one divine purpose of salvation for humankind. The Father in love arranged for the salvation of His people, and the Son in love freely gave His all to accomplish salvation for His people. Naturally, the Father's everlasting love always endures for the Son. However, His death is the supreme manifestation of His sacrificial obedience to the will of God the Father.

18 No man taketh it from me, but I lay it down of myself. I have power to lay it down, and I have power to take it again. This commandment have I received of my Father.

In choosing to die for the sins of the world, Jesus once again proved His sovereign authority over His own destiny. If Christ had not chosen to die, no one would have had the power to kill Him. The work of redemption is done by the Father through the Son. Jesus laid down His life in order to take it up again. In Jesus' death, the penalty for sin is paid in full, and the Resurrection is the vindication of the Son as the atonement for sin. In death, the Son becomes the sacrifice for our sins and reconciles us to God. In resurrection, the Son is glorified and the victory of God's kingdom is announced.

Sources:
New Testament Greek Lexicon. Bible Study Tools.com. http://www.biblestudytools.com/lexicons/greek (accessed January 10, 2011).
Passage Lookup. Bible Gateway.com. http://www.bible-gateway.com/passage (accessed January 10, 2011).

Say It Correctly

Debauchery. De-BAW-cher-e.
Ezekiel. E-ZEE-ke-el.
Palestinian. Pal-e-STIN-e-en.

Daily Bible Readings

MONDAY
Sheep without a Shepherd
(2 Chronicles 18:12–22)

TUESDAY
A New Shepherd for Israel
(Numbers 27:12–20)

WEDNESDAY
The Shepherd David
(Psalm 78:67–72)

THURSDAY
Lord, Be Our Shepherd
(Psalm 28)

FRIDAY
Shepherd of Israel, Restore Us
(Psalm 80:1–7)

SATURDAY
The Sheep Follow
(John 10:1–6)

SUNDAY
I Am the Good Shepherd
(John 10:7–18)

Notes

_____

_____

_____

_____

Teaching Tips

Words You Should Know

A. Resurrection (John 11:25) *anastasis* (Gk.)—A rising from the dead.

B. Life (v. 25) *zoe* (Gk.)—Denotes life in the fullest sense; life as God has it.

C. Believeth (v. 25) *pisteuo* (Gk.)—To put confidence in; to trust or be persuaded.

Teacher Preparation

Unifying Principle—Life That Does Not End. People often think that death separates us from everything we know. Jesus promised that those who believe in Him will—even though they die—have a new relationship with God.

A. Prepare for this lesson by reading the entire lesson.

B. Meditate on the Keep in Mind verse, and ask the Lord to give you a clear understanding of His Word.

C. Complete the companion lesson in the *Precepts For Living Personal Study Guide®*.

O—Open the Lesson

A. Take prayer requests and open with prayer.

B. Read the poem from the In Focus section. Discuss.

C. Pray that the Lord would use the class time to speak through His Word to the hearts of His people.

P—Present the Scriptures

A. Ask for volunteers to read the Focal Verses; The People, Places, and Times; Background; and In Depth sections aloud.

B. Answer the Search the Scriptures questions. Discuss.

E—Explore the Meaning

A. Answer Discuss the Meaning questions in class.

B. Have the students read the Lesson in Our Society section. Then ask them to give examples of times when the Lord demonstrated His power in their lives.

N—Next Steps for Application

A. Read the Make It Happen section, and challenge the students to take any hopeless situation that they may currently face to the Lord.

B. Instruct the class to read the Daily Bible Readings in preparation for next week's lesson.

C. Close with prayer.

Worship Guide

For the Superintendent or Teacher
Theme: The Resurrection
and the Life
Theme Song: "The Strife Is O'er"
Devotional Reading:
1 Corinthians 15:50–58
Prayer

MAY 20th

The Resurrection and the Life

Bible Background • JOHN 11:1–27
Printed Text • JOHN 11:17–27 | Devotional Reading • 1 CORINTHIANS 15:50–58

—————— Aim for Change ——————

By the end of the lesson, we will: DISCUSS what the Resurrection and the Life in Christ means for us; RECALL a time when we experienced joy in a situation that looked hopeless; and SHARE with others the Good News that Jesus is the Resurrection and the Life.

———— In Focus ————

The Power of God

Dear Lord,

Your Resurrection Power makes possible the impossible. You and only You have just what we need: Power to live a holy life, Power to walk with You and succeed. You can re-create us, make us new creations inside out; make us all brand new. You can deliver the inner man so that we are blessed in all that we do.

Thank You for making Your power available to us! Thank You for the Cross. Without Your love and tender mercy, we would be forever lost. Amen.

—Evangeline Carey

Jesus is the Resurrection and the Life. In the book of John, we are reminded that He is the Giver of physical as well as spiritual life.

—————— Keep in Mind ——————

"Jesus said unto her, I am the resurrection, and the life: he that believeth in me, though he were dead, yet shall he live" (John 11:25).

"Jesus said unto her, I am the resurrection, and the life: he that believeth in me, though he were dead, yet shall he live" (John 11:25).

Focal Verses

KJV **John 11:17** Then when Jesus came, he found that he had lain in the grave four days already.

18 Now Bethany was nigh unto Jerusalem, about fifteen furlongs off:

19 And many of the Jews came to Martha and Mary, to comfort them concerning their brother.

20 Then Martha, as soon as she heard that Jesus was coming, went and met him: but Mary sat still in the house.

21 Then said Martha unto Jesus, Lord, if thou hadst been here, my brother had not died.

22 But I know, that even now, whatsoever thou wilt ask of God, God will give it thee.

23 Jesus saith unto her, Thy brother shall rise again.

24 Martha saith unto him, I know that he shall rise again in the resurrection at the last day.

25 Jesus said unto her, I am the resurrection, and the life: he that believeth in me, though he were dead, yet shall he live:

26 And whosoever liveth and believeth in me shall never die. Believest thou this?

27 She saith unto him, Yea, Lord: I believe that thou art the Christ, the Son of God, which should come into the world.

NLT **John 11:17** When Jesus arrived at Bethany, he was told that Lazarus had already been in his grave for four days.

18 Bethany was only a few miles down the road from Jerusalem,

19 and many of the people had come to pay their respects and console Martha and Mary on their loss.

20 When Martha got word that Jesus was coming, she went to meet him. But Mary stayed at home.

21 Martha said to Jesus, "Lord, if you had been here, my brother would not have died.

22 But even now I know that God will give you whatever you ask."

23 Jesus told her, "Your brother will rise again."

24 "Yes," Martha said, "when everyone else rises, on resurrection day."

25 Jesus told her, "I am the resurrection and the life. Those who believe in me, even though they die like everyone else, will live again.

26 They are given eternal life for believing in me and will never perish. Do you believe this, Martha?"

27 "Yes, Lord," she told him. "I have always believed you are the Messiah, the Son of God, the one who has come into the world from God."

The People, Places, and Times

Martha. It is thought by some scholars that Martha was the elder sister of Mary and Lazarus. This is because she is referred to as the owner of the house (Luke 10:38). In an earlier meeting with Jesus, it was Martha who became distraught when her sister Mary sat at Jesus' feet instead of helping her serve (Luke 10:39–42).

Bethany. This is a village on the eastern slope of the Mount of Olives, two miles east of Jerusalem. It appears that Jesus preferred to lodge there instead of in Jerusalem. Today, it is known as *el-Azariyeh* (i.e., "place of Lazarus").

Background

Only in the book of John do we find the recounting of Jesus raising Lazarus from the dead. This is a family that Jesus loved, and He was loved by them. When He needed a rest, He knew He could find it with these three adults.

At-A-Glance

1. Jesus Is in Control
(John 11:17–20)

2. Jesus Is Always Right on Time
(vv. 21–24)

3. Jesus Is the Resurrection and the Life
(vv. 25–27)

In Depth

1. Jesus Is in Control (John 11:17–20)

At the start of John 11, Martha and Mary notify Jesus that their brother Lazarus is very sick (v. 3). But instead of rushing to Bethany, Jesus stays where He is for two more days. In biblical times, it was common to bury the dead either on the same day or very close to the time of death. It was also believed that a person's soul hovered around the body for three days after physical death. But by the time Jesus finally arrives in Bethany, Lazarus has been dead four days.

Obviously, Jesus was not in a rush to get to Bethany. He informs His disciples that Lazarus is in fact dead and that He is glad that He was not there to keep Lazarus from dying, so that they may believe (John 11:15). This statement shapes the theological heart of today's lesson.

When Jesus arrives in Bethany, Lazarus had already been dead four days. The professional mourners had arrived, and the situation looked hopeless to the human eye. Everything around Martha and Mary was telling them that it was time to give up hope—that there was nothing more to be done. Mary and Martha must have begun to wonder whether Jesus had forgotten about them or, worse yet, had decided not to do anything about their brother's condition. But in John 11:14, Jesus provides confirmation that He is well aware of Lazarus' condition. He knows exactly what is taking place in the lives of Mary and Martha. But why does He linger and not rush to the scene? Could it be that He waited to demonstrate His power until all hope in human effort was exhausted? Ultimately, Jesus is in complete control of the situation. His delay is for the benefit of His disciples and Lazarus' sisters, Martha and Mary, so they may come to trust in the Lord with all their hearts, instead of leaning on their own understanding (compare [cf.] Proverbs 3:5).

Jesus wants us to put our complete confidence in Him because He is in control of all the affairs of life. When things look bad and we cannot see any way out, Jesus wants us to run to Him, like Martha, and place all of our trust in Him alone.

2. Jesus Is Always Right on Time (vv. 21–24)

Martha expects Jesus to do something. She says, "'Lord, if You had been here, my brother would not have died'" (John 11:21, NKJV). Mary also challenged Jesus. "Then when Mary was come where Jesus was, and saw him, she fell down at his feet, saying unto him, Lord, if thou hadst been here, my brother had not died" (John 11:32, KJV). Some scholars suggest that Martha's remarks to Jesus were ones of reproach instead of words of grief. Some consider Martha a woman of practical duty, eager to put everybody in their rightful place. After all, it was Martha who questioned Jesus regarding her sister Mary's lack of service when Jesus visited their home (see Luke 10:38–41). But here in John 11:22, we realize that Martha's faith in Jesus' ability to heal her brother is undiminished. She tells Jesus, "I know" that God will do whatever we ask, which implies that intuitively Martha's assessment of Jesus is that of a righteous man to whom God listens and for whom nothing is impossible.

In response to Martha's statement, Jesus tells her, "Thy brother shall rise again" (v. 23). Judging from Martha's response to Jesus, it appears that she is disappointed. She says, "'I know that he will rise again in the resurrection on the last day'" (v. 24, ESV). Martha's response to the Master implies that she does not yet grasp the full implication of what Jesus was saying. She understood that in the "last day" all would rise, but Martha yearned for a more immediate solution—she wanted her brother back!

Initially, the way Martha addressed Jesus is similar to how we often address Him when things do not go the way we think they should. Oftentimes we ask, "Lord, where were You? If You would have showed up when I called You, this might not have happened." The Lord may not show up when we think He ought to, but we can be sure that He is always right on time.

3. Jesus Is the Resurrection and the Life (vv. 25–27)

When Jesus heard Martha's reply, He responded to her by stating emphatically, "I am the resurrection and the life" (v. 25, NIV). In essence, Jesus was telling Martha, "You keep looking forward to some event in the future, but what you are looking for is standing right in front of you." Jesus challenged Martha to place her trust in Him as the One who holds the power of life and death in His hands.

The word Jesus used for "life" is the Greek word *zoe* (**dzo-AY**), which speaks of life in the fullest sense. Jesus has the power to give life because He is Life itself. The power that Jesus has extends beyond merely the physical; He also holds the power to give life to the spiritually dead. Ephesians 2:1 (NKJV) says that we "were dead in trespasses and sins," and God "made us alive" or raised us from our spiritual death (2:5). On another occasion, addressing a mob of angry Jews, Jesus said, "For as the Father raises the dead and gives them life, so also the Son gives life to whom he will" (John 5:21, ESV). The Lord wants us to know that all power in heaven and on earth is in Jesus' hand (Matthew 28:18), and for this reason we should place all of our trust in Him.

Placing faith in Jesus has implications for the present and is not relegated to some "pie in the sky, we'll do better in the sweet by and by" mind-set. Jesus wants to effect change in our lives right now. As Christians, we must reach the point where our trust in Christ transcends our understanding of the world around us. When things look impossible from a human perspective, we cannot let this diminish our faith in the One who "upholds the universe by the word of his power" (Hebrews 1:3, ESV). Jesus cares about the troubles of our lives, and more important than that, He has the power and desire to do something about it.

Search the Scriptures

1. What is the first thing Martha says to Jesus when she meets Him (John 11:21)?

2. How does Martha understand Jesus' words about her brother rising again (v. 24)?

3. What does Jesus say are the results of believing in Him (vv. 25–26)?

4. What is Martha's response to Jesus' statement in verses 25 and 26 (v. 27)?

Discuss the Meaning

1. Jesus tells Martha, "Your brother will rise again" (John 11:23, NIV), and raises him from death that same day. Do you think that Jesus wants to demonstrate His resurrecting power in our lives even today? Give some examples of His power at work in your life.

2. What did Jesus mean when He said, "He who believes in me will live, even though he dies" (from John 11:25, NIV)? How does this affect our lives right now?

3. Why is it important not to panic or jump to conclusions when faced with a difficult situation? How might those kinds of reactions affect your walk?

Lesson in Our Society

When a wife gave birth to her son, she had complications that threatened her life. Her uterus ruptured, and she was losing a tremendous amount of blood. The doctors were doing everything they could, but the situation was looking worse by the minute. Her husband had a choice to make: either put his hope solely in the impersonal practices of medical science or primarily trust in the personal Lord and Savior, Jesus Christ. He expected the physicians to do their best, but he relied on the Lord for the healing. When faced with tough circumstances, let us look to Jesus, the One who is able not only to raise us from the dead, but also to powerfully intervene in the dead circumstances of our lives.

Make It Happen

We have all been in situations that looked hopeless. Undoubtedly, we have been tempted to give up hope and count our losses. Think about some of the times that you have given up hope and the Lord came in and "resurrected" the situation. Think about the effect this had on you and what effect it should have on your faith.

Follow the Spirit

What God wants me to do:

_____

_____

_____

_____

Remember Your Thoughts

Special insights I have learned:

_____

_____

_____

_____

More Light on the Text

John 11:17–27

17 Then when Jesus came, he found that he had lain in the grave four days already. 18 Now Bethany was nigh unto Jerusalem, about fifteen furlongs off: 19 And many of the Jews came to Martha and Mary, to comfort them concerning their brother.

Lazarus had been dead and buried for four days. Bethany (now called *el-Azariyeh*, or "place of Lazarus") is approximately two miles east of Jerusalem. This fact is significant because it shows how close Jesus was to Jerusalem. The nearness of Bethany to Jerusalem accounts for the large presence of Jews at the scene of this miracle. Jewish custom provided for a 30-day period of mourning. To console the bereaved during this period of mourning was considered a pious act among the Jews. Here, John draws attention to two things. First, Jesus' proximity to Jerusalem would have allowed Him to get to Lazarus' house within the first three days of his death. Second, because Bethany was so close to Jerusalem, there were many Jews present to witness the great miracle that was about to take place.

20 Then Martha, as soon as she heard that Jesus was coming, went and met him: but Mary sat still in the house.

Upon hearing of Jesus' arrival, Martha hastened to meet Him, while Mary sat in the house. The different responses of Martha and Mary may indicate their personality types: Martha was the outgoing activist and Mary was the contemplative type. It can also be said that because Martha was the older of the two sisters, it was her duty to go out to meet Jesus, while Mary stayed home to continue the mourning rituals with the other mourners.

21 Then said Martha unto Jesus, Lord, if thou hadst been here, my brother had not died. 22 But I know, that even now, whatsoever thou wilt ask of God, God will give it thee.

Martha's words were a confession of her faith in the Lord; they were not intended as a reproach of Jesus, but were the response of a person in great grief. It is probable that the sisters expressed the same ideas to one another as they awaited the coming of Jesus.

Martha believed that through Christ nothing was impossible with God. She firmly believed that Jesus would have saved Lazarus from death had He been present. But even now that Lazarus was dead, she believed that Jesus could still bring him back to life. In verse 22, the use of the phrase "thou wilt ask" (Gk. *aiteo*, **ahee-TEH-o**), which means "desire, call for, or crave" implies that she hoped that Jesus would and that He should pray for an immediate resurrection in spite of Lazarus' decomposing body.

23 Jesus saith unto her, Thy brother shall rise again. 24 Martha saith unto him, I know that he shall rise again in the resurrection at the last day.

The phrase "shall rise" (Gk. *anistemi*, **an-IS-tay-mee**) means to "stand up." This statement has a double meaning. It relates to the recall of Lazarus from death to life that was about to take place, as well as to his final resurrection at the close of time. Martha seems to understand Jesus' words to mean that her brother will rise again during the last days. If she understood Jesus' words only in this sense, the assumption is that she had no thought of Lazarus' immediate resurrection (v. 22).

25 Jesus said unto her, I am the resurrection, and the life: he that believeth in me, though he were dead, yet shall he live: 26 And whosoever liveth and believeth in me shall never die. Believest thou this?

Like most Jews, Martha believed in the final resurrection of the dead and the coming rule of God. Therefore, when Jesus stated, "I am the resurrection, and the life," He was saying that the promise of resurrection and life is not only some future event, but also was immediately available. To Martha, this would have been a startlingly new revelation. Christ embodies that kingdom with all of its blessings for humankind for which Martha and her people hoped. The power to initiate eternal life and resurrection through which humankind may gain entry into life resides in Jesus. This revelation was both an assurance of resurrection to the eschatological kingdom of God and of life in the present through Him who is Life.

It was crucial that Martha grasp the full importance of what Christ was about to do for Lazarus. In Christ, death will never triumph over the believer. Moreover, Jesus was saying that the person who believes in Him, though they die, will live; and the person who lives and believes in Him will never die.

In verse 26, Jesus asks Martha a question that is the basis for determining her faith and the faith of all believers. Jesus asked, "Believest thou this?" Jesus was asking Martha if she had the faith to believe what He said. Did she believe that He (Jesus) is the Resurrection, and that He has the power of life over death? That is, does she believe in His sovereignty? Unless a person believes in Jesus and His Word, the eternal life He offers cannot be found.

27 She saith unto him, Yea, Lord: I believe that thou art the Christ, the Son of God, which should come into the world.

Here, Martha's reply is a full-fledged confession of her faith in Jesus. In her confession, Martha states, "I believe" (Gk. *pisteuo*, **pist-YOO-o**), which means "accept as true, be persuaded of, credit, or place confidence in." This is a belief that includes commitment. Martha was agreeing with Jesus' exposition about eternal life for those who believe in Him. Martha's magnificent confession contains some principal elements of the Person of Christ: He is the Christ (God's anointed One) and the Son of God.

Sources:
Adeyemo, Tokunboh, ed. *Africa Bible Commentary*. Grand Rapids, MI: Zondervan, 2006.
Barclay, William. *The Gospel of John. Vol. 2*. Philadelphia, PA: The Westminster Press, 1956.
"Bethany." *Smith's Bible Dictionary*. Bible Study Tools.com. http://www.biblestudytools.com/dictionaries/smiths-bible-dictionary/bethany.html (accessed January 8, 2011).
Carson, D. A. *The Gospel According to John*. Grand Rapids, MI: William B. Eerdmans Publishing Company, 1991.
New Testament Greek Lexicon. Bible Study Tools.com. http://www.biblestudytools.com/lexicons/greek (accessed January 10, 2011).
Passage Lookup. Bible Gateway.com. http://www.biblegateway.com/passage (accessed January 10, 2011).
Strong's Exhaustive Concordance of the Bible. McLean, VA: MacDonald Publishing Company. n.d.

Say It Correctly

Didymus. DID-e-mus.
Furlongs. FUR-longs.

Daily Bible Reading

MONDAY
The Power of Christ's Resurrection
(Philippians 3:7–11)

TUESDAY
The Son Gives Life
(John 5:19–24)

WEDNESDAY
Life or Condemnation
(John 5:25–29)

THURSDAY
"I Give Eternal Life"
(John 10:22–28)

FRIDAY
For God's Glory
(John 11:1–10)

SATURDAY
So That You May Believe
(John 11:11–16)

SUNDAY
The Resurrection and the Life
(John 11:17–27)

Teaching Tips

Words You Should Know
A. Troubled (John 14:1) *tarasso* (Gk.)—Agitated, anxious, or causing commotion.

B. Mansions (v. 2) *mone* (Gk.)—Abodes or dwellings.

C. Works (v. 12) *ergon* (Gk.)—Denotes a deed or act.

Teacher Preparation
Unifying Principle—Finding Direction for Life. People always try to find direction in their lives. Jesus proclaimed that He was the way to God, because He was in God and God was in Him.

A. Pray and ask the Lord for insight while preparing to teach the lesson.

B. Study and meditate on the entire text.

C. Complete the companion lesson in the *Precepts For Living Personal Study Guide®*.

O—Open the Lesson
A. Begin the class with prayer, using the Lesson Aim as a guide.

B. Read the In Focus story aloud and ask the class to list ways God is leading them in their lives.

C. Write the At-A-Glance outline on the chalkboard.

D. Allow time for the class to read silently the Background section and The People, Places, and Times. Discuss.

P—Present the Scriptures
A. Divide the class into three groups, and assign each group an In Depth section and a Search the Scriptures question based on the At-A-Glance outline.

B. Reassemble the class, and ask a representative from each group to identify ways Jesus plays a central role in the life of the believer.

E—Explore the Meaning
A. Initiate discussion based on the questions found in the Discuss the Meaning section.

B. Summarize Lesson in Our Society.

N—Next Steps for Application
A. Encourage the class to follow through on the Make It Happen section in the upcoming week.

B. Instruct the class to read the Daily Bible Readings for class next week.

C. Close the class with prayer.

Worship Guide
For the Superintendent or Teacher
Theme: The Way, the
Truth, and the Life
Theme Song: "I Am the Way, the Truth,
and the Life"
Devotional Reading: Matthew 7:13–20
Prayer

The Way, the Truth, and the Life

Bible Background • JOHN 14:1–14
Printed Text • JOHN 14:1–14 | Devotional Reading • MATTHEW 7:13–20

Aim for Change

By the end of the lesson, we will: KNOW why Jesus is the Word in our lives; REFLECT on how Jesus gives us direction; and DECIDE to affirmly trust Jesus as "the way, the truth, and the life" for the world.

 In Focus

D. J. was taking a comparative religions class in college. He was ready to display his superior knowledge to his granny. "All religions are the same," he said. "They just call God by different names. We are all going the same direction. If we say Christianity is the only way, we are being so narrow-minded!"

Granny answered, "D. J.—Child, if there was any other way to God, Jesus would not have died on the Cross. Why would He do that if He did not have to?"

D. J. sat there thinking quietly.

Jesus said that He is the only way. Was He merely on an ego trip? If so, why did He go to the Cross? And if He was just another martyr, why did God raise Him from the dead? Let's look at the words of Jesus for ourselves and contemplate them today.

Keep in Mind

"Jesus saith unto him, I am the way, the truth, and the life: no man cometh unto the Father, but by me" (John 14:6).

MAY 27th

"Jesus saith unto him, I am the way, the truth, and the life: no man cometh unto the Father, but by me" (John 14:6).

Focal Verses

KJV **John 14:1** Let not your heart be troubled: ye believe in God, believe also in me.

2 In my Father's house are many mansions: if it were not so, I would have told you. I go to prepare a place for you.

3 And if I go and prepare a place for you, I will come again, and receive you unto myself; that where I am, there ye may be also.

4 And whither I go ye know, and the way ye know.

5 Thomas saith unto him, Lord, we know not whither thou goest; and how can we know the way?

6 Jesus saith unto him, I am the way, the truth, and the life: no man cometh unto the Father, but by me.

7 If ye had known me, ye should have known my Father also: and from henceforth ye know him, and have seen him.

8 Philip saith unto him, Lord, show us the Father, and it sufficeth us.

9 Jesus saith unto him, Have I been so long time with you, and yet hast thou not known me, Philip? he that hath seen me hath seen the Father; and how sayest thou then, Show us the Father?

10 Believest thou not that I am in the Father, and the Father in me? the words that I speak unto you I speak not of myself: but the Father that dwelleth in me, he doeth the works.

11 Believe me that I am in the Father, and the Father in me: or else believe me for the very works' sake.

12 Verily, verily, I say unto you, He that believeth on me, the works that I do shall he do also; and greater works than these shall he do; because I go unto my Father.

NLT **John 14:1** "Don't be troubled. You trust God, now trust in me.

2 There are many rooms in my Father's home, and I am going to prepare a place for you. If this were not so, I would tell you plainly.

3 When everything is ready, I will come and get you, so that you will always be with me where I am.

4 And you know where I am going and how to get there."

5 "No, we don't know, Lord," Thomas said. "We haven't any idea where you are going, so how can we know the way?"

6 Jesus told him, "I am the way, the truth, and the life. No one can come to the Father except through me.

7 If you had known who I am, then you would have known who my Father is. From now on you know him and have seen him!"

8 Philip said, "Lord, show us the Father and we will be satisfied."

9 Jesus replied, "Philip, don't you even yet know who I am, even after all the time I have been with you? Anyone who has seen me has seen the Father! So why are you asking to see him?

10 Don't you believe that I am in the Father and the Father is in me? The words I say are not my own, but my Father who lives in me does his work through me.

11 Just believe that I am in the Father and the Father is in me. Or at least believe because of what you have seen me do.

12 "The truth is, anyone who believes in me will do the same works I have done, and even greater works, because I am going to be with the Father.

KJV Cont.

13 And whatsoever ye shall ask in my name, that will I do, that the Father may be glorified in the Son.

14 If ye shall ask any thing in my name, I will do it.

NLT Cont.

13 You can ask for anything in my name, and I will do it, because the work of the Son brings glory to the Father.

14 Yes, ask anything in my name, and I will do it!

The People, Places, and Times

Philip. He was one of the 12 disciples whom Jesus called directly. Philip, along with Peter and Andrew, was from Bethsaida of Galilee (John 1:44).

Thomas. Also called Didymus, or "the twin," Thomas was one of Jesus' 12 disciples. He is the one who said that he would not believe that Jesus was resurrected from the dead unless he could touch the nail prints in Jesus' hands and the wound from the spear in His side.

Background

During His ministry, Jesus repeatedly prepared the disciples for His suffering and death. In John 13, Jesus tells the disciples that one of them would betray Him (v. 21). At the same time, He also informs the disciples that He will soon be leaving them and that they could not follow Him (v. 33). Undoubtedly, these things disturbed the disciples. When Peter asks Jesus where He was going, Jesus responds, "Where I am going you cannot follow me now, but you will follow afterward" (John 13:36, ESV). It is not difficult to see why the disciples would have been troubled. They were coming to grips with the fact that the One they had given up everything to follow was now telling them that He was about to leave them to go to a place where they could not follow. It must have seemed as though they were losing the very reason for which they had existed for the past three years.

At-A-Glance

1. Jesus, the Way to Comfort
(John 14:1–4)

2. Jesus, the Way to the Father
(vv. 5–11)

3. Jesus, the Way to Powerful Living
(vv. 12–14)

In Depth

1. Jesus, the Way to Comfort (John 14:1–4)

In John 13, Jesus told His disciples of His approaching suffering and departure. Now, He aims to calm the turmoil raging in their hearts. Jesus encourages them by telling them, "Let not your hearts be troubled" (John 14:1, ESV). Jesus' news apparently throws the disciples' minds into disarray and sends them into a spiritual tailspin, but Jesus provides the key that will lead them out of their mental anguish. He points to Himself as the basis for sustaining peace in the midst of the storm of difficult circumstances by telling them if "you believe in God, believe also in Me" (v. 1, NKJV). Even though He will no longer be present with the disciples physically, He assures them that where He is going, He is preparing a place for them. This provides great comfort, not only for the apostles, but also for us. Even though Jesus no longer walks the earth in bodily form, we have His promise that He is with us "even to the end of the age" (Matthew 28:20, NLT), and that He still has the power to calm the storms that rage in our lives. In our times of anxiety and uncertainty, we are directed to place our faith not in our own ingenuity, wit, or financial savvy, but in Jesus Christ, the Sovereign Lord, who is in control of all the circumstances of our lives.

2. Jesus, the Way to the Father (vv. 5–11)

We live in a religiously pluralistic society. The overarching theme preached from some pulpits is tolerance. To some, it is considered nothing short of arrogance to claim that a religion has the exclusive right to the truth. The mainstream view—that all religions worship the same God—is best expressed in a statement made by nineteenth-century Indian saint Sri Ramakrishna: "God has made different religions to suit different aspirations, times, and countries. All doctrines are only so many paths, but a path is by no means God Himself. Indeed, one can reach God if one follows any of the paths with wholehearted devotion" (Smith, 1991).

However, what Ramakrishna expresses is in direct opposition to what Jesus Himself says: "I am the way, the truth, and the life: no man cometh unto the Father but by me" (John 14:6). Jesus declares that there are not many ways to God; there is only one way. Therefore, no matter how sincere one is in following a particular path, if it is not the one true path, it will ultimately lead to a dead end.

Jesus, unlike Ramakrishna, does not point His followers to a path but to a person, namely, Himself: "I am the way." Jesus is not claiming to have uncovered some hidden truth. He is not telling His disciples, "I have experienced enlightenment and now I am able to point you in the direction you must travel." He is claiming something much stronger than

that. Jesus declares, "Anyone who has seen me has seen the Father" (v. 9, NIV). Jesus reveals the character and personality of God to us, just as John writes earlier in chapter 1, "No one has seen God at any time. The only begotten Son, who is in the bosom of the Father, He has declared Him" (John 1:18, NKJV). We are to place faith in Christ as the way to the Father because it is only through Him that we can know the Father.

3. Jesus, the Way to Powerful Living (vv. 12–14)

In verses 12 through 14, Christ notifies His disciples that placing their faith in Him will cause them to lead lives that exhibit the power of God. He says, "He who believes in Me, the works that I do he will do also; and greater works than these he will do, because I go to My Father" (v. 12, NKJV). It is important to note that Jesus says that the works testified of His relationship with the Father: "Believe Me that I am in the Father and the Father in Me, or else believe Me for the sake of the works themselves" (v. 11, NKJV). These were not gratuitous or pointless displays of power, but a demonstration of His authenticity as the Son of God. Furthermore, Jesus lets us know that it is the Father who is at work through Him: "The words that I speak to you I do not speak on My own authority; but the Father who dwells in Me does the works" (v. 10, NKJV). This reveals the unity of Jesus and the Father.

Placing all our trust in Jesus produces two results. First, faith in Christ yields fruitful lives that both demonstrate our relationship with Him and glorify the Father. "This is to my Father's glory, that you bear much fruit, showing yourselves to be my disciples" (John 15:8, NIV). Christ comes to give us "abundant life," promising to do anything we ask in His name, to the glory of the Father. Of course, this is not a blank check given to us with which we can expect to receive all of our wildest desires. What it means to "ask in Christ's name" is made clearer in John 15:7 (ESV), "If you abide in me, and my words abide in you, ask whatever you wish, and it will be done for you." When we ask for things in Jesus' name, we are to ask for things that are consistent with His character and purpose. Putting all our trust in Christ guarantees that we will experience power-filled lives because He aims to glorify His Father's name.

Second, placing faith in Christ gives us the power we need to live out the Christian life. Before ascending into heaven, Jesus delivers a parting promise to His disciples: "But you will receive power when the Holy Spirit comes on you; and you will be my witnesses in Jerusalem, and in all Judea and Samaria, and to the ends of the earth" (Acts 1:8, NIV). The only way we can live powerful lives that reflect Christ's presence is by being indwelt with the Holy Spirit. It is the Holy Spirit who gives us power to live the Christian life, and it is only accessible through faith in Christ.

Search the Scriptures

1. How did Jesus tell the disciples to deal with anxiety in their hearts (John 14:1)?

2. According to Jesus, how can we know the Father (vv. 6–7)?

3. What does it mean to "ask in Jesus' name" (vv. 13–14; 15:7)?

Discuss the Meaning

Suppose you are having a conversation with someone and he or she tells you, "I believe all religions worship the same God. It's just that each one does it in its own way." How would you respond?

Lesson in Our Society

In our society, many believe science is the only way by which we can access the truth about the world around us. Many of our scientists believe that faith is a superstitious concept embraced by those who are weak. In what ways does Jesus' declaration, "I am the way, the truth, and the life" challenge that notion? What are some ways that we can share with our family, neighbors, and coworkers the importance of this declaration?

Make It Happen

This week, share with someone that Jesus is the only way to a relationship with God and that He wants to reconcile him or her to God. Also, pray that God will give you the faith to trust Him and allow Him to guide you throughout your everyday life.

Follow the Spirit

What God wants me to do:

_____

_____

_____

_____

Remember Your Thoughts

Special insights I have learned:

_____

_____

_____

_____

More Light on the Text

John 14:1–14

1 Let not your heart be troubled: ye believe in God, believe also in me.

In his letter to the Romans, the apostle Paul says, "Whatsoever is not of faith is sin"

(14:23). Many have included worry in this list to counter those who treat worry as if it falls somehow harmlessly between sin and virtue. Jesus emphasizes this truth by pointing to faith as the relief or antidote for worry or anxiety. Here, Jesus tells the disciples not to let their hearts become troubled. In Greek, the word "troubled" is *tarasso* (**tar-AS-so**), and it means "agitated, disquieted, or stirred up."

In the context of this passage, Jesus ushers in faith as a comfort to relieve the anxious disciples, much like a welcome medicine for a nagging illness or parental reassurance about a child's nightmare. In this scenario, the disciples' concern was well founded, since they had just learned that one would betray Jesus, that one would deny Him, and that they couldn't go with Him wherever it was He was going (John 13). Jesus' own heart was "troubled" when He announced that one would betray Him (13:21). It is remarkable that Jesus ministered to them with compassion in spite of the fact that His much more serious anguish was now only hours away.

Peter must have been the most visibly shocked to learn he would deny Jesus, since Jesus immediately responded to his concern with His declaration that Peter would be disloyal (John 13:38). Jesus immediately follows this with His words of comfort. When our hearts are troubled, when things look their worst, our best response is faith or belief in our Lord; nothing less will open the door to His peace and comfort (Psalm 42:5). Nothing is more important than guarding our hearts (Proverbs 4:23; 1 Corinthians 16:13–14; 2 Peter 3:17), but at the same time, we as believers have good reason to take courage, unlike those without the hope that is ours.

2 In my Father's house are many mansions: if it were not so, I would have told you. I go to prepare a place for you.

The hope of a home in heaven was given as a source of comfort, not only for the disciples, but also for countless believers through the ages, confronting all the multiple anxieties they as individuals and the church as a whole would face. Jesus' intent was to minister comfort in the face of potentially overwhelming distress; His response (begun in v. 1) was thorough and multifaceted. Added to faith in God and Himself was the reminder of the disciples' (and our) final reward. Here, Jesus reassures them that He would not deceive them by promising them something that was so grand but wasn't the truth. Along with having our name written in the book of life (Isaiah 62:2; Revelation 2:17; 3:12; 21:27), everything becomes new in Christ (2 Corinthians 5:17), including our coming new home in God's kingdom.

3 And if I go and prepare a place for you, I will come again, and receive you unto myself; that where I am, there ye may be also.

This isn't an impersonal second coming to which Jesus refers; He won't be sending a butler, an angel, or anyone else to escort us to our heavenly home. He will come Himself and receive us personally (1 Thessalonians 4:17). In John 14:3, the phrase "I will come" is a common, single word in Greek (*erchomai*, **ER-khom-ahee**) and refers to individuals arriving or returning, appearing or making an appearance. The emphasis is on "again," just as being born is common but being born "again" is noteworthy (John 3:3).

As many have said, "Heaven is where Jesus is, and it wouldn't be heaven without Him." According to Acts 7:31, 49 (KJV), the voice of the Lord came unto Moses saying, "Heaven is my throne, and earth is my footstool." Then according to Revelation 11:19, "And the temple of God was opened in heaven." Indeed, heaven would be sufficient if we just got to be with Him. Wherever He is should be where we want to be; wherever He is not should be the place to avoid at all costs. Nonetheless, it is to His Father's house that we will be going, the home of the King of kings and Lord of lords, the Creator of the universe—being ushered by Christ at His Second Coming to God's eternal home will be glorious beyond words (Luke 22:30; Revelation 21).

4 And whither I go ye know, and the way ye know.

Matthew Henry said, "As the resurrection of Christ is the assurance of our resurrection, so his ascension, victory, and glory, are an assurance of ours" (*Commentary on the Whole Bible*). Jesus is trying to tell or remind His disciples that they already know in their hearts where He is going and how to get there. Surely this would be one of the things of which the coming Comforter would continue to remind them after Jesus' departure, and about which He would continue to teach them (cf. John 14:26).

5 Thomas saith unto him, Lord, we know not whither thou goest; and how can we know the way?

With childlike innocence, Thomas asks about what Jesus just told them that they already knew. Perhaps Thomas's response is an illustration of our own level of spiritual awareness, in reality knowing more than we think we do and being less in the dark than we believe we are at times. The disciples had received a full load of bad news, and perhaps, had they had more time to digest Jesus' discourse, they might have been less reactive. In any case, Jesus doesn't entrust the matter to their faulty memories and previous knowledge, but continues to explain in order to be certain they do in fact know what they need to know.

6 Jesus saith unto him, I am the way, the truth, and the life: no man cometh unto the Father, but by me.

The most common reading of this verse puts the emphasis on the key words "way" (Gk. *hodos*, **hod-OS**), "truth" (Gk. *aletheia*, **al-AY-thi-a**), and "life" (Gk. *zoe*, **dzo-AY**). Yet this most famous statement of all the ages was in response to Thomas's question—to which the disciples should have known the answer. In this light, surely the emphasis was on the word "I" at the beginning of the sentence. "*I* am the way; *I* am the truth; *I* am the life: no man cometh unto the Father, but by *ME*." One can imagine Jesus stopping just short of exasperation; one can see Him explicitly trying to hammer home His point to those closest to Him, who soon would be without Him, who soon would need to teach others about Him—yet who still didn't seem to understand.

Scripture states that there are two gates and two ways in life; there is a straight gate and a narrow way that leads to life, and a wide gate and a broad way that leads to destruction (Matthew 7:13). Acts talks about the way of salvation, the way of God, and the Way as the early church had been called (Acts 16:17; 18:26; 24:14). By His blood, Jesus opened up for us the "new and living way" into the Holy of Holies (Hebrews 10:20). Even the Old Testament speaks of there being only one way: "Ask for the old paths, where is the good way, and walk therein, and ye shall find rest for your souls" (Jeremiah 6:16). In Greek, the word "way" is *hodos* and refers to a traveler's way or a way of thinking, feeling, and deciding; it is used over 100 times in the New Testament and normally has the aforementioned common interpretation—until Jesus says He is *the* way.

John clearly establishes that the Word is God (1:1), the Word became flesh (1:14), and the Word is truth (17:17). "Thy word is true from the beginning" (Psalm 119:160). Jesus completes the circle by stating that He is the truth and is one with God (John 10:30); other writers are more explicit regarding His deity (Colossians 1:16; 2:9; Philippians 2:6; 1 John 5:20). It is truth that sets us free (John 8:32) and that leads us to salvation (Ephesians 1:13). Even His critics know that, as truth, Jesus would never deceive anyone (Luke 20:21). However, people are able to deceive themselves (1 John 1:8). As the embodiment of truth, Jesus stands in perfect contrast to the devil, in whom there is no truth (John 8:44). In Greek, the word "truth" is *aletheia* and is used in a variety of contexts, including references to personal excellence and to truth pertaining to God. Again, it is a common word that is used in these ways over 100 times in the New Testament—until Jesus says He is *the* truth.

Only because of Christ, we are "dead indeed unto sin, but alive unto God" (Romans 6:11); likewise, He is the only cure for sin (Romans 6:23). No one can ever accuse Jesus of having made mediocre claims. Just in John's Gospel alone, preceding His ultimate statement in 14:6, Jesus similarly stated that He was the Bread of Life (6:35); that He came to give life, and life more abundantly (10:10); that He gives eternal life to His sheep (10:28); and that He is the Resurrection and the Life (11:25). In the Greek, the word "life" is *zoe*, the meaning of which includes the state of living, every living soul, and the absolute fullness of life. Like the words "way" and "truth," "life" is a common word used well over 100 times in the New Testament—until Jesus says He is *the* life.

The latter part of 14:6 is what is known as an "exceptive statement," meaning "all and only." All may come to the Father through Jesus, and only those coming through Jesus may come to the Father. No matter how politically incorrect His statements may seem, Jesus was, is, and always will be the true and only way to God the Father and life everlasting.

7 If ye had known me, ye should have known my Father also: and from henceforth ye know him, and have seen him.

Jesus' words are a not-so-subtle rebuke of the disciples' for their lack of awareness of just who had been with them for so long. Regardless of the disciples' shortsightedness, Jesus patiently continues to explain that in seeing and knowing Him, they have already seen and known the Father. Almost before they can realize they have been rebuked for their lack of awareness, Jesus immediately extends comfort in His reassurance that, at least from this point forward, they no longer need to be unaware of the Father. As Jesus stated (John 10:30), He and the Father are one. Jesus is God and reveals God to us. The disciples' common awakening experience, which came soon enough and was similar in essence for all of them (and us), is captured by the apostle Paul's pen: "God . . . hath shined in our hearts, to give the light of the knowledge of the glory of God in the face of Jesus Christ" (2 Corinthians 4:6; cf. 4:4; Colossians 1:15). God does this by sending the Holy Spirit after Jesus ascended to heaven.

8 Philip saith unto him, Lord, show us the Father, and it sufficeth us. 9 Jesus saith unto him, Have I been so long time with you, and yet hast thou not known me, Philip? he that hath seen me hath seen the Father; and how sayest thou then, Show us the Father? 10 Believest thou not that I am in the Father, and the Father in me? the words that I speak unto you I speak not of myself: but the Father that dwelleth in me, he doeth the works.

Philip wanted a sign. One cannot help but empathize with Philip, since he sounds like so many today who, no matter how much they know or are told, insist on saying, "If I could just see God once, that would settle it for me. If just once I could witness a real miracle, then I'd become a believer. Why can't God just show His face for one split second?" Just like Philip, modern skeptics ignore what is before them. In Philip's case, it was the living Jesus, God in the flesh, worker of miracles, standing before him and talking to him. Yet he didn't understand what he was hearing. In this light, Jesus' response (verse 9) is both understandable and appropriate.

On closer examination, it seems evident that more of Jesus' exasperation is showing. Jesus is asking Philip, "How could you not know after all this time? Haven't you been paying attention at all? Do you really not get it? If you've seen Me, you've seen the Father. How can you look right at Me and ask to see the Father?"

Jesus' response continues (v. 10): "Philip, do you really not comprehend that I am in the Father, and the Father is in Me? The Father lives in Me; it is He who does the works I do." Jesus stresses His unity with the Father once again. When we read these passages consecutively, we see the patient Teacher gently guiding His future apostles, who soon will faithfully carry out His Great Commission to the four corners of the world—that is, once they get it straight who He is.

11 Believe me that I am in the Father, and the Father in me: or else believe me for the very works' sake.

Although Jesus' conversation is in response to questions from Thomas and Philip, all the disciples are present and Jesus is addressing all of them in His typical teaching fashion. In this passage, Jesus continues in the same "read-my-lips" tone: "Philip—all of you—it is imperative that you listen very closely and hear Me well. Again, I repeat, I am in the Father and the Father is in Me." It is no wonder that the early church continued to struggle with the essence of Jesus' words. One can hardly imagine how He could have communicated His deity any more clearly than He did. At first, it was hard for even the disciples to grasp that Jesus was deity; then, after He ascended, whether or not He had really been human became the prime issue of the Gnostics (thus the emphasis on Jesus' human birth and physical crucifixion in the Apostles' Creed). There were many struggles about Jesus' divinity and humanity through the fifth century, when the Council of Chalcedon finally set the boundaries for orthodox doctrine about the union of divine and human natures in Christ. Today, there are still people who have no problem with Jesus' humanity but struggle greatly with His deity, and sects like the Jehovah's Witnesses, who deny Christ's divinity.

12 Verily, verily, I say unto you, He that believeth on me, the works that I do shall he do also; and greater works than these shall he do; because I go unto my Father.

At this point, Jesus moves on to a different subject, one of many He would address on that auspicious night. One has to wonder if the disciples grasped the fact that the "greater works" to which Jesus referred in verse 12 would not be possible if He had stayed with them, but were only going to be possible because He was leaving them. Jesus' words were not only about the fantastic advances in ministry that they were going to accomplish when the Holy Spirit came. He also offered them another facet of His multilayered message of comfort and courage regarding His impending death and subsequent departure. His message was entirely about comfort, assurances, and taking heart for the great things that awaited them. These 11 men—the original pillars of the faith and the architects of the New Testament church—needed at that moment to hear some words of encouragement, reassurance, and hope from their departing Master.

13 And whatsoever ye shall ask in my name, that will I do, that the Father may be glorified in the Son.

Jesus would deny these particular men nothing. He left in their charge the greatest task ever given to any human, and He knew what they would need in order to accomplish the work He had given them. Many people have heard some preacher at some time try to interpret this as some kind of mysterious combination or formula by implying or claiming that all you have to do is say all the right words and include all the potential caveats and specific disclaimers, and God is almost obliged to accommodate you. Unfortunately, many in the church have a gross misconception of what it means to abide in Christ, which impairs their understanding of how things work in God's kingdom.

When we abide in Christ, His power flows through us to accomplish His purposes in the world. The Holy Spirit is the agent, sent by the resurrected Christ, and we are the vehicles through which He flows. It is not our confession or religious invocation that garners the forces of heaven to do our bidding. It is only when our hearts are surrendered, when we are living in and for God, when our will is attuned to His, and when our prayers are for His purposes, in His name, and for His glory that He will answer, even beyond all we ask or think (Ephesians 3:20).

14 If ye shall ask any thing in my name, I will do it.

It is here that we find some of the most poignant parting words known to humankind. Jesus, the Savior, is preparing for His death, burial, and resurrection. He is equipping His disciples with the most important things they will need to know as they carry out His work without His physical presence. The reiteration of John 14:13 must be heard in the context of the whole passage. This kind of repetitive reassurance is the type one gives a loved one who needs comfort. We tend to say things more than once when we want someone to believe us, especially if there is an impending separation.

Yes, when our hearts become one heart like that of the disciples (v. 1), when our faith is sure and steady, when our will is surrendered to Christ, and when our purpose is completely for God's glory, most certainly we, too, can believe like the disciples that our prayers will be answered.

Sources:

Henry, Matthew. *Commentary on the Whole Bible.* Christian Classics Ethereal Library.org. http://www.ccel.org/h/henry/mhc5John.xv.html (accessed October 1, 2010).

New Testament Greek Lexicon. Bible Study Tools.com. http://www.biblestudytools.com/lexicons/greek (accessed January 10, 2011).

Passage Lookup. Bible Gateway.com. http://www.biblegateway.com/passage (accessed January 10, 2011).

Smith, Huston. *The World's Religions.* San Francisco, CA: Harper, 1991. 56.

Tenney, Merrill C. *The Expositor's Bible Commentary.* Edited by Frank E. Gaebelein. Grand Rapids, MI: Zondervan Publishing House, 1981.

Say It Correctly

Sri Ramakrishna. SRE Ra-ma-KRISH-na.

Daily Bible Readings

MONDAY
Making Known the Way of God
(Exodus 18:13–23)

TUESDAY
Turning Aside from the Way
(Exodus 32:7–14)

WEDNESDAY
Seeking Truth Within
(Psalm 51:1–7)

THURSDAY
Speaking Truth from the Heart
(Psalm 15)

FRIDAY
Telling the Whole Message
(Acts 5:17–21)

SATURDAY
Choosing the Hard Road
(Matthew 7:13–20)

SUNDAY
"How Can We Know the Way?"
(John 14:1–14)

Notes

_____

_____

_____

_____

God Calls for Justice: Old Testament Survey

This quarter's study offers an Old Testament survey following the theme of justice in the early church. This quarter also offers insight into God's ongoing relationship with Israel and all the people He created.

UNIT 1 • JUSTICE DEFINED

The four lessons in this unit explore the fundamental teachings of the Law. They help us to define the biblical principles of justice expressed in the books of Exodus, Leviticus, and Deuteronomy.

Lesson 1: June 3, 2012
Rules for Just Living
Exodus 23:1–9

This passage is part of what is known as "the book of the covenant" (Exodus 20:22—23:33), which is the oldest extant record of Jewish law. Unlike other ancient law codes of the ancient Near East, it rests on the authority of God rather than on that of a king.

Lesson 2: June 10, 2012
Living as God's Just People
Leviticus 19:9–18, 33–37

This chapter begins with a call to reflect the nature of God: "You shall be holy, for I the LORD your God am holy" (v. 2, NKJV).

Lesson 3: June 17, 2012
Celebrate Jubilee
Leviticus 25:8–12, 25, 35–36, 39–40, 47–48, 55

The jubilee year was a year of "release" when people returned to their homes and property reverted to its ancestral owners. The jubilee year began when the ram's horn sounded on the Day of Atonement (v. 9). By observing a year of jubilee, those who are oppressed are given the means for making a fresh start.

Lesson 4: June 24, 2012
The Heart of the Law
Deuteronomy 10:12–22; 16:18–20

The principle underlying justice in this passage does not originate in humankind, but in the nature of God. Loving God involves more than a sentimental response; it means serving God with one's heart and soul.

UNIT 2 • JUSTICE ENACTED

The five lessons of Unit II look at the justice of God as it is enacted through some of Israel's righteous leaders. The first lesson considers Samuel. The next three lessons study David and Solomon. The final lesson of the unit examines the judicial reforms carried out under Jehoshaphat.

Lesson 5: July 1, 2012
Samuel Administers Justice
1 Samuel 7:3–11, 15–17

Israel's repentance at Samuel's urging is a repetition of its behavior on many previous occasions. The period of the judges is marked by cycles of prosperity, sin and idolatry, divine punishment at the hands of an invader, and the raising of a judge who leads in repentance and deliverance.

Lesson 6: July 8, 2012
David Embodies God's Justice
2 Samuel 23:1–7; 1 Chronicles 18:14

People want to have a meaningful existence. Acknowledging God's authority in our lives enables us to become the person God created us to be.

Lesson 7: July 15, 2012
Solomon Judges with Wisdom and Justice
1 Kings 3:16–28; 2 Chronicles 9:8

People need a just and wise mediator when life presents unjust situations. Because of Solomon's relationship with God, he was able to make just and wise choices.

Lesson 8: July 22, 2012
A King Acts on a Widow's Behalf
2 Kings 8:1–6

People who are estranged from their families may long to return home. By acting in a benevolent manner, we can offer hope to those seeking justice and restoration.

Lesson 9: July 29, 2012
Jehoshaphat Makes Judicial Reforms
2 Chronicles 19:4–11

People want to be judged fairly. When human judges adhere to God's standards and fearlessly apply God's laws, there is no perversion of justice.

UNIT 3 • JUSTICE PROMISED

These last four passages examine some of the Old Testament texts that prophesy God's coming judgments. The first lesson is from Psalm 146. The remaining lessons are from the Major Prophets: Isaiah, Jeremiah, and Ezekiel.

Lesson 10: August 5, 2012
Praise for God's Justice
Psalm 146:1–10

Psalm 146 is the first of five hallelujah psalms that conclude the Psalter. Its opening directive to the soul—to praise the Lord and promise to praise God throughout life—is a response to the commitment to lifelong praise at the end of Psalm 145.

Lesson 11: August 12, 2012
God Promised a Righteous Lord
Isaiah 9:2–7

Christ was born to be our Lord and Savior. He would ultimately redeem the world. As our hope, the prediction of the birth of a child finds fulfillment in the birth of Christ (Matthew 4:12–16).

Lesson 12: August 19, 2012
God Promised a Righteous Branch
Jeremiah 23:1–6; 33:14–18

The prophet expresses the hope that a king will be raised up, one who will bear the name "The LORD is our righteousness" (23:6, ESV).

Lesson 13: August 26, 2012
God Promised To Be with Us
Ezekiel 34:23–31

The kings of Israel and Judah were self-serving and neglected the needs of the people. The result of the shepherds' neglect is that the sheep are scattered and unprotected. In this lesson, we learn about God restoring order and justice.

God Calls for Justice

"Though ye offer me burnt offerings
and your meat offerings,
I will not accept them:
neither will I regard
the peace offerings of your fat beasts.
Take thou away from me
the noise of thy songs;
for I will not hear the melody of thy viols.
But let judgment run down as waters,
and righteousness as a mighty stream"
(Amos 5:22–24).

Walking in the Light We Share through Forgiveness

by Rukeia Draw-Hood, Ph.D.

As God's Word tells us, God so loved the world that He sent His only begotten Son as a sacrifice to amend for their sins so that forgiveness could be offered and reconciliation achieved. As the story continues, those who accept this reality are to extend this forgiveness and love to one another and be reconciled (Matthew 6:14; Mark 11:25; 2 Corinthians 2:10; Ephesians 4:32, 5:2; Colossians 3:13). So why is it that the world recognizes believers more by their hypocrisy than by their love for one another?

Alexander Pope is famous for saying, "To err is human, but to forgive is divine." Elizabeth Large agrees that it is human nature to respond to an offense with anger, grudges, or vengeance; and in spite of religious instruction, many believers respond with all three. Lots of Christians have lives controlled by anger and bitterness. Many are touchy and eagerly provoked. Others don't know how to let go of grudges. Like the second grader who is full of rage and yells, "I don't forget anything" to his teacher, like the abused woman who has rehearsed the acts of molestation and retaliation in her mind a million times over the past 20 years, like the streetwise young man who refuses to let go of payback for the business venture gone sour with his childhood friend, how is it that many of God's children never adequately learned how to cope with the disappointments and injuries experienced at the hands of others?

The church should dedicate more resources to facilitating forgiveness. Let me give an exam-

ple that starts with the theologians, the great minds whose task it is to challenge the church to reflect on issues of great importance. There are many systematic theology textbooks, and although they are supposed to cover all the major authoritative teachings of the church, they rarely, if ever, address the topic of love. This trend continues among distinguished Black theologians, with the exception of J. Deotis Roberts and Dwight Hopkins. In contemporary Black theology, forgiveness and reconciliation are overshadowed by freedom and justice. There is, however, ample preaching on forgiveness in local churches. In spite of this, many believers have not moved beyond knowing about forgiveness and believing in its goodness. Christian education in the local church has not typically given congregants the educational experiences they need to practice forgiveness in their daily lives.

Forgiveness helps Christians fulfill God's commandment to love one another (Matthew 22:39; John 13:34; 1 John 3:23). To love another brother or sister in Christ is to walk in the light they share (1 John 2:10). Love is the bond that holds Christian communities together, and forgiveness is an expression of that love. Mother Theresa said, "If we want to love, we must learn how to forgive." Paul confirms this when he writes that love keeps no record of wrongs (1 Corinthian 13:5). Healthy love relationships are impossible without forgiveness because as Peter Ustinov says, "Love is an act of endless forgiveness." Jesus tries to communicate this to Peter in Matthew 18:22 when he encourages him to forgive one person 77 times.

Forgiveness is a moral response to injustice. It's a choice to lay down the right to pay an offender back, absorbing the evil and suffering the pain of an injury instead. Based on the merciful character of God and the forgiveness He has already extended to the believer for far greater offenses; such a choice is informed by a conviction that unwillingness to forgive another Christian is hypocritical (Luke 6:36; Ephesians 4:32). The International Forgiveness Institute says forgiveness also reaches out to the offender in moral love by seeking the rehabilitation and betterment of the injurer.

An unforgiving believer walks in darkness because every part of his or her being is negatively affected—mind, body, and spirit. One guy said, "If you licked my heart, you'd die from poisoning." Like this guy, an unforgiving person drinks poison and expects someone else to die from it. The point is that harboring hostility can be deadly for individuals and those who come too close to them!

Projects looking at the benefits of forgiveness have received millions of dollars in funding lately. These studies have found that people who hold grudges have diminished health compared to those in the general population. They have more visits to the doctor, more stress-related disorders (anxiety, restlessness, sadness, and depression), lower immune system functioning, and higher rates of cardiovascular disease (high blood pressure, heart disease, low heart rate).

Jesus warns that God is like the lender who forgave an enormous debt (Matthew 18:35) because He expects a believer's character and treatment of others to reflect His own character and treatment toward you in some small measure. Forgiven people forgive others, and there are consequences when they don't.

Believers are an integral part of a loving community, linked by the Spirit of God. Everyone will inevitably, if not regularly, be offended in this imperfect community. Love can only prosper where there is forgiveness. To walk in the light of love and facilitate forgiveness in your life or congregation, consider assigning/keeping gratitude journals, providing/attending training in communication skills and conflict resolution, using/participating in role plays and simulations, emphasizing/completing weekly the REMEMBER YOUR THOUGHTS, MAKE IT HAPPEN, and FOLLOW THE SPIRIT, seeing a professional (minister, therapist, social worker, life coach) who can accompany you through the process, researching a forgiveness curriculum for congregational use, hiring a consultant to design an intervention, formulating a personal/congregation theology of forgiveness through honest dialogue and Bible study (please address reconciliation, repentance, process, and abuse cycles).

Practicing forgiveness allows believers to be healthy and whole, therefore contributing to the stability, unity, and maturity of the entire Christian community. Remember unforgiveness has serious consequences. Begin using what resources you have to let go of grudges or help others do so today!

Sources:

James, Larry. *How to Really Love the One You're With.* http://www.celebratelove.com (accessed July 7, 2005).

Large, Elizabeth. "Forgiveness is hot: Researchers cite health, personal benefits." Reprint. *Baltimore Sun.* January 12, 2005. http://www.azcentral.com/health/wellness/articles/0112forgiveness12.html (accessed July 5, 2005).

Rhodes-Wickett, Sharon. "Judge Not—Forgive A Lot" [sermon online]. Westwood United Methodist Church. September 15, 2002. http://www.westwoodumc.org/sermons/2002sermons/s091502.htm (July 5, 2005).

Xenos Christian Fellowship. "Christian Community: Part #6 Forgive One Another." http://www.xenos.org/ct_outln/forgive1another.htm (July 6, 2005).

Rukeia Draw-Hood, Ph.D., *received a Master of Arts in Christian Education from Oral Roberts University and a Doctor of Philosophy in Educational Studies from Trinity International University. She is an active member of The Church Without Walls in Houston, Texas.*

FREEDOM

Can I be free,
If I pursue it with all that God has given me,
But I encroach upon my fellow man's
Right to that same freedom?
No, I cannot be free,
For one truth I can never deny,
And it is that an Omnipotent God
Has plotted my course,
And He has seen to it that my freedom
And my fellow man's are entwined.
Therefore, I cannot seek life's fulfillment,
I cannot seek the beauty and wonders of living
When it causes my fellow man to still be in bondage.
I have found that I must give up some of my freedom
In order to deny him his,
So with each passing moment,
I have come to realize and appreciate,
That the realities of my freedom
Rest upon my pursuing my fellow man's as well.

—Evangeline Carey

Nathaniel R. Jones

1926–

Just a few blocks from the Smoky Hollow community in Youngstown, Ohio, where Nathaniel R. Jones grew up, stands the Nathaniel R. Jones federal courthouse. This was certainly not something that Jones had dreamed of.

He was a good student and caught the eye of African American newspaper publisher, Maynard Dickerson, while he was still in high school. Jones was soon writing a sports column for the *Buckeye Review*. When Jones finished high school, he was enlisted into the U.S. Army Air Corps and served in Dayton, Ohio.

After his army experience, he returned home and attended Youngstown State University, followed by Youngstown State University Law School. He worked for four years as a private practice lawyer and then was appointed Executive Director of the Fair Employment Practices Commission, where he could work on assuring that African Americans had equal opportuni-ties in employment. After this, he served on the Kerner Commission, which was investigating the causes of the race riots that began with the assassination of Dr. Martin Luther King Jr.

Then Roy Wilkins, the Executive Director of the NAACP, asked him to lead their law team. In his acceptance speech, he said, "We still live in the basement of the great society." As general counsel for the NAACP, he worked for integration of northern schools, affirmative action, and equality in the U.S. armed services.

In 1979, President Jimmy Carter nominated Jones as judge of the U.S. Court of Appeals, and he served in this position for 23 years. He retired in 2002, and he continues to work as a lawyer in private practice. He has a wife and five children.

Source:

The History Makers. http://www.thehistorymakers.com/biographyasp?bioindex= 1274&category=La (accessed September 12, 2010).

463

Teaching Tips

Words You Should Know

A. Gift (Exodus 23:8) *shachad* (Heb.)—This word means the same in Hebrew and English, but the context is a present being used as a bribe.

B. Oppress (Exodus 23:9) *lachats* (Heb.)—To take advantage of, restrict, or pervert justice regarding someone's human rights.

Teacher Preparation

Unifying Principle—Justice for All. When God's people act with justice and mercy—whether toward a friend or foe—they reflect the heart and character of God.

A. Pray for your students and that God will bring clarity to this lesson.

B. Study and meditate on the entire text.

C. Complete the companion lesson in the *Precepts For Living Personal Study Guide®*.

D. Prepare a PowerPoint or bring news clippings of incidents involving injustice.

O—Open the Lesson

A. Open with prayer, including the Aim for Change.

B. Introduce today's subject.

C. Read the Aim for Change and Keep in Mind verse in unison. Discuss.

D. Share your presentation.

E. Then ask, "Have you ever personally experienced injustice?"

F. Share testimonies.

G. Have a volunteer summarize the In Focus story. Discuss.

P—Present the Scriptures

A. Have volunteers read the Focal Verses.

B. Now use The People, Places, and Times; Background; Search the Scriptures; At-A-Glance outline; In Depth; and More Light on the Text to clarify the verses.

E—Explore the Meaning

A. Have volunteers summarize the Discuss the Meaning, Lesson in Our Society, and Make It Happen sections.

B. Connect these sections to the Aim for Change and the Keep in Mind verse.

N—Next Steps for Application

A. Write some easy-to-remember take-away principles under the Follow the Spirit or Remember Your Thoughts section.

B. Close with prayer and praise God for giving us details of His laws that reflect His holy and just character.

Worship Guide

For the Superintendent or Teacher
Theme: Rules for Just Living
Theme Song: "Amazing Grace"
Devotional Reading:
Deuteronomy 32:1–7
Prayer

Rules for Just Living

Bible Background • EXODUS 22:1–23:9
Printed Text • EXODUS 23:1–9 | Devotional Reading • DEUTERONOMY 32:1–7

——————— Aim for Change ———————

By the end of the lesson, we will: KNOW that God is not pleased with injustice; FEEL the joy that comes from observing justice; and SEEK justice for all.

——————— 🦋 In Focus ———————

One day when I was little, my mom screamed. Everybody in the house ran to see what was the matter. Ants.

Lots of annoying ants. Black ants—together . . . moving in a line, in the same direction—toward the window . . . toward our kitchen. My father commanded me to get the water hose, and my sister to turn on the water—then we watched as those ants were sprayed off of the house and onto the ground. No more ants marching toward our kitchen.

One day in the 1960s, a White person must have screamed. Everybody ran to see what was the matter. Blacks. Lots of annoying Blacks—united . . . moving toward the same direction . . . toward Freedom.

A policeman commanded a fireman to get his water hose and to turn on the water.

Then the world watched those Blacks sprayed off their feet and tumble onto the ground. No more Blacks marching for their Freedom.

The focus of this week's lesson is on the horizontal aspect of the Covenant Code, addressing one's behavior toward others. A just and righteous God expects His children to do justice and righteousness.

Keep in Mind

"Thou shalt not follow a multitude to do evil; neither shalt thou speak in a cause to decline after many to wrest judgment" (Exodus 23:2).

"Thou shalt not follow a multitude to do evil; neither shalt thou speak in a cause to decline after many to wrest judgment" (Exodus 23:2).

Focal Verses

KJV **Exodus 23:1** Thou shalt not raise a false report: put not thine hand with the wicked to be an unrighteous witness.

2 Thou shalt not follow a multitude to do evil; neither shalt thou speak in a cause to decline after many to wrest judgment:

3 Neither shalt thou countenance a poor man in his cause.

4 If thou meet thine enemy's ox or his ass going astray, thou shalt surely bring it back to him again.

5 If thou see the ass of him that hateth thee lying under his burden, and wouldest forbear to help him, thou shalt surely help with him.

6 Thou shalt not wrest the judgment of thy poor in his cause.

7 Keep thee far from a false matter; and the innocent and righteous slay thou not: for I will not justify the wicked.

8 And thou shalt take no gift: for the gift blindeth the wise, and perverteth the words of the righteous.

9 Also thou shalt not oppress a stranger: for ye know the heart of a stranger, seeing ye were strangers in the land of Egypt.

NLT **Exodus 23:1** "Do not pass along false reports. Do not cooperate with evil people by telling lies on the witness stand.

2 "Do not join a crowd that intends to do evil. When you are on the witness stand, do not be swayed in your testimony by the opinion of the majority.

3 And do not slant your testimony in favor of a person just because that person is poor.

4 "If you come upon your enemy's ox or donkey that has strayed away, take it back to its owner.

5 If you see the donkey of someone who hates you struggling beneath a heavy load, do not walk by. Instead, stop and offer to help.

6 "Do not twist justice against people simply because they are poor.

7 "Keep far away from falsely charging anyone with evil. Never put an innocent or honest person to death. I will not allow anyone guilty of this to go free.

8 "Take no bribes, for a bribe makes you ignore something that you clearly see. A bribe always hurts the cause of the person who is in the right.

9 "Do not oppress the foreigners living among you. You know what it is like to be a foreigner. Remember your own experience in the land of Egypt.

The People, Places, and Times

A Covenant People. For the first time, the people of Israel under Moses' leadership were ready to pledge themselves in covenant with the God who had delivered them from slavery to the Egyptians. In Walter Brueggemann's words, "The *proclamation of commands* and the *oath of allegiance* are the defining elements of the covenant that bind Israel to YHWH in obedience" (61). Along with the new laws that God gave to Moses came instructions for the construction of a holy place where God's presence would confirm his faithfulness to the new covenant.

Time for a Covenant. This was a foundational, formative time for God's people. During their "sojourn tradition," they had just been miraculously delivered from the horrible oppression in Egypt. Now they were ready to commit to a covenantal relationship with God. The giving of the Decalogue (the Ten Commandments) and the Covenant Code that followed define the formation of God's nation of Israel.

Background

The Covenant Code of Exodus 20:22–23:33, also known as "The Book of the Covenant," follows and expands on the Decalogue (the Ten Commandments) that God gave to Moses on Mt. Sinai. This was not a one-way relationship because Israel had readily agreed to obey God's laws (Exodus 19:2–8). It was their voluntary agreement to follow and obey God that caused Israel to suffer God's judgment when they disobeyed the Covenant laws. Implicit in any law forbidding something is a judgment for disobedience. It is because of justice and mercy being part of God's character and part of His Covenant Code that His anger was kindled when His people engaged in injustice and did not show mercy to others.

At-A-Glance

1. Five Judicial Imperatives
(Exodus 23:1–3)

2. Two Case Studies (vv. 4–6)

3. Five More Judicial Imperatives
(vv. 7–9)

In Depth

1. Five Judicial Imperatives (Exodus 23:1–3)

The lesson Scriptures focus on the arena of law called "social justice" legislation. The first set of judicial imperatives is addressed

to witnesses in a legal proceeding. These are given as examples of the types of things that constitute injustice, which are to be avoided under penalty of judgment. The list was not meant to be exhaustive, and there are many other similar situations that would involve the same principles of not only avoiding injustice, but also doing justice.

(A): *"Thou shalt not raise a false report"* (v. 1). This refers to someone being an untruthful witness. Today, before witnesses may testify during a trial, they must swear to "tell the truth, the whole truth, and nothing but the truth." This reinforces the law of perjury, and if violated and proven that one has lied under oath, it carries a serious penalty. In non-legal settings, the justice principle of speaking truthfully about others extends to gossip and slander.

(B): *"Put not thine hand with the wicked to be an unrighteous witness"* (v. 1). This means *do not* cooperate with wicked people and give false testimony about someone who is guilty. This is the inverse of the previous. Just as one must not testify falsely if someone is innocent, by the same justice principle, one must not testify falsely if someone is guilty.

(C): *"Thou shalt not follow a multitude to do evil"* (v. 2). This means *do not* go along with the crowd if justice is being perverted. God holds each person to a personal standard of holiness and justice, and it is no excuse to say that one was just going along to get along. The child of God must be willing to refuse to follow the majority when he or she sees injustice being committed.

(D): *"Neither shalt thou speak in a cause to decline after many to wrest judgment"* (v. 2). This means *do not* fail to speak up when you see injustice, even if your voice is outnumbered or unpopular. This is the inverse of the third injunction. Not only must the just person not follow the crowd to participate in injustice, but also he or she must be willing to speak out against it.

(E): *"Neither shalt thou countenance a poor man in his cause"* **(v. 3).** This means *do not* automatically show partiality for a poor person, just because he or she is poor; the same goes for a rich person. The poor are not always innocent, nor are the rich always guilty. Such axiomatic statements were true in Old Testament times, and they are still true today. People tend to believe in stereotypes regarding a certain type or class of people for whom they have reason to disagree. The just child of God must be blind to both poverty and wealth when called on to make such a judgment.

2. Two Case Studies (vv. 4–5)

These two examples are outside of a legal environment and uniquely refer to how one treats one's enemies.

(A): *"If thou meet thine enemy's ox or his ass going astray, thou shalt surely bring it back to him again"* **(v. 4).** The meaning is clear that the just person is to help a man whose donkey has strayed, even if that person is an enemy. Through the ages, this has been the testimony that often has won converts because they saw God's people being kind and just, even to their enemies.

(B): *"If thou see the ass of him that hateth thee lying under his burden, and wouldest forbear to help him, thou shalt surely help with him"* **(v. 5).** Similar to the above point, the just person is to help a person whose donkey has fallen with a load, even if that person is an enemy. The parable of the good Samaritan is a perfect New Testament parallel to this Old Testament injunction. If, for example, a person is lying trapped under a fallen animal, the just person is compelled to help—the principle is timeless, whether it is someone trapped under a car, a tree, or in a burning building. The just person must act justly in all situations, whether the person needing help is a friend or foe.

3. Five More Judicial Imperatives (vv. 6–9)

The final five judicial imperatives of this portion of Scripture are addressed specifically to judges. After all, who other than a judge is more often in a position to determine the fate of others and to exercise either justice or injustice?

(A): *"Thou shalt not wrest the judgment of thy poor in his cause"* **(v. 6).** Just as one should not deny justice to a rich person, just because he or she is rich, so the just person must not deny justice to a poor person, just because he or she is poor.

(B): *"Keep thee far from a false matter"* **(v. 7).** The just person must at all costs avoid evil and injustice. One must consciously and deliberately steer clear of such things. Conversely, the clear implication is to maintain God's standard of justice.

(C): *"And the innocent and righteous slay thou not, for I will not justify the wicked"* **(v. 7).** This passage could not be clearer. A judge must never falsely charge anyone and must never put an innocent person to death. Particularly when it comes to matters of life and death, God specifically will not excuse the one with innocent blood on his or her hands. This is the only injunction in the passage that comes with an attached warning that such wickedness will not go unpunished. God will judge the unjust judge.

(D): *"And thou shalt take no gift: for the gift blindeth the wise, and perverteth the words of the righteous"* **(v. 8).** Sadly, bribing judges and other officials is a sin that has been committed countless times through the centuries. The frequency of the sin, however, does not relieve the sinners of the responsibility. If that were the case, then God would be guilty of going along with the crowd! No one who is in a position of authority should take a bribe, especially a judge who is often solely responsible for the fate of others. Bribes blind judges to justice, when instead judges are to be blind to partiality.

(E): *"Also thou shalt not oppress a stranger: for ye know the heart of a stranger, seeing ye were strangers in the land of Egypt"* (v. 9). As with the previous verse, this injunction comes with an explanation. Just as the Israelites once were oppressed strangers in Egypt, so they are not to oppress strangers (e.g., foreigners and travelers). Referring specifically to judges, again few others are so often responsible for the fate of so many others, and in this case, the person on trial must not be judged by their nationality or ethnicity.

Search the Scriptures

1. Where is the Decalogue found in Scripture (Exodus 20)?

2. Were the laws in the Covenant Code exhaustive?

Discuss the Meaning

Compare the examples of injustice given in the Covenant Code. Try to find modern examples that would parallel the same principles. Have you ever witnessed injustice firsthand or participated in it?

Lesson in Our Society

One hears a lot about social justice in the news, and it is only natural for victims of injustice to cry out for justice in every aspect of society. Studying the Scriptures on social justice presents a clear picture of what it means for God's people to embody justice in society—how they are to both avoid injustice and exercise justice. This clear picture must be preserved in a world where so many believe that only political solutions or new laws will fulfill God's requirements for justice. While governments are capable of doing things that individuals cannot, according to God's Word, individuals are always responsible for their own actions and decisions. Even governments are made up of individuals, and each will give an account of every decision, whether it was just or unjust. Ultimately, no one will be excused for inflicting or enabling injustice.

Make It Happen

Even though today's believers live in the New Covenant, God's holy character and standards have not changed. He still does not tolerate injustice among His people. He still calls His people to be holy and to come out from among those in the world who commit such evil, as stated in 1 Peter 2:9, "But ye are a chosen generation, a royal priesthood, an holy nation, a peculiar people; that ye should shew forth the praises of him who hath called you out of darkness into his marvellous light." The challenge for believers today is to correct injustices when they are found and to act justly, even when there is compelling reason or temptation to do otherwise.

Follow the Spirit

What God wants me to do:

_____

_____

_____

_____

Remember Your Thoughts
Special insights I have learned:

_____

_____

_____

_____

More Light on the Text
Exodus 23:1–9
Introduction

The Covenant Code of Exodus (20:18–23:33) immediately follows the Decalogue in 20:1–17. This portion of that code addresses behavior toward others, focusing on the arenas of justice and mercy. Walter Kaiser unequivocally connects the Covenant Code of Exodus with the Holiness Code of Leviticus, which is the subject of Lessons 2 and 3. Kaiser writes, "Whereas most of the previous sections of the covenant code have stressed love and compassion toward the weak, the poor, and the alien, this section exhorts Israel to practice another virtue: justice" (442).

1 Thou shalt not raise a false report: put not thine hand with the wicked to be an unrighteous witness.

Interestingly, the Hebrew word for "report" is *shema`* (**SHAY-mah**), which means "tidings," and can even refer to God's words (Habakkuk 3:2). *Shema`* comes from the root of the Hebrew word *shama`* (**shaw-MAW**) from the famous passage in Deuteronomy 6:4, which means to hear and obey. In Exodus 23:1, the phrase "Put not thine hand with the wicked to be an unrighteous witness" in the NLT reads, "Do not cooperate with evil people by telling lies on the witness stand."

This verse adds detail to the ninth commandment (20:13; see also Leviticus 19:11; Deuteronomy 19:15–21) and indicates a courtroom situation, but it is not limited to that context. Any "raising up" of an "unrighteous" witness or testimony in any context is to be avoided. This includes even telling the truth in an unrighteous way (i.e., bringing harm to a person or damaging them in any way). It is common knowledge that there are countless scenarios where gossip has caused great injury and injustice. The entire spectrum of gossip—from inappropriate truth telling, to minor exaggerations, to outright fabrications—is to be avoided by God's people.

Exodus 23:1 also specifically addresses giving false testimony about someone who is guilty, which would include helping cover up an evil person's deeds. Doing so enables the "wicked" person to continue in his or her evil and directly contributes to any future harm that comes to others as a result of the false testimony. According to Old Testament law, any false or unrighteous report (also in v. 8, "perverteth the words of the righteous") deserves the same punishment that was intended for the other (see Deuteronomy 19:15–21). "What is in view here is a conspiracy to pervert the course of justice and to deprive an innocent individual of his rights," notes John Mackay (*Exodus: A Mentor Commentary*, 398; see also commentary on Leviticus 19:16 in *Precepts For Living Bible Study Guide®* for June 10, 2012; and the story of Jezebel and Naboth in 1 Kings 21:10–13).

2 Thou shalt not follow a multitude to do evil; neither shalt thou speak in a cause to decline after many to wrest judgment:

Justifications such as "majority rule" or "popular consensus" do not relieve a child of God from the responsibility of speaking out against the doing of evil. When it comes to the weighty matter of injustice, God expects His people to take a stand—even if it means swimming against the current or enduring the pressure of the crowd attempting to pervert justice. "Multitude" in Hebrew is *rab* (**rab**) and means "many," but also can mean "mighty" or "chief," which is a sharp contrast to the plight of the vulnerable poor person whose welfare is at stake. The NIV reads, "Do not follow the crowd in doing wrong . . . do not pervert justice by siding with the crowd."

In verse 1, the prohibition was against personally engaging in the evil; verse 2 prohibits not speaking up for the truth even when one's opinion is outnumbered. Again, the verse implies primarily a courtroom setting, but can extend universally. These injunctions are amplifications of the Decalogue but do not and cannot cover all possible cases for doing evil and committing injustice. In a modern application, even if the other 11 jurors are tired and want to throw the accused under the bus so they can be done with him or her, God's people are held to a higher standard and must uphold justice, no matter how unpopular.

3 Neither shalt thou countenance a poor man in his cause.

"Countenance" in the Hebrew is *hadar* (**ha-DAR**) and means to honor. This verse should be viewed with the illumination of Leviticus 19:15 (see Lesson 2), which addresses the same matter of partiality or favoritism— which perverts justice—but specifies both rich and poor. The NLT of Exodus 23:3 reads, "Do not slant your testimony in favor of a person just because that person is poor." In other words, sympathy for a poor person should not be allowed to influence justice anymore than partiality for the rich might

subvert justice. The message, especially for judges, is simply to never show partiality.

4 If thou meet thine enemy's ox or his ass going astray, thou shalt surely bring it back to him again. 5 If thou see the ass of him that hateth thee lying under his burden, and wouldest forbear to help him, thou shalt surely help with him.

Verses 4 and 5 are two case laws showing examples of impartiality, which uniquely address justice for one's enemies. Apparently, it was a common misunderstanding—and still is—to think that the Old Testament taught people to hate their enemies. On the contrary, benevolence and mercy were frequent themes (see 2 Kings 6:18–23; Proverbs 25:21–22; Jeremiah 29:7). Even the famous "eye for an eye" assertion (Exodus 21:24) was a matter of straight justice and not revenge or hatred. In reality, vengeance often far exceeds the original incident. What Jesus clarified and overruled in Matthew 5:38–39 was a misinterpreted oral tradition and not a matter of actual law. Exodus 23:4–5 are examples of the practical application of justice, a dominant and explicit theological theme of the Old Testament.

Even when the circumstance involves an "enemy," which in Hebrew is *'oyeb* (**o-YABE**)—a common word in the Old Testament used nearly 300 times, which can also mean one who hates you—God's standards clearly are to dispense justice for all. In today's world, helping someone with his or her donkey that has strayed or fallen with a load would be a direct parallel to helping someone change a tire. In this case, it would be helping someone who perhaps had mistreated you, or flat out despised you. As emphasized in Proverbs 25:22, doing a good thing for him or her would heap coals of shame on his or her head for hating you. Jesus illustrated the principle with the parable of the good Samaritan. An act of compassion or kindness, which is commanded in Proverbs 25:21–22 (see also 24:17), is what Jesus meant when He refuted the mistaken oral tradition of hatred toward one's enemies, and instead embraced the greater and also explicit commands for justice and mercy, even for enemies (Matthew 5:43–45; 23:23; Luke 6:27–38).

6 Thou shalt not wrest the judgment of thy poor in his cause. 7 Keep thee far from a false matter; and the innocent and righteous slay thou not: for I will not justify the wicked.

The injunction now returns to courtroom procedural laws, this time addressing corrupt judges who put vulnerable people at a great disadvantage. There are two types of poor in this section: "poor" in Exodus 23:3 in Hebrew is *dal* (**dal**), a basic term, while "poor" in verse 6 in Hebrew is *'ebyown* (**eb-YONE**) and refers to an extremely needy person, in danger of oppression and abuse; someone who is destitute or indigent. The NLT reads, "Do not twist justice against people simply because they are poor. Keep far away from falsely charging anyone with evil."

Again, God's people are called to a higher standard, and even the poorest of the poor must be treated fairly and justly. Since such matters frequently fall to judges to determine, they are singled out for these holy proscriptions. Even more specific is the injunction to see to it that no innocent person ("innocent or honest," NLT) is ever put to death, which begins by staying far away from anything false or evil. In this case, God warns that He will not spare judgment on the judge. The warning is trans-cultural on principle to all who occupy positions of power or influence, not only judges, but any who abuse their positions by acting unjustly.

No matter how high their offices, they are not the ultimate authorities—even for Supreme Court judges.

8 And thou shalt take no gift: for the gift blindeth the wise, and perverteth the words of the righteous. 9 Also thou shalt not oppress a stranger: for ye know the heart of a stranger, seeing ye were strangers in the land of Egypt.

As if the above is still not explicit enough, verse 8 specifies taking bribes. In verse 8, the word "gift" in Hebrew is *shachad* (**SHAKH-ad**) and means, as it does in English, a bribe or present for a corrupt official (a gift with the intent of gaining some kind of favor). The Old Testament has many such warnings (see the close parallel in Deuteronomy 16:19, "a gift doth blind the eyes of the wise, and pervert the words of the righteous"; see also Proverbs 17:8, 23; 21:14).

There are several nearly identical passages to Exodus 23:9, one of which is found in 22:21: "Thou shalt neither vex a stranger, nor oppress him: for ye were strangers in the land of Egypt" (for others, see Leviticus 19:34; Deuteronomy 10:19). The latter verse in the list goes far above and beyond not oppressing: "Love ye therefore the stranger: for ye were strangers in the land of Egypt." See Lessons 2 and 3 for commentary on strangers and sojourners (aliens).

To "oppress the alien, the orphan, or the widow" in ancient Israel (Jeremiah 7:6, NASB; see also Deuteronomy 24:13–15, NASB) was not the same as today's frequently misunderstood situation regarding people in a country without legal documents for visiting, working, or residence. It is not unjust to expect visitors to follow the laws of the land, which makes them either travelers (sojourners) or those seeking legal immigration. Likewise, straightforward prosecution of lawbreakers, regardless of residency status, is not unjust. What is unjust, as pointed out in Exodus 23:9, is to "oppress" (Heb. *lachats*, **LAKH-ats**), meaning to take advantage of or pervert justice for people of any residency status, but especially if they are following the laws (if they are "innocent or honest," v. 7, NLT).

Ultimately, why should Israel not oppress or commit injustice? Why should they exercise justice, even for enemies and aliens? God reminds them it is because they should remember how they were treated and how it felt when they were in Egypt. The greater truth is that justice is the embodiment of God's holiness within His people. God did not simply deliver His laws to His people, and then leave them to their own devices to interpret and apply it. Rather, He is personally involved with the lives of His people, even judging individual cases, and He hears the cries of the oppressed (see also Exodus 22:22–24; Judges 2:18; Nehemiah 9:27).

Sources:
Bruckner, James K. *Exodus. Old Testament Series. New International Biblical Commentary.* Peabody, MA: Hendrickson Publishers, 2008. 216–17.
Brueggemann, Walter. *An Introduction to the Old Testament: The Canon and Christian Imagination.* Louisville, KY: Westminster John Knox Press, 2003. 60–66.
Hebrew and Greek Lexicons. Bible Study Tools.com. http://www.biblestudytools.com/lexicons (accessed November 5, 2010).
Kaiser, Walter C. *Genesis, Exodus, Leviticus, Numbers. The Expositor's Bible Commentary, vol. 2.* Edited by Frank E. Gaebelein. Grand Rapids, MI: Zondervan, 1990. 442–43.
Mackay, John L. Exodus: A Mentor Commentary. Ross-Shire, Great Britain: Christian Focus Publications, 2001. 398–401.
Merriam-Webster Online Dictionary. Merriam-Webster, Inc. http://www.merriam-webster.com (accessed November 5, 2010).
Old and New Testament Concordances, Lexicons, Dictionaries, Commentaries, Images, and Bible Versions. Blue Letter Bible. org. http://www.blueletterbible.org/ (accessed July 10, 2010).
Passage Lookup. Bible Gateway.com. http://www.biblegateway.com/passage (accessed January 17, 2011).
Rogerson, John, and Philip Davies. *The Old Testament World.* Englewood Cliffs, NJ: Prentice Hall, 1989. 238–42.

Say It Correctly

Decalogue. DEK-uh-log.
Deuteronomy. Doo'tuh-RON-uh-mee.
Sinai. SI-ni.

Daily Bible Readings

MONDAY
Punishment for False Witnesses
(Deuteronomy 19:15–20)

TUESDAY
God Holds Court
(Psalm 82)

WEDNESDAY
The Day of Punishment
(Isaiah 10:1–4)

THURSDAY
Rescued from the Wicked and Unjust
(Psalm 71:1–6)

FRIDAY
A God of Justice
(Isaiah 30:18–22)

SATURDAY
God's Ways Are Just
(Deuteronomy 31:30–32:7)

SUNDAY
Justice for All
(Exodus 23:1–9)

Teaching Tips

June 10
Bible Study Guide 2

Words You Should Know

A. Stranger (Leviticus 19:10) *ger* (Heb.)—A sojourner; a newcomer, or a foreigner.

B. Unrighteousness (Lev. 19:15) *`evel* (Heb.)—Injustice, iniquity, and wickedness.

Teacher Preparation

Unifying Principle—Acting with Compassion. Those who reflect God's holy nature and love others as they love themselves, which includes treating them fairly, justly, and respectfully.

A. Pray for lesson clarity.

B. Study and meditate on the entire text.

C. Prepare a PowerPoint presentation or bring news clippings of incidents involving justice and compassion.

D. Complete the companion lesson in the *Precepts For Living Personal Study Guide®*.

O—Open the Lesson

A. Open with prayer, including the Aim for Change.

B. After prayer, introduce today's subject of the lesson.

C. Read the Aim for Change and Keep in Mind verse in unison. Discuss.

D. Share your presentation.

E. Then ask, "Have you ever personally experienced injustice?"

F. Share testimonies.

G. Have a volunteer summarize the In Focus story. Discuss.

H. Ask, "Knowing how painful injustice feels, how careful should we be to avoid inflicting others with injustice?" Discuss.

P—Present the Scriptures

A. Have volunteers read the Focal Verses.

B. Now use The People, Places, and Times; Background; Search the Scriptures; At-A-Glance outline; In Depth; and More Light on the Text to clarify the verses.

E—Explore the Meaning

A. Have volunteers summarize the Discuss the Meaning, Lesson in Our Society, and Make It Happen sections.

B. Connect these sections to the Aim for Change and the Keep in Mind verse.

N—Next Steps for Application

A. Summarize the lesson.

B. Close with prayer.

Worship Guide

For the Superintendent or Teacher
Theme: Living as God's Just People
Theme Song: "Standing on Holy Ground"
Devotional Reading: Luke 10:25–37
Prayer

Living as God's Just People

Bible Background • LEVITICUS 19:9–18, 33–37
Printed Text • LEVITICUS 19:9–18, 33–37 | Devotional Reading • LUKE 10:25–37

— Aim for Change —

By the end of the lesson, we will: KNOW what it means to love one's neighbor as one's self; REFLECT on ways to act with compassion; and PRAY to live a life of justice and compassion.

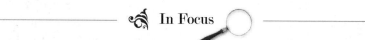

— 🔍 In Focus —

In the March 6, 1994, issue of *Our Daily Bread*, Haddon W. Robinson wrote: "In his autobiography, Mahatma Gandhi [the preeminent political and spiritual leader of India during the Indian Independence Movement] wrote that during his student days he read the Gospels seriously and considered converting to Christianity. He believed that in the teachings of Jesus he could find the solution to the caste system that was dividing the people of India. So one Sunday he decided to attend services at a nearby church and talk to the minister about becoming a Christian. When he entered the sanctuary, however, the usher refused to give him a seat and suggested that he go worship with his own people. Gandhi left the church and never returned.

"'If Christians have caste differences also,'" he said, "'I might as well remain a Hindu.'"

"That usher's prejudice not only betrayed Jesus but also turned a person away from trusting Him as Savior."

Our lesson today deals with loving and respecting people for whom God has made them to be.

— Keep in Mind —

"But the stranger that dwelleth with you shall be unto you as one born among you, and thou shalt love him as thyself; for ye were strangers in the land of Egypt: I am the LORD your God" (Leviticus 19:34).

"But the stranger that dwelleth with you shall be unto you as one born among you, and thou shalt love him as thyself; for ye were strangers in the land of Egypt: I am the LORD your God" (Leviticus 19:34).

Focal Verses

KJV **Leviticus 19:9** And when ye reap the harvest of your land, thou shalt not wholly reap the corners of thy field, neither shalt thou gather the gleanings of thy harvest.

10 And thou shalt not glean thy vineyard, neither shalt thou gather every grape of thy vineyard; thou shalt leave them for the poor and stranger: I am the LORD your God.

11 Ye shall not steal, neither deal falsely, neither lie one to another.

12 And ye shall not swear by my name falsely, neither shalt thou profane the name of thy God: I am the LORD.

13 Thou shalt not defraud thy neighbour, neither rob him: the wages of him that is hired shall not abide with thee all night until the morning.

14 Thou shalt not curse the deaf, nor put a stumblingblock before the blind, but shalt fear thy God: I am the LORD.

15 Ye shall do no unrighteousness in judgment: thou shalt not respect the person of the poor, nor honour the person of the mighty: but in righteousness shalt thou judge thy neighbour.

16 Thou shalt not go up and down as a talebearer among thy people: neither shalt thou stand against the blood of thy neighbour: I am the LORD.

17 Thou shalt not hate thy brother in thine heart: thou shalt in any wise rebuke thy neighbour, and not suffer sin upon him.

18 Thou shalt not avenge, nor bear any grudge against the children of thy people, but thou shalt love thy neighbour as thyself: I am the LORD.

19:33 And if a stranger sojourn with thee in your land, ye shall not vex him.

34 But the stranger that dwelleth with you shall be unto you as one born among you,

NLT **Leviticus 19:9** "When you harvest your crops, do not harvest the grain along the edges of your fields, and do not pick up what the harvesters drop.

10 It is the same with your grape crop—do not strip every last bunch of grapes from the vines, and do not pick up the grapes that fall to the ground. Leave them for the poor and the foreigners who live among you, for I, the LORD, am your God.

11 "Do not steal.

"Do not cheat one another.

"Do not lie.

12 "Do not use my name to swear a falsehood and so profane the name of your God. I am the LORD.

13 "Do not cheat or rob anyone.

"Always pay your hired workers promptly.

14 "Show your fear of God by treating the deaf with respect and by not taking advantage of the blind. I am the LORD.

15 "Always judge your neighbors fairly, neither favoring the poor nor showing deference to the rich.

16 "Do not spread slanderous gossip among your people.

"Do not try to get ahead at the cost of your neighbor's life, for I am the LORD.

17 "Do not nurse hatred in your heart for any of your relatives.

"Confront your neighbors directly so you will not be held guilty for their crimes.

18 "Never seek revenge or bear a grudge against anyone, but love your neighbor as yourself. I am the LORD.

19:33 "Do not exploit the foreigners who live in your land.

34 They should be treated like everyone else, and you must love them as you love yourself. Remember that you were once

KJV Cont.

and thou shalt love him as thyself; for ye were strangers in the land of Egypt: I am the LORD your God.

35 Ye shall do no unrighteousness in judgment, in meteyard, in weight, or in measure.

36 Just balances, just weights, a just ephah, and a just hin, shall ye have: I am the LORD your God, which brought you out of the land of Egypt.

37 Therefore shall ye observe all my statutes, and all my judgments, and do them: I am the LORD.

NLT Cont.

foreigners in the land of Egypt. I, the LORD, am your God.

35 "Do not use dishonest standards when measuring length, weight, or volume.

36 Your scales and weights must be accurate. Your containers for measuring dry goods or liquids must be accurate. I, the LORD, am your God, who brought you out of the land of Egypt.

37 You must be careful to obey all of my laws and regulations, for I am the LORD."

The People, Places, and Times

A Holy People. God's people have always had a special relationship with Him, one that is based on God's nature and character. When Israel agreed to be God's people and to obey His covenant—following His miraculous deliverance of them from the Egyptians—they bound themselves to ethical and religious responsibilities. These were delivered to them in the form of legal codes (i.e., the Covenant Code and the Holiness Code), which included both positive and negative injunctions. The vertical relationship of God's people was outlined in the Decalogue (the Ten Commandments) and was fairly simple and straightforward—they were to have no other gods, they were not to use the Lord's name in vain, and they were to honor the Sabbath. The horizontal relationship was more complicated and came in the form of numerous specific injunctions, all provided as guiding examples and principles for how they were to govern themselves both at home and in the world.

Background

The Holiness Code of Leviticus 18:1–24:9 was given to the Israelites as a set of ethical and religious responsibilities, which includes both positive and negative injunctions. John Rogerson and Philip Davies write, "The basis of the regulations in 19:11–18 about fair dealing with one's neighbours [sic] is not so much social solidarity as mutual religious responsibility" (145). A large part of Leviticus deals with priestly matters, while chapters 18 and 20 address sexual relations. Chapter 19, the focus of today's lesson, deals primarily with Israel's horizontal relationships with others, particularly addressing justice and fairness as examples of holiness.

At-A-Glance

1. Social Justice: Treating Others Right
(Leviticus 19:9–16)

2. Social Justice: Starts in the Heart
(vv. 17–18)

3. Social Justice: Cares for Strangers
(vv. 33–34)

4. Social Justice: Being Fair in Business
and Law (vv. 35–37)

In Depth

1. Social Justice: Treating Others Right (Leviticus 19:9–16)

Jesus summarized the horizontal part of a proper relationship with God as "love thy neighbour as thyself" (see Matthew 22:38–39; Luke 10:27). Inherent in every aspect of God's holy nature and His laws regarding holiness is His heart of love. Every injunction contained in the entire Sinai Tradition reflects God's heart of love. Treating others right, or loving one's neighbor, is the ultimate expression of social justice. Contained within this overriding principle are the following details:

Proper handling of the land (vv. 9–10). Inherent in treating others right is the matter of strangers (e.g., travelers), but also includes the ubiquitous poor and those who perhaps once were better off but have fallen on hard times. By generously leaving the corners of one's fields or vines for those less fortunate, the Israelite demonstrated a godly attitude toward others. Today, one's surplus can be shared with others in any number of ways.

Honesty with everyone (vv. 11–13). It might seem obvious at first, but the injunctions against committing perjury, stealing, and lying (which parallel the third, eighth, and ninth commandments respectively) are sometimes harder to obey when the boundaries are less clear. When the cases are obvious, the choices between right and wrong are clear. But often deception, deceit, and fraud can take very subtle and more easily justified forms. The godly person avoids all such acts, however minor, that dishonor God and harm others.

Not taking advantage of others (vv. 14–16). Much like the previous injunctions, these specify taking advantage of the disadvantaged. In particular, singling out weak or easy "marks," such as the handicapped or someone in a desperate situation, is injustice defined. The opposite type of person is also included—God's holy people also are not to act dishonorably toward the privileged. An easy example would be filing unjust lawsuits against "deep pockets." In all cases, embodying social justice excludes all forms of gossip, backstabbing, and slander, as these are harmful to others and dishonoring to God.

2. Social Justice: Starts in the Heart (vv. 17–18)

Don't hate and don't seek revenge. Jesus was very clear when He commanded in Matthew 5:43–44 to love even one's enemies, which would more than encompass these verses speaking primarily about "neighbors." Jesus knew that murder started with hate and frequently originated with a grudge that morphed into vengeance. An injunction against this evil root would preclude much trouble, grief, and heartache, not to mention it would spare lives. God is fully capable of exercising vengeance, as eloquently captured in the prayer of Psalm 94:1, "O Lord God, to whom vengeance belongeth; O God, to whom vengeance belongeth, shew thyself." In verse 3, Psalm 94 asks the timeless question, "How long shall the wicked triumph?" The answer is that however long it is, their judgment belongs to God and God alone.

Love your neighbor as yourself. The second greatest commandment is reiterated in both testaments and reinforced by Jesus and others (see More Light on the Text). This is presented as one of several positive injunctions, but it happens to capture the heart of the entire Holiness Code—in fact all the law codes. Nothing better defines the child of God or social justice than loving one's neighbor as one's self.

3. Social Justice: Cares for Strangers (vv. 33–34)

Strangers are sojourners (travelers). Strangers also may be newcomers or foreigners (aliens), and God's children are to treat them as they would be treated—again invoking the second greatest commandment. This clarifies beyond question the New Testament rhetorical question, "Who is my neighbour?" (Luke 10:29). The answer is abundantly clear—everyone! None are excluded from the injunction, as clarified by the various specific examples. Whether they are visitors just passing through, settlers from another culture, or foreign outsiders, all are to be treated like blood relatives and loved as one's self.

Israel once was a stranger in Egypt. Considering that the great Exodus from Egypt had not happened very long before the time of these injunctions, the reminder should have been a very familiar example. Nothing drives a point home better than a personal example, especially a recent one. For Christians, the parallel is with their personal deliverance from the bondage of sin, which more often than not is remembered with great fondness, no matter how many years transpire. Occasionally, however, some need to be reminded that they once had been delivered from oppression and bondage, and they should not even consider mistreating others or inflicting them with any kind of injustice.

4. Social Justice: Being Fair in Business and Law (vv. 35–37)

Just scales, righteous dealings, and fairness toward all. Occasionally, some Old Testament laws translate perfectly into modern society without need for any kind of cultural filter. The injunction about unjust scales is preceded by a general command of not doing any unrighteousness in "judgment" or in weighing any matter, but specifically when scales determine values and deception is difficult to detect. This could find countless modern applications, such as gas stations not setting their pumps accurately; taxi drivers "running up the meter"; expense accounts or invoices being "padded"; accountants doing "creative" bookkeeping.

Obeying God's just ordinances is evidence for righteousness. Even where there is an unbridgeable cultural distance between the laws of the "Sinai Tradition" and today, God's people are still called to a standard of holiness measured against God's own holiness. Nothing demonstrates personal righteousness more than being faithful to living in a way that honors God. Nothing more explicitly defines such a life as one who is committed to loving others through practical expressions of social justice.

Search the Scriptures

1. Where is the Holiness Code found in Scripture (Leviticus 19)?

2. Were the laws in the Holiness Code exhaustive?

Discuss the Meaning

Locate some of the examples given in the Holiness Code of specific examples of injustice. Try to find modern examples that would parallel the same principles. Now think about some of your personal experiences with injustice or unrighteousness. How did these experiences make you feel? Now contrast these memories and feelings with a memorable time when you witnessed holiness, justice, or righteousness. Finish by thinking about how you have treated others justly and unjustly.

Lesson in Our Society

Often, the lofty matters of holiness and justice become elusive principles when confronted with complex, emotional, and controversial events and circumstances—such as the nation's concern for border security and how that should be translated into laws and actions. As much as one wants to obey God's Word and love one's neighbor, how are those realities impacted when a neighbor is breaking the law? Should everyone crossing the border illegally be granted unlimited freedom to enter the U.S., even if some of them are criminals from the Mexican drug cartel, murderers, kidnappers, and drug and weapons dealers? How should the thinking of law-abiding Christians be balanced to reflect the concerns for the innocent poor seeking a better life as well as the safety of fellow American citizens? These are not easy questions or simple issues. God's people must be careful to weigh (judge) the issues and allow themselves to be driven by principles of biblical justice and not let God's definitions be confused by the vested interests of politics.

Make It Happen

God's people are to be in the world but not of it. Theirs is a higher calling to the kingdom of God and to holy living as defined by Scripture—which translates to a timeless command to treating others as we would be treated, to love others as we would be loved, and a determination to be just and fair in all one's human relationships. Surely, there are enough challenges in this one paragraph to last a lifetime.

Follow the Spirit

What God wants me to do:

_____

_____

_____

_____

Remember Your Thoughts

Special insights I have learned:

_____

_____

_____

_____

More Light on the Text
Leviticus 19:9–18, 33–37
Introduction

Just in this lesson, the phrase "I am the LORD" appears eight times. With other verses in chapter 19, it appears a total of 16 times and 162 times within the entire Bible. Within the lesson, the phrase expands in verses 10, 34, and 36 as "I am the LORD your God" (see also vv. 3, 4, 7, 24). All of the above are abbreviations of the full first use in the chapter, "Ye shall be holy: for I the LORD your God am holy" (19:2), which serves as the introduction to the chapter and this lesson. These words are the simple but all-sufficient reason that Israel (and the church) is to obey. This portion of Scripture is all about God's holiness and His requirements for our holiness, and thus has been called the "Holiness Code."

The chapter spells out Israel's ethical and religious responsibilities. Some injunctions are negative (to be avoided) while others are positive (to be embraced), which together "say both *yes* to what God requires and *no* to what God forbids," in the words of Samuel Balentine (160, emphasis added). As a whole, this chapter underscores and elaborates the Ten Commandments (Decalogue) given to Moses in Exodus 20:2–17 and reiterated in Deuteronomy 5:6–21.

9 And when ye reap the harvest of your land, thou shalt not wholly reap the corners of thy field, neither shalt thou gather the gleanings of thy harvest. 10 And thou shalt not glean thy vineyard, neither shalt thou gather every grape of thy vineyard; thou shalt leave them for the poor and stranger: I am the LORD your God.

Jesus quoted from the Law to confirm that the greatest command is vertical, to love God (Deuteronomy 6:5, right after the great "*shema*" verse in 6:4), while the second greatest command is horizontal, to love one's neighbor (see commentary here on Leviticus 19:18 and 19:34; also Matthew 22:38–39; Luke 10:27). Virtually all of Leviticus 19 deals with the horizontal, which includes proper handling of the land in order to care for the needs of the poor. In 19:10, the Hebrew word for "poor" is `aniy (**aw-NEE**) and has been consistently interpreted among most versions. The Hebrew word for "stranger" is *ger* (**gare**), but this word has been interpreted as "foreigner," "alien," and "sojourner." The point is to *not* pick the fields or vines clean and to *not* think only of oneself or one's own profits. The point is to act generously with every harvest and crop and to consciously think of others, especially those less fortunate, like the poor and those who are away from home—the travelers— and to care about their needs in a practical and tangible way.

11 Ye shall not steal, neither deal falsely, neither lie one to another. 12 And ye shall not swear by my name falsely, neither shalt thou profane the name of thy God: I am the LORD. 13 Thou shalt not defraud thy neighbour, neither rob him: the wages of him that is hired shall not abide with thee all night until the morning.

This part of the Holiness Code of Leviticus is cast in the negative, by way of prohibitions, just as there were both positive and negative injunctions in the Decalogue. It is all about social justice, which involves much more than economic justice, as some might think incorrectly. To steal, deceive, or lie is squarely denounced in the eighth and ninth commandments (do not steal and do not bear false witness), but in this context it seems to apply especially to the poor. Later verses in this lesson directly include all who are in a state of vulnerability and indirectly include everyone. Ultimately, the prohibition is against deception and deceit of any kind, against anyone, for any reason. Paralleling the third commandment (do not take the name of the Lord in vain) with different words in Leviticus 19:12 refers to using God's name in an oath that one does not intend to keep. Today's swearing on a Bible in a courtroom, but planning to commit perjury, specifically would violate this injunction. Dishonesty compromises both the individual and the entire human community, and it is contrary to and destructive of God's holiness.

Oppression of any kind does not reflect God's holiness, which demands a higher standard and values even the "least of these" as the same thing as serving God Himself (Matthew 25:31–40). In Leviticus 19:13, the Hebrew word for "neighbour" is *rea`* (**RAY-ah**) and ultimately refers to everyone (see commentary here on verses 18 and 34).

14 Thou shalt not curse the deaf, nor put a stumblingblock before the blind, but shalt fear thy God: I am the LORD. 15 Ye shall do no unrighteousness in judgment: thou shalt not respect the person of the poor, nor honour the person of the mighty: but in righteousness shalt thou judge thy neighbour. 16 Thou shalt not go up and down as a talebearer among thy people: neither shalt thou stand against the blood of thy neighbour: I am the LORD.

None are more vulnerable than the handicapped, and even in ancient times it was clear that God would not tolerate injustice of any kind inflicted upon them. In fact, this specific injunction is followed by the familiar and powerful rationalization, as if to say, "Do this, just because I the Lord say it." Verse 15 is a more general reference; as if verse 14 needed another blanket for those who might find exceptions to "do no unrighteousness" of any kind in judgment (negative injunction)— whether it involves the poor or the rich—but rather "judge" your neighbor righteously (positive injunction). "Judge" comes from the Hebrew word *shaphat* (**shaw-FAT**) and can mean to govern, vindicate, or punish, but it can also mean to either decide a controversy or enter into one. "Judgment" in Hebrew is *mishpat* (**mish-PAWT**) and means a just ordinance; it is a little more specific (with the "just" element) than "statute" (see commentary on v. 37). The context of this entire section speaks to men acting like wolves who single out the weak, or sickly, or those most likely to be easy marks. A child of the holy God is not to do these things—or risk God's anger.

Slander is another specific type of evil or injustice, which in Ezekiel 22:9 is connected to murder. In modern times, the legal definition of slander is publishing something about someone else that is not true and doing it with malice. The biblical injunction refers to gossip, which can involve either true or untrue statements that are spread perniciously. Because it causes so much damage, and because it is so far from holiness, slander or gossip is singled out for prohibition in Scripture (see also Jeremiah 6:28; 9:4; Proverbs 11:13; 20:19). Gossip or slander also violates the eighth commandment.

17 Thou shalt not hate thy brother in thine heart: thou shalt in any wise rebuke thy neighbour, and not suffer sin upon him. 18 Thou shalt not avenge, nor bear any grudge against the children of thy people, but thou shalt love thy neighbour as thyself: I am the LORD.

In Matthew 5:43, Jesus quoted Leviticus 19:17–18 (part of the Mosaic Law), understanding clearly that hate in one's heart is what leads to murder. Thus, hate has always been condemned in both testaments of Scripture, with or without the act of murder. The specific expressions of revenge and bearing a grudge in verse 18 are a sharper focus of the general injunction against hatred. Other parts of the Old Testament zoom in even further on the subject of revenge, specifying repeatedly that God alone has the right, and God alone is able to exact perfect justice, regardless of the severity of the act or actions that inspired the hate and revenge (see Jeremiah 15:15; Nahum 1:2; Psalm 94:1). It is common knowledge that resentment and anger fester and invariably result in unholy expressions and deeds. It is also commonly known that such attitudes often harm the bearers more than their targets.

Juxtaposed against, and antithetical to, all forms of injustice, hatred, and evil, love stands as the quintessential solution and antidote. In Leviticus 19:18 the Hebrew word for "love" is *'ahab* (**AH-hab**). The do's and don'ts of loving one's neighbor could have been listed by the thousands, but this list in Leviticus, expanded from the Decalogue in Exodus, should have served as sufficient extension to make the clear point that love for God translates into love for neighbors, and that love does not inflict injustice, hatred, vengeance, and so on. Jesus quoted from the now famous citation of the second greatest commandment, captured by all three Synoptic Gospel writers (Matthew 5:43; 19:19; 22:39; Mark 12:31; Luke 10:27), Paul (Romans 13:9; Galatians 5:14), and James (James 2:8). Again, the only rationale needed is that God is God.

19:33 And if a stranger sojourn with thee in your land, ye shall not vex him. 34 But the stranger that dwelleth with you shall be unto you as one born among you, and thou shalt love him as thyself; for ye were strangers in the land of Egypt: I am the LORD your God.

As stated, the Hebrew word for "stranger" is *ger* (**gare**) and can include a sojourner; in verse 33, the phrase "stranger sojourn" is interpreted from the Hebrew *guwr* (**goor**). Thus, the phrase easily could have been a bit of humorous alliteration (i.e., spelled phonetically, "the *ger guwr*").

It is easy to see the proper way to treat strangers in a brief sentence: "Love them as you love yourself." In a literal sense, the Israelites had been "stranger sojourners" in Egypt not long before, so the reference in verse 34 to their former place of slavery was appropriate and the connection vivid. God loved the Israelites when they were sojourners in the foreign land of Egypt, and He also loved them when they rebelled against Him and practiced evil. Likewise, He loves us while we have been strangers and sinners to Him.

35 Ye shall do no unrighteousness in judgment, in meteyard, in weight, or in measure. 36 Just balances, just weights, a just ephah, and a just hin, shall ye have: I am the LORD your God, which brought you out of the land of Egypt.

`Evel (**EH-vel**) is the Hebrew word for "unrighteousness," and it sounds remarkably like our word "evil." Indeed, the meaning is synonymous with injustice, iniquity, and wickedness, and it can include violent deeds of injustice. In verse 36 the Hebrew word for "just" is *tsedeq* (**TSEH-dek**) and means justice, rightness, and righteousness—the exact opposite of *evel* from verse 35. Few Old Testament theological concepts emerge quite as strongly as the twin themes of justice and righteousness (see Proverbs 21:3; Isaiah 16:5; Amos 5:24). We are to embody or model our love and obedience to God through our love for and service to others, without exception.

Jesus further underscored the Levitical amplifications of the Decalogue by removing all listed specifics and replacing them with an even more impossible-to-achieve holiness— namely that to simply think about acting unjustly would make one guilty of the whole law (Matthew 5:22). In contrast to unjust weights used in unrighteousness, those in Leviticus 19:36 who use "just weights" both exercise justice and are evidence of righteousness.

37 Therefore shall ye observe all my statutes, and all my judgments, and do them: I am the LORD.

Again, the word "judgments" in Hebrew is *mishpat* and means just ordinances, an equivalent of "statutes," although that word in the Hebrew is *choq* (**khoke**), which refers to God's laws in this use, but does not contain the clear, "just" element of *mishpat*. We must obey God's commands!

Sources:

Balentine, Samuel E. *Leviticus. Interpretation: A Bible Commentary for Teaching and Preaching.* 2nd ed. Louisville, KY: John Knox Press, 2002. 160–67.

Bellender, W. H., Jr. *Leviticus, Numbers. Old Testament Series. New International Biblical Commentary.* Peabody, MA: Hendrickson Publishers, 2001. 116–21.

Bible Pronunciation Chart. Better Days Are Coming.com. http://www.betterdaysarecoming/bible/pronunciation.html (accessed January 29, 2011).

Brueggemann, Walter. *An Introduction to the Old Testament: The Canon and Christian Imagination.* Louisville, KY: Westminster John Knox Press, 2003. 67–74.

Harris, R. Laird. *Genesis, Exodus, Leviticus, Numbers. The Expositor's Bible Commentary,* vol. 2. Edited by Frank E. Gaebelein. Grand Rapids, MI: Zondervan, 1990. 604–09.

Hebrew and Greek Lexicons. Bible Study Tools.com. http://www.biblestudytools.com/lexicons (accessed November 8, 2010).

Merriam-Webster Online Dictionary. Merriam-Webster, Inc. http://www.merriam-webster.com (accessed November 8, 2010).

Old and New Testament Concordances, Lexicons, Dictionaries, Commentaries, Images, and Bible Versions. Blue Letter Bible. org. http://www.blueletterbible.org/ (accessed July 10, 2010).

Passage Lookup. Bible Gateway.com. http://www.biblegateway.com/passage (accessed January 17, 2011).

Robinson, Haddon W. "A Prejudiced Usher." *Our Daily Bread.* March 6, 1994. http://www.odb.org/1994/03/06/a-prejudiced-usher/ (accessed January 29, 2011).

Rogerson, John, and Philip Davies. *The Old Testament World.* Englewood Cliffs, NJ: Prentice Hall, 1989. 242–45.

Daily Bible Readings

MONDAY
God's Indignation over Injustice
(Ezekiel 22:23–31)

TUESDAY
No Safety for Sinners
(Jeremiah 7:8–15)

WEDNESDAY
Deliver Me from Evildoers
(Psalm 140:1–8)

THURSDAY
Occasions for Stumbling
(Matthew 18:1–9)

FRIDAY
If You Truly Amend Your Ways
(Jeremiah 7:1–7)

SATURDAY
"Who Is My Neighbor?"
(Luke 10:25–37)

SUNDAY
"I Am the LORD"
(Leviticus 19:9–18, 33–37)

Say It Correctly

Decalogue. DEK-uh-log.
Ephah. EE-fuh, EE-fah.
Leviticus. Lih-VI-tih-kuhs.
Zechariah. Zek'uh-RI-ah.

Notes

Teaching Tips

June 17
Bible Study Guide 3

JUNE
17th

Words You Should Know

A. Jubile (Leviticus 25:10, 11, 12, 40) *teruw`ah, yowbel* (Heb.)—Also spelled "jubilee"; a season of celebration; a year of emancipation and restoration.

B. Hallow (v. 10) *qadash* (Heb.)—To consecrate or sanctify.

Teacher Preparation

Unifying Principle—Making a Fresh Start. Some people are oppressed because of the unjust circumstances into which they are born and live. By observing a year of jubilee, those who are oppressed are given the means for making a fresh start.

A. Pray for your students and that God will bring clarity to this lesson.

B. Study and meditate on the entire text.

C. Complete the companion lesson in the *Precepts For Living Personal Study Guide®*.

D. Research statistics and other information about the number of housing foreclosures, joblessness, etc., in America and tie that in with the "Year of Jubilee" discussed in today's lesson.

O—Open the Lesson

A. Open with prayer, including the Aim for Change.

B. Introduce today's subject.

C. Share your information on joblessness, "the Year of Jubilee," etc.

D. Share testimonies.

E. Have a volunteer summarize the In Focus story. Discuss.

P—Present the Scriptures

A. Have volunteers read the Focal Verses.

B. Now use The People, Places, and Times; Background; Search the Scriptures; At-A-Glance outline; In Depth; and More Light on the Text to clarify the verses.

E—Explore the Meaning

A. Have volunteers summarize the Discuss the Meaning, Lesson in Our Society, and Make It Happen sections.

B. Connect these sections to the Aim for Change and the Keep in Mind verse.

N—Next Steps for Application

A. Summarize the lesson.

B. Close with prayer and praise to God for Jubilee.

Worship Guide

For the Superintendent or Teacher
Theme: Celebrate Jubilee
Theme Song: "Jubilee"
Devotional Reading:
Nehemiah 1:5–11
Prayer

Celebrate Jubilee

Bible Background • LEVITICUS 25:8–55
Printed Text • LEVITICUS 25:8–12, 25, 35–36, 39–40, 47–48, 55
Devotional Reading • NEHEMIAH 1:5–11

—————————— Aim for Change ——————————

By the end of the lesson, we will: EXPLAIN why jubilee was an opportunity to begin anew; REFLECT on a time when we needed to begin again; and SUMMARIZE the principles of jubilee.

—————————— In Focus ——————————

There is a vintage song of the church entitled, "He Broke the Chains." This very heart-stirring song extols what God has done for humanity when He gave His life on that cruel Cross at Calvary. One verse says, "My life was lost in sin and shame, The way I could not see, But Jesus came, oh, bless His name, And set my spirit free." The chorus proclaims, "I can't forget the day He spoke to my troubled soul, Words of peace that made my burdens roll, He broke the chains that bound and set all my joybells ringing, Praise to His matchless name."

"He Broke the Chains" should remind us that we were in captivity, as well. We needed a Savior to set us free, and we needed to believe in the Lord Jesus Christ so that we could be saved. It should also remind us that sometimes even after we are saved, we can find ourselves in captivity to bills, credit cards, jobs, families, busy schedules, etc. Still, we need that same God to help set us free.

Yes, captivity sometimes comes in the lives of Christians. We must know that God is still on our side and in due season He will deliver us. Our mission is to continue to believe God, trust God, and know that everything will work out for our good.

—————————— Keep in Mind ——————————

"And ye shall hallow the fiftieth year, and proclaim liberty throughout all the land unto all the inhabitants thereof: it shall be a jubile unto you; and ye shall return every man unto his possession, and ye shall return every man unto his family" (Leviticus 25:10).

"And ye shall hallow the fiftieth year, and proclaim liberty throughout all the land unto all the inhabitants thereof: it shall be a jubile unto you; and ye shall return every man unto his possession, and ye shall return every man unto his family" (Leviticus 25:10).

Focal Verses

KJV **Leviticus 25:8** And thou shalt number seven sabbaths of years unto thee, seven times seven years; and the space of the seven sabbaths of years shall be unto thee forty and nine years.

9 Then shalt thou cause the trumpet of the jubile to sound on the tenth day of the seventh month, in the day of atonement shall ye make the trumpet sound throughout all your land.

10 And ye shall hallow the fiftieth year, and proclaim liberty throughout all the land unto all the inhabitants thereof: it shall be a jubile unto you; and ye shall return every man unto his possession, and ye shall return every man unto his family.

11 A jubile shall that fiftieth year be unto you: ye shall not sow, neither reap that which groweth of itself in it, nor gather the grapes in it of thy vine undressed.

12 For it is the jubile; it shall be holy unto you: ye shall eat the increase thereof out of the field.

25:25 If thy brother be waxen poor, and hath sold away some of his possession, and if any of his kin come to redeem it, then shall he redeem that which his brother sold.

25:35 And if thy brother be waxen poor, and fallen in decay with thee; then thou shalt relieve him: yea, though he be a stranger, or a sojourner; that he may live with thee.

36 Take thou no usury of him, or increase: but fear thy God; that thy brother may live with thee.

25:39 And if thy brother that dwelleth by thee be waxen poor, and be sold unto thee; thou shalt not compel him to serve as a bondservant:

40 But as an hired servant, and as a sojourner, he shall be with thee, and shall serve thee unto the year of jubile:

NLT **Leviticus 25:8** "In addition, you must count off seven Sabbath years, seven years times seven, adding up to forty-nine years in all.

9 Then on the Day of Atonement of the fiftieth year, blow the trumpets loud and long throughout the land.

10 This year will be set apart as holy, a time to proclaim release for all who live there. It will be a jubilee year for you, when each of you returns to the lands that belonged to your ancestors and rejoins your clan.

11 Yes, the fiftieth year will be a jubilee for you. During that year, do not plant any seeds or store away any of the crops that grow naturally, and do not process the grapes that grow on your unpruned vines.

12 It will be a jubilee year for you, and you must observe it as a special and holy time. You may, however, eat the produce that grows naturally in the fields that year.

25:25 If any of your Israelite relatives go bankrupt and are forced to sell some inherited land, then a close relative, a kinsman redeemer, may buy it back for them.

25:35 "If any of your Israelite relatives fall into poverty and cannot support themselves, support them as you would a resident foreigner and allow them to live with you.

36 Do not demand an advance or charge interest on the money you lend them. Instead, show your fear of God by letting them live with you as your relatives.

25:39 "If any of your Israelite relatives go bankrupt and sell themselves to you, do not treat them as slaves.

40 Treat them instead as hired servants or as resident foreigners who live with you, and they will serve you only until the Year of Jubilee.

KJV Cont.

25:47 And if a sojourner or stranger wax rich by thee, and thy brother that dwelleth by him wax poor, and sell himself unto the stranger or sojourner by thee, or to the stock of the stranger's family:

48 After that he is sold he may be redeemed again; one of his brethren may redeem him:

25:55 For unto me the children of Israel are servants; they are my servants whom I brought forth out of the land of Egypt: I am the LORD your God.

NLT Cont.

25:47 "If a resident foreigner becomes rich, and if some of your Israelite relatives go bankrupt and sell themselves to such a foreigner,

48 they still retain the right of redemption. They may be bought back by a close relative—

25:55 For the people of Israel are my servants, whom I brought out of the land of Egypt. I, the LORD, am your God.

The People, Places, and Times

Moses. "Moses belonged to the tribe of Levi, to the clan of Kohath, and to the house or family of Amram (Exodus 6:16ff)" (*The New Bible Dictionary*, 795). To save her baby son from Pharaoh's command to destroy all male infants of Hebrew descent, Moses' mother put him in a basket next to a stream, his sister Miriam kept watch, and a daughter of Pharaoh found the baby. She took the baby home with her and became his adoptive mother (Exodus 2:1–10). Years later, after Moses discovered his true Hebrew heritage, he left Pharaoh's house and became the leader that God used to bring the Hebrews out of Egypt and toward the Promised Land (*The New Bible Dictionary*, 794–795).

Levites. The tribe of Levi was separated by God from the other tribes and placed in charge of the dismantling, carrying, and erecting of the tabernacle (Numbers 1:47–54). The Levites were dedicated to the ministry of priesthood, especially in regards to caring for the tabernacle. A representative function of the Levites is symbolized in the rituals of cleansing and dedication (*MacArthur Study Bible*, 217).

Exodus. The Exodus of the people of Israel from enslavement in Egypt occurred in 1445 B.C. The Israelites' tabernacle was completed in 1444 B.C. After its completion, the book of Leviticus begins telling the story of the Children of Israel, most likely during the start of the second year after the Exodus (*MacArthur Study Bible*, 150–153).

Background

Moses had been instructed to teach the Children of Israel about the Feasts and what was required in each (Leviticus 23). He then speaks to them on the proper care of the Tabernacle lamps and the bread for the Tabernacle (Leviticus 24). The Children of Israel were also warned about blaspheming God and how any person committing this act would be handled. So leading into chapter 25, the people were receiving instructions from their leader, Moses. In Leviticus 25–27, Moses gives the Israelites practical guidelines for holiness.

At-A-Glance

1. The Appointed Time
   (Leviticus 25:8–12)

2. It's Yours! (25:25)

3. Help the Poor (25:35–36)

4. From Slave to Servant (25:39–40)

5. Redeemed (25:47–48)

6. Our Deliverer (25:55)

In Depth

1. The Appointed Time (Leviticus 25:8–12)

Moses begins this portion of his message by informing the Levites that there is a time for everything in their lives, even a time of release from their circumstance. All prisoners and captives obtained their liberties, slaves were declared free, and debtors were absolved. It is wonderful to know that God has an appointed time in which He will deliver. We must remember that He will not leave us in our condition forever, just like He did not leave the Israelites. When we find ourselves wavering in our faith and ready to give up, we must remember that God promised us, "All things work together for good to them that love God, to them who are the called according to his purpose" (Romans 8:28). So, "Wait on the LORD: be of good courage, and he shall strengthen thine heart" (Psalm 27:14).

Sound the alarm (**Leviticus 25:9**). Moses informs the people that they have to sound the trumpet of jubilee. The sounding of the trumpet proclaimed the universal day of release for the people. Sometimes in our lives, when things are coming to an end, we have to declare its closure. If we take God at His word, if we trust Him and know that He cannot lie, if He tells us something has come to completion, then we must receive it in our spirits.

Shout the victory (**vv. 10–11**). The instruction to the Levites is to proclaim liberty throughout the land. When we have been released from the enemy's strongholds, this is something to shout about. When we have been released from bondage and the yokes that were placed upon our necks, this is something to shout about. When we have been released from sickness, disease, bad habits, bad attitudes, foul mouths, abusive relationships, parasitic friendships, and infested households, this is something to shout about. And when you've been released, you ought to tell the world what the Lord has done in your life.

Your blessing is here (**v. 12**). Moses begins this verse by telling the people, "It is the jubile." "Jubilee" (its modern spelling) means "a joyful shout or clangor of trumpets." It is the name of the great semicentennial festival of the Hebrews, which lasted for a year. During this time, all that the ground yielded could be eaten out of necessity, but no one could hoard or compile a private inventory with what came forth. The Year of Jubilee came to afford a fresh opportunity to those whose lives were reduced by adverse circumstances. It released them from situations that would have held them captive forever.

2. It's Yours! (25:25)

Moses informs the people that if a person has become poor and has sold his or her possessions, a family member may come and redeem what was sold. We must always know that God has a way to restore us. Even when we have given up our best and given our all, God can restore us.

3. Help the Poor (25:35–36)

We must always help those who are poor among us. We must treat the poor just as we would treat our own brothers or sisters— lend a helping hand to them. Don't take advantage of their condition; instead, fear God and treat them as we would want to be treated. When we fall on hard times, the same hand that we reached out to others can be extended to us.

4. From Slave to Servant (25:39–40)

Sometimes, the Israelites were compelled to mortgage their inheritance and even themselves, due to financial crises. If this was the case, they could not be treated as a slave, but must be treated as a hired servant, because they had gained their liberty. We must be mindful of the things people sometimes must do to survive. We never want to treat them as though they are our slaves because of hard times they have fallen upon. God calls for us to show them kindness and courtesy, just as we would to a person that we respect and honor. They are due this because of the year of release that has come in their lives. They are due this because God commands it.

5. Redeemed (25:47–48)

When they sold themselves to someone who was rich, slaves could be bought back or redeemed by family members or persons who were willing to pay the price. God will and has made provision for us to be spiritually redeemed. Jesus paid the price for our salvation and redeemed us from a path of unrighteousness.

6. Our Deliverer (25:55)

God brought the Israelites out of Egypt, and He expected them to serve Him only— He was to be their only God. We must also remember our deliverance and whom we are to honor with our lives. God is the One we owe our all to for everything that He has done for us, and He is to be our one true God.

Search the Scriptures

1. How many Sabbaths were the Israelites to count for themselves (Leviticus 25:8)?

2. On what day of the seventh month were they to sound the trumpet (v. 9)?

3. To whom were they to proclaim liberty in the 50th year (v. 10)?

4. What year is the Year of Jubilee (v. 11)?

Discuss the Meaning

If the Year of Jubilee is scriptural, how would it play out in our day? Think about how many people would experience financial liberty. Could it be that the hungry among us would be fed, the homeless would be housed, the abused would be helped, and God would get the glory?

Lesson in Our Society

One of the biggest problems facing persons in our society today is credit card debt. There is school loan debt, property debt, and debt to stores. As a society, we like to buy now and pay later. We enjoy the power of the credit card. Unfortunately, this pay-later mentality puts us into financial bondage and literally gives loan institutions power over our financial choices and our economic well-being. Borrowers in essence allow the yokes and chains to be put on them, just because they often want what they cannot afford. Break the bondage and live within your means.

Make It Happen

Today many people are experiencing tremendous financial bondage and discouragement in their lives. Some have lost homes, jobs, cars, savings, and even hope. But we must know that God is a God who never fails us. We must begin to seek God's face and ask Him to help us break this bondage so that our jubilee can come, as well.

Follow the Spirit

What God wants me to do:

_____

_____

_____

_____

Remember Your Thoughts

Special insights I have learned:

_____

_____

_____

_____

More Light on the Text

Leviticus 25:8–12, 25, 35–36, 39–40, 47–48, 55

Introduction

Too often, the Mosaic Law is viewed with 21st century eyes and is not sufficiently appreciated for the pivotal and normative role it played in the lives of our faith's ancestors. As Samuel Balentine writes about the Holiness Code of Leviticus (18:1–24:9), "[It is] an integral part of the instructions that undergird God's covenantal relationship with Israel" (193). In addition to the many prohibitions of the Law in general and in the Holiness Code, God included many positive injunctions and did not neglect celebrations such

as the Sabbath year (just prior to this lesson, explained in 25:2–7). In this climactic portion of Leviticus, the Jubilee year is in focus, which is the ultimate Sabbath year. God's ongoing desire for liberty and justice for all continues in the laws regarding the Jubilee (see also Exodus 23:10–11 and Deuteronomy 15:1–6).

8 And thou shalt number seven sabbaths of years unto thee, seven times seven years; and the space of the seven sabbaths of years shall be unto thee forty and nine years. 9 Then shalt thou cause the trumpet of the jubile to sound on the tenth day of the seventh month, in the day of atonement shall ye make the trumpet sound throughout all your land.

In the prelude to this lesson, God expanded the Sabbath rest for people to include a Sabbath rest for the land (Leviticus 25:1–7). People rested every seventh day, and the land now would rest every seven years. In such a year, none would starve as the land would still produce naturally (vv. 6–7) and all were welcome to enjoy its bounty. As the lesson opens, the Sabbath year itself now is extended to seven cycles, each lasting seven years, after which, in the 50th year, a type of super Sabbath would ensue, appropriately named the Year of Jubilee. The Sabbath was held in very high regard as the sign of the Mosaic Covenant (Exodus 31:12–17; Ezekiel 20:12). A seventh Sabbath would invoke an even higher respect, and a Jubilee year would be a high point in the life of an Israelite.

Leviticus 25:9 specifies the day and month for the blowing of the shofar "trumpet," proclaiming the commencement of the ultimate Sabbath. There are two uses for the word "jubile" in Hebrew. The first in Leviticus 25 is in the phrase "trumpet of the jubile" in verse 9, *teruw`ah* (**ter-oo-AW**), and it means "a shout or blast of warning or joy." The announcement appropriately came on the Day of Atonement, which was a somber occasion for national repentance that continues to the present. It appears that God's plans and schedule put people—especially sellers and creditors—in the right frame of mind for generosity. There is an indication in 2 Chronicles 36:21 that the Jubilees and Sabbaths occasionally were not observed. (See also Isaiah 61:1; Jeremiah 34:8, 15, 17; Ezekiel 46:17 for releasing of those enslaved for debt.)

10 And ye shall hallow the fiftieth year, and proclaim liberty throughout all the land unto all the inhabitants thereof: it shall be a jubile unto you; and ye shall return every man unto his possession, and ye shall return every man unto his family.

"Hallow" in Hebrew is *qadash* (**kaw-DASH**), and it means to consecrate or sanctify. To "hallow the fiftieth year" is to make the entire year holy, to set it apart, as God's people are to be holy and set apart (Leviticus 20:26). "Liberty" in Hebrew is *derowr* (**der-ORE**). In this use, "liberty throughout all the land" refers to the mass relief regarding land mortgages, which many would have undertaken (as many still do) in order to survive hard economic times. The "jubile" in 25:10 is *yowbel* (**yo-BALE**) and comes from the root word *yabal* (**yaw-BAL**), meaning "to lead, bring, or carry." Put together, the jubilee trumpet is sounded to carry forth the joyful news. In the Year of Jubilee, so appropriately named, there would be much expected celebration as properties were either reclaimed or repurchased, and those who had been forced to move now could come back home.

It must be noted that such national sharing and communal wealth redistribution was a far cry from communism, which is government-forced redistribution. By the same token, New Testament communal sharing also was not communism (Acts 4:32). A social unit as small as a family can have unity when all are in agreement; likewise, Israel enjoyed God's blessing when everyone for the most part obeyed and engaged properly with the Levitical Jubilee. As time passed, the more self-seeking people everywhere became, including Israelites, the less the passages were observed.

At the same time, the principles of not taking advantage of one another, of looking out for the poor, and of acting generously out of fear and reverence for God are still wise attitudes and practices.

11 A jubile shall that fiftieth year be unto you: ye shall not sow, neither reap that which groweth of itself in it, nor gather the grapes in it of thy vine undressed. 12 For it is the jubile; it shall be holy unto you: ye shall eat the increase thereof out of the field.

Not only were mortgages renegotiated to return land to the original owners or to assist with interest free loans to help reunite owners with property, but the Year of Jubilee also was a yearlong vacation from work, during which both planting and harvesting ceased. Ultimately, the message from God is a reminder that even landowners and property owners in reality are only stewards or custodians, dwelling on God's land and God's property—all of creation belongs to Him (see v. 23, "the land is mine").

"Holy unto you" in verse 12 is another reminder that this is part of God's Holiness Code and Law, which clearly contains good news along with its prohibitions. No one could harvest, yet everyone could eat, including slaves, the poor, and animals. Not only that, God would see to it that the year prior to the Jubilee yielded an abundant enough crop to sustain them through the Jubilee year and until the harvest of the following year—a total of three years. At the same time, it was not entirely a vacation, as the law was to be read to the people, perhaps resembling a kind of national year of study (see Deuteronomy 31:10–13).

25:25 If thy brother be waxen poor, and hath sold away some of his possession, and if any of his kin come to redeem it, then shall he redeem that which his brother sold.

In Leviticus 25:25, "redeem" in Hebrew is *ga'al* (**gaw-AL**), a familiar concept of Old Testament times in the person of the "kinsman-redeemer" (see Ruth 4:4, 6). In ancient Israel, the well-being of the community was more important than that of the individual. This theme resonates throughout the Holiness Code.

Three specific cases are presented in Leviticus 25:25, 35–36, and 39–40. In each case, there is a person who has fallen on hard times (is "waxen poor" or "go(es) bankrupt," NLT). In today's volatile economic climate, many have lost their homes to foreclosure. What if America had a Jubilee year, where all would have the right (or their descendants) to repurchase, refinance, or "redeem" their home at a fair and just price?

25:35 And if thy brother be waxen poor, and fallen in decay with thee; then thou shalt relieve him: yea, though he be a stranger, or a sojourner; that he may live with thee. 36 Take thou no usury of him, or increase: but fear thy God; that thy brother may live with thee.

"Usury," found in verse 36, is *neshek* (**NEH-shek**) in the Hebrew and means the added charge of interest, which is forbidden in the Jubilee year. Even in the majority of normal years, general protections for the poor were in place, of which any excessive interest was prohibited (see Deuteronomy 23:20; Ezekiel 18:8; 22:12). In ancient times (as today), interest on loans was collected in advance, and if the loan was not paid off on time, more

interest was added. Since many borrowers could never repay the accruing total, they often became indentured servants.

In this second case (which includes Leviticus 25:37–38), rather than a home having been sold, someone had been forced to surrender the property's title to a creditor but remained as a tenant or renter, working off his debt by tending his own crops. Unlike greedy modern financial institutions that evict families without showing an ounce of compassion, the people of God, who had been set free from slavery, did not in turn exploit their fellow Israelites, and the Holiness Code ensured that this would not happen. In verse 36, a kind of no-interest loan is granted—out of fear of God—in order that the unity of God's people might not be broken. Imagine this in the modern world!

25:39 And if thy brother that dwelleth by thee be waxen poor, and be sold unto thee; thou shalt not compel him to serve as a bondservant: 40 But as an hired servant, and as a sojourner, he shall be with thee, and shall serve thee unto the year of jubile:

In another variation of the same case, the owner who is unable to maintain his payments or work off his debt often would become a "bondservant" to the creditor. In Hebrew, this is *`ebed* (**EH-bed**) and means slave but not in the anachronistic (old-fashioned) sense. The creditor would "own" him, much like the term continues in use even today. For the Israelites, however, anything more than financially driven indentured servitude was not to be permitted. Bellinger writes, "The notion of one Israelite owning another and putting the slave to hard service is anathema" (153). While, technically, servitude to repay a debt is a form of slavery, what clearly was prohibited was the element of harshness. Rather, whatever the person was able to earn was to be applied to his debt, and he was not to be mistreated. Also, his "contract" could not be unending—as many today experience hopeless indebtedness, where they will never be free of the debt regardless of how long or hard they work.

At the onset of the Year of Jubilee, this debtor is relieved of the outstanding balance. When God's Word includes "all the inhabitants," it means it literally.

25:47 And if a sojourner or stranger wax rich by thee, and thy brother that dwelleth by him wax poor, and sell himself unto the stranger or sojourner by thee, or to the stock of the stranger's family: 48 After that he is sold he may be redeemed again; one of his brethren may redeem him:

The third case is similar to the others, but involves a debt relationship with a Gentile. Amazingly, the same basic proscription applies even to non-Israelites, that the Israelite be released in the Year of Jubilee. Balentine offers this insight: "Israelites must not be treated harshly; they are servants to God alone and owe ultimate allegiance to no other power" (197). Verse 49 has an interesting statement that a slave might amass the funds to redeem himself, which speaks to the much different status of slaves in ancient times compared to the modern association with the word. In a sense, it was not a lot different from modern contracts, which "bind" one to another for the term of the contract.

25:55 For unto me the children of Israel are servants; they are my servants whom I brought forth out of the land of Egypt: I am the LORD your God.

Verse 47 supports verse 55—God delivered Israel, Israel belongs to God, and Israel's allegiance belongs to none other (see also v. 53). The rationale was clean and simple: because God is the Lord and it was His will. Any non-Israelite who wished to contest the Hebrew Scriptures surely would be quickly reminded of how things had gone for Israel's enemies through the years. Since the God of the Old Testament is the same God of the New Testament, one would expect similar principles to be found in both testaments. Consider the close parallel here with Colossians 4:1: "Masters, give unto your servants that which is just and equal; knowing that ye also have a Master in heaven."

God calls His people to holiness, which involves horizontal relationships with others. God instituted the Year of Jubilee at a time when liberty and justice for all was imbedded in the law of the land. Among its inherent provisions for the land were those involving crop rotation, not allowing anyone to ever be indebted for a lifetime. There was also a forbidding the of the kind of enslavement as they had experienced in Egypt; and, further, no one would be permitted to mistreat others, even enemies, or God would judge them because of His perfect compassion (for the oppressed) and justice (for oppressors).

Sources:
Balentine, Samuel E. *Leviticus. Interpretation: A Bible Commentary for Teaching and Preaching.* Louisville, KY: John Knox Press, 2002. 193–97.
Bellenger, W. H., Jr. *Leviticus, Numbers. Old Testament Series. New International Biblical Commentary.* Peabody, MA: Hendrickson Publishers, 2001. 140–54.
Brown, David, A. R. Fausset, and Robert Jamieson. *A Commentary, Critical and Explanatory on Old and New Testaments.* Logos Bible Software.
Evans, Tony. *Tony Evans' Book of Illustrations.* Chicago, IL: Moody Publishers, 2009. 113–14.
Hebrew and Greek Lexicons. Bible Study Tools.com. http://www.biblestudytools.com/lexicons (accessed November 8, 2010).
Harris, R. Laird. *Genesis, Exodus, Leviticus, Numbers. The Expositor's Bible Commentary,* vol. 2. Edited by Frank E. Gaebelein. Grand Rapids, MI: Zondervan, 1990. 632–40.
MacArthur, John. *The MacArthur Study Bible: NASB.* Nashville, TN: Thomas Nelson, 2006. 150–53.
Merriam-Webster Online Dictionary. Merriam-Webster, Inc. http://www.merriam-webster.com (accessed November 8, 2010).
Douglas, James D., et al., eds. *The New Bible Dictionary.* London, U.K.: InterVarsity Press, 1962. 794–99, 1120–21.
Old and New Testament Concordances, Lexicons, Dictionaries, Commentaries, Images, and Bible Versions. Blue Letter Bible. org. http://www.blueletterbible.org/ (accessed July 10, 2010).

Passage Lookup. Bible Gateway.com. http://www.biblegateway.
com/passage (accessed January 28, 2011).

Say It Correctly

Levite. LEE-vit.

Daily Bible Reading

MONDAY
Turning Back from Repentance
(Jeremiah 34:8–17)

TUESDAY
If You Return to Me
(Nehemiah 1:5–11)

WEDNESDAY
Walking at Liberty
(Psalm 119:41–48)

THURSDAY
The Spirit and Freedom
(2 Corinthians 3:12–18)

FRIDAY
When Liberty Becomes a Stumbling
Block
(1 Corinthians 8)

SATURDAY
The Perfect Law of Liberty
(James 1:19–27)

SUNDAY
Proclaiming Liberty throughout
the Land
(Leviticus 25:8–12, 25, 35–36, 39–40,
47–48, 55)

Teaching Tips

June 24
Bible Study Guide 4

Words You Should Know

A. Fear (Deuteronomy 10:12, 20) *yare'* (Heb.)—Dreading punishment or destruction; feeling overwhelming awe, wonder and amazement.

B. Heart (v. 12) *lebab* (Heb.)—The seat of thought and will.

Teacher Preparation

Unifying Principle—Loving as We Are Loved. People respond in various ways to being loved. As recipients of God's love, we are expected to be fair, act justly, and love others.

A. Pray for your students and the immigration concerns of our country.

B. Study and meditate on the entire lesson.

C. Complete the companion lesson in the *Precepts For Living Personal Study Guide®*.

D. Bring a "love poem" or greeting card (e.g., husband-wife, mother-child, etc.) to class.

O—Open the Lesson

A. After taking prayer requests, lead the class in prayer.

B. Read your "love poem" and tie it into today's lesson.

C. Have a volunteer read the In Focus story aloud. Discuss.

D. Discuss the Lesson Aim after reading it out loud.

E. Read the Keep in Mind verse in unison, and then encourage the class to commit the verse to memory during the week.

P—Present the Scriptures

A. Discuss the Focal Verses according to the At-A-Glance outline and More Light on the Text.

B. Reflect on God's unconditional love for us and what Jesus did for us on the Cross.

E—Explore the Meaning

A. Divide the class into groups to answer the Search the Scriptures questions.

B. Read and discuss each Discuss the Meaning question.

C. Review the Lesson in Our Society section. Discuss.

N—Next Steps for Application

A. Challenge students to complete the Make It Happen assignment.

B. Close in prayer, thanking God for His unconditional love.

Worship Guide

For the Superintendent or Teacher
Theme: The Heart of the Law
Theme Song: "Love Lifted Me"
Devotional Reading: Micah 6:1–8
Prayer

The Heart of the Law

Bible Background • DEUTERONOMY 10:1-22; 16:18-20
Printed Text • DEUTERONOMY 10:12-22; 16:18-20 | Devotional Reading • MICAH 6:1-8

Aim for Change

By the end of the lesson, we will: EXPLAIN what our response should be to God's unconditional love; REFLECT on God's love and justice; and EVALUATE how loving and just we are toward others.

In Focus

A renowned singer and minister, Shirley Caesar, tells the story in one of her compelling, soul-stirring songs entitled, "No Charge," of how a little boy presented his mother with a list of charges for the chores he had done for her and the family. The patient mother read the list and then began to numerate all the things she had done for him. She included carrying him for 9 months and nursing him through illnesses. Then she said, "No Charge." By the time Shirley had finished this song; many people were in tears, especially if they listened to it around or on Mother's Day.

Across this country and around the world, many parents and grandparents have spent countless hours, days, and years doing things for their families because they love them. They showed and show the unconditional love that our Lord and Savior has for humanity.

Our lesson today reiterates that love is sweet, love is kind, love is understanding, and love conquers all. God's love for us is so great that He gave His only begotten Son, Jesus, to die for our sins. There is no greater love.

Keep in Mind

"And now, Israel, what doth the LORD thy God require of thee, but to fear the LORD thy God, to walk in all his ways, and to love him, and to serve the LORD thy God with all thy heart and with all thy soul, To keep the commandments of the LORD, and his statutes, which I command thee this day for thy good?" (Deuteronomy 10:12–13).

"And now, Israel, what doth the LORD thy God require of thee, but to fear the LORD thy God, to walk in all his ways, and to love him, and to serve the LORD thy God with all thy heart and with all thy soul, To keep the commandments of the LORD, and his statutes, which I command thee this day for thy good?" (Deuteronomy 10:12–13).

Focal Verses

KJV **Deuteronomy 10:12** And now, Israel, what doth the LORD thy God require of thee, but to fear the LORD thy God, to walk in all his ways, and to love him, and to serve the LORD thy God with all thy heart and with all thy soul,

13 To keep the commandments of the LORD, and his statutes, which I command thee this day for thy good?

14 Behold, the heaven and the heaven of heavens is the LORD's thy God, the earth also, with all that therein is.

15 Only the LORD had a delight in thy fathers to love them, and he chose their seed after them, even you above all people, as it is this day.

16 Circumcise therefore the foreskin of your heart, and be no more stiffnecked.

17 For the LORD your God is God of gods, and Lord of lords, a great God, a mighty, and a terrible, which regardeth not persons, nor taketh reward:

18 He doth execute the judgment of the fatherless and widow, and loveth the stranger, in giving him food and raiment.

19 Love ye therefore the stranger: for ye were strangers in the land of Egypt.

20 Thou shalt fear the LORD thy God; him shalt thou serve, and to him shalt thou cleave, and swear by his name.

21 He is thy praise, and he is thy God, that hath done for thee these great and terrible things, which thine eyes have seen.

22 Thy fathers went down into Egypt with threescore and ten persons; and now the LORD thy God hath made thee as the stars of heaven for multitude.

16:18 Judges and officers shalt thou make thee in all thy gates, which the LORD thy God giveth thee, throughout thy tribes: and they shall judge the people with just judgment.

NLT **Deuteronomy 10:12** "And now, Israel, what does the LORD your God require of you? He requires you to fear him, to live according to his will, to love and worship him with all your heart and soul,

13 and to obey the LORD's commands and laws that I am giving you today for your own good.

14 The highest heavens and the earth and everything in it all belong to the LORD your God.

15 Yet the LORD chose your ancestors as the objects of his love. And he chose you, their descendants, above every other nation, as is evident today.

16 Therefore, cleanse your sinful hearts and stop being stubborn.

17 "The LORD your God is the God of gods and Lord of lords. He is the great God, mighty and awesome, who shows no partiality and takes no bribes.

18 He gives justice to orphans and widows. He shows love to the foreigners living among you and gives them food and clothing.

19 You, too, must show love to foreigners, for you yourselves were once foreigners in the land of Egypt.

20 You must fear the LORD your God and worship him and cling to him. Your oaths must be in his name alone.

21 He is your God, the one who is worthy of your praise, the one who has done mighty miracles that you yourselves have seen.

22 When your ancestors went down into Egypt, there were only seventy of them. But now the LORD your God has made you as numerous as the stars in the sky!

16:18 "Appoint judges and officials for each of your tribes in all the towns the LORD your God is giving you. They will judge the people fairly throughout the land.

KJV Cont.

19 Thou shalt not wrest judgment; thou shalt not respect persons, neither take a gift: for a gift doth blind the eyes of the wise, and pervert the words of the righteous.

20 That which is altogether just shalt thou follow, that thou mayest live, and inherit the land which the LORD thy God giveth thee.

NLT Cont.

19 You must never twist justice or show partiality. Never accept a bribe, for bribes blind the eyes of the wise and corrupt the decisions of the godly.

20 Let true justice prevail, so you may live and occupy the land that the LORD your God is giving you.

The People, Places, and Times

God. Known as YHWH (YAHWEH), Lord of Hosts, Almighty, Spirit of the Lord, Holy One, God Most High, Master, Sovereign Lord.

Israelites. An Israelite can be: (a) a descendant of the patriarch Jacob; (b) a member of the holy and inclusive community of those who follow the God of Israel, keeping the laws divinely revealed to the prophet Moses, without any ethnic identification; (c) a member of the holy and exclusive community of Israel defined by ethnic and religious purity.

Background

"The book of Deuteronomy concentrates on the events that took place in the final weeks of Moses' life. The major event of that period was the verbal communication of divine revelation from Moses to the people of Israel" (*MacArthur Study Bible*, 243). These speeches were then written and given to the priests and elders to pass on to future generations of Israel. It is estimated that they were written somewhere in the 11th month of the 40th year after the Exodus from Egypt. Some other scholars place the time frame from January-February, 1405 B.C. "Having shown the impossibility of self-dependence (chapter 8) and the impossibility of spiritual pride in light of her rebellious history (9:1—10:11), Moses called Israel to exercise her only option for survival: total commitment to the LORD" (Walvoord, 281).

At-A-Glance

1. Let Your Love Show
(Deuteronomy 10:12–22)

2. God's Administrators (16:18–20)

In Depth

1. Let Your Love Show (Deuteronomy 10:12–22)

Moses lets the Children of Israel know that God requires some things of them. There must be a fear of God because of who He is—His greatness. When the Israelites are instructed to fear God, Moses is not telling them to be afraid. He simply wants them to hold God in awe and submit to Him. We, too, must surrender and submit to God, who should be the Head of our lives. Moses also instructs the people to love God. We know that God is love, and He loved us first. But because of all that God has done for us, we need to love Him in return. And if we truly love Him, we will willingly serve and obey Him. Our love for God will move us to serve Him with our whole heart and soul. And while serving Him, we will have a true desire to walk in all His ways. In addition, when our love for God is pure, it will be our desire to please Him in all that we do. One thing that always pleases God is our obedience. When we are obedient, we demonstrate our sincere love for God.

Remove it (v. 16). Moses instructs the people to "circumcise...the foreskin" of their hearts. We must cut away all the sin in our hearts today—pull back all the unrighteousness inside of us and totally surrender to the Lord. When we remove that which is blocking our heart from being true, then we can turn ourselves over to the Lord and have a loving relationship with Him.

There's enough love for everybody (vv. 18–19). Moses reminds the people that God is a just (righteous) God. He also reminds them that they were once strangers in the land. Therefore they must treat everyone with love. Even those whom they didn't know personally, they were to show them love—those whom they had never seen before and might not ever see again, they were to treat them with love. They were to help the stranger in whatever way they could. If strangers needed food, feed them. If they needed clothes, clothe them. If they needed money, give to them. The people were to show God's love to everyone, because God constantly showed love to them.

God should be the Receiver of our praise (vv. 21–22). Moses lets the Israelites know that God should be the Recipient of their praises; He has done great and awesome things for them. God multiplied 70 persons to be as numerous as the stars in the sky. Sometimes we, too, lose sight of all that God has done in our lives. We wrongfully give humanity the praise for what goes on in our lives and in the world. But we must always remember that God should be the Receiver of our praise—"Bless the LORD, O my soul, and forget not all his benefits: Who forgiveth all thine iniquities; who healeth all thy diseases; Who redeemeth thy life from destruction; who crowneth thee *with* lovingkindness and tender mercies; Who satisfieth thy mouth

with good things; so that thy youth is renewed like the eagle's" (Psalm 103:2–5).

2. God's Administrators (16:18–20)

Moses instructs the people on how to select the judges and officials in the land. He lets them know that God has a say in this selection as well. There are judges that the Lord gives that will provide righteous judgment. We must make sure that we seek God's advice on persons that we put in leadership positions. Those who are called to serve must serve through the leading of God's Spirit. God does not want His leaders being bought and bribed by persons who want things to always go their way. There must be justice in the world, and this comes through those who judge with the Spirit of God leading them. Those who are just in their judging will be blessed by God.

Search the Scriptures

1. What five things does the Lord require of the Israelites (Deuteronomy 10:12–13)?

2. Who did the Lord delight in loving (v. 15)?

3. Which body organ were the people to circumcise, metaphorically (v. 16)?

4. Who shall be appointed to judge the people in just judgment (16:18)?

Discuss the Meaning

Today, do people really fear (reverence) the Lord? Can we serve God without loving Him? If we love Him, then why aren't we (the church) collectively obedient to Him and His Word?

Lesson in Our Society

In America we have many who were not born on American soil, but have begun to call America home. We must not mistreat others just because they are foreign to this land. It is our duty to treat everyone with love and kindness, as God has treated us. If we love God, we will follow His command and serve Him with our hearts and souls. God commands that we love one another, including all of those who have come to live in our community as well.

Make It Happen

Begin to show love everywhere that you go. Recipients of your love shouldn't always have to be family members or friends. God calls for us to love one another, as He has loved us. That means we must love all of our neighbors, near and far. Love is what makes the world a better place. Let people see the love of God in you each day.

Follow the Spirit

What God wants me to do:

_____

_____

_____

_____

Remember Your Thoughts

Special insights I have learned:

_____

_____

_____

_____

More Light on the Text

Deuteronomy 10:12–22; 16:18–20

12 And now, Israel, what doth the LORD thy God require of thee, but to fear the LORD thy God, to walk in all his ways, and to love him, and to serve the LORD thy God with all thy heart and with all thy soul. 13 To keep the commandments of the LORD, and his statutes, which I command this day for thy good?

After Moses spent a second 40 days on top of Mt. Sinai, he brought down a second pair of stone tablets inscribed by God with the Ten Commandments. He had thrown down and shattered the first set when he came down from the mountain and discovered Aaron and the Israelite encampment worshiping a gold idol shaped like a calf (Exodus 32:2–6, 19; Deuteronomy 9:15–17). In today's passage, Moses detailed a fitting response to God's deliverance of the Israelites from slavery in Egypt and provision for them in the Sinai wilderness.

He began by asking the question that God's prophets asked the Israelites repeatedly in different ways: "What doth the LORD thy God require of thee . . . ?" (Deuteronomy 10:12; Micah 6:8). In essence, Moses' question was, "If you're going to be one of God's people, what does that involve? What does God expect of you?" Then in verses 12–13, he listed five responses that honored God's grace to them.

The first is to "fear" Him (Heb. *yare'*, **yaw-RAY**). Fear could mean "dreading punishment or destruction," but just as often, it meant "feeling overwhelming awe, wonder and amazement." The second meaning fits better here for those who choose to include themselves as one of God's people. As children, we may fear Daddy's disapproval because of his size and strength. His size and strength are also our basis for confidence when we face problems or danger.

Second, Moses said God asked His people "to walk in all his ways" (v. 12). "To walk" indicates the Israelites' actions. Trudging through the hot, dry desert was exhausting. Imagine doing that for 40 years, thirsty, hungry, or in danger (Numbers 21:1–6). The word "ways" (Heb. *derek*, **DEH-rek**) could refer literally to "a path or a road," but also figuratively to "habits or behavior." Moses said God wanted His people to model themselves after Him and His behavior toward them in all their relationships (Ephesians 5:1, NLT, NIV).

In Deuteronomy 10:12, the third instruction for the Israelites was "to love the LORD thy God" by trusting Him, being thankful for their deliverance from slavery and His forgiveness of their stubborn rebellion (9:5–8, 26–27).

Moses's fourth instruction in Deuteronomy 10:12 tells how to express that loving trust and gratitude: "serve the LORD thy God with all thy heart and with all thy soul." It's easy to miss what Moses meant here. In English we connect the "heart" (Heb. *lebab*, **lay-BAWB**) with feelings. But the Israelites viewed the heart as "the seat of thought and will." The "soul" (Heb. *nephesh*, **NEH-fesh**) referred here to a person's seat of human passion and energy. Moses urged the Israelites to show their love for God by faithfully obeying God's will with all their energy and determination.

In Deuteronomy 10:13, Moses summed up God's instructions in practical terms: "keep the commandments of the LORD, and his statutes." Commandments gave basic general principles; "statutes" (Heb. *choq*, **khoke**) referred to specific ways of applying those laws in various situations. To keep the Ten Commandments, the heart of God's law and other laws He gave for applying them, meant to "obey" them (NLT), to "observe" them (NIV), and "keep" them (NASB).

Moses saved the most important truth for last. God said the intent behind all His instructions was "for thy good." Who would want to live in a world where it was okay for people to steal, to lie to or about each other, or to kill each other? God wanted to pattern life among His chosen people on His caring and generous attitude toward them, to create a just world where each of them cared about each other like He cared about them.

14 Behold, the heavens and the heaven of heavens is the LORD's thy God, the earth also, with all therein is. 15 Only the LORD had a delight in thy fathers to love them, and he chose their seed after them, even you above all people, as it is this day.

Until recent times, few people even imagined how immense our world is, much less the universe. Barely 500 years ago, most people on Earth assumed the world was flat and the sun revolved around the Earth, rather than vice versa. During the 1800s, Rev. John Jasper preached for 20 years as a slave and for 20 more as a free man after the Civil War. Crowds of thousands, Black and White, came to hear him preach his famous sermon, "The Sun Do Move." But 3,000 years ago, God inspired Moses to imagine a reality beyond what anyone could see or imagine—a heaven beyond the heavens.

Likewise, Paul described his other-worldly vision as being "caught up to the third heaven" (2 Corinthians 12:2). The Gospel of Mark didn't give numbers but assumed more than one (Mark 13:27, NIV, "the ends of the heavens"). Ephesians 4:10 affirms Jesus' ascension, that He "ascended higher than all the heavens, so that he might fill the entire universe" (NLT). Moses declared what seldom crosses the minds of most of the world's population even today—that God is the Creator and Owner of all anyone can see and what we can still only imagine.

Deuteronomy 10:15, in the KJV, begins with the word "only." At least four modern translations start the verse with "yet" (e.g., NLT, NIV, CEV, and NASB). Both words are weaker than the one Moses used: *raq* (Heb. **rak**), which indicated a complete contrast with what was just stated. He "had a 'delight' (Heb. *chashaq*, **khaw-SHAK**) in thy fathers to 'love' (Heb. *'ahab*, **AH-hab**) them." The word *chashaq* is often translated "love," but meant more than strong affection. Rather, it involved being actively committed to what you love. From all God created, He was especially tied to the Israelites, not just to one generation of ex-slaves wandering in the wilderness. God wanted the Israelites to understand that He chose them from everything He made as His chosen people.

16 Circumcise therefore the foreskin of your heart, and be no more stiffnecked.

In Israel's early days, circumcision was performed on not only baby boys, but also on young men approaching puberty and marriage as they became part of God's covenant people (Genesis 17:9–25; 34:14–15; Exodus 4:25–26). Here circumcision symbolized the intentional commitment to God, the knowing choice of an adult, not an act performed on a helpless newborn infant. To circumcise the heart symbolized a covenantal agreement and was intended to be a permanent, life-altering change, a spiritual transformation in how an Israelite, especially a man, thought of a relationship with God.

Moses used the word "stiffnecked" repeatedly to describe an obstinate unwillingness by Israel toward giving God the love, faith, and obedience His grace toward them deserved (Exodus 32:9; 33:5; Deuteronomy 9:6,13).

17 For the LORD your God is God of gods and Lord of lords, a great God, a mighty, a terrible, which rewardeth not persons, nor taketh reward. 18 He doth execute the judgment of the fatherless and widow, and loveth the stranger, in giving him food and raiment.

As the Israelites plodded through the Sinai desert, they encountered many nations. Each group worshiped a different god, some Molek, others Ashtoreth, more still Chemosh. Moses emphasized that whatever other gods there were, their God, the LORD (Heb. *YHWH*, **yah-WEH**) was the one true God. The people passed through the territories of many kings, including Balak, king of Moab (Numbers 22:2-5); Og, king of Bashan (Numbers 21:33-35); and Sihon, king of the Amorites (Numbers 21:21). Moses declared that many kings exerted lordly power over peoples and nations, but the Israelites' God was "Lord" (Heb. *'adown*, **ah-DOHN**) supreme of all other lords.

Here Moses explained the reasons for that claim. Their LORD was the only true God, not a minor god, and thus "great" in the extent of His influence (see Deuteronomy 11:7). "Mighty" was used in Deuteronomy 10:17 to describe a warrior in battle whose breadth of power could overcome whatever opposition he faced (Psalm 65:5-8a). The word "terrible" (or "awesome," NLT) in Deuteronomy 10:17 (Heb. *yare'*, **yaw-RAY**), had the basic meaning of "fearful," but here Moses referred to a trusting awe of their God because of His past powerful acts (Exodus 34:10).

Too often their treatment of other Israelites was influenced by the status of people seeking justice or by the possibility of material inducements. Their God's actions or judgments could not be swayed in these ways (Psalm 96:10, 13). To the contrary, their God "shows no partiality" (Deuteronomy

10:17c, NIV). Without a father or a husband, children and women were especially vulnerable to abuse and injustice, but when God acts, He does so without any partiality for one person over another.

That fairness applied even to the "stranger" (Heb. *ger*, **gare**), a word in v. 18 which is often translated "alien" (NASB,) or "foreigner" (NIV, NLT). However, it didn't necessarily mean the person wasn't an Israelite. It could refer to an Israelite from another tribe, anyone who was an outsider, someone with no property rights, living temporarily or permanently in their midst. Not only could the outsider expect fair treatment from their God, Moses told them that God "'loveth' (Heb. *'ahab*, **AH-hab**) the stranger," using the same term he used toward the Israelites in verse 15.

19 Love ye therefore the stranger: for ye were strangers in the land of Egypt.

To share in God's holiness required sharing His merciful attitude toward people (Deuteronomy 5:15). Jesus made this the heart of the Gospel: "By this shall all men know that ye are my disciples, if ye have love one to another" (John 13:35). Again using the same word that referred to His love for them, He instructs them to have love for the outsider. He reminds them that for hundreds of years they had been homeless, penniless outsiders in Egypt. They knew the injustice and abuse such people went through (Exodus 2:19-24). The NLT of Deuteronomy 10:19 pinpoints their duty as God's chosen people to embody love for the powerless outsider: "You, too, must show love to foreigners, for you yourselves were once foreigners."

20 Thou shalt fear the LORD thy God: him shalt thou serve, and to him shalt thou cleave, and swear by his name.

To uphold God's awe-inspiring greatness confirmed belief in His fearful power. Faithful pursuit of His expressed will and purposes nailed down the reality of that belief. Taking a sworn oath in the LORD's name declared acceptance of God as their highest authority. Talk about God's grandeur meant little unless it was backed up "in truth or righteousness" (Isaiah 48:1, NIV). In Deuteronomy 10:20, Moses urged them to "cleave" (Heb. *dabaq*, **daw-BAK**), or hold tightly to that belief. Later in Deuteronomy 30:20 (NIV), he charged them to "hold fast to him. For the LORD is your life."

21 He is thy praise, and he is thy God, that hath done for thee these great and terrible things, which thine eyes have seen. 22 Thy fathers went down into Egypt with threescore and ten persons; and now the LORD thy God hath made thee as the stars of heaven for multitude.

The word "praise" in Deuteronomy 10:21 (Heb. *tehillah*, **teh-hil-LAW**), meant hymn of praise; the word "hallelujah" is derived from the Hebrew. Scholars debate whether the praise mentioned here was for God or Israel. Both were true. God's acts of delivering them from slavery and sustaining them in spite of hunger, thirst, and enemies brought them wary respect. Yet in spite of their fearful stubbornness, their lifesaving deliverance came about only because of God's grace through visible acts of power (Exodus 19:4).

It was undeniable that God miraculously engineered their exodus from Egypt and provided for them during their sojourn in the Sinai desert. Moses reminded them that God had sustained them through years of abusive treatment and multiplied their numbers and strength for a new future. God had braced the Israelites through centuries of slavery and mistreatment for a greater future. By doing so, He demonstrated His great love and power.

16:18 Judges and officers shalt thou make thee in all thy gates, which the LORD thy God giveth thee, throughout thy tribes: and they shall judge the people with just judgment.

This brief passage lays out the guidelines God gave in His covenant with Israel at Mt. Sinai for building a just society (Exodus 23:1–9). "Judges and officers" referred to those who decided how to settle disputes and those who enforced judges' decisions. Several modern translations of Deuteronomy 16:18, such as NLT, NIV, and NKJV say "appoint" (Heb. *nathan*, **naw-THAWN**) judges and officers, which specified intentionally setting persons in a particular place. In other words, both judges and their assistants were to be chosen with care for fairness and honesty.

Moses inserted a reminder that their land was a gift from God. By their covenant with God, they obligated themselves to abide by its laws and apply them to all persons and circumstances (Exodus 19:8; 23:1–9; 24:3). The mention in Deuteronomy 16:18 of "all thy gates" and "throughout thy tribes" shows that God intended to ensure justice both locally and nationally.

19 Thou shalt not wrest judgment; thou shalt not respect persons, neither take a gift: for a gift doth blind the eyes of the wise, and pervert the words of the righteous.

The word "wrest" (Heb. *natah*, **naw-TAW**) means "to bend or twist something away from its intended use." In other words, God said: "Don't twist My law around to say whatever you want it to say." Proverbs 17:23 says only a wicked person does that (see, for example, 1 Samuel 8:3).

To "not respect persons" (Deuteronomy 16:19) literally meant "do not...show partiality" (NIV). When a judge learned that a dispute involved one of his friends or someone rich or influential from his community, Moses said he should not allow that recognition to influence how he interpreted the law or how it was enforced.

Another warning to judges was not to accept a "gift" (Heb. *shachad*, **shaw-KHAD**). Most modern translations such as NIV and NASB use the word "bribe" because accepting gifts can often create a sense of obligation on the part of the recipient. Gifts could cause a judge to say what wasn't true or look away from what he or she was smart enough to see wasn't right.

20 That which is altogether just thou shalt follow, that thou mayest live, and inherit the land which the LORD thy God giveth thee.

Only "justice (that) is a joy to the godly" (Heb. *tsedeq tsdeq*, **TSEH-dek TSEH-dek**) could ensure the stability of the community God wanted His chosen people to show the rest of the world (Proverbs 21:15, NLT). Only certainty of fairness for all could ensure life at its fullest, not for one generation but for those who inherit what the Israelites left behind.

Sources:

Bible Pronunciation Chart. Better Days Are Coming.com. http://www.betterdaysarecoming/bible/pronunciation.html (accessed January 29, 2011).

Brown, Francis, et al. *The New Brown-Driver-Briggs-Gesenius Hebrew and English Lexicon*. Peabody, MA: Hendrickson Publishers, 1985.

Evans, Tony. *Tony Evans' Book of Illustrations*. Chicago, IL: Moody Publishers, 2009. 199.

Hebrew and Greek Lexicons. Bible Study Tools.com. http://www.biblestudytools.com/lexicons (accessed November 8, 2010).

MacArthur, John. *The MacArthur Study Bible: NASB*. Nashville, TN: Thomas Nelson, 2006. 243.

Mayes, A. D. H. *New Century Bible: Deuteronomy*. London, England: Morgan, Marshall & Scott Publications, 1979. 207–212, 264-265.

Sockman, Ralph W. *Date with Destiny: A Preamble to Christian Culture*. New York, NY: Abingdon-Cokesbury Press, 1944. 8.

Takadi, Midori. "Jasper, John J. (1812–1901)." Black Past.org. http://www.blackpast.org/?q=aah/jasper-john-j-1812-

1901 (accessed January 29, 2011).

Von Rad, Gerhard. *The Old Testament Library: Deuteronomy, A Commentary*. Philadelphia, PA: Westminster Press, 1966. 83-84, 114-115.

Walvoord, John F., and Roy B. Zuck. *The Bible Knowledge Commentary: An Exposition of the Scriptures, Old Testament*. Wheaton, IL: Victor Books, 1985. 281. Logos Bible Software – Dallas Theological Seminary.

Say It Correctly

Amorite. A-mə-rīt.
Ashtoreth. ASH-tuh-reth.
Balak. BAY-lak.
Bashan. BAY-shuhn.
Chemosh. KEE-mosh.
Moab. MO-ab.
Molech. MOH-lok.

Daily Bible Reading

MONDAY
God of Gods, Lord of Lords
(Psalm 136:1–9)

TUESDAY
Spiritual Matters of the Heart
(Romans 2:25–29)

WEDNESDAY
God's Faithfulness and Justice
(Romans 3:1–9)

THURSDAY
Hold Fast to the Traditions
(2 Thessalonians 2:13–17)

FRIDAY
What the Lord Requires
(Micah 6:1–8)

SATURDAY
Just and True Are Your Ways
(Revelation 15:1–4)

SUNDAY
Loving God and Justice
(Deuteronomy 10:12–22; 16:18–20)

Notes

_____

_____

_____

_____

Teaching Tips

Words You Should Know

A. Pray (1 Samuel 7:5) *palal* (Heb.)—To plead, to intervene, to interpose, to arbitrate, or even judge.

B. Sinned (v. 6) *chata'* (Heb.)—Missed the mark; erred.

Teacher Preparation

Unifying Principle—Rescued! People want to feel safe. Samuel taught the people that their security was a direct result of their loyalty and obedience to God.

A. Pray for your students, and ask God for lesson clarity.

B. Study and meditate on the lesson.

C. Research the life of Samuel and be prepared to present.

D. Complete the companion lesson in the *Precepts For Living Personal Study Guide®*.

O—Open the Lesson

A. After taking prayer requests, lead the class in prayer.

B. Have a volunteer read the In Focus story aloud. Discuss.

C. Discuss the Lesson Aim after reading it aloud.

D. Read the Keep in Mind verse in unison, and then encourage the class to commit the verse to memory during the week.

E. Introduce the students to Samuel and point out his role as Israel's last judge—God's spokesperson.

P—Present the Scriptures

A. Discuss the Focal Verses according to the At-A-Glance outline and More Light on the Text.

B. Reflect on God's justice and the role of believers in helping to bring about His justice on earth.

E—Explore the Meaning

A. Divide the class into groups to answer the Search the Scriptures questions.

B. Read and discuss each Discuss the Meaning question.

C. Review the Lesson in Our Society section. Discuss.

N—Next Steps for Application

A. Challenge students to complete the Make It Happen assignment.

B. Close in prayer, thanking God for His justice.

Worship Guide

For the Superintendent or Teacher
Theme: Samuel Administers Justice
Theme Song: "I Need Thee Every Hour"
Devotional Reading: Ezekiel 18:25–32
Prayer

Samuel Administers Justice

Bible Background • 1 SAMUEL 7:3–17
Printed Text • 1 SAMUEL 7:3–11, 15–17 | Devotional Reading • EZEKIEL 18:25–32

Aim for Change

By the end of the lesson, we will: KNOW the power of prayer and the purpose of praying for justice; SENSE God's call for justice in our community; and PRAY for justice in our community (the country).

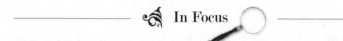

In Focus

After graduating from college, Tamara planned to enter law school. She was on the dean's list and was included in Who's Who Among College Students. Tamara believed that she would be an excellent lawyer. Although she had not decided what aspect of law she would pursue, she knew that she wanted to be financially independent.

Tamara was raised in a Christian home. The entire family regularly attended Bible study, Sunday School, and Sunday service. As a result, Tamara had a strong foundation in God's Word, and she had seen the power of prayer. When Tamara went away to college, her family prayed continually for her. They had a family prayer hour every Friday night. Even when not everyone was under the same roof, they went to God in prayer as a family at the same hour.

As she filled out applications for law school, Tamara remembered the day she had received a full scholarship to attend college. We can accomplish anything God desires for us when we have a strong relationship with Him.

In today's lesson, we see that just as Tamara's church and family prayed on her behalf, Samuel prayed to God on the Israelites' behalf, and God saved them—He brought justice.

Keep in Mind

"And Samuel took a sucking lamb, and offered it for a burnt offering wholly unto the LORD: and Samuel cried unto the LORD for Israel: and the LORD heard him"
(1 Samuel 7:9).

"And Samuel took a sucking lamb, and offered it for a burnt offering wholly unto the LORD: and Samuel cried unto the LORD for Israel: and the LORD heard him" (1 Samuel 7:9).

Focal Verses

KJV **1 Samuel 7:3** And Samuel spake unto all the house of Israel, saying, If ye do return unto the LORD with all your hearts, then put away the strange gods and Ashtaroth from among you, and prepare your hearts unto the LORD, and serve him only: and he will deliver you out of the hand of the Philistines.

4 Then the children of Israel did put away Baalim and Ashtaroth, and served the LORD only.

5 And Samuel said, Gather all Israel to Mizpeh, and I will pray for you unto the LORD.

6 And they gathered together to Mizpeh, and drew water, and poured it out before the LORD, and fasted on that day, and said there, We have sinned against the LORD. And Samuel judged the children of Israel in Mizpeh.

7 And when the Philistines heard that the children of Israel were gathered together to Mizpeh, the lords of the Philistines went up against Israel. And when the children of Israel heard it, they were afraid of the Philistines.

8 And the children of Israel said to Samuel, Cease not to cry unto the LORD our God for us, that he will save us out of the hand of the Philistines.

9 And Samuel took a sucking lamb, and offered it for a burnt offering wholly unto the LORD: and Samuel cried unto the LORD for Israel; and the LORD heard him.

10 And as Samuel was offering up the burnt offering, the Philistines drew near to battle against Israel: but the LORD thundered with a great thunder on that day upon the Philistines, and discomfited them; and they were smitten before Israel.

NLT **1 Samuel 7:3** Then Samuel said to all the people of Israel, "If you are really serious about wanting to return to the LORD, get rid of your foreign gods and your images of Ashtoreth. Determine to obey only the LORD; then he will rescue you from the Philistines."

4 So the Israelites destroyed their images of Baal and Ashtoreth and worshiped only the LORD.

5 Then Samuel told them, "Come to Mizpah, all of you. I will pray to the LORD for you."

6 So they gathered there and, in a great ceremony, drew water from a well and poured it out before the LORD. They also went without food all day and confessed that they had sinned against the LORD. So it was at Mizpah that Samuel became Israel's judge.

7 When the Philistine rulers heard that all Israel had gathered at Mizpah, they mobilized their army and advanced. The Israelites were badly frightened when they learned that the Philistines were approaching.

8 "Plead with the LORD our God to save us from the Philistines!" they begged Samuel.

9 So Samuel took a young lamb and offered it to the LORD as a whole burnt offering. He pleaded with the LORD to help Israel, and the LORD answered.

10 Just as Samuel was sacrificing the burnt offering, the Philistines arrived for battle. But the LORD spoke with a mighty voice of thunder from heaven, and the Philistines were thrown into such confusion that the Israelites defeated them.

11 The men of Israel chased them from Mizpah to Beth-car, slaughtering them all along the way.

KJV Cont.

11 And the men of Israel went out of Mizpeh, and pursued the Philistines, and smote them, until they came under Bethcar.

7:15 And Samuel judged Israel all the days of his life.

16 And he went from year to year in circuit to Bethel, and Gilgal, and Mizpeh, and judged Israel in all those places.

17 And his return was to Ramah; for there was his house; and there he judged Israel; and there he built an altar unto the LORD.

NLT Cont.

7:15 Samuel continued as Israel's judge for the rest of his life.

16 Each year he traveled around, setting up his court first at Bethel, then at Gilgal, and then at Mizpah. He judged the people of Israel at each of these places.

17 Then he would return to his home at Ramah, and he would hear cases there, too. And Samuel built an altar to the LORD at Ramah.

The People, Places, and Times

Samuel. Samuel was the son of Elkanah and Hannah. He served as prophet, judge, and priest. He was born in answer to the prayers of his barren mother, Hannah. Hannah gave Samuel to Eli, the high priest at Shiloh, for dedicated service to God. When Samuel was dedicated to God, he listened to God. Samuel was the last judge in Israel, and he encouraged the Israelites to commit themselves to God and serve Him only.

Mizpah, Mizpeh. The name means "watchtower" or "lookout." Samuel called the Israelites to come to Mizpah to pray and fast in sorrow for their sins. Mizpah was the capital of Judah after the fall of Jerusalem. Later, Saul would be chosen at Mizpah as Israel's first king. Saul had the blessings but not the approval of God and Samuel.

Ashtaroth. The name of the Canaanite goddess of fertility, sexuality, and war, she was the companion of Baal. Ashtaroth worship usually involved prostitution. The ground was believed to be fertile when she was worshiped in sexual rituals.

Background

Samuel was a judge, prophet, and priest who was obedient to God. He was familiar with the power of God. Samuel knew that the Israelites were worshiping false gods; they were not committed to the true and living God.

The Israelites had suffered defeat by the Philistines when they had tried to use the power of the Ark of the Covenant to gain victory in battle. The Lord had given the Children of Israel strict instructions concerning the Ark. Instead of keeping the Ark in the most holy place, they were disobedient by moving it to the battlefield. Earlier, God had killed the men of Beth-shemesh because they had gazed upon the Ark. The Israelites had experienced 20 years of sorrow because they had not repented of their sins. Samuel urged the Israelites to repent and called them to meet him at Mizpah so that he could pray on their behalf. The Israelites believed that God had left them, but they did not do anything about it. Samuel urged them to make a change—to repent.

At-A-Glance

1. Samuel Leads Israel to Repent
(1 Samuel 7:3–7)

2. Samuel Leads Israel to Victory
(vv. 8–11, 15–17)

In Depth

1. Samuel Leads Israel to Repent (1 Samuel 7:3–7)

Eleazar, whose name means "God is power" or "God is help," had been selected to take care of the Ark of the Covenant. The Ark was taken to a city named Kirjath-jearim, which was near the battlefield, because the Israelites wanted to be victorious in battle. Unfortunately, their faith was focused on the Ark of the Covenant, not on God. Therefore, they believed it would bring them victory if it was nearby when they fought the Philistines. In essence, the Ark had become an idol for them. God Himself should have been the focus of their faith, not the Ark. Because God will not tolerate such misplaced faith, they were defeated. Because of this defeat, the Israelites realized that God was no longer blessing them. They needed to repent and return to God. Samuel, who was judge, called the assembly at Mizpah. He directed the Israelites to pray and ask God for forgiveness.

The Israelites prayed and fasted in sorrow for their sins. Fasting is a religious practice associated with making a request of God. Fasting is an act of humbling oneself before God prior to purification. The fasting and prayer represented acts of repentance—acts of turning from idolatry and turning to God. The Israelites desired to remove any obstacles or sins that had led to their defeat and subjection by the Philistines. They needed to reaffirm their covenantal loyalty to God in order to receive His blessings.

Samuel directed the Israelites to gather at Mizpah and pray. He was active in all his roles as prophet, priest, and judge for the Children of Israel. Samuel prayed to God on behalf of the Israelites and urged them to turn from their sins and turn to God in obedience. After Samuel prayed, he poured out water. The act of pouring the water was a sign of repentance. The Israelites no longer desired to worship false gods and so to sin. They wanted to return to God by obeying, serving, and worshiping Him. As judge, Samuel made decisions and settled disputes. Although God was the true leader of Israel, Samuel was His spokesperson. Samuel was obedient to God's direction and judged the Israelites.

As with Samuel, our commitment to God should be continual. If we are distracted and place anything before God, we should seek Him and repent. When we follow God, there will be distractions; but we must focus on Him. We can easily make excuses, but we must follow God. When we seek God daily with a sincere heart, we can endure and keep our focus on Him.

2. Samuel Leads Israel to Victory (vv. 8–11, 15–17)

The Philistines knew that the Israelites were not gathered at Mizpah for a religious observance; they suspected that the Israelites were united in an uprising. The Philistines planned to attack the Israelites, who wanted Samuel to continue to pray for them. The Israelites wanted Samuel to pray for their victory. At Aphek, they had depended on the Ark for victory. Now the Israelites depended on the power of God for victory.

Samuel offered a 1-year-old lamb (a spring lamb with the tenderest meat) to God. According to Levitical law, an animal could not be offered unless it was at least 8 days old. When Samuel offered the sacrifice, he prayed to God, who heard him. God responded with thunder and lightning, which are associated with the presence of a deity. As God thundered from heaven, He stood for the Children of Israel, and the Philistines were confused and defeated. Israel had strength under the leadership of Samuel, who redirected the Israelites to renew their covenant with God—this was the just thing to do. God intervened and gave the

Israelites the victory. The Israelites chased the Philistines to Beth-car, which was a high place overlooking the Philistine territory.

After the battle, Samuel set up a memorial of stone between Mizpah and Shen and named the place Ebenezer, which means "stone of help." God had delivered the Israelites from the hand of the Philistines. Like Joshua, Samuel commemorated God's victories for the Children of Israel with a stone marker (Joshua 4). The Philistines had endured a final defeat at the hands of God. There were no other battles between the Israelites and the Philistines during the time when Samuel was judge. Because of the Israelites' obedience, then, God executed justice through Samuel.

Like the Philistines, we may need to remember the personal victories that God has given us. When we are experiencing difficult moments, the memories will help us to endure. When we remember the victories that God has given us, we can endure the present suffering with confidence. We have faith that God has already given us the victory if we endure.

Search the Scriptures

1. What false god was Ashtaroth associated with (1 Samuel 7:4)?

2. What did the pouring of water by the Israelites mean (v. 6)?

Discuss the Meaning

1. Samuel knew that God hears the prayers of His children. Samuel called the Israelites to Mizpeh to pray to God on their behalf. Do you believe that intercessory prayer is effective? Discuss the importance of praying for others in today's society.

2. Society offers many temptations and distractions that cause humanity to be disobedient to God. What are some false idols in our society today? Discuss how we can stay obedient and focused on God while we live in this world. Discuss the encouragement that others have given you or that you have given others to live for God in all situations.

Lesson in Our Society

The Israelites believed that God had abandoned them. In reality, the Israelites had turned from God. God does not change; humanity changes. God continually waits for sinners with open arms and calls out to those who have turned from Him to return.

As humans, we live in a world of sin. As believers, we serve a loving God, who hears our prayers and knows our need for help. When we are disobedient, we cannot stay in our current state. We must make a change. We must repent—turn from our sin, and return to God. If you know someone who has stopped seeking God's guidance, pray for that person. Encourage him or her to return to God.

Make It Happen

Seek God at all times. The standards of the world are different from God's standards. Remember that God has complete control; therefore, we can be victorious in all situations. Success defined by the world's standards cannot compare with success as a child of God. While we live in the world, we can be strengthened to endure difficult situations by associating with others who will encourage and pray for us.

Seek out a Christian group that has community involvement, or support a community group that encourages those who are alone or homeless. We receive strength when we pray for others and encourage them with our actions and lifestyles. Seek to help those in need; by so doing, you are serving God. When you join a group that prays and seeks to help those in need, you will stay encouraged to do God's will.

Follow the Spirit

What God wants me to do:

_____

_____

_____

_____

Remember Your Thoughts

Special insights I have learned:

_____

_____

_____

_____

More Light on the Text

1 Samuel 7:3–11, 15–17

3 And Samuel spake unto all the house of Israel, saying, If ye do return unto the LORD with all your hearts, then put away the strange gods and Ashtaroth from among you, and prepare your hearts unto the LORD, and serve him only: and he will deliver you out of the hand of the Philistines.

The Ark of the Covenant was returned to Israel and brought to Kirjath-jearim, "and all the house of Israel lamented after the LORD" (v. 2). Afterward, Samuel, functioning as judge, prophet, and priest (and king) over God's chosen people, sets forth the condition for deliverance, whereby covenantal fellowship may be restored with the true and living God. That covenantal fellowship had been broken because of their sin. The phrase in verse 3 "with all your hearts" in Hebrew is *lebab* (**lay-BAWB**), meaning "seat of emotions and passions; the seat of courage" (Strong, 1994).

As judge, Samuel wants the Israelites to give their hearts back to the one true God. He guides the house of Israel through the prescription of consecrating themselves before God. As God's chosen people, they must walk in obedience to the stipulations in order to receive His promise of mercy and favor (Exodus 19:5).

4 Then the children of Israel did put away Baalim and Ashtaroth, and served the LORD only.

God fashions, through tests and discipline, the hearts and minds of His people as they turn toward Him. After a period of estrangement because of their rebellion and apostasy, during which the promise of blessing and protection is deferred, the Israelites return to their God as prodigals— not just agreeing to abide by the dictates of God's Law, but wholeheartedly committing themselves to having no other god and to serve Him only. They readily comply with Samuel's call to repentance. "Baalim" is the plural in Hebrew for *Ba`al* (**BAH-al**), the son of Dagon, the god of the sky who brought forth thunder and rain to fertilize the earth. Of the many strange gods, Baal and Ashtoreth were perhaps the most popular and therefore the most prevalent.

5 And Samuel said, Gather all Israel to Mizpeh, and I will pray for you unto the LORD.

Samuel directs the people to gather at Mizpeh ("Mizpah" in other translations) that he might intercede for them before God. Mizpeh, several miles north of Jerusalem, is a familiar setting. It was the place of national assembly where the people of Israel conferred to bring the Benjamites to justice for the atrocity committed against the concubine of a Levite (see Judges 20:1). Mizpeh would also be the place for the national convention of all the tribes of Israel at which Saul would be elected king, and it would become the capital of Judah after the fall of Jerusalem (1 Samuel 10:17; 2 Kings 25:21–24).

6 And they gathered together to Mizpeh, and drew water, and poured it out before the LORD, and fasted on that day, and said there, We have sinned against the LORD. And Samuel judged the children of Israel in Mizpeh.

That the people would pour water on the ground is an acknowledgment that they deserved to be cursed for violating the terms of the covenant—they had sinned. In Hebrew, the word "sin" is *chata'* (**khaw-TAW**), meaning "miss the mark; to bring into guilt or condemnation or punishment" (Strong, 1994).

But underlying this act is the appeal for mercy and the knowledge that God honors a contrite heart that knows its bankruptcy. He is a merciful God who says that "the soul that sinneth, it shall die" (Ezekiel 18:4). But He also provides a legal refuge—with Samuel as His leader and judge of Israel at Mizpeh—whereby He remains true to His word; some transgressors find refuge by the means of grace He provides. Thus, the people fasted and confessed their sin. The word "fasted" in Hebrew is *tsuwm* (**tsoom**), meaning "abstain(ed) from food" (Strong, 1994). The Israelites felt compelled to also abstain from food in acknowledgment of their sin and repentance.

7 And when the Philistines heard that the children of Israel were gathered together to Mizpeh, the lords of the Philistines went up against Israel. And when the children of Israel heard it, they were afraid of the Philistines.

Perhaps the Philistines sensed an opportunity, now that all the Israelites have gathered at Mizpeh, to decimate the Israelites once and for all; or perhaps they felt threatened and mobilized their army. Certainly, the reality of the attack of the enemy becomes more evident when God's people turn away from and against the evil influence of the world. God's way is never without opposition and challenge. In any case, the people are afraid. (Fear is the potential enemy within because it tempts us with getting momentary expediency of relief without waiting on God.)

8 And the children of Israel said to Samuel, Cease not to cry unto the LORD our God for us, that he will save us out of the hand of the Philistines.

The people look to and beseech Samuel, God's provision and chosen instrument, as mediator on their behalf. Samuel, in this sense, is a type of Christ, and the deliverance sought from the Philistines foreshadows the greater deliverance and salvation affected in the Person of Christ.

9 And Samuel took a sucking lamb, and offered it for a burnt offering wholly unto the LORD: and Samuel cried unto the LORD for Israel; and the LORD heard him.

Acting as priest, Samuel sacrifices a lamb. The stage is set. The Lord's face and the promise of His mercies are no longer eclipsed by the iniquity of His people. When Samuel cries out, God accepts and answers his prayer.

10 And as Samuel was offering up the burnt offering, the Philistines drew near to battle against Israel: but the LORD thundered with a great thunder on that day upon the Philistines, and discomfited them; and they were smitten before Israel.

The Philistines are poised for attack, but the Lord's hand against the Philistines is sure, swift, and unmistakable—they were smitten before Israel. The Israelites—as they had done so many times before, from the day of their liberation from the hand of Pharaoh—see the miracle of what the Lord has done.

11 And the men of Israel went out of Mizpeh, and pursued the Philistines, and smote them, until they came under Bethcar.

"Who is this King of glory? the LORD strong and mighty, the LORD mighty in battle" (Psalm 24:8). So it is when the battle is the Lord's, and all that is left for the Israelites to do is to pursue the scattered Philistines and slay them.

7:15 And Samuel judged Israel all the days of his life. 16 And he went from year to year in circuit to Bethel, and Gilgal, and Mizpeh, and judged Israel in all those places. 17 And his return was to Ramah; for there was his house; and there he judged Israel; and there he built an altar unto the LORD.

God won the battle for the Israelites and He used Samuel until Samuel's death to continue to judge the Israelites. In Hebrew, the word "judged" is *shaphat* (**shaw-FAHT**), meaning ruled, governed; decided about a controversy; exercised judgment. Therefore, Samuel administered justice when he helped the people to repent and turn their hearts back to the true and living God.

Sources:
Bible Pronunciation Chart. Better Days Are Coming.com. http://www.betterdaysarecoming/bible/pronunciation.html (accessed January 29, 2011).
Hebrew and Greek Lexicons. Bible Study Tools.com. http://www.biblestudytools.com/lexicons (accessed June 18, 2010).
Life Application Study Bible: New Living Translation. Wheaton, IL: Tyndale House Publishers, 1996. 402–18.
Merriam-Webster Online Dictionary. Merriam-Webster, Inc. http://www.merriam-webster.com (accessed October 20, 2010).
Passage Lookup. Bible Gateway.com. http://www.biblegateway.com/passage (accessed January 17, 2011).
Strong, James. *New Exhaustive Strong's Numbers and Concordance with Expanded Greek-Hebrew Dictionary.* Seattle, WA: Biblesoft, and International Bible Translators, 1994.

Say It Correctly

Ashtaroth. ASH-tuh-reth.
Mizpah. MIZ-puh.
Philistine. fuh-LIS-teen.
Shiloh. SHI-loh.

Daily Bible Readings

MONDAY
Repent and Turn
(Ezekiel 18:25–32)

TUESDAY
An Earnest Petition
(1 Samuel 1:12–20)

WEDNESDAY
A Gift to the Lord
(1 Samuel 2:11–21)

THURSDAY
A Voice in the Night
(1 Samuel 3:1–14)

FRIDAY
A Trustworthy Prophet
(1 Samuel 3:15–4:1a)

SATURDAY
A Revered Prophet
(Psalm 99)

SUNDAY
A Faithful Judge
(1 Samuel 7:3–11, 15–17)

Teaching Tips

Words You Should Know

A. Anointed (2 Samuel 23:1) *mashiyach* (Heb.)—A consecrated person, such as a king or priest; can refer to the Messiah.

B. Just (v. 3) *tsaddiyq* (Heb.)—Lawful, righteous.

Teacher Preparation

Unifying Principle—True to the End. People want to have a meaningful existence. Acknowledging God's authority in our lives enables us to become the persons God created us to be.

A. Pray for each student by name every day this week.

B. Phone or write each student that missed last week's class.

C. Study and meditate on the entire text in both translations.

D. Complete the companion lesson in the *Precepts For Living Personal Study Guide®*.

E. Bring an obituary that you can read and discuss in class.

O—Open the Lesson

A. Open with prayer.

B. After prayer, read an obituary, perhaps from a newspaper. Ask your students what type of obituary they would like written about themselves. "What things would you like to be remembered for?" Tell them that today they will see how King David summarized his life.

P—Present the Scriptures

A. Have volunteers read the Focal Verses.

B. Summarize the verses, using The People, Places, and Times; Background; Search the Scriptures; At-A-Glance outline; In Depth; and More Light on the Text to clarify the verses.

E—Explore the Meaning

A. Have volunteers summarize the Discuss the Meaning, Lesson in Our Society, and Make It Happen sections.

B. Connect these sections to the Aim for Change and the Keep in Mind verse.

N—Next Steps for Application

A. Allow time for the students to create an obituary that might be written for their lives thus far.

B. Close with prayer and ask God to help each student to live in such a way that people can see his or her righteousness and his or her relationship with Jesus Christ.

Worship Guide

For the Superintendent or Teacher
Theme: David Embodies God's Justice
Theme Song: "My Tribute"
Devotional Reading: Isaiah 32:1–8
Prayer

David Embodies God's Justice

Bible Background • 2 SAMUEL 22:1–23:7; 1 CHRONICLES 18:14
Printed Text • 2 SAMUEL 23:1–7; 1 CHRONICLES 18:14
Devotional Reading • ISAIAH 32:1–8

—————————— Aim for Change ——————————

By the end of the lesson, we will: UNDERSTAND the importance of promoting justice and equity in our relationships; BE ASSURED that God has a covenant with us; and BE A VOICE for God and justice in our church and community.

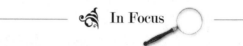

—————————— In Focus ——————————

Bishop Arthur M. Brazier died on October 22, 2010, at age 89. Through the power of God, he built up the Apostolic Church of God in Chicago, Illinois, to an impressive 20,000 active members worshiping in a large modern building that fills an entire city block. But beyond the love and respect of church members, the entire African American community paused to honor him when he died because of his tremendous fight for social justice and community revitalization. Although few of us will achieve the things that this man of God was able to do, when we get to the end of our lives, what will be said about us? What will we have accomplished?

Today's Scripture passage looks at King David's final words and what he thought was the most important legacy he had to leave behind.

—————————— Keep in Mind ——————————

"So David reigned over all Israel, and executed judgment and justice among all his people" (1 Chronicles 18:14).

"So David reigned over all Israel, and executed judgment and justice among all his people" (1 Chronicles 18:14).

Focal Verses

KJV **2 Samuel 23:1** Now these be the last words of David. David the son of Jesse said, and the man who was raised up on high, the anointed of the God of Jacob, and the sweet psalmist of Israel, said,

2 The Spirit of the LORD spake by me, and his word was in my tongue.

3 The God of Israel said, the Rock of Israel spake to me, He that ruleth over men must be just, ruling in the fear of God.

4 And he shall be as the light of the morning, when the sun riseth, even a morning without clouds; as the tender grass springing out of the earth by clear shining after rain.

5 Although my house be not so with God; yet he hath made with me an everlasting covenant, ordered in all things, and sure: for this is all my salvation, and all my desire, although he make it not to grow.

6 But the sons of Belial shall be all of them as thorns thrust away, because they cannot be taken with hands:

7 But the man that shall touch them must be fenced with iron and the staff of a spear; and they shall be utterly burnt with fire in the same place.

1 Chronicles 18:14 So David reigned over all Israel, and executed judgment and justice among all his people.

NLT **2 Samuel 23:1** These are the last words of David:

"David, the son of Jesse, speaks—David, the man to whom God gave such wonderful success, David, the man anointed by the God of Jacob, David, the sweet psalmist of Israel.

2 "The Spirit of the LORD speaks through me; his words are upon my tongue.

3 The God of Israel spoke. The Rock of Israel said to me: 'The person who rules righteously, who rules in the fear of God,

4 he is like the light of the morning, like the sunrise bursting forth in a cloudless sky, like the refreshing rains that bring tender grass from the earth.'

5 "It is my family God has chosen! Yes, he has made an everlasting covenant with me. His agreement is eternal, final, sealed. He will constantly look after my safety and success.

6 But the godless are like thorns to be thrown away, for they tear the hand that touches them.

7 One must be armed to chop them down; they will be utterly consumed with fire."

1 Chronicles 18:14 David reigned over all Israel and was fair to everyone.

The People, Places, and Times

David, The Psalmist. We first meet a teenage David when Samuel anointed him as the future king. The next time we meet him is as a musician. Music seems to have always been a big part of David's life. We can imagine him as he spent long days minding the sheep as he sang and composed songs. He probably took his portable harp with him to the pasturelands. Sometime after his anointing, he sang and played his harp to calm the troubled heart of King Saul. Evidently, the news of his musical talent had reached all the way to the king's palace. As the narrative of David's life is recorded in 1 and 2 Samuel and 1 Chronicles, we see little of the thoughts in David's mind. But many of the psalms are inscribed to tell us where they fit in David's life and so we enter his thoughts and heart. In today's Scripture passage, he calls himself "the sweet psalmist of Israel" (2 Samuel 23:1). Psalms are the prayer and praise songs of the Bible. We have little idea about the tunes and types of music for the psalms, but the God-inspired words are preserved for us, so we are free to interpret the musical style as fits our culture, history, and personal taste.

The United Kingdom. Only three kings ruled over the united kingdom of Israel and Judah—King Saul, King David, and King Solomon. Just a little over a thousand years before the birth of Christ (1050 B.C.), Saul was anointed to be king over all of Israel. God had already planned for the Israelites to have a king, but not by setting aside the Lord God as their true King. Tall and impressive Saul was just who people might choose for a king, but soon after his reign began, it became obvious that Saul was going to do things his way, not God's way. Twenty-five years later, David was anointed king, but another 15 years passed before he actually took possession of the kingdom. David reigned as king in Hebron for seven years and over all Israel for 33 years . . . a total of 40 years (1 Kings 2:11), until his son, Solomon, became the king. Solomon reigned for 40 years. He started well, but by marrying 700 wives and having 300 concubines, he was clearly disobedient to the Lord and his heart was turned away from following God. Under Solomon's son, Rehoboam, the kingdom was divided into Israel and Judah and that was the end of the united kingdom.

Background

God called David a man who followed Him with all his heart (1 Kings 14:8). David did some terrible things, but his heart was tender toward God, so that when he sinned, he repented deeply. Before his sin with

Bathsheba and his murder of her husband, Uriah, David had a desire to build a beautiful temple for the Lord. God denied his desire because as a warrior David had blood on his hands. But God had a far greater blessing for David. God promised to send Jesus, the eternal King, through the ancestry of David. For a complete account of this story and all the many blessings promised to David, see 2 Samuel 7.

At-A-Glance

1. David, the Singer of Songs
   (2 Samuel 23:1)

2. David, Inspired by God
   (vv. 2–3a)

3. David, Ruling in Justice
   (vv. 3b–4)

4. David, the Ideal King
   (vv. 5–7)

5. David, a Reign Summarized by Justice
   (1 Chronicles 18:14)

In Depth

1. David, the Singer of Songs (2 Samuel 23:1)

David was aware that the words of this psalm were probably his last as a composer of songs. Before the beginning of the psalm, we read in verse 1 a brief biographical description of David, the composer. The bio begins with his father, Jesse. Perhaps David was thinking of how he began life as the youngest son (the oldest son was usually the one with the most prestige), the one who cared for the sheep, and yet he was the one whom God chose and raised up to be the king of Israel and the ancestor of His Son, Jesus.

2. David, Inspired by God (vv. 2–3a)

David was also aware that as he composed many psalms, God was inspiring the words he wrote. This is consistent with other biblical writers, who also were aware that their words were God-breathed. This is one of many reasons why we know the Word of God is inspired and can trust in it.

3. David, Ruling in Justice (vv. 3b–4)

Politicians who exercise their offices with integrity and justice sometimes seem to be rare. But David ruled in righteousness because of his relationship with God. The fear of God may be defined as a profound sense of the holiness of God. This fear leads us to worship God and obey Him. Leaders of any sort, who are keenly aware of God's omniscience (all knowing), His omnipotence (all powerful), and His omnipresence (everywhere present), would be very careful to do what is right. Such leaders know that God knows everything we think, say, and do. And having such great knowledge of God causes us to desire to please Him and obey Him. We pray that our leaders will rule in justice because they have a true sense of who God is.

Leaders who rule with justice are beautiful to see—as beautiful as the sun coming up on a cloudless day, or like the sun coming out after a rainy day. Not only is the sun lovely to look at, but it causes green plants to sprout forth from the earth. Therefore, we are happy to see compassionate and just rulers, but we are also happy with the results of their leadership.

4. David, the Ideal King (vv. 5–7)

Is David the ideal king, like the sunlight coming up, the new growth after the rain? No,

David was not perfect and Scripture makes sure that we see him in all his weaknesses. But because David loved God and repented when he did wrong, God loved David and made a special covenant with him. This covenant was made before David sinned with Bathsheba and Uriah. And because the covenant was with God, God was keeping His word. In spite of the fact that Solomon did not follow God to the end and most of the rulers after him did not follow God, God kept His promise to send His Son through the lineage of David. David was well aware of the awesomeness of God's promises to him.

But those who refuse to live in covenant with God are just the opposite of the beautiful sunny day. Instead of lush grass, their lives are patches of thorns. You can't use your hands to pull them up. You must use some sort of tool to pull them up, and then you burn them so they cannot reseed themselves.

5. David, a Reign Summarized by Justice (1 Chronicles 18:14)

King David's rule is summarized as just and right. Other nations may be richer and stronger, but the nation of Israel is to be special because it is governed according to God's justice.

Search the Scriptures

1. What are some of the phrases that King David uses to describe himself (2 Samuel 23:1–4)?

2. What are some of the phrases used to describe God (v. 3)?

3. What is the fate of evil men (vv. 6–7)?

Discuss the Meaning

What does "the fear of God" mean? How does the fear of God rightly understood help us to do what is right? How does this differ from being afraid of an evil character who will harm you if you are not doing what the evil person wants you to do?

Lesson in Our Society

During the recent economic meltdown, many bankers and other people in high-placed financial positions were caught doing things that were illegal or at least seemed to be very unethical. The things they did destroyed the pensions of elderly people, took away the homes of families, and otherwise caused economic ruin for their wealthy peers. Not only did they not seem to care about the poor and middle class, but they seemed to have no concept that God knows and sees everything they are doing and have done. Why do you think they are so indifferent to the situations of others, especially those who have much less than they do? How can they have forgotten about God?

Make It Happen

It's easy to criticize the rich and famous, but if we examine ourselves, we will discover some of those same tendencies within us. How can we demonstrate justice and compassion toward our coworkers or neighbors this week?

Follow the Spirit

What God wants me to do:

_____

_____

_____

_____

Remember Your Thoughts

Special insights I have learned:

_____

_____

_____

More Light on the Text

2 Samuel 23:1–7; 1 Chronicles 18:14

Introduction

As our lives here on earth come to an end, every person wants to sum up his or her life at its best. King David was no different.

These first seven verses in 2 Samuel 23 are written in the Hebrew form of poetry. This was used often in the Old Testament in order to make it easier to remember. Until Gutenberg invented the printing press and produced the first printed Bible in 1440, every Bible prior to that time was hand-copied. Priests and elders in the temple were among the few with access to a Bible (2 Chronicles 34:14; 2 Kings 22:8–12). As a result, most people only learned God's Word by hearing it read in worship and classes and then memorizing what they heard (Exodus 24:7; Deuteronomy 31:11; Nehemiah 8:1–5, 13). This emphasizes how important the writer of 2 Samuel thought it was for all Israelites, both priests and laypeople, to remember David's final words.

23:1 Now these be the last words of David. David the son of Jesse said, and the man who was raised up on high, the anointed of the God of Jacob, and the sweet psalmist of Israel, said, 2 The Spirit of the LORD spake by me, and his word was in my tongue.

Many nations revere their founders and first great leaders. David was both. He was an unlikely soldier, much less a military leader. He was the youngest of eight sons of Jesse, a shepherd from the village of Bethlehem. His three oldest brothers were already in Israel's army. Four other older brothers were still at home. His father Jesse made use of David to care for his sheep and to carry supplies to replenish the needs of his older brothers in the army (1 Samuel 17:13–22).

Yet, God told the prophet Samuel that He had chosen young David for a special purpose. In 2 Samuel 23:1 we read that God ordered young David to be "anointed" (Heb. *mashiyach,* **maw-SHEE-akh**) with oil, marking him as God's choice to become the next king of Israel. Decades later, David had been "raised up" (Heb. *quwm,* **koom**) from a simple shepherd and errand boy to his nation's exalted leader. God endowed David with bravery, aptitude as a warrior, and great leadership skills. Being called "the sweet psalmist of Israel" indicates that he was also blessed with musical and poetic talents, as 1 Samuel 16:23 and 2 Samuel 22:1–51 show.

In spite of his moral failings, the memory of what God brought about through David's life at his best symbolized the fulfillment of God's promise through David's ancestors Abraham, Isaac, and Jacob.

Second Samuel 23:1 begins with "the last words of David." "Words" here (Heb. *dabar,* **daw-BAW**) referred to human words or statements. Verse 2 refers to "spake" (Heb. *ne'um,* **neh-OOM**), primarily found in the Old Testament, meaning a message or utterance by God, often with "the LORD" or some other reference to God attached (1 Samuel 2:30; Amos 6:8). Many modern versions translate "spake" or "said" as "oracle" (NIV, NRSV). This indicates that what David said was not just his opinion of himself, but God's evaluation of his reign as king. Thus, David said, "The Spirit of the LORD spake by me" (2 Samuel 23:2).

3 The God of Israel said, the Rock of Israel spake to me, He that ruleth over men must be just, ruling in the fear of God.

Once again David emphasized that he was declaring not his own point of view but God's. By calling God "the Rock" (Heb. *tsuwr,* **tsoor**), he pictured God as a great cliff of protection in the storms of life, a place of security on which to mount a defense against an enemy or an unmovable foundation when crushing problems threatened to wash him away (2 Samuel 22:1–2; Psalm 61:2–3). He remains so for today's believers.

David's comments in these first three verses provide a great opportunity for teaching those seeking guidance for living from God's Word. As 2 Samuel 23:1 declares, this was written at the very end of David's life after he was a known and admitted adulterer and murderer. These verses show that God's people must constantly guard against the universal inclination and temptation to sin in every person (Romans 3:23). No matter how powerful, wealthy, or talented a person becomes, and David certainly was all three, none of us ever escapes the reality that "sin is crouching at the door, eager to control you" (Genesis 4:7, NLT; see also 1 Peter 5:8–9a; 1 Corinthians 10:12). These verses also show that despite the seriousness of our sins, God can speak and work through our lives to bring enrichment to individuals and society as a whole and bring honor to Himself. But, for that to happen, a person must be willing to return to God in repentance as David did (Psalm 51).

In the middle of 2 Samuel 23:3, David stated God's inventory of the importance of his reign as king. God concludes that as head of state, the most important quality of David's reign was that Israel's governance under him was just. In spite of David's personal moral failings, his reign was characterized by judgments on national issues that were "just"

(Heb. *tsaddiyq*, **tsad-DEEK**). (See 2 Samuel 8:15; Jeremiah 23:5.)

What enabled a ruler to do that then, as well as officials in authority today, is a fearful concern for honoring and acting in keeping with God's unchanging nature and values. Righteousness did not require that justice be harsh. Zechariah prophesied of God's revelation of Himself in the coming of His Messiah: "Look, your king is coming to you. He is righteous and victorious, yet he is humble (KJV, "lowly"), riding on a donkey" (Zechariah 9:9, NLT). Likewise, Psalm 89:14 declared, "Justice and judgment are the habitation of thy throne: mercy and truth shall go before thy face."

4 And he shall be as the light of the morning, when the sun riseth, even a morning without clouds; as the tender grass springing out of the earth by clear shining after rain.

Bible translators have struggled with getting the meaning out of this verse. The King James Version gets the meaning across as well as most modern translations. David starts by picturing a bright sunrise on a cloudless day. The sky is clear. But then he talks about rain on the grass. From a sunny cloudless sky? For some, the imagery might seem perplexing.

The lesson from this verse is that when a ruler is committed to doing what's right, the assurance of justice makes life better. That's true whether everything's perfect as on a bright, clear morning, or in difficult times such as on a rainy day. Right after it rains, leaves of grass are rising up from the ground and "shining" (Heb. *nogah*, **NO-gah**) with glittering raindrops on them. David's point was that commitment to God's righteous will and faithfulness in executing justice in human relations had positive effects in easy or difficult times (Leviticus 19:14–15; Isaiah 55:10–11; Jeremiah 21:10–16; 22:16).

5 Although my house be not so with God; yet he hath made with me an everlasting covenant, ordered in all things, and sure; for this is all my salvation, and all my desire, although he did not make it to grow.

This is another verse with many layers of meaning. The key to understanding its truths is keeping in mind that God was speaking through David and David responded to what God inspired him to say. First, David admitted that his royal family, "my house," had not all bought into his commitment to doing God's righteous will. Several examples could be cited, but two involving David's children illustrate why David said this. David's son, Ammon, raped David's daughter, Tamar, Ammon's half-sister (2 Samuel 13:14). In revenge David's son Absalom, Tamar's brother, had Ammon murdered (2 Samuel 13:22, 28–29).

In spite of his own and his family's failure to follow God's purposes fully, 2 Samuel 23:5 points out that David was convinced of the enduring certainty of God's "covenant" (Heb. *beriyth*, **ber-EETH**) with him and his descendants. David cited that the basis for his confidence about his family's future was God's purposes and pleasure. God had a plan "ordered . . . and sure." The "salvation" of God's purposes through David's descendants lay in God's power to rescue them from whatever difficulty they encountered and ensure their welfare, generation after generation. That was God's desire, which gave David pleasure to fulfill. That, however, did not mean that God caused to prosper those things in David's life or in his family that were contrary to His nature.

6 But the sons of Belial shall be all of them as thorns thrust away, because they cannot be taken with hands: 7 But the man that shall touch them must be fenced with iron and

the staff of a spear; and they shall be utterly burnt with fire in the same place.

Second Samuel 23:6 begins with the phrase "the sons of Belial"; this is the one time in the Old Testament that Belial is mentioned as an individual. The translator of the KJV likely added the phrase here because all the other 14 times that Belial is mentioned, the biblical writers speak of the sons, daughters, or children of Belial. The Hebrew word *Beliya`al* (**bel-e-YAH-al**) meant a worthless, witless person who causes needless destruction or evil events. The Israelites did not have as clear an image of the evil spiritual being who opposed God's involvement with humanity as the New Testament writers did. Belial was a personal name used in the Old Testament similar to Satan. Satan, which means "adversary," was often used as a descriptive title, "the Satan," rather than as a personal name.

God's purpose in verses 6 and 7 was to illustrate that the lives of David's descendants would only have lasting meaning if they maintained a just society and followed David's example of trying to implement God's righteous values in their lives. He compared an unjust ruler to thorny vines. He said briar vines should be chopped down with a stout, durable tool, taking care not to be pierced by their thorns. Once cut off, they should be moved out of the way using a spear's wooden shaft. A pile of chopped-down, thorny briars was worthless. Their only value after that was to serve as fuel for a fire (John 15:6). Likewise, unjust rulers or officials remained a constant danger to society. These verses were David's poetic way of saying they should be dealt with carefully and pushed aside where they could cause no harm.

1 Chronicles 18:14 So David reigned over all Israel, and executed judgment and justice among all his people.

The two books of Chronicles were written after the Israelites returned from exile and captivity in Babylon. They show that even hundreds of years after David lived and the monarchy David founded had collapsed, the justice experienced during David's reign was still held up as a model that society should aspire to.

Sources:

Bible Pronunciation Chart. Better Days Are Coming.com. http://www.betterdaysarecoming/bible/pronunciation.html (accessed January 29, 2011).

Brown, Francis, et al. *The New Brown-Driver-Briggs-Gesenius Hebrew and English Lexicon.* Peabody, MA: Hendrickson Publishers, 1985.

Hertzberg, Hans Wilhelm. *The Old Testament Library: I & II Samuel, A Commentary.* 4th ed. Philadelphia, PA: Westminster Press, 1976. 398–402.

Mauchline, John. *New Century Bible: 1 and 2 Samuel.* London, England: Morgan, Marshall & Scott Publications, 1971. 312–15.

Merriam-Webster Online Dictionary. Merriam-Webster, Inc. http://www.merriam-webster.com (accessed January 29, 2011).

Passage Lookup. Bible Gateway.com. http://www.biblegateway.com/passage (accessed January 17, 2011).

Peterson, Eugene H. *First and Second Samuel.* Louisville, KY: Westminster John Knox Press, 1999.

Robinson, Gnana. *Let Us Be Like the Nations: A Commentary on the Books of 1 and 2 Samuel.* Grand Rapids, MI: William B. Eerdmans Publishing Co., 1993.

Wilcock, Michael. *The Message of Chronicles: One Church, One Faith, One Lord.* Downers Grove, IL: InterVarsity Press, 1987. 13–18, 78.

Williamson, Hugh G. M. *New Century Bible Commentary: 1 and 2 Chronicles.* Grand Rapids, MI: William B. Eerdmans Publishing Co., 1982. 15–17.

Say It Correctly

Ammon. AM-uhn.
Belial. BEE-lee-uhl.
Tamar. TAY-mahr.

Daily Bible Readings

MONDAY
Inquiring of the Lord
(2 Samuel 2:1–7)

TUESDAY
Rejoicing in God's Deliverance
(2 Samuel 22:8–20)

WEDNESDAY
Depending on God's Guidance
(2 Samuel 22:26–31)

THURSDAY
Living in God's Strength
(2 Samuel 22:32–37)

FRIDAY
Praising God's Steadfast Love
(2 Samuel 22:47–51)

SATURDAY
Reigning in Righteousness
(Isaiah 32:1–8)

SUNDAY
Ruling in the Fear of God
(2 Samuel 23:1–7; 1 Chronicles 18:14)

Notes

_____

_____

_____

_____

Teaching Tips

July 15
Bible Study Guide 7

Words You Should Know

A. Wisdom (1 Kings 3:28) *chokmah* (Heb.)—Ability to discern inner qualities and relationships.

B. Judgment (v. 28; 2 Chronicles 9:8) *mishpat* (Heb.)—A formal utterance of an authoritative opinion.

Teacher Preparation

Unifying Principle—Wisdom and Justice. People need a just and wise mediator when life presents unjust situations. To whom may we go to receive justice? Because of Solomon's relationship with God, he was able to make just and wise choices.

A. Pray for your students and that God will bring lesson clarity.

B. Study and meditate on the entire text.

C. Complete the companion lesson in the *Precepts For Living Personal Study Guide®*.

O—Open the Lesson

A. Open with prayer, including the Aim for Change.

B. After prayer, introduce today's subject of the lesson.

C. Have your students read the Aim for Change and Keep in Mind verse in unison. Discuss.

D. Then ask, "Like Solomon, have you ever prayed to God for wisdom?"

E. Share testimonies.

F. Now have a volunteer summarize the In Focus story. Discuss.

P—Present the Scriptures

A. Have volunteers read the Focal Verses.

B. Now use The People, Places, and Times; Background; Search the Scriptures; At-A-Glance outline; In Depth; and More Light on the Text to clarify the verses.

E—Explore the Meaning

A. Have volunteers summarize the Discuss the Meaning, Lesson in Our Society, and Make It Happen sections.

B. Connect these sections to the Aim for Change and the Keep in Mind verse.

N—Next Steps for Application

A. Summarize the lesson.

B. Close with prayer and praise God for the victory He's won in their lives and for who He is.

Worship Guide

For the Superintendent or Teacher
Theme: Solomon Judges with
Wisdom and Justice
Theme Song: "Walk in the Light!"
Devotional Reading: Psalm 37:27–34
Prayer

Solomon Judges with Wisdom and Justice

Bible Background • 1 KINGS 3; 2 CHRONICLES 9:8
Printed Text • 1 KINGS 3:16–28; 2 CHRONICLES 9:8 | Devotional Reading • PSALM 37:27–34

—————— Aim for Change ——————

By the end of the lesson, we will: UNDERSTAND the importance of seeking divine wisdom; REFLECT on a time when acting with compassion and justice brought about a fair result; and CHOOSE to act with wisdom and justice.

—————  In Focus —————

Dwight was only 35 when his father died unexpectedly and then Dwight **JULY 15th** became president of the family's real estate firm. On top of all that, it was not a good economic time to be in that business. Banks were foreclosing on many homeowners. Times were especially hard for African Americans who were the first homeowners in their families. Some had bought homes with mortgages that were too big for their incomes, and then they lost their jobs on top of it all. Every morning, Dwight read his Bible and then earnestly sought the wisdom of God on how to run his business. He could get out of the business and save his own family's finances, but what about the Black community where he lived? How could he be a man of integrity and compassion?

What circumstances have you found yourself in that called for wisdom that seemed to be beyond your own abilities? What did you do about the situation? Today's lesson is about executing wisdom and justice.

—————— Keep in Mind ——————

"And all Israel heard of the judgment which the king had judged; and they feared the king: for they saw that the wisdom of God was in him, to do judgment" (1 Kings 3:28).

"And all Israel heard of the judgment which the king had judged; and they feared the king: for they saw that the wisdom of God was in him, to do judgment" (1 Kings 3:28).

Focal Verses

KJV **1 Kings 3:16** Then came there two women, that were harlots, unto the king, and stood before him.

17 And the one woman said, O my lord, I and this woman dwell in one house; and I was delivered of a child with her in the house.

18 And it came to pass the third day after that I was delivered, that this woman was delivered also: and we were together; there was no stranger with us in the house, save we two in the house.

19 And this woman's child died in the night; because she overlaid it.

20 And she rose at midnight, and took my son from beside me, while thine handmaid slept, and laid it in her bosom, and laid her dead child in my bosom.

21 And when I rose in the morning to give my child suck, behold, it was dead: but when I had considered it in the morning, behold, it was not my son, which I did bear.

22 And the other woman said, Nay; but the living is my son, and the dead is thy son. And this said, No; but the dead is thy son, and the living is my son. Thus they spake before the king.

23 Then said the king, The one saith, This is my son that liveth, and thy son is the dead: and the other saith, Nay; but thy son is the dead, and my son is the living.

24 And the king said, Bring me a sword. And they brought a sword before the king.

25 And the king said, Divide the living child in two, and give half to the one, and half to the other.

26 Then spake the woman whose the living child was unto the king, for her bowels yearned upon her son, and she said, O my lord, give her the living child, and in no wise slay it. But the other said, Let it be neither mine nor thine, but divide it.

NLT **1 Kings 3:16** Some time later, two prostitutes came to the king to have an argument settled.

17 "Please, my lord," one of them began, "this woman and I live in the same house. I gave birth to a baby while she was with me in the house.

18 Three days later, she also had a baby. We were alone; there were only two of us in the house.

19 But her baby died during the night when she rolled over on it.

20 Then she got up in the night and took my son from beside me while I was asleep. She laid her dead child in my arms and took mine to sleep beside her.

21 And in the morning when I tried to nurse my son, he was dead! But when I looked more closely in the morning light, I saw that it wasn't my son at all."

22 Then the other woman interrupted, "It certainly was your son, and the living child is mine."

"No," the first woman said, "the dead one is yours, and the living one is mine." And so they argued back and forth before the king.

23 Then the king said, "Let's get the facts straight. Both of you claim the living child is yours, and each says that the dead child belongs to the other.

24 All right, bring me a sword." So a sword was brought to the king.

25 Then he said, "Cut the living child in two and give half to each of these women!"

26 Then the woman who really was the mother of the living child, and who loved him very much, cried out, "Oh no, my lord! Give her the child—please do not kill him!"

But the other woman said, "All right, he will be neither yours nor mine; divide him between us!"

KJV Cont.

27 Then the king answered and said, Give her the living child, and in no wise slay it: she is the mother thereof.

28 And all Israel heard of the judgment which the king had judged; and they feared the king: for they saw that the wisdom of God was in him, to do judgment.

2 Chronicles 9:8 Blessed be the LORD thy God, which delighted in thee to set thee on his throne, to be king for the LORD thy God: because thy God loved Israel, to establish them for ever, therefore made he thee king over them, to do judgment and justice.

NLT Cont.

27 Then the king said, "Do not kill him, but give the baby to the woman who wants him to live, for she is his mother!"

28 Word of the king's decision spread quickly throughout all Israel, and the people were awed as they realized the great wisdom God had given him to render decisions with justice.

2 Chronicles 9:8 The LORD your God is great indeed! He delights in you and has placed you on the throne to rule for him. Because God loves Israel so much and desires this kingdom to last forever, he has made you king so you can rule with justice and righteousness."

The People, Places, and Times

Prostitution. Prostitution is defined as selling sexual favors. Even in the Bible, people seemed to have a double standard regarding the female prostitute and the male who patronizes her. In Genesis 38 we read that Judah paid for sex from a woman he thought was a prostitute, but who was actually his widowed daughter-in-law. He acted as though he were scandalized when she became pregnant, but had a change of attitude when it came out that he was the father of the baby. However, the Bible always condemns any sex outside of marriage.

Prostitutes in every culture are looked down upon, and it is very surprising seeing Solomon, the king of Israel, judging a case with two such women. This incident highlights the wisdom of Solomon, but it also shows that every human being deserves justice and fair treatment.

Wisdom. Wisdom is more than mere book knowledge; it involves knowing the right thing to do and doing it. Social scientists today have observed that the heads of major corporations are rarely younger than 50 years old. There are certain mental processes that seem to come only with maturity. This was something that young King Solomon was lacking, but God granted him wisdom at the beginning of his reign (1 Kings 3:3–15). True wisdom comes from God. We read in James 1:5 that if we lack wisdom, we should ask God and He will give it to us. At many points in life, we are challenged to make decisions, and if we are wise, we will ask God for His help.

Background

At 20 years of age, King Solomon felt very young and unprepared to assume the throne of his father, the great King David. (We only need to look at Solomon's son, Rehoboam, as he ascended to the throne, to see how some youths can make very unwise decisions.) Solomon had already married Pharaoh's daughter—not a wise decision—and here he was worshiping at a high place, another forbidden thing. But God was able to see that in his heart, Solomon was worshiping the true God. Therefore, when young Solomon lay down to sleep that night, God appeared to him in a dream. God made the wonderful offer to Solomon that He would give him whatever he wanted God to give him.

Solomon could have asked for riches and fame, for long life and for the death of his enemies. Instead, he asked God to give him wisdom to rule Israel. This answer showed that already Solomon was wise enough to know that he needed the Lord's help to govern the nation. God was delighted with Solomon's answer. He promised to make him wiser than any other king of that time. God also gave him riches and fame. He promised to give Solomon long life, too, if he would obey God all his life. Unfortunately, he was distracted from obeying the Lord by his many wives and their foreign gods, and his story ends in a lamentable fashion.

Today's Scripture passage shows how God answered Solomon's request and gave him great wisdom in governing the people.

At-A-Glance

In Depth

1. Two Prostitutes with Two Babies (1 Kings 3:16–18)

A pregnant prostitute has a dilemma. Pregnancy and child care prevent her from working. She probably also knows that bringing a child into her world gives a child a poor environment in which to grow up. The two women in the narrative probably lived in a brothel. Brothels have always been common in cities, and they may provide some protection and company for the women in a very lonely business. A baby will also provide some solace to a prostitute.

The men who pay for the body of the prostitute do not love her. Society looks down upon her. But a child will love its mother, and she can lavish her love on her child. God has created a nurturing instinct in the heart of a mother. In the mother's eyes, her baby is the most beautiful child in the entire world.

2. Two Prostitutes with a Problem (vv. 19–22)

Evidently, during the night, one of the sleeping mothers rolled over on her baby and suffocated the child. When she discovered that her baby was dead, she went over to the other sleeping mother and substituted her own dead child for the other mother's living baby. The second mother woke up during the night to nurse her baby and was horrified to find the baby dead. But, when morning came, she looked closely at the baby and realized that the dead child was not hers. The living baby in the arms of the other woman was her child.

So now, the two mothers are before King Solomon arguing their cases. Both claim to be the mother of the living baby. We are surprised that a case of two prostitutes would come up before the king of the land. But perhaps they went before a lower court first, and no solution could be found. So they are appearing before the "Supreme Court," so to speak.

3. King Solomon's Proposal (vv. 23–25)

This story appears right after God has agreed to make Solomon the wisest king of his day, and it demonstrates how wise Solomon was. Solomon called for a sword and threatened to cut the baby in half and give half of a dead baby to each mother. Was Solomon taking a risk? No, God gave him insight into a mother's heart.

4. King Solomon's Judgment (vv. 26–28)

For the protection of the human race, God puts love in a mother's heart for her baby. "Good" mothers would do anything to protect their children. God gave King Solomon the wisdom to understand this. There are many kinds of wisdom and one type is the ability to understand human emotions, which Solomon displayed in this situation.

5. King Solomon's Wisdom Recognized (2 Chronicles 9:8)

This verse appears in the midst of the visit of the African Queen of Sheba to King Solomon. She had come to Israel to see if he was as wise as people were saying. She found his wisdom to be overwhelming, and she praised God for giving Solomon such wisdom. She said that God gave Solomon and his wisdom to Israel because He was delighted with Solomon and because God loves Israel. Although Solomon displayed his wisdom in many areas—botany, zoology, commerce, writing, and so forth—the Queen of Sheba rightly saw what type of wisdom was most important for a king. She said that God gave this wisdom to Solomon so that he would rule with justice and righteousness.

Search the Scriptures

1. Who came to King Solomon for justice (1 Kings 3:16)?

2. What problem did they bring to Solomon (vv. 17–22)?

3. How did Solomon demonstrate justice in his ruling (vv. 24–25)?

Discuss the Meaning

1. Name some of the different kinds of wisdom. What kind of wisdom is most important for the ruler of a nation? Why do you think this kind of wisdom is most important?

2. Give some examples of other types of wisdom needed in other areas. What type of wisdom is needed for a schoolteacher? A business executive? A mother or a father? Name as many examples as time allows.

Lesson in Our Society

There are many kinds of leaders in society today. There are arrogant leaders, corrupt leaders, and many other types of persons in charge who are not showing justice and righteousness in their leadership. We always can use more leaders who are full of wisdom. Read Romans 13:1–7 to see what we can do to encourage our leaders to operate as God wants them to.

Make It Happen

Reflect on question two of the Discuss the Meaning section. What kind of wisdom do you need in your life? Look up James 1:5. This verse tells us that if we lack wisdom, we should ask God to give it to us and He will do so. Start at the same place as young Solomon—recognizing that you need God's wisdom.

Follow the Spirit

What God wants me to do:

_____

_____

_____

_____

Remember Your Thoughts

Special insights I have learned:

_____

_____

_____

_____

More Light on the Text

1 Kings 3:16–28; 2 Chronicles 9:8

16 Then came there two women, that were harlots, unto the king, and stood before him.

In the time of Israel's first kings, "to rule" meant "to judge, to make life-changing decisions, to be society's final authority." Few matters could be more important than the custody of a child. Direct access to a nation's king was a widespread practice then. So, two women brought their dispute over a baby boy's rightful custody for King Solomon to settle. His responsibility was to referee and decide the baby's true mother.

Although prostitution was never viewed as an attractive occupation, and by definition requires behavior contrary to God's standards, it was accepted then as lawful, permissible work. For example, there is no hint of censure when Hebrew spies went to scout out Canaan and "went . . . into an harlot's house . . . and lodged there" (Joshua 2:1). Nor is there any condemnation of the widowed Judah, when he hired a woman he thought was a prostitute, only to learn later that it was his daughter-in-law in disguise (Genesis 38:13–17, 24–26).

Both "harlots" as well as Judah were included in Jesus' genealogy in the first verses of the New Testament's first chapter (Matthew 1:3, 5). By Jesus' time, prostitution was still legal, but it was classified on the same low level of respectability as tax collectors. Prostitution was viewed as a tawdry trade even in Solomon's time, yet the two harlots were accepted by Israel's king and their dispute received his full attention. The lesson for our time from this incident is that regardless of a person's social standing, he or she deserves the full benefits of the government's system of justice.

17 And the one woman said, O my lord, I and this woman dwell in one house; and I was delivered of a child with her in the house. 18 And it came to pass the third day after I was delivered, that this woman was delivered also: and we were together; there was no stranger with us in the house, save we two in the house.

The first woman makes clear Solomon's task: whom to believe. Only two people were present. Being prostitutes, the women were young and unmarried. No husbands or children were present to confirm or contradict either woman's claim. Both women gave birth to a child; both babies were boys.

19 And this woman's child died in the night; because she overlaid it. 20 And she rose at midnight, and took my son from beside me, while thy handmaid slept, and laid it in her bosom, and laid her dead child in my bosom.

wise justice was not simply a matter of will or talent. It was God's gift to him. That gift was endowed on Solomon for a purpose: "to do judgment" (Heb. *mishpat*, **mish-PAWT**). That meant not simply giving a legal ruling, but a just one (2 Chronicles 9:8, "judgment and justice"). Mere knowledge of facts according to testimony could not ensure a just ruling for the baby's true mother. Only a commitment to justice at their nation's highest level and a desire among leaders to know and follow God's leading made that a reality.

2 Chronicles 9:8 Blessed be the LORD thy God, which delighted in thee to set thee on his throne, to be king for the LORD thy God: because thy God loved Israel, to establish them for ever, therefore made he thee king over them, to do judgment and justice.

From over a thousand miles away, the queen of Sheba had heard about Solomon's incredible insight into personal, relational, and governmental affairs. So she brought a great store of wealth to persuade him to share its benefits with her (1 Kings 10:1–8; 2 Chronicles 9:1–7). Her conclusions are distilled in 2 Chronicles 9:8.

She first concluded that God deserved praise as the source of Solomon's success as king. In 2 Chronicles 9:8 the chronicler adds one letter to the Hebrew word for "throne" (Heb. *kicce'*, **kis-SAY**) and changes the emphasis from Solomon's rule over Israel to God's rule over them as His people (Williamson, 234; see also 1 Chronicles 17:14). Then, to make clear what so many of Israel's kings after David's and Solomon's reigns had missed, he adds, "to be king for the LORD thy God" (2 Chronicles 9:8). God's purpose went far beyond simply making Solomon the sovereign ruler of God's people. God's purpose in installing him was in order that Solomon might implement God's just,

merciful, and righteous purposes. Ultimately, Solomon's task was to make decisions that fully implemented the purposes of a merciful and just Creator.

Sources:

Adeyemo, Tokunboh, et al., eds. *Africa Bible Commentary*. Grand Rapids, MI: Zondervan, 2006.

Bible Pronunciation Chart. Better Days Are Coming.com. http://www.betterdaysarecoming/bible/pronunciation.html (accessed January 29, 2011).

Brown, Francis, et al. *The New Brown-Driver-Briggs-Gesenius Hebrew and English Lexicon*. Peabody, MA: Hendrickson Publishers, 1985.

Gray, John. *Old Testament Library: I & II Kings, A Commentary*. 2nd ed., revised. Philadelphia, PA: The Westminster Press, 1970. 127–29.

Morris, Wilda W. "Prostitution." *Holman Illustrated Bible Dictionary*. Chad Brand, et al., eds. Nashville, TN: Holman Bible Publishers, 2003. 1336–37.

Passage Lookup. Bible Gateway.com. http://www.biblegateway.com/passage (accessed January 17, 2011).

The Revised English Bible (REB). New York, NY: Oxford University Press, 1989. 288.

Williamson, Hugh G. M. *1 and 2 Chronicles: New Century Bible Commentary*. Grand Rapids, MI: Wm. B. Eerdmans Publishing Co., 1982. 233–34.

Say It Correctly

Chronicles. KRON-ih-kuhlz.
Babylonian. Bab'uh-LOH-nee-uhn.
Sheba. SHE-bah.

Daily Bible Readings

MONDAY
A Prayer for Wisdom
(Ephesians 1:15–23)

TUESDAY
The Lord Loves Justice
(Psalm 37:27–34)

WEDNESDAY
Jedidiah—Beloved of the Lord
(2 Samuel 12:20–25)

THURSDAY
Solomon Anointed Israel's King
(1 Kings 1:28–37)

FRIDAY
Grace for a Competitor
(1 Kings 1:41–53)

SATURDAY
Solomon's Unsurpassed Wisdom
(1 Kings 4:29–34)

SUNDAY
Solomon Puts Wisdom into Practice
(1 Kings 3:16–28; 2 Chronicles 9:8)

Notes

_____

_____

_____

_____

Teaching Tips

Words You Should Know

A. Servant (2 Kings 8:4) `ebed` (Heb.)—A minister, ambassador, and a worshiper of God.

B. Officer (v. 6) *cariyc* (Heb.)—A man in the royal court who is a "eunuch"; a castrated male.

Teacher Preparation

Unifying Principle—Restorative Justice. People who are estranged from their families may long to return home. By acting in a benevolent manner, we can offer hope to those seeking justice and restoration.

A. Pray for your students and lesson clarity.

B. Study and meditate on the entire text.

C. Prepare to share examples of how God's Word restores—how God's Word restores us, how God's Word can restore our relationships.

D. Complete the companion lesson in the *Precepts For Living Personal Study Guide®*.

O—Open the Lesson

A. Open with prayer, including the Aim for Change.

B. After prayer, introduce today's subject, Aim for Change, and Keep in Mind verse. Discuss.

C. Share your presentation.

D. Then ask, "Has God restored you?"

E. Share testimonies.

F. Now, have a volunteer summarize the In Focus story. Discuss.

P—Present the Scriptures

A. Have volunteers read the Focal Verses.

B. Now use The People, Places, and Times; Background; Search the Scriptures; At-A-Glance outline; In Depth; and More Light on the Text to clarify the verses.

E—Explore the Meaning

A. To answer questions in the Discuss the Meaning, Lesson in Our Society, and Make It Happen sections, divide the class into groups. Assign one or two questions to each.

B. Have them select a representative to report their responses to the rest of the class.

N—Next Steps for Application

A. Summarize the lesson.

B. Close with prayer and praise God for how He restores us.

Worship Guide

For the Superintendent or Teacher
Theme: *A King Acts on a Widow's Behalf*
Theme Song: "I Surrender All"
Devotional Reading: Luke 15:11–24
Prayer

A King Acts on a Widow's Behalf

Bible Background • 2 KINGS 4:1–37; 8:1–6
Printed Text • 2 KINGS 8:1–6 | Devotional Reading • LUKE 15:11–24

—— Aim for Change ——

By the end of the lesson, we will: IDENTIFY scriptural support that justice can restore people and communities; FEEL blessed and appreciate the wonderful things we have seen accomplished by God's power; and PRAISE God for guiding us to pursue justice when we have been deprived of it.

In Focus

I wished I had not promised Grandma that I would go to church with her. Doesn't she realize it's time for me to feed my habit? But here I am because Grandma is the only one in my family who treats me like I'm someone. I know my grandma loves me because she cooks for me and even gives me money to support my habit. I have even heard Grandma praying for me, something like, "Save my grandbaby; put her back together again."

JULY 22nd

What my grandma does not realize is that it is too late for me. Not even God can put me back together. Grandma does not know the things I have done. If the preacher knew, he would have me escorted out of the church. Plus, I'm not sure if God is still listening to me. But that preacher is still talking about how God can put you back together again. Maybe I should listen to what he is saying. Maybe if I ask God myself to restore me, He will. I sure am tired of living like this. Who knows? Maybe if I go back to God, God will help me.

Renewal begins by asking for God's help to put back together what needs to be restored. In today's lesson, we see how the Shunammite woman sought to have her house and land restored. God abundantly restored more than what the woman asked for.

—— Keep in Mind ——

"And when the king asked the woman, she told him. So the king appointed unto her a certain officer, saying, Restore all that was hers, and all the fruits of the field since the day that she left the land, even until now" (2 Kings 8:6).

"And when the king asked the woman, she told him. So the king appointed unto her a certain officer, saying, Restore all that was hers, and all the fruits of the field since the day that she left the land, even until now" (2 Kings 8:6).

Focal Verses

KJV **2 Kings 8:1** Then spake Elisha unto the woman, whose son he had restored to life, saying, Arise, and go thou and thine household, and sojourn wheresoever thou canst sojourn; for the LORD hath called for a famine; and it shall also come upon the land seven years.

2 And the woman arose, and did after the saying of the man of God: and she went with her household, and sojourned in the land of the Philistines seven years.

3 And it came to pass at the seven years' end, that the woman returned out of the land of the Philistines: and she went forth to cry unto the king for her house and for her land.

4 And the king talked with Gehazi the servant of the man of God, saying, Tell me, I pray thee, all the great things that Elisha hath done.

5 And it came to pass, as he was telling the king how he had restored a dead body to life, that, behold, the woman, whose son he had restored to life, cried to the king for her house and for her land. And Gehazi said, My lord, O king, this is the woman, and this is her son, whom Elisha restored to life.

6 And when the king asked the woman, she told him. So the king appointed unto her a certain officer, saying, Restore all that was hers, and all the fruits of the field since the day that she left the land, even until now.

NLT **2 Kings 8:1** Elisha had told the woman whose son he had brought back to life, "Take your family and move to some other place, for the LORD has called for a famine on Israel that will last for seven years."

2 So the woman did as the man of God instructed. She took her family and lived in the land of the Philistines for seven years.

3 After the famine ended she returned to the land of Israel, and she went to see the king about getting back her house and land.

4 As she came in, the king was talking with Gehazi, the servant of the man of God. The king had just said, "Tell me some stories about the great things Elisha has done."

5 And Gehazi was telling the king about the time Elisha had brought a boy back to life. At that very moment, the mother of the boy walked in to make her appeal to the king.

"Look, my lord!" Gehazi exclaimed. "Here is the woman now, and this is her son—the very one Elisha brought back to life!"

6 "Is this true?" the king asked her. And she told him that it was. So he directed one of his officials to see to it that everything she had lost was restored to her, including the value of any crops that had been harvested during her absence.

The People, Places, and Times

Famine. A famine is an extreme shortage of food that God oftentimes used on the Israelites in response to their continued disobedience. One of the common forms of famine was a drought, which is the excessive dryness of the land. Famines and droughts are recorded throughout the Bible during the time of Abraham (Genesis 12:10), Isaac (Genesis 26:1), Joseph (Genesis 41:27), the Judges (Ruth 1:1), and the Israelites in the days of David (2 Samuel 21:1), Elijah (1 Kings 18:2), Elisha (2 Kings 4:38), Haggai (Haggai 1:11), and Nehemiah (Nehemiah 5:3).

Some famines were predicted by prophets, as seen in 2 Kings 8:1 when Elisha tells the Shunammite woman to take her household and leave the land, because the Lord has called for a famine that will last seven years. Famines appeared also as a natural cause. Joel 1:2–4 states, "Hear this you elders, And give ear, all you inhabitants of the land! Has anything like this happened in your days, or even in the days of your fathers? Tell your children about it, Let your children tell their children, and their children another generation. What the chewing locust left, the swarming locust has eaten; What the swarming locust left, the crawling locust has eaten; And what the crawling locust left, the consuming locust has eaten" (NKJV).

Wind, hail, and mildew were other ways that famine appeared. Warfare as experienced by the Israelites was another example of famines. "Now it came to pass in the ninth year of his reign, in the tenth month, on the tenth day of the month, that Nebuchadnezzar king of Babylon and all his army came against Jerusalem and encamped against it; and they built a siege wall against it all around. So the city was besieged until the eleventh year of King Zedekiah. By the ninth day of the fourth month the famine had become so severe in the city that there was no food for the people of the land" (2 Kings 25:1–3, NKJV). Either because of disobedience to God or natural causes or war, families frequently migrated from one place to another seeking food and water because of the frequent famines on the land.

Background

The woman mentioned in 2 Kings 8 is the same Shunammite woman who earlier identified Elisha as a holy man and persuaded him to eat. The Bible records her as a woman of wealth (2 Kings 4:8) who said to her husband, "'Look now, I know that this is a holy man of God, who passes by us regularly. Please, let us make a small upper room on the wall; and let us put a bed for him there, and a table and a chair and a lampstand; so it will be, whenever he comes to us, he can turn in there'" (2 Kings 4:9–10, NKJV).

The Shunammite woman already has a relationship with Elisha from when he restored her son back to life (2 Kings 4:34–35). So it is not unusual for the Shunammite woman to be obedient to Elisha when he told her, "'Arise and go, you and your household, and stay wherever you can; for the LORD has called for a famine'" (2 Kings 8:1, NKJV).

At-A-Glance

1. The Process of Seeking Restoration
(2 Kings 8:3–4)

2. The Fulfillment of Restoration
(vv. 5–6)

In Depth

1. The Process of Seeking Restoration (2 Kings 8:3–4)

"It came to pass, at the end of seven years, that the woman returned from the land of the Philistines; and she went to make an appeal to the king for her house and for her land" (2 Kings 8:3, NKJV). The beginning of restoration is obedience to the will of God and obedience to the leaders God sends for us. The people of God have a history just as we do today of obeying God, disobeying God, following false teachings, worshiping false gods, only to eventually return back to God. Because of God's continuous faithfulness for us, God provides leaders to help us to obey God's will in our lives. "And He Himself gave some to be apostles, some prophets, some evangelists, and some pastors and teachers, for the equipping of the saints for the work of ministry, for the edifying of the body of Christ, till we all come to the unity of the faith" (Ephesians 4:11–13a, NKJV).

The Shunammite woman accepted Elisha as a holy man because of the relationship she had built with him. With our verbal confession of faith in Jesus Christ and belief in our heart of His resurrection, we begin to participate in a life of faith, which is our *faith walk*. Our faith walk is based on a life of obedience to God's purpose for our lives. Our faith walk matures as we actively begin a prayer life and daily renewal of our minds from reading the Word of God. As our faith in God and His Son, Jesus Christ, grows, we can learn to accept and desire restoration.

After the famine, which lasted seven years, the Shunammite woman returns to her land to discover that her property has been taken. There is no recording of how her property was taken. Despite no record of Elisha's presence or of Elisha directing the woman to go to the king to petition for her property, the woman goes to the king to appeal to him to have her property restored to her.

The king says to Gehazi, the servant of Elisha, "'Tell me, please, all the great things Elisha has done'" (2 Kings 8:4, NKJV). As Gehazi tells the king how Elisha restored the woman's son from the dead to life, the woman appears to ask the king for her property.

2. The Fulfillment of Restoration (vv. 5–6)

Gehazi says, "'My lord, O king, this is the woman, and this is her son whom Elisha restored to life'" (2 Kings 8:5, NKJV). After the king asks the woman if she is indeed that woman whose son was restored back to life by Elisha, the king appoints a certain man and says, "'Restore all that was hers, and all the proceeds of the field from the day that she left the land until now'" (2 Kings 8:6, NKJV).

Restoration is based on faith and trust. For the believer, trust involves faith in Jesus Christ, the Son of God, trusting that Jesus Christ can and will renew us. This point is illustrated by the woman with an issue of blood: "Now a certain woman had a flow of blood for twelve years, and had suffered many things from many physicians. She had spent all that she had and was no better, but rather grew worse. When she heard about Jesus, she came behind Him in the crowd and touched His garment. For she said, 'If only I may touch His clothes, I shall be made well'" (Mark 5:25–28, NKJV).

Therefore, faith is believing. The Shunammite woman, because of her faith in Elisha, believed the king would give back her land. All she had to do was ask. Jesus Christ assures those who believe in Him, "'If you have faith and do not doubt, . . . whatever things you ask in prayer, believing, you will receive'" (Matthew 21:21–22, NJKV). Faith in Jesus Christ is the desire to become whole. "If anyone is in Christ, he is a new creation; old things have passed away" (2 Corinithians 5:17, NKJV).

Search the Scriptures

1. Why did the woman go to the king (2 Kings 8:3)?

2. How did the king know of the woman (v. 5)?

Discuss the Meaning

While God offers restoration and demonstrates examples in the Bible of how He does restore, why do so many Christians seek to be renewed elsewhere?

Lesson in Our Society

For many years, the Black community has been under siege: Black on Black crime is destroying our nuclear family unit; a large percentage of our children are being raised in single parent homes; we as a people seem to have lost hope as evidenced by those who self-medicate and engage in substance abuse. Yet Jesus Christ is still saying, "Come to Me, all you who labor and are heavy laden, and I will give you rest. Take My yoke upon you and learn from Me, for I am gentle and lowly in heart, and you will find rest for your souls" (Matthew 11:28–29, NKJV). We need to turn to God rather than give in to desperation.

Make It Happen

Many people are seeking to be restored. The obstacle they encounter is they are unable to forgive themselves for actions they have committed. Instead of seeking help, they find themselves drawn to self-destructive behavior. They have lost their hope in God, and they are no longer able to trust God. As believers in God, our challenge must show them the love of God. We are to show them it is God who "blots out your transgressions . . . and . . . will not remember your sins" (Isaiah 43:25, NKJV). It is God who can and does restore you. God used Elisha to restore the woman's son from death to life. God will also restore us. "For I will restore health to you and heal you of your wounds, says the LORD" (Jeremiah 30:17, NKJV).

Follow the Spirit

What God wants me to do:

_____

_____

_____

_____

Remember Your Thoughts

Special insights I have learned:

_____

_____

_____

_____

More Light on the Text
2 Kings 8:1–6
Introduction

The author of 2 Kings focuses on the history of the divided kingdoms of Israel and Judah. One of the main prophetic characters in the early part of the book was Elisha, the servant of Elijah, and he was endowed with a "double portion" of His spirit (see 2 Kings 2:8–9). Some suggest that Elisha's ministry continued where Elijah's left off, but with a greater anointing and effect, especially during the apostasy that was prevalent in Israel. Elisha's ministry seems to have centered on Gilgal and Shunem. The Gilgal mentioned in the earlier part of 2 Kings indicates that this was in the hill country of Ephraim, north of Bethel. Shunem was a town in the territory of Issachar near Jezreel on the slopes of Mount Moriah, overlooking the eastern end of the Jezreel Valley.

It was here that Elisha had a divine contact with the Shunammite woman, a woman of great wealth and social prominence. The prophet, and his servant Gehazi, stayed in her home and, through the power of God, caused the woman to conceive a child, though her husband was old.

1 Then spake Elisha unto the woman, whose son he had restored to life, saying, Arise, and go thou and thine household, and sojourn wheresoever thou canst sojourn: for

the LORD hath called for a famine; and it shall also come upon the land seven years.

The text says that Elisha warned the Shunammite woman, "Leave immediately with your family and go sojourn somewhere else; for the LORD has decreed a seven-year famine upon the land, and it has already begun" (v. 1, *The Jewish Study Bible*).

In Hebrew, the phrase "hath called" is *qara* (**kaw-RAW**) and it has the idea of giving a specific message for a particular purpose. Thus, God made it clear through the prophet that He would pronounce a curse in the form of a famine on the land, because of Israel's constant disobedience of the Mosaic covenant.

Famines happened as a matter of course in the ancient Near East (see Genesis 47:13–20; 1 Kings 17:1–13; 2 Kings 4:38), and sometimes people migrated to escape them (see Genesis 12:10; 26:1). A woman of such influence and wealth as the one in 2 Kings 8 and 9 could have survived the famine by selling her olive oil, for instance; Elisha suggested this in 2 Kings 4:1–4. Perhaps the real reason behind the warning from Elisha for her to leave was the impending bloodbath that Jehu was to bring upon the land (see 2 Kings 9:1–37). However, John MacArthur and others hint that 2 Kings 8:1–6 is out of chronological order from the preceding events of the Syrian famine and occurred earlier in the reign of King Jehoram of Israel, before the events of 2 Kings 5:1–7:20 (*MacArthur Study Bible*, 518–519).

2 And the woman arose, and did after the saying of the man of God: and she went with her household, and sojourned in the land of the Philistines seven years.

How important it is for us to heed God's Word. The woman did just as Elisha commanded, and left Shunem. She settled for seven years in the "land of the Philistines,"

an area located southwest of Israel along the Mediterranean Sea coastal plain between the Jarkon River in the North and the Besor Brook in the South. Wayne Meeks and John MacArthur point to the fact that the famine was not as widespread as one might think, specifically because God had called for it to be a localized punishment upon His people (*The Harper Collins Study Bible, NRSV*, 571; *MacArthur Study Bible*, 519).

3 And it came to pass at the seven years' end, that the woman returned out of the land of the Philistines: and she went forth to cry unto the king for her house and for her land.

The author says that once the seven-year famine ended, the woman returned "from the land of the 'Philistines'" (Heb. *Pelishtiy*, **puh-lish-TEE**) "and went to lodge a claim with the king for her house and lands" (v. 3, *Old Testament of the Jewish Bible*).

While the woman was away, it appeared that her land and home were confiscated, although the specific cause of the seizure is unclear. MacArthur says that because the woman was "only a resident alien in a foreign land," her return within the seven-year time frame may have helped her reclaim legal right to her property (519; see also Exodus 21:2; 23:10–11; Leviticus 25:1–7; Deuteronomy 15:1–6). Meeks thinks that her property may have been taken by the kingdom, or a neighbor who expanded his borders to include her land (571).

The text is clear that, as soon as the seven years ended, the woman returned to her homeland and went directly to the king to make a legal appeal to support her ownership claim of her land, property, and home—what rightfully belonged to her.

4 And the king talked with Gehazi the servant of the man of God, saying, Tell me, I pray thee, all the great things that Elisha hath done. 5 And it came to pass, as he was telling the king how he had restored a dead body to life, that, behold, the woman, whose son he had restored to life, cried to the king for her house and for her land. And Gehazi said, My lord, O king, this *is* the woman, and this is her son, whom Elisha restored to life.

The Bible says that Gehazi was Elisha's personal servant, in much the same manner that Elisha served Elijah, and Joshua served Moses. The Hebrew word for "servant" is `ebed (**EH-bed**), and part of its meaning includes "minister," a courtier of the king, ambassador, and a worshiper of God. Gehazi knew well of Elisha's ministry, especially with the Shunammite woman. He was there when the woman invited them to her home, when Elisha prophesied that she would receive a son, and when the prophet raised the son from death. Gehazi was also in the presence of Elisha when he healed Naaman of leprosy. Because of Gehazi's greed and lack of ability to believe that God could provide for them, the prophet pronounced leprosy on him (see 2 Kings 5:20–27).

The text does not say how, as a leper, Gehazi was able to stand before the king, when the law specifically states that a leper must not come in contact with others because of his uncleanness (see Leviticus 13–14). Some commentators advocate that at the time of this event, Elisha was already dead and had become a national legend among the people, and the king was intrigued at the stories of the prophet's work. Other scholars affirm that the king idolized Elisha and wanted to know details about the prophet. Who better to give the king an account of Elisha than Gehazi?

As Gehazi told about Elisha's exploits, providentially the woman arrived to appeal to the king about her "property." Gehazi turned and proclaimed, "My lord, . . . this is the woman and this is her son whom Elisha revived" (2 Kings 8:5b–c, JSB).

As Gehazi shared how Elisha raised the young boy from the dead, the same woman, who cried out for Elisha to help her (see 2 Kings 4:30–37), now had the attention of the king who wanted to hear her story and had the power to restore her farm and other property.

Although the text does not say, we can assume that the king was "floored" at the providential nature of all that took place. In similar manner, we are often stunned when God works in our lives in ways that seem impossible. But we must always remember that what is impossible with people, is possible with God (see Luke 1:37).

6 And when the king asked the woman, she told him. So the king appointed unto her a certain officer, saying, Restore all that was hers, and all the fruits of the field since the days that she left the land, even unto now.

Certainly, the woman had a personal testimony to share with the king. Not only was she intimately involved in the ministry of Elisha, but she also received specific instructions from the prophet to leave her home and property and spend seven years in the land of the Philistines to escape the famine. God's hand was upon this woman in a powerful manner, because of her obedience and trust in the ministry of Elisha.

The king was overjoyed at the news of the work of the prophet in the life of the Shunammite and appointed "a certain officer for her" (2 Kings 8:6a). The Hebrew word for "officer" is *cariyc* (**saw-REECE**), and the meaning is "to castrate." Therefore, the noun means "a man in the royal court who is a eunuch, a castrated male." Kings of the ancient Near East usually assigned castrated males over the care of their affairs of the court (see Esther 1:10, 12; Daniel 1:3) to ensure loyalty to them.

The king commanded the eunuch to act on his behalf; everything the woman had lost—her home, farm, and personal possession—was to be restored in the same quantity that it was taken from her during the seven-year famine.

The Hebrew word for "restore" is *shuwb* (**shoob**) and means "to turn back, to repeal, to cause to return, give back, or to return to the point of departure." In this manner, the woman received the blessing of the Lord in the form of her property, because of her faithfulness to the man of God and the king.

The Shunammite woman's testimony is ours, as well. We, too, have a King acting on our behalf as we share our stories and declare His truth with those we encounter in our life journeys.

Sources:
Berlin, Adele, and Marc Brettler. *The Jewish Study Bible.* New York, NY: Oxford University Press, 1999. 740.
Bible Pronunciation Chart. Better Days Are Coming.com. http://www.betterdaysarecoming/bible/pronunciation.html (accessed January 29, 2011).
Bruce, F. F., gen. ed. *Zondervan Bible Commentary.* Grand Rapids, MI: Zondervan Publishing Company, 2008. 373.
Hayford, Jack W., Litt.D., et al., eds. *The New Spirit-Filled Life Bible, NKJV.* Nashville, TN: Thomas Nelson Publishers, 2002. 357.
Hebrew and Greek Lexicons. Bible Study Tools.com. http://www.biblestudytools.com/lexicons (accessed November 9, 2010).
MacArthur, John. *The MacArthur Study Bible: NASB.* Nashville, TN: Thomas Nelson Publishing Company, 2006. 511–13, 519.
Meeks, Wayne, et al. *The Harper Collins Study Bible, NRSV.* New York, NY: HarperCollins Publishers, 1993. 565–71.
Myers, Allen C., ed. *The Eerdmans Bible Dictionary.* Grand Rapids, MI: William B. Eerdmans Publishing Company, 1996.
Old and New Testament Concordances, Lexicons, Dictionaries, Commentaries, Images, and Bible Versions. Blue Letter Bible.org. http://www.blueletterbible.org/ (accessed January 29, 2011).
The Old Testament of the Jewish Bible. Alexander Jones, gen. ed. Garden City, NY: Doubleday, 1966. 463.
Zodhiates, Spiros. *The Hebrew-Greek Key Word Study Bible, King James Version.* Chattanooga, TN: AMG Publishers, 1991. 1666.

Say It Correctly

Elisha. Ih-LI-shuh.
Gehazi. Ge-HA-zi.
Philistine. FIL-uh-steen.
Shunammite. SHOO-na-mite.

Daily Bible Readings

MONDAY
A Son Restored
(Luke 15:11–24)

TUESDAY
The Protector of Widows
(Psalm 68:1–6)

WEDNESDAY
Greed and Generosity
(Luke 20:45–21:4)

THURSDAY
A Promised Son
(2 Kings 4:8–17)

FRIDAY
Seeking Help from the Prophet
(2 Kings 4:18–27)

SATURDAY
A Child Restored
(2 Kings 4:28–37)

SUNDAY
Justice for a Widow
(2 Kings 8:1–6)

Teaching Tips

July 29
Bible Study Guide 9

Words You Should Know

A. Judges (2 Chronicles 19:5) *mishpat* (Heb.)—Men chosen to exercise authority over God's chosen people to lead them back to the one true God.

B. Judgment (v. 6) *mishpat* (Heb.)—A verdict that is pronounced judicially; a formal decree or ordinance.

Teacher Preparation

Unifying Principle—Return to Justice. When human judges adhere to God's standards and fearlessly apply God's laws, there is no perversion of justice.

A. Pray for your students and that God will bring clarity to this lesson.

B. Study and meditate on the entire text.

C. Prepare an example of how human judges should adhere to God's standards.

D. Complete the companion lesson in the *Precepts For Living Personal Study Guide®*.

O—Open the Lesson

A. Open with prayer, including the Aim for Change.

B. After prayer, introduce today's subject of the lesson.

C. Have your students read the Aim for Change and Keep in Mind verse in unison Discuss.

D. Share your presentation on human judges.

E. Then ask, "Has God permitted you to be fairly judged?"

F. Share testimonies.

G. Now, have a volunteer summarize the In Focus story. Discuss.

P—Present the Scriptures

A. Have volunteers read the Focal Verses.

B. Now use The People, Places, and Times; Background; Search the Scriptures; At-A-Glance outline; In Depth; and More Light on the Text to clarify the verses.

E—Explore the Meaning

A. Have volunteers summarize the Discuss the Meaning, Lesson in Our Society, and Make It Happen sections.

B. Connect these sections to the Aim for Change and the Keep in Mind verse.

N—Next Steps for Application

A. Summarize the lesson.

B. Close with prayer and praise God for how He restores us.

Worship Guide

For the Superintendent or Teacher
Theme: Jehoshaphat Makes
Judicial Reforms
Theme Song: "Must Jesus
Bear the Cross"
Devotional Reading: James 2:1–5
Prayer

Jehoshaphat Makes Judicial Reforms

Bible Background • 2 Chronicles 18:28–19:11
Printed Text • 2 Chronicles 19:4–11 | Devotional Reading • James 2:1–5

———— Aim for Change ————

By the end of the lesson, we will: UNDERSTAND that God is the ultimate authority to whom we are accountable; REFLECT on a time when choosing the "fair" or "just" option worked out for good; and JUDGE fairly when given the responsibility.

 In Focus

Sitting in his courtroom, a judge thought to himself, "There he is again, back before me accused of shoplifting." What he didn't understand was that this person was well dressed, appeared to be articulate, yet he was constantly stealing food. The judge reasoned that maybe he should stop being lenient with the young man and give him a maximum sentence. He thought that the state would surely feed him, if he needed food. However, before he made his ruling, this judge took the defendant to his chambers to further examine the matter.

In his chambers, the young man told a story of living in an expensive house with one parent because the other parent, who was the breadwinner, left. Even though the expensive house was paid for, the parent who was abandoned was too embarrassed to seek help. The judge was humbled as the young man opened a notebook that showed how he and his parent kept a ledger of the money they owed the grocery store. The young man told the judge, "We plan to pay the store back as soon as one of us gets a job."

Judging begins with first seeking the facts and then providing a solution. In today's lesson, we see how Jehoshaphat did not judge the people of Judah for their disobedience to God. He put into place a way for them to return back to God.

JULY
29th

———— Keep in Mind ————

"And said to the judges, Take heed what ye do: for ye judge not for man, but for the LORD, who is with you in the judgment" (2 Chronicles 19:6).

"And said to the judges, Take heed what ye do: for ye judge not for man, but for the LORD, who is with you in the judgment" (2 Chronicles 19:6).

Focal Verses

KJV **2 Chronicles 19:4** And Jehoshaphat dwelt at Jerusalem: and he went out again through the people from Beersheba to mount Ephraim, and brought them back unto the LORD God of their fathers.

5 And he set judges in the land throughout all the fenced cities of Judah, city by city,

6 And said to the judges, Take heed what ye do: for ye judge not for man, but for the LORD, who is with you in the judgment.

7 Wherefore now let the fear of the Lord be upon you; take heed and do it: for there is no iniquity with the LORD our God, nor respect of persons, nor taking of gifts.

8 Moreover in Jerusalem did Jehoshaphat set of the Levites, and of the priests, and of the chief of the fathers of Israel, for the judgment of the LORD, and for controversies, when they returned to Jerusalem.

9 And he charged them, saying, Thus shall ye do in the fear of the LORD, faithfully, and with a perfect heart.

10 And what cause soever shall come to you of your brethren that dwell in their cities, between blood and blood, between law and commandment, statutes and judgments, ye shall even warn them that they trespass not against the LORD, and so wrath come upon you, and upon your brethren: this do, and ye shall not trespass.

11 And, behold, Amariah the chief priest is over you in all matters of the LORD; and Zebadiah the son of Ishmael, the ruler of the house of Judah, for all the king's matters: also the Levites shall be officers before you. Deal courageously, and the LORD shall be with the good.

NLT **2 Chronicles 19:4** So Jehoshaphat lived in Jerusalem, but he went out among the people, traveling from Beersheba to the hill country of Ephraim, encouraging the people to return to the LORD, the God of their ancestors.

5 He appointed judges throughout the nation in all the fortified cities,

6 and he gave them these instructions: "Always think carefully before pronouncing judgment. Remember that you do not judge to please people but to please the LORD. He will be with you when you render the verdict in each case that comes before you.

7 Fear the LORD and judge with care, for the LORD our God does not tolerate perverted justice, partiality, or the taking of bribes."

8 Jehoshaphat appointed some of the Levites and priests and clan leaders in Israel to serve as judges in Jerusalem for cases concerning both the law of the LORD and civil disputes.

9 These were his instructions to them: "You must always act in the fear of the LORD, with integrity and with undivided hearts.

10 Whenever a case comes to you from fellow citizens in an outlying town, whether a murder case or some other violation of God's instructions, commands, laws, or regulations, you must warn them not to sin against the LORD, so that his anger will not come against you and them. Do this and you will not be guilty.

11 "Amariah the high priest will have final say in all cases concerning the LORD. Zebadiah son of Ishmael, a leader from the tribe of Judah, will have final say in all civil cases. The Levites will assist you in making sure that justice is served. Take courage as you fulfill your duties, and may the LORD be with those who do what is right."

The People, Places, and Times

Jehoshaphat. As the son of Asa and his successor as king of Judah (1 Kings 15:24), Jehoshaphat was "a faithful worshiper of Yahweh (1 Kings 22:42–43). He occupied the throne for 25 years" (*Holman Illustrated Bible Dictionary,* 877). Jehoshaphat's concern was that the people of Judah would receive the Word of the Lord. To help them accomplish this, he sent Levites and priests into the cities of Judah to teach the people the law of the Lord (2 Chronicles 17:7–9).

Mountains of Ephraim. This was hill country where Scripture records where the following cities were located: Bethel (Judges 4:5); Gibeah (Joshua 24:33); Ramah (Judges 4:5); Shamir (Judges 10:1); Sechem (Joshua 20:7); and Timnath-serah (Joshua 19:50; Judges 2:9).

Background

Jehoshaphat created a system of reform by establishing judges for the people of Judah. "Also in the third year of his reign he sent his leaders, . . . to teach in the cities of Judah. So they taught in Judah, and had the Book of the Law of the LORD with them; they went throughout all the cities of Judah and taught the people" (2 Chronicles 17:7, 9, NKJV). Jehoshaphat reminded the judges: "'Take heed to what you are doing, for you do not judge for man but for the LORD, who is with you in the judgment'" (19:6, NKJV).

The system of reform was established in levels to prevent abuse of power. Jehoshaphat taught the Levites and priests to "act in the fear of the LORD, faithfully and with a loyal heart" (v. 9, NKJV). He reminded the Levites and the priests that some of the decisions would be made by others. "And take notice: Amariah the chief priest is over you in all matters of the LORD; and Zebadiah the son of Ishmael, the ruler of the house of Judah,

for all the king's matters; also the Levites will be officials before you" (v. 11, NKJV).

With the creation of a layered system of reforms, Jehoshaphat was able to bring the people of Judah back to the authority of God. We also see this divine concern for justice expressed in the New Testament: "Let every soul be subject to the governing authorities. For there is no authority except God, and the authorities that exist are appointed by God. Therefore whoever resists the authority resists the ordinance of God, and those who resist will bring judgment on themselves" (Romans 13:1–2, NKJV).

At-A-Glance

1. God's People Return to Justice
(2 Chronicles 19:4–7)

2. The Equipping of the Judges
(vv. 8–11)

In Depth

1. God's People Return to Justice (2 Chronicles 19:4–7)

The people of Judah forsook the Law of the Lord. They engaged in the worship of foreign gods, built altars for those gods, and built wooden images of those gods. Many of us, because we are under His grace and mercy, have also disobeyed God. Like the people of Judah, each of us with our disobedience has experienced God's wrath and ultimately God's forgiveness. "Now when the LORD saw that they humbled themselves, the word of the LORD came to Shemaiah, saying, 'They have humbled themselves; therefore I will not destroy them, but I will grant them some deliverance. My wrath shall not be poured out on Jerusalem by the hand of Shishak'" (2 Chronicles 12:7, NKJV).

Similar to the people of Judah, as each of us has learned to humble ourselves and seek God's forgiveness, God has placed people into our lives to turn us back to Him. "So Jehoshaphat dwelt at Jerusalem; and he went out again among the people from Beersheba to the mountains of Ephraim, and brought them back to the LORD God of their fathers" (19:4, NKJV).

2. The Equipping of the Judges (vv. 8–11)

God places people in our lives to equip us for service to Him. "So they taught in Judah, and had the Book of the Law of the LORD with them; they went throughout all the cities of Judah and taught the people" (2 Chronicles 17:9, NKJV). When we are prepared to go out and serve, God tells us what our assignment is. "'Take heed to what you are doing, for you do not judge for man but for the LORD, who is with you in the judgment'" (2 Chronicles 19:6, NKJV). God instructs us on our assignment and cautions us to not abuse the authority He has placed within us. "And he commanded them, saying, 'Thus you shall act in the fear of the LORD, faithfully and with a loyal heart'" (v. 9, NKJV). God reminds each of us that we are accountable for what God has instructed us to do. "And take notice: Amariah the chief priest is over you in all matters of the LORD; and Zebadiah the son of Ishmael, the ruler of the house of Judah, for all the king's matters; also the Levites will be officials before you. Behave courageously, and the LORD will be with the good" (v. 11, NKJV).

Search the Scriptures

1. Why did Jehoshaphat send judges to the people of Judah (2 Chronicles 19:4)?

2. What warning did Jehoshaphat give to the judges (v. 6)?

Discuss the Meaning

With the authority each of us may have over another's life, each of us has a responsibility to obtain all of the facts and to judge fairly. Why do some Christians find themselves unfairly judging, which may lead to all Christians being judged unfairly?

Lesson in Our Society

Many of our young men are being judged unfairly, because they have chosen to adopt a dress code of wearing their pants far below their waists and without a belt, which suggests time spent in prison. Instead of judging our young men, perhaps the elder men of our community should explain some of the consequences of this clothing choice (attracts negative attention; likely to prevent long-term, well-paying employment; reinforces isolation from benefits society as a whole could offer; etc.). Jehoshaphat's concern for the people of Judah returning back to God was demonstrated when he sent out the leaders of the community, equipped with the Word of God to teach. "In the third year of his reign he sent his leaders, . . . So they taught in Judah, and had the Book of the Law of the LORD with them; they went throughout all the cities of Judah and taught the people" (2 Chronicles 17:7, 9, NKJV).

Make It Happen

Many people within the African American community are being judged unfairly, simply because of choices related to their lifestyles. Perhaps those of us within our community who are doing the judging should go back to emphasizing that God and education are the keys to a positive lifestyle. Perhaps those of us who are judging should become positive roles models by mentoring, going back to the community, and sharing the stories of our successes. For instance, we should tell the story of the importance of obtaining and maintaining a strong work ethic. In addition, we should make a commitment to avoid condemnation without truly understanding the person's situation. "So Jehoshaphat dwelt at Jerusalem, and he went out again among the people from Beersheba to the mountains of Ephraim, and brought them back to the LORD God of their fathers" (2 Chronicles 19:4, NKJV). Maybe God can use us in restoring many of our people.

Follow the Spirit

What God wants me to do:

_____

_____

_____

_____

Remember Your Thoughts

Special insights I have learned:

_____

_____

_____

_____

More Light on the Text

2 Chronicles 19:4–11

4 And Jehoshaphat dwelt at Jerusalem: and he went out again through the people from Beersheba to mount Ephraim, and brought them back unto the LORD God of their fathers.

In today's study, God used "Jehoshaphat" (Heb. *Yehowshaphat*, **yeh-ho-shaw-FAWT**, meaning "the Lord has judged"), the

king of Judah, and son of King Asa, in the lineage of David and Solomon (see 2 Chronicles 17:1–3). Though the Bible says that Jehoshaphat "followed the . . . ways of . . . David . . . but worshiped the God of his father and followed His commandments" (2 Chronicles 17:3–4, *Jewish Study Bible*), he aligned himself with Ahab, the northern kingdom's wicked ruler, in an attempt to rout the land of Ramoth-Gilead. In the ensuing battle, Ahab died and Jehoshaphat was spared (see 2 Chronicles 18:1–34), but was sharply rebuked by the prophet Jehu for disobeying God (see 2 Chronicles 19:1–3).

Jehu declared in the Word of the Lord that "good things" were found in the king (v. 3, NKJV); consequently, the king returned to Jerusalem and began spiritual and judicial reformation among the people, who had previously been taught the law (2 Chronicles 17:7–9).

It takes spiritual audacity to be a reformer as one must inaugurate change in the hearts of people and the life of religious organizations, such as the church. The reformer must be brave and committed to God, despite the criticism he or she will face from those who will fight change, even though the change is for everyone's (and God's) benefit.

5 And he set judges in the land throughout all the fenced cities of Judah, city by city, 6 And said to the judges, Take heed what ye do: for ye judge not for man, but for the LORD, who is with you in the judgment.

John MacArthur acknowledges that "Jehoshaphat put God's kingdom in greater spiritual order than at any time since Solomon" (*MacArthur Study Bible*, 605). To make sure that reformation prevailed, Jehoshaphat set "judges in the land" (2 Chronicles 19:5). Wayne Meeks and other

Bible scholars suggest that Jehoshaphat delegated judicial authority and extended his own jurisdiction, yet he still restricted the influence of local courts (*The HarperCollins Study Bible, NRSV,* 670).

Jehoshaphat set the judges in the "fenced cities of Judah," indicating that he was establishing not just a main court in Jerusalem, but also smaller courts throughout the region that would report directly to him. He gave each judge a specific command to follow. He instructed them, "Give due thought to your duties, since you are not judging in the name of men but in the name of Yahweh, who is with you whenever you pronounce sentence" (v. 6, *Old Testament of the Jewish Bible*).

In 2 Chronicles 19:6, the word "judgment" is *mishpat* (**mish-PAWT**) in Hebrew and the idea is a verdict that is pronounced judicially; a formal decree or ordinance. *Mishpat* is a very important word for the proper understanding of all governments, whether human or divine.

7 Wherefore now let the fear of the LORD be upon you; take heed and do it: for there is no iniquity with the LORD our God, nor respect of persons, nor taking of gifts.

The king continued to remind the appointees of two of the most important principles of God's character: righteousness and godly fear. The word "fear" is *pachad* (**PAKH-ad**) in Hebrew, and it means "terror, dread, or an object of fear". Sometimes, it is the terror which Jehovah causes (see 2 Chronicles 14:14). Another specific meaning is "fear of God" (see Psalm 36:1). Jehoshaphat's command was simple: Each judge must realize that God is *omniscient,* which means He knows all things, and *omnipresent,* meaning He is everywhere. No judge would be able to get away with bribery or deceit in his courtroom.

Jehoshaphat also used the word "iniquity." Here, the Hebrew is `evel (**EH-vel**) or 'aven (**aw-VEN**), and it means "perversion, dishonest, wrongdoing, or unrighteousness." Meeks states that the Lord's own sense of integrity and justice was to be the foundation of the behavior of each judge (*The HarperCollins Study Bible, NRSV,* 670; see also Deuteronomy 10:17-18; 16:19), while MacArthur explains that the judge's main role was "to rule by . . . integrity and honesty" (*MacArthur Study Bible,* 605). "For there is no injustice or favoritism or bribe-taking with the LORD our God" (2 Chronicles 19:7, JSB; see also Romans 2:11).

8 Moreover in Jerusalem did Jehoshaphat set of the Levites, and *of* the priests, and of the chief of the fathers of Israel, for the judgment of the LORD, and for controversies, when they returned to Jerusalem. 9 And he charged them, saying, Thus shall ye do in the fear of the LORD, faithfully, and with a perfect heart.

F. F. Bruce asserts that Jehoshaphat set up "a central court in Jerusalem to deal with major cases, including homicide and appeals" (*Zondervan Bible Commentary,* 426). The word "controversies" found in 2 Chronicles 19:8 is *riyb* (**reeb**) in Hebrew and the idea is judicial or forensic in nature; a lawsuit or some sort of litigation. Notice that Jehoshaphat wanted these cases to be heard by the Levites and chiefs of Israel, and only in Jerusalem. Meeks says, "These cases could be resolved by the establishment of precedents or the formulation of new law" (*The HarperCollins Study Bible, NRSV,* 670).

The cases were to be brought before those who could interpret the religious laws and the civil laws. This would imply that the cases had civil and religious overtones. The king's primary objectives were that all judgment must be done in the fear of the Lord and with a heart that is focused on justice and "truth" (Heb. *shalem*, **shaw-LAME**).

10 And what cause soever shall come to you of your brethren that dwell in their cities, between blood and blood, between law and commandment, statutes and judgments, ye shall even warn them that they trespass not against the LORD, and so wrath come upon you, and upon your brethren: this do, and ye shall not trespass.

It would appear that the king reminded the judges of the law that Moses had established in Deuteronomy 17. Berlin and Brettler help us understand that during "the pre-Deuteronomic period, the local sanctuaries served a judicial function in addition to providing a place for the sacrificial worship of God" (*The Jewish Study Bible*, 404). In legal cases where there was no physical evidence or witnesses, the court could not make a ruling. Such cases were remanded (sent back for judgment) to divine jurisdiction at the local sanctuary on the assumption that God could determine guilt or innocence and not be bound by empirical conditions. The parties swore a judicial oath at the altar and symbolically "before the LORD" (see Deuteronomy 17:12).

Jehoshaphat warns the judges that all matters, whether civil or religious must be impartial because, as with Moses who shared with Jethro the basis of the law, all disputes are to be brought before God. Though He uses human vessels to judge cases, it is God who is the final arbiter (see Exodus 18:16).

Additionally, the king uses two familiar terms in 2 Chronicles 19:10, "law" and "commandments." The Hebrew word for "law" is *towrah* (**tow-RAW**), and the essential meaning is teaching, especially God's instruction of His children through His Word or the regulations He has provided

through priests, elders, and others. Israel clearly understood the meaning of *towrah* and adhered to this principle throughout its history.

The Hebrew word for "commandment" is *mitsvah* (**mits-VAW**), and here the meaning is an ordinance or precept, or to describe the particular condition of God's covenant with Israel. Consequently, the king's reforms were all-encompassing from both judicial and religious perspectives.

11 And, behold, Amariah the chief priest is over you in all matters of the LORD; and Zebadiah the son of Ishmael, the ruler of the house of Judah, for all the king's matters: also the Levites shall be officers before you. Deal courageously, and the LORD shall be with the good.

In *Zondervan Bible Commentary*, Bruce notes that the court's system was divided in the following manner: Amariah, the chief priest dealt with the religious affairs, while Zebadiah was in charge of all civil cases; that is, "the administration of uncodified traditional law" (426). We are not told who specifically Amariah was. Meeks suggests that he was "probably the third high priest after Solomon had built the temple" (*The HarperCollins Study Bible, NRSV,* 671; see also 1 Chronicles 6:11). Or maybe Amariah had an important role in the king's palace before the reformation took place, and the king felt comfortable promoting him to this new duty. However, Zebadiah was the son of Ishmael, one of the leaders of the tribe of Judah. In his new position, Zebadiah and the other Levites were given the jobs of bailiff and other officers of the court.

Bruce states that Zebadiah's specific position was not clear (*Zondervan Bible Commentary,* 426). However, the reform that King Jehoshaphat instituted involved a delegation of responsibility from the king to his officials and a possible regaining by the priests of some of the authority they had lost in the highly centralized days of David and Solomon.

Note the king's final word to the judges as the reformation is put in place: "Be resolute, carry out these instructions, and Yahweh will be there to bring success" (2 Chronicles 19:11c, *Old Testament of the Jewish Bible*)

Sources:
Berlin, Adele, and Marc Brettler. *The Jewish Study Bible*. New York, NY: Oxford University Press, 2004. 144, 404–5, 1790–94.
Bible Pronunciation Chart. Better Days Are Coming.com. http://www.betterdaysarecoming/bible/pronun-ciation.html (accessed January 29, 2011).
Brand, Chad, and Charles Draper, eds. *Holman Illustrated Bible Dictionary*. Nashville, TN: Holman Bible Publishers, 2003. 500, 877–78.
Bruce, F. F., gen. ed. *Zondervan Bible Commentary*. Grand Rapids, MI: Zondervan Publishing Company, 2008. 426.
Hebrew and Greek Lexicons. Bible Study Tools.com. http://www.biblestudytools.com/lexicons (accessed November 11, 2010).
MacArthur, John. *The MacArthur Study Bible: NASB*. Nashville, TN: Thomas Nelson Publishing Company, 2006. 605.
Meeks, Wayne, et al., eds. *The HarperCollins Study Bible, NRSV*. New York, NY: HarperCollins Publishers, 1993. 667–71.
Myers, Allen C., ed. *The Eerdmans Bible Dictionary*. Grand Rapids, MI: William B. Eerdmans Publishing Company, 1996.
The Old Testament of the Jewish Bible. Alexander Jones, gen. ed. Garden City, NY: Doubleday, 1966. 547.
Passage Lookup. Bible Gateway.com. http://www.biblegateway.com/passage (accessed January 24, 2011).
Zodhiates, Spiros. *The Hebrew-Greek Key Word Study Bible, King James Version*. Chattanooga, TN: AMG Publishers, 1991. 1632, 1674.

Say It Correctly

Amariah. Am'uh-RI-uh.
Beer-sheba. Bee'uhr-SHEE-buh.
Jehoshaphat. Juh-HOSH-uh-fat.

Daily Bible Readings

MONDAY
The Lord Is Our Judge
(Isaiah 33:13–22)

TUESDAY
May Righteousness Flourish
(Psalm 72:1–7)

WEDNESDAY
Steadfast in Keeping God's Statutes
(Psalm 119:1–8)

THURSDAY
Fear the Lord, Depart from Evil
(Job 28:20–28)

FRIDAY
The Battles Is God's
(2 Chronicles 20:5–15)

SATURDAY
Walking in God's Commandments
(2 Chronicles 17:1–6)

SUNDAY
Judging on the Lord's Behalf
(2 Chronicles 19:4–11)

Teaching Tips

Words You Should Know

A. Executes (Psalm 146:7) `asah (Heb.)—Undertakes a deliberate action with a specific or distinct purpose.

B. Oppressed (v. 7) `ashaq (Heb.)—Someone who has been cheated or otherwise exploited.

Teacher Preparation

Unifying Principle—Executing Justice. People appreciate receiving lasting justice. Where can we look to find unshakable justice? God is the source of steadfast justice.

A. Pray for lesson clarity.

B. Study and meditate on the entire text.

C. Prepare a PowerPoint presentation or bring news clippings of historical, justice-related incidents that you and others have prayed about.

D. Complete the companion lesson in the *Precepts For Living Personal Study Guide*®.

O—Open the Lesson

A. Open with prayer.

B. Ask the class to read the Aim for Change in unison.

C. Ask a volunteer to read the Keep in Mind verse.

D. Ask your students to give you examples of injustice they have personally witnessed.

E. Share your presentation. Discuss.

F. Ask for a volunteer to read the In Focus story aloud. Discuss.

P—Present the Scriptures

A. Have volunteers read the Focal Verses.

B. Now use The People, Places, and Times; Background; Search the Scriptures; At-A-Glance outline; In Depth; and More Light on the Text to clarify the verses.

E—Explore the Meaning

A. Divide the students into small groups and ask each group to discuss the Discuss the Meaning, Lesson in Society, and Make It Happen sections. Then have a representative from each group report their group's response to the entire class.

B. Connect these sections to the Aim for Change and the Keep in Mind verse.

N—Next Steps for Application

A. Summarize the lesson.

B. Close with prayer, thanking God for His justice.

Worship Guide

For the Superintendent or Teacher
Theme: Praise for God's Justice
Theme Song: "Great Is
Thy Faithfulness"
Devotional Reading: Luke 4:16–21
Prayer

Praise for God's Justice

Bible Background • PSALM 146:1–10; EXODUS 21–23; ISAIAH 58
Printed Text • PSALM 146:1–10 | Devotional Reading • LUKE 4:16–21

--------------------- Aim for Change ---------------------

By the end of the lesson, we will: EXPLAIN how prayer and faith can bring about justice; REFLECT upon God's role as Promise Keeper; and AFFIRM that God has promised to help people who are oppressed.

------------------------- In Focus -------------------------

In December 2008, after Bernard Madoff was arrested and charged with fraud, the scandal tied to his firm, Bernard L. Madoff Investment Securities, made front-page headlines across the country in various media. This already wealthy man not only caused other rich people to lose their fortunes, but he may also have affected "pensioners, municipal workers, students on scholarship, and middle-class Americans. . . . The scandal has been estimated to cost investors upward of $50 billion and it may be one of the biggest Ponzi schemes on record" ("Did Bernie Madoff Steal Your Money?" *Newsweek*, December 16, 2008).

Many unsuspecting investors put their trust in this man, and their trust was abused.

In today's lesson, we will see that trust is a crucial component of humankind's covenant relationship with God. The writer of Psalm 146 exposes for us foolishness and limitations associated with placing our confidence in humans. Instead, we are encouraged to trust the Lord, our God, implicitly. He alone is capable of righting every wrong, and breaking the yoke of unforgiven sin on our lives.

AUG 5th

-------------------- Keep in Mind --------------------

"Happy is he that hath the God of Jacob for his help, whose hope is in the LORD his God: Which executeth judgment for the oppressed: which giveth food to the hungry. The LORD looseth the prisoners" (Psalm 146:5, 7).

"Happy is he that hath the God of Jacob for his help, whose hope is in the LORD his God: Which executeth judgment for the oppressed: which giveth food to the hungry. The LORD looseth the prisoners" (Psalm 146:5, 7).

Focal Verses

KJV **Psalm 146:1** Praise ye the LORD. Praise the LORD, O my soul.

2 While I live will I praise the LORD: I will sing praises unto my God while I have any being.

3 Put not your trust in princes, nor in the son of man, in whom there is no help.

4 His breath goeth forth, he returneth to his earth; in that very day his thoughts perish.

5 Happy is he that hath the God of Jacob for his help, whose hope is in the LORD his God:

6 Which made heaven, and earth, the sea, and all that therein is: which keepeth truth for ever:

7 Which executeth judgment for the oppressed: which giveth food to the hungry. The LORD looseth the prisoners:

8 The LORD openeth the eyes of the blind: the LORD raiseth them that are bowed down: the LORD loveth the righteous:

9 The LORD preserveth the strangers; he relieveth the fatherless and widow: but the way of the wicked he turneth upside down.

10 The LORD shall reign for ever, even thy God, O Zion, unto all generations. Praise ye the LORD.

NLT **Psalm 146:1–10 1** Praise the LORD! Praise the LORD, I tell myself.

2 I will praise the LORD as long as I live. I will sing praises to my God even with my dying breath.

3 Don't put your confidence in powerful people; there is no help for you there.

4 When their breathing stops, they return to the earth, and in a moment all their plans come to an end.

5 But happy are those who have the God of Israel as their helper, whose hope is in the LORD their God.

6 He is the one who made heaven and earth, the sea, and everything in them. He is the one who keeps every promise forever,

7 who gives justice to the oppressed and food to the hungry. The LORD frees the prisoners.

8 The LORD opens the eyes of the blind. The LORD lifts the burdens of those bent beneath their loads. The LORD loves the righteous.

9 The LORD protects the foreigners among us. He cares for the orphans and widows, but he frustrates the plans of the wicked.

10 The LORD will reign forever. O Jerusalem, your God is King in every generation! Praise the LORD!

The People, Places, and Times

Hallelujah Psalms. The book of Psalms, as we know it, was central to the worship of the Jews. Different genres or styles are incorporated in their composition. Some psalms reflect thanksgiving, praise, confession of sin, pursuit of wisdom, or devotion; others concentrate on prayer or petitions. Psalms 113–118 are known as the *Hallel* psalms, which focus on the Exodus and on praising God. These psalms have been used as part of commemorative services during Passover and other holidays. Of the five groupings of psalms, the last group, Psalms 107–150 are unique in that they each begin and end with the exuberant exclamation of both joy and gratitude "Praise ye the LORD," which is derived from the Hebrew phrase *Hallelu Yah.* The term "Hallelujah" only appears in the book of Psalms.

Background

The concepts of oppression and justice are both universal and ancient. Access to abundance and fair judgment are often reserved for the powerful. This means that equity and justice are frequently denied to the oppressed. In the ancient world, human-made social order dictated the "haves" and the "have nots." The widows, orphans, and strangers occupied the lowest stratum of society; hence, justice was not within their reach. In today's lesson, the psalmist recognizes that God reverses this perverse pecking order, and the psalmist praises God for His righteous judgment and affirms his trust in the Lord. The psalmist expresses his confidence that because He is righteous in nature, our God will bless those whom people had found insignificant. God will listen to and fairly judge the petitions of those that humankind has ignored. In the presence of an all-knowing, ever-present, all-powerful Creator, the poor and needy will be exalted, while the wealthy and powerful will be rendered frail and useless. This blessed assurance gives us reason to place our trust in God and in God alone.

At-A-Glance

1. A Promise of Praise
(Psalm 146:1–2)

2. Perils of Misplaced Trust
(vv. 3–4)

3. Declaration of God's Righteousness
(vv. 5–9)

4. Confidence in the Eternity of the
Righteous Judge (v. 10)

In Depth

1. A Promise of Praise (Psalm 146:1–2)

This psalm begins with an undeniable declaration of praise. Praise is reserved generally for someone that we recognize as great. In today's world, we sometimes praise our friends or family for kind or notable actions or deeds. We even praise politicians or celebrities for their works or performances. This type of praise is subjective. These people do something that benefits us, and we express our gratitude by praising them. Unfortunately, we are equally quick to censure and even condemn these same people if they do something that evokes our disapproval.

The subject of the psalmist's adoration is neither fleeting nor capricious. The earnestness of the psalmist is apparent to us in the very personalization of the praise. With his entire being (his "soul," v. 1), the psalmist will *halal* or "praise" *Yah. Yah* is one of the Hebrew names for God that is often translated as "Lord." The use of God's covenant name is especially significant. This praise is leveled at God who has covenanted to love and protect His people. The psalmist's praise echoes the Israelites' covenant to obey, honor, and love God with all of their being. Unconditional praise should be our response as Christians to our understanding that Jesus, the Christ, is our Savior, and it is only through Him that we are reconciled to the one, true, and righteous God. As mature Christians, we should begin and maintain a pattern of praise in our lives, which will continue through all eternity like the psalmist's.

2. The Perils of Misplaced Trust (vv. 3–4)

The psalmist now turns his attention from praise to issue an important warning. We are instructed not to place our trust in human leadership. When we "trust" (v. 3), we have confidence and assurance that someone will do what he or she promises to do. In the ancient world of the psalmist, the "princes" were the kings and rulers. The equivalent for present-day saints would be people in authority. While many in authority do as they promise, many others do not. In recent years, failure to exercise proper authority led to a global financial crisis and an unprecedented oil spill that resulted in catastrophic ecological and economic damage. We must always remember that those in authority only hold temporary positions. Because they are human, they will eventually "perish" or die (v. 4).

Here, we are reminded of Isaiah's declaration: "All flesh is grass, and all the goodliness thereof is as the flower of the field: The grass withereth, the flower fadeth: because the spirit of the LORD bloweth upon it: surely the people is grass. The grass withereth, the flower fadeth: but the word of our God shall stand for ever" (Isaiah 40:6–8). While highly positioned men and women may hold authority in government or be in positions that assist in our employment, education, finances, and so on, not one of them can offer us help after we die!

3. Declaration of God's Righteousness (vv. 5–9)

The psalmist's reference to "the God of Jacob" probably means the God of the people of Israel (Psalm 146:5). The psalmist identifies God as the Creator of everything (heaven, earth, and the seas) and everyone. Clearly, God is worthy of praise not only because He is the Creator, but because He makes provision for the most beloved of His creations: human beings. The psalmist goes on to list some of the ways God cares for the "oppressed" or those who most need His care and protection. God feeds the hungry, sets prisoners free, makes the blind to see, and lifts up the fallen (v. 7).

It is important to note that God's provisional care goes beyond the poor and downtrodden. These are people who have been abused, usually by someone in power who took advantage of them. The psalmist tells us that God will bring judgment upon the people who are responsible for these abuses. Those who think they are getting away with oppressing others will encounter God, who protects and vindicates the righteous.

We should also note that our righteous God acknowledges His creation as righteous, too. "The righteous" refers to those who are faithful to God's covenant (v. 8); after Christ's advent, we obtain righteousness through faith in Christ. The reference to "strangers" in verse 9 refers to people who were from other countries living among the Jews. God's provisional care is extended to these immigrants and refugees, too.

4. Confidence in the Eternity of the Righteous Judge (v. 10)

As the psalmist concludes his thoughts, he circles back to where he began: an outburst of praise and a proclamation that our God, our righteous Judge, will reign over us forever. This sentiment is echoed in Exodus 15:18, "The LORD shall reign for ever and ever." Similarly, the eternity of God's reign is confirmed when we read, "And the seventh angel sounded; and there were great voices in heaven, saying, The kingdoms of this world are become the kingdoms of our Lord, and of his Christ; and he shall reign for ever and ever" (Revelation 11:15). This is a promise to all generations who hear and respond to the message of salvation revealed in Jesus.

Search the Scriptures

Fill in the blanks.

1. "While I live will I _____ the LORD: I will sing praises unto my God while I have any _____" (Psalm 146:2).

2. "_____ is he that hath the God of _____for his help, whose hope is in the LORD his God" (v. 5).

Discuss the Meaning

The notion of justice is sometimes a tricky one. When we face unfair situations, we often try to use common sense or logic to rectify things. Sometimes we take on the operation of judgment ourselves—"to get even." The very term "getting even" implies making someone else carry the appropriate weight so that there is an even distribution. Compare and contrast our understanding of justice with the justice described in Psalm 146.

Lesson in Our Society

True believers know that the God of heaven became a man in order to become our salvation. We also know that although He died on the Cross for our sins and was laid in the grave, His commitment to us did not perish; He rose again and secured our reconciliation with God. This confidence in the Lord as our only source of salvation not only prompts us to praise Him, but it also should encourage us to stir up each other to praise His holy and righteous name.

Make It Happen

One need only listen to friends, family members, and coworkers to hear the discouragement of those around us. Many of the people we see every day are without hope and trust in anything and anyone. Make it a point to reach out to someone this week. Share your testimony with them, and more importantly, share the Word of God with them. Encourage them to put their confidence in God.

Follow the Spirit

What God wants me to do:

_____

_____

_____

_____

Remember Your Thoughts

Special insights I have learned:

_____

_____

_____

_____

More Light on the Text

Psalm 146:1–10

1 Praise ye the LORD. Praise the LORD, O my soul. 2 While I live will I praise the LORD: I will sing praises unto my God while I have any being.

The Hebrew Bible identifies the last five groupings of psalms in the book of Psalms as *tehilim* (**teh-HEE-lem**), a Hebrew word meaning "song of praise." Each of these psalms has the superscription "Hallelujah" (*The Jewish Study Bible*, 1280). The word "praise" is translated *halal* (**haw-LAL**) in Hebrew, and it has a variety of meanings, including "celebration," "boastful," "shining," and "radiance." However, the most common meaning for Christians is "hallelujah," ebullience for giving glory and honor to God.

We are not given the identity of the psalmist who wrote the doxology (expression of praise). Some scholars conclude that David was the writer (see 2 Samuel 23:1), as evident in the style and content of the writing. David often extolled the majesty and justice of God, while fleeing from Saul (see Psalms 52–54), his son Absalom (see Psalm 64), and his own sin (see Psalms 32; 51). The common theme of these and many other psalms that David wrote is God's efficacy (great capacity to function) in the midst of human frailty.

As the psalmist begins the doxology, he calls for his soul to praise the Lord and to "praise Yahweh all my life" (146:2, *Old Testament of the Jewish Bible*).

The Hebrew word for "Lord" is *Adonai* (**aw-DONE**) and literally represents God. The tetragrammation, the Hebrew name for God, consists of the four letters *Yud-Heh-Vav-Heh (YHWH)*, and it is sometimes rendered in English as *Jehovah* or *Yahweh*.

The phrase "sing praise" is *zamar* (**zaw-MAR**) in Hebrew, and here, the psalmist declares his ability to make music or poetry in songs, which is another possible clue that the doxology has a Davidic authorship.

3 Put not your trust in princes, nor in the son of man, in whom there is no help. 4 His breath goeth forth, he returneth to his earth; in that very day his thoughts perish.

In verse 3, the psalmist warns his audience of the absurdity of trusting in human beings as life's foundation and source of justice, whether they are "princes" (Heb. *nadiyb*, **naw-DEEB**) or common persons. All are the same in that they cannot provide help or safety. If David was the author of this psalm, perhaps he reflected on his despair about his weakness and sin, such as when his adultery with Bathsheba, resulted in a child who then died at a very young age. No matter how much the king fasted and wept for the child, he did not have the ability to preserve his life (see 2 Samuel 12:15–23). If the psalmist is David, then indeed we can understand his admonition: When mortal man "yields his breath and goes back to the earth he came from, . . . on that day all his schemes perish," they breathe their last, they return to dust, on that very day, all their plans are gone" (Psalm 146:4, JSB).

5 Happy is he that hath the God of Jacob for his help, whose hope is in the LORD his God: 6 Which made heaven and earth, the sea, and all that therein is: which keepeth truth for ever:

The psalmist declares that Jehovah God is Creator (see Genesis 1:1; Revelation 14:7), Sustainer, and Keeper of all life—a God of firmness, stability, and faithfulness ("truth," Psalm 146:6).

We are called to trust in God no matter how tempestuous or uncertain life's storms can be. One theme that runs throughout all of God's Word is His faithfulness to His people, even in the most difficult test. God has never let His people down. Even when we become faithless and want to run from God, He remains faithful. He will never deny those who trust Him (see 2 Timothy 2:13).

7 Which executeth judgment for the oppressed: which giveth food to the hungry. The LORD looseth the prisoners: 8 The LORD openeth the eyes of the blind: the LORD raiseth them that are bowed down: the LORD loveth the righteous: 9 The LORD preserveth the strangers; he relieveth the fatherless and widow: but the way of the wicked he turneth upside down.

The psalmist gives his audience eight specific reasons to believe in God's faithfulness, especially the poor and indigent of Israel who had no one to turn to when faced with injustice and oppression.

A. God became their advocate and defense, executing swift justice on the oppressor. The word "judgment" or "justice" comes from the Hebrew word *mishpat* (**mish-PAWT**). Some of its meanings include: "a formal sentence, decree, ordinance, law, or what is due." Justice is an attribute of God, and it is rooted in His divine nature and must also be demonstrated by those who love God.

B. God is faithful because He relieves His people's hunger (Psalm 146:7b; 107:9). Perhaps the psalmist recalled when God miraculously fed His people for 40 years as they marched through the wilderness on the way to the Promised Land (see Exodus 16:13–15, 35). In an earlier psalm, David declared that he never saw the righteous forsaken, nor God's people beg for bread (see Psalm 37:25). Indeed, God takes care of His own.

C. God demonstrates His faithfulness by releasing prisoners from their bondage. Berlin and Brettler make it clear that the author of Psalm 146 refers in verse 7 to the

exiles that God will restore in the millennium (JSB, 1443; see also Isaiah 49:8–9), while the writer highlights the same themes as David in Psalm 68:6, "God setteth the solitary in families; he bringeth out those which are bound with chains" (see Psalm 107:10, 14). Because of God's mercy, those who have done wrong shall be set free from their prisons as they confess their sins and trust the Lord for deliverance (Psalm 146:7; see 1 John 1:8–9).

D. God opens and restores blinded eyes. The Hebrew Bible affirms that *Adonai* (The Lord our God) has the ability to touch the physically blind and make them see. In both Matthew 9:27–30 and John 9:1–7, *Yeshua* (**YESH-oo-ah**) or Jesus, meaning "Jehovah Saves," caused people to see by the touch of His hand. As believers and followers of Christ, we have had our "spiritual sight" restored and walk in revelation of truth because we have confessed Jesus as our Savior and Lord.

E. "Yahweh straightens the bent" (Psalm 146:8b, JSB). In Psalm 145:14, David states the same, and in Psalm 3:3 the psalmist says, "But thou, O LORD, art a shield for me; my glory, and the lifter up of mine head." We have ample evidence in the Scriptures that God heals by the word of His power (see Exodus 15:26), the touch of His garment (see Mark 5:25–34), and the stripes on His back (see 1 Peter 2:24).

F. *Adonai* means "loves the virtuous" (Psalm 146:8c, JSB). In the KJV, the word "righteous" comes from the Hebrew *tsadaq* (**tsaw-DAK**), and several of its meanings include: "straight," "lawful," "honest," and "right." Once again, David declares the same in Psalm 145:17, "The LORD is righteous in all his ways, and holy in all his works." In this manner, Jehovah is the just Judge because He is the standard of all morality. Jeremiah affirms to the exiles of His day that when they are returned to the land, they will call their God *Yehovih tsidqenuw* (**yeh-ho-VEH**

tsid-KAY-noo, meaning, "The Lord [is] our Righteousness, Jeremiah 23:6). The psalmist urges that we must be righteous people if we want to serve a righteous God.

G. *Adonai* means "protects the stranger, [and] he keeps (sustains) the orphan and widow" (Psalm 146:9a–b, JSB). The psalmist quotes this promise from Leviticus 19:33–34 and Deuteronomy 10:18–19, where God reminds the Children of Israel of His care and concern for them when they were strangers in Egypt. Both David in the Old Testament (Psalm 68:5) and the apostle Paul to the church (1 Timothy 5:3–5) make known God's concern and love for widows and the fatherless. In our modern society, we must do the same.

H. "Yahweh . . . frustrates the wicked" (Psalm 146:9c, JSB). The word "wicked" comes from the Hebrew *rasha`* (**raw-SHAH**) and it conveys "moral wrong, bad, lawless, or viciousness." Because God is righteous and demands righteous justice, those who practice immoral and bad behavior and oppress the righteous, especially the fatherless and widows, will be judged severely. God will "bend" them to His own pleasure.

10 The LORD shall reign for ever, even thy God, O Zion, unto all generations. Praise ye the LORD.

Like David in Psalm 10:16 and 145:13, and at the end of Moses' song (Exodus 15:18), in Psalm 146:10 the psalmist sings of the majesty of a mighty God who will "reign" (Heb. *malak*, **maw-LAK**) to the end of days. In Revelation 11:15, the apostle John affirms, "The kingdoms of this world are become the kingdoms of our Lord, and of his Christ; and he shall reign for ever and ever."

Though wickedness abounds today, we who are Christians have the assurance of an everlasting God who shall reign in "Zion"

(Heb. *Tsiyown*, **tsee-YONE**) throughout all of life. Hallelujah!

Sources:
Berlin, Adele, and Marc Brettler. *The Jewish Study Bible.* New York, NY: Oxford University Press, 2004. 17–18, 1280–81, 1398, 1442–43.
Bible Pronunciation Chart. Better Days Are Coming.com. http://www.betterdaysarecoming/bible/pronunciation.html (accessed January 29, 2011).
Blank, Wayne, ed. *Daily Bible Study.* http://www.keyway.ca (accessed June 17, 2010).
"Did Bernie Madoff Steal Your Money?" Newsweek.com. December 16, 2008. http://www.newsweek.com/2008/12/16/did-bernie-steal-your-money.html (accessed June 14, 2010).
Exploring the Word of God. Psalms: Thematic Collections. http://www.wcg.org/lit/bible/poetry/psalms5.htm (accessed June 1, 2010).
"Hallel." Answers.com. http://www.answers.com/topic/hallel (accessed January 29, 2011).
Hebrew and Greek Lexicons. Bible Study Tools.com. http://www.biblestudytools.com/lexicons (accessed November 11, 2010).
Merriam-Webster Online Dictionary. Merriam-Webster, Inc. http://www.merriam-webster.com (accessed January 29, 2011).
The Old Testament of the Jewish Bible. Alexander Jones, gen. ed. Garden City, NY: Doubleday, 1966. 927–28.
Stern, David H. *Complete Jewish Bible: An English Version of the Tanakh and B'rit Hadashah.* Clarksville, MD: Jewish New Testament Publications, 1998. 937,1234, 1558, 1576, 1599–1600.
Wigram, George V. *The Englishman's Hebrew and Chaldee Concordance of the Old Testament.* Nashville, TN: Broadman Press, 1980. 614.
Zodhiates, Spiros. *The Hebrew-Greek Key Word Study Bible, King James Version.* Chattanooga, TN: AMG Publishers, 1991. 798, 1569, 1608, 1652.

Say It Correctly

Hallelujah. Ha'lul-LOO-yuh.
Nehemiah. Nee'(h)uh-MI-uh.

Daily Bible Readings

MONDAY
Where Is the God of Justice?
(Malachi 2:10–17)

TUESDAY
God's Ways Are Justice
(Daniel 4:34–37)

WEDNESDAY
The Fast That God Chooses
(Isaiah 58:1–9b)

THURSDAY
God's Continued Guidance
(Isaiah 58:9c–14)

FRIDAY
God Will Grant Justice
(Luke 18:1–8)

SATURDAY
Love God and Establish Justice
(Amos 5:8–15)

SUNDAY
Happy Are Those Who Execute Justice
(Psalm 146)

Notes

_____

_____

_____

_____

Teaching Tips

August 12
Bible Study Guide 11

Words You Should Know
A. Shadow of Death (Isaiah 9:2) *tsalmaveth* (Heb.)—Distress or extreme danger.

B. Yoke (v. 4) `ol (Heb.)—Denotes a condition of servitude or slavery.

Teacher Preparation
Unifying Principle—Hope in Spite of Darkness. Discouraged people look for hope. Our hope is found in the coming Messiah who established a just and right kingdom.

A. Pray for lesson clarity.

B. Study and meditate on the entire text.

C. Research this period in Judah's history (see The People, Places, and Times and Background sections).

D. Complete the companion lesson in the *Precepts For Living Personal Study Guide®*.

E. Prepare to share a PowerPoint presentation or pictures of hopeless faces and circumstances.

O—Open the Lesson
A. Open with prayer.

B. Ask the class to read the Keep in Mind verse in unison.

C. Share your presentations. Discuss.

D. Ask a volunteer to read the In Focus story. Discuss.

P—Present the Scriptures
A. Have volunteers read the Focal Verses.

B. Now use The People, Places, and Times; Background; Search the Scriptures; At-A-Glance outline; In Depth; and More Light on the Text to clarify the verses.

E—Explore the Meaning
A. Divide the students into small groups and ask each group to discuss the Discuss the Meaning, Lesson in Our Society, and Make It Happen sections. They should have a representative from each group report their group's responses to the entire class.

B. Connect these sections to the Aim for Change and the Keep in Mind verse.

N—Next Steps for Application
A. Write some takeaway principles under the Follow the Spirit or Remember Your Thoughts section.

B. Ask for a volunteer to close the class in prayer.

Worship Guide

For the Superintendent or Teacher
Theme: God Promised
a Righteous Lord
Theme Song: "Breathe on Me,
Breath of God"
Devotional Reading: John 8:12–19
Prayer

God Promised a Righteous Lord

Bible Background • ISAIAH 9:1–7
Printed Text • ISAIAH 9:2–7 | Devotional Reading • JOHN 8:12–19

Aim for Change

By the end of the lesson, we will: KNOW the relationship between Isaiah's prophecy and its fulfillment in Jesus Christ; REFLECT on God's promise of justice to those who are without hope; and IDENTIFY signs of hope in conflict-ridden areas such as inner cities and our government.

In Focus

He Is Dead, So I Cry

by Evangeline Carey

They call him, Another statistic, another burden on society . . . DEAD!

They call him, Another Black criminal killed in rage . . . TORMENT!

A Black woman calls him, Gentle, warm, and compassionate . . . HER BROTHER!

Another Black woman calls him, A great loss, a sensitive human being . . . HER SON!

He is dead, so I cry!

Just like many Black families who live in gang-war zones and see their children dying, and need hope and comforting, in today's lesson, the prophet Isaiah delivers words of hope and comfort to a nation that had lived with war and the threat of war for many years. Isaiah assures them that God has not forgotten them and that help was on the way.

(Copyright © 1996 by Evangeline Carey. All rights reserved. Used by permission.)

Keep in Mind

"For unto us a child is born, unto us a son is given: and the government shall be upon his shoulder: and his name shall be called Wonderful, Counsellor, The mighty God, The everlasting Father, The Prince of Peace" (Isaiah 9:6).

"For unto us a child is born, unto us a son is given: and the government shall be upon his shoulder: and his name shall be called Wonderful, Counsellor, The mighty God, The everlasting Father, The Prince of Peace" (Isaiah 9:6).

Focal Verses

KJV Isaiah 9:2 The people that walked in darkness have seen a great light: they that dwell in the land of the shadow of death, upon them hath the light shined.

3 Thou hast multiplied the nation, and not increased the joy: they joy before thee according to the joy in harvest, and as men rejoice when they divide the spoil.

4 For thou hast broken the yoke of his burden, and the staff of his shoulder, the rod of his oppressor, as in the day of Midian.

5 For every battle of the warrior is with confused noise, and garments rolled in blood; but this shall be with burning and fuel of fire.

6 For unto us a child is born, unto us a son is given: and the government shall be upon his shoulder: and his name shall be called Wonderful, Counsellor, The mighty God, The everlasting Father, The Prince of Peace.

7 Of the increase of his government and peace there shall be no end, upon the throne of David, and upon his kingdom, to order it, and to stablish it with judgment and with justice from henceforth even for ever. The zeal of the LORD of hosts will perform this.

NLT Isaiah 9:2 The people who walk in darkness will see a great light—a light that will shine on all who live in the land where death casts its shadow.

3 Israel will again be great, and its people will rejoice as people rejoice at harvesttime. They will shout with joy like warriors dividing the plunder.

4 For God will break the chains that bind his people and the whip that scourges them, just as he did when he destroyed the army of Midian with Gideon's little band.

5 In that day of peace, battle gear will no longer be issued. Never again will uniforms be bloodstained by war. All such equipment will be burned.

6 For a child is born to us, a son is given to us. And the government will rest on his shoulders. These will be his royal titles: Wonderful Counselor, Mighty God, Everlasting Father, Prince of Peace.

7 His ever expanding, peaceful government will never end. He will rule forever with fairness and justice from the throne of his ancestor David. The passionate commitment of the LORD Almighty will guarantee this!

The People, Places, and Times

Isaiah. One of the most influential Old Testament prophets, Isaiah lived and ministered in the southern kingdom of Judah for 58 years. Isaiah lived through one of his nation's most turbulent periods during which he witnessed Judah's defeat by the Babylonian Empire and actually saw his fellow citizens taken into captivity. He prophesizes during the reign of five kings: Uzziah, Jotham, Ahaz, Hezekiah, and Manasseh. His free access to the palace in Jerusalem and his familiarity with court life imply that Isaiah belonged to Judah's wealthy class and may have been related to the ruling family. However, this did not keep Isaiah from verbally attacking the aristocracy in defense of the common people. Scripture refers to his wife as a "prophetess" and identifies him as the father of at least two sons: Shear-jashub and Maher-shalal-hash-baz (Isaiah 7:1–3; 8:1–3).

Background

Much of Isaiah's writings strongly criticize the people of Judah for their sinfulness and unwillingness to be faithful to the one true God. During the reign of King Ahaz, the kings of Israel and Damascus waged war against Judah. Instead of looking to God for support, King Ahaz foolishly allied himself with the Assyrian king, Tiglath-pileser. Judah soon found itself a vassal state under the Assyrians. In 721 B.C., Israel was invaded and the capital city of Samaria was destroyed. The tribute demanded by the Assyrians from Judah was so great that Ahaz's successor and son, King Hezekiah, formed an alliance with the nations of Egypt, Moab, and Edom, and plotted with them to revolt against the Assyrians. The revolt was squashed in 711 B.C. Isaiah warned that their continued refusal to be faithful to God would result in disaster for the entire nation. King Hezekiah didn't listen, and in 705 B.C., he participated in another attempted revolt, this time enlisting the aid of the Babylonians. King Hezekiah refused to heed the prophet, and Judah was almost destroyed before the people turned back to God and begged Him to come to their aide. Throughout his ministry, Isaiah repeatedly called on the nation to rely on God, rather than military strength or political alliances. The northern kingdom had refused to listen to their prophets, Amos and Hosea. Instead, Israel had resorted to military might to assert their nationhood, and as a result had been soundly defeated and no longer existed as a nation. By the grace of God, Judah was for a time spared.

At-A-Glance

1. End of the Darkness
(Isaiah 9:2–5)

2. Gift of Forthcoming Peace
(vv. 6–7)

In Depth

1. End of the Darkness (Isaiah 9:2–5)

During the time Isaiah lived, Assyria was a major military force that was defeating many countries. It is understandable that the future appeared foreboding and hopeless to the people of Judah. In the previous chapter, the prophet Isaiah describes the bleak spiritual conditions when he writes, "When they say to you, 'Consult the mediums and the spiritists who whisper and mutter,' should not a people consult their God? Should they consult the dead on behalf of the living? They will pass through the land hard-pressed and famished, and it will turn out that when they are hungry, they will be enraged and curse their king and their God as they face upward. Then they will look to the earth, and behold, distress and darkness, the gloom of anguish; and they will be driven away into darkness" (Isaiah 8:19, 21–22, NASB). It is reasonable to assume that this text occurs after Assyria invaded Syria and Israel around 734–32 B.C. Judah was in a state of spiritual darkness and political distress as it helplessly watched the scorched earth policy of the invading Assyrians in the northern portion of Palestine.

It is onto this scene that the prophet Isaiah introduces a wonderful prophecy of hope. Isaiah makes it clear that he is addressing Judah. They are the people who had walked in "darkness" and dwelled "in the land of the shadow of death" (Isaiah 9:2). It is ironic that the people, who dwell in the Promised Land, have been plunged into spiritual darkness. This kind of darkness is a frightening but apt description of sin. The lost person foolishly believes that he "understands" or is in the light, when he actually operates in perpetual darkness. It is this spiritual darkness that contributes to the encompassing sense of hopelessness and helplessness.

Conversely, God's presence is equated with light. "God is light, and in Him is no darkness at all" (1 John 1:5b, NKJV). The great light that will appear is Jesus, *Christ* Jesus, the Messiah. Seven hundred years later, Jesus would begin His ministry and bring light into this very land that is now plunged into darkness. It is Jesus who will stand in the Temple and declare, "I am the light of the world; he who follows Me shall not walk in darkness, but shall have the light of life" (John 8:12, NKJV). Isaiah insists that because a Messiah is coming, there will be "gladness" and joy instead of the gloom (Isaiah 9:3, NASB). The hope of the people is to be placed in the Lord, not in reliance on military strength or political savvy. Their "joy" would come from the Messiah, not human allies. Only then would they be able to rejoice. Present-day saints should be reminded that we are not bound by our present conditions and circumstances; we can rejoice in our hope in the only One who can remove the gloom from our lives. From his dark and dank Roman prison cell, the apostle Paul rejoiced in his chains: "Rejoice in the Lord always; again I will say, rejoice!" (Philippians 4:4, NASB).

2. Gift of Forthcoming Peace (vv. 6–7)

How wonderful it is to Christians to note that the birth of this child, introduced by Isaiah, is a gift to us from God Himself. A child, but not just any child—He will be the Son of God. Here, Isaiah's prophecy recognizes that the Messiah will be a legitimate heir to the Davidic throne, a point of paramount importance to the people living in the time of this writing. Even though the Messiah would be "born" as human beings are, Isaiah stresses that He will "be given" (Isaiah 9:6). The King of whom Isaiah speaks will be both human and divine, possessing the power of the Creator (God) and the frailties and characteristics of the creation (humankind). However, He was without sin. When we read "the government will rest on his shoulders" (9:6, NLT), we see Isaiah's poetic description of the Messiah as a capable and sovereign Ruler, not to be confused with a mere human king.

Isaiah further identifies the Messiah as "Wonderful, Counsellor" (v. 6). Here, we are assured that the Messiah will rule with infinite wisdom that exceeds human limitations. He will be efficient and effective in the planning and implementation of His divine plans. It is in this role that Jesus invites us, "Come to me, all who are weary and burdened, and I will give you rest. Take my yoke upon you and learn from me, for I am gentle and humble in heart, and you will find rest for your souls. For my yoke is easy and my burden is light" (Matthew 11:28–30, NIV).

In Isaiah 9:6, the prophet's description of the Messiah as "mighty God" recognizes the full omnipotence (having all-power) and absolute deity of the Savior. The qualities of eternal tenderness and protection are evoked with the title "The everlasting Father." Jesus offers us the same compassion and provision that the loving and caring Father shows toward His children who love, fear, and obey Him.

Finally, Isaiah declares that the Messiah is the "Prince of Peace" (v. 6). Not only will He bring peace, but He will rule with peace. Christians have the blessed assurance that at the very moment we place our trust in Jesus, He gives us His perfect peace. This does not mean that all of our problems will go away. Rather, it means that we can have confidence that we will never face our problems alone—He will always be with us, guiding and providing protection through our darkest hours. His promise to us is the same promise He gave to the disciples following His resurrection, "My peace I give unto you" (John 14:27a).

Search the Scriptures

Fill in the blanks.

1. "The people that walked in _____ have seen a great light: they that dwell in the land of the shadow of _____, upon them hath the _____ shined" (Isaiah 9:2).

2. "For every _____ of the warrior is with confused noise, and _____ rolled in blood; but this shall be with burning and fuel of fire" (v. 5).

3. "For unto us a _____ is born, unto us a Son is given: and the _____ shall be upon his shoulder: and his name shall be called Wonderful, _____, The mighty God, The everlasting Father, The _____ of Peace" (v. 6).

Discuss the Meaning

Do you think that our society is suffering from the effects of spiritual darkness? In what ways? How does our near worship of materialism contribute to this spiritual darkness?

Lesson in Our Society

The growing number of global military conflicts and an economic meltdown that has left millions jobless and homeless only add to a growing sense of helplessness throughout the world. The alarming crime rates have also left many frightened and insecure.

Few if any leave their doors unlocked, and many are afraid to travel. Every day we see examples of people with money, power, and position afforded one form of treatment within the judicial system and the poor and disadvantaged are treated radically different. There are some rich people who steal millions and get away with little more than a slap on the wrist, and often the poor are sentenced to prison for stealing hundreds.

What a joy to know that in this fast-paced, restless, and insecure world we live in, we can still turn to Jesus for hope, comfort, and perfect peace.

Make It Happen

The prophet Isaiah lived in a time of political turmoil and spiritual confusion. The people of Judah were understandably anxious as the powerful Assyrian army gathered at the gates of Jerusalem. Their world was very similar to ours in some ways. Many people are stressed out and feel powerless, hopeless, and helpless. Similar to Isaiah, reach out to someone this week and let them know that God is still in control. Speak words of comfort to them and let them know that God knows and He cares.

Follow the Spirit

What God wants me to do:

_____

_____

_____

_____

Remember Your Thoughts

Special insights I have learned:

_____

_____

_____

_____

More Light on the Text
Isaiah 9:2–7
Introduction

In Isaiah 9:1, God's initial treatment of Zebulun and Napthali ("he lightly afflicted" them) referred to the first invasion by Assyria's King Tiglath-pileser in 733 or 732 B.C., during which the king annexed a large part of the kingdom of Samaria (see 2 Kings 15:29). Only a decade later, in 722 B.C., the Assyrians would return to capture the entire northern kingdom. The first captured territory stretched from the Jezreel Valley north to Mount Herman (today's Huleh Valley). The Jordan River flows through this area before emptying into the Sea of Galilee. It was (and still is) a lush, agricultural area and a main trade route at the time; thus, it was a high priority conquest. The three areas of Isaiah 9:1 were renamed as Assyrian provinces: the "way of the sea" became Dor, the land "beyond Jordan" became Gilead, and "Galilee of the nations" became Megiddo.

2 The people that walked in darkness have seen a great light: they that dwell in the land of the shadow of death, upon them hath the light shined.

The Hebrew word for "darkness" here is *choshek* (**kho-SHEK**), and it is the same term used at Creation (Genesis 1:2). Isaiah used the term frequently (5:20, 30; 42:7; 60:2); the meaning is clear that this is not just nighttime,

as clarified above, but rather dangerous spiritual obscurity at best and the definition of evil at worst. As it is here, the reference of 60:2 (worded even more strongly as "gross darkness") is framed in stark contrast, both before and after, with the brightness of God's glory. In Isaiah 9:2 the Hebrew word for "light" is `owr (**ore**), which also is the same word used in Creation (Genesis 1:3–5).

Note how Isaiah 9:2 is cast in what is called prophetic perfect tense; even as the prophecy is penned, it secures future events with certainty.

Although Israel rejected God, directly and through His prophets, He still planned redemption for them—in due time. Matthew did not miss the glorious reality that, in his day, Jesus fulfilled God's promises delivered through Isaiah, even quoting the prophet's words (Matthew 4:15–16; see also Luke 1:79; John 8:12).

3 Thou hast multiplied the nation, and not increased the joy: they joy before thee according to the joy in harvest, and as men rejoice when they divide the spoil.

In ancient times, the enlarging of a nation and the goods from both crops and spoils of war were considered signs of God's blessing. Compare this with Isaiah's messianic reference to Jesus' "spoils" in 53:12, NIV. The Hebrew word for "spoil" is *shalal* (**shaw-LAL**) and refers specifically to the booty or plunder of war, sometimes translated as "prey" (Judges 8:24–25; Isaiah 10:2, 6; 33:4, 23).

4 For thou hast broken the yoke of his burden, and the staff of his shoulder, the rod of his oppressor, as in the day of Midian.

Multiple comparisons can be made between Isaiah's reference to the Messiah and Gideon's victory over the Midianites. The yoke, staff, and rod are images of oppression (see Isaiah 10:5, 24, 27; 14:25), which in Gideon's case came from an army of 120,000 (Judges 8:10). God reduced the Israelite army from 32,000 to a mere 300, or one percent of the original force, making them outnumbered 400 to one. The whole purpose, as stated in Judges 7:2, was so there was no way the Israelites would receive the glory. Clearly, the sovereign God secured the victory.

Likewise, Isaiah compares the Assyrian army to a flooding river (Isaiah 8:7–8). In Gideon's story, he sought the Lord for a sign (Judges 6:17–22; actually, he sought sign after sign!). Isaiah prophesied a sign in the form of a child born of a virgin who would be called Immanuel (Isaiah 7:11–14). The lesson of Gideon is a lesson of trust and faith in God (Judges 7), and the lesson of Isaiah is one of faith (Isaiah 7:9). God overcame the Midianites and delivered Israel with Gideon's tiny army—in the same way He would ultimately break the power of sin and bring redemption to the world through a tiny infant.

God never afflicts (Isaiah 9:1) or humbles (2:11; 10:33) a person or nation without reason; He always has a higher purpose for all people (see 25:6–9). Sadly, not all learn the lessons of humbling oneself in trust and faith (as even Jesus did, Philippians 2:8), in order to avoid being involuntarily humbled.

5 For every battle of the warrior is with confused noise, and garments rolled in blood; but this shall be with burning and fuel of fire.

Other versions of Isaiah 9:5 refer to the soldier's trampling boots or sandals, which along with the blood-soaked garments of those slain would be burned when the battle was finished. Along with the epic light versus darkness theme, another major theme of Isaiah is the end of war or end of hostilities—the advent of peace. Indeed, "they shall beat their swords into plowshares" (Isaiah 2:4) and "the wolf also shall dwell with the lamb" (11:6) are among the prophet's best-loved passages. It must be noted that the end of hostilities is a precondition of peace, but peace is not limited to putting down arms (see 32:17). Joseph Blenkinsopp writes, "Peace is what happens when a righteous order prevails" (251).

6 For unto us a child is born, unto us a son is given: and the government shall be upon his shoulder: and his name shall be called Wonderful, Counsellor, The mighty God, The everlasting Father, The Prince of Peace.

The promise of a child named Immanuel in Isaiah 7:14 (see also 8:8, 10) is fulfilled by the promised birth in 9:6 of the Son, who was both God and King. It is beyond question that both prophecies foretell Jesus. "Immanuel" in Hebrew is `Immanuw'el (**im-maw-noo-EL**), and it means "God with us" or literally "with us is God." God did not come as an even greater oppressor, but rather as a child. As the son of David, He would reign from David's throne, but as the Son of God, He would be "God with us."

Interestingly, the child who would bear the righteous rule on His shoulders would remove the burden from the shoulders of the oppressed (v. 4; see also Isaiah 22:22–24). The one who was beaten would deliver humankind from the rod of injustice; the one who bore the yoke of the Cross would deliver people from their impossible burdens.

The one named Immanuel received a royal investiture, complete with the conferring of throne-names, which followed the protocol of Egyptians celebrating a new pharaoh's accession. These are the "emblems of sovereignty" in Blenkinsopp's words (250).

In Isaiah 9:6, the phrase "Wonderful, Counsellor" in Hebrew is *pele' ya`ats* (**PEH-**

leh yaw-ATS), and these are attributes of Yahweh (see Isaiah 5:19; 25:1). There is a supernatural, extraordinary overtone of divine wisdom and power (see Isaiah 11:2).

"Mighty God"—in Hebrew this is *gibbowr el* (**ghib-BORE el**), a divine title (see Nehemiah 9:32; Isaiah 10:21; Jeremiah 32:18). This parallels the Isaiah 7:14 passage about Immanuel, meaning "God (*el*) with us"— or `*Immanuw'el*, "with us is God" (see also Daniel 11:3).

"Everlasting Father"—in Hebrew this is `*ad 'ab* (**ad awb**). Yahweh, the divine Father, cares for the orphans and widows (Psalm 68:5) and also loves and cares for all His people (103:13). Isaiah uses similar language in 63:16: "O LORD, art our father, our redeemer; thy name is from everlasting" (see also 2 Thessalonians 2:16).

"Prince of Peace"—in Hebrew this is *sar shalowm* (**sar shaw-LOME**); the royal God-child will bring the blessings of peace with righteousness (see Isaiah 11:1–9). Blenkinsopp notes that this phrase is a "messianic designation by both Christians and Jews" (250). *Shalowm* (**shaw-LOME**), commonly spelled *shalom*, is a stronger word than the English word "peace," which can simply mean "an absence of war" (see note here on 9:5). Isaiah's classic verse regarding "perfect peace" (26:3) has guided many Christians through troubled times; another classic most have heard in song is Isaiah 55:12. At the same time, there is no peace for the wicked (Isaiah 48:22; 57:21). Altogether, Isaiah uses *shalowm* 25 times.

Shalom can mean many things: contentment or fulfillment (Genesis 15:15); health and well-being (29:6); confidence and freedom from anxiety (1 Samuel 1:17); goodwill, harmony, or tranquility (Exodus 4:18); and favor or peace with God (see Numbers 6:26; also Isaiah 53:5, prophetically speaking of Jesus creating this peace).

7 Of the increase of his government and peace there shall be no end, upon the throne of David, and upon his kingdom, to order it, and to stablish it with judgment and with justice from henceforth even for ever. The zeal of the LORD of hosts will perform this.

As an elaboration of the divine names of the Child, the implications also are nothing short of supernatural. A king might enlarge a kingdom (e.g., David, 2 Samuel 8), but only a divine king can enlarge His kingdom infinitely—this kingdom will be so much greater than the kingdoms of Israel or David. Not only that, everything will be built on righteousness (see again Isaiah 11:1–9). In Isaiah 9:7, "government" in Hebrew is *misrah* (**mis-RAW**) and refers to a rule or dominion. Nothing will corrupt this princely administration. The last sentence of verse 7 changes the prior prophetic perfect tense to simple future tense: It *will* happen— God Himself will make sure it happens (see parallel language in Isaiah 37:32).

Just as the Pharisees in Jesus' day struggled with Isaiah's words, unable to make the leap from the human son of David to the divine Son of God named Immanuel, "God with us," so modern Pharisees are equally confounded and reject what they cannot comprehend.

Sources:

Bible Pronunciation Chart. Better Days Are Coming.com. http://www.betterdaysarecoming/bible/pronunciation.html (accessed January 29, 2011).

Blenkinsopp, Joseph. *Isaiah 1–39: A New Translation with Introduction and Commentary. The Anchor Bible, vol. 19.* New York, NY: Doubleday, 2000. 245–51.

Grogan, Geoffrey W. *Isaiah–Ezekiel. The Expositor's Bible Commentary*, vol. 6. Edited by Frank E. Gaebelein. Grand Rapids, MI: Zondervan, 1986. 73–75.

"Isaiah." Biblical Resources. www.biblicalresources.info/pages/isaiah/biography.html (accessed June 24, 2010).

Merriam-Webster Online Dictionary. Merriam-Webster, Inc. http://www.merriam-webster.com (accessed January 29, 2011).

Old and New Testament Concordances, Lexicons, Dictionaries, Commentaries, Images, and Bible Versions. Blue Letter Bible.org. http://www.blueletterbible.org/ (accessed November 17, 2010).

Passage Lookup. Bible Gateway.com. http://www.biblegateway.com/passage (accessed January 24, 2011).

Seitz, Christopher R. *Isaiah 1–39. Interpretation: A Bible Commentary for Teaching and Preaching.* Louisville, KY: John Knox Press, 1993. 84–87.

Say It Correctly

Gideon. GID-ee-uhn.
Hezekiah. Hez'uh-KI-uh.
Jotham. JOH-thuhm.
Midian. MID-ee-uhn.
Tiglath-pileser. Tig'lath-puh-LEE-
zuhr.
Zebulun. ZEB-yuh-luhn.

Daily Bible Readings

MONDAY
A Heart Hardened to God's
Righteousness
(Exodus 9:27–35)

TUESDAY
Before God in Our Guilt
(Ezra 9:10–15)

WEDNESDAY
Take Your Stand
(1 Samuel 12:6–16)

THURSDAY
If We Confess Our Sins
(1 John 1:5–9)

FRIDAY
The Righteous Judge
(2 Timothy 4:1–8)

SATURDAY
The Light of the World
(John 8:12–19)

SUNDAY
The Promise of a Righteous King
(Isaiah 9:2–7)

Notes

_____

_____

_____

_____

Teaching Tips

August 19
Bible Study Guide 12

Words You Should Know

A. Fruitful (Jeremiah 23:3) *para'* (Heb.)—Abundant, successful, showing an ability to bear fruit.

B. Righteous (v. 5) *tsaddiyq* (Heb.)—Just, lawful, righteous.

Teacher Preparation

Unifying Principle—The Just Leader. Leaders may betray the people whom they serve. God promises to send leaders who will administer justice in God's name.

A. Pray for your students and lesson clarity.

B. Study and meditate on the entire text.

C. Research the bios on some "good" leaders and be prepared to share their outstanding leadership qualities.

D. Complete the companion lesson in the *Precepts For Living Personal Study Guide®*.

O—Open the Lesson

A. Open with prayer, including the Aim for Change.

B. After prayer, introduce today's subject of the lesson.

C. Have your students read the Aim for Change and Keep in Mind verse in unison. Discuss.

D. Share your presentation. Discuss.

E. Review the In Focus story. Discuss.

P—Present the Scriptures

A. Read the Focal Verses.

B. Use The People, Places, and Times; Background; Search the Scriptures; At-A-Glance outline; and In Depth to explain the verses.

E—Explore the Meaning

A. Discuss the Search the Scriptures questions and Discuss the Meaning.

B. Ask for a volunteer to read Lesson in Our Society. Discuss.

C. Summarize with the Make It Happen section.

D. Connect these sections to the Aim for Change and the Keep in Mind verse in order to sum up.

N—Next Steps for Application

A. Ask students to complete the Follow the Spirit and Remember Your Thoughts sections with "points to remember."

B. Close with prayer.

KJV Cont.

18 Neither shall the priests the Levites want a man before me to offer burnt offerings, and to kindle meat offerings, and to do sacrifice continually.

NLT Cont.

18 And there will always be Levitical priests to offer burnt offerings and grain offerings and sacrifices to me."

The People, Places, and Times

Kings. The Old Testament tells many stories of how kings ruled over the Israelites in the northern kingdom and the southern nation of Judah, but most of them did not obey God. All of the northern kings were evil and a number of Judah's kings worshiped idols, married heathens, sacrificed children, and committed other sins that disobeyed God's Law and the keeping of His way. Judah's bad kings promoted their own self-serving interests with little regard for the people they served. God put the practice of kingship in place so they could watch over the Children of Israel, His people. Instead, they were corrupt, unjust, and led the people away from God—into sin and wrongdoing.

Zedekiah, the last king to reign over Judah, disobeyed God as so many who came before him. He acted prideful and sinned greatly, which caused a heathen nation to conquer Judah and force them into exile after slavery. Zedekiah would not submit to God's way and led the nation into utter collapse and ruin, which marked the end of Judah reigning as a free and self-governing country (*Nelson's Illustrated Bible Dictionary*, 1986). As a result, Judah no longer held its former fame and honor.

Background

The plight of Judah looked hopeless when other nations pummeled everything linked to their beliefs, way of life, and society. The prospect of rebuilding or restoring themselves looked impossible. Before Zedekiah, a handful of kings did right in the sight of God. When these kings reigned, they led the people and the nation back to God. At other times, when the ungodly kings ruled, God raised prophets to foretell blessings if the king and nation repented, or judgment if they did not.

During the reign of Zedekiah, God called Jeremiah as a prophet to speak against the rampant sin occurring in the nation of Judah and declare His judgment. Zedekiah's name means the "the righteousness of Yahweh." However, instead of Zedekiah ruling Judah in righteousness as his name suggests, under Zedekiah's rule, the nation adopted many strange ways that did not align with God's direction for them. They rebelled against the Law of God.

So Jeremiah's woe stresses the atrocities of their time. He cries out, "Woe be unto the pastors that destroy and scatter the sheep of my pasture! saith the LORD" (Jeremiah 23:1). The language used highlights the prophets and God's sorrow and distress at the cruelty, idolatry, evil, and selfishness of the leaders. However, as we will see later in his prophecy, all was not lost and a promise of a better future and idyllic king would come.

At-A-Glance

1. Promise of Restoration (Jeremiah 23:1–4)

2. The Righteous Branch (23:5–6; 33:14–18)

God Promised
a Righteous Branch

Bible Background • JEREMIAH 23:1–6; 33:14–18
Printed Text • JEREMIAH 23:1–6; 33:14–18 | Devotional Reading • PSALM 33:1–5

————————— Aim for Change —————————

By the end of the lesson, we will: UNDERSTAND the relationship between the "Righteous Branch" in Jeremiah and the coming of Jesus; REFLECT on examples of good leaders; and LIST ways we can become better leaders.

—————————  In Focus —————————

Ryan felt God leading him to participate in the leadership of his local church. He discussed this with his pastor, and the pastor urged him to attend their church's leadership classes. Ryan attended the classes, did very well, and received a certificate of leadership upon completion of his course work. Ryan then took responsibility for a ministry where he led a group weekly. He led this ministry while working his secular full-time job.

After spending the large part of his day at his secular job, in order to minister effectively in the group, Ryan spent several evenings weekly preparing. After several months of juggling both positions, Ryan began responding crossly to the people he worked with and started lashing out at them. He also treated them poorly, which led to them protesting to the pastor for Ryan's removal. The pastor decided to meet with Ryan. As a result of meeting with the pastor, Ryan learned his role as a leader should not include lording his position over people or abusing them.

True leaders possess a servant heart and a commitment to live uprightly before God.

————————— **Keep in Mind** —————————
AUG
19th

"Behold, the days come, saith the LORD, that I will raise unto David a righteous Branch, and a King shall reign and prosper, and shall execute judgment and justice in the earth" (Jeremiah 23:5).

In Depth

1. Promise of Restoration (Jeremiah 23:1–4)

"Therefore thus saith the LORD God of Israel against the pastors that feed my people; Ye have scattered my flock, and driven them away, and have not visited them: behold, I will visit upon you the evil of your doings, saith the LORD" (Jeremiah 23:2). God promised to step in and take control over the scattered nation in spite of the lack of care and attention and despite the harm they suffered. God takes ownership and calls them "my people" and "my flock." Repetition of the word "my" emphasizes the importance of Judah to God and the seriousness of their state.

"And I will gather the remnant of my flock out of all countries whither I have driven them, and will bring them again to their folds; and they shall be fruitful and increase" (v. 3). Regardless of how far the people scattered, how far they strayed or how damaged they were, Jeremiah prophesizes hope. No longer did they need to suffer at the hands of ungodly leaders. God says, "I Myself" (v. 3, NASB)—He is concerned and will move on their behalf. God, who is holy, faithful, and righteous in contrast to Zedekiah and other Old Testament kings who acted unrighteously will provide and lead His people back to a location of fruitfulness and increase.

Under the unrighteous kings, the nation no longer lived within their inheritance or the right location—their exile deprived them of their true heritage. With the promise of restoration and a change of leadership back to God's rule, He would bring them to their pasture ("their folds")—a place of covering, accountability, purpose, destiny, and fellowship.

"And I will set up shepherds over them which shall feed them: and they shall fear no more, nor be dismayed, neither shall they be lacking, saith the LORD" (v. 4). A further distinction between Old Testament leadership, which scattered the nation versus the promised coming leadership, relates to God's Headship, which gathers and unites. Zedekiah abused his charge, but God will attend to and care for His flock and will even raise up other leaders to tend them.

2. The Righteous Branch (23:5–6; 33:14–18)

"Behold, the days come, saith the LORD, that I will raise unto David a righteous Branch, . . . and this is his name whereby he shall be called, THE LORD OUR RIGHTEOUSNESS" (from Jeremiah 23:5–6). At first glance, God's promise of a shepherd could potentially look like nothing would change from Zedekiah. If God raised more shepherds, they possibly would also be subject to human failures, which could fall into the same lack of control as those who came before them, like Zedekiah—after all, his name means "the righteousness of Yahweh." However, a shift occurs from the promise of more individual shepherds to the promise of a "righteous Branch" whose very nature cannot tolerate sin. Unlike Zedekiah, His name, "the Lord our Righteousness," defines the very core of His existence. The character of the "righteous Branch" would exude everything related to righteousness, truth, and purity. Jeremiah's prophecy about the righteous Branch refers to the coming of Jesus Christ, the only Leader and Shepherd who cannot and will not fail. Jesus would spring forth from the line of King David to fulfill the promise to David that the throne will not lack any man sitting on the throne to rule over the Children of Israel.

The Hebrew root for "righteous" refers to an ethical or moral standard, which portrays the nature and will of God (R. Laird Harris, *Theological Wordbook of the Old Testament*, 1980). Psalm 145:17 says, "The LORD is righteous in all his ways, and holy in all his works." Therefore, the people of God and His leaders, who rule or lead on His behalf, should exhibit righteousness or "conformity to an ethical or moral standard" as presented in God's Word (Harris, 752). Jeremiah's lament further reflects this ideal about the offense of Judah's kings: "Shalt thou reign, because thou closest thyself in cedar? did not thy father eat and drink, and do judgment and justice, and then it was well with him? He judged the cause of the poor and needy; then it was well with him: was not this to know me? saith the LORD" (Jeremiah 22:15–16).

As the righteous Branch, Jesus embodies the true character of a king and leader. Jesus would show justice and righteousness, instead of corruption and sin. Jesus would save His people from trouble, delivering them from their enemies, while providing safety and security. Christ's coming would fulfill God's promise to David and His promise of restoration to His people from exile back into their rightful place in their inheritance.

Search the Scriptures

1. What does God say He will raise up over the nation of Judah (Jeremiah 23:4)?

2. Describe the differences between an ungodly king and a righteous king (vv. 2, 5).

Discuss the Meaning

If God manifests His righteousness in believers and leaders through faith in Jesus Christ, why do many leaders fall into constant sin, which can negatively impact the people they serve in ministry?

Lesson in Our Society

We hear, through Christian media, about the alarming trend in the church regarding the large number of leaders' moral and ethical failures occurring across the nation. It would seem that the principle of righteous-

ness is taboo and accountability no longer required. Does the level of righteousness required for leaders need to keep pace and change as the times change, or does the standard of righteousness still stand as a required principle as indicated in Romans 6:12–14?

Make It Happen

As leaders and believers, our uprightness should be defined in God's terms, not ours. When we accept Christ, we accept the "the Lord our righteousness." Jesus is our righteousness. Just as God promised restoration through the coming of Christ to the nation of Judah, we possess an even greater hope for experiencing fruitfulness and success because He actually lives within us; He is with and in us. God accredits the virtue of Jesus' character to us when we believe in Him. You have the power this week and every week to obey and commit to God's will and way for your life.

Over the next week, review the quality of your relationships with others and how you interact. Decide if you are demonstrating God's conduct. Did your actions demonstrate fairness or justice? Did they reflect truthfulness or uprightness? Make a commitment this week to mirror the character and righteousness of Jesus Christ.

Follow the Spirit

What God wants me to do:

_____

_____

_____

_____

Remember Your Thoughts

Special insights I have learned:

_____

_____

_____

_____

More Light on the Text

Jeremiah 23:1–6; 33:14–18

23:1 Woe be unto the pastors that destroy and scatter the sheep of my pasture! saith the LORD.

The "woe oracles," which are indictments and judgments, started in the previous chapter against all who were unrighteous, then singled out individual kings (Jeremiah 22:13ff), and then mentioned shepherds coming to judgment (22:22). This "woe oracle" singles out pastors (shepherds), representative of all kings and leaders, which would include prophets and priests. In Charles Feinberg's words, they were "guilty of gross dereliction of duty" (*Isaiah–Ezekiel*, 517). Shepherds are supposed to lead and feed; these did the opposite. They did all the things that shepherds are supposed to prevent. The possessive "my pasture" in Jeremiah 23:1 underlines Yahweh's voice and the gravity of the offense. The wicked shepherds will regret their actions with bitter tears (see Jeremiah 25:36). "Pasture" in Hebrew is *mir`iyth* (**meer-EETH**) and in several usages is within similar phrases "sheep of thy pasture," "sheep of his hand," "his people and the sheep of his pasture," and others (see Psalms 74:1; 79:13; 95:7).

2 Therefore thus saith the LORD God of Israel against the pastors that feed my people; Ye have scattered my flock, and driven them away, and have not visited them: behold, I will visit upon you the evil of your doings, saith the LORD.

In the beginning of 23:2, Jeremiah uses a play on words, which is only evident in the Hebrew. "Pastors" in Hebrew is *ra`ah* (**raw-AW**), a verb that can mean either to shepherd or feed. "Feed" thus uses the same Hebrew word—in other words, shepherds who shepherd, or in modern language, feeders who feed or leaders who lead. In Genesis 4:2, Abel was a *ra`ah* (shepherd) of the sheep; in Genesis 37:2, Joseph *ra`ah* (fed) the sheep. In reverse, which was the case in Jeremiah's indictment, they were shepherds who didn't shepherd, feeders who didn't feed, and leaders who didn't lead. In Jeremiah 23:2, "visited" in Hebrew is *paqad* (**paw-KAD**) and in this use means attended or bestowed care. The shepherds did not attend or bestow care to the sheep, so now God would attend to or bestow on them His judgment (from the same oracle, see Jeremiah 21:14; 22:22).

3 And I will gather the remnant of my flock out of all countries whither I have driven them, and will bring them again to their folds; and they shall be fruitful and increase.

After more than two chapters of indictments, Jeremiah's tone abruptly changes to one of hope. His prophecy came during Zedekiah's reign, which if one can imagine hearing it in his time, in those circumstances, it gives it that much more contrast. Would it even be possible for the endless evil reigns to end? Who could accomplish such a thing?

Regardless of how many sheep or shepherds rebelled against God, throughout history a remnant remained faithful to Him. Unfortunately, they, too, were caught up in the scattering and God's judgment on the nation. Regardless of where they landed, however, they were still God's people and He never forgot about them. Not only will God gather them again (see also Jeremiah 29:14; 31:8, 10; 32:37), He will bless them as well, and they will experience blessings of being fruitful and increasing (multiplying); see similar descriptions in Jeremiah 3:16; 29:6; 30:19. In the Hebrew, "fruitful" and "increase" are two rhyming words, *para'* (**paw-RAW**) and *rabah* (**raw-BAW**), which may explain why they are often used together (Genesis 1:22, 28; 8:17). These words of blessing have "cosmic implications" according to Terence Fretheim and fulfill ancient promises dating back to creation and the first covenants (*Jeremiah*, 325; see also Genesis 17:1–8, 20; 28:3; 48:4; Isaiah 35; 40–55).

4 And I will set up shepherds over them which shall feed them: and they shall fear no more, nor be dismayed, neither shall they be lacking, saith the LORD.

Again, Jeremiah uses the twin meanings of *ra`ah* together, this time in the positive. While bad shepherds scatter, good shepherds gather. While bad shepherds don't do their job, don't feed the sheep, and don't protect them, good shepherds will do their job well, and the fears and terrors of the sheep will subside; all their needs will be met and they will be content.

Interestingly, Jeremiah uses the same Hebrew word, *paqad*, for "lacking" as for the previous word "visited." One of the possible meanings has to do with numbering. The NLT of Jeremiah 23:4 is "Not a single one of them will be lost or missing," perhaps tapping the ancient custom of a shepherd counting sheep as they come into the fold at night. In a New Testament parallel, Jesus said, "I have not lost a single one" (John 18:9, NLT). Just as God knows the number of sparrows (Matthew 10:29), He knows the number of His faithful remnant.

5 Behold, the days come, saith the LORD, that I will raise unto David a righteous Branch, and a King shall reign and prosper, and shall execute judgment and justice in the earth.

Jeremiah uses the phrase "the days come" ("the days are coming," NKJV; "the time is coming," NLT) 15 times. It is a "messianic formula" in Feinberg's words, which was a popular theme among Old Testament Jews (518). For Jews who had lost everything to the Babylonians, the Messiah offered hope for a future golden age that would be ruled by a future Davidic king, who would judge all their oppressors and create a permanent, worldwide *shalom*. A parallel but more elaborate passage is Isaiah 11:1–9. Various Old Testament writers envisioned the restored Davidic rule (see Amos 9:11; Isaiah 9:6–7; Psalm 89:28–37).

The New Testament reveals that Jesus, Son of David, was the Christ, the anointed one (*Christos* in Greek), the Son of God, the Messiah (see Matthew 1:1, 16; John 1:41; 4:25).

In Jeremiah 23:5, "raise" in Hebrew is *quwm* (**koom**), which among its 629 Old Testament uses can mean to rouse, stir up, or constitute. Most versions use "raise," but uniquely, the NLT uses "place" instead. In an almost identical verse in 33:15, Jeremiah used a different Hebrew word translated "grow": "I will cause the Branch of righteousness to grow up unto David." The same verse in NIV is "make a righteous Branch sprout from David's line."

The phrase "righteous Branch" in Hebrew is *tsaddiyq tsemach* (**tsad-DEEK TSEH-makh**), for which alternate synonyms easily could be "rightful sprout" or "righteous shoot" (see Isaiah 4:2, "branch of the LORD"; Zechariah 3:8, "my servant, the Branch"; 6:12, NIV, "the man whose name is the Branch").

Above all, the "righteous Branch," the Messiah sitting on David's throne, will rule with justice and righteousness (see Jeremiah 21:12; 22:3, and 22:15, referring to Josiah). In stark contrast to the unwise, uncaring, and unjust shepherds and kings, the wise, just shepherd-king will rule like God rules (Isaiah 9:7; 11:1–5; Ezekiel 34:23–24).

6 In his days Judah shall be saved, and Israel shall dwell safely: and this is his name whereby he shall be called, THE LORD OUR RIGHTEOUSNESS.

Both Judah and Israel will be saved, which clearly will be a restored nation (see also Ezekiel 37:19), safe and secure in God (Jeremiah 32:37; see also Isaiah 30:15; 32:17). Even with a divided nation, even when oppressed and taken into captivity, even when their precious Jerusalem had been destroyed, still they were and never ceased to be one people—God's people (Jeremiah 32:38).

Jeremiah makes yet another play on words with his wording of the name of the coming righteous Branch: "The Lord our righteousness." In Hebrew this is two words, *Yehovah tsidqenuw* (**yeh-ho-VAW tsid-KAY-noo**), and it is only found here and in the next portion of this lesson (33:16). Conversely, Zedekiah's name meant the same but in reverse, "Righteousness is our Lord," a name he clearly did not live up to. Many commentators believe Jeremiah's reversal was deliberate, as if to say the future king will be the opposite of Zedekiah (and all similar wicked leaders)—a complete turnaround. Compare the similarity of the Hebrew spelling of Zedekiah's name, *Tsidqiyah* (**tsid-kee-YAW**).

33:14 Behold, the days come, saith the LORD, that I will perform that good thing which I have promised unto the house of Israel and to the house of Judah. 15 In those days, and at that time, will I cause the Branch of righteousness to grow up unto David; and he shall execute judgment and righteousness in the land. 16 In those days shall Judah be saved, and Jerusalem shall dwell safely: and this is the name wherewith she shall be called, The LORD our righteousness.

These verses are an almost exact parallel to the previous section. The oracle expands and modifies the messianic oracle just discussed, with some notable parallel constructs, such as the phrases "The days come" or "the time is coming" (23:5). Verse 15 has the same name for the branch; verse 16 contains the same play on Zedekiah's name (23:6). Clearly, the passage has a messianic interpretation.

One major difference is that "the LORD our righteousness" here is applied to Jerusalem instead of the future king (as in 23:6). Compare Isaiah 1:26, "the city of righteousness," and Ezekiel 48:35, "the name of the city from that day shall be, 'The LORD is there.'" The focus shifts from Israel and Judah to Judah and Jerusalem, where the city takes the new name.

17 For thus saith the LORD; David shall never want a man to sit upon the throne of the house of Israel; 18 Neither shall the priests the Levites want a man before me to offer burnt offerings, and to kindle meat offerings, and to do sacrifice continually.

The complete oracle (vv. 14–26) refers primarily to the royal and priestly offices, while the prior oracle (vv. 4–13) refers primarily to the nation and people. Jack Lundbrom notes that God will not only restore Israel and Jerusalem, but He also will restore the royal (Davidic) and priestly (Levite) lineages and offices (*Jeremiah 21–36: A New Translation with*

Introduction and Commentary, 540–541; see also Isaiah 61:6; Jeremiah 31:14). This is a fulfillment of God's unconditional covenants in 2 Samuel 7. Even with no king and no temple, the priestly line survived the Babylonian exile (see Ezekiel 43:19; 44:15). Even with the great disappointments of Judah's wicked kings, God's promise in 2 Samuel remained fixed with the renewed hope of the messianic Davidic king. David's dynasty never would be permanently cut off (Luke 1:32–33).

Sources:

Bible Pronunciation Chart. Better Days Are Coming.com. http://www.betterdaysarecoming.com/bible/pronunciation.html#z (accessed December 3, 2010).

Clements, R. E. *Jeremiah. Interpretation: A Bible Commentary for Teaching and Preaching.* Atlanta, GA: John Knox Press, 1988. 137–40, 199–201.

Feinberg, Charles L. *Isaiah–Ezekiel. The Expositor's Bible Commentary,* vol. 6. Edited by Frank E. Gaebelein. Grand Rapids, MI: Zondervan, 1986. 517–20, 590–92.

Fretheim, Terence E. Jeremiah. *Smyth & Helwys Bible Commentary.* Macon, GA: Smyth & Helwys, 2002. 324–330, 477–81.

Lundbom, Jack R. *Jeremiah 21–36: A New Translation with Introduction and Commentary. The Anchor Bible, vol. 21B.* New York, NY: Doubleday, 2004. 164–76, 537–42.

Merriam-Webster Online Dictionary. Merriam-Webster, Inc. http://www.merriam-webster.com (accessed January 29, 2011).

Old and New Testament Concordances, Lexicons, Dictionaries, Commentaries, Images, and Bible Versions. Blue Letter Bible. org. http://www.blueletterbible.org/ (accessed November 18, 2010).

"Saddiq." *Theological Wordbook of the Old Testament.* R. Laird Harris, gen. ed. Chicago, IL: Moody Press, 1980. 752–55 (accessed through PC Study Bible, September 1, 2010).

"Zedekiah." *Merriam-Webster Online Dictionary.* http://www.merriam-webster.com/dictionary/zedekiah (accessed December 3, 2010).

"Zedekiah." *Nelson's Illustrated Bible Dictionary.* Herbert Lockyer, Sr., gen. ed. Nashville, TN: Thomas Nelson Publishers, 1986. 1326–27 (accessed through PC Study Bible, September 1, 2010).

Say It Correctly

Jehoahaz. Juh-HOH-uh-haz.
Jehoiachin. Juh-HOI-uh-kin.
Judah. JOO-duh.
Levite. LEE-vite.
Nebuchadnezzar. Neb'uh-kuhd-NEZ-uhr.
Zedekiah. Zed'uh-KI-uh.

Daily Bible Readings

MONDAY
Pursue Righteousness
(1 Timothy 6:11–16)

TUESDAY
God's Children Now
(1 John 2:28–3:3)

WEDNESDAY
The Righteous Will Flourish
(Proverbs 11:27–31)

THURSDAY
All Shall Be Righteous
(Isaiah 60:17–22)

FRIDAY
The Lord Loves Righteousness
and Justice
(Psalm 33:1–5)

SATURDAY
The Gracious and Righteous Lord
(Psalm 116:5–19)

SUNDAY
The Lord Is Our Righteousness
(Jeremiah 23:1–6; 33:14–18)

Teaching Tips

Words You Should Know

A. Shepherd (Ezekiel 34:23) *ra`ah* (Heb.)—Pastor, ruler, teacher.

B. Prince (v. 24) *nasiy', nasa'* (Heb.)—Captain, leader.

Teacher Preparation

Unifying Principle—Meeting Our Deepest Need. People are searching for tranquility and wholeness. Where can these things be found? A lasting relationship with God and an assurance that God is with us meets our deepest need.

A. Pray for your students and that God will bring lesson clarity.

B. Study and meditate on the entire text.

C. Complete the companion lesson in the *Precepts For Living Personal Study Guide®*.

D. Be prepared to share a testimony on how God met a dire need in your life.

O—Open the Lesson

A. Open with prayer, including the Aim for Change.

B. Introduce today's subject.

C. Read the Aim for Change and Keep in Mind verse in unison. Discuss.

D. Share your testimony and allow others to share.

E. Now, have a volunteer summarize the In Focus story. Discuss.

P—Present the Scriptures

A. Have volunteers read the Focal Verses.

B. Now use The People, Places, and Times; Background; Search the Scriptures; At-A-Glance outline; In Depth; and More Light on the Text to clarify the verses.

E—Explore the Meaning

A. Have volunteers summarize the Discuss the Meaning, Lesson in Our Society, and Make It Happen sections.

B. Connect these sections to the Aim for Change and the Keep in Mind verse.

N—Next Steps for Application

A. Write some easy-to-remember takeaway principles under the Follow the Spirit or Remember Your Thoughts section.

B. Close with prayer, and praise God for promising to be with us and keeping His word.

Worship Guide

For the Superintendent or Teacher
Theme: God Promised To Be with Us
Theme Song: "I Will Trust in the Lord!"
Devotional Reading: Psalm 23
Prayer

AUG
26th

597

God Promised To Be with Us

Bible Background • EZEKIEL 34
Printed Text • EZEKIEL 34:23–31 | Devotional Reading • PSALM 23

———————————— Aim for Change ————————————

By the end of the lesson we will: KNOW and understand the new covenant between God and God's people; FEEL the tranquility of a lasting relationship with Christ; and PERFORM acts of justice so that others can find peace and wholeness.

——————————  In Focus ——————————

As a recent graduate from college, Rhonda finally decided to move out of her parents' house into her own apartment. With her newfound job, Rhonda felt it appropriate to stand on her own by getting her own place. She rented an apartment close to her job, bought a dog, and began to settle into her new home. Rhonda did not live on a budget, and within a couple months she began to suffer financially in meeting her monthly bills. In her attempt to meet all of her expenses, she stopped paying her tithes. Soon, her financial situation became even more chaotic as random expenses or a crisis would always arise. Rhonda could not figure out why she could not get ahead.

While visiting her parents for Easter dinner, Rhonda opened up and shared her financial problems. Her parents reiterated with her the importance of ordering her financial priorities, including tithing, which demonstrates our trust and gratitude to God. Rhonda realized she had been unwise, leaving God out of her situation while trying to fix it on her own. She discovered that her life would be more peaceful if she kept God at the center.

In today's lesson, we will learn that God is with us and will supply all of our needs as long as we depend and trust in Him. We do not need to fear or feel alone in any situation as long as we allow Him to be Lord and God in our lives.

———————————— Keep in Mind ————————————

"And I will set up one shepherd over them, and he shall feed them, even my servant David; he shall feed them, and he shall be their shepherd"
(Ezekiel 34:23).

"And I will set up one shepherd over them, and he shall feed them, even my servant David; he shall feed them, and he shall be their shepherd." (Ezekiel 34:23).

Focal Verses

KJV **Ezekiel 34:23** And I will set up one shepherd over them, and he shall feed them, even my servant David; he shall feed them, and he shall be their shepherd.

24 And I the LORD will be their God, and my servant David a prince among them; I the LORD have spoken it.

25 And I will make with them a covenant of peace, and will cause the evil beasts to cease out of the land: and they shall dwell safely in the wilderness, and sleep in the woods.

26 And I will make them and the places round about my hill a blessing; and I will cause the shower to come down in his season; there shall be showers of blessing.

27 And the tree of the field shall yield her fruit, and the earth shall yield her increase, and they shall be safe in their land, and shall know that I am the LORD, when I have broken the bands of their yoke, and delivered them out of the hand of those that served themselves of them.

28 And they shall no more be a prey to the heathen, neither shall the beast of the land devour them; but they shall dwell safely, and none shall make them afraid.

29 And I will raise up for them a plant of renown, and they shall be no more consumed with hunger in the land, neither bear the shame of the heathen any more.

30 Thus shall they know that I the LORD their God am with them, and that they, even the house of Israel, are my people, saith the Lord GOD.

31 And ye my flock, the flock of my pasture, are men, and I am your God, saith the Lord GOD.

NLT **Ezekiel 34:23** And I will set one shepherd over them, even my servant David. He will feed them and be a shepherd to them.

24 And I, the LORD, will be their God, and my servant David will be a prince among my people. I, the LORD, have spoken!

The LORD's Covenant of Peace

25 "I will make a covenant of peace with them and drive away the dangerous animals from the land. Then my people will be able to camp safely in the wildest places and sleep in the woods without fear.

26 I will cause my people and their homes around my holy hill to be a blessing. And I will send showers, showers of blessings, which will come just when they are needed.

27 The orchards and fields of my people will yield bumper crops, and everyone will live in safety. When I have broken their chains of slavery and rescued them from those who enslaved them, then they will know that I am the LORD.

28 They will no longer be prey for other nations, and wild animals will no longer attack them. They will live in safety, and no one will make them afraid.

29 "And I will give them a land famous for its crops, so my people will never again go hungry or be shamed by the scorn of foreign nations.

30 In this way, they will know that I, the LORD their God, am with them. And they will know that they, the people of Israel, are my people, says the Sovereign LORD.

31 You are my flock, the sheep of my pasture. You are my people, and I am your God, says the Sovereign LORD."

The People, Places, and Times

Shepherding. A key occupation of the Children of Israel, shepherding was also used as a term to compare the reign of the Old Testament kings to their reign over God's people—the Israelites. God's Law charged the kings to care for the people. However, throughout the Old Testament we see many examples of kings disobeying God and adopting the practices of non-believing nations. They did not keep their charge and often abused their authority. Because of their "bad shepherding," the Israelites did whatever they wanted with little guidance or direction. They behaved like sheep without a shepherd to guide them.

As a result, other nations conquered Israel and forced them into exile away from the land God gave to them as an inheritance. These heathen nations took over and ripped their land away from them, while forcing the Israelites into slavery and bondage. The Israelites lived in constant fear as they faced war, conflict, and defeat. The Israelites' defeat and ruin annulled any opportunity to recover on their own.

Background

A lack of good leadership points to the primary reason for Israel's downfall. Many of the Old Testament kings did not lead well, because they did not obey God's edicts or commands. They did not shepherd properly. Scriptures use the shepherding allegory throughout based on its familiarity among the people of its times to clarify or describe a truth. The Hebrew root for "shepherding" means "to pasture" and denotes the key term for feeding domestic animals. Figuratively, the shepherd signifies a leader, and sheep symbolized the people under his rule.

Historically, not only were shepherds responsible for the physical survival and welfare of their own or their master's flocks, but they also had to provide shelter, medication, and provision for lameness and weariness. Because the shepherd watched over, cared for, and met the sheep's needs to keep them safe, the sheep were helpless without the shepherd's guidance and protection. Thus, if the shepherds could not perform these basic tasks, the sheep could not survive. Thus, the shepherd must maintain a clear understanding of his role to watch and tend the sheep. The kings of Israel and Judah failed to live up to this standard.

At-A-Glance

1. The Good Shepherd
(Ezekiel 34:23–24)

2. God Supplies All of Our Needs
(vv. 25–31)

In Depth

1. The Good Shepherd (Ezekiel 34:23–24)

"And I will set up one shepherd over them, and he shall feed them, even my servant David; he shall feed them, and he shall be their shepherd. And I the LORD will be their God, and my servant David a prince among them; I the Lord have spoken it" (Ezekiel 34:23–24). In contrast to the kings of Judah and Israel, who did not shepherd or pasture the people properly, God declares that He will restore order and everything taken from these nations. Order would come through God as He reestablished His rule over His people. Ezekiel uses the shepherd imagery to describe His leadership and the restoration of His kingdom. Of course, God is the supreme Good Shepherd (Psalm 23). Whereas many Old Testament kings failed and sinned greatly due to their self-serving interests and inevitably scattered the people, God as their Shepherd is infallible. He rules perfectly without constraints of human frailty or human error.

The New Testament also uses shepherd imagery as described in John 10:11–15, "I am the good shepherd: the good shepherd giveth his life for the sheep. But he that is an hireling, and not the shepherd, whose own the sheep are not, seeth the wolf coming, and leaveth the sheep, and fleeth: and the wolf catcheth them, and scattereth the sheep. The hireling fleeth, because he is an hireling, and careth not for the sheep. I am the good shepherd, and know my sheep, and am known of mine. As the Father knoweth me, even so know I the Father: and I lay down my life for the sheep."

The attributes described in the Old Testament interconnect with the New Testament description of Jesus as the Good Shepherd. Jesus is caring and selfless to the point of laying down His life for the sheep.

2. God Supplies All of Our Needs (vv. 25–31)

Now that we know about the character of the Shepherd, what does He do on behalf of the sheep?

He protects. "And I will make with them a covenant of peace, and will cause the evil beasts to cease out of the land: and they shall dwell safely in the wilderness, and sleep in the woods" (Ezekiel 34:25). No one likes to live in fearful or traumatic conditions. Fear can become a normal part of life depending on where one lives, negative experiences, or enemies we confront. When God committed to a covenant of peace, He reversed His people's status as the bane of society. The covenant established His role to protect the Israelites, prevent their enemies from pillaging and defeating them, and allow

them to feel safe. Security, a basic human need, frees us from living in anxiety and fear.

He blesses. "And I will make them and the places round about my hill a blessing; and I will cause the shower to come down in his season; there shall be showers of blessing" (Ezekiel 34:26). A "blessing" is the "pronouncement of the favor of God upon an assembled congregation." A blessing is also "based upon the widespread biblical precedent" (see Genesis 27:27–29; Numbers 6:22–27) (*Tyndale Bible Dictionary,* 226–227). When God shepherds, He not only meets the basic needs of the sheep or His people, but He also blesses them or puts them in a position of favor. As His people, when we allow God to shepherd, lead, guide, and direct us, we can enjoy a state of spiritual favor. We can rest securely in Him for He cares for us and desires for us to live abundantly, successfully, and productively.

He frees. "And (they) shall know that I am the LORD, when I have broken the bands of their yoke, and delivered them out of the hand of those that served themselves of them" (from Ezekiel 34:27). Under the Shepherd's care, He will break the yoke of bondage from the Israelites' captors. No longer would they be enslaved, restricted, or subject to another nation's rule. Under the Good Shepherd they would possess freedom—from slavery, fear, and worry, free to live.

He feeds. "And I will raise up for them a plant of renown, and they shall be no more consumed with hunger in the land, neither bear the shame of the heathen any more" (Ezekiel 34:29). All creatures must eat in order to survive, but if they do not maintain the means to find food, this can prove difficult. Forced into exile, the Israelites fended for themselves for the basic necessity of food. God promised that they would no longer hunger or question where their food would come from as He would allow their barren land to produce again. Food provides the basic foundation for strength and sustenance in order to function effectively. We can see not only the literal aspect, but the spiritual implication, as well. If Christians do not properly feed on the Word of God, we will weaken spiritually.

Search the Scriptures

1. How did God promise to bless His sheep (Ezekiel 24:26–27)?

2. Describe the various ways that God refers to His people (vv. 23–31).

Discuss the Meaning

If God considers us to be His sheep and He is our Good Shepherd, do we owe Him any obligation or is our relationship with Him without a debt on our part?

Lesson in Our Society

The past few decades reflect a slow shift in Black America away from Christian principles to a reliance on self, which is also evident across all cultural groups. Historically, Blacks held strong spiritual relationships as we needed to depend on God for basic needs. But as the country has increased in wealth, our tendency to rely on our jobs and our education for food, shelter, and safety for our families increased, as well. How can the Black church maintain our dependence on God and a rich relationship with Him when, for most of us, so many of our basic daily needs, such as food and shelter, are already met?

Make It Happen

"For He is our God, And we are the people of His pasture, And the sheep of His hand" (Psalm 95:7, NKJV). As the sheep of God's pasture, we must completely depend upon God for our well-being, endurance, and our lives. Take time this week to acknowledge Him in everything you do. Do not allow the busyness of life to overwhelm you where you do not seek direction from Him and obtain your strength to accomplish all that He purposes for you.

Follow the Spirit

What God wants me to do:

_____

_____

_____

_____

Remember Your Thoughts

Special insights I have learned:

_____

_____

_____

_____

More Light on the Text

Ezekiel 34:23–31

23 And I will set up one shepherd over them, and he shall feed them, even my servant David; he shall feed them, and he shall be their shepherd.

Our passage begins with a promise from the God of Israel to His people. The promise of a single "shepherd" (Heb. *ra`ah*, **raw-AW**), which means "pastor, ruler, teacher," must have been unspeakably sweet for Ezekiel's hearers. Why? Would not many shepherds be better? Not when those many shepherds of the people Israel—their kings, their priests, their prophets—had been such faithless leaders. Of them, God says, "Ye eat the fat, and ye clothe you with the wool, ye kill them that are fed: but ye feed not the flock" (Ezekiel 34:3). One commentator helpfully sums up Ezekiel 34:3–6: "As a result, diseased sheep had died, the wounded had been untended, the wandering had been lost, and the flock decimated. Meanwhile, the shepherds had continued in their selfish way of life while the sheep were gobbled up by the wild beasts" (Briscoe, 125). Of course, God is not talking about literal sheep; God is comparing His people to creatures that are helpless without someone to guide them and care for them. We know that Ezekiel spoke to the people at the lowest point of their history, after Jerusalem and its temple had been overrun by enemies and its people sent into exile in far away Babylon. Into this dismal situation, God speaks the hopeful words of one shepherd: one that could not be more different than the false prophets, compromised priests, and cruel kings that have failed to shepherd them into God's way of flourishing.

24 And I the LORD will be their God, and my servant David a prince among them; I the LORD have spoken it.

God now approaches His people using His covenant name, *Yahweh*: the name that points back to Exodus 3 and the call of Moses in the burning bush. Translated in the King James Version as "LORD" (always with capital letters), this name would have reminded the people of the promises God had made to them through Moses (see Exodus 19:4–6) and His other covenant messengers. One of those covenant messengers was David, a reminder of Israel's golden age. Interestingly, in Ezekiel 34:24 he is called a "prince" (Heb. *nasiy'*, *nasa'*, **naw-SEE, naw-SAW**), meaning "captain, leader" rather than a king. Perhaps Ezekiel uses "prince" instead of "king" for the

reason mentioned above in the discussion of verse 23: Israel had had enough of kings! God makes it clear that this rescue by David will not come through the merely human line of King David's authority. Rather, this "prince" stands at the right side of the true King in heaven and will come to bring about His will. The Redeemer's presence in the people's midst will be the everlasting proof that God is with them. And there is nothing conditional or uncertain about this promise, for the same God who spoke heaven and earth into being now finishes the promise with finality: "I the LORD have spoken it."

25 And I will make with them a covenant of peace, and will cause the evil beasts to cease out of the land: and they shall dwell safely in the wilderness, and sleep in the woods.

Alongside the presence of their Messiah, the people of promise will enjoy a "covenant of peace." A covenant in the ancient Near East was a binding contract between two parties sealed with some visible symbol of their mutual promise. God's covenant with Moses, similarly, involved obligations to both parties. But other covenants, like the Abrahamic covenant, took place solely because of God's gracious promise. This "covenant of peace" seems to be more of the latter kind. Whereas the covenant with Moses brought much futility because of Israel's disobedience, God will now institute a covenant that brings wholeness and the enduring blessing of peace—*shalom*—to His people.

As a result, Israel will enjoy unprecedented safety. The promise about freedom from "evil beasts" echoes that given in Leviticus 26:6, with the Mosaic covenant: "And I will give peace in the land, and ye shall lie down, and none shall make you afraid: and I will rid evil beasts out of the land, neither shall the sword go through your land." In the Bible, the wilderness is always a place of danger and distress (think of the Israelites wandering in the desert, or Jesus facing Satan in the wild places). The "woods," as mentioned in Ezekiel 34:25, were hardly better—full of darkness and peril. But when God's ruler is on the throne and His covenant of *shalom* in place, these terrifying places become safe places, and God's people are able to go to those places and perform the ultimate sign of safety and trust—falling asleep!

26 And I will make them and the places round about my hill a blessing; and I will cause the shower to come down in his season; there shall be showers of blessing.

The previous verse shows us that God's blessing is powerful and pervasive enough to reach the most empty and dangerous places of the world. But throughout the Old Testament, God's power for Israel is especially profound in the heart of what is often called His "dwelling place." That dwelling place is often known as "Zion," which is also called the "holy hill"—or, as it is here, "my hill." Israel, languishing far from their home in a lonely exile, would have taken unspeakable comfort from the promise that God's own dwelling place among them—"my hill"—would be restored. And just as we see in Isaiah 2, Micah 4, and other places, the blessing of God's presence on that hill blesses not only chosen Israel but also the nations that surround it. So, says Ezekiel, the "the places about my hill" (34:26) will find abundance and salvation, as well.

27 And the tree of the field shall yield her fruit, and the earth shall yield her increase, and they shall be safe in their land, and shall know that I am the LORD, when I have broken the bands of their yoke, and

delivered them out of the hand of those that served themselves of them.

In case there was any doubt that Ezekiel was speaking of a return out of exile to the holy land of Palestine, this verse removes it. The agricultural pictures continue, all pointing to abundance and security: trees blooming and yielding good things; the soil springing forth with food for the harvest; utter safety in the land of promise. But unlike previous generations, who forgot the Lord in the midst of their comfort and prosperity, "They . . . shall know that I am the LORD." Essentially, this verse promises another Exodus. Just as God at one time miraculously took His people out from bondage in Egypt, so now He will once again deliver them from their captors. Ezekiel's words show that God has not forgotten His people, though their experience might appear to show otherwise.

28 And they shall no more be a prey to the heathen, neither shall the beast of the land devour them; but they shall dwell safely, and none shall make them afraid.

God's continuing promise makes it clearer that His people have been profoundly oppressed. In addition to the threatening "beast of the land," of which we have already spoken, we find the claim that Israel has been "a prey to the heathen." The use of the strong word "prey" implies, of course, that there is a predator and that God's helpless people have been devoured. The cruelty of the Babylonians was well known (see Daniel 2:5; 3:6), and it is not difficult to imagine the wandering, scattered Jews at the mercy of Babylonian predators. But in Ezekiel 34:28 these "heathen"—those not given the covenant promise of God—will not prey on the Jews forever, and the rule of the King on the hill of Zion will restore blessed security to the people of God. The fear that these

Jews have known as a constant presence for years and years will be gone, says Ezekiel, when the Lord reestablishes His kingdom in their midst.

29 And I will raise up for them a plant of renown, and they shall be no more consumed with hunger in the land, neither bear the shame of the heathen any more.

The unusual phrase "plant of renown" suggests more than one possibility for interpretation. In Hebrew the phrase is *matta` shem* (**mat-TAW shame**), and it literally means "a planting-place for a name" and could, therefore, refer to the promise of a return to the land and a place for the Jews to plant themselves once again—but in such a glorious way that the surrounding nations will also know God's glory, or "renown." Beyond this, the verse continues to celebrate the prosperity and wholeness Israel will enjoy; hunger, which in Ezekiel's time was likely a frequent problem, would be heard of no more. Further, in Ezekiel 34:29 the "heathen" is mentioned again, but this time it is his or her "shame" that will no longer be borne. This probably means not the shame that the heathen felt, but rather the shame the Jews felt at being wanderers in the heathen's land, rootless and exposed to whatever oppression and violence the Babylonians felt inclined to inflict.

30 Thus shall they know that I the LORD their God am with them, and that they, even the house of Israel, are my people, saith the Lord GOD.

"Thus," meaning that "in this way" (NLT)—because of all the blessings mentioned in verses 23 and 29—the people of Israel will know that their exile is ended and that the blessing of God's presence has returned. This is consistent with the patterns of the Mosaic covenant: God promised bless-ings in response to faithfulness and curses in response to unfaithfulness (see Deuterono-my 28). Under the new covenant, the picture is more complicated. Following their Master, God's people often receive suffering, and not material blessing, in response to their faith-fulness––for this is the path blazed for them by Jesus Himself. Such thoughts are relevant to Ezekiel 34 because, as these verses promise the better David to come, they anticipate the days in which God's people would have a bet-ter hope than material blessing. One thing never changes, throughout the Scriptures: the promise of God that He is with them, and they are His people. This promise brings im-mense comfort to people in exile, both Israel in the days of Babylon and the church today.

31 And ye my flock, the flock of my pasture, are men, and I am your God, saith the Lord GOD.

Having given such wondrous promises to Israel, God now brings the message full circle. By calling Israel His "flock," He reminds them that they will not always be vulnerable to shepherds, who only feed themselves and neglect the care of the sheep. He will be their Shepherd and will send His Prince, the new David, to shepherd the people on His behalf. The reminder that the flock "are men, and I am your God" may be intended to remind Israel that they exist through Him and are helpless without Him. As the bumper sticker phrase puts it, "I am God, and you are not." But the context shows most clearly that the emphasis is on the word "your": "I am your God." The overriding lesson of this passage, then, is that God is with His people at all times, without any exception, even when He might least seem to be with them.

edeem (buy back) from, to pay
erson. It is commonly used as a
e to free slaves.
nsomed, purchaseed.
of shelter; stronghold or
ce to which we can run when the
ns and be secure; a shelter from
danger.
ange (be transformed) or turn
and turn to God in faith.
be declared "not guilty."
God's justness and rightness,
s as a gift also in His people; refers
y to live as opposed to a lifestyle
rs unfairly or unjustly.

brew, *shabbath* means "ceasing
day set aside to worship God.
ord which means "holy" when
ctive. The "holy place" of which
the tabernacle, the portable
der Moses' leadership after the
gypt.
ue, safety, deliverance.
rsary or devil.
der, rescuer, deliverer.
vere secretaries, recorders, men
w.
refuge, place of safety and a
ll forms of destructive elements
ck or destroy the children of God
us from experiencing the fullness
gs, peace, and divine providence.
consider, discern, perceive.
rew expression (**SEH-lah**) is
xclusively in the book of Psalms.
at Selah denotes a pause or a
nging of the psalm or recitation,
n of an instrumental musical
Greek Septuagint renders the
meaning "a musical interlude."
k that the word *Selah* signaled
of singing and allowed for
n.
eans "seventy," and it is the
ranslation of the Hebrew Old
Jewish scholars.
subject, worshiper.
"peace."
The awesome presence of the
fame, and reputation.

Shofar (sho-FAR): Means "ram's horn," and was used in celebration as well as in signaling armies or large groups of people in civil assembly.
Soul: Refers to the immaterial part of the human being (what leaves the body when death occurs), or to the whole being—the self, one's life.
Stiffnecked: Obstinate and difficult.
Strengthen: To secure, make firm, make strong.
Strive: To struggle, to exert oneself.
Supplications: Seeking, asking, entreating, pleading, imploring, and petitioning God.

T
Tabernacles: Literally means "dwelling places," the name of the portable temple constructed by Moses and the people of Israel.
Teaching: Instruction in Christian living.
Tetragrammaton: Hebrew name for God (YHWH).
Torah: The Law, which means "instrument" or "direction"; the first five books of the Old Testament (Genesis, Exodus, Leviticus, Numbers, and Deuteronomy).
Transfigured: To change or transform.
Transgressions: Include sins, rebellion, breaking God's Law.
Tried: Smelted or refined, purified.
Trumpet: A ram's horn that was used in celebration as well as in signaling armies or large groups of people in civil assembly.

U
Understand: To consider, have wisdom.

W
Wisdom: "Prudence, an understanding of ethics" (Strong).
Woe: An exclamation of grief.
Worship: Bow down deeply, show obeisance and reverence.
Wrath: "Burning anger, rage" (Strong).

Y
Yahweh: Many scholars simply use the Hebrew spelling with consonants only, *YHWH*, which is God's name.

Source:
Strong, James. *New Exhaustive Strong's Numbers and Concordance with Expanded Greek-Hebrew Dictionary*. Seattle, WA: Biblesoft, and International Bible Translators, 1994. 2003.

Sources:
"Bless, Blessing." *Tyndale Bible Dictionary*. Walter A. Elwell and Philip W. Comfort, eds. Wheaton, IL: Tyndale House Publishers, 2001. 226–27.
"Blessing." *Nelson's Illustrated Bible Dictionary*. Herbert Lockyer, Sr., gen. ed. Nashville, TN: Thomas Nelson Publishers, 1986 (accessed through PC Study Bible, September 1, 2010).
Briscoe, Stuart. *All Things Weird and Wonderful: Ezekiel and His Mysterious Book of Whirling Wheels and Dry Bones Can Help You Be a Better Communicator to a Spiritually Dead Generation*. Wheaton, IL: Victor Books, 1977. 125.
Merriam-Webster Online Dictionary. Merriam-Webster, Inc. http://www.merriam-webster.com (accessed January 29, 2011).
"Ra`ah." *Theological Wordbook of the Old Testament, vol. 2*. R. Laird Harris, gen. ed. Chicago, IL: Moody Press, 1980. 852-853 (accessed through PC Study Bible, September 1, 2010).
Taylor, John B. *Ezekiel: An Introduction & Commentary*. Downers Grove, IL: InterVarsity Press, 1969. 223–24.

Say It Correctly

Babylonian. Bab'uh-LOH-nee-uhn.
Ezekiel. Ih-ZEE-kee-uhl.
Judah. JOO-duh.
Yahweh. YAH-weh.

Daily Bible Readings

MONDAY
The Lord Is My Shepherd
(Psalm 23)

TUESDAY
I Will Be with You
(Genesis 28:10–17)

WEDNESDAY
God Will Be with You
(Genesis 48:17–21)

THURSDAY
I AM Has Sent Me
(Exodus 3:9–15)

FRIDAY
I Am with You
(Haggai 1:7–14)

SATURDAY
I Am with You Always
(Matthew 28:16–20)

SUNDAY
"I Am Your God"
(Ezekiel 34:23–31)

Notes

_____

_____

_____

A

Abomination: A foul and detestable thing.

Affliction: Anguish, burden, persecution, tribulation, or trouble.

Angels: God's messengers; they are not eternal or all-knowing, and are sometimes referred to as winged creatures known as "cherubim" and "seraphim."

Atonement: To "propitiate" (to satisfy the demands of an offended holy God) or "atone" (being reconciled to a holy God) because of sin.

Avenger: One who takes revenge, one who punishes.

B

Be Baptized: To dip repeatedly, to immerse, to submerge.

Blameless: Irreproachable, faultless, flawless.

Blessedness: Happiness, joy, prosperity. It is not based on circumstance, but is rooted in the deep abiding hope shared by all who have received salvation through Jesus Christ.

Bless the Lord: To simply speak well of Him.

Blood of the Lamb: The blood that Jesus shed on the Cross of Calvary when He suffered and died for humanity's sin.

Bowels: The place of emotions, distress, or love.

C

Called: Appointed or commissioned by God to fulfill a task.

Charge: Admonish, order, command.

Chosen: To be elected, be selected.

Christ: The Anointed One.

Commandments: God's mandates; the entire body of Laws issued by God to Moses for Israel.

Conduct: Manner of living.

Confess: To acknowledge or to fully agree.

Consider: To determine, make out.

Covenant: An agreement with God based on God's character, strength, and grace; an agreement and promise between God and humankind.

Crucifixion: Jesus suffered and died on the Cross.

D

Decalogue: The Ten Commandments; the words translated "Ten Commandments" literally mean "ten words."

Desolation: Making something deserted, uninhabited.

Disciples: Learners, pupils.

Dominion: Rule or reign.

Dwelling place: A location that is a person's refuge, home.

E

El: The Hebrew word for "god" or "mighty one."

Even from everlasting to everlasting: "Indefinite or unending future, eternity" (Strong).

Evil: To do "bad, unpleasant, displeasing" things.

Evil doer: A malefactor, wrongdoer, criminal, troublemaker.

Evil spirits: Messengers and ministers of the devil.

Exalt: To raise up; to raise to the highest degree possible.

Exhortation: Giving someone motivation to change his or her behavior. It can imply either rebuke or encouragement.

F

Faithfulness: Steadfastness, steadiness.

Fear of the Lord: Reverence or awe of who God is.

G

Gittith: A musical instrument resembling a Spanish guitar that, in ancient times, provided a musical tune or tempo during a ceremony or festival.

Glory: Splendor, unparalleled honor, dignity, or distinction; to honor, praise, and worship.

God called: To commission, appoint, endow.

God's Bride: The Church.

God's own hand: God's strength, power.

God's protection: Conveys the idea of staying in God's abode, staying constantly in His presence, getting completely acquainted or connected with Him, and resting permanently in Him.

Gospel: "The glad tidings of the kingdom of God soon to be set up, and later also of Jesus the Messiah, the founder of this kingdom" (Strong).

Graven image: An idol or likeness cut from stone, wood, or metal and then worshiped as a god.

Great Tribulation: A time of great suffering (Daniel 12:1, Revelation 6–18).

H

Hallowed: Consecrated, dedicated, or set apart.

Hear: Listen to, yield to, to be obedient.

Hearken: Pay attention to, give attention to.

Heart: The place, figuratively, where our emotions and passions exist.

Heathen: Literally means "nations," and is used in the Old Testament to refer to the Gentiles, all those who are not a part of the people of God.

Holy: Anything consecrated and set aside for sacred use; the place made sacred because of God's presence; set apart from sin.

Honor: To revere, value.

Hosts: Those which go forth; armies.

I

Idolatry: The worship of anything other than God, our Creator.

Infidel: One who is unfaithful, unbelieving, not to be trusted.

Iniquities: Perversity, depravity, guilt.

In vain: A waste, a worthless thing, or simply emptiness.

J

Jesus' ascension: Forty days after Jesus' death, burial, and resurrection, He ascended or went back to heaven to sit at the right hand of the Father (Acts 1:9–11).

Jesus' transfiguration: While on the Mount of Olives with His closest disciples—Peter, James, and John—Jesus changed into another form. His face shone with the brightness like the sun and His raiment was white as snow (cf. Matthew 17:2; Mark 9:2; Luke 9:29).

Just: A word often rendered as "righteous"; that which is right and fair.

Justice: Righteousness in government.

K

Kingdom of Christ: It is the same as the "Kingdom of Heaven (Matthew 18:1–4); it is where Jesus reigns in "glory" (i.e., in "dignity or honor").

Know: To ascertain by seeing, have understanding, to acknowledge.

Knowledge: Discernment, understanding, wisdom.

L

Labor: To toil to the point of exhaustion or weariness.

Logos (LOG-os): The entire Word of God.

M

"Make a joyful noise": A command that literally means "shout."

Manna: Food fro

Messiah: The Pr

Minister: "A serv executes the co

O

Omnipotent: Al

Omnipresent: A

Omniscient: Al

Ordained: Esta founded, fixed

P

Parousia (par-
Second Comin

Path: Connote
dynamic steps

Peace: Denote
contentment,
it is far more
problems, bu
be blessed.

Pentateuch: T
The first five
well as the O
the entire se
which God g
people. Terr
include com
legal regula
and teachin

People(s): N
"people" as
Translation
world bless

Power: Bol
especially C

Prophets: T
and under
pleaded G
be saved.

Profit: To
Prosperou
especially
refer to p
move for

Proved: F
Psalm: A
Purity: "S

R

Ranso
a price
purcha

Redee

Refuge
fortress
enemy
rain, sto

Repent
back fro

Righteo
Righteo
which H
to the ri
that trea

S

Sabbath:
from wor

Sanctuary
used as a
David spe
temple b
Exodus fr

Salvation:
Satan: An
Savior: A
Scribes: T
skilled in t

Secret plac
covering fr
that seek t
and to prev
of God's bl

See: To beh
Selah: This
found almc
Some believ
suspension
and the inse
interlude. T
word *dia'psa*
Still others t
a holding ba
silent medita

Septuagint:
ancient Gree
Testament by

Servant: A sla

Shalom: Mea

Shekinah Glc

Lord: His ho

Notes

Notes